INTERNATIONAL DISPUTE RESOLUTION

Volume I: Materials

AUSTRALIA
Law Book Co.
Sydney

CANADA and USA
Carswell
Toronto

HONG KONG
Sweet & Maxwell Asia

NEW ZEALAND
Brooker's
Wellington

SINGAPORE and MALAYSIA
Sweet and Maxwell Asia
Singapore and Kuala Lumpur

INTERNATIONAL DISPUTE RESOLUTION

Volume I: Materials

Leila Anglade
and
John Tackaberry

LONDON
SWEET & MAXWELL
2004

Published in 2004 by
Sweet & Maxwell Limited, of
100 Avenue Road,
Swiss Cottage,
NW3 3PF
Typeset by Servis Filmsetting Ltd
and printed and bound in Great Britain by
Creative Print and Design (Wales) Ebbw Vale

No natural forests were destroyed to make this product; only farmed timber was used and replanted.

A CIP catalogue record for this book is available from the British Library

ISBN 0421 887001

© Leila Anglade 2004

All rights reserved. Crown Copyright material is reproduced with the permission of the Controller of HMSO and the Queen's Printer for Scotland.

Whilst every care has been taken to establish and acknowledge copyright, and contact the copyright owners, the publishers tender their apologies for any accidental infringement. They would be pleased to come to a suitable arrangement with the owners in each case.

No part of this publication may be reproduced in any form or by any means, or stored in any retrieval system of any nature without prior written permission, except for permitted fair dealing under the Copyright, Designs and Patents Act 1988, or in accordance with the terms of a licence issued by the Copyright Licensing Agency in respect of photocopying and/or reprographic reproduction.
Application for permission for other use of copyright material including permission to reproduce extracts in other published works shall be made to the publishers. Full acknowledgment of author, publisher and source must be given.

Preface

As the world economic order is globalising so also must the legal order. Courts engaged in civil litigation are striving to achieve this but often find themselves constrained by issues surrounding jurisdiction and applicable law. Sometimes these difficulties touch on the sensitive subject of national sovereignty. Whereas there are recent signs of judges coming to terms with such problems, a harmonising global approach requiring judges to apply a careful balance of robustness and restraint is yet a long way off.

However, for many years now, and especially during the past decade, international arbitration has become the method of choice for those wishing to resolve their disputes without resorting to courts exercising a civil law jurisdiction. Such courts are required to become involved only when there is a need to enforce an award under the New York Convention.

The resolution of international disputes, whether they be political or commercial, contribute enormously to stability, peace and prosperity. The practitioners, often lawyers, who engage in these exercises, provide the legal frameworks into which international political and commercial agreements can rest. I have seen these experts at their work and, by their skills, resolving conflicts and reducing the risk of political turmoil. This is true whether the context is the Good Friday Agreement or the next WTO Round.

Such skills also promote the harmonious resolution of commercial disputes through ADR and arbitration. The tools used by these experts are international conventions, statutes and other legal instruments. With the inexorable growth of international commercial arbitration, these instruments proliferate. However, our two distinguished authors, Leila Anglade and John Tackaberry Q.C., rescue us from ever more tedious research and the ever more increasing risk of error by placing this two volume book in our hands. The first volume gives easy access to the full text of all major arbitration laws and conventions from all regions of the world. The second volume contains an exhaustive table of cases in alphabetical order, each one easily found by casename or by referring to the comprehensive subject index.

This publication, as a single point of reference, is of enormous value to the arbitrator, the practitioner and indeed, the student.

Its scope is truly global, its reach comprehensive and its construction concise and convenient. All of us with an interest in International arbitration will be grateful.

David Byrne S.C. F.C.I.Arb
Commissioner of the European Union
September 2004

To Pàdraig

The authors would like to acknowledge the following people:

Cécile Trochu
Nicky Meech and Steven Jackson

Authors' Note

Dispute resolution is a growing industry both internationally and within national boundaries. It is important for those who are interested in these disputes but do not specialise in them full time to be able to have access to basic materials and to see how issues which are common to both the domestic and the international arena have been approached in particular jurisdictions.

Accordingly Volume 1 of this work seeks to provide ready access to a great deal of basic worldwide source materials, which cover all aspects of international commercial dispute resolution. Volume 2 takes a selection of cases from different jurisdictions and highlights some of the issues that those cases have thrown up and the way the relevant tribunal has responded to them.

This work is the second in the latest Sweet and Maxwell series of dispute resolution books, of which the first was *Bernstein's Handbook of Arbitration and Dispute Resolution Practice*.

Whilst writing, we take the opportunity to express our gratitude to Cécile Trochu for her work on Volume 1; to Gareth Reeds who did an enormous amount of very helpful work on Volume 2; and to Declan O'Mahony who rallied round in the later stages of the preparation, to Richard Milsom, Nicky Meech and Tessa Norton who patiently and courteously provided us with wisdom and guidance on the arcane matters of publishing, to Alison Ho who has taken on the task of marketing this great work; to Kate Auer, Catherine Redmond and Richard Greener who intervened when needed; and to Steven Jackson who carried through the editing in the final stages. We very much appreciate all that all the above did.

Lastly, we emphasise that this work is intended to provide material for discussion and consideration. It is not advice; and anyone who is involved in an actual dispute must seek or take proper advice specific to that case rather than blindly following any general observations to be found in our texts!

Leila Anglade
John Tackaberry
September 2004

London and Dublin

Foreword

by Professor Pieter Sanders, the conceiver and author of the
New York Convention and founder of the International Council for
Commercial Arbitration.

The appearance of a publication such as the one I am honoured to introduce is to be welcomed. For resolving disputes, arising out of international trade, arbitration is generally preferred for reasons which I do not need to repeat. However, a wealth of material has to be consulted by the lawyers as well as the arbitrators before the award can be rendered.

Not all of them will have readily available the material assembled in Volume I and certainly not the case material contained in Volume II. Publication of arbitral awards occur and a lex mercatoria is appearing thanks to arbitration. But where can one find the material? In my Quo Vadis Arbitration (1999) I suggested the assembly, in a loose-leaf edition, of arbitral awards of general interest. These 150 cases may provide the start for such edition.

Source Acknowledgement

The Publishers would like to thank the following:

We wish to acknowledge Cameron May Ltd for kindly granting permission to reproduce 'Arbitration Act 1996 (Chapter 23)' (England), 'Arbitration Act 1980' (Ireland), 'Law of the Russian Federation on International Commercial Arbitration, 1993' (Russia), 'Arbitration Law of the People's Republic of China, 1994' (China), 'European Convention on International Commercial Arbitration, Geneva, 1961', 'Convention on the Settlement of Investment Disputes Between States and Nationals of Other States' and 'Arab Convention on Commercial Arbitration' (see *www.jus.uio.no/lm/*).

We are grateful to the United Nations Commission on International Trade Law (UNCITRAL)for granting permission to reproduce 'UNCITRAL Model Law on International Commercial Arbitration', 'UNCITRAL Model Law on International Commercial Conciliation', 'United Nations Convention on the Recognition and Enforcement of Foreign Arbitral Awards', 'UNCITRAL Notes on Organising Arbitral Proceedings' and 'UNCITRAL Arbitration Rules' (see *www.uncitral.org/*).

We are grateful to the International Bar Association for granting permission to reproduce 'International Bar Association's Guidelines on Impartiality, Independence and Disclosure in International Commercial Arbitration' and 'International Bar Association's Rules on the Taking of Evidence in International Commercial Arbitration'(see *www.ibanet.org/*).

We wish to acknowledge World Trade Organization for kindly granting permission to reproduce 'WTO Understanding on Rules and Procedures governing the Settlement of Disputes (Annex 2 of the WTO Agreement)' (see *www.wto.org/*).

We wish to acknowledge OHADA for kindly granting permission to reproduce 'OHADA Uniform Act on Arbitration' (see *www.ohada.com*).

We are grateful to Ola Lando at the Copenhagen Business School for granting permission to reproduce 'The Principles of European Contract Law'. This article was prepared by the Commission on European Contract Law. Part I and II, 1999 edited by Ole Lando and Hugh Beale, and Part III, 2003 edited by Ole Lando, Eric Clive, André Prüm and Reinhard Zimmermann. Part I and II l999 and Part III 2003 containing the articles, comments and notes, may be procured from Kluwer Law International PLO Box 85889, 2508 CNN Hague, The Netherlands (see *www.cbs.dk*).

We wish to acknowledge Robert Umbricht for kindly granting permission to reproduce 'Federal Code on Private International Law,1987 (Chapter 12)' (Switzerland). Copyright © 1987 Robert P. Umbricht, Attorney at Law, Bahnhofstrasse 22, CH-8022 Zurich, Switzerland. All rights reserved. (see *www.umbricht.ch*)

We wish to acknowledge the Australian Government for kindly granting permission to reproduce 'International Arbitration Law, 1974'. All legislative material herein is reproduced by permission but does purport to be the official or authorised versions. They are subject to Commonwealth of Australia copyright. The *Copyright Act 1968* permits certain reproduction and publication of Commonwealth legislation and judgements. In particular, section 182A of the Act enables a complete copy to be made by or on behalf of a particular person. For reproduction or publication beyond that permitted by the Act, permission should be sought in writing. Requests should be addressed to Commonwealth Copyright Administration, Australian Government Department of Communications, Information Technology and the Arts, GPO Box 2154, Canberra ACT 2601, or posted at *http://www.dcita.gov.au/cca*.

We wish to acknowledge the American Society of International Law for kindly granting permission to reproduce 'France: International Arbitration Provisions of Decree Amending Code of Civil Procedure, Reproduced from the English Translation and annotation of Messrs. W. Laurence Craig and Jan Paulsson, Coudert Frères, Paris, and Prof. William W. Park, Boston University School of Law (20 ILM 917).

While every care has been taken to establish and acknowledge copyright, and contact the copyright owners, the publishers tender their apologies for any accidental infringement. They would be pleased to come to a suitable arrangement with the rightful owners in each case.

Contents

Preface	*v*
Acknowledgement	*ix*
Author Note	*xi*
Foreword	*xiii*
Source Acknowledgement	*xv*
Contents	*xvii*
Curricula Vitae of the Authors	*xx*
Table of Cases	*xxv*
Table of Materials	*xxxiii*

CHAPTER 1: INTERNATIONAL ARBITRATION AND ADR STATUTES

A.	***English and Irish Statutes***	1–001
	England: Arbitration Act, 1996 (Chapter 23)	1–001
	Ireland: Arbitration Act, 1998	1–112
B.	***Foreign Statutes: European Jurisdictions***	1–167
	Switzerland: Federal Code on Private International Law, 1987 (Chapter 12)	1–167
	France: New Code of Civil Procedure, 1981 (Book 4)	1–186
	Germany: Arbitration Law of 1998	1–202
	Russia: Law of the Russian Federation on International Commercial Arbitration, 1993	1–244
C.	***Foreign Statutes: Non-European Jurisdictions***	1–281
	USA: Federal Arbitration Act, 1925, as amended	1–281
	Australia: International Arbitration Law, 1974, as amended	1–312
	China: Arbitration Law, 1994	1–326
	Egypt: Egyptian Arbitration Act in Civil and Commercial Matters, 1994	1–406

D.	*Uniform and Model Laws*	1–469
	UNCITRAL Model Law on International Commercial Arbitration	1–469
	UNCITRAL Model Law on International Commercial Conciliation	1–506
	European Convention Providing a Uniform Law on Arbitration	1–520
	OHADA Uniform Act on Arbitration	1–569

CHAPTER 2: INTERNATIONAL ARBITRATION CONVENTIONS

A.	*World-wide Multilateral Conventions*	2–001
	United Nations Convention on the Recognition and Enforcement of Foreign Arbitral Awards, New York, 1958	2–001
	ICSID Convention on the Settlement of Investment Disputes Between States and Nationals of Other States, Washington, 1965	2–017
	WTO Understanding on Rules and Procedures governing the Settlement of Disputes, 1994	2–092
B.	*Regional Multilateral Conventions*	2–123
	European Convention on International Commercial Arbitration, Geneva 1961	2–123
	Inter-American Convention on International Commercial Arbitration, Panama City, 1975	2–135
	Arab Convention on Commercial Arbitration, Amman 1987	2–149
	North American Free Trade Agreement, 1992	2–192

CHAPTER 3: INTERNATIONAL ARBITRATION PROCEDURAL AND ETHICAL RULES

A.	*Code of Ethics For Arbitrators in International Arbitration*	3–001
	American Arbitration Association's Code of Ethics for Arbitrators in Commercial Disputes	3–001
	IBA Guidelines on Conflict of Interest in International Arbitration	3–017
B.	*Rules of Procedure*	3–029
	UNCITRAL Notes on Organizing Arbitral Proceedings	3–029
	UNCITRAL Arbitration Rules	3–084
	International Bar Association's Rules on the Taking of Evidence in International Commercial Arbitration	3–126

CHAPTER 4: INTERNATIONAL CONTRACTUAL INSTRUMENTS

A. *Transnational Contract Principles* — 4–001

    UNIDROIT Principles for International Commerical Contracts, 1994 — 4–001

    Principles for European Contract Law, as revised in 1999 and supplemented in 2002 — 4–120

B. *Rules of Conflict* — 4–318

    Convention on the Law Applicable to Contractual Obligations, Rome, 1980 — 4–318

    Inter-American Convention on the Law Applicable to International Contracts, Mexico City, 1994 — 4–360

Index — 625

Curricula Vitae of the Authors

LEILA SOPHIE ANGLADE

M.B.A. (ECS Lyon), Licence (Paris I), Maîtrise (Paris I), D.E.S.S. (Paris I), D.E.A. (Paris I), LL.M. (Harvard), C.A.P.A. (Bar of Paris)

University College Dublin, Faculty of Law, Roebuck Castle,
Dublin 4, IRELAND
Telephone: 716-8781 (W); Facsimile: 269-2655
E-Mail: Leila.Anglade@ucd.ie

Leila Anglade is admitted to the Bar of Paris and is a graduate of the Lyon Graduate School of Business, Pantheon Sorbonne – Paris I and Harvard Law School. She has practiced international dispute resolution and international commercial law in both the Common and Civil Law Systems and is College Lecturer in International Arbitration and International Commercial Transactions at University College Dublin. She is also the Director of the Diploma in International Arbitration at University College Dublin.

Ms. Anglade specialises in international arbitration and is extensively experienced in the field both academically and as a practitioner. She has acted in international arbitrations involving the United States, France, Germany, Libya, Madagascar, Tanzania, Hong Kong, Algeria and Iraq. She also acted in the Iraq-Kuwait dispute following the Gulf War. She is a member of the Chartered Institute of Arbitrators.

She has complimentary expertise in international commercial transactions in which her areas of specialty include transnational contracts, mergers & acquisitions, joint ventures, transfer of technology, distribution and bankruptcy.

PROFESSIONAL

UNIVERSITY COLLEGE DUBLIN, Ireland
Lecturer at Law

Subjects Taught:

International Arbitration

- Postgraduate Diploma in International Arbitration (Programme Director)
- International Arbitration for Master's (LL.M.) Degree

International Business Law

- International Business Law for Master's (LL.M.) Degree
- International Business Law for B.C.L. and B.B.L.S. Degrees

French Legal Theory

- French Legal Theory for BCL Law with French Law Degree (Programme Director for this degree)

FORDHAM LAW SCHOOL, New York
Invited Professor of International Dispute Resolution

EDUCATION

1989 to 1990
HARVARD LAW SCHOOL, Cambridge, MA
LL.M. (MASTER OF LAWS DEGREE)

1988 to 1989
PANTHEON-SORBONNE – Paris I
D.E.A. (POSTGRADUATE DEGREE IN U.K. & U.S. BUSINESS LAW)

1987 to 1988
PARIS BAR SCHOOL
C.A.P.A. (PROFESSIONAL QUALIFICATION & ADMISSION TO THE BAR OF PARIS)

1986 to 1987
PANTHEON-SORBONNE – Paris I
D.E.S.S. (POSTGRADUATE DEGREE IN FRENCH INTERNATIONAL COMMERCIAL LAW)

1985 to 1986
PANTHEON-SORBONNE – Paris I
Maitrise en Droit des Affaires (Master of Laws specialized in business law)

1984 to 1985
PANTHEON-SORBONNE – Paris I
Licence en Droit des Affaires

1981 to 1984
ECOLE SUPERIEURE DE COMMERCE DE LYON (LYON GRADUATE SCHOOL OF BUSINESS)
M.B.A.

ACADEMIC HONOURS

- Harvard Club of France Scholarship
- Fullbright Scholar
- Bar of Paris Scholarship
- French Ministry of Foreign Affairs Scholarship
- Dorothea L. Beckwith Scholarship

PROFESSIONAL ADMISSIONS AND ACTIVITIES

1988	Bar of Paris
1997 – present	Member of the panel of arbitrators of the International Chamber of Commerce (ICC)
2001 – present	Member of the Advisory Council of the International Centre for Dispute Resolution (ICDR)
2003 – present	Member of the ICC Taskforce on Arbitrating Competition Law Issues
2003 – present	Member of the European Group on Comparative Cultural Heritage Laws

SELECTED PUBLICATIONS

"The Use of Transnational Rules in International Arbitration", Vol. The Irish Jurist 2004

"Ireland as a place for International arbitration", American Review of International Arbitration, Volume 12, No.2

"Developing International Arbitration in Ireland", the Bar Review, December 1999.

"Challenge, Recognition and Enforcement of Domestic and Foreign International Arbitral Awards under the New Irish Arbitration (International Commercial) Act" [1998] I.C.C.L.R., Issue 5, Sweet & Maxwell

"The Arbitration (International Commercial) Act, 1998", Irish Law Statutes Annotated, October 1998, Sweet & Maxwell

"Chronicle of a Death Foretold: the decline of the importance of the law of the seat in the enforcement of international arbitral awards", The Irish Jurist December 1998, Round Hall Sweet and Maxwell, Dublin

"Art Law and the Holocaust: the French Situation", Art Antiquity and Law, December 1999.

"The Portrait of Adrianus Tegularius: A landmark decision by French courts", Art Antiquity and Law, March 2003

"A Special Jurisdiction: France" in Norman Palmer, "Museums and the Holocaust", London, IAL October 2000.

"Anti-seizure Statutes in Art Law: The Influence of '*La Danse*' on French Law" in *Liber Memorialis* for Professor James C. Brady, Round Hall Sweet & Maxwell May 2001.

With John Tackaberry, Q.C., International Dispute Resolution, Volumes I and II, Thompson Sweet& Maxwell, London 2004.

JOHN TACKABERRY QC MA LLM FCIArb FFB

Arbitration Chambers, 22 Willes Road, London, NW5 3DS
DX 46454 Kentish Town
E-Mail JATQC@atack.demon.co.uk
Tel: 00 44 (0)20 7267 2137
Fax: 00 44 (0)20 7482 1018

Present Position: QC, Recorder, Registered Chartered Arbitrator, Former UNCC Commissioner
Date of Birth 13 November 1939

1967   Called to the Bar of England and Wales (Grays Inn).
1982   Appointed to be one of Her Majesty's Counsel (England & Wales).
Admitted (ad hoc) to the Bar of Malaysia.
1987   Admitted to the Bar of Ireland
1988   Admitted to the Bar of California.
Admitted (ad hoc) to the Bar of Hong Kong.
Appointed a Recorder of the Crown Court.
1989   Admitted to the Bar of New South Wales (also QC).
Appointed visiting Professor in Construction Law, Queensland University of Technology.
1998   Appointed a Commissioner by the United Nations Compensation Commission (until July 2003).

Positions and memberships Past Chairman of the Chartered Institute of Arbitrators and first chairman of its Executive Committee. Also a principal architect of the Chartered Institute of Arbitrators' international activities and of its Special Fellowship courses. Founding President of the Society of Construction Law and Past President of the European Society of Construction Law. A principal editor of the Handbook of Arbitration Practice. Past or present member of many international arbitration panels. CEDR Mediator. Vice President of the Arbitration Club. Adjudication and D.R.B [Dispute Resolution Board] work also undertaken. A member of ADR Chambers. A Member of the Construction Disputes Division, European Court of Arbitration.

Recent work has involved a major gas storage and pumping station in Poland, an LPG plant in Malaysia, underground storage of LPG in Australia, a dispute about a catcracker (refinery equipment) in Australia, a mining collapse dispute, a share dealing dispute in HK, an undersea cable dispute (North Sea), a barge mounted generating plant in Bangladesh, a shipping dispute in India, a commission dispute arising out of Westland v Saudi Arabia (a major case in the 90s), a follow on dispute to the CME television rights dispute, an industrial boiler and water treatment installation plant in England; a major building dispute in HK; an aircraft servicing dispute in Africa – involving serious corruption issues – a gypsum plant in Jordan; a steel mill in Egypt. A very recent case concerned the conversion of the Solitaire into the world's largest dynamically positioned pipelaying vessel.

Work at the UNCC involved five years of intensive dispute resolution on a paper only basis utilising a locally based legal team.

A Principal Editor of Bernstein, Handbook of Arbitration and Dispute Resolution Practice.

Earlier cases concerned a substantial glass walling contract in London; a major offshore fabrication dispute in the gulf; a lift installation contract in Hong Kong; prefabricated housing in Saudi Arabia; Mercury Court in Liverpool; the construction of Fantasy Land in Paris; an hotel project in the Gambia; the Westminster and Chelsea Hospital; a taxi franchise in the High Court; a bus contract in Turkey; Connah's Quay and other combined cycle gas turbine power stations; copyright in architects' designs; local authority housing rehabilitation schemes; a coastal defence project; and the British Library mech and eng contract.

A more detailed CV can be supplied if desired.

Also at:
ADR Chambers (UK) Ltd, Equity House, Blackbrook Park Avenue, Taunton, TA1 2LR;
Director: Frances Burton; Senior Litigation Secretary: Stephen Ward – Email: ward@adrchambers.co.uk

Assize Court Chambers	Dublin International Arbitration Centre
14 Small Street	Distillery Building
Bristol BS1 1DE	145–151 Church Street
DX 78134 Bristol	Dublin 7
Tel: 0117 926 4587	DX 2512 Dublin
Fax: 0117 922 6835	Tel: 353 1 817 4663
E-mail chambers@assize-court-chambers.co.uk	Fax: 353 1 817 5150
Head Clerk: Mr Jonathan Smith	Attn: Harry McQuaid

40 King Street, Manchester M26BA, DX 718188 Manchester
Tel: 0161 832 9082   Fax: 0161 835 2139
E-mail: kingst40@aol.com
Head Clerk: William Brown

Table of Cases

This Table refers to both volumes. Paragraph numbers prefixed with a number refer to Volume 1: Materials. Paragraph numbers prefixed with a 'C' refer to Volume 2: Cases.

A/S Det Dansk-Franske Dampskibselskab v Compagnie Financière D'Investissements Transatlantiques SA (Compafina) (The Himmerland) [1965] 2 Lloyd's Rep. 353 .... C-005, C-019
AAOT Foreign Economic Association (VO) Technostroy-export ("Technostroy") v International Development and Trade Services, Inc. ("IDTS"), 139 F. 3d 980 (2d Cir., 1998) C-001, C-015, C-050, C-058
AT & T Corp v Saudi Cable Co [2000] EWCA Civ 154; [2000] 2 Lloyd's Rep. 127; [2000] 2 All E.R. (Comm) 625; [2000] C.L.C. 1309; [2000] B.L.R. 743 . C-021, C-041, C-050, C-058
ATSA of California Inc v Continental Insurance Co and Cairo General Contracting Co; Hamed Abulhassan v Cairo General Contracting Co, 702 F. 2d 172 (9th Cir., 1983) (Note: amended 754 F. 2d 1394 (9th Cir., 1985)) C-022, C-023
Abu Dhabi Gas Liquefaction Co Ltd v Eastern Bechtel Corp and Chiyoda Chemical Engineering & Construction Co Ltd; Eastern Bechtel Corp and Chiyoda Chemical Engineering & Construction Co Ltd v Ishikawajima-Harima Heavy Industries Co Ltd [1982] 2 Lloyd's Rep. 425; [1982] 126 S.J. 524; [1982] Com.L.R. 215 .... C-002, C-003
Aggeliki Charis Compania Maritima SA v Pagnan SpA (The Angelic Grace) [1995] 1 Lloyd's Rep. 87, CA C-004, C-047, C-130
Agios Lazaros, The. See Nea Agrex SA v Baltic Shipping Co Ltd (The Agios Lazaros)
Agro Company of Canada Ltd v Richmond Shipping Ltd (The Simonburn) [1973] 1 Lloyd's Rep. 392 .... C-005, C-019
Al Wahab, The. See Amin Rasheed Shipping Corp v Kuwait Insurance Co (The Al Wahab)
Alcom Ltd v Republic of Colombia [1984] A.C. 580; [1984] 2 W.L.R. 750; [1984] 2 Lloyd's Rep. 24 .... C-006
Almare Prima, The. See Almare Societa di Navigazione SpA v Derby and Co Ltd (The Almare Prima)
Almare Societa di Navigazione SpA v Derby and Co Ltd (The Almare Prima) [1989] 2 Lloyd's Rep. 376 .... C-007
Am. Dredging Co v Miller, 510 U.S. 443 (1994) C-090
American International Group v Islamic Republic of Iran and Central Insurance of Iran (Bimeh Markazi Iran), 493 F. Supp. 522 (D.D.C. 1980) C-008
American Safety Equipment Corp v J.P. Maguire & Co, Inc, a Delaware Corp; American Safety Equipment Corp v Hickok Manufacturing Co, Inc., 391 F. 2d 821 (2d Cir., 1968) C-009, C-010
Amin Rasheed Shipping Corp v Kuwait Insurance Co (The Al Wahab) [1984] A.C. 50; [1983] 3 W.L.R. 241; [1983] 127 S.J. 492; [1983] 2 All E.R. 884; [1983] 2 Lloyd's Rep. 365, HL C-011

Anangel Peace, The. *See* Anangel Peace Compania Naviera SA v Bacchus International Commerce Corp (The Anangel Peace)
Anangel Peace Compania Naviera SA v Bacchus International Commerce Corp (The Anangel Peace) [1981] 1 Lloyd's Rep. 452 .... C-012
Andros Compania Maritima, SA v André & Cie, 430 F. Supp. 88; 1977 A.M.C. 668 (S.D.N.Y. 1977) C-037
Angelic Grace, The. *See* Aggeliki Charis Compania Maritima SA v Pagnan SpA (The Angelic Grace)
Antaios, The. *See* Antaios Cia Naviera SA v Salen Rederierna AB (The Antaios)
Antaios Cia Naviera SA v Salen Rederierna AB (The Antaios) [1985] A.C. 191; [1984] 3 W.L.R. 592; [1984] 3 All E.R. 229; [1984] 2 Lloyd's Rep. 235; (1984) 81 L.S.G. 2776; (1984) 128 S.J. 564 .... C-013, C-078
Application of Antco Shipping Company Ltd v Sidermar SpA. In the matter of the arbitration between Sidermar SpAm, Cross-Petitioner, and Antco Shipping Company Ltd and New England Petroleum Corp ("Nepco"), Cross-Respondents, 417 F. Supp. 207 (S.D.N.Y. 1976) C-014
Application of Technostroy-export ("Technostroy"), a foreign Economic Association organised under the laws of the Russian Federation, 853 F. Supp. 695 (S.D.N.Y. 1994) C-015
Arab African Energy Corp Ltd v Olie Produkten Nederland BV [1983] 2 Lloyd's Rep. 419; [1983] Com.L.R. 195 .... C-016, C-086
Arab Republic of Egypt v Southern Pacific Properties Ltd (1984) 23 I.L.M. 1048; 86 I.L.R. 475 (1984) C-017
Arenson v Casson Beckman Rutley & Co [1977] A.C. 405; [1975] 3 W.L.R. 815; [1975] 3 All E.R. 901; [1976] 1 Lloyd's Rep. 179; 119 S.J. 810, HL C-0185
Ashville Investments Ltd v Elmer Contractors Ltd [1989] Q.B. 488; [1988] 3 W.L.R. 867; [1988] 2 All E.R. 577; [1988] 2 Lloyd's Rep. 73 (Note); 37 B.L.R. 55; 10 Con. L.R. 72; (1987) 3 Const. L.J. 193; (1988) 132 S.J. 1553 .... C-004, C-020, C-076
Associate General Contractors, NY State Chapter (Savin Bros), 36 N.Y. 2d 957 ... C-075
Atlas Chartering Services v World Trade Group, 453 F. Supp. 861; 1978 A.M.C. 2033 (S.D.N.Y. 1978) C-037
Att.-Gen. of New Zealand v Mobil Oil NZ Ltd [1989] 2 N.Z.L.R. 649 .... C-024
Bank Mellat v Helléniki Techniki SA [1984] Q.B. 291; [1983] 3 W.L.R. 783; [1983] 3 All E.R. 428; [1983] Com. L.R. 273; (1983) 133 N.L.J. 597; (1983) 127 S.J. 618, CA C-025, C-056
Base Metal Trading Ltd v OJSC "Novokuznetsky Aluminium" Factory, 283 F. 3d 208 (4th Cir., 2002) C-026
Bergesen v Joseph Muller Corp, 710 F. 2d 928 (2nd Cir., 1983) C-094
Bernhardt v Polygraphic Company of America Inc, 350 U.S. 198 (1956); 76 S.Ct. 273; 100 L.Ed. 199 .... C-027
Bianchi v Commissioner, 553 F. 2d 93 (2d Cir., 1977) C-014
Birch Shipping Corp v The Embassy of the United Republic of Tanzania, 507 F. Supp. 311 (D.D.C. 1980) C-028
Bomar Oil NV ("Bomar") (Neth. Antilles) v Enterprise Tunisienne d'Activités Petrolières ("ETAP") (Tunisia), Bulletin 1993 No.313, 218; (1994) Revue de l'arbitrage 108 .... C-029
Bonar v Dean Witter Reynolds, Inc, 835 F. 2d 1378 (11th Cir., 1988) C-129
Boucraa, The. *See* L'Office Cherifien des Phosphates v Yamashita-Shinnihon Steamship Co Ltd (The Boucraa)
Brandeis Instel Ltd v Calabrian Chemicals Corp, 656 F. Supp. 160 (S.D.N.Y. 1987); (1988) XIII Yearbook Commercial Arbitration 543 ..... C-030, C-080
Braspetro Oil Services Co-Brasoil (Cayman Islands) v The Management and Implementation Authority of the Great Man-Made River Project (Libya) (1999) XXIV Yearbook Commercial Arbitration 296; (1999) Revue de l'arbitrage 835, 847 .... C-031, C-054

Bremen v Zapata Off-Shore Co, 407 U.S. 1; 92 S.Ct. 1907; 32 L.Ed. 2d 513
(1972) C-032, C-109
Bremer Vulkan Schiffbau und Maschinenfabrik v South India Shipping Corp
[1984] Q.B. 291; [1983] 3 W.L.R. 783; [1983] 3 All E.R. 428; [1983] Com. L.R.
273; (1983) 133 N.L.J. 597; (1983) 127 S.J. 618, CA C-033
British Airways Board v Laker Airways Ltd [1985] A.C. 58; [1984] 3 W.L.R. 413;
[1984] 3 All E.R. 39; [1985] E.C.C. 49; (1984) 81 L.S.G. 2849; (1984) 134
N.L.J. 746; (1984) 128 S.J. 531, HL; reversing [1984] Q.B. 142; [1983] 3 W.L.R.
544; [1983] 3 All E.R. 375; [1983] Com. L.R. 254; [1984] E.C.C. 36; (1983) 80
L.S.G. 2437; (1983) 127 S.J. 646, CA C-030, C-034, C-050
Brown (Christopher) Ltd v Genossenschaft Österreichischer Waldbestzer
Holzwirtschaftsbetriebe Registrierte GmbH [1954] 1 Q.B. 8; [1953] 3 W.L.R.
689; [1953] 2 All E.R. 1039; [1953] 2 Lloyd's Rep. 373; 97 S.J. 744 .... C-035
CMA CGM SA v Beteiligungs-Kommanditgesellschaft MS "Northern Pioneer"
Schiffahrtgesellschaft mbH [2002] EWCA Civ 1878; [2003] 1 W.L.R. 1015;
[2003] 3 All E.R. 330; [2003] 1 All E.R. (Comm) 204; [2003] 1 Lloyd's Rep.
212; (2003) 100(9) L.S.G. 28 .... C-104
California Inc v Continental Insurance Co, 702 F. 2d 172 (9th Cir., 1983) C-007
Carlisle Place Investments Ltd v Wimpey Construction (UK) Ltd [1980] 15
B.L.R. 109 .... C-033, C-036
Carolina Power & Light Co v Uranex (groupement d'interet economique), 451
F. Supp. 1044 (N.D.Cal. 1977) C-037, C-087
Carte Blanche (Singapore) Pte, Ltd v Carte Blanche International Ltd, 888 F. 2d
260 (2d Cir., 1989) 2 Arbitration Materials 118 (No. 1, 1990) C-038
Cero Navigation Corp v Jean Lion & Cie (The Solon) [2000] EWHC Comm;
[2000] 1 Lloyd's Rep. 292; [2000] 1 All E.R. (Comm) 214 .... C-085
Channel Tunnel Group Ltd v Balfour Beatty Construction Ltd [1993] A.C. 334;
[1993] 2 W.L.R. 262; [1993] 1 All E.R. 664; [1993] 1 Lloyd's Rep. 291; 61
B.L.R. 1; 32 Con. L.R. 1; [1993] I.L.Pr. 607; (1993) 137 S.J.L.B. 36; [1993]
N.P.C. 8 .... C-039
China National Metal Products Import Export Company v Apex Digital, Inc,
May 1, 2002, US [Federal] District Court for the Central District of
California C-037
Chloe Z Fishing Co Inc v Odyssey Re (London) Ltd, 2000 A.M.C. 2409
(D.Cal. 2000); (2001) XXIV Yearbook Commercial Arbitration 910 .... C-087
Christiani & Nielsen Ltd v The Lowry Development Co Ltd, unreported, June
29, 2000, TCC C-035
Chromalloy Aeroservices, a Division of Chromalloy Gas Turbine Corp v The
Arab Republic of Egypt, 939 F. Supp. 907 (D.D.C. 1996) C-040, C-046
City of Parkersburg v Turner Construction Co, 612 F. 2d 155 (4th Cir., 1980) C-073
Commonwealth Coatings Corp v Continental Casualty Co, 393 U.S. 145;
89 S.Ct. 337 (1968) C-041
Compagnie d'Armement Maritime SA v Compagnie Tunisienne de Navigation
SA [1971] A.C. 572; [1970] 3 W.L.R. 389; [1970] 3 All E.R. 71; [1970] 2 Lloyd's
Rep. 99; (1970) 114 S.J. 618 .... C-042
Compania de Navegacion v Financiera Bosnia SA v National Unity Marine
Salvage Corp, 457 F. Supp. 1013 (S.D.N.Y. 1978) C-087
—— v National Unity Marine Salvage Corp, 457 F. Supp. 1013 (S.D.N.Y.
1978) C-037
Compania Espanola de Petroleos SA v Nereus Shipping SA, 527 F. 2d 966 (2d
Cir., 1975) C-014
Cooper Ateliers de la Motobecane, 57 N.Y. 2d 408; 456 N.Y.S. 2d 728 (1982) .. C-087
Coppée-Lavalin SA/NV v Ken-Ren Chemicals and Fertilizers Ltd (In liquidation
in Kenya); Voest Alpine Aktiengesellschaft v Ken-Ren Chemicals and
Fertilizers Ltd (In liquidation in Kenya) [1995] 1 A.C. 38; [1994] 2 W.L.R. 631;

[1994] 2 All E.R. 449; [1994] 2 Lloyd's Rep. 109; (1994) 91(23) L.S.G. 27;
(1994) 144 N.L.J. 636; (1994) 138 S.J.L.B. 103 .... C-025, C-043
Czarnikow v Roth, Schmidt & Co [1922] 2 K.B. 478; (1922) 12 Ll. L. Rep. 195 .... C-104
Dalmia Dairy Industries Ltd v National Bank of Pakistan [1978] 2 Lloyd's
Rep. 223; [1977] 121 S.J. 442 .... C-045
Deutsche Schachtbau- und Tiefbohrgesellschaft mbH ("DST") v Ras Al
Khaimah National Oil Co ("Ratokil") [1990] 1 A.C. 295; [1988] 3 W.L.R.
230; [1988] 2 All E.R. 833; [1988] 2 Lloyd's Rep. 293; (1988) 85(28) L.S.G.
45 .... C-046, C-064
Ethiopian Oilseeds & Pulses Export Corp v Rio Del Mar Foods Inc [1990] 1
Lloyd's Rep. 86 .... C-020, C-047, C-076
European Gas Turbines SA (France) v Westman International Ltd (UK) (1995)
XX Yearbook Commercial Arbitration 198 .... C-048
Everglade Maritime Inc v Schiffahrtgesellschaft Detlef von Appen mbH (The
Maria) [1993] Q.B. 780; [1993] 3 W.L.R. 176; [1993] 3 All E.R. 748; [1993] 2
Lloyd's Rep. 168 .... C-049
Fertilizer Corp of India v IDI Management Inc, 530 F. Supp. 542 (1982) C-050,
C-058
Filia Compania Naviera v Petroship SA, 1982 A.M.C. 1217 at 1222–1223
(S.D.N.Y. 1982) C-037
Fillite (Runcorn) Ltd v Aqua-Lift (a firm), 45 B.L.R. 27; [1989] 5 Const.L.J. 197,
CA C-020, C-051, C-076
First Options of Chicago, Inc v Kaplan, et uxor and MK Investments, Inc, 514
U.S. 938 (1995) C-052
Fotochrome Inc v Copal Company Ltd, 517 F. 2d 512 (2d Cir. 1975) C-053
Fougerolle SA (France) v Procofrance SA (France) (1994) XIX Yearbook
Commercial Arbitration 205 .... C-054
Frota Oceanica Brasiliera SA v Steamship Mutual Underwriting Association
(Bermuda) Ltd (The Frotanorte) [1996] 2 Lloyd's Rep. 461; [1997] C.L.C.
230 .... C-055
Garrity v Lyle Stuart, Inc, 48 A.D. 2d 814 .... C-075
Gemanco v SAEPA, June 2, 1989 .... C-001
General National Maritime Transport Company ("GMTC"), as legal successor
of Libyan General Maritime Transport Organization (GMTO) (Libyan) v AB
Götaverken Arendal (Swedish) (1981) VI Yearbook Commercial Arbitration
221; 20 I.L.M. 883; (1980) Revue de l'arbitrage 524 .... C-056
Genesco, Inc v T. Kakiuchi & Co, Ltd, T. Kakiuchi America, Inc; Peel Textiles
Ltd and Frederick H. Schmeling, 815 F. 2d.830 (2d.Cir., 1987) C-057
Ghirardosi v Minister of Highways for British Columbia [1966] S.C.R. 367; 56
D.L.R. (2d) 469 .... C-058
Halki Shipping Corp v Sopex Oils Ltd (The Halki) [1997] EWCA Civ 3062;
[1998] 1 W.L.R. 726; [1998] 2 All E.R. 23; [1998] 1 Lloyd's Rep. 465; [1998]
C.L.C. 583; (1998) 142 S.J.L.B. 44; [1998] N.P.C. 4 .... C-059
Harbour Assurance Co Ltd v Kansa General Insurance Ltd [1993] Q.B. 701; [1993]
3 W.L.R. 42; [1993] 3 All E.R. 897; [1993] 1 Lloyd's Rep. 455 .... C-051, C-060, C-064
Hebei Import and Export Corp v Polytek Engineering Co Ltd [1999] H.K.C.
205 .... C-001
Heyman v Darwins Ltd [1942] A.C. 356; 11 L.J.K.B. 241; [1942] 1 All E.R. 337;
166 L.T. 306; 58 T.L.R. 169; (1942) 72 Ll.L. Rep. 65, HL C-024, C-061, C-064
Himmerland, The. See A/S Det Dansk-Franske Dampskibselskab v Compagnie
Financière D'Investissements Transatlantiques SA (Compafina) (The
Himmerland)
Hiscox v Outhwaite (No.1) [1992] 1 A.C. 562; [1991] 3 W.L.R. 297; [1991] 3 All
E.R. 641; [1991] 2 Lloyd's Rep. 435, HL; affirming [1991] 2 W.L.R. 1321;
[1991] 3 All E.R. 124; [1991] 2 Lloyd's Rep. 1, CA C-056, C-062

Home and Overseas Insurance Co Ltd v Mentor Insurance Co (UK) Ltd (In liquidation) [1990] 1 W.L.R. 153; [1989] 3 All E.R. 74; [1989] 1 Lloyd's Rep. 473; (1989) 86(7) L.S.G. 36; (1989) 133 S.J. 44 .... C-063
Hub Power Company Ltd ("HUBCO") v Pakistan Water and Power Development Authority ("WAPDA") and Federation of Pakistan, P.L.D. 2000 S.C. 841; (1999) C.L.C. Karachi 1320 .... C-064
I.T.A.D. Associates Inc (Respondent) v Podar Bros (Appellant), 636 F. 2d 75 (4th Cir., 1981) C-073
International Bulk Shipping and Services Ltd v Minerals and Metals Trading Corp of India; International Bulk Shipping and Services Ltd v President of India; Himoff Maritime Enterprises Ltd v President of India [1996] 1 All E.R. 1017; [1996] 2 Lloyd's Rep. 474 .... C-065, C-066, C-067
International Shoe Co v Washington, 326 U.S. 310 (1945) C-037
International Standard Electric Corp v Bridas Sociedad Anonima Petrolera, Industrial Y Commercial, 745 F. Supp. 172 (S.D.N.Y. 1990) C-068
International Tank and Pipes AK v Kuwait Aviation Fuelling Co KSC [1975] Q.B. 224; [1974] 3 W.L.R. 721; [1975] 1 All E.R. 242; [1975] 1 Lloyd's Rep. 8; 5 B.L.R. 147; 118 S.J. 752 .... C-069
Ipitrade International SA v Federal Republic of Nigeria, 465 F. Supp. 824 (1978) 17 ILM 1395 (1979) C-070, C-082
Ipswich Borough Council v Fisons plc [1990] Ch. 709; [1990] 2 W.L.R. 108; [1990] 1 All E.R. 730; [1990] 04 E.G. 127; (1990) 87(7) L.S.G. 32; (1990) 134 S.J. 517 .... C-078
Iran Aircraft Industries and Iran Helicopter Support and Renewal Co v Avco Corp, 980 F. 2d 141 (2d Cir., 1992) C-071
Island Archon, The. *See* Triad Shipping Co v Stellar Chartering & Brokerage Inc (The Island Archon)
Island Territory of Curacao v Solitron Devices Inc, 356 F. App. 1 (S.D.N.Y. 1973) C-072
Joan Garrity v Lyle Stuart Inc, 40 N.Y. 2d 354 (1976); 353 N.E. 2d 793; 386 N.Y.S. 2d 831 (1976) C-075, C-129
K/S Norjarl A/S v Hyundai Heavy Industries Co Ltd [1992] Q.B. 863; [1991] 3 W.L.R. 1025; [1991] 3 All E.R. 211; [1991] 1 Lloyd's Rep. 524; [1991] E.G.C.S. 20; (1991) 141 N.L.J. 343 .... C-077
Kalamazoo Spice Extraction Co v Provisional Military Government of Socialist Ethiopia, 729 F. 2d 422 (6th Cir., 1984) at 426 .... C-008
Kalliopi, The. *See* Marc Rich & Co Ltd v Tourloti Compania Naviera SA (The Kalliopi A)
Kaverit Steel and Crane Ltd v Kone Corp, 87 D.L.R. (4th) 129, CA; (1992) 120 A.R. 346; 85 Alta.L.R. (2d) 287; 4 C.P.C. (3d) 99; 40 C.P.R. (2d) 161, CA; (1994) XVII Yearbook Commercial Arbitration 346 .... C-020, C-076
Kyocera Corp v Prudential-Bache Trade Services Inc; LaPine Technology Corp v Kyocera Corp (Lapine II), 341 F. 3d 987 (9th Cir. 2003, en banc) cert. dismissed 124S.Ct. (1980) (2004) C-078
La Société Nationale pour la Recherche v Shaheen Natural Resources Co, 585 F. Supp. 57 (S.D.N.Y. 1983); affirmed 733 F. 2d 260 (2d Cir., 1984), cert. denied, 469 U.S. 883 (1984) C-014
Laker Airways Inc v FLS Aerospace Ltd and Burnton [2000] 1 W.L.R. 113; [1999] 2 Lloyd's Rep. 45; [1999] C.L.C. 1124 .... C-079
Laminoirs-Trefileries-Cableries de Lens SA v Southwire Company and Southwire International Corp, 484 F. Supp. 1063 (N.D.Ga. 1980) C-030, C-080
LaPine Technology Corp v Kyocera Corp (LaPine I), 130 F. 3d 884 (9th Cir.1997) C-078
Lewis v Eliades [2003] EWCA Civ 1758; [2004] 1 All E.R. 1196 .... C-030, C-034
Liamco v Libya, 62 I.L.R. 225, 228; 20 I.L.M. 893, (1981) C-082

Liberian Eastern Timber Company v Government of the Republic of Liberia,
    650 F. Supp. 73 (S.D.N.Y. 1986) 26 ILM 695 (1987) C-006, C-081
Libyan American Oil Co v Socialist People's Libyan Arab Jamahirya (formerly
    Libyan Arab Republic), 482 F. Supp. 1175 (D.D.C. 1980); 62 I.L.R. 220; 20
    I.L.M. 161 (1981) C-082
Lindner Ceilings Floors and Partitions Plc v How Engineering Services Ltd
    [2001] B.L.R. 90; [2000] All E.R.(D) 2012 .... C-049
Loewen Group, Inc and Raymond L. Loewen v United States of America, Case
    No.ARB (AF)/98/3 (ICSID); Vol. 7 ISID Reports, (Nov 2004); 4 J. World
    Investment 675 (2003) C-083
L'Office Cherifien des Phosphates v Yamashita-Shinnihon Steamship Co Ltd
    (The Boucraa) [1994] 1 A.C. 486; [1994] 2 W.L.R. 39; [1994] 1 All E.R. 20;
    [1994] 1 Lloyd's Rep. 251; (1994) 138 S.J.L.B. 19 .... C-084
McCreary Tire & Rubber Co v CEAT SpA, 501 F. 2d 1032 (3d Cir., 1974) C-037,
                                                                                            C-073, C-087
Marc Rich & Co Ltd v Tourloti Compania Naviera SA (The Kalliopi A) [1988]
    2 Lloyd's Rep. 101 .... C-085
Marine Contractors Inc v Shell Petroleum Development Co of Nigeria Ltd
    [1984] 2 Lloyd's Rep. 77; 81 L.S.Gaz.1044 .... C-086
Matter of Paver & Wildfoerster [Catholic High School Assn] 38 N.Y. 2d 669,
    677 .... C-075
Matter of Stalinski [Pyramid Elec. Co] 6 N.Y. 2d 159 .... C-075
Mernill Lynch, Pierce, Fenner & Smith, Inc v Bobker, 808 F. 2d 930 (2d
    Cir., 1986) C-038
Metropolitan World Tanker Corp v P.N. Pertambangan Minjakdangas Bumi
    Nacional, 427 F. Supp. 2 (S.D.N.Y. 1975) C-087
Michaels v Mariforum Shipping SA, 624 F. 2d 411 (2d Cir., 1980) C-117
Minmetals Germany GmbH v Ferco Steel Ltd [1999] 1 All E.R. (Comm) 315;
    [1999] C.L.C. 647 .... C-056, C-088
Mitsubishi Motors Corp v Soler Chrysler-Plymouth, Inc, 473 U.S. 614; 105
    S.Ct. 3346; 87 L.Ed. 2d. 444 (1985) 24 ILM 1064 (1985) C-024, C-089
Mobil Oil Corp, Mobil Petroleum Company Inc, Mobil Oil New Zealand v
    Her Majesty the Queen in Right of New Zealand (Case No.ARB/87/2) C-024
Monagasque De Reassurances SAM (Monde Re) v Nak Naftogaz of
    Ukraine (Naftogaz) and State of Ukraine (Ukraine), 311 F. 3d 488 (2d Cir.,
    2002) C-090
Moses H. Cone Memorial Hospital v Mercury Construction Corp, 460 U.S. 1
    (1983) C-129
Myron, The. *See* Owners of the MV Myron v Tradax Export SA Panama City
    RP (The Myron)
Nagasaki Spirit, The. *See* Semco Salvage & Marine Pte Ltd v Lancer Navigation
    Co. Ltd; Lancer Navigation Co Ltd v Semco Salvage & Marine Pte Ltd (The
    Nagasaki Spirit)
Naviera Amazonica Peruana SA v Compania Internacional de Seguros del Peru
    [1988] 1 Lloyd's Rep. 116 .... C-091, C-125
Nea Agrex SA v Baltic Shipping Co Ltd (The Agios Lazaros) [1976] Q.B. 933; [1976]
    2 W.L.R. 925; [1976] 2 All E.R. 842; [1976] 2 Lloyd's Rep. 47; 120 S.J. 351 .... C-092
Nema, The. *See* Pioneer Shipping Ltd v BTP Tioxide Ltd (The Nema)
Norsolor SA (French Company) v Pabalk Ticaret Ltd (Turkish Company) 8 Ob
    520/82; (1984) IX Yearbook Commercial Arbitration 159 .... C-093
North Range Shipping v Seatrans Shipping [2002] EWCA Civ 405; [2002] 1
    W.L.R. 2397; [2002] 4 All E.R. 390; [2002] 2 All E.R. (Comm) 193; [2002] 2
    Lloyd's Rep. 1; [2002] C.L.C. 992; (2002) 99(20) L.S.G. 31 .... C-013
Northrop Corp v Triad Financial Establishment and Triad International Market-
    ing SA, 811 F. 2d 1265 (9th Cir., 1987) cert. denied, 484 U.S. 914 (1987) C-094

Nova (Jersey) Knit Ltd v Kammgarn Spinnerei GmbH [1977] 1 W.L.R. 713; [1977] 2 All E.R. 463; [1977] 1 Lloyd's Rep. 463; 121 S.J. 170 .... C-095
Ofelia Rodriquez Quijas v Shearson/American Express Inc, 490 U.S. 477; 109 S.Ct.1917 (1989) C-096, C-128
Orion Compania Espanola de Seguros v Belfort Maatschappij Voor Algemene Verzekgringeen [1962] 2 Lloyd's Rep. 257 .... C-097
Overseas Union Insurance Ltd v AA Mutual International Insurance Co Ltd [1988] 2 Lloyd's Rep. 63; [1988] F.T.L.R. 421 .... C-020, C-076, C-098
Owners of the MV Myron v Tradax Export SA Panama City RP (The Myron) [1970] 1 Q.B. 527; [1969] 3 W.L.R. 292; [1969] 2 All E.R. 1263; [1969] 1 Lloyd's Rep. 411; 113 S.J. 404 .... C-099
Pabalk Ticaret Ltd Sirketi (Turkey) v Norsolor SA (France) (1986) XI Yearbook Commercial Arbitration 484; [1985] Dalloz 101; (1985) 24 I.L.M.360 .... C-100
Pando Compania Naviera SA v Filmo SAS [1975] Q.B. 742; [1975] 2 W.L.R. 636; [1975] 2 All E.R. 515; [1975] 1 Lloyd's Rep. 560; 119 S.J. 253 .... C-101
Paramount Carriers Corp v Cook Industries, 465 F. Supp. 599; 1979 A.M.C. 875 (S.D.N.Y. 1979) C-037
Parsons & Whittemore Overseas Co Inc v Société Générale de l'Industrie de Papier, and Bank of America, 508 F. 2d 969 (2d.Cir. 1974) C-102
Patel v Patel [1999] B.L.R.227 .... C-073, C-108
Paul Smith Ltd v H & S International Holding Inc [1991] 2 Lloyd's Rep. 127 .... C-056, C-103
Pennzoil Exploration and Production Co v Ramco Energy Ltd, 139 F. 3d 1061 (5th Cir., 1998) C-047
Peterson Farms Inc v C&M Farms Ltd [2004] EWHC Comm 121 .... C-052
Pioneer Shipping Ltd v BTP Tioxide Ltd (The Nema) [1982] A.C. 724; [1981] 3 W.L.R. 292; [1981] 2 All E.R. 1030; [1981] 2 Lloyd's Rep. 239; [1981] Com. L.R. 197; 125 S.J. 542, HL; affirming [1980] Q.B. 547; [1980] 3 W.L.R. 326; [1980] 3 All E.R. 117; [1980] 2 Lloyd's Rep. 339; [1980] E.C.C. 467 .... C-078, C-097, C-104
Prima Paint Corp v Flood & Conklin Manufacturing Co, 388 U.S. 395; 18 L.Ed. 2d 1270; 87 S.Ct. 1801 (1967) C-027, C-072, C-105
Rena K, The [1979] Q.B. 377; [1978] 3 W.L.R. 431; [1979] 1 All E.R. 397; [1978] 1 Lloyd's Rep. 545; 122 S.J. 315 .... C-106
Rhone Mediterranée Compagnia Francese di Assicurazioni e Riassicurazioni v Achille Lauro, dba Achille Lauro Armatore, aka Achille Lauro, dba Flotta Lauro, aka Achille Lauro, dba Lauro Lines, X company, 712 F. 2d 50 (3d Cir., 1983) C-107
Richard Hoeft III v MVL Group, Inc 343 F.3d57 (2d.Cir.2003) C-078
Roussel-Uchaf v G.D. Searle & Co Ltd and G.D. Searle & Co [1978] 1 Lloyd's Rep. 225; [1978] F.S.R. 95; [1978] R.P.C. 747 .... C-076, C-108
Royal Bank of Canada v Cooperatieve Centrale Raiffeisen-Boerenleenbank BA [2004] EWCA Civ 7; 148 Sol.Jo.L.B.147; [2004] All E.R.(D) 216 .... C-004
Ryan (J.J.) & Sons Inc v Rhone Poulenc Textile SA, 863 F. 2d 315 (4th Cir., 1988) C-074
Sam Reisfeld & Son Import Co v SA Eteco, 530 F. 2d 679 (5th Cir., 1976) C-074
Santa Clara, The. See Vitol SA v Norlef Ltd (The Santa Clara)
Scheffer v Heitner, 433 U.S. 186 (1977) C-026, C-037
Scherk v Alberto-Culver Co, 417 U.S. 506 (1974); 94 S.Ct. 2449; 41 L.Ed. 2d. 270 (1974) C-014, C-024, C-073, C-076, C-087, C-090, C-094, C-109, C-128
Sea Containers Ltd v ICT Pty [2002] N.S.W.C.A. 84 .... C-077
Sellar v Highland Railway Co [1918] S.C. 838; [1919] S.C. (H.L.) 19 .... C-058
Semco Salvage & Marine Pte Ltd v Lancer Navigation Co. Ltd; Lancer Navigation Co. Ltd v Semco Salvage & Marine Pte Ltd (The Nagasaki Spirit) [1996] 1 Lloyd's Rep. 449; [1996] C.L.C. 658; [1996] 5 Re. L.R. 70; (1996) 140 S.J.L.B. 35 .... C-110, C-111, C-112

Shearson/American Express Inc and Mary Ann McNulty v Eugene McMahon,
   482 U.S. 220; 107 S.Ct. 2332; 96 Led. 2d 185 (1987) C-096, C-113, C-128
Shenzhen Nan Da Industrial and Trade United Company Ltd (nationality not
   indicated) v FM International Ltd (Hong Kong); [1992] HKCFI 49; (1993)
   XVIII Yearbook Commercial Arbitration 377 .... C-114
Simonburn, The. *See* Agro Company of Canada Ltd v Richmond Shipping Ltd
   (The Simonburn)
Société Grands Moulins de Strasbourg (France) v Cie Continentale France
   (France) (1991) XVI Yearbook Commercial Arbitration 129 .... C-115
Solon, The. *See* Cero Navigation Corp v Jean Lion & Cie (The Solon)
Soules CAF v Louis Dreyfus Negoce SA [2000] 2 All E.R. (Comm) 154; [2000]
   2 Lloyd's Rep. 307; [2001] C.L.C. 797 .... C-116
Southern Seas Navigation Ltd of Monrovia, as owner of the Messiniaki Floga
   v Petroleos Mexicanos of Mexico City, 606 F. Supp. 692 (S.D.N.Y. 1985)
   [1985] AMC 2190; (1986) XI Yearbook Commercial Arbitration 209 .... C-117
Sperry International Trade v Government of Israel, 689 F. 2d 301 (2d
   Cir., 1982) C-117, C-118
Star Shipping AS v China National Foreign Trade Transportation Corp (The
   Star Texas) [1993] 2 Lloyd's Rep. 445 .... C-119
Star Texas, The. *See* Star Shipping AS v China National Foreign Trade
   Transportation Corp (The Star Texas)
State of New York Department of Taxation and Finance v Saverio J. Valenti, 57
   A.D. 2d 174; 393 N.Y.S. 2d 797 .... C-120
Succula Ltd and Pomona Shipping Co Ltd v Harland and Wolff Ltd [1980] 2
   Lloyd's Rep. 381 .... C-121
Sumitomo Heavy Industries Ltd v Oil and Natural Gas Commission [1994] 1
   Lloyd's Rep. 45 .... C-122
Szilard v Szaz [1955] 1 D.L.R. 370; S.C.R. 3 .... C-058
Tennessee Imports Inc v Filippi, 745 F. Supp. 1314 (M.D. Tenn. 1990) C-087
Triad Shipping Co v Stellar Chartering & Brokerage Inc (The Island Archon)
   [1995] 1 All E.R. 595; [1994] 2 Lloyd's Rep. 227 .... C-123
Turner v Stevenage Borough Council [1997] EWCA Civ 1184; [1998] Ch. 28;
   [1997] 3 W.L.R. 309; [1997] 16 L.S.Gaz.R. 29 .... C-077
Underhill v Hernandez, 168 U.S. 250 (1897); 18 S.Ct. C-082
UNESCO – United Nations Educational, Scientific and Cultural Organisation,
   in the person of its legal representatives (France) v Max-Henri Boulois
   (France) (1999) XXIV Yearbook Commercial Arbitration 294 .... C-124
Union of India v McDonnell Douglas Corp [1993] 2 Lloyd's Rep. 48 ... C-091, C-125
United Steelworkers of America v Enterprise Wheel & Car Corp, 363 U.S. 593,
   598; 80 S.Ct.1343; 4 L.Ed2d 1403 (1960) C-126, C-128
Vitol SA v Norlcf Ltd (The Santa Clara) [1996] A.C. 800; [1996] 3 W.L.R. 105;
   [1996] 3 All E.R. 193; [1996] 2 Lloyd's Rep. 225; [1996] C.L.C. 1159; (1996)
   15 Tr. L.R. 347; (1996) 93(26) L.S.G. 19; (1996) 146 N.L.J. 957; (1996) 140
   S.J.L.B. 147 .... C-127
Wilko v Swan, doing Business as Hayden, Stone & Co, 346 U.S. 427 (1953); 74
   S.Ct. 182 (1953) C-038, C-089, C-096, C-109, C-113, C-128
Willoughby Roofing and Supply Company Inc v Kajima International Inc, 776
   F. 2d 269 (11th Cir., 1985) C-075, C-129
XL Insurance Ltd v Owens Corning [2001] 1 All E.R. (Comm) 530; [2000] 2
   Lloyd's Rep. 500; [2001] C.P. Rep. 22; [2001] C.L.C. 914 .... C-130

Table of Materials

This Table refers to both volumes. Paragraph numbers prefixed with a number refer to Volume 1: Materials. Paragraph numbers prefixed with a 'C' refer to Volume 2: Cases

International Arbitration and A.D.R. Statutes
ENGLISH AND IRISH STATUTES
England
1889 Arbitration Act (52 & 53 Vict. c.49)
   s.4 ....C–061
1930 Arbitration (Foreign Awards) Act (20 & 21 Geo.5 c.15)............................C–059
1950 Arbitration Act (14 Geo. 6 c.27) C–025, C–055, C–062, C–069, C–077, C–092
   s.1 ....C–121
   s.4 ....C–063
   s.7 ....C–101
   s.9 ....C–101
   s.10 ....C–002, C–055, C–121
      (b) C–121
   s.12(6)...C–039
      (a).......................C–025, C–044
      (h) C–039
   s.13(3)..C–121
   s.13A C–084
   s.18(1) C–049
   s.22..C–062
   s.23..C–021
      (1) C–077
   s.24(2) C–020
      (4) C–020
   s.27 ....C–005, C–019, C–069, C–092
1975 Arbitration Act (c.3) C–062, C–108
   s.1 ....C–039, C–047, C–060, C–095, C–098, C–108, C–119
      (1) C–039, C–095, C–106
   s.3(2) C–062
   s.5(2) C–062
      (5) C–062
   s.7(1) C–062

International Arbitration and A.D.R. Statutes—cont.
ENGLISH AND IRISH STATUTES—cont.
England—cont.
1979 Arbitration Act (c.42).........C–062, C–097, C–104
   s.1 ....C–016
      (3) C–078
      (b) C–013, C–062, C–104
      (4) C–078
      (5) C–062
      (6A) C–013
      (7) C–127
   s.3 ....C–104
      (1) **C–016**
   s.4 ....C–104
   s.5 ....C–122
1996 Arbitration Act (c.23) **1–001**, C–055, C–059, C–097, C–104, C–107, C–126
   s.1 ....C–044
   ss.1–5 General principles 1–002–1–006
   s.3 ....C–062
   s.5 ....C–061, C–130
      (3) C–016
   ss.6–8 The arbitration agreement 1–007–1–009
   s.7 ....C–061, C–105
   s.9 ....C–059
      (2) C–039
      (4) C–059
   ss.9–11 Stay of legal proceedings......................1–010–1–012
   s.12 ....C–005, C–019, C–036, C–069, C–092
   ss.12–14 Commencement of arbitral proceedings....1–013–1–015
   s.15(2)...C–107

International Arbitration and A.D.R. Statutes—*cont.*
ENGLISH AND IRISH STATUTES—*cont.*
England—*cont.*
1996 Arbitration Act (c.23)—*cont.*
  ss.15–29 The arbitral tribunal 1–016–1–030
  s.24(1)(a) C–079
  s.29 .... C–018
  s.30 .... C–130
  ss.30–32 Jurisdiction of the arbitral tribunal 1–031–1–033
  s.33 .... C–044
  ss.33–41 The arbitral proceedings 1–034–1–042
  s.38 .... C–025, C–044
  s.42 .... C–084
  ss.42–45 Powers of court in relation to arbitral proceedings 1–043–1–046
  s.44 .... C–025, C–044
  s.45 .... C–126
  ss.46–58 The award 1–047–1–059
  s.49 .... C–080
  s.54 .... C–126
  ss.59–65 Costs of the arbitration 1–060–1–066
  ss.66–71 Powers of the court in relation to the award ... 1–067–1–072
  s.67 .... C–052
  s.69 .... C–086, C–104, C–126
  ss.72–75 Miscellaneous .. 1–073–1–076
  s.73 .... C–080
  ss.76–84 Supplementary . 1–077–1–085
  ss.85–88 Domestic arbitration agreements 1–086–1–089
  ss.89–91 Consumer arbitration agreements 1–090–1–092
  s.92 Small claims arbitration in the county court 1–093
  s.93 Appointment of judges as arbitrators 1–094
  ss.94–98 Statutory arbitrations 1–095–1–099
  s.99 Enforcement of Geneva Convention awards 1–100
  ss.100–104 Recognition and enforcement of New York Convention awards 1–101–1–105
  s.101 .... C–088
  s.102 .... C–069
  s.103 .... C–088
    (2)(c) C–088
  ss.105–110 General provisions 1–106–1–111

International Arbitration and A.D.R. Statutes—*cont.*
ENGLISH AND IRISH STATUTES—*cont.*
Ireland
1998 Arbitration (International Commercial) Act **1–112**
  ss.1, 2 Pt I Preliminary and General 1–113–1–114
  ss.3–16 Pt II International Commercial Arbitration 1–115–1–127
  ss.17, 18 Pt III Amendments to Arbitration Acts 1–128– 1–129
  Sch. Text of UNCITRAL Model Law on International Commercial Arbitration 1–130–1–166

OTHER ENGLISH STATUTES
1906 Marine Insurance Act (6 Edw. 7 c.41)
  Sch.1 .... C–011
1939 Limitation Act (2 & 3 Geo. 6 c.21)
  s.27(3) C–092
1967 Misrepresentation Act (c.7)
  s.2(1) C–051
1974 Insurance Companies Act (c.49) C–060
1978 State Immunity Act (c33) C–005
  s.3(1) C–006
   (3) C–006
  s.13(2) C–005
   (b) C–006
   (4) C–006
  s.17(1) C–005
1980 Protection of Trading Interests Act (c.11)
  s.5 .... C–034
   (1) C–034
1981 Insurance Companies Act (c.31) C–060
1981 Supreme Court Act (c.54)
  s.37 .... C–039
1982 Civil Jurisdiction and Judgments Act (c.27)
  s.26 .... C–106
1994 Merchant Shipping (Salvage and Pollution) Act (c.28) C–112
1998 Human Rights Act (c.42) C–013

STATUTORY INSTRUMENTS
1965 Rules of the Supreme Court (SI 1965/1776)
Ord.11, r.1 ....C–119
    (f)(iii) C–011
    r.4(2) C–011
Ord.14 ....C–063, C–103
Ord.15, r.6 ....C–067
Ord.20, r.5 ....C–067
    (3) C–067
Ord.75, r.13(4) C–106

FOREIGN STATUTES: EUROPEAN JURISDICTIONS
Austria
1983 Code of Civil Procedure
Art. 595, s.5 ....C–093
    s.6 ....C–093

France
1981 New Code of Civil Procedure (Book 4)
Art.12......................................C–100
Title V International Arbitration Arts 1492–1497...1–186–1–190a
Title V International Arbitration Art.1502........................C–017
    (5) C–001, C–115
Title V International Arbitration Art.1504........................C–017
Title V International Arbitration Art.1507........................C–017, C–054
Title VI Chapter I The recognition and enforcement of arbitral awards rendered abroad or in international arbitration Arts 1498–1500 1–191–1–194
Title VI Chapter II Challenge of arbitral awards rendered abroad or in international arbitration Arts 1501–1507 1–195–1–201

Germany
1998 German Arbitration Law
s.1025 Scope of application..1–202
s.1026 Extent of court intervention 1–203
s.1027 Loss of right to object.....1–204
s.1028 Receipt of written communications in case of unknown whereabouts 1–205
s.1029 Definition.......................1–206
s.1030 Arbitrability 1–207

FOREIGN STATUTES: EUROPEAN JURISDICTIONS—cont.
Germany—cont.
1998 German Arbitration Law—cont.
s.1031 Form of arbitration agreement 1–208
s.1032 Arbitration agreement and substantive claim before court 1–209
s.1033 Arbitration agreement and interim measures by court.....................................1–210
s.1034 Composition of arbitral tribunal 1–211
s.1035 Appointment of arbitrators 1–212
s.1036 Challenge of an arbitrator 1–213
s.1037 Challenge procedure.......1–214
s.1038 Failure or impossibility to act 1–215
s.1039 Appointment of substitute arbitrator......................1–216
s.1040 Competence of arbitral tribunal to rule on its jurisdiction 1–217
s.1041 Interim measures of protection 1–218
s.1042 General rules of procedure.......................................1–219
s.1043 Place of arbitration 1–220
s.1044 Commencement of arbitral proceedings 1–221
s.1045 Language of proceedings ..1–222
s.1046 Statements of claim and defence.........................1–223
s.1047 Oral hearings and written proceedings................1–224
s.1048 Default of a party...........1–225
s.1049 Expert appointed by arbitral tribunal 1–226
s.1050 Court assistance in taking evidence and other judicial acts..........................1–227
s.1051 Rules applicable to substance of dispute...................1–228
s.1052 Decision making by panel of arbitrators...............1–229
s.1053 Settlement 1–230
s.1054 Form and contents of award...................................1–231
s.1055 Effect of arbitral award...1–232
s.1056 Termination of proceedings...............................1–233
s.1057 Decision on costs............1–234

FOREIGN STATUTES: EUROPEAN JURISDICTIONS—*cont.*
Germany—*cont.*
1998 German Arbitration Law—*cont.*
 s.1058 Correction and interpretation of award 1–235
 s.1059 Application for setting aside 1–236
 s.1060 Domestic awards 1–237
 s.1061 Foreign awards 1–238
 s.1062 Competence 1–239
 s.1063 General provisions 1–240
 s.1064 Particularities regarding the enforcement of awards 1–241
 s.1065 Legal remedies 1–242
 s.1066 Mutatis mutandis application of the provisions of the Tenth Book 1–243
Russia
1993 Law of the Russian Federation on International Commercial Arbitration
 Art.1 Scope of Application 1–245
 Art.2 Definitions and Rules of Interpretation 1–246
 Art.3 Receipt of Written Communications 1– 247
 Art.4 Waiver of Right to Object .. 1–248
 Art.5 Extent of Court Intervention 1–249
 Art.6 Authority for Certain Functions of Arbitration Assistance and Control 1–250
 Art.7 Definition and Form of Arbitration Agreement 1–251
 Art.8 Arbitration and Agreement and Substantive Claim Before Court 1–252
 Art.9 Arbitration and Agreement and Interim Measures by Court 1–253
 Art.10 Number of Arbitrators ... 1–254
 Art.11 Appointment of Arbitrators 1–255
 Art.12 Grounds for Challenge of Arbitrator 1–256
 Art.13 Challenge Procedure 1–257
 Art.14 Termination of Authority (Mandate) of Arbitrator 1–258
 Art.15 Substitution of Arbitrator 1–259
 Art.16 Competence of Arbitral Tribunal to Rule on its Jurisdiction 1–260

FOREIGN STATUTES: EUROPEAN JURISDICTIONS—*cont.*
Russia—*cont.*
1993 Law of the Russian Federation on International Commercial Arbitration—*cont.*
 Art.17 Power of Arbitral Tribunal to Order Interim Measures 1–261
 Art.18 Equal Treatment of Parties 1–262
 Art.19 Determination of Rules of Procedure 2–263
 Art.20 Place of Arbitration 1–264
 Art.21 Commencement of Arbitral Proceedings 1–265
 Art.22 Language 1–266
 Art.23 Statements of Claim and Defence 1–267
 Art.24 Hearings and Written Proceedings 1–268
 Art.25 Failure to Submit Documents or to Appear at Hearing 1–269
 Art.26 Expert Appointed by Arbitral Tribunal 1–270
 Art.27 Court Assistance in Taking Evidence 1–271
 Art.28 Rules Applicable to Substance of Dispute 1–272
 Art.29 Decision Making by Panel of Arbitrators 1–273
 Art.30 Settlement 1–274
 Art.31 Form and Contents of Award 1–275
 Art.32 Termination of Arbitral Proceedings 1–276
 Art.33 Correction and Interpretation of Award 1–277
 Art.34 Application for Setting Aside as Exclusive Recourse Against Arbitral Award 1–278
 Art.35 Recognition and Enforcement 1–279
 Art.36 Grounds for Refusing Recognition or Enforcement of Arbitral Award 1–280
Switzerland
1987 Federal Code on Private International Law (c.12)
 Art.176 Scope of application; seat of the arbitral tribunal ... 1–167
 Art.177 Arbitrability 1–168

FOREIGN STATUTES: EUROPEAN JURISDICTIONS—cont.
Switzerland —cont.
1987 Federal Code on Private International Law (c.12)—cont.
    Art.178 Arbitration agreement ..1–169
    Art.179 Arbitral tribunal..........1–170
    Art.180 Challenge of arbitrators..1–171
    Art.181 Lis pendens 1–172
    Art.182 General rule 1–173
    Art.183 Provisional and protective measures 1–174
    Art.184 Taking of evidence 1–175
    Art.185 Further assistance by the judge 1–176
    Art.186 Jurisdiction 1–177
    Art.187 Applicable law.............1–178
    Art.188 Partial award................1–179
    Art.189 Arbitral award.............1–180
    Art.190 General rule 1–181
    Art.191 Court of appeal............1–182
    Art.192 Waiver of appeal 1–183
    Art.193 Deposit and certificate of enforceability.............1–184
    Art.194 Foreign arbitral awards 1–185

FOREIGN STATUTES: NON-EUROPEAN JURISDICTIONS
Australia
1974 International Arbitration Act
    s.1 Short title of Principal Act ...1–313
    s.2 Commencement...................1–314
    s.2A Territories.........................1–315
    s.2B Crown to be bound............1–316
    s.2C Carriage of goods by sea ...1–317
    s.3 Interpretation 1–318
    s.4 Accession to Convention......1–319
    s.7 Enforcement of foreign arbitration agreements 1–320
    s.8 Recognition of foreign awards 1–321
    s.9 Evidence of awards and arbitration agreements 1–322
    s.10 Evidence relating to Convention 1–323
    s.10A Delegation by Secretary to the Department of Foreign Affairs and Trade 1–324
    s.12 Effect of this Part on other laws 1–325
    s.13 Judiciary Act...................1–325/1

FOREIGN STATUTES: NON-EUROPEAN JURISDICTIONS—cont.
Australia—cont.
1974 International Arbitration Act—cont.
    s.14 Application of Part 1–325/2
    s.15 Interpretation..................1–325/3
    s.16 Model Law to have force of law 1–325/4
    s.17 Interpretation of Model Law—use of extrinsic material 1–325/5
    s.18 Courts specified for purposes of Article 6 of Model Law 1–325/6
    s.19 Articles 34 and 36 of Model Law—public policy...............................1–325/7
    s.20 Chapter VIII of Model Law not to apply in certain cases 1–325/8
    s.21 Settlement of dispute otherwise than in accordance with Model Law.................1–325/9
    s.22 Application of optional provisions........................1–325/10
    s.23 Orders under Article 17 of the Model Law 1–325/11
    s.24 Consolidation of arbitral proceedings 1–325/12
    s.25 Interest up to making of award 1–325/13
    s.26 Interest on debt under award 1–325/14
    s.27 Costs...........................1–325/14a
    s.28 Liability of arbitrator 1–325/15
    s.29 Representation in proceedings 1–325/16
    s.30 Application of Part........1–325/17
    s.31 Interpretation................1–325/18
    s.32 Application of Investment Convention to Australia 1–325/19
    s.33 Award is binding..........1–325/19a
    s.34 Investment Convention awards to prevail over other laws 1–325/20
    s.35 Recognition of awards 1–325/21
    s.36 Evidence relating to Investment Convention 1–325/22
    s.37 Representation in proceedings 1–325/23
    s.38 Judiciary Act.................1–325/24

FOREIGN STATUTES: NON-EUROPEAN JURISDICTIONS—*cont.*
Australia—*cont.*
1974 International Arbitration Act—*cont.*
  Sch. 1—United Nations Conference on International Commercial Arbitration Convention on the Recognition and Enforcement of Foreign Arbitral Awards 1–325/24a–1–325/39
  Sch. 2—UNCITRAL Model Law on International Commercial Arbitration (as adopted by the United Nations Commission on International Trade Law on 21 June 1985) 1–325/40–1–325/74
  Sch. 3—Convention on the Settlement of Investment Disputes Between States and Nationals of Other States 1–325/75–1–325/98
Canada
1985 Companies' Creditors Arrangement Act..................C–083
1986 International Commercial Arbitration Act (Alberta)......C–076
  s.2 ....C–076
China
1994 Arbitration Law of the People's Republic of China
  Arts 1–9 Chapter I General Principles 1–326–1–334
  Arts 10–15 Chapter II The Arbitration Commission and Arbitration Association 1–335–1–340
  Arts 16–20 Chapter III Arbitration Agreement 1–341–1–345
  Arts 21–29 Chapter IV Arbitration Procedure Section 1 Application and Acceptance 1–346–1–354
  Arts 30–38 Section 2 The Formation of an Arbitration Tribunal..............1–355–1–363
  Arts 39–57 Section 3 Hearing and Ruling 1–364–1–382
  Arts 58–61 Chapter V Request to Repeal a Ruling 1–380–1–386

FOREIGN STATUTES: NON-EUROPEAN JURISDICTIONS—*cont.*
China —*cont.*
1994 Arbitration Law of the People's Republic of China —*cont.*
  Arts 62–64 Chapter VI Execution 1–387–1–389
  Arts 65–73 Chapter VII Special Provision for Arbitrations Involving Foreign Concerns 1–390–1–398
  Arts 74–80 Chapter VIII Supplementary Articles ...1–399–1–405
China Rules
  China International Economic Trade Arbitration Commission Rules.................C–114
  Art.14......................................C–088
  Art.20......................................C–088
  Art.53......................................C–088
Egypt
1994 Egyptian Arbitration Act in Civil and Commercial Matters
Law No. 27 for 1994 promulgating the Law concerning Arbitration in Civil and Commercial Matters
  Arts 1–4.........................1–407–1–410
  Arts (1)–(9) Pt I General Provisions 1–411–1–419
  Arts (10)–(14) Pt II The Arbitration Agreement 1–420–1–424
  Arts (15)–(24) Pt III The Arbitral Panel 1–425–1–434
  Arts (25)–(38) Pt IV Conduct of the Arbitral Proceedings 1–435–1–448
  Arts (39)–(51) Pt V The Arbitral Award and the Closing of the Procedures 1–449–1–461
  Arts (52)–(54) Pt VI Nullity of the Arbitral Award 1–462–1–464
  Arts (55)–(58) Pt VII Recognition and Enforcement of Arbitral Awards 1–465–1–468
India
1940 Arbitration Act...................C–125
  s.33..C–122
1987 Finance Act C–122
New Zealand
1908 Arbitration Act
  s.5 ....C–024
1979 Arbitration (International Investment Disputes) Act
  s.8 ....C–024

FOREIGN STATUTES: NON-EUROPEAN JURISDICTIONS—*cont.*
New Zealand—*cont.*
1982 Arbitration (Foreign Agreements and Awards) Act
s.4 ....C–024
1986 Commerce Act
s.27..C–024
s.88..C–024
s.89..C–024
United States of America
1925 Federal Arbitration Act as amended, (codified at 9 U.S.C.) C–009, **C–010**, C–027, C–057, C–072, C–073, C–078, C–087, C–089, C–113, C–129
Ch.2 ....C–014, C–027, C–072
Ch.3 ....C–027
s.1–14 ....C–027
s.1 Maritime transactions and commerce defined 1–281
s.2 Validity, irrevocability and enforcement of agreements to arbitrate 1–282
s.3 Stay of proceedings where issue therein referable to arbitration................1–283, C–027, C–105, C–128
s.4 Failure to arbitrate under agreement 1–284
s.5 Appointment of arbitrators or umpire 1–285, C–022
s.6 Application heard as motion..................................1–286
s.7 Witnesses before arbitrators..1–287
s.8 Proceedings begun by libel in admiralty and seizure of vessel or property 1–288
s.9 Award of arbitrators; confirmation; jurisdiction; procedure............1–289, C–028, C–039
s.10 Same; vacation; grounds; rehearing..................1–290, C–027, C–041
(b) C–041
s.11 Same; modification or correction; grounds; order 1–291
s.12 Notice of motions to vacate or modify; service; stay of proceedings 1–292
s.13 Papers filed with order on motions 1–293

FOREIGN STATUTES: NON-EUROPEAN JURISDICTIONS—*cont.*
United States of America—*cont.*
1925 Federal Arbitration Act, as amended—*cont.*
s.14 Contracts not affected........1–294
s.15 Inapplicability of the Act of State doctrine 1–295
s.16 Appeals 1–296
s.201 Enforcement of Convention..1–297
s.202 Agreement or award falling under the Convention 1–298
s.203 Jurisdiction: amount in controversy 1–299
s.204 Venue..............................1–300
s.205 Removal of cases from State courts..........................1–301
s.206 Order to compel arbitration..1–302
s.207 Award of arbitrators 1–303
s.208 Chapter 1; residual application...........................1–304
s.301 Enforcement of Convention..1–305
s.302 Incorporation by reference 1–306
s.303 Order to compel arbitration..1–307
s.304 Recognition and enforcement of foreign arbitral decisions and awards 1–308
s.305 Relationship between the Inter-American Convention and the Convention on the Recognition and Enforcement of Foreign Arbitral Awards 1–309
s.306 Applicable rules of Inter-American Commercial Arbitration Commission 1–310
s.307 Chapter 1; residual application 1–311

Other U.S. Legislation
1890 Sherman Anti-Trust Act
....................C–009, C–010, C–089
1898 Bankruptcy Act C–053
Ch.XI C–053
1933 Securities Act C–089, C–096, C–128
s.12(2)......................................C–128
s.14...C–128

FOREIGN STATUTES: NON-EUROPEAN JURISDICTIONS—*cont.*
United States of America—*cont.*
Other U.S. Legislation—*cont.*
1934 Securities Exchange Act C–096, C–109, C–113
   s.10b..C–113
   s.27...C–113
   s.29(a)..C–113
1964 Foreign Assistance Act C–082
   s.2370 ....C–082
1969 Export Administration Act (50 U.S.C.App.)..............C–014
   s.3 ....C–014
     (5) C–014
1971 Restatement (Second) of Conflict of Laws
   s.66, comment a C–037
   s.187(2) C–094
     (b) C–094
1976 Arms Export Control Act....C–094
1976 Foreign Sovereign Immunities Act (codified at 28 U.S.C.) C–028, C–070, C–074, C–081, C–082
1977 Foreign Corrupt Practices Act..C–094
1978 Bankruptcy Reform Act C–053
1982 Racketeer Influenced and Corrupt Organisations Act (RICO) (codified at 18 U.S.C.) C–057, C–113
1982 Robinson-Patman Price Discrimination Act...............C–057
United States Code
   Title 9 (Arbitration) C–073, C–087
      Ch.2................C–014, C–027, C–072
       s.1 .... C–014, C–027, C–037, C–129
       s.1–3 ....**C–027**
       s.2................................C–027
       s.3 ....C–027, C–125
       s.4................................C–014
       s.9 ....C–028, C–039, C–053
       s.10 ....C–027, C–038, C–041, C–117
         (d) C–072
       s.201 ....C–001, C–070
       ss. 201–208 ....C–072, C–082
       s.202.............................C–107
       s.203 ....C–072
       s.204 ....C–070
       s.205 ....C–073, **C–087**

FOREIGN STATUTES: NON-EUROPEAN JURISDICTIONS—*cont.*
United States of America—*cont.*
United States Code—*cont.*
       s.206 ....C–014, C–073
       s.207 ....C–053, C–090
       ss. 5301–5309 ....C–072
   Title 11 (Bankruptcy),
       s.11(a)(15) C–053
       s.701 ....C–053
   Title 15 (Commerce and Trade),
       s.78dd–1(a) C–094
   Title 18 (Crimes and Criminal Procedure) C–057
       s.1962(c).......................C–113
       s.1964(c).......................C–113
   Title 22 (Foreign Relations and Intercourse), s.1603........C–082
       s.2370(e)(2) C–082
       s.2751..........................C–094
   Title 28 (Judiciary and Judicial Procedure) C–087
       ss. 201–208 ....C–087
       s.1292(a)(1)......C–074, C–117
         (b) C–087
       s.1330...C–070, C–074, C–082
         (a) C–082
         (b) C–082
       s.1331..........................C–001
       s.1332(a)(2)–(4) C–082
       s.1391(f) C–082
         (4) C–070
   Title 28, s.1441(d) C–082
       s.1602.............C–008, C–028
       s.1602–1611 ....C–028, C–082
       s.1603(d) C–028
       s.1605(a)(1) C–070
         (2) C–008
       ss.1605–1607 ....C–070
       s.1608(e)......................C–070
       s.1609...........................C–028
       s.1610..........................C–028
         (a) C–081
       s.1782..........................C–015
         (a) C–015
       s.1963..........................C–028
   Title 50, s.2402........................C–014
Rules and Codes of Procedure
   New York Civil Practice Laws and Rules (CPLR) C–072, C–120
   Art.53......................................C–072
   s.7507 ....C–120
   s.7511(b)................................C–120
   Federal Rules of Civil Procedure (FRCP)

FOREIGN STATUTES: NON-EUROPEAN JURISDICTIONS—*cont.*
United States of America—*cont.*
Rules and Codes of Procedure—*cont.*
Federal Rules of Civil Procedure—*cont.*
Rule 4(k)(2) C–026
Rule 12(b)(1) C–068
       (6) C–068
Rule 24 .... C–037
Rule 59(b) C–050
Rule 60(b)(2) C–050

UNIFORM AND MODEL LAWS
1966 European Convention Providing A Uniform Law on Arbitration
Arts 1–5 1–521–1–525
Arts 6–10 1–526–1–530
Arts 11–15 1–531–1–535
Annex I, Arts 1–31 1–536–1–566
Annex II 1–567
Annex III 1–568

1985 UNCITRAL Model Law on International Commercial Arbitration
Art.1 Scope of Application 1–470, C–061
Art.2 Definitions and rules of interpretation 1–471
Art.3 Receipt of written communications 1–472
Art.4 Waiver of right to object .. 1–473
Art.5 Extent of court intervention 1–474
Art.6 Court or other authority for certain functions of arbitration assistance and supervision 1–475
Art.7 Definition and form of arbitration agreement 1–476
Art.8 Arbitration agreement and substantive claim before court 1–477
Art.9 Arbitration agreement and interim measures by court 1–478
Art.10 Number of arbitrators 1–479
Art.11 Appointment of arbitrators 1–480
Art.12 Grounds for challenge 1–481
Art.13 Challenge procedure 1–482
Art.14 Failure or impossibility to act 1–483
Art.15 Appointment of substitute arbitrator ....

UNIFORM AND MODEL LAWS—*cont.*
1985 UNCITRAL Model Law on International Commercial Arbitration—*cont.*
Art.16 Competence of arbitral tribunal to rule on its jurisdiction 1–485
Art.17 Power of arbitral tribunal to order interim measures 1–486
Art.18 Equal treatment of parties 1–487
Art.19 Determination of rules of procedure 1–488
Art.20 Place of arbitration 1–489
Art.21 Commencement of arbitral proceedings 1–490
Art.22 Language 1–491
Art.23 Statements of claim and defence 1–492
Art.24 Hearings and written proceedings 1–493
Art.25 Default of a party 1–494
Art.26 Expert appointed by arbitral tribunal 1–495
Art.27 Court assistance in taking evidence 1–496
Art.28 Rules applicable to substance of dispute 1–497
Art.29 Decision making by panel of arbitrators 1–498
Art.30 Settlement 1–499
Art.31 Form and contents of award 1–500
Art.32 Termination of proceedings 1–501
Art.33 Correction of interpretation of award 1–502
Art.34 Application for setting aside as exclusive recourse against arbitral award 1–503
Art.35 Recognition and enforcement 1–504
Art.36 Grounds for refusing recognition or enforcement 1–505

1999 OHADA Uniform Act on Arbitration
Arts 1–4 Chapter I Scope of Application 1–569–1–572
Arts 5–8 Chapter II Constitution of the Arbitral Tribunal 1–573–1–576
Arts 9–18 Chapter III The Arbitral Hearing 1–577–1–586

UNIFORM AND MODEL LAWS—*cont.*
1999 OHADA Uniform Act on Arbitration—*cont.*
Arts 19–24 Chapter IV The Arbitral Award 1–587–1–592
Arts 25–29 Chapter V Recourse Against the Arbitral Award 1–593–1–597
Arts 30–34 Chapter VI Recognition and Enforcement of Arbitral Awards.......... 1–598–1–602
Arts 35, 36 Chapter VII Final Provisions 1–603–1–604
2003 UNCITRAL Model Law on International Commercial Conciliation
Art.1 Scope of application and definitions 1–506
Art.2 Interpretation 1–507
Art.3 Variation by agreement 1–508
Art.4 Commencement of conciliation proceedings 1–509
Art.5 Number and appointment of conciliators 1–510
Art.6 Conduct of conciliation ... 1–511
Art.7 Communication between conciliator and parties............ 1–512
Art.8 Disclosure of information .. 1–513
Art.9 Confidentiality................. 1–514
Art.10 Admissibility of evidence in other proceedings 1–515
Art.11 Termination of conciliation proceedings................ 1–516
Art.12 Conciliator acting as arbitrator.............................. 1–517
Art.13 Resort to arbitral or judicial proceedings 1–518
Art.14 Enforceability of settlement agreement 1–519

INTERNATIONAL ARBITRATION CONVENTIONS
World-wide Multilateral Conventions
1958 United Nations Convention on the Recognition and Enforcement of Foreign Arbitral Awards ("New York Convention") C–014, C–029, C–037, C–050, C–053, C–056, C–057, C–059, C–070, C–071, C–072, C–074, C–076, C–082, C–087, C–088, C–090, C–094, C–102, C–107
Arts I–IV 2–001–2–004

INTERNATIONAL ARBITRATION CONVENTIONS—*cont.*
World-wide Multilateral Conventions—*cont.*
1958 United Nations Convention on the Recognition and Enforcement of Foreign Arbitral Awards—*cont.*
Art.II C–073
(3) C–014, C–073, C–074, C–075, C–087
Art.III C–053, C–068
Art.V ... C–001, C–053, C–068, C–070, C–070, C–088, C–090, C–114
(1) C–090
(b) C–071
(d) C–068
(2) C–090
(a) C–082
(b) C–001, C–014, C–050, C–080
Arts V–VIII.................... 2–005–2–008
Art.VI..................................... C–100
(e) C–068, C–100
Art.VII C–100
Art.IX C–053
Arts IX–XII 2–009–2–012
Arts XIII–XVI 2–013–2–016
1965 Convention on the Settlement of Investment Disputes Between States and Nationals of Other States C–081
Arts 1–3 Chapter I Section 1: Establishment and Organization 2–018–2–020
Arts 4–8 Section 2: The Administrative Council ... 2–021–2–025
Arts 9–11 Section 3: The Secretariat........................ 2–026–2–028
Arts 12–16 Section 4: The Panels 2–029–2–033
Art.17 Section 5: Financing the Center 2–034
Arts 18–24 Section 6: Status, Immunities and Privileges 2–035–2–041
Arts 25–27 Chapter II 2–042–2–044
Art. 28 Chapter III Request for Conciliation........................... 2–045
Arts 29–31 Constitution of the Conciliation Committee 2–046–2–048
Arts 32–35 Conciliation Proceedings 2–049–2–052
Art.36 Chapter IV Request for Arbitration 2–053

INTERNATIONAL ARBITRATION
CONVENTIONS—*cont.*
World-wide Multilateral Conventions—*cont.*
1965 Convention on the Settlement of Investment Disputes Between States and Nationals of Other States—*cont.*
   Arts 37–40 Constitution of the Tribunal 2–054–2–057
   Arts 41–47 Powers and Functions of the Tribunal ... 2–058–2–064
   Arts 48, 49 The Award ... 2–065–2–066
   Arts 50–52 Interpretation, Revision and Annulment of the Award 2–067–2–069
   Arts 53–55 Recognition and Enforcement of the Award 2–070–2–072
   Art.54 .... C–081
   Arts 56–58 Chapter V Replacement and Disqualification of Conciliators and Arbitrators 2–073–2–075
   Arts 59–61 Chapter VI Cost of Proceedings 2–076–2–078
   Arts 62, 63 Chapter VII Place of Proceedings 2–079–2–080
   Art.64 Chapter VIII Disputes between Contracting States 2–081
   Arts 65, 66 Chapter IX Amendment 2–082–2–083
   Arts 67–74 Chapter X Final Provisions 2–084–2–091
1994 WTO Understanding on Rules and Procedures Governing the Settlement of Disputes
   Art.1 Coverage and Application 2–092
   Art.2 Administration 2–093
   Art.3 General Provisions 2–094
   Art.4 Consultations 2–095
   Art.5 Good Offices, Conciliation and Mediation 2–096
   Art.6 Establishment of Panels 2–097
   Art.7 Terms of Reference of Panels 2–098
   Art.8 Composition of Panels 2–099
   Art.9 Procedures for Multiple Complainants 2–100
   Art.10 Third Parties 2–101
   Art.11 Function of Panels 2–102
   Art.12 Panel Procedures 2–103

INTERNATIONAL ARBITRATION
CONVENTIONS—*cont.*
World-wide Multilateral Conventions—*cont.*
1994 WTO Understanding on Rules and Procedures Governing the Settlement of Disputes—*cont.*
   Art.13 Right to Seek Information 2–104
   Art.14 Confidentiality 2–105
   Art.15 Interim Review Stage 2–106
   Art.16 Adoption of Panel Reports 2–107
   Art.17 Appellate Review 2–108
   Art.18 Communications with the Panel or Appellate Body .. 2–109
   Art.19 Panel and Appellate Body Recommendations 2–110
   Art.20 Time-frame for DSB Decisions 2–111
   Art.21 Surveillance of Implementation of Recommendations and Rulings 2–112
   Art.22 Compensation and the Suspension of Concessions 2–113
   Art.23 Strengthening of the Multilateral System 2–114
   Art.24 Special Procedures Involving Least Developed Country Members 2–115
   Art.25 Arbitration 2–116
   Art.26 2–117
   Art.27 Responsibilities of the Secretariat 2–118
   Appendix 1 Agreements Covered by the Understanding 2–119
   Appendix 2 Special or Additional Rules and Procedures Contained in the Covered Agreements 2–120
   Appendix 3 Working Procedures 2–121
   Appendix 4 Expert Review Groups 2–122

REGIONAL MULTILATERAL CONVENTIONS
1961 European Convention on International Commercial Arbitration
   Art.I Scope of the Convention 2–124
   Art.II Right of Legal Persons of Public Law to Resort to Arbitration 2–125

REGIONAL MULTILATERAL CONVENTIONS—*cont.*

1961 European Convention on International Commercial Arbitration—*cont.*
 Art.III Right of Foreign Nationals to be Designated as Arbitrators 2–126
 Art.IV Organization of the Arbitration 2–127
 Art.V Pleas as to Arbitral Jurisdiction 2–128
 Art.VI Jurisdiction of Courts of Law 2–129
 Art.VII Applicable Law 2–130
 Art.VIII Reasons for the Award 2–131
 Art.IX Setting Aside of the Arbitral Award 2–132
 Art.X Final Clauses 2–133
 Annex Composition and Procedure of the Special Committee 2–134

1975 Inter-American Convention on International Commercial Arbitration
 Arts 1–6 2–136–2–141
 Arts 7–13 2–142–2–148

1987 Arab Convention on Commercial Arbitration
 Arts 1–3 Chapter 1 General Provisions 2–150–2–152
 Arts 4–13 Chapter 2 The Arab Centre for Commercial Arbitration 2–153–2–162
 Arts 14, 15 Chapter 3 The arbitral tribunal 2–163–2–164
 Arts 16–30 Chapter 4 The arbitral proceedings 2–165–2–179
 Arts 31–35 Chapter 5 The Award 2–180–2–184
 Art.36 Transitory provisions 2–185
 Arts 37–42 Chapter 6 Final Provisions 2–186–2–191

1992 North American Free Trade Agreement (Investment Provisions) C–083
 Ch.11 .... C–083
 Art.1102 .... C–083
   (3) C–083
 Art.1105 .... C–083
 Art.1107 .... C–083
 Art.1110 .... C–083
 Art.1115 Purpose 2–192

REGIONAL MULTILATERAL CONVENTIONS—*cont.*

1992 North American Free Trade Agreement (Investment Provisions)—*cont.*
 Art.1116 Claim by an Investor of a Party on Behalf of Itself 2–193
 Art.1117 Claim by an Investor of a Party on Behalf of an Enterprise 2–194
 Art.1118 Settlement of a Claim Through Consultation and Negotiation 2–195
 Art.1119 Notice of Intent to Submit a Claim to Arbitration 2–196
 Art.1120 Submission of a Claim to Arbitration 2–197
 Art.1121 Conditions Precedent to Submission of a Claim to Arbitration 2–198
 Art.1122 Consent to Arbitration 2–199
 Art.1123 Number of Arbitrators and Method of Appointment 2–200
 Art.1124 Constitution of Tribunal When a Party Fails to Appoint an Arbitrator or the Disputing Parties Are Unable to Agree on a Presiding Arbitrator 2–201
 Art.1125 Consolidation 2–202
 Art.1126 Notice 2–203
 Art.1127 Participation by a Party 2–204
 Art.1128 Documents 2–205
 Art.1129 Place of Arbitration 2–206
 Art.1130 Governing Law 2–207
 Art.1131 Interpretation of Annexes 2–208
 Art.1132 Report from an Expert 2–209
 Art.1133 Interim Measures of Protection 2–210
 Art.1134 Final Award 2–211
 Art.1135 Finality and Enforcement of Award 2–212
 Art.1136 General 2–213
 Art.1137 Exclusions 2–214
 Art.1138 Definitions 2–215
 Annex 1120.1 Submission of Claims to Arbitration 2–216

REGIONAL MULTILATERAL CONVENTIONS—cont.
1992 North American Free Trade Agreement (Arbitration Provisions)—cont.
Annex 1137.2 Exclusions from Dispute Settlement 2–217

INTERNATIONAL ARBITRATION PROCEDURAL AND ETHICAL RULES
Code of Ethics for Arbitrators in International Arbitration
American Arbitration Association's Code of Ethics for Arbitrators in Commercial Disputes
Preamble 3–002
Canon I An Arbitrator Should Uphold The Integrity and Fairness of The Arbitration Process...............................3–003
Canon II An Arbitrator Should Disclose Any Interest or Relationship Likely to Affect Impartiality or Which Might Create An Appearance of Partiality or Bias 3–004
Canon III An Arbitrator in Communicating With the Parties Should Avoid Impropriety or the Appearance of Impropriety 3–006
Canon IV An Arbitrator Should Conduct the Proceedings Fairly and Diligently 3–007
Canon V An Arbitrator Should Make Decisions In a Just, Independent and Deliberate Manner 3–008
Canon VI An Arbitrator Should Be Faithful To The Relationship of Trust and Confidentiality Inherent in That Office 3–009
Canon VII Ethical Considerations Relating to Arbitrators Appointed by One Party.....................................3–010
A–F Obligations under Canons I–VI...............3–011–3–016

IBA Guidelines on conflict of Interest in International Arbitrations
Introduction 3–017

INTERNATIONAL ARBITRATION PROCEDURAL AND ETHICAL RULES—cont.
IBA Guidelines on Conflict of Interest in International Arbitrations—cont.
Pt I General Standards Regarding Impartiality, Independence and Disclosure 3–018
Pt II Explanatory Notes Concerning The General Standards 3–021
1. Non-Waivable Red List..........3–023
2. Waivable Red List...................3–024
3. Orange List...........................3–026
4. Green List..............................3–028

RULES OF PROCEDURE
IBA Rules on the Taking of Evidence in International Commercial Arbitration
Preamble 3–126
Art.1 Definitions......................3–127
Art.2 Scope of Application........3–128
Art.3 Documents 3–129
Art.4 Witnesses of Fact 3–130
Art.5 Party Appointed Experts.................................3–131
Arts 6, 7 Tribunal Appointed Experts 3–132–3–133
Art.8 Evidentiary Hearing.........3–134
Art.9 Admissibility and Assessment of Evidence.........3–135

UNCITRAL Arbitration Rules
....C–029
Art.1 Scope of application 3–085
Art.2 Notice, calculation of periods of time......................3–086
Art.3 Notice of arbitration 3–087
Art.4 Representation and assistance...............................3–088
Art.5 Number of arbitrators 3–089
Arts 6–8 Appointment of arbitrators........................3–090–3–092
Arts 9–12 Challenge of arbitrators........................3–093–3–096
Art.13 Replacement of an arbitrator..............................3–097
Art.14 Repetition of hearings in the event of the replacement of an arbitrator 3–098
Art.15 General provisions 3–099

RULES OF PROCEDURE—*cont.*
UNCITRAL Arbitration Rules—*cont.*
    Art.16 Place of arbitration 3–100
    Art.17 Language 3–101
    Art.18 Statement of claim 3–102
    Art.19 Statement of defence 3–103
    Art.20 Amendments to the claim of defence....................3–104
    Art.21 Pleas to the jurisdiction of the arbitral tribunal 3–105
    Art.22 Further written statements...................................3–106
    Art.23 Periods of time...............3–107
    Arts 24, 25 Evidence and hearings...........................3–108–3–109
    Art.26 Interim measures of protection 3–110
    Art.27 Experts 3–111
    Art.28 Default 3–112
    Art.29 Closure of hearings 3–113
    Art.30 Waiver of rules................3–114
    Art.31 Decisions 3–115
    Art.32 Form and effect of the award......................................3–116
    Art.33 Applicable law, amiable composition.........................3–117
    Art.34 Settlement or the grounds for termination 3–118
    Art.35 Interpretation of the award.....................................3–119
    Art.36 Correction of the award....3–120
    Art.37 Additional award 3–121
    Arts 38–40 Costs.............3–122–3–124
    Art.41 Deposit of the costs........3–125
UNCITRAL Notes on Organizing Arbitral Proceedings
    Introduction 3–029
    List of Matters For Possible Consideration in Organizing Arbitral Proceedings 3–035
    1. Set of arbitration rules 3–036
    2. Language of proceedings.......3–037
    3. Place of arbitration 3–041
    4. Administrative services that may be needed for the arbitral tribunal to carry out its functions...........................3–043
    5. Deposits in respect of costs 3–044
    6. Confidentiality of information relating to the arbitration.................................3–047
    7. Routing of written communications among the parties and arbitrators.....................3–048

RULES OF PROCEDURE—*cont.*
UNCITRAL Notes on Organizing Arbitral Proceedings—*cont.*
    8. Telefax and other electronic means of sending documents 3–049
    9. Arrangements for the exchange of written submissions 3–051
    10. Practical details concerning written submissions and evidence 3–054
    11. Defining points at issue....3–054A
    12. Possible settlement negotiations and their effect on scheduling proceedings..........3–057
    13. Documentary evidence 3–058
    14. Physical evidence other than documents 3–062
    15. Witnesses 3–065
    16. Experts and expert witnesses 3–071
    17. Hearings 3–074
    18. Multi-party arbitration 3–082
    19. Possible requirements concerning filing or delivering of award 3–083
International Rules
International Convention for the Unification of Certain Rules of Law relating to Bills of Lading ("Hague Rules") 1924........................C–092
    Art.III, r.6 ....C–092
Rules of Arbitration of the International Chambers of Commerce (ICC) Court of Arbitration ("ICC Rules") (as amended from time to time) C–021, C–022, C–086, C–103
    Art.8(5) C–044
    Art.11......................................C–056
    Art.13......................................C–093
        (3)....................................C–093
    Art.18(2)..................................C–080
    Art.21......................................C–031
    Art.23......................................C–031
    Art.24 ....C–016, C–086
    Art.28(6)..................................C–046
GAFTA Arbitration Rules 125 (as amended from time to time) 047
    r.2..C–047
        2(a) C–047

RULES OF PROCEDURE—*cont.*
  Arbitration (Additional Facility) Rules of the International Centre for Settlement of Investment Disputes ("ICSID Additional Facility Rules") (as amended from time to time) C–083
INTERNATIONAL CONTRACTUAL INSTRUMENTS
Transnational Contract Principles
1994 UNIDROIT Principles for International Commercial Contracts
  Preamble 4–001
  Art.1.1 Freedom of Contract.....4–002
  Art.1.2 No Form Required 4–003
  Art.1.3 Binding Character of Contract...........................4–003A
  Art.1.4 Mandatory Rules 4–004
  Art.1.5 Exclusion or Modification by the Parties............4–005
  Art.1.6 Interpretation and Supplementation of the Principles............................4–006
  Art.1.7 Good Faith and Fair Dealing................................4–007
  Art.1.8 Usages and Practices 4–008
  Art.1.9 Notice 4–009
  Art.1.10 Definitions 4–010
  Art.2.1 Manner of Formation ...4–011
  Art.2.2 Definition of Offer........4–012
  Art.2.3 Withdrawal of Offer......4–013
  Art.2.4 Revocation of Offer 4–014
  Art.2.5 Rejection of Offer 4–105
  Art.2.6 Mode of Acceptance 4–016
  Art.2.7 Time of Acceptance 4–017
  Art.2.8 Acceptance Within a Fixed Period of Time 4–018
  Art.2.9 Late Acceptance. Delay in Transmission 4–019
  Art. 2.10 Withdrawal of Acceptance 4–020
  Art.2.11 Modified Acceptance 4–021
  Art.2.12 Writings in Confirmation....................................4–022
  Art.2.13 Conclusion of Contract Dependent on Agreement on Specific Matter or in a Specific Form..................4–023
  Art.2.14 Contract with Terms Deliberately Left Open..........4–024
  Art.2.15 Negotiations in Bad Faith 4–025

INTERNATIONAL CONTRACTUAL INSTRUMENTS—*cont.*
Transnational Contract Principles—*cont.*
1994 UNIDROIT Principles for International Commercial Contracts—*cont.*
  Art.2.16 Duty of Confidentiality...............................4–026
  Art.2.17 Merger Clause.............4–027
  Art.2.18 Written Modification Clauses 4–028
  Art.2.19 Contracting Under Standard Terms....................4–029
  Art.2.20 Surprising Terms 4–030
  Art.2.21 Conflict Between Standard Terms and Non-Standard Terms....................4–031
  Art.2.22 Battle of Forms 4–032
  Art.3.1 Matters Not Covered 4–033
  Art.3.2 Validity of Mere Agreement 4–034
  Art.3.3 Initial Impossibility.......4–035
  Art.3.4 Definition of Mistake 4–036
  Art.3.5 Relevant Mistake..........4–037
  Art.3.6 Error in Expression or Transmission 4–038
  Art.3.7 Remedies for Non-Performance.......................4–039
  Art.3.8 Fraud 4–040
  Art.3.9 Threat 4–041
  Art 3.10 Gross Disparity 4–042
  Art.3.11 Third Persons..............4–043
  Art.3.12 Confirmation 4–044
  Art.3.13 Loss of Right to Avoid 4–045
  Art.3.14 Notice of Avoidance 4–046
  Art.3.15 Time Limits 4–047
  Art.3.16 Partial Avoidance 4–048
  Art.3.17 Retroactive Effect of Avoidance 4–049
  Art.3.18 Damages 4–050
  Art.3.19 Mandatory Character of the Provisions 4–051
  Art.3.20 Unilateral Declarations 4–052
  Art.4.1 Intention of the Parties..4–053
  Art.4.2 Interpretation of Statements and Other Conduct.....................................4–054
  Art.4.3 Relevant Circumstances...............................4–055

INTERNATIONAL CONTRACTUAL
  INSTRUMENTS—*cont.*
Transnational Contract Principles—
  cont.
1994 UNIDROIT Principles for
  International Commercial
  Contracts—*cont.*
  Art.4.4 Reference to Contract
    or Statement as a Whole........4–056
  Art.4.5 All Terms to be Given
    Effect 4–057
  Art.4.6 Contra Proferentem
    Rule 4–058
  Art.4.7 Linguistic Discrepancies 4–059
  Art.4.8 Supplying an Omitted
    Term...4–060
  Art.5.1 Express and Implied
    Obligations..............................4–061
  Art.5.2 Implied Obligations 4–062
  Art.5.3 Co-operation between
    the Parties..............................4–063
  Art.5.4 Duty to Achieve a
    Specific Result. Duty of Best
    Efforts 4–064
  Art.5.5 Determination of
    Kind of Duty Involved...........4–065
  Art.5.6 Determination of
    Quality of Performance.........4–066
  Art.5.7 Price Determination 4–067
  Art.5.8 Contract for an Indefinite period 4–068
  Art.6.1.1 Time of Performance...4–069
  Art.6.1.2 Performance at one
    Time or in Instalments 4–070
  Art.6.1.3 Partial Performance....4–071
  Art.6.1.4 Order of Performance......................................4–072
  Art.6.1.5 Earlier Performance....4–073
  Art.6.1.6 Place of Performance......................................4–074
  Art.6.1.7 Payment by Cheque
    or other Instrument...............4–075
  Art.6.1.8 Payment by Funds
    Transfer 4–076
  Art.6.1.9 Currency of Payment...4–077
  Art.6.1.10 Currency Not
    Expressed 4–078
  Art.6.1.11 Costs of Performance......................................4–079
  Art.6.1.12 Imputation of Payments...4–080
  Art.6.1.13 Imputation of Non-
    Monetary Obligations...........4–081

INTERNATIONAL CONTRACTUAL
  INSTRUMENTS—*cont.*
Transnational Contract Principles—
  cont.
1994 UNIDROIT Principles for
  International Commercial
  Contracts—*cont.*
  Art.6.1.14 Application for
    Public Permission 4–082
  Art.6.1.15 Procedure in Applying for Permission 4–083
  Art.6.1.16 Permission Neither
    Granted Nor Refused 4–084
  Art.6.1.17 Permission Refused...4–085
  Art.6.2.1 Contract to be
    Observed 4–086
  Art.6.2.2 Definition of Hardship 4–087
  Art.6.2.3 Effects of Hardship 4–088
  Art.7.1.1 Non-Performance
    Defined 4–089
  Art.7.1.2 Interference by the
    Other Party............................4–090
  Art.7.1.3 Withholding Performance...................................4–091
  Art.7.1.4 Cure by Non-Performing Party 4–092
  Art.7.1.5 Additional Period
    for Performance 4–093
  Art.7.1.6 Exemption Clauses.....4–094
  Art.7.1.7 Force Majeure 4–095
  Art.7.2.1 Performance of
    Monetary Obligation 4–096
  Art.7.2.2 Performance of Non-
    Monetary Obligation 4–097
  Art.7.2.3 Repair and Replacement of Defective Performance......................................4–098
  Art.7.2.4 Judicial Penalty 4–099
  Art.7.2.5 Change of Remedy 4–100
  Art.7.3.1 Right to Terminate
    the Contract 4–101
  Art.7.3.2 Notice of Termination..4–102
  Art.7.3.3 Anticipatory Non-
    Performance..........................4–103
  Art.7.3.4 Adequate Assurance
    of Due Performance 4–104
  Art.7.3.5 Effects of Termination in General......................4–105
  Art.7.3.6 Restitution 4–106
  Art.7.4.1 Right to Damages........4–107
  Art.7.4.2 Full Compensation 4–108
  Art.7.4.3 Certainty of Harm 4–109

INTERNATIONAL CONTRACTUAL INSTRUMENTS—*cont.*
Transnational Contract Principles—*cont.*

1994 UNIDROIT Principles for International Commercial Contracts—*cont.*
Art.7.4.4 Foreseeability of Harm 4–110
Art.7.4.5 Proof of Harm in case of Replacement Transaction 4–111
Art.7.4.6 Proof of Harm by Current Price 4–112
Art.7.4.7 Harm Due in Part to Aggrieved Party 4–113
Art.7.4.8 Mitigation of Harm 4–114
Art.7.4.9 Interest for Failure to Pay Money 4–115
Art.7.4.10 Interest on Damages 4–116
Art.7.4.11 Manner of Monetary Redress 4–117
Art.7.4.12 Currency in which to Access Damages 4–118
Art.7.4.13 Agreed Payment for Non-Performance 4–119

1999/2002 Principles of European Contract Law (Commission on European Contract Law)
Art.1.101 Application of the Principles 4–120
Art.1.102 Freedom of Contract 4–121
Art.1.103 Mandatory Law 4–122
Art.1.104 Application to Questions of Consent 4–123
Art.1.105 Usages and Practices 4–124
Art.1.106 Interpretation and Supplementation 4–125
Art.1.107 Application of the Principles by Way of Analogy 4–126
Art.1.201 Good Faith and Fair Dealing 4–127
Art.1.202 Duty to Co-operate 4–128
Art.1.301 Meaning of Terms 4–129
Art.1.302 Reasonableness..........4–130
Art.1.303 Notice 4–131
Art.1.304 Computation of Time ...4–132
Art.1.305 Imputed Knowledge and Intention 4–133

INTERNATIONAL CONTRACTUAL INSTRUMENTS—*cont.*
Transnational Contract Principles—*cont.*

1999/2002 Principles of European Contract Law (Commission on European Contract Law)—*cont.*
Art.2.101 Conditions for the Conclusion of a Contract 4–134
Art.2.102 Intention 4–135
Art.2.103 Sufficient Agreement 4–136
Art.2.104 Terms Not Individually Negotiated 4–137
Art.2.105 Merger Clause 4–138
Art.2.106 Written Modification Only 4–139
Art.2.107 Promise Binding without Acceptance 4–140
Art.2.201 Offer 4–141
Art.2.202 Revocation of an Offer 4–142
Art.2.203 Rejection 4–143
Art.2.204 Acceptance 4–144
Art.2.205 Time and Conclusion of the Contract 4–145
Art.2.206 Time Limit for Acceptance 4–146
Art.2.207 Late Acceptance 4–147
Art.2.208 Modified Acceptance...4–148
Art.2.209 Conflicting General Conditions..........................4–149
Art.2.210 Professional's Written Confirmation............4–150
Art.2.211 Contracts not Concluded through Offer and Acceptance 4–151
Art.2.301 Negotiations Contrary to Good Faith 4–152
Art.2.302 Breach of Confidentiality 4–153
Art.3.101 Scope of the Chapter..4–154
Art.3.102 Categories of Representation 4–155
Art.3.201 Express, Implied and Apparent Authority 4–156
Art.3.202 Agent acting in Exercise of its Authority 4–157
Art.3.203 Unidentified Principal 4–158
Art.3.204 Agent acting without or outside its Authority 4–159
Art.3.205 Conflict of Interest 4–160

INTERNATIONAL CONTRACTUAL INSTRUMENTS—*cont.*
Transnational Contract Principles—*cont.*
1999/2002 Principles of European Contract Law (Commission on European Contract Law)—*cont.*
Art.3.206 Subagency 4–161
Art.3.207 Ratification by Principal 4–162
Art.3.208 Third Party's Right with Respect to Confirmation of Authority...................4–163
Art.3.209 Duration of Authority 4–164
Art.3.301 Intermediaries not acting in the name of a Principal 4–165
Art.3.302 Intermediary's Insolvency or Fundamental Non-performance to Principal 4–166
Art.3.303 Intermediary's insolvency or Fundamental Non-performance to Third Party 4–167
Art.3.304 Requirement of Notice 4–168
Art.4.101 Matters not Covered ...4–169
Art.4.102 Initial Impossibility 4–170
Art.4.103 Fundamental Mistake as to Facts or Law 4–171
Art.4.104 Inaccuracy in Communication 4–172
Art.4.105 Adaptation of Contract...................................4–173
Art.4.106 Incorrect Information..4–174
Art.4.107 Fraud 4–175
Art.4.108 Threats 4–176
Art.4.109 Excessive Benefit or Unfair Advantage 4–177
Art.4.110 Unfair Terms not Individually Negotiated.........4–178
Art.4.111 Third Persons 4–179
Art.4.112 Notice of Avoidance..4–180
Art.4.113 Time Limits 4–181
Art.4.114 Confirmation 4–182
Art.4.115 Effect of Avoidance....4–183
Art.4.116 Partial Avoidance.......4–184
Art.4.117 Damages 4–185
Art.4.118 Exclusion or Restriction of Remedies..............4–186
Art.4.119 Remedies for Non-performance 4–187

INTERNATIONAL CONTRACTUAL INSTRUMENTS—*cont.*
Transnational Contract Principles—*cont.*
1999/2002 Principles of European Contract Law (Commission on European Contract Law)—*cont.*
Art.5.101 General Rules of Interpretation 4–188
Art.5.102 Relevant Circumstances.................................4–189
Art.5.103 Contra Proferentem Rule....................................4–190
Art.5.104 Preference to Negotiated Terms.........................4–191
Art.5.105 Reference to Contract as a Whole 4–192
Art.5.106 Terms to Be Given Effect................................4–193
Art.5.107 Linguistic Discrepancies 4–194
Art.6.101 Statements giving rise to Contractual Obligations 4–195
Art.6.102 Implied Terms 4–196
Art.6.103 Simulation.................4–197
Art.6.104 Determination of Price 4–198
Art.6.105 Unilateral Determination by a Party...............4–199
Art.6.106 Determination by a Third Person 4–200
Art.6.107 Reference to a Non-Existent Factor......................4–201
Art.6.108 Quality of Performance.................................4–202
Art.6.109 Contract for an Indefinite Period...................4–203
Art.6.110 Stipulation in Favour of a Third Party 4–204
Art.6.111 Change of Circumstances.................................4–205
Art.7.101 Place of Performance...4–206
Art.7.102 Time of Performance 4–206A
Art.7.103 Early Performance 4–207
Art.7.104 Order of Performance...............................4–208
Art.7.105 Alternative Performance...............................4–209
Art.7.106 Performance by a Third Party 4–210
Art.7.107 Form of Payment.......4–211
Art.7.108 Currency of Payment 4–212

INTERNATIONAL CONTRACTUAL
   INSTRUMENTS—*cont.*
Transnational Contract Principles—
   cont.
1999/2002 Principles of European
   Contract Law (Commission on
   European Contract Law)—*cont.*
   Art.7.109 Appropriation of
      Performance..........................4–213
   Art.7.110 Property Not
      Accepted..................................4–214
   Art.7.111 Money Not
      Accepted..................................4–215
   Art.7.112 Costs of Perfor-
      mance 4–215A
   Art.8.101 Remedies Available 4–216
   Art.8.102 Cumulation of
      Remedies 4–217
   Art.8.103 Fundamental Non-
      Performance..........................4–218
   Art.8.104 Cure by Non-Perfor-
      ming Party 4–219
   Art.8.105 Assurance of Perfor-
      mance......................................4–220
   Art.8.106 Notice Fixing Addi-
      tional Period for Perfor-
      mance......................................4–221
   Art.8.107 Performance En-
      trusted to Another 4–222
   Art.8.108 Excuse Due to an
      Impediment 4–223
   Art.8.109 Clause Excluding or
      Restricting Remedies.............4–224
   Art.9.101 Monetary Obliga-
      tions 4–225
   Art.9.102 Non-Monetary Obli-
      gations....................................4–226
   Art.9.103 Damages Not
      Precluded...............................4–227
   Art.9.201 Right to Withhold
      Performance..........................4–228
   Art.9.301 Right to Terminate
      the Contract 4–229
   Art.9.302 Contract to be Per-
      formed in Parts 4–230
   Art.9.303 Notice of Termina-
      tion..4–231
   Art.9.304 Anticipatory Non-
      Performance..........................4–232
   Art.9.305 Effects of Termina-
      tion in General......................4–233
   Art.9.306 Property Reduced in
      Value 4–234
   Art.9.307 Recovery of Money
      Paid 4–235

INTERNATIONAL CONTRACTUAL
   INSTRUMENTS—*cont.*
Transnational Contract Principles—
   cont.
1999/2002 Principles of European
   Contract Law (Commission on
   European Contract Law)—*cont.*
   Art.9.308 Recovery of Propert.....4–236
   Art.9.309 Recovery for Per-
      formance that Cannot be
      Returned................................4–237
   Art.9.401 Right to Reduce the
      Price 4–238
   Art.9.501 Right to Damages.......4–239
   Art.9.502 General Measure of
      Damages.................................4–240
   Art.9.503 Foreseeability 4–241
   Art.9.504 Loss Attributable to
      Aggrieved Party 4–242
   Art.9.505 Reduction of Loss......4–243
   Art.9.506 Substitute Trans-
      action 4–244
   Art.9.507 Current Price.............4–245
   Art.9.508 Delay in Payment of
      Money....................................4–246
   Art.9.509 Agreed Payment for
      Non-Performance..................4–247
   Art.9.510 Currency by which
      Damages to be Measured 4–248
   Art.10.101 Solidary, Separate
      and Communal Obligations
     4–249
   Art.10.102 When Solidary
      Obligations Arise..................4–250
   Art.10.103 Liability under
      Separate Obligations............4–251
   Art.10.104 Communal Obli-
      gations....................................4–252
   Art.10.105 Apportionment
      between Solidary Debtors......4–253
   Art.10.106 Recourse between
      Solidary Debtors...................4–254
   Art.10.107 Performance, Set-
      off and Merger in Solidary
      Obligations............................4–255
   Art.10.108 Release or Settle-
      ment in Solidary Obliga-
      tions 4–256
   Art.10.109 Effect of Judgment
      in Solidary Obligations 4–257
   Art.10.110 Prescription in
      Solidary Obligations............4–258
   Art.10.111 Opposability of
      other Defences in Solidary
      Obligations............................4–259

INTERNATIONAL CONTRACTUAL
INSTRUMENTS—*cont.*
Transnational Contract Principles—*cont.*
1999/2002 Principles of European Contract Law (Commission on European Contract Law)—*cont.*
Art.10.201 Solidary, Separate and Communal Claims 4–260
Art.10.202 Apportionment of Separate Claims 4–261
Art.10.203 Difficulties of executing a Communal Claim 4–262
Art.10.204 Apportionment of Solidary Claims 4–263
Art.10.205 Regime of solidary Claims 4–264
Art.11.101 Scope of Chapter 4–265
Art.11.102 Contractual Claims Generally Assignable 4–266
Art.11.103 Partial Assignment 4–267
Art.11.104 Form of Assignment 4–268
Art.11.201 Rights Transferred to Assignee 4–269
Art.11.202 When Assignment Takes Effect 4–270
Art.11.203 Preservation of Assignee's Rights Against Assignor 4–271
Art.11.204 Undertakings by Assignor 4–272
Art.11.301 Contractual Prohibition of Assignment 4–273
Art.11.302 Other Ineffective Assignments 4–274
Art.11.303 Effect on Debtor's Obligation 4–275
Art.11.304 Protection of Debtor 4–276
Art.11.305 Competing Demands 4–277
Art.11.306 Place of Performance 4–278
Art.11.307 Defences and Rights of Set-off 4–279
Art.11.308 Unauthorised Modification not Binding on Assignee 4–280
Art.11.401 Priorities 4–281
Art.12.101 Substitution: General rules 4–282

INTERNATIONAL CONTRACTUAL
INSTRUMENTS—*cont.*
Transnational Contract Principles—*cont.*
1999/2002 Principles of European Contract Law (Commission on European Contract Law)—*cont.*
Art.12.102 Effects of Substitution on Defences and Securities 4–283
Art.12.201 Transfer of Contract 4–284
Art.13.101 Requirements for Set-Off 4–285
Art.13.102 Unascertained Claims 4–286
Art.13.103 Foreign Currency Set-Off 4–287
Art.13.104 Notice of Set-Off 4–288
Art.13.105 Plurality of Claims and Obligations 4–289
Art.13.106 Effect of Set-Off 4–290
Art.13.107 Exclusion of Right of Set-Off 4–291
Art.14.101 Claims subject to Prescription 4–292
Art.14.201 General Period 4–293
Art.14.202 Period for a Claim Established by Legal Proceedings 4–294
Art.14.203 Commencement 4–295
Art.14.301 Suspension in Case of Ignorance 4–296
Art.14.302 Suspension in Case of Judicial and Other Proceedings 4–297
Art.14.303 Suspension in Case of Impediment beyond Creditor's Control 4–298
Art.14.304 Postponement of Expiry in case of Negotiations 4–299
Art.14.305 Postponement of Expiry in case of Incapacity 4–300
Art.14.306 Postponement of Expiry; Deceased's Estate 4–301
Art.14.307 Maximum Length of Period 4–302
Art.14.401 Renewal by Acknowledgment 4–303
Art.14.402 Renewal by Attempted Execution 4–304
Art.14.501 General Effect 4–305
Art.14.502 Effect on Ancillary Claims 4–306

INTERNATIONAL CONTRACTUAL INSTRUMENTS—cont.
Transnational Contract Principles—cont.
1999/2002 Principles of European Contract Law (Commission on European Contract Law)—cont.
Art.14.503 Effect on Set-Off......4–307
Art.14.601 Agreements Concerning Prescription 4–308
Art.15.101 Contracts Contrary to Fundamental Principles 4–309
Art.15.102 Contracts Infringing Mandatory Rules...........4–310
Art.15.103 Partial Ineffectiveness 4–311
Art.15.104 Restitution...............4–312
Art.15.105 Damages 4–313
Art.16.101 Types of Condition...4–314
Art.16.102 Interference with Conditions...........................4–315
Art.16.103 Effect of Conditions 4–316
Art.17.101 When Interest to be Added to Capital 4–317

RULES OF CONFLICT
1980 Convention on the Law Applicable to Contractual Obligations
Preamble 4–318
Art.1 Scope of the Convention ..4–319
Art.2 Application of law of non-contracting States...........4–320
Art.3 Freedom of choice............4–321
Art.4 Applicable law in the absence of choice 4–322
Art.5 Certain consumer contracts 4–323
Art.6 Individual employment contracts..............................4–324
Art.7 Mandatory rules..............4–325
Art.8 Material validity 4–326
Art.9 Formal validity 4–327
Art.10 Scope of applicable law ...4–328
Art.11 Incapacity 4–329
Art.12 Voluntary assignment.....4–330
Art.13 Subrogation 4–331
Art.14 Burden of proof etc........4–332
Art.15 Exclusion of convoy 4–333
Art.16 Ordre public 4–334
Art.17 No retrospective effect....4–335

RULES OF CONFLICT—cont.
1980 Convention on the Law Applicable to Contractual Obligations—cont.
Art.18 Uniform interpretation...4–336
Art.19 States with more than one legal system 4–337
Art.20 Precedence of Community Law...........................4–338
Art.21 Relationship with other conventions.................4–339
Art.22 Reservations...................4–340
Arts 23–33 4–341–4–351
Protocol 4–352
Joint Declaration 4–353–4–354

1994 Inter American Convention on the Law Applicable to International Contracts
Arts 1–6 Scope of Application............
................................4–361–4–366
Arts 7– 11 Determination of Applicable Law 4–367–4–371
Arts 12, 13 Existence and Validity of the Contract
................................4–372– 4–373
Arts 14–18 Scope of the Applicable Law 4–374– 4–378
Arts 19–24 General Provisions
................................4–379– 4–384
Arts 25–30 Final Clauses
................................4–385–4–390

OTHER CONVENTIONS AND TREATIES
1950 European Convention for the Protection of Human Rights and Fundamental Liberties
Art.6..C–124
(1) C–124
1954 France-UNESCO Agreement
Art.12..C–124
1955 Treaty of Amity, Economic Relations and Consular Rights between the United States of America and Iran
Art.IV, s.2 ....C–008
Art.XI, s.4 ....C–008
1989 International Convention on Salvage
Art.13.......................................C–110
Art.14.......................................C–110
Art.14.3....................................C–110

CHAPTER 1

International Arbitration and ADR Statutes

A. ENGLISH AND IRISH STATUTES

ENGLAND

Arbitration Act 1996
1996 Chapter 23

ARRANGEMENT OF SECTIONS

PART I—ARBITRATION PURSUANT TO AN ARBITRATION AGREEMENT

Introductory

Section.
1. General principles
2. Scope of application of provisions.
3. The seat of the arbitration.
4. Mandatory and non-mandatory provisions.
5. Agreements to be in writing.

The arbitration agreement

6. Definition of arbitration agreement.
7. Separability of arbitration agreement.
8. Whether agreement discharged by death of a party.

Stay of legal proceedings

9. Stay of legal proceedings.
10. Reference of interpleader issue to arbitration.
11. Retention of security where Admiralty proceedings stayed.

Commencement of arbitral proceedings

12. Power of court to extend time for beginning arbitral proceedings, &c.
13. Application of Limitation Acts.
14. Commencement of arbitral proceedings.

The arbitral tribunal

15. The arbitral tribunal.
16. Procedure for appointment of arbitrator.
17. Power in case of default to appoint sole arbitrator.
18. Failure of appoint procedure.
19. Court to have regard to agreed qualifications.
20. Chairman.
21. Umpire.
22. Decision-making where no chaiman or umpire.
23. Revocation of arbitrator's authority.
24. Power of court to remove arbitrator.
25. Resignation of arbitrator.
26. Death of arbitrator or person appointing him.
27. Filling of vacancy, &c.
28. Joint and several liability of parties to arbitrators for fees and expenses.
29. Immunity of arbitrator.

Jurisdiction of the arbitral tribunal

30. Competence of tribunal to rule on its own jurisdiction.
31. Objection to substantive jurisdiction of tribunal.
32. Determination of preliminary point of jurisdiction.

The arbitral proceedings

33. General duty of the tribunal.
34. Procedural and evidential matters.
35. Consolidation of proceedings and concurrent hearings.
36. Legal or other representation.
37. Power to appoint experts, legal advisers or assessors.
38. General powers exercisable by the tribunal.
39. Power to make provisional awards.
40. General duty of parties.
41. Powers of tribunal in case of party's default.

Powers of court in relation to arbitral proceedings

42. Enforcement of peremptory orders of tribunal.
43. Securing the attendance of witnesses.
44. Court powers exercisable in support of arbitral proceedings.
45. Determination of preliminary point of law.

The award

46. Rules applicable to substance of dispute.
47. Awards on different issues, &c.
48. Remedies.
49. Interest.
50. Extension of time for making award.
51. Settlement.
52. Form of award.
53. Place where award treated as made.
54. Date of award.
55. Notification of award.
56. Power to withold award in case of non-payment.
57. Correction of award or additional award.
58. Effect of award.

Costs of the arbitration

59. Costs of the arbitration.
60. Agreement to pay costs in any event.
61. Award of costs.
62. Effect of agreement or award about costs.
63. The recoverable costs of the arbitration.
64. Recoverable fees and expenses of arbitrators.
65. Power to limit recoverable costs.

Powers of the court in relation to award

66. Enforcement of the award.
67. Challenging the award: substantive jurisdiction.
68. Challenging the award: serious irregularity.
69. Appeal on point of law.
70. Challenge or appeal: supplementary provisions.
71. Challenge or appeal: effect of order of court.

Miscellaneous

72. Saving for rights of person who takes no part in proceedings.
73. Loss of right to object.
74. Immunity of arbitral institutions, &c.
75. Charge to secure payment of solicitors' costs.

Supplementary

76. Service of notices, &c.
77. Powers of court in relation to service of documents.
78. Reckoning periods of time.
79. Power of court to extend time limits relating to arbitral proceedings
80. Notice and other requirements in connection with legal proceedings.
81. Saving for certain matters governed by common law.

82. Minor definitions.
83. Index of defined expressions: Part I.
84. Transitional provisions.

PART II—OTHER PROVISIONS RELATING TO ARBITRATION

Domestic arbitration agreements

85. Modification of Part I in relation to domestic arbitration agreement.
86. Staying of legal proceedings.
87. Effectiveness of agreement to exclude court's jurisdiction.
88. Power to repeal or amend sections 85 to 87.

Consumer arbitration agreements

89. Application of unfair terms regulations to consumer arbitration agreements.
90. Regulations apply where consumer is a legal person.
91. Arbitration agreement unfair where modest amount sought.

Small claims arbitration in the county court

92. Exclusion of Part I in relation to small claims arbitration in the county court.

Appointment of judges as arbitrators

93. Appointment of judges as arbitrators

Statutory arbitrations

94. Application of Part I to statutory arbitrations.
95. General adaptation of provisions in relation to statutory arbitrations.
96. Specific adaptations of provisions in relation to statutory arbitrations.

97. Provisions excluded from applying to statutory arbitrations.
98. Power to make further provision by regulations.

PART III—RECOGNITION AND ENFORCEMENT OF CERTAIN FOREIGN AWARDS

Enforcement of Geneva Convention awards

99. Continuation of Part II of the Arbitration Act 1950.

Recognition and enforcement of New York Convention awards

100. New York Convention awards.
101. Recognition and enforcement awards.
102. Evidence to be produced by party seeking recognition or enforcement.
103. Refusal of recognition or enforcement.
104. Saving for other bases of recognition or enforcement.

PART IV—GENERAL PROVISIONS

105. Meaning of "the court": jurisdiction of High Court and county court.
106. Crown application.
107. Consequential amendments and repeals.
108. Extent.
109. Commencement.
110. Short title.

SCHEDULES

Schedule 1—Mandatory provisions of Part I.
Schedule 2—Modifications of Part I in relation to judge-arbitrators.
Schedule 3—Consequential amendments.
Schedule 4—Repeals.

Arbitration Act 1996
1996 Chapter 23 [17th June 1996]

Arbitration Her Majesty's Stationary Office;
LM toc LM 20**

1—001 An Act to restate and improve the law relating to arbitration pursuant to an arbitration agreement; to make other provision relating to arbitration and arbitration awards; and for connected purposes. Be it enacted by the Queen's most Excellent Majesty, by and with the advice and consent of the Lords Spiritual and Temporal, and Commons, in this present Parliament assembled, and by the authority of the same, as follows:—

Part I—Arbitration Pursuant to an Arbitration Agreement

Introductory

1—002   General principles

1.—The provisions of this Part are founded on the following principles, and shall be construed accordingly—

  (a) the object of arbitration is to obtain the fair resolution of disputes by an impartial tribunal without unnecessary delay or expense;

  (b) the parties should be free to agree how their disputes are resolved, subject only to such safeguards as are necessary in the public interest;

  (c) in matters governed by this Part the court should not intervene except as provided by this Part.

1—003   Scope of application of provisions

2.—(1) The provisions of this Part apply where the seat of the arbitration is in England and Wales or Northern Ireland.

  (2) The following sections apply even if the seat of the arbitration is outside England and Wales or Northern Ireland or no seat has been designated or determined—

    (a) sections 9 to 11 (stay of legal proceedings, &c.), and
    (b) section 66 (enforcement of arbitral awards).

(3) The powers conferred by the following sections apply even if the seat of the arbitration is outside England and Wales or Northern Ireland or no seat has been designated or determined—

   (a) section 43 (securing the attendance of witnesses), and
   (b) section 44 (court powers exercisable in support of arbitral proceedings); but the court may refuse to exercise any such power if, in the opinion of the court, the fact that the seat of the arbitration is outside England and Wales or Northern Ireland, or that when designated or determined the seat is likely to be outside England and Wales or Northern Ireland, makes it inappropriate to do so.

(4) The court may exercise a power conferred by any provision of this Part not mentioned in subsection (2) or (3) for the purpose of supporting the arbitral process where—

   (a) no seat of the arbitration has been designated or determined, and
   (b) by reason of a connection with England and Wales or Northern Ireland the court is satisfied that it is appropriate to do so.

(5) Section 7 (separability of arbitration agreement) and section 8 (death of a party) apply where the law applicable to the arbitration agreement is the law of England and Wales or Northern Ireland even if the seat of the arbitration is outside England and Wales or Northern Ireland or has not been designated or determined.

1—004   **The seat of the arbitration**

3.—In this Part "the seat of the arbitration" means the juridical seat of the arbitration designated—

   (a) by the parties to the arbitration agreement, or
   (b) by any arbitral or other institution or person vested by the parties with powers in that regard, or
   (c) by the arbitral tribunal if so authorised by the parties, or determined, in the absence of any such designation, having regard to the parties' agreement and all the relevant circumstances.

1—005 Mandatory and non-mandatory provisions

4.—(1) The mandatory provisions of this Part are listed in Schedule 1 and have effect notwithstanding any agreement to the contrary.

(2) The other provisions of this Part (the "non-mandatory provisions") allow the parties to make their own arrangements by agreement but provide rules which apply in the absence of such agreement.

(3) The parties may make such arrangements by agreeing to the application of institutional rules or providing any other means by which a matter may be decided.

(4) It is immaterial whether or not the law applicable to the parties' agreement is the law of England and Wales or, as the case may be, Northern Ireland.

(5) The choice of a law other than the law of England and Wales or Northern Ireland as the applicable law in respect of a matter provided for by a non-mandatory provision of this Part is equivalent to an agreement making provision about that matter. For this purpose an applicable law determined in accordance with the parties' agreement, or which is objectively determined in the absence of any express or implied choice, shall be treated as chosen by the parties.

1—006 Agreements to be in writing

5.—(1) The provisions of this Part apply only where the arbitration agreement is in writing, and any other agreement between the parties as to any matter is effective for the purposes of this Part only if in writing. The expressions "agreement", "agree" and "agreed" shall be construed accordingly.

(2) There is an agreement in writing—

(a) if the agreement is made in writing (whether or not it is signed by the parties),
(b) if the agreement is made by exchange of communications in writing, or
(c) if the agreement is evidenced in writing.

(3) Where parties agree otherwise than in writing by reference to terms which are in writing, they make an agreement in writing.

(4) An agreement is evidenced in writing if an agreement made otherwise than in writing is recorded by one of the parties, or

by a third party, with the authority of the parties to the agreement.

(5) An exchange of written submissions in arbitral or legal proceedings in which the existence of an agreement otherwise than in writing is alleged by one party against another party and not denied by the other party in his response constitutes as between those parties an agreement in writing to the effect alleged.

(6) References in this Part to anything being written or in writing include its being recorded by any means.

Definition of arbitration agreement

1—007 The arbitration agreement

6.—(1) In this Part an "arbitration agreement" means an agreement to submit to arbitration present or future disputes (whether they are contractual or not).

(2) The reference in an agreement to a written form of arbitration clause or to a document containing an arbitration clause constitutes an arbitration agreement if the reference is such as to make that clause part of the agreement.

1—008 Separability of arbitration agreement

7.—Unless otherwise agreed by the parties, an arbitration agreement which forms or was intended to form part of another agreement (whether or not in writing) shall not be regarded as invalid, non-existent or ineffective because that other agreement is invalid, or did not come into existence or has become ineffective, and it shall for that purpose be treated as a distinct agreement.

1—009 Whether agreement discharged by death of a party

8.—(1) Unless otherwise agreed by the parties, an arbitration agreement is not discharged by the death of a party and may be enforced by or against the personal representatives of that party.

(2) Subsection (1) does not affect the operation of any enactment or rule of law by virtue of which a substantive right or obligation is extinguished by death.

Stay of legal proceedings

1—010 **Stay of legal proceedings**

9.—(1) A party to an arbitration agreement against whom legal proceedings are brought (whether by way of claim or counterclaim) in respect of a matter which under the agreement is to be referred to arbitration may (upon notice to the other parties to the proceedings) apply to the court in which the proceedings have been brought to stay the proceedings so far as they concern that matter.

(2) An application may be made notwithstanding that the matter is to be referred to arbitration only after the exhaustion of other dispute resolution procedures.

(3) An application may not be made by a person before taking the appropriate procedural step (if any) to acknowledge the legal proceedings against him or after he has taken any step in those proceedings to answer the substantive claim.

(4) On an application under this section the court shall grant a stay unless satisfied that the arbitration agreement is null and void, inoperative, or incapable of being performed.

(5) If the court refuses to stay the legal proceedings, any provision that an award is a condition precedent to the bringing of legal proceedings in respect of any matter is of no effect in relation to those proceedings.

1—011 **Reference of interpleader issue to arbitration**

10.—(1) Where in legal proceedings relief by way of interpleader is granted and any issue between the claimants is one in respect of which there is an arbitration agreement between them, the court granting the relief shall direct that the issue be determined in accordance with the agreement unless the circumstances are such that proceedings brought by a claimant in respect of the matter would not be stayed.

(2) Where subsection (1) applies but the court does not direct that the issue be determined in accordance with the arbitration agreement, any provision that an award is a condition precedent to the bringing of legal proceedings in respect of any matter shall not affect the determination of that issue by the court.

1—012 Retention of security where Admiralty proceedings stayed

11.—(1) Where Admiralty proceedings are stayed on the ground that the dispute in question should be submitted to arbitration, the court granting the stay may, if in those proceedings property has been arrested or bail or other security has been given to prevent or obtain release from arrest—

(a) order that the property arrested be retained as security for the satisfaction of any award given in the arbitration in respect of that dispute, or

(b) order that the stay of those proceedings be conditional on the provision of equivalent security for the satisfaction of any such award.

(2) Subject to any provision made by rules of court and to any necessary modifications, the same law and practice shall apply in relation to property retained in pursuance of an order as would apply if it were held for the purposes of proceedings in the court making the order.

Commencement of arbitral proceedings

1—013 Power of court to extend time for beginning arbitral proceedings, &c

12.—(1) Where an arbitration agreement to refer future disputes to arbitration provides that a claim shall be barred, or the claimant's right extinguished, unless the claimant takes within a time fixed by the agreement some step—

(a) to begin arbitral proceedings,

(b) to begin other dispute resolution procedures which must be exhausted before arbitral proceedings can be begun, the court may by order extend the time for taking that step.

(2) Any party to the arbitration agreement may apply for such an order (upon notice to the other parties), but only after a claim has arisen and after exhausting any available arbitral process for obtaining an extension of time.

(3) The court shall make an order only if satisfied—

(a) that the circumstances are such as were outside the reasonable contemplation of the parties when they agreed the provision in question, and that it would be just to extend the time, or

(b) that the conduct of one party makes it unjust to hold the other party to the strict terms of the provision in question.

(4) The court may extend the time for such period and on such terms as it thinks fit, and may do so whether or not the time previously fixed (by agreement or by a previous order) has expired.

(5) An order under this section does not affect the operation of the Limitation Acts (see section 13).

(6) The leave of the court is required for any appeal from a decision of the court under this section.

1—014 Application of Limitation Acts

13.—(1) The Limitation Acts apply to arbitral proceedings as they apply to legal proceedings.

(2) The court may order that in computing the time prescribed by the Limitation Acts for the commencement of proceedings (including arbitral proceedings) in respect of a dispute which was the subject matter:—

(a) of an award which the court orders to be set aside or declares to be of no effect, or
(b) of the affected part of an award which the court orders to be set aside in part, or declares to be in part of no effect, the period between the commencement of the arbitration and the date of the order referred to in paragraph (a) or (b) shall be excluded.

(3) In determining for the purposes of the Limitation Acts when a cause of action accrued, any provision that an award is a condition precedent to the bringing of legal proceedings in respect of a matter to which an arbitration agreement applies shall be disregarded.

(4) In this Part "the Limitation Acts" means:—

(a) in England and Wales, the Limitation Act 1980, the Foreign Limitation Periods Act 1984 and any other enactment (whenever passed) relating to the limitation of actions;
(b) in Northern Ireland, the Limitation (Northern Ireland) Order 1989, the Foreign Limitation Periods (Northern Ireland) Order 1985 and any other enactment (whenever passed) relating to the limitation of actions.

1—015 Commencement of arbitral proceedings

14.—(1) The parties are free to agree when arbitral proceedings are to be regarded as commenced for the purposes of this Part and for the purposes of the Limitation Acts.

(2) If there is no such agreement the following provisions apply.

(3) Where the arbitrator is named or designated in the arbitration agreement, arbitral proceedings are commenced in respect of a matter when one party serves on the other party or parties a notice in writing requiring him or them to submit that matter to the person so named or designated.

(4) Where the arbitrator or arbitrators are to be appointed by the parties, arbitral proceedings are commenced in respect of a matter when one party serves on the other party or parties notice in writing requiring him or them to appoint an arbitrator or to agree to the appointment of an arbitrator in respect of that matter.

(5) Where the arbitrator or arbitrators are to be appointed by a person other than a party to the proceedings, arbitral proceedings are commenced in respect of a matter when one party gives notice in writing to that person requesting him to make the appointment in respect of that matter.

The arbitral tribunal

1—016 The arbitral tribunal

15.—(1) The parties are free to agree on the number of arbitrators to form the tribunal and whether there is to be a chairman or umpire.

(2) Unless otherwise agreed by the parties, an agreement that the number of arbitrators shall be two or any other even number shall be understood as requiring the appointment of an additional arbitrator as chairman of the tribunal.

(3) If there is no agreement as to the number of arbitrators, the tribunal shall consist of a sole arbitrator.

1—017 Procedure for appointment of arbitrators

16.—(1) The parties are free to agree on the procedure for appointing the arbitrator or arbitrators, including the procedure for appointing any chairman or umpire.

(2) If or to the extent that there is no such agreement, the following provisions apply.

(3) If the tribunal is to consist of a sole arbitrator, the parties shall jointly appoint the arbitrator not later than 28 days after service of a request in writing by either party to do so.

(4) If the tribunal is to consist of two arbitrators, each party shall appoint one arbitrator not later than 14 days after service of a request in writing by either party to do so.

(5) If the tribunal is to consist of three arbitrators—

   (a) each party shall appoint one arbitrator not later than 14 days after service of a request in writing by either party to do so, and
   (b) the two so appointed shall forthwith appoint a third arbitrator as the chairman of the tribunal.

(6) If the tribunal is to consist of two arbitrators and an umpire—

   (a) each party shall appoint one arbitrator not later than 14 days after service of a request in writing by either party to do so, and
   (b) the two so appointed may appoint an umpire at any time after they themselves are appointed and shall do so before any substantive hearing or forthwith if they cannot agree on a matter relating to the arbitration.

(7) In any other case (in particular, if there are more than two parties) section 18 applies as in the case of a failure of the agreed appointment procedure.

1—018 **Power in case of default to appoint sole arbitrator**

17.—(1) Unless the parties otherwise agree, where each of two parties to an arbitration agreement is to appoint an arbitrator and one party ("the party in default") refuses to do so, or fails to do so within the time specified, the other party, having duly appointed his arbitrator, may give notice in writing to the party in default that he proposes to appoint his arbitrator to act as sole arbitrator.

(2) If the party in default does not within 7 clear days of that notice being given—

   (a) make the required appointment, and
   (b) notify the other party that he has done so, the other party may appoint his arbitrator as sole arbitrator whose

award shall be binding on both parties as if he had been so appointed by agreement.

(3) Where a sole arbitrator has been appointed under subsection (2), the party in default may (upon notice to the appointing party) apply to the court which may set aside the appointment.

(4) The leave of the court is required for any appeal from a decision of the court under this section.

1—019 Failure of appointment procedure

18.—(1) The parties are free to agree what is to happen in the event of a failure of the procedure for the appointment of the arbitral tribunal. There is no failure if an appointment is duly made under section 17 (power in case of default to appoint sole arbitrator), unless that appointment is set aside.

(2) If or to the extent that there is no such agreement any party to the arbitration agreement may (upon notice to the other parties) apply to the court to exercise its powers under this section.

(3) Those powers are—
   (a) to give directions as to the making of any necessary appointments;
   (b) to direct that the tribunal shall be constituted by such appointments (or any one or more of them) as have been made;
   (c) to revoke any appointments already made;
   (d) to make any necessary appointments itself.

(4) An appointment made by the court under this section has effect as if made with the agreement of the parties.

(5) The leave of the court is required for any appeal from a decision of the court under this section.

1—020 Court to have regard to agreed qualifications

19.—In deciding whether to exercise, and in considering how to exercise, any of its powers under section 16 (procedure for appointment of arbitrators) or section 18 (failure of appointment procedure), the court shall have due regard to any agreement of the parties as to the qualifications required of the arbitrators.

A. English and Irish Statutes

1—021   Chairman

20.—(1) Where the parties have agreed that there is to be a chairman, they are free to agree what the functions of the chairman are to be in relation to the making of decisions, orders and awards.

(2) If or to the extent that there is no such agreement, the following provisions apply.

(3) Decisions, orders and awards shall be made by all or a majority of the arbitrators (including the chairman).

(4) The view of the chairman shall prevail in relation to a decision, order or award in respect of which there is neither unanimity nor a majority under subsection (3).

1—022   Umpire

21.—(1) Where the parties have agreed that there is to be an umpire, they are free to agree what the functions of the umpire are to be, and in particular—

(a) whether he is to attend the proceedings, and
(b) when he is to replace the other arbitrators as the tribunal with power to make decisions, orders and awards.

(2) If or to the extent that there is no such agreement, the following provisions apply.

(3) The umpire shall attend the proceedings and be supplied with the same documents and other materials as are supplied to the other arbitrators.

(4) Decisions, orders and awards shall be made by the other arbitrators unless and until they cannot agree on a matter relating to the arbitration. In that event they shall forthwith give notice in writing to the parties and the umpire, whereupon the umpire shall replace them as the tribunal with power to make decisions, orders and awards as if he were sole arbitrator.

(5) If the arbitrators cannot agree but fail to give notice of that fact, or if any of them fails to join in the giving of notice, any party to the arbitral proceedings may (upon notice to the other parties and to the tribunal) apply to the court which may order that the umpire shall replace the other arbitrators as the tribunal with power to make decisions, orders and awards as if he were sole arbitrator.

(6) The leave of the court is required for any appeal from a decision of the court under this section.

1—023 Decision-making where no chairman or umpire

22.—(1) Where the parties agree that there shall be two or more arbitrators with no chairman or umpire, the parties are free to agree how the tribunal is to make decisions, orders and awards.

(2) If there is no such agreement, decisions, orders and awards shall be made by all or a majority of the arbitrators.

1—024 Revocation of arbitrator's authority

23.—(1) The parties are free to agree in what circumstances the authority of an arbitrator may be revoked.

(2) If or to the extent that there is no such agreement the following provisions apply.

(3) The authority of an arbitrator may not be revoked except—

   (a) by the parties acting jointly, or
   (b) by an arbitral or other institution or person vested by the parties with powers in that regard.

(4) Revocation of the authority of an arbitrator by the parties acting jointly must be agreed in writing unless the parties also agree (whether or not in writing) to terminate the arbitration agreement.

(5) Nothing in this section affects the power of the court—

   (a) to revoke an appointment under section 18 (powers exercisable in case of failure of appointment procedure), or
   (b) to remove an arbitrator on the grounds specified in section 24.

1—025 Power of court to remove arbitrator

24.—(1) A party to arbitral proceedings may (upon notice to the other parties, to the arbitrator concerned and to any other arbitrator) apply to the court to remove an arbitrator on any of the following grounds—

   (a) that circumstances exist that give rise to justifiable doubts as to his impartiality;
   (b) that he does not possess the qualifications required by the arbitration agreement;

(c) that he is physically or mentally incapable of conducting the proceedings or there are justifiable doubts as to his capacity to do so;

(d) that he has refused or failed—

(i) properly to conduct the proceedings, or

(ii) to use all reasonable despatch in conducting the proceedings or making an award, and that substantial injustice has been or will be caused to the applicant.

(2) If there is an arbitral or other institution or person vested by the parties with power to remove an arbitrator, the court shall not exercise its power of removal unless satisfied that the applicant has first exhausted any available recourse to that institution or person.

(3) The arbitral tribunal may continue the arbitral proceedings and make an award while an application to the court under this section is pending.

(4) Where the court removes an arbitrator, it may make such order as it thinks fit with respect to his entitlement (if any) to fees or expenses, or the repayment of any fees or expenses already paid.

(5) The arbitrator concerned is entitled to appear and be heard by the court before it makes any order under this section.

(6) The leave of the court is required for any appeal from a decision of the court under this section.

1—026 Resignation of arbitrator

25.—(1) The parties are free to agree with an arbitrator as to the consequences of his resignation as regards—

(a) his entitlement (if any) to fees or expenses, and

(b) any liability thereby incurred by him.

(2) If or to the extent that there is no such agreement the following provisions apply.

(3) An arbitrator who resigns his appointment may (upon notice to the parties) apply to the court—

(a) to grant him relief from any liability thereby incurred by him, and

(b) to make such order as it thinks fit with respect to his entitlement (if any) to fees or expenses or the repayment of any fees or expenses already paid.

(4) If the court is satisfied that in all the circumstances it was reasonable for the arbitrator to resign, it may grant such relief as is mentioned in subsection (3)(a) on such terms as it thinks fit.

(5) The leave of the court is required for any appeal from a decision of the court under this section.

1—027 Death of arbitrator or person appointing him

26.—(1) The authority of an arbitrator is personal and ceases on his death.

(2) Unless otherwise agreed by the parties, the death of the person by whom an arbitrator was appointed does not revoke the arbitrator's authority.

1—028 Filling of vacancy, &c

27.—(1) Where an arbitrator ceases to hold office, the parties are free to agree—

(a) whether and if so how the vacancy is to be filled,
(b) whether and if so to what extent the previous proceedings should stand, and
(c) what effect (if any) his ceasing to hold office has on any appointment made by him (alone or jointly).

(2) If or to the extent that there is no such agreement, the following provisions apply.

(3) The provisions of sections 16 (procedure for appointment of arbitrators) and 18 (failure of appointment procedure) apply in relation to the filling of the vacancy as in relation to an original appointment.

(4) The tribunal (when reconstituted) shall determine whether and if so to what extent the previous proceedings should stand. This does not affect any right of a party to challenge those proceedings on any ground which had arisen before the arbitrator ceased to hold office.

(5) His ceasing to hold office does not affect any appointment by him (alone or jointly) of another arbitrator, in particular any appointment of a chairman or umpire.

A. English and Irish Statutes

1—029 Joint and several liability of parties to arbitrators for fees and expenses

28.—(1) The parties are jointly and severally liable to pay to the arbitrators such reasonable fees and expenses (if any) as are appropriate in the circumstances.

(2) Any party may apply to the court (upon notice to the other parties and to the arbitrators) which may order that the amount of the arbitrators' fees and expenses shall be considered and adjusted by such means and upon such terms as it may direct.

(3) If the application is made after any amount has been paid to the arbitrators by way of fees or expenses, the court may order the repayment of such amount (if any) as is shown to be excessive, but shall not do so unless it is shown that it is reasonable in the circumstances to order repayment.

(4) The above provisions have effect subject to any order of the court under section 24(4) or 25(3)(b) (order as to entitlement to fees or expenses in case of removal or resignation of arbitrator).

(5) Nothing in this section affects any liability of a party to any other party to pay all or any of the costs of the arbitration (see sections 59 to 65) or any contractual right of an arbitrator to payment of his fees and expenses.

(6) In this section references to arbitrators include an arbitrator who has ceased to act and an umpire who has not replaced the other arbitrators.

1—030 Immunity of arbitrator

29.—(1) An arbitrator is not liable for anything done or omitted in the discharge or purported discharge of his functions as arbitrator unless the act or omission is shown to have been in bad faith.

(2) Subsection (1) applies to an employee or agent of an arbitrator as it applies to the arbitrator himself.

(3) This section does not affect any liability incurred by an arbitrator by reason of his resigning (but see section 25).

Jurisdiction of the arbitral tribunal

1—031 Competence of tribunal to rule on its own jurisdiction

30.—(1) Unless otherwise agreed by the parties, the arbitral tribunal may rule on its own substantive jurisdiction, that is, as to—

(a) whether there is a valid arbitration agreement,
(b) whether the tribunal is properly constituted, and
(c) what matters have been submitted to arbitration in accordance with the arbitration agreement.

(2) Any such ruling may be challenged by any available arbitral process of appeal or review or in accordance with the provisions of this Part.

1—032 Objection to substantive jurisdiction of tribunal

31.—(1) An objection that the arbitral tribunal lacks substantive jurisdiction at the outset of the proceedings must be raised by a party not later than the time he takes the first step in the proceedings to contest the merits of any matter in relation to which he challenges the tribunal's jurisdiction. A party is not precluded from raising such an objection by the fact that he has appointed or participated in the appointment of an arbitrator.

(2) Any objection during the course of the arbitral proceedings that the arbitral tribunal is exceeding its substantive jurisdiction must be made as soon as possible after the matter alleged to be beyond its jurisdiction is raised.

(3) The arbitral tribunal may admit an objection later than the time specified in subsection (1) or (2) if it considers the delay justified.

(4) Where an objection is duly taken to the tribunal's substantive jurisdiction and the tribunal has power to rule on its own jurisdiction, it may—

(a) rule on the matter in an award as to jurisdiction, or
(b) deal with the objection in its award on the merits. If the parties agree which of these courses the tribunal should take, the tribunal shall proceed accordingly.

(5) The tribunal may in any case, and shall if the parties so agree, stay proceedings whilst an application is made to the court under section 32 (determination of preliminary point of jurisdiction).

1—033 Determination of preliminary point of jurisdiction

32.—(1) The court may, on the application of a party to arbitral proceedings (upon notice to the other parties), determine any question as to the substantive jurisdiction of the tribunal. A party may lose the right to object (see section 73).

(2) An application under this section shall not be considered unless—

(a) it is made with the agreement in writing of all the other parties to the proceedings, or
(b) it is made with the permission of the tribunal and the court is satisfied—

(i) that the determination of the question is likely to produce substantial savings in costs,
(ii) that the application was made without delay, and
(iii) that there is good reason why the matter should be decided by the court.

(3) An application under this section, unless made with the agreement of all the other parties to the proceedings, shall state the grounds on which it is said that the matter should be decided by the court.

(4) Unless otherwise agreed by the parties, the arbitral tribunal may continue the arbitral proceedings and make an award while an application to the court under this section is pending.

(5) Unless the court gives leave, no appeal lies from a decision of the court whether the conditions specified in subsection (2) are met.

(6) The decision of the court on the question of jurisdiction shall be treated as a judgment of the court for the purposes of an appeal. But no appeal lies without the leave of the court which shall not be given unless the court considers that the question involves a point of law which is one of general importance or is one which for some other special reason should be considered by the Court of Appeal.

The Arbitral Proceedings

1—034 General duty of the tribunal

33.—(1) The tribunal shall—

(a) act fairly and impartially as between the parties, giving each party a reasonable opportunity of putting his case and dealing with that of his opponent, and

(b) adopt procedures suitable to the circumstances of the particular case, avoiding unnecessary delay or expense, so as to provide a fair means for the resolution of the matters falling to be determined.

(2) The tribunal shall comply with that general duty in conducting the arbitral proceedings, in its decisions on matters of procedure and evidence and in the exercise of all other powers conferred on it.

1—035 **Procedural and evidential matters**

34.—(1) It shall be for the tribunal to decide all procedural and evidential matters, subject to the right of the parties to agree any matter.

(2) Procedural and evidential matters include—

(a) when and where any part of the proceedings is to be held;
(b) the language or languages to be used in the proceedings and whether translations of any relevant documents are to be supplied;
(c) whether any and if so what form of written statements of claim and defence are to be used, when these should be supplied and the extent to which such statements can be later amended;
(d) whether any and if so which documents or classes of documents should be disclosed between and produced by the parties and at what stage;
(e) whether any and if so what questions should be put to and answered by the respective parties and when and in what form this should be done;
(f) whether to apply strict rules of evidence (or any other rules) as to the admissibility, relevance or weight of any material (oral, written or other) sought to be tendered on any matters of fact or opinion, and the time, manner and form in which such material should be exchanged and presented;
(g) whether and to what extent the tribunal should itself take the initiative in ascertaining the facts and the law;
(h) whether and to what extent there should be oral or written evidence or submissions.

(3) The tribunal may fix the time within which any directions given by it are to be complied with, and may if it thinks fit extend the time so fixed (whether or not it has expired).

1—036 Consolidation of proceedings and concurrent hearings

35.—(1) The parties are free to agree—

    (a) that the arbitral proceedings shall be consolidated with other arbitral proceedings, or

    (b) that concurrent hearings shall be held, on such terms as may be agreed.

(2) Unless the parties agree to confer such power on the tribunal, the tribunal has no power to order consolidation of proceedings or concurrent hearings.

1—037 Legal or other representation

36.—Unless otherwise agreed by the parties, a party to arbitral proceedings may be represented in the proceedings by a lawyer or other person chosen by him.

1—038 Power to appoint experts, legal advisers or assessors

37.—(1) Unless otherwise agreed by the parties—

    (a) the tribunal may—

        (i) appoint experts or legal advisers to report to it and the parties, or

        (ii) appoint assessors to assist it on technical matters,

    and may allow any such expert, legal adviser or assessor to attend the proceedings; and

    (b) the parties shall be given a reasonable opportunity to comment on any information, opinion or advice offered

(2) The fees and expenses of an expert, legal adviser or assessor appointed by the tribunal for which the arbitrators are liable are expenses of the arbitrators for the purposes of this Part.

1—039 General powers exercisable by the tribunal

38.—(1) The parties are free to agree on the powers exercisable by the arbitral tribunal for the purposes of and in relation to the proceedings.

(2) Unless otherwise agreed by the parties the tribunal has the following powers.

(3) The tribunal may order a claimant to provide security for the costs of the arbitration. This power shall not be exercised on the ground that the claimant is—

(a) an individual ordinarily resident outside the United Kingdom, or

(b) a corporation or association incorporated or formed under the law of a country outside the United Kingdom, or whose central management and control is exercised outside the United Kingdom.

(4) The tribunal may give directions in relation to any property which is the subject of the proceedings or as to which any question arises in the proceedings, and which is owned by or is in the possession of a party to the proceedings—

(a) for the inspection, photographing, preservation, custody or detention of the property by the tribunal, an expert or a party, or

(b) ordering that samples be taken from, or any observation be made of or experiment conducted upon, the property.

(5) The tribunal may direct that a party or witness shall be examined on oath or affirmation, and may for that purpose administer any necessary oath or take any necessary affirmation.

(6) The tribunal may give directions to a party for the preservation for the purposes of the proceedings of any evidence in his custody or control.

1—040   Power to make provisional awards

39.—(1) The parties are free to agree that the tribunal shall have power to order on a provisional basis any relief which it would have power to grant in a final award.

(2) This includes, for instance, making—

(a) a provisional order for the payment of money or the disposition of property as between the parties, or

(b) an order to make an interim payment on account of the costs of the arbitration.

(3) Any such order shall be subject to the tribunal's final adjudication; and the tribunal's final award, on the merits or as to costs, shall take account of any such order.

(4) Unless the parties agree to confer such power on the tribunal, the tribunal has no such power. This does not affect its powers under section 47 (awards on different issues, &c.).

1—041 General duty of parties

40.—(1) The parties shall do all things necessary for the proper and expeditious conduct of the arbitral proceedings.

(2) This includes—

(a) complying without delay with any determination of the tribunal as to procedural or evidential matters, or with any order or directions of the tribunal, and
(b) where appropriate, taking without delay any necessary steps to obtain a decision of the court on a preliminary question of jurisdiction or law (see sections 32 and 45).

1—042 Powers of tribunal in case of party's default

41.—(1) The parties are free to agree on the powers of the tribunal in case of a party's failure to do something necessary for the proper and expeditious conduct of the arbitration.

(2) Unless otherwise agreed by the parties, the following provisions apply.

(3) If the tribunal is satisfied that there has been inordinate and inexcusable delay on the part of the claimant in pursuing his claim and that the delay—

(a) gives rise, or is likely to give rise, to a substantial risk that it is not possible to have a fair resolution of the issues in that claim, or
(b) has caused, or is likely to cause, serious prejudice to the respondent, the tribunal may make an award dismissing the claim.

(4) If without showing sufficient cause a party—

(a) fails to attend or be represented at an oral hearing of which due notice was given, or
(b) where matters are to be dealt with in writing, fails after due notice to submit written evidence or make written submissions, the tribunal may continue the proceedings in the absence of that party or, as the case may be, without any written evidence or submissions on his behalf, and may make an award on the basis of the evidence before it.

(5) If without showing sufficient cause a party fails to comply with any order or directions of the tribunal, the tribunal may make a peremptory order to the same effect, prescribing such time for compliance with it as the tribunal considers appropriate.

(6) If a claimant fails to comply with a peremptory order of the tribunal to provide security for costs, the tribunal may make an award dismissing his claim.

(7) If a party fails to comply with any other kind of peremptory order, then, without prejudice to section 42 (enforcement by court of tribunal's peremptory orders), the tribunal may do any of the following—

(a) direct that the party in default shall not be entitled to rely upon any allegation or material which was the subject matter of the order;
(b) draw such adverse inferences from the act of non-compliance as the circumstances justify;
(c) proceed to an award on the basis of such materials as have been properly provided to it;
(d) make such order as it thinks fit as to the payment of costs of the arbitration incurred in consequence of the non-compliance.

Powers of Court in Relation to Arbitral Proceedings

1—043 Enforcement of peremptory orders of tribunal

42.—(1) Unless otherwise agreed by the parties, the court may make an order requiring a party to comply with a peremptory order made by the tribunal.

(2) An application for an order under this section may be made—

(a) by the tribunal (upon notice to the parties),
(b) by a party to the arbitral proceedings with the permission of the tribunal (and upon notice to the other parties), or
(c) where the parties have agreed that the powers of the court under this section shall be available.

(3) The court shall not act unless it is satisfied that the applicant has exhausted any available arbitral process in respect of failure to comply with the tribunal's order.

(4) No order shall be made under this section unless the court is satisfied that the person to whom the tribunal's order was directed has failed to comply with it within the time prescribed in the order or, if no time was prescribed, within a reasonable time.

(5) The leave of the court is required for any appeal from a decision of the court under this section.

1—044 Securing the attendance of witnesses

43.—(1) A party to arbitral proceedings may use the same court procedures as are available in relation to legal proceedings to secure the attendance before the tribunal of a witness in order to give oral testimony or to produce documents or other material evidence.

(2) This may only be done with the permission of the tribunal or the agreement of the other parties.

(3) The court procedures may only be used if—

 (a) the witness is in the United Kingdom, and
 (b) the arbitral proceedings are being conducted in England and Wales or, as the case may be, Northern Ireland.

(4) A person shall not be compelled by virtue of this section to produce any document or other material evidence which he could not be compelled to produce in legal proceedings.

1—045 Court powers exercisable in support of arbitral proceedings

44.—(1) Unless otherwise agreed by the parties, the court has for the purposes of and in relation to arbitral proceedings the same power of making orders about the matters listed below as it has for the purposes of and in relation to legal proceedings.

(2) Those matters are—

 (a) the taking of the evidence of witnesses;
 (b) the preservation of evidence;
 (c) making orders relating to property which is the subject of the proceedings or as to which any question arises in the proceedings—

  (i) for the inspection, photographing, preservation, custody or detention of the property, or
  (ii) ordering that samples be taken from, or any observation be made of or experiment conducted upon, the property; and for that purpose authorising any person to enter any premises in the possession or control of a party to the arbitration;

 (d) the sale of any goods the subject of the proceedings;
 (e) the granting of an interim injunction or the appointment of a receiver.

(3) If the case is one of urgency, the court may, on the application of a party or proposed party to the arbitral proceedings,

make such orders as it thinks necessary for the purpose of preserving evidence or assets.

(4) If the case is not one of urgency, the court shall act only on the application of a party to the arbitral proceedings (upon notice to the other parties and to the tribunal) made with the permission of the tribunal or the agreement in writing of the other parties.

(5) In any case the court shall act only if or to the extent that the arbitral tribunal, and any arbitral or other institution or person vested by the parties with power in that regard, has no power or is unable for the time being to act effectively.

(6) If the court so orders, an order made by it under this section shall cease to have effect in whole or in part on the order of the tribunal or of any such arbitral or other institution or person having power to act in relation to the subject-matter of the order

(7) The leave of the court is required for any appeal from a decision of the court under this section.

1—046 Determination of preliminary point of law

45.—(1) Unless otherwise agreed by the parties, the court may on the application of a party to arbitral proceedings (upon notice to the other parties) determine any question of law arising in the course of the proceedings which the court is satisfied substantially affects the rights of one or more of the parties. An agreement to dispense with reasons for the tribunal's award shall be considered an agreement to exclude the court's jurisdiction under this section.

(2) An application under this section shall not be considered unless—

  (a) it is made with the agreement of all the other parties to the proceedings, or

  (b) it is made with the permission of the tribunal and the court is satisfied—

    (i) that the determination of the question is likely to produce substantial savings in costs, and

    (ii) that the application was made without delay.

(3) The application shall identify the question of law to be determined and, unless made with the agreement of all the other parties to the proceedings, shall state the grounds on which it is said that the question should be decided by the court.

(4) Unless otherwise agreed by the parties, the arbitral tribunal may continue the arbitral proceedings and make an award while an application to the court under this section is pending.

(5) Unless the court gives leave, no appeal lies from a decision of the court whether the conditions specified in subsection (2) are met.

(6) The decision of the court on the question of law shall be treated as a judgment of the court for the purposes of an appeal. But no appeal lies without the leave of the court which shall not be given unless the court considers that the question is one of general importance, or is one which for some other special reason should be considered by the Court of Appeal.

The Award

1—047 Rules applicable to substance of dispute

46.—(1) The arbitral tribunal shall decide the dispute—

    (a) in accordance with the law chosen by the parties as applicable to the substance of the dispute, or
    (b) if the parties so agree, in accordance with such other considerations as are agreed by them or determined by the tribunal.

(2) For this purpose the choice of the laws of a country shall be understood to refer to the substantive laws of that country and not its conflict of laws rules.

(3) If or to the extent that there is no such choice or agreement, the tribunal shall apply the law determined by the conflict of laws rules which it considers applicable.

1—048 Awards on different issues, &c

47.—(1) Unless otherwise agreed by the parties, the tribunal may make more than one award at different times on different aspects of the matters to be determined.

(2) The tribunal may, in particular, make an award relating—

    (a) to an issue affecting the whole claim, or
    (b) to a part only of the claims or cross-claims submitted to it for decision.

(3) If the tribunal does so, it shall specify in its award the issue, or the claim or part of a claim, which is the subject matter of the award.

1—049 Remedies

48.—(1) The parties are free to agree on the powers exercisable by the arbitral tribunal as regards remedies.

(2) Unless otherwise agreed by the parties, the tribunal has the following powers.

(3) The tribunal may make a declaration as to any matter to be determined in the proceedings.

(4) The tribunal may order the payment of a sum of money, in any currency.

(5) The tribunal has the same powers as the court—

    (a) to order a party to do or refrain from doing anything;
    (b) to order specific performance of a contract (other than a contract relating to land);
    (c) to order the rectification, setting aside or cancellation of a deed or other document.

1—050 Interest

49.—(1) The parties are free to agree on the powers of the tribunal as regards the award of interest.

(2) Unless otherwise agreed by the parties the following provisions apply

(3) The tribunal may award simple or compound interest from such dates, at such rates and with such rests as it considers meets the justice of the case—

    (a) on the whole or part of any amount awarded by the tribunal, in respect of any period up to the date of the award;
    (b) on the whole or part of any amount claimed in the arbitration and outstanding at the commencement of the arbitral proceedings but paid before the award was made, in respect of any period up to the date of payment.

(4) The tribunal may award simple or compound interest from the date of the award (or any later date) until payment, at such rates and with such rests as it considers meets the justice of the case, on the outstanding amount of any award (including any award of interest under subsection (3) and any award as to costs).

(5) References in this section to an amount awarded by the tribunal include an amount payable in consequence of a declaratory award by the tribunal.

(6) The above provisions do not affect any other power of the tribunal to award interest.

1—051 Extension of time for making award

50.—(1) Where the time for making an award is limited by or in pursuance of the arbitration agreement, then, unless otherwise agreed by the parties, the court may in accordance with the following provisions by order extend that time.

(2) An application for an order under this section may be made—
   (a) by the tribunal (upon notice to the parties), or
   (b) by any party to the proceedings (upon notice to the tribunal and the other parties), but only after exhausting any available arbitral process for obtaining an extension of time.

(3) The court shall only make an order if satisfied that a substantial injustice would otherwise be done.

(4) The court may extend the time for such period and on such terms as it thinks fit, and may do so whether or not the time previously fixed (by or under the agreement or by a previous order) has expired.

(5) The leave of the court is required for any appeal from a decision of the court under this section.

1—052 Settlement

51.—(1) If during arbitral proceedings the parties settle the dispute, the following provisions apply unless otherwise agreed by the parties.

(2) The tribunal shall terminate the substantive proceedings and, if so requested by the parties and not objected to by the tribunal, shall record the settlement in the form of an agreed award.

(3) An agreed award shall state that it is an award of the tribunal and shall have the same status and effect as any other award on the merits of the case.

(4) The following provisions of this Part relating to awards (sections 52 to 58) apply to an agreed award.

(5) Unless the parties have also settled the matter of the payment of the costs of the arbitration, the provisions of this Part relating to costs (sections 59 to 65) continue to apply.

1—053 Form of award

52.—(1) The parties are free to agree on the form of an award.

(2) If or to the extent that there is no such agreement, the following provisions apply.

(3) The award shall be in writing signed by all the arbitrators or all those assenting to the award.

(4) The award shall contain the reasons for the award unless it is an agreed award or the parties have agreed to dispense with reasons.

(5) The award shall state the seat of the arbitration and the date when the award is made.

1—054 Place where award treated as made

53.—Unless otherwise agreed by the parties, where the seat of the arbitration is in England and Wales or Northern Ireland, any award in the proceedings shall be treated as made there, regardless of where it was signed, despatched or delivered to any of the parties.

1—055 Date of award

54.—(1) Unless otherwise agreed by the parties, the tribunal may decide what is to be taken to be the date on which the award was made.

(2) In the absence of any such decision, the date of the award shall be taken to be the date on which it is signed by the arbitrator or, where more than one arbitrator signs the award, by the last of them.

1—056 Notification of award

55.—(1) The parties are free to agree on the requirements as to notification of the award to the parties.

(2) If there is no such agreement, the award shall be notified to the parties by service on them of copies of the award, which shall be done without delay after the award is made.

(3) Nothing in this section affects section 56 (power to withhold award in case of non-payment).

1—057   Power to withhold award in case of non-payment

56.—(1) The tribunal may refuse to deliver an award to the parties except upon full payment of the fees and expenses of the arbitrators.

   (2) If the tribunal refuses on that ground to deliver an award, a party to the arbitral proceedings may (upon notice to the other parties and the tribunal) apply to the court, which may order that—

   (a) the tribunal shall deliver the award on the payment into court by the applicant of the fees and expenses demanded, or such lesser amount as the court may specify,
   (b) the amount of the fees and expenses properly payable shall be determined by such means and upon such terms as the court may direct, and
   (c) out of the money paid into court there shall be paid out such fees and expenses as may be found to be properly payable and the balance of the money (if any) shall be paid out to the applicant.

   (3) For this purpose the amount of fees and expenses properly payable is the amount the applicant is liable to pay under section 28 or any agreement relating to the payment of the arbitrators.

   (4) No application to the court may be made where there is any available arbitral process for appeal or review of the amount of the fees or expenses demanded.

   (5) References in this section to arbitrators include an arbitrator who has ceased to act and an umpire who has not replaced the other arbitrators.

   (6) The above provisions of this section also apply in relation to any arbitral or other institution or person vested by the parties with powers in relation to the delivery of the tribunal's award. As they so apply, the references to the fees and expenses of the arbitrators shall be construed as including the fees and expenses of that institution or person.

   (7) The leave of the court is required for any appeal from a decision of the court under this section.

   (8) Nothing in this section shall be construed as excluding an application under section 28 where payment has been made to the arbitrators in order to obtain the award.

1—058 Correction of award or additional award

57.—(1) The parties are free to agree on the powers of the tribunal to correct an award or make an additional award.

(2) If or to the extent there is no such agreement, the following provisions apply.

(3) The tribunal may on its own initiative or on the application of a party—

(a) correct an award so as to remove any clerical mistake or error arising from an accidental slip or omission or clarify or remove any ambiguity in the award, or

(b) make an additional award in respect of any claim (including a claim for interest or costs) which was presented to the tribunal but was not dealt with in the award. These powers shall not be exercised without first affording the other parties a reasonable opportunity to make representations to the tribunal.

(4) Any application for the exercise of those powers must be made within 28 days of the date of the award or such longer period as the parties may agree.

(5) Any correction of an award shall be made within 28 days of the date the application was received by the tribunal or, where the correction is made by the tribunal on its own initiative, within 28 days of the date of the award or, in either case, such longer period as the parties may agree.

(6) Any additional award shall be made within 56 days of the date of the original award or such longer period as the parties may agree.

(7) Any correction of an award shall form part of the award.

1—059 Effect of award

58.—(1) Unless otherwise agreed by the parties, an award made by the tribunal pursuant to an arbitration agreement is final and binding both on the parties and on any persons claiming through or under them.

(2) This does not affect the right of a person to challenge the award by any available arbitral process of appeal or review or in accordance with the provisions of this Part.

Costs of the arbitration

1—060 Costs of the arbitration

59.—(1) References in this Part to the costs of the arbitration are to—
    (a) the arbitrators' fees and expenses,
    (b) the fees and expenses of any arbitral institution concerned, and
    (c) the legal or other costs of the parties.

(2) Any such reference includes the costs of or incidental to any proceedings to determine the amount of the recoverable costs of the arbitration (see section 63).

1—061 Agreement to pay costs in any event

60.—An agreement which has the effect that a party is to pay the whole or part of the costs of the arbitration in any event is only valid if made after the dispute in question has arisen.

1—062 Award of costs

61.—(1) The tribunal may make an award allocating the costs of the arbitration as between the parties, subject to any agreement of the parties.

(2) Unless the parties otherwise agree, the tribunal shall award costs on the general principle that costs should follow the event except where it appears to the tribunal that in the circumstances this is not appropriate in relation to the whole or part of the costs.

1—063 Effect of agreement or award about costs

62.—Unless the parties otherwise agree, any obligation under an agreement between them as to how the costs of the arbitration are to be borne, or under an award allocating the costs of the arbitration, extends only to such costs as are recoverable.

1—064 The recoverable costs of the arbitration

63.—(1) The parties are free to agree what costs of the arbitration are recoverable.

(2) If or to the extent there is no such agreement, the following provisions apply.

(3) The tribunal may determine by award the recoverable costs of the arbitration on such basis as it thinks fit. If it does so, it shall specify—

(a) the basis on which it has acted, and
(b) the items of recoverable costs and the amount referable to each.

(4) If the tribunal does not determine the recoverable costs of the arbitration, any party to the arbitral proceedings may apply to the court (upon notice to the other parties) which may—

(a) determine the recoverable costs of the arbitration on such basis as it thinks fit, or
(b) order that they shall be determined by such means and upon such terms as it may specify.

(5) Unless the tribunal or the court determines otherwise—

(a) the recoverable costs of the arbitration shall be determined on the basis that there shall be allowed a reasonable amount in respect of all costs reasonably incurred, and
(b) any doubt as to whether costs were reasonably incurred or were reasonable in amount shall be resolved in favour of the paying party.

(6) The above provisions have effect subject to section 64 (recoverable fees and expenses of arbitrators).

(7) Nothing in this section affects any right of the arbitrators, any expert, legal adviser or assessor appointed by the tribunal, or any arbitral institution, to payment of their fees and expenses.

1—065 **Recoverable fees and expenses of arbitrators**

64.—(1) Unless otherwise agreed by the parties, the recoverable costs of the arbitration shall include in respect of the fees and expenses of the arbitrators only such reasonable fees and expenses as are appropriate in the circumstances.

(2) If there is any question as to what reasonable fees and expenses are appropriate in the circumstances, and the matter is not already before the court on an application under section 63(4), the court may on the application of any party (upon notice to the other parties)—

(a) determine the matter, or
(b) order that it be determined by such means and upon such terms as the court may specify.

(3) Subsection (1) has effect subject to any order of the court under section 24(4) or 25(3)(b) (order as to entitlement to fees or expenses in case of removal or resignation of arbitrator).

(4) Nothing in this section affects any right of the arbitrator to payment of his fees and expenses.

1—066   **Power to limit recoverable costs**

65.—(1) Unless otherwise agreed by the parties, the tribunal may direct that the recoverable costs of the arbitration, or of any part of the arbitral proceedings, shall be limited to a specified amount.

(2) Any direction may be made or varied at any stage, but this must be done sufficiently in advance of the incurring of costs to which it relates, or the taking of any steps in the proceedings which may be affected by it, for the limit to be taken into account.

Powers of the court in relation to award

1—067   **Enforcement of the award**

66.—(1) An award made by the tribunal pursuant to an arbitration agreement may, by leave of the court, be enforced in the same manner as a judgment or order of the court to the same effect.

(2) Where leave is so given, judgment may be entered in terms of the award.

(3) Leave to enforce an award shall not be given where, or to the extent that, the person against whom it is sought to be enforced shows that the tribunal lacked substantive jurisdiction to make the award. The right to raise such an objection may have been lost (see section 73). #488 1950 c. 27.

(4) Nothing in this section affects the recognition or enforcement of an award under any other enactment or rule of law, in particular under Part II of the Arbitration Act 1950 (enforcement of awards under Geneva Convention) or the provisions of Part III of this Act relating to the recognition and enforcement of awards under the New York Convention or by an action on the award.

1—068   **Challenging the award: substantive jurisdiction**

67.—(1) A party to arbitral proceedings may (upon notice to the other parties and to the tribunal) apply to the court—

(a) challenging any award of the arbitral tribunal as to its substantive jurisdiction; or

(b) for an order declaring an award made by the tribunal on the merits to be of no effect, in whole or in part, because the tribunal did not have substantive jurisdiction. A party may lose the right to object (see section 73) and the right to apply is subject to the restrictions in section 70(2) and (3).

(2) The arbitral tribunal may continue the arbitral proceedings and make a further award while an application to the court under this section is pending in relation to an award as to jurisdiction.

(3) On an application under this section challenging an award of the arbitral tribunal as to its substantive jurisdiction, the court may by order—

(a) confirm the award,
(b) vary the award, or
(c) set aside the award in whole or in part.

(4) The leave of the court is required for any appeal from a decision of the court under this section.

1—069 Challenging the award: serious irregularity

68.—(1) A party to arbitral proceedings may (upon notice to the other parties and to the tribunal) apply to the court challenging an award in the proceedings on the ground of serious irregularity affecting the tribunal, the proceedings or the award. A party may lose the right to object (see section 73) and the right to apply is subject to the restrictions in section 70(2) and (3).

(2) Serious irregularity means an irregularity of one or more of the following kinds which the court considers has caused or will cause substantial injustice to the applicant—

(a) failure by the tribunal to comply with section 33 (general duty of tribunal);

(b) the tribunal exceeding its powers (otherwise than by exceeding its substantive jurisdiction: see section 67);

(c) failure by the tribunal to conduct the proceedings in accordance with the procedure agreed by the parties;

(d) failure by the tribunal to deal with all the issues that were put to it;

(e) any arbitral or other institution or person vested by the parties with powers in relation to the proceedings or the award exceeding its powers;

A. ENGLISH AND IRISH STATUTES 41

- (f) uncertainty or ambiguity as to the effect of the award;
- (g) the award being obtained by fraud or the award or the way in which it was procured being contrary to public policy;
- (h) failure to comply with the requirements as to the form of the award; or
- (i) any irregularity in the conduct of the proceedings or in the award which is admitted by the tribunal or by any arbitral or other institution or person vested by the parties with powers in relation to the proceedings or the award.

(3) If there is shown to be serious irregularity affecting the tribunal, the proceedings or the award, the court may—

- (a) remit the award to the tribunal, in whole or in part, for reconsideration,
- (b) set the award aside in whole or in part, or
- (c) declare the award to be of no effect, in whole or in part. The court shall not exercise its power to set aside or to declare an award to be of no effect, in whole or in part, unless it is satisfied that it would be inappropriate to remit the matters in question to the tribunal for reconsideration.

(4) The leave of the court is required for any appeal from a decision of the court under this section.

1—070 **Appeal on point of law**

69.—(1) Unless otherwise agreed by the parties, a party to arbitral proceedings may (upon notice to the other parties and to the tribunal) appeal to the court on a question of law arising out of an award made in the proceedings. An agreement to dispense with reasons for the tribunal's award shall be considered an agreement to exclude the court's jurisdiction under this section.

(2) An appeal shall not be brought under this section except—

- (a) with the agreement of all the other parties to the proceedings, or
- (b) with the leave of the court. The right to appeal is also subject to the restrictions in section 70(2) and (3).

(3) Leave to appeal shall be given only if the court is satisfied—

- (a) that the determination of the question will substantially affect the rights of one or more of the parties,

(b) that the question is one which the tribunal was asked to determine,

(c) that, on the basis of the findings of fact in the award—

  (i) the decision of the tribunal on the question is obviously wrong, or

  (ii) the question is one of general public importance and the decision of the tribunal is at least open to serious doubt, and

(d) that, despite the agreement of the parties to resolve the matter by arbitration, it is just and proper in all the circumstances for the court to determine the question.

(4) An application for leave to appeal under this section shall identify the question of law to be determined and state the grounds on which it is alleged that leave to appeal should be granted.

(5) The court shall determine an application for leave to appeal under this section without a hearing unless it appears to the court that a hearing is required.

(6) The leave of the court is required for any appeal from a decision of the court under this section to grant or refuse leave to appeal.

(7) On an appeal under this section the court may by order—

  (a) confirm the award,
  (b) vary the award,
  (c) remit the award to the tribunal, in whole or in part, for reconsideration in the light of the court's determination, or
  (d) set aside the award in whole or in part. The court shall not exercise its power to set aside an award, in whole or in part, unless it is satisfied that it would be inappropriate to remit the matters in question to the tribunal for reconsideration.

(8) The decision of the court on an appeal under this section shall be treated as a judgment of the court for the purposes of a further appeal. But no such appeal lies without the leave of the court which shall not be given unless the court considers that the question is one of general importance or is one which for some other special reason should be considered by the Court of Appeal.

1—071 Challenge or appeal: supplementary provisions

70.—(1) The following provisions apply to an application or appeal under section 67, 68 or 69.

(2) An application or appeal may not be brought if the applicant or appellant has not first exhausted—

(a) any available arbitral process of appeal or review, and
(b) any available recourse under section 57 (correction of award or additional award).

(3) Any application or appeal must be brought within 28 days of the date of the award or, if there has been any arbitral process of appeal or review, of the date when the applicant or appellant was notified of the result of that process.

(4) If on an application or appeal it appears to the court that the award—

(a) does not contain the tribunal's reasons, or
(b) does not set out the tribunal's reasons in sufficient detail to enable the court properly to consider the application or appeal, the court may order the tribunal to state the reasons for its award in sufficient detail for that purpose.

(5) Where the court makes an order under subsection (4), it may make such further order as it thinks fit with respect to any additional costs of the arbitration resulting from its order.

(6) The court may order the applicant or appellant to provide security for the costs of the application or appeal, and may direct that the application or appeal be dismissed if the order is not complied with. The power to order security for costs shall not be exercised on the ground that the applicant or appellant is—

(a) an individual ordinarily resident outside the United Kingdom, or
(b) a corporation or association incorporated or formed under the law of a country outside the United Kingdom, or whose central management and control is exercised outside the United Kingdom.

(7) The court may order that any money payable under the award shall be brought into court or otherwise secured pending the determination of the application or appeal, and may direct that the application or appeal be dismissed if the order is not complied with.

(8) The court may grant leave to appeal subject to conditions to the same or similar effect as an order under subsection (6) or (7). This does not affect the general discretion of the court to grant leave subject to conditions.

1—072 **Challenge or appeal: effect of order of court**

71.—(1) The following provisions have effect where the court makes an order under section 67, 68 or 69 with respect to an award.

(2) Where the award is varied, the variation has effect as part of the tribunal's award.

(3) Where the award is remitted to the tribunal, in whole or in part, for reconsideration, the tribunal shall make a fresh award in respect of the matters remitted within three months of the date of the order for remission or such longer or shorter period as the court may direct.

(4) Where the award is set aside or declared to be of no effect, in whole or in part, the court may also order that any provision that an award is a condition precedent to the bringing of legal proceedings in respect of a matter to which the arbitration agreement applies, is of no effect as regards the subject matter of the award or, as the case may be, the relevant part of the award.

Miscellaneous

1—073 **Saving for rights of person who takes no part in proceedings**

72.—(1) A person alleged to be a party to arbitral proceedings but who takes no part in the proceedings may question—

(a) whether there is a valid arbitration agreement,
(b) whether the tribunal is properly constituted, or
(c) what matters have been submitted to arbitration in accordance with the arbitration agreement, by proceedings in the court for a declaration or injunction or other appropriate relief.

(2) He also has the same right as a party to the arbitral proceedings to challenge an award—

(a) by an application under section 67 on the ground of lack of substantive jurisdiction in relation to him, or
(b) by an application under section 68 on the ground of serious irregularity (within the meaning of that section)

A. English and Irish Statutes

affecting him; and section 70(2) (duty to exhaust arbitral procedures) does not apply in his case.

1—074 **Loss of right to object**

73.—(1) If a party to arbitral proceedings takes part, or continues to take part, in the proceedings without making, either forthwith or within such time as is allowed by the arbitration agreement or the tribunal or by any provision of this Part, any objection—

    (a) that the tribunal lacks substantive jurisdiction,
    (b) that the proceedings have been improperly conducted,
    (c) that there has been a failure to comply with the arbitration agreement or with any provision of this Part, or
    (d) that there has been any other irregularity affecting the tribunal or the proceedings, he may not raise that objection later, before the tribunal or the court, unless he shows that, at the time he took part or continued to take part in the proceedings, he did not know and could not with reasonable diligence have discovered the grounds for the objection.

  (2) Where the arbitral tribunal rules that it has substantive jurisdiction and a party to arbitral proceedings who could have questioned that ruling—

    (a) by any available arbitral process of appeal or review, or
    (b) by challenging the award, does not do so, or does not do so within the time allowed by the arbitration agreement or any provision of this Part, he may not object later to the tribunal's substantive jurisdiction on any ground which was the subject of that ruling.

1—075 **Immunity of arbitral institutions, &c**

74.—(1) An arbitral or other institution or person designated or requested by the parties to appoint or nominate an arbitrator is not liable for anything done or omitted in the discharge or purported discharge of that function unless the act or omission is shown to have been in bad faith.

  (2) An arbitral or other institution or person by whom an arbitrator is appointed or nominated is not liable, by reason of having appointed or nominated him, for anything done or omitted by the arbitrator (or his employees or agents) in the discharge or purported discharge of his functions as arbitrator.

(3) The above provisions apply to an employee or agent of an arbitral or other institution or person as they apply to the institution or person himself.

1—076 Charge to secure payment of solicitors' costs

75.—The powers of the court to make declarations and orders under section 73 of the Solicitors Act 1974 or Article 71H of the Solicitors (Northern Ireland) Order 1976 (power to charge property recovered in the proceedings with the payment of solicitors' costs) may be exercised in relation to arbitral proceedings as if those proceedings were proceedings in the court.

Supplementary

1—077 Service of notices, &c

76.—(1) The parties are free to agree on the manner of service of any notice or other document required or authorised to be given or served in pursuance of the arbitration agreement or for the purposes of the arbitral proceedings.

(2) If or to the extent that there is no such agreement the following provisions apply.

(3) A notice or other document may be served on a person by any effective means.

(4) If a notice or other document is addressed, pre-paid and delivered by post—

(a) to the addressee's last known principal residence or, if he is or has been carrying on a trade, profession or business, his last known principal business address, or
(b) where the addressee is a body corporate, to the body's registered or principal office, it shall be treated as effectively served.

(5) This section does not apply to the service of documents for the purposes of legal proceedings, for which provision is made by rules of court.

(6) References in this Part to a notice or other document include any form of communication in writing and references to giving or serving a notice or other document shall be construed accordingly.

1—078 **Powers of court in relation to service of documents**

77.—(1) This section applies where service of a document on a person in the manner agreed by the parties, or in accordance with provisions of section 76 having effect in default of agreement, is not reasonably practicable.

(2) Unless otherwise agreed by the parties, the court may make such order as it thinks fit—

(a) for service in such manner as the court may direct, or
(b) dispensing with service of the document.

(3) Any party to the arbitration agreement may apply for an order, but only after exhausting any available arbitral process for resolving the matter.

(4) The leave of the court is required for any appeal from a decision of the court under this section.

1—079 **Reckoning periods of time**

78.—(1) The parties are free to agree on the method of reckoning periods of time for the purposes of any provision agreed by them or any provision of this Part having effect in default of such agreement.

(2) If or to the extent there is no such agreement, periods of time shall be reckoned in accordance with the following provisions.

(3) Where the act is required to be done within a specified period after or from a specified date, the period begins immediately after that date.

(4) Where the act is required to be done a specified number of clear days after a specified date, at least that number of days must intervene between the day on which the act is done and that date.

(5) Where the period is a period of seven days or less which would include a Saturday, Sunday or a public holiday in the place where anything which has to be done within the period falls to be done, that day shall be excluded. In relation to England and Wales or Northern Ireland, a "public holiday" means Christmas Day, Good Friday or a day which under the Banking and Financial Dealings Act 1971 is a bank holiday.

1—080 Power of court to extend time limits relating to arbitral proceedings

79.—(1) Unless the parties otherwise agree, the court may by order extend any time limit agreed by them in relation to any matter relating to the arbitral proceedings or specified in any provision of this Part having effect in default of such agreement. This section does not apply to a time limit to which section 12 applies (power of court to extend time for beginning arbitral proceedings, &c.).

(2) An application for an order may be made—

(a) by any party to the arbitral proceedings (upon notice to the other parties and to the tribunal), or
(b) by the arbitral tribunal (upon notice to the parties).

(3) The court shall not exercise its power to extend a time limit unless it is satisfied—

(a) that any available recourse to the tribunal, or to any arbitral or other institution or person vested by the parties with power in that regard, has first been exhausted, and
(b) that a substantial injustice would otherwise be done.

(4) The court's power under this section may be exercised whether or not the time has already expired.

(5) An order under this section may be made on such terms as the court thinks fit.

(6) The leave of the court is required for any appeal from a decision of the court under this section.

1—081 Notice and other requirements in connection with legal proceedings

80.—(1) References in this Part to an application, appeal or other step in relation to legal proceedings being taken "upon notice" to the other parties to the arbitral proceedings, or to the tribunal, are to such notice of the originating process as is required by rules of court and do not impose any separate requirement.

(2) Rules of court shall be made—

(a) requiring such notice to be given as indicated by any provision of this Part, and
(b) as to the manner, form and content of any such notice.

(3) Subject to any provision made by rules of court, a requirement to give notice to the tribunal of legal proceedings shall be construed—

   (a) if there is more than one arbitrator, as a requirement to give notice to each of them; and
   (b) if the tribunal is not fully constituted, as a requirement to give notice to any arbitrator who has been appointed.

(4) References in this Part to making an application or appeal to the court within a specified period are to the issue within that period of the appropriate originating process in accordance with rules of court.

(5) Where any provision of this Part requires an application or appeal to be made to the court within a specified time, the rules of court relating to the reckoning of periods, the extending or abridging of periods, and the consequences of not taking a step within the period prescribed by the rules, apply in relation to that requirement.

(6) Provision may be made by rules of court amending the provisions of this Part—

   (a) with respect to the time within which any application or appeal to the court must be made,
   (b) so as to keep any provision made by this Part in relation to arbitral proceedings in step with the corresponding provision of rules of court applyig in relation to proceedings in the court, or
   (c) so as to keep any provision made by this Part in relation to legal proceedings in step with the corresponding provision of rules of court applying generally in relation to proceedings in the court.

(7) Nothing in this section affects the generality of the power to make rules of court.

1—082 **Saving for certain matters governed by common law**

81.—(1) Nothing in this Part shall be construed as excluding the operation of any rule of law consistent with the provisions of this Part, in particular, any rule of law as to—

   (a) matters which are not capable of settlement by arbitration;
   (b) the effect of an oral arbitration agreement; or
   (c) the refusal of recognition or enforcement of an arbitral award on grounds of public policy.

(2) Nothing in this Act shall be construed as reviving any jurisdiction of the court to set aside or remit an award on the ground of errors of fact or law on the face of the award.

1—083   Minor definitions

82.—(1) In this Part—

"arbitrator", unless the context otherwise requires, includes an umpire;

"available arbitral process", in relation to any matter, includes any process of appeal to or review by an arbitral or other institution or person vested by the parties with powers in relation to that matter;

"claimant", unless the context otherwise requires, includes a counterclaimant, and related expressions shall be construed accordingly;

"dispute" includes any difference;

"enactment" includes an enactment contained in Northern Ireland legislation;

"legal proceedings" means civil proceedings in the High Court or a county court;

"peremptory order" means an order made under section 41(5) or made in exercise of any corresponding power conferred by the parties;

"premises" includes land, buildings, moveable structures, vehicles, vessels, aircraft and hovercraft;

"question of law" means—

(a) for a court in England and Wales, a question of the law of England and Wales, and
(b) for a court in Northern Ireland, a question of the law of Northern Ireland;

"substantive jurisdiction", in relation to an arbitral tribunal, refers to the matters specified in section 30(1)(a) to (c), and references to the tribunal exceeding its substantive jurisdiction shall be construed accordingly.

(2) References in this Part to a party to an arbitration agreement include any person claiming under or through a party to the agreement.

1—084   Index of defined expressions: Part I

83.— In this Part the expressions listed below are defined or otherwise

explained by the provisions indicated—

agreement, agree and agreed section 5(1)

agreement in writing section 5(2) to (5)

arbitration agreement sections 6 and 5(1)

arbitrator section 82(1)

available arbitral process section 82(1)

claimant section 82(1)

commencement (in relation to arbitral proceedings) section 14

costs of the arbitration section 59

the court section 105

dispute section 82(1)

enactment section 82(1)

legal proceedings section 82(1)

Limitation Acts section 13(4)

notice (or other document) section 76(6) party—

— in relation to an arbitration agreement section 82(2)
— where section 106(2) or (3) applies section 106(4)

peremptory order section 82(1) (and see section 41(5))

premises section 82(1)

question of law section 82(1)

recoverable costs sections 63 and 64

seat of the arbitration section 3

serve and service (of notice or other document) section 76(6)

substantive jurisdiction (in relation to an arbitral tribunal) section 82(1) (and see section 30(1)(a) to (c))

upon notice (to the parties or the tribunal) section 80

written and in writing section 5(6)

1—085 Transitional provisions

84.—(1) The provisions of this Part do not apply to arbitral proceedings commenced before the date on which this Part comes into force.

(2) They apply to arbitral proceedings commenced on or after that date under an arbitration agreement whenever made.

(3) The above provisions have effect subject to any transitional provision made by an order under section 109(2) (power to include transitional provisions in commencement order).

PART II—OTHER PROVISIONS RELATING TO ARBITRATION

Domestic arbitration agreements

1—086 Modification of Part I in relation to domestic arbitration agreement

85.—(1) In the case of a domestic arbitration agreement the provisions of art I are modified in accordance with the following sections.

(2) For this purpose a "domestic arbitration agreement" means an arbitration agreement to which none of the parties is—

(a) an individual who is a national of, or habitually resident in, a tate other than the United Kingdom, or
(b) a body corporate which is incorporated in, or whose central control and management is exercised in, a state other than the United Kingdom,
(c) and under which the seat of the arbitration (if the seat has been esignated or determined) is in the United Kingdom.

(3) In subsection (2) "arbitration agreement" and "seat of the arbitration" have the same meaning as in Part I (see sections 3, 5(1) and 6).

1—087 Staying of legal proceedings

86.—(1) In section 9 (stay of legal proceedings), subsection (4) (stay unless the arbitration agreement is null and void, inoperative, or incapable of being performed) does not apply to a domestic arbitration agreement.

(2) On an application under that section in relation to a domestic arbitration agreement the court shall grant a stay unless satisfied—

    (a) that the arbitration agreement is null and void, inoperative, or incapable of being performed, or

    (b) that there are other sufficient grounds for not requiring the parties to abide by the arbitration agreement.

(3) The court may treat as a sufficient ground under subsection (2)(b) the fact that the applicant is or was at any material time not ready and willing to do all things necessary for the proper conduct of the arbitration or of any other dispute resolution procedures required to be exhausted before resorting to arbitration.

(4) For the purposes of this section the question whether an arbitration agreement is a domestic arbitration agreement shall be determined by reference to the facts at the time the legal proceedings are commenced.

1—088 Effectiveness of agreement to exclude court's jurisdiction

87.—(1) In the case of a domestic arbitration agreement any agreement to exclude the jurisdiction of the court under—

    (a) section 45 (determination of preliminary point of law), or

    (b) section 69 (challenging the award: appeal on point of law), is not effective unless entered into after the commencement of the arbitral proceedings in which the question arises or the award is made.

(2) For this purpose the commencement of the arbitral proceedings has the same meaning as in Part I (see section 14).

(3) For the purposes of this section the question whether an arbitration agreement is a domestic arbitration agreement shall be determined by reference to the facts at the time the agreement is entered into.

1—089 Power to repeal or amend sections 85 to 87

88.—(1) The Secretary of State may by order repeal or amend the provisions of sections 85 to 87.

(2) An order under this section may contain such supplementary, incidental and transitional provisions as appear to the Secretary of State to be appropriate.

(3) An order under this section shall be made by statutory instrument and no such order shall be made unless a draft of it has been laid before and approved by a resolution of each House of Parliament.

Consumer arbitration agreements

1—090 **Application of unfair terms regulations to consumer arbitration agreements**

89.—(1) The following sections extend the application of the Unfair Terms in Consumer Contracts Regulations 1994 in relation to a term which constitutes an arbitration agreement. For this purpose "arbitration agreement" means an agreement to submit to arbitration present or future disputes or differences (whether or not contractual). S.I. 1994/3159

(2) In those sections "the Regulations" means those regulations and includes any regulations amending or replacing those regulations.

(3) Those sections apply whatever the law applicable to the arbitration agreement.

1—091 **Regulations apply where consumer is a legal person**

90.—The Regulations apply where the consumer is a legal person as they apply where the consumer is a natural person.

1—092 **Arbitration agreement unfair where modest amount sought**

91.—(1) A term which constitutes an arbitration agreement is unfair for the purposes of the Regulations so far as it relates to a claim for a pecuniary remedy which does not exceed the amount specified by order for the purposes of this section.

(2) Orders under this section may make different provision for different cases and for different purposes.

(3) The power to make orders under this section is exercisable—

(a) for England and Wales, by the Secretary of State with the concurrence of the Lord Chancellor,
(b) for Scotland, by the Secretary of State with the concurrence of the Lord Advocate, and
(c) for Northern Ireland, by the Department of Economic Development for Northern Ireland with the concurrence of the Lord Chancellor.

(4) Any such order for England and Wales or Scotland shall be made by statutory instrument which shall be subject to annulment in pursuance of a resolution of either House of Parliament.

(5) Any such order for Northern Ireland shall be a statutory rule for the purposes of the Statutory Rules (Northern Ireland) Order 1979 and shall be subject to negative resolution, within the meaning of section 41(6) of the Interpretation Act (Northern Ireland) 1954. Small claims arbitration in the county court

1—093 Exclusion of Part I in relation to small claims arbitration in the county court

92.—Nothing in Part I of this Act applies to arbitration under section 64 of the County Courts Act 1984. 1984 c. 28.

1—094 Appointment of judges as arbitratorsAppointment of judges as arbitrators

93.—(1) A judge of the Commercial Court or an official referee may, if in all the circumstances he thinks fit, accept appointment as a sole arbitrator or as umpire by or by virtue of an arbitration agreement.

(2) A judge of the Commercial Court shall not do so unless the Lord Chief Justice has informed him that, having regard to the state of business in the High Court and the Crown Court, he can be made available.

(3) An official referee shall not do so unless the Lord Chief Justice has informed him that, having regard to the state of official referees' business, he can be made available.

(4) The fees payable for the services of a judge of the Commercial Court or official referee as arbitrator or umpire shall be taken in the High Court.

(5) In this section—

"arbitration agreement" has the same meaning as in Part I; and 1981 c. 54.
"official referee" means a person nominated under section 68(1)(a) of the Supreme Court Act 1981 to deal with official referees' business.

(6) The provisions of Part I of this Act apply to arbitration before a person appointed under this section with the modifications specified in Schedule 2.

Statutory arbitrations

1—095 Application of Part I to statutory arbitrations

94.—(1) The provisions of Part I apply to every arbitration under an enactment (a "statutory arbitration"), whether the enactment was passed or made before or after the commencement of this Act, subject to the adaptations and exclusions specified in sections 95 to 98.

(2) The provisions of Part I do not apply to a statutory arbitration if or to the extent that their application—

(a) is inconsistent with the provisions of the enactment concerned, with any rules or procedure authorised or recognised by it, or

(b) is excluded by any other enactment.

(3) In this section and the following provisions of this Part "enactment"— 1978 c. 30.

(a) in England and Wales, includes an enactment contained in subordinate legislation within the meaning of the Interpretation Act 1978; 1954 c. 33 (N.I.).

(b) in Northern Ireland, means a statutory provision within the meaning of section 1(f) of the Interpretation Act (Northern Ireland) 1954.

1—096 General adaptation of provisions in relation to statutory arbitrations

95.—(1) The provisions of Part I apply to a statutory arbitration—

(a) as if the arbitration were pursuant to an arbitration agreement and as if the enactment were that agreement, and

(b) as if the persons by and against whom a claim subject to arbitration in pursuance of the enactment may be or has been made were parties to that agreement.

(2) Every statutory arbitration shall be taken to have its seat in England and Wales or, as the case may be, in Northern Ireland.

1—097 Specific adaptations of provisions in relation to statutory arbitrations

96.—(1) The following provisions of Part I apply to a statutory arbitration with the following adaptations.

(2) In section 30(1) (competence of tribunal to rule on its own jurisdiction), the reference in paragraph (a) to whether there is a valid arbitration agreement shall be construed as a reference to whether the enactment applies to the dispute or difference in question.

(3) Section 35 (consolidation of proceedings and concurrent hearings) applies only so as to authorise the consolidation of proceedings, or concurrent hearings in proceedings, under the same enactment.

(4) Section 46 (rules applicable to substance of dispute) applies with the omission of subsection (1)(b) (determination in accordance with considerations agreed by parties).

1—098 **Provisions excluded from applying to statutory arbitrations**

97.—The following provisions of Part I do not apply in relation to a statutory arbitration—

(a) section 8 (whether agreement discharged by death of a party);

(b) section 12 (power of court to extend agreed time limits);

(c) sections 9(5), 10(2) and 71(4) (restrictions on effect of provision that award condition precedent to right to bring legal proceedings).

1—099 **Power to make further provision by regulations**

98.—(1) The Secretary of State may make provision by regulations for adapting or excluding any provision of Part I in relation to statutory arbitrations in general or statutory arbitrations of any particular description.

(2) The power is exercisable whether the enactment concerned is passed or made before or after the commencement of this Act.

(3) Regulations under this section shall be made by statutory instrument which shall be subject to annulment in pursuance of a resolution of either House of Parliament.

Part III—Recognition and Enforcement of Certain Foreign Awards

Enforcement of Geneva Convention awards

1—100 Continuation of Part II of the Arbitration Act 1950

99.—Part II of the Arbitration Act 1950 (enforcement of certain foreign awards) continues to apply in relation to foreign awards within the meaning of that Part which are not also New York Convention awards. 1950 c. 27.

Recognition and enforcement of New York Convention awards

1—101 New York Convention awards

100.—(1) In this Part a "New York Convention award" means an award made, in pursuance of an arbitration agreement, in the territory of a state (other than the United Kingdom) which is a party to the New York Convention.

(2) For the purposes of subsection (1) and of the provisions of this Part relating to such awards—

(a) "arbitration agreement" means an arbitration agreement in writing, and
(b) an award shall be treated as made at the seat of the arbitration, regardless of where it was signed, despatched or delivered to any of the parties. In this subsection "agreement in writing" and "seat of the arbitration" have the same meaning as in Part I.

(3) If Her Majesty by Order in Council declares that a state specified in the Order is a party to the New York Convention, or is a party in respect of any territory so specified, the Order shall, while in force, be conclusive evidence of that fact.

(4) In this section "the New York Convention" means the Convention on the Recognition and Enforcement of Foreign Arbitral Awards adopted by the United Nations Conference on International Commercial Arbitration on 10th June 1958.

1—102 Recognition and enforcement of awards

101.—(1) A New York Convention award shall be recognised as binding on the persons as between whom it was made, and may accordingly be relied on by those persons by way of defence, set-off or otherwise in any legal proceedings in England and Wales or Northern Ireland.

(2) A New York Convention award may, by leave of the court, be enforced in the same manner as a judgment or order of the court to the same effect. As to the meaning of "the court" see section 105.

(3) Where leave is so given, judgment may be entered in terms of the award.

1—103 **Evidence to be produced by party seeking recognition or enforcement**

102.—(1) A party seeking the recognition or enforcement of a New York Convention award must produce—

(a) the duly authenticated original award or a duly certified copy of it, and
(b) the original arbitration agreement or a duly certified copy of it.

(2) If the award or agreement is in a foreign language, the party must also produce a translation of it certified by an official or sworn translator or by a diplomatic or consular agent.

1—104 **Refusal of recognition or enforcement**

103.—(1) Recognition or enforcement of a New York Convention award shall not be refused except in the following cases.

(2) Recognition or enforcement of the award may be refused if the person against whom it is invoked proves—

(a) that a party to the arbitration agreement was (under the law applicable to him) under some incapacity;
(b) that the arbitration agreement was not valid under the law to which the parties subjected it or, failing any indication thereon, under the law of the country where the award was made;
(c) that he was not given proper notice of the appointment of the arbitrator or of the arbitration proceedings or was otherwise unable to present his case;
(d) that the award deals with a difference not contemplated by or not falling within the terms of the submission to arbitration or contains decisions on matters beyond the scope of the submission to arbitration (but see subsection (4));
(e) that the composition of the arbitral tribunal or the arbitral procedure was not in accordance with the agreement

of the parties or, failing such agreement, with the law of the country in which the arbitration took place;

(f) that the award has not yet become binding on the parties, or has been set aside or suspended by a competent authority of the country in which, or under the law of which, it was made.

(3) Recognition or enforcement of the award may also be refused if the award is in respect of a matter which is not capable of settlement by arbitration, or if it would be contrary to public policy to recognise or enforce the award.

(4) An award which contains decisions on matters not submitted to arbitration may be recognised or enforced to the extent that it contains decisions on matters submitted to arbitration which can be separated from those on matters not so submitted.

(5) Where an application for the setting aside or suspension of the award has been made to such a competent authority as is mentioned in subsection (2)(f), the court before which the award is sought to be relied upon may, if it considers it proper, adjourn the decision on the recognition or enforcement of the award. It may also on the application of the party claiming recognition or enforcement of the award order the other party to give suitable security.

1—105 Saving for other bases of recognition or enforcement

104.—Nothing in the preceding provisions of this Part affects any right to rely upon or enforce a New York Convention award at common law or under section 66.

Part IV — General Provisions

1—106 Meaning of "the court": jurisdiction of High Court and county court

105.—(1) In this Act "the court" means the High Court or a county court, subject to the following provisions.

(2) The Lord Chancellor may by order make provision—

(a) allocating proceedings under this Act to the High Court or to county courts; or

(b) specifying proceedings under this Act which may be

commenced or taken only in the High Court or in a county court.

(3) The Lord Chancellor may by order make provision requiring proceedings of any specified description under this Act in relation to which a county court has jurisdiction to be commenced or taken in one or more specified county courts. Any jurisdiction so exercisable by a specified county court is exercisable throughout England and Wales or, as the case may be, Northern Ireland.

(4) An order under this section—

   (a) may differentiate between categories of proceedings by reference to such criteria as the Lord Chancellor sees fit to specify, and
   (b) may make such incidental or transitional provision as the Lord Chancellor considers necessary or expedient.

(5) An order under this section for England and Wales shall be made by statutory instrument which shall be subject to annulment in pursuance of a resolution of either House of Parliament.

(6) An order under this section for Northern Ireland shall be a statutory rule for the purposes of the Statutory Rules (Northern Ireland) Order 1979 which shall be subject to annulment in pursuance of a resolution of either House of Parliament in like manner as a statutory instrument and section 5 of the Statutory Instruments Act 1946 shall apply accordingly.

1—107 Crown application

106.—(1) Part I of this Act applies to any arbitration agreement to which Her Majesty, either in right of the Crown or of the Duchy of Lancaster or otherwise, or the Duke of Cornwall, is a party.

(2) Where Her Majesty is party to an arbitration agreement otherwise than in right of the Crown, Her Majesty shall be represented for the purposes of any arbitral proceedings—

   (a) where the agreement was entered into by Her Majesty in right of the Duchy of Lancaster, by the Chancellor of the Duchy or such person as he may appoint, and
   (b) in any other case, by such person as Her Majesty may appoint in writing under the Royal Sign Manual.

(3) Where the Duke of Cornwall is party to an arbitration agreement, he shall be represented for the purposes of any arbitral proceedings by such person as he may appoint.

(4) References in Part I to a party or the parties to the arbitration agreement or to arbitral proceedings shall be construed, where subsection (2) or (3) applies, as references to the person representing Her Majesty or the Duke of Cornwall.

1—108 Consequential amendments and repeals

107.—(1) The enactments specified in Schedule 3 are amended in accordance with that Schedule, the amendments being consequential on the provisions of this Act.

(2) The enactments specified in Schedule 4 are repealed to the extent specified.

1—109 Extent

108.—(1) The provisions of this Act extend to England and Wales and, except as mentioned below, to Northern Ireland.

(2) The following provisions of Part II do not extend to Northern Ireland—

— section 92 (exclusion of Part I in relation to small claims arbitration in the county court), and
— section 93 and Schedule 2 (appointment of judges as arbitrators).

(3) Sections 89, 90 and 91 (consumer arbitration agreements) extend to Scotland and the provisions of Schedules 3 and 4 (consequential amendments and repeals) extend to Scotland so far as they relate to enactments which so extend, subject as follows.

(4) The repeal of the Arbitration Act 1975 extends only to England and Wales and Northern Ireland.

1—110 Commencement

109.—(1) The provisions of this Act come into force on such day as the Secretary of State may appoint by order made by statutory instrument, and different days may be appointed for different purposes.

(2) An order under subsection (1) may contain such transitional provisions as appear to the Secretary of State to be appropriate.

1—111 Short title

110.—This Act may be cited as the Arbitration Act 1996.

IRELAND

Arbitration (International Commercial) Act, 1998

ARRANGEMENT OF SECTIONS

PART I—PRELIMINARY AND GENERAL

Section

1. Short title and collective citation.
2. References.

PART II—INTERNATIONAL COMMERCIAL ARBITRATION

3. Interpretation of this Part.
4. Adoption of Model Law.
5. Construction of Model Law.
6. Functions of High Court.
7. Court powers exercisable in support of international commercial arbitration proceedings.
8. Powers of arbitral tribunal in relation to examination of witnesses, etc.
9. Consolidation of arbitral proceedings and concurrent hearings.
10. Interest.
11. Recoverable costs of arbitration and recoverable fees and expenses of arbitral tribunal.
12. Restriction on liability of arbitrators, etc.
13. Time limits for setting aside award.
14. Effect of award.
15. Transitional provisions.
16. Non-application of Arbitration Acts

PART III—AMENDMENTS TO ARBITRATION ACTS, 1954 AND 1980

17. Amendment to Arbitration Act, 1954.

18. Amendment to Arbitration Act, 1980.

SCHEDULE

TEXT OF UNCITRAL MODEL LAW ON INTERNATIONAL COMMERCIAL ARBITRATION

ACTS REFERRED TO

Arbitration Act, 1954	1954, No. 26
Arbitration Act, 1980	1980, No. 7
Arbitration Acts, 1954 and 1980	
Patents Act, 1992	1992, No. 1
Property Values (Arbitration and Appeals) Act, 1960	1960, no. 45
Trade Marks Act, 1996	1996, No. 6

Arbitration (International Commercial) Act, 1998

1—112 AN ACT TO ENABLE EFFECT TO BE GIVEN IN THE STATE TO THE UNCITRAL MODEL LAW ON INTERNATIONAL COMMERCIAL ARBITRATION (AS ADOPTED BY THE UNITED NATIONS COMMISSION ON INTERNATIONAL TRADE LAW ON 21 JUNE 1985) AND TO AMEND THE ARBITRATION ACTS; 1954 AND 1980, AND TO MAKE FURTHER AND BETTER PROVISION IN RESPECT OF ARBITRATIONS. [20th May, 1998]

BE IT ENACTED BY THE OIREACHTAS AS FOLLOWS:

PART I—PRELIMINARY AND GENERAL

1—113 **Short title and collective citation**

1.—(1) This Act may be cited as the Arbitration (International Commercial) Act, 1998.

(2) The Arbitration Acts, 1954 and 1980 and this Act may be cited together as the Arbitration Acts, 1954 to 1998.

1—114   References

2.— In this Act—

(a) a reference to any other enactment is to that enactment as amended by or under any other enactment including this Act, unless the context otherwise requires,

(b) a reference to a section, Part or Schedule is to a section or Part of, or Schedule to, this Act unless it is indicated that reference to some other enactment is intended,

(c) a reference to a subsection is to a subsection of the provision in which the reference occurs, unless it is indicated that reference to some other provision is intended, and

(d) a reference to an Article is to an Article of the Model Law.

PART II — INTERNATIONAL COMMERCIAL ARBITRATION

1—115   Interpretation of this Part

3.—(1) In this Part, unless the context otherwise requires—

"arbitration agreement" means an arbitration agreement concerning international commercial arbitration; "award" includes an interim award;

"international commercial arbitration" means arbitration to which the Model Law applies;

"the Model Law" means the UNCITRAL Model Law on International Commercial Arbitration (as adopted by the United Nations Commission on International Trade Law on 21 June 1985), the text in the English language of which is set out in the Schedule.

(2) Terms and expressions that are used in this Part and defined in the Model Law have the same meaning in this Part as in that Law unless the context otherwise requires.

1—116   Adoption of Model Law

4.— Subject to this Part, the Model Law shall apply in the State.

1—117 Construction of Model Law

5.—(1) The reference to an agreement in Article 1(1) shall be construed as referring only to an agreement which has the force of law in the State.

(2) The documents of the United Nations Commission on International Trade Law and its working group relating to the preparation of the Model Law may be considered in ascertaining the meaning or effect of any provision of the Model Law.

1—118 Functions of High Court

6.—(1) The High Court is specified for the purposes of Article 6 and is the court for the purposes of Article 9 and the court of competent jurisdiction for the purposes of Articles 27, 35 and 36.

(2) The functions of the High Court under an Article referred to in subsection (1) and its functions under sections 7, 11 (7) and (9) and 14(1) shall be performed by—

(a) the President of the High Court, or
(b) such Judge of the High Court as may be nominated by the President, subject to any rules of court made in that behalf.

(3) An application may be made in a summary manner to the President of the High Court or to a judge referred to in subsection (2)(b) to exercise any of the functions referred to in subsection (2).

1—118a Court powers exercisable in support of international commercial arbitration proceedings

7.—(1) For the purposes of giving effect to Article 9 or 27, the High Court may, on application under section 6(3), make, in relation to an international commercial arbitration, any order in respect of—

(a) the preservation, interim custody or sale of any goods which are the subject matter of the arbitral proceedings,
(b) securing the amount at issue in the arbitral proceedings,
(c) security for costs,
(d) interim injunctions,
(e) the appointment of a receiver,
(f) the detention, preservation or inspection of any property or thing which is the subject matter of the arbitral proceedings and authorising—

(i) for any of those purposes any person to enter any land or building in the possession of a party, or

(ii) any sample to be taken, any observation to be made or any experiment to be tried which may be necessary or expedient for obtaining full information or evidence,

(g) securing the attendance of witnesses before the arbitral tribunal in order that evidence be given or documents be produced,

(h) the examination on oath or affirmation of any witness before an officer of the Court or other person,

(i) the issue of a commission or request for the examination of a witness outside the State, or

(j) the discovery and inspection of documents and interrogatories,that it has power to make for the purpose of and in relation to an action or other matter before the High Court.

(2) A party shall not be ordered under this section to provide security for costs solely on the ground that the party is—

(a) an individual who is ordinarily resident outside the State, or

(b) a corporation or association incorporated or formed under a law other than the law of the State or whose central management and control is exercised outside the State.

(3) Nothing in this section shall be taken to prejudice—

(a) the generality of Articles 9 and 27, or

(b) any power of an arbitral tribunal to make orders in respect of any of the matters mentioned in subsection (1).

1—119 Powers of arbitral tribunal in relation to examination of witnesses, etc

8.—Unless otherwise agreed by the parties, the arbitral tribunal may—

(a) direct that a party to an arbitration agreement or a witness who gives evidence in proceedings before the arbitral tribunal be examined on oath or affirmation, and

(b) administer any oaths or take any affirmations necessary for the purposes of the examination.

1—120 **Consolidation of arbitral proceedings and concurrent hearings**

9.—(1) The parties to an arbitration agreement may agree—

 (a) that the arbitral proceedings shall be consolidated with other arbitral proceedings, or
 (b) that concurrent hearings shall be held on such terms as may be agreed.

 (2) The arbitral tribunal has no power to order consolidation of proceedings or concurrent hearings unless the parties agree to confer such power on that tribunal.

1—121 **Interest**

10.—(1) The parties to an arbitration agreement may agree on the arbitral tribunal's powers regarding the award of interest.

 (2) Unless otherwise agreed by the parties, the arbitral tribunal may award simple or compound interest from the dates, at the rates and with the rests that it considers meet the justice of the case—

 (a) on all or part of any amount awarded by the arbitral tribunal, in respect of any period up to the date of the award;
 (b) on all or part of any amount claimed in the arbitration and outstanding at the commencement of the arbitration but paid before the award was made, in respect of any period up to the date of payment.

 (3) Unless otherwise agreed by the parties, the arbitral tribunal may award simple or compound interest from the date of the award (or any later date) until payment, at the rates and with the rests that it considers meet the justice of the case, on the outstanding amount of any award (including any award of interest under subsection (2) and any award of costs).

 (4) References in this section to an amount awarded by the arbitral tribunal include an amount payable in consequence of a declaratory award by the arbitral tribunal.

 (5) This section shall not affect any other power of the arbitral tribunal to award interest.

1—122 Recoverable costs of arbitration and recoverable fees and expenses of arbitral tribunal

11.—(1) The parties to an arbitration agreement are free to agree on how the costs of the international commercial arbitration are to be allocated and on the costs that are recoverable.

(2) An agreement of the parties to arbitrate subject to the rules of an arbitral institution shall be deemed to be an agreement to abide by the rules of that institution as to how costs are to be allocated and as to the costs that are recoverable.

(3) References in subsections (1) and (2) to "costs" include the costs as between the parties and the fees and expenses of the arbitral tribunal.

(4) Where there is no agreement of the parties as to the recoverable costs of the international commercial arbitration as between the parties, the arbitral tribunal may, with the consent of the parties to the arbitral proceedings, determine by award those costs on the basis it thinks fit.

(5) Where there is no agreement of the parties as to the recoverable fees and expenses of the arbitral tribunal, the tribunal may determine by award those fees and expenses on the basis it thinks fit.

(6) Where the tribunal makes a determination under subsection (4) or (5), it shall specify—

(a) the basis on which it acted,
(b) the items of recoverable costs, fees or expenses, as appropriate, and the amount referable to each, and
(c) by and to whom they shall be paid.

(7) Where a party does not consent to the arbitral tribunal making a determination under subsection (4) or where for any other reason the arbitral tribunal does not make that determination—

(a) any party to the arbitral proceedings may apply to the High Court within 30 days after receipt of the award, or such further time as the Court may direct, for a determination of the recoverable costs as between the parties, and
(b) the Court may determine those costs on the basis it thinks fit or may order that they be determined by the means and on the terms it specifies.

(8) Notice of an application to the High Court under subsection (7) or subsection (9) shall be given to the arbitral tribunal and to the other parties to the arbitral proceedings.

(9) Where the arbitral tribunal makes a determination under subsection (5)—

   (a) any party to the arbitral proceedings may apply to the High Court within 30 days after receipt of the determination, and
   (b) the Court may order that the amount of the arbitral tribunal's fees and expenses be reviewed and adjusted by the means and on the terms the Court specifies.

(10) Subject to an order under subsection (9)(b), nothing in this section affects any right of the arbitral tribunal to payment of its fees and expenses.

(11) References in this section to the fees and expenses of the arbitral tribunal include the fees and expenses of any expert appointed by the tribunal.

1—123   Restriction on liability of arbitrators, etc

12.—(1) An arbitrator shall not be liable for anything done or omitted in the discharge or purported discharge of his or her functions as arbitrator unless the act or omission is shown to have been in bad faith.

   (2) Subsection (1) shall apply to an employee, agent or advisor of an arbitrator and to an expert appointed under Article 26, as it applies to the arbitrator.

   (3) An arbitral or other institution or person designated or requested by the parties to appoint or nominate an arbitrator shall not be liable for anything done or omitted in the discharge or purported discharge of that function unless the act or omission is shown to have been in bad faith.

   (4) An arbitral or other institution or person by whom an arbitrator is appointed or nominated shall not be liable for anything done or omitted by the arbitrator (or his or her employees or agents) in the discharge or purported discharge of his or her functions as arbitrator.

   (5) Subsections (3) and (4)) shall apply to an employee or agent of an arbitral or other institution or person as they apply to the institution or person himself or herself.

   (6) A witness who gives evidence in proceedings before an arbitral tribunal shall have the same privileges and immunities as witnesses have in proceedings before the High Court.

(7) A person who—
  (a) is a barrister or solicitor or holds qualifications that have been obtained in another jurisdiction and are equivalent to those of a barrister or solicitor, and
  (b) appears in proceedings before an arbitral tribunal, shall have the same privileges and immunities as barristers and solicitors have in proceedings before the High Court.

(8) A person who is a patent agent as defined in section 94(3) of the Patents Act, 1992, or a registered agent as defined in section 91(3) of the Trade Marks Act, 1996, shall have the same privileges and immunities referred to in subsection (7) when appearing in proceedings before an arbitral tribunal on —
  (a) in the case of a patent agent, any matter concerning the protection of an invention, patent, design or technical information or any matter involving passing off, and
  (b) in the case of a registered agent, any matter relating to the protection of a trade mark or any matter involving passing off.

1—124 **Time limits for setting aside award**

13.—The time limit specified in Article 34(3) shall not apply to an application to the High Court to have an arbitral award set aside on the grounds that the award is in conflict with the public policy of the State.

1—125 **Effect of award**

14.—(1) An award made by an arbitral tribunal under an arbitration agreement shall be enforceable in the State either by action or, by leave of the High Court, in the same manner as a judgment or order of that Court to the same effect and, where leave is given, judgment may be entered in terms of the award.

(2) An award referred to in subsection (1) shall be treated as binding for all purposes on the parties between whom it was made, and may accordingly be relied on by any of those parties by way of defence, set-off or otherwise in any legal proceedings in the State, and any reference in this section to the enforcement of an award shall be construed as including a reference to the reliance on such an award.

(3) Unless otherwise agreed by the parties, Articles 35 and 36 shall apply to orders made by an arbitral tribunal under Article 17 as if a reference in Articles 35 or 36 to an award were a reference to such an order and subsections (1) and (2) shall apply accordingly.

(4) Nothing in this section affects the recognition or enforcement of an award under—

(a) Part V of the Arbitration Act, 1954 (enforcement of awards under the Geneva Convention), or
(b) Parts III and IV of the Arbitration Act, 1980 (enforcement of awards under the New York and Washington Conventions).

1—126 **Transitional provisions**

15.—(1) This Part shall not apply to an international commercial arbitration commenced before the day on which this Act comes into operation unless—

(a) the arbitration is concluded after that day, and
(b) the parties agree that this Part shall apply.

(2) This Part shall apply to an international commercial arbitration commenced on or after the day on which this Act comes into operation—

(a) under an arbitration agreement entered into on or after that day, or
(b) if the parties so agree, under an arbitration agreement entered into before that day.

1—127 **Non-application of Arbitration Acts**

16.—Subject to section 14(4), the Arbitration Acts, 1954 and 1980, shall not apply to an arbitration to which this Part applies.

PART III—AMENDMENTS TO ARBITRATION ACTS, 1954 AND 1980

1—128 **Amendment to Arbitration Act, 1954**

17.—The Arbitration Act, 1954, is hereby amended by substituting the following for section 34: "Interest on awards.

34.—(1) The parties to an arbitration agreement may agree on the powers of the arbitrator or umpire as regards the award of interest.

(2) Unless otherwise agreed by the parties, the arbitrator or umpire may award simple or compound interest from the dates, at the rates and with the rests that he or she considers meet the justice of the case—

(a) on all or part of any amount awarded by the arbitrator or umpire, in respect of any period up to the date of the award;

(b) on all or part of any amount claimed in the arbitration and outstanding at the commencement of the arbitration but paid before the award was made, in respect of any period up to the date of payment.

(3) Unless otherwise agreed by the parties, the arbitrator or umpire may award simple or compound interest from the date of the award (or any later date) until payment, at the rates and with the rests that he or she considers meet the justice of the case, on the outstanding amount of any award (including an award of interest under subsection (2) and an award of costs).

(4) References in this section to an amount awarded by an arbitrator or umpire include an amount payable in consequence of a declaratory award by the arbitrator or umpire.

(5) This section shall not apply to an arbitration commenced before the day on which the Arbitration (International Commercial) Act, 1998, comes into operation unless—

(a) the arbitration is concluded after that day, and
(b) the parties agree that this section shall apply.

(6) This section shall apply to an arbitration commenced on or after the day on which the Arbitration (International Commercial) Act, 1998 comes into operation—

(a) under an arbitration agreement entered into on or after that day, or
(b) if the parties so agree, under an arbitration agreement entered into before that day.

(7) This section shall not apply to an arbitration conducted by a property arbitrator appointed under section 2 of the Property Values (Arbitration and Appeals) Act, 1960.".

1—129 Amendment to Arbitration Act, 1980

18.—Section 5 of the Arbitration Act, 1980, is hereby amended by the insertion of the following subsection after subsection (2):

"(3) Nothing in this section shall prevent any party to an arbitration agreement from invoking the alternative method, provided by the Rules of Court (as amended from time to time), of commencing and dealing with a civil proceeding in respect of a small claim."

SCHEDULE

1—130 Text of UNCITRAL MODEL LAW ON INTERNATIONAL COMMERCIAL ARBITRATION as adopted by the United Nations Commission on International Trade Law on 21 June 1985

(UNCITRAL) Model Law

CHAPTER I: GENERAL PROVISIONS

1—131 Article 1—Scope of application

1. This Law applies to international commercial 2 arbitration, subject to any agreement in force between this State and any other State or States.

2. The provisions of this Law, except articles 8, 9, 35 and 36, apply only if the place of arbitration is in the territory of this State.

3. An arbitration is international if:

    (a) the parties to an arbitration agreement have, at the time of the conclusion of that agreement, their places of business in different States; or
    (b) one of the following places is situated outside the State in which the parties have their places of business:

        (i) the place of arbitration if determined in, or pursuant to, the arbitration agreement;
        (ii) any place where a substantial part of the obligations of the commercial relationship is to be performed or the place with which the subject-matter of the dispute is most closely connected; or

    (c) the parties have expressly agreed that the subject-matter of the arbitration agreement relates to more than one country.

4. For the purposes of paragraph (3) of this article:

    (a) if a party has more than one place of business, the place of business is that which has the closest relationship to the arbitration agreement;
    (b) if a party does not have a place of business, reference is to be made to his habitual residence.

5. This Law shall not affect any other law of this State by virtue of which certain disputes may not be submitted to arbitration or may be submitted to arbitration only according to provisions other than those of this Law.

1—132   Article 2—Definitions and rules of interpretation

For the purposes of this Law:

(a) "arbitration" means any arbitration whether or not administered by a permanent arbitral institution;

(b) "arbitral tribunal" means a sole arbitrator or a panel of arbitrators;

(c) "court" means a body or organ of the judicial system of a State;

(d) where a provision of this Law, except article 28, leaves the parties free to determine a certain issue, such freedom includes the right of the parties to authorize a third party, including an institution, to make that determination;

(e) where a provision of this Law refers to the fact that the parties have agreed or that they may agree or in any other way refers to an agreement of the parties; such agreement includes any arbitration rules referred to in that agreement;

(f) where a provision of this Law, other than in articles 25 (a) and 32

(2) (a), refers to a claim, it also applies to a counter-claim, and where it refers to a defence, it also applies to a defence to such counter-claim.

1—133   Article 3—Receipt of written communications

1. Unless otherwise agreed by the parties:

(a) any written communication is deemed to have been received if it is delivered to the addressee personally or if it is delivered at his place of business, habitual residence or mailing address; if none of these can be found after making a reasonable inquiry, a written communication is deemed to have been received if it is sent to the addressee's last-known place of business, habitual residence or mailing address by registered letter or any other means which provides a record of the attempt to deliver it;

(b) the communication is deemed to have been received on the day it is so delivered.

2. The provisions of this article do not apply to communications in court proceedings.

1—134   Article 4—Waiver of right to object

A party who knows that any provision of this Law from which the parties may derogate or any requirement under the arbitration agreement has not been complied with and yet proceeds with the arbitration without stating his objection to such non-compliance without undue delay or, if a time-limit is provided therefor, within such period of time, shall be deemed to have waived his right to object.

1—135   Article 5—Extent of court intervention

In matters governed by this Law, no court shall intervene except where so provided in this Law.

1—136   Article 6—Court or other authority for certain functions of arbitration assistance and supervision

The functions referred to in articles 11(3), 11(4), 13(3),14,16 (3) and 34 (2) shall be performed by . . . [Each State enacting this model law specifies the court, courts or, where referred to therein, other authority competent to perform these functions.]

CHAPTER II: ARBITRATION AGREEMENT

1—137   Article 7—Definition and form of arbitration agreement

1. "Arbitration agreement" is an agreement by the parties to submit to arbitration all or certain disputes which have arisen or which may arise between them in respect of a defined legal relationship, whether contractual or not. An arbitration agreement may be in the form of an arbitration clause in a contract or in the form of a separate agreement.

2. The arbitration agreement shall be in writing. An agreement is in writing if it is contained in a document signed by the parties or in an exchange of letters, telex, telegrams or other means of telecommunication which provide a record of the agreement, or in an exchange of statements of claim and defence in which the existence of an agreement is alleged by one party and not denied by another. The reference in a contract to a document containing an arbitration clause

constitutes an arbitration agreement provided that the contract is in writing and the reference is such as to make that clause part of the contract.

1—138 Article 8—Arbitration agreement and substantive claim before court

1. A court before which an action is brought in a matter which is the subject of an arbitration agreement shall, if a party so requests not later than when submitting his first statement on the substance of the dispute, refer the parties to arbitration unless it finds that the agreement is real and void, inoperative or incapable of being performed.

2. Where an action referred to in paragraph (1) of this article has been brought, arbitral proceedings may nevertheless be commenced or continued, and an award may be made, while the issue is pending before the court.

1—139 Article 9—Arbitration agreement and interim measures by court

It is not incompatible with an arbitration agreement for a party to request, before or during arbitral proceedings, from a court an interim measure of protection and for a court to grant such measure.

CHAPTER III: COMPOSITION OF ARBITRAL TRIBUNAL

1—140 Article 10—Number of arbitrators

1. The parties are free to determine the number of arbitrators.

2. Failing such determination, the number of arbitrators shall be three.

1—141 Article 11—Appointment of arbitrators

1. No person shall be precluded by reason of his nationality from acting as an arbitrator, unless otherwise agreed by the parties.

2. The parties are free to agree on a procedure of appointing the arbitrator or arbitrators, subject to the provisions of paragraphs (4) and (5) of this article.

3. Failing such agreement,

(a) in an arbitration with three arbitrators, each party shall appoint one arbitrator, and the two arbitrators thus appointed shall appoint the third arbitrator; if a party fails to appoint the arbitrator within thirty days of receipt of a request to do so from the other party, or if the two arbitrators fail to agree on the third arbitrator within thirty days of their appointment, the appointment shall be made, upon request of a party, by the court or other authority specified in article 6;

(b) in an arbitration with a sole arbitrator, if the parties are unable to agree on the arbitrator, he shall be appointed, upon request of a party, by the court or other authority specified in article 6.

4. Where, under an appointment procedure agreed upon by the parties,

(a) a party fails to act as required under such procedure, or

(b) the parties, or two arbitrators, are unable to reach an agreement expected of them under such procedure, or

(c) a third party, including an institution, fails to perform any function entrusted to it under such procedure, any party may request the court or other authority specified in article 6 to take the necessary measure, unless the agreement on the appointment procedure provides other means for securing the appointment.

5. A decision on a matter entrusted by paragraph (3) and (4) of this article to the court or other authority specified in article 6 shall be subject to no appeal. The court or other authority, in appointing an arbitrator, shall have due regard to any qualifications required of the arbitrator by the agreement of the parties and to such considerations as are likely to secure the appointment of an independent and impartial arbitrator and, in the case of a sole or third arbitrator, shall take into account as well the advisability of appointing an arbitrator of a nationality other than those of the parties.

1—142   Article 12—Grounds for challenge

1. When a person is approached in connection with his possible appointment as an arbitrator, he shall disclose any circumstances likely to give rise to justifiable doubts as to his impartiality or independence. An arbitrator, from the time of his appointment and throughout the arbitral proceedings, shall without delay disclose any such circumstances to the

parties unless they have already been informed of them by him.

2. An arbitrator may be challenged only if circumstances exist that give rise to justifiable doubts as to his impartiality or independence, or if he does not possess qualifications agreed to by the parties. A party may challenge an arbitrator appointed by him, or in whose appointment he has participated, only for reasons of which he becomes aware after the appointment has been made.

1—143   Article 13—Challenge procedure

1. The parties are free to agree on a procedure for challenging an arbitrator, subject to the provisions of paragraph (3) of this article.

2. Failing such agreement, a party which intends to challenge an arbitrator shall, within fifteen days after becoming aware of the constitution of the arbitral tribunal or after becoming aware of any circumstance referred to in article 12(2), send a written statement of the reasons for the challenge to the arbitral tribunal. Unless the challenged arbitrator withdraws from his office or the other party agrees to the challenge, the arbitral tribunal shall decide on the challenge.

3. If a challenge under any procedure agreed upon by the parties or under the procedure of paragraph (2) of this article is not successful, the challenging party may request, within thirty days after having received notice of the decision rejecting the challenge, the court or other authority specified in article 6 to decide on the challenge, which decision shall be subject to no appeal; while such a request is pending, the arbitral tribunal, including the challenged arbitrator, may continue the arbitral proceedings and make an award.

1—144   Article 14—Failure or impossibility to act

1. If an arbitrator becomes de jure or de facto unable to perform his functions or for other reasons fails to act without undue delay, his mandate terminates if he withdraws from his office or if the parties agree on the termination. Otherwise, if a controversy remains concerning any of these grounds, any party may request the court or other authority specified in article 6 to decide on the termination of the mandate, which decision shall be subject to no appeal.

2. If, under this article or article 13 (2), an arbitrator withdraws from his office or a party agrees to the termination of the mandate of an arbitrator, this does not imply acceptance of the validity of any ground referred to in this article or article 12 (2).

1—145   Article 15—Appointment of substitute arbitrator

Where the mandate of an arbitrator terminates under article 13 or 14 or because of his withdrawal from office for any other reason or because of the revocation of his mandate by agreement of the parties or in any other case of termination of his mandate, a substitute arbitrator shall be appointed according to the rules that were applicable to the appointment of the arbitrator being replaced.

CHAPTER IV: JURISDICTION OF ARBITRAL TRIBUNAL

1—146   Article 16—Competence of arbitral tribunal to rule on its jurisdiction

1. The arbitral tribunal may rule on its own jurisdiction, including any objections with respect to the existence or validity of the arbitration agreement. For that purpose, an arbitration clause which forms part of a contract shall be treated as an agreement independent of the other terms of the contract. A decision by the arbitral tribunal that the contract is null and void shall not entail ipso jure the invalidity of the arbitration clause.

2. A plea that the arbitral tribunal does not have jurisdiction shall be raised not later than the submission of the statement of defence. A party is not precluded from raising such a plea by the fact that he has appointed, or participated in the appointment of, an arbitrator. A plea that the arbitral tribunal is exceeding the scope of its authority shall be raised as soon as the matter alleged to be beyond the scope of its authority is raised during the arbitral proceedings. The arbitral tribunal may, in either case, admit a later plea if it considers the delay justified.

3. The arbitral tribunal may rule on a plea referred to in paragraph (2) of this article either as a preliminary question or in an award on the merits. If the arbitral tribunal rules as a preliminary question that it has jurisdiction, any party may request, within thirty days after having received notice of that

ruling, the court specified in article 6 to decide the matter, which decision shall be subject to no appeal; while such a request is pending, the arbitral tribunal may continue the arbitral proceedings and make an award.

1—147   Article 17—Power of arbitral tribunal to order interim measures

Unless otherwise agreed by the parties, the arbitral tribunal may, at the request of a party, order any party to take such interim measure of protection as the arbitral tribunal may consider necessary in respect of the subject-matter of the dispute. The arbitral tribunal may require any party to provide appropriate security in connection with such measure.

Chapter V: Conduct of Arbitral Proceedings

1—148   Article 18—Equal treatment of parties

The parties shall be treated with equality and each party shall be given a full opportunity of presenting his case.

1—149   Article 19—Determination of rules of procedure

1. Subject to the provisions of this Law, the parties are free to agree on the procedure to be followed by the arbitral tribunal in conducting the proceedings.

2. Failing such agreement, the arbitral tribunal may, subject to the provisions of this Law, conduct the arbitration in such manner as it considers appropriate. The power conferred upon the arbitral tribunal includes the power to determine the admissibility, relevance, materiality and weight of any evidence.

1—150   Article 20—Place of arbitration

1. The parties are free to agree on the place of arbitration. Failing such agreement, the place of arbitration shall be determined by the arbitral tribunal having regard to the circumstances of the case, including the convenience of the parties.

2. Notwithstanding the provisions of paragraph (1) of this article, the arbitral tribunal may, unless otherwise agreed by the parties, meet at any place it considers appropriate for

consultation among its members, for hearing witnesses, experts or the parties, or for inspection of goods, other property or documents.

1—151   Article 21—Commencement of arbitral proceedings

Unless otherwise agreed by the parties, the arbitral proceedings in respect of a particular dispute commence on the date on which a request for that dispute to be referred to arbitration is received by the respondent.

1—152   Article 22—Language

1. The parties are free to agree on the language or languages to be used in the arbitral proceedings. Failing such agreement, the arbitral tribunal shall determine the language or languages to be used in the proceedings. This agreement or determination, unless otherwise specified therein, shall apply to any written statement by a party, any hearing and any award, decision or other communication by the arbitral tribunal.

2. The arbitral tribunal may order that any documentary evidence shall be accompanied by a translation into the language or languages agreed upon by the parties or determined by the arbitral tribunal.

1—153   Article 23—Statements of claim and defence

1. Within the period of time agreed by the parties or determined by the arbitral tribunal, the claimant shall state the facts supporting his claim, the points at issue and the relief or remedy sought, and the respondent shall state his defence in respect of these particulars, unless the parties have otherwise agreed as to the required elements of such statements. The parties may submit with their statements all documents they consider to be relevant or may add a reference to the documents or other evidence they will submit.

2. Unless otherwise agreed by the parties, either party may amend or supplement his claim or defence during the course of the arbitral proceedings, unless the arbitral tribunal considers it inappropriate to allow such amendment having regard to the delay in making it.

1—154   Article 24—Hearings and written proceedings

1. Subject to any contrary agreement by the parties, the arbitral tribunal shall decide whether to hold oral hearings for the

presentation of evidence or for oral argument, or whether the proceedings shall be conducted on the basis of documents and other materials. However, unless the parties have agreed that no hearings shall be held, the arbitral tribunal shall hold such hearings at an appropriate stage of the proceedings, if so requested by a party.

2. The parties shall be given sufficient advance notice of any hearing and of any meeting of the arbitral tribunal for the purposes of inspection of goods, other property or documents.

3. All statements, documents or other information supplied to the arbitral tribunal by one party shall be communicated to the other party. Also any expert report or evidentiary document on which the arbitral tribunal may rely in making its decision shall be communicated to the parties.

1—155   Article 25—Default of a party

Unless otherwise agreed by the parties, if, without showing sufficient cause,

(a) the claimant fails to communicate his statement of claim in accordance with article 23 (1), the arbitral tribunal shall terminate the proceedings;

(b) the respondent fails to communicate his statement of defence in accordance with article 23 (1), the arbitral tribunal shall continue the proceedings without treating such failure in itself as an admission of the claimant's allegations;

(c) any party fails to appear at a hearing or to produce documentary evidence, the arbitral tribunal may continue the proceedings and make the award on the evidence before it.

1—156   Article 26—Expert appointed by arbitral tribunal

1. Unless otherwise agreed by the parties, the arbitral tribunal

   (a) may appoint one or more experts to report to it on specific issues to be determined by the arbitral tribunal;

   (b) may require a party to give the expert any relevant information or to produce, or to provide access to, any relevant documents, goods or other property for his inspection.

2. Unless otherwise agreed by the parties, if a party so requests or if the arbitral tribunal considers it necessary, the expert

shall, after delivery of his written or oral report, participate in a hearing where the parties have the opportunity to put questions to him and to present expert witnesses in order to testify on the points at issue.

1—157 Article 27—Court assistance in taking evidence

The arbitral tribunal or a party with the approval of the arbitral tribunal may request from a competent court of this State assistance in taking evidence. The court may execute the request within its competence and according to its rules on taking evidence.

Chapter V: Making of Award and Termination of Proceedings

1—158 Article 28—Rules applicable to substance of dispute

1. The arbitral tribunal shall decide the dispute in accordance with such rules of law as are chosen by the parties as applicable to the substance of the dispute. Any designation of the law or legal system of a given State shall be construed, unless otherwise expressed, as directly referring to the substantive law of that State and not to its conflict of laws rules.

2. Failing any designation by the parties, the arbitral tribunal shall apply the law determined by the conflict of laws rules which it considers applicable.

3. The arbitral tribunal shall decide ex aequo et bono or as amiable compositeur only if the parties have expressly authorized it to do so.

4. In all cases, the arbitral tribunal shall decide in accordance with the terms of the contract and shall take into account the usages of the trade applicable to the transaction.

1—159 Article 29—Decision-making by panel of arbitrators

In arbitral proceedings with more than one arbitrator, any decision of the arbitral tribunal shall be made, unless otherwise agreed by the parties, by a majority of all its members. However, questions of procedure may be decided by a presiding arbitrator, if so authorized by the parties or all members of the arbitral tribunal.

1—160   Article 30—Settlement

1. If, during arbitral proceedings, the parties settle the dispute, the arbitral tribunal shall terminate the proceedings and, if requested by the parties and not objected to by the arbitral tribunal, record the settlement in the form of an arbitral award on agreed terms.

2. An award on agreed terms shall be made in accordance with the provisions of article 31 and shall state that it is an award. Such an award has the same status and effect as any other award on the merits of the case.

1—161   Article 31—Form and contents of award

1. The award shall be made in writing and shall be signed by the arbitrator or arbitrators. In arbitrator proceedings with more than one arbitrator, the signatures of the majority of all members of the arbitral tribunal shall suffice, provided that the reason for any omitted signature is stated.

2. The award shall state the reasons upon which it is based, unless the parties have agreed that no reasons are to be given or the award is an award on agreed terms under article 30.

3. The award shall state its date and the place of arbitration as determined in accordance with article 20 (1). The award shall be deemed to have been made at that place.

4. After the award is made, a copy signed by the arbitrators in accordance with paragraph (1) of this article shall be delivered to each party.

1—162   Article 32—Termination of proceedings

1. The arbitral proceedings are terminated by the final award or by an order of the arbitral tribunal in accordance with paragraph (2) of this article.

2. The arbitral tribunal shall issue an order for the termination of the arbitral proceedings when:

    (a) the claimant withdraws his claim, unless the respondent objects thereto and the arbitral tribunal recognizes a legitimate interest on his part in obtaining a final settlement of the dispute;

    (b) the parties agree on the termination of the proceedings;

(c) the arbitral tribunal finds that the continuation of the proceedings has for any other reason become unnecessary or impossible.

3. The mandate of the arbitral tribunal terminates with the termination of the arbitral proceedings, subject to the provisions of articles 33 and 34 (4).

1—163   Article 33—Correction of interpretation of award; additional award

1. Within thirty days of receipt of the award, unless another period of time has been agreed upon by the parties:

   (a) a party, with notice to the other party, may request the arbitral tribunal to correct in the award any error in computation, any clerical or typographical errors or any errors of similar nature;

   (b) if so agreed by the parties, a party, with notice to the other party, may request the arbitral tribunal to give an interpretation of a specific point or part of the award.
   If the arbitral tribunal considers the request to be justified, it shall make the correction or give the interpretation within thirty days of receipt of the request. The interpretation shall form part of the award.

2. The arbitral tribunal may correct any error of the type referred to in paragraph (1) (a) of this article on its own initiative within thirty days of the day of the award.

3. Unless otherwise agreed by the parties, a party, with notice to the other party, may request, within thirty days of receipt of the award, the arbitral tribunal to make an additional award as to claims presented in the arbitral proceedings but omitted from the award. If the arbitral tribunal considers the request to be justified, it shall make the additional award within sixty days.

4. The arbitral tribunal may extend, if necessary, the period of time within which it shall make a correction, interpretation or an additional award under paragraph (1) or (3) of this article.

5. The provisions of article 31 shall apply to a correction or interpretation of the award or to an additional award.

CHAPTER VII: RECOURSE AGAINST AWARD

1—164 **Article 34—Application for setting aside as exclusive recourse against arbitral award**

1. Recourse to a court against an arbitral award may be made only by an application for setting aside in accordance with paragraphs (2) and (3) of this article.

2. An arbitral award may be set aside by the court specified in article 6 only if:

   (a) the party making the application furnishes proof that:

   (i) a party to the arbitration agreement referred to in article 7 was under some incapacity; or the said agreement is not valid under the law to which the parties have subjected it or, failing any indication thereon, under the law of this State; or

   (ii) the party making the application was not given proper notice of the appointment of an arbitrator or of the arbitral proceedings or was otherwise unable to present his case; or

   (iii) the award deals with a dispute not contemplated by or not falling within the terms of the submission to arbitration, or contains decisions on matters beyond the scope of the submission to arbitration, provided that, if the decisions on matters submitted to arbitration can be separated from those not so submitted, only that part of the award which contains decisions on matters not submitted to arbitration may be set aside; or

   (iv) the composition of the arbitral tribunal or the arbitral procedure was not in accordance with the agreement of the parties, unless such agreement was in conflict with a provision of this Law from which the parties cannot derogate, or, failing such agreement, was not in accordance with this Law; or

   (b) the court finds that:

   (i) the subject-matter of the dispute is not capable of settlement by arbitration under the law of this State; or

   (ii) the award is in conflict with the public policy of this State.

3. An application for setting aside may not be made after three months have elapsed from the date on which the party

making that application had received that award or, if a request had been made under article 33, from the date on which that request had been disposed of by the arbitral tribunal.

4. The court, when asked to set aside an award, may, where appropriate and so requested by a party, suspend the setting aside proceedings for a period of time determined by it in order to give the arbitral tribunal an opportunity to resume the arbitral proceedings or to take such other action as in the arbitral tribunal's opinion will eliminate the grounds for setting aside.

CHAPTER VIII: RECOGNITION AND ENFORCEMENT OF AWARDS

1—165 Article 35—Recognition and enforcement

1. An arbitral award, irrespective of the country in which it was made, shall be recognized as binding and, upon application in writing to the competent court, shall be enforced subject to the provisions of this article and of article 36.

2. The party relying on an award or applying for its enforcement shall supply the duly authenticated original award or a duly certified copy thereof, and the original arbitration agreement referred to in article 7 or a duly certified copy thereof. If the award or agreement is not made in an official language of this State, the party shall supply a duly certified translation thereof into such language.

1—166 Article 36—Grounds for refusing recognition or enforcement

1. Recognition or enforcement of an arbitral award, irrespective of the country in which it was made, may be refused only:

    (a) at the request of the party against whom it is invoked, if that party furnishes to the competent court where recognition or enforcement is sought proof that:

       (i) a party to the arbitration agreement referred to in article 7 was under some incapacity; or the said agreement is not valid under the law to which the parties have subjected it or, failing any indication thereon, under the law of the country where the award was made; or

(ii) the party against whom the award is invoked was not given proper notice of the appointment of an arbitrator or of the arbitrator proceedings or was otherwise unable to present his case; or

(iii) the award deals with a dispute not contemplated by or not falling within the terms of the submission to arbitration, or it contains decisions on matters beyond the scope of the submission to arbitration, provided that, if the decisions on matters submitted to arbitration can be separated from those not so submitted, that part of the award which contains decisions on matters submitted to arbitration may be recognized and enforced; or

(iv) the composition of the arbitral tribunal or the arbitral procedure was not in accordance with the agreement of the parties or, failing such agreement, was not in accordance with the law of the country where the arbitration took place; or

(v) the award has not yet become binding on the parties or has been set aside or suspended by a court of the country in which, or under the law of which, that award was made; or

(b) if the court finds that:

(i) the subject-matter of the dispute is not capable of settlement by arbitration under the law of this State; or

(ii) the recognition or enforcement of the award would be contrary to the public policy of this State.

2. If an application for setting aside or suspension of an award has been made to a court referred to in paragraph (1) (a) (v) of this article, the court where recognition or enforcement is sought may, if it considers it proper, adjourn its decision and may also, on the application of the party claiming recognition or enforcement of the award, order the other party to provide appropriate security.

B. Foreign Statutes

1. European Jurisdictions

Switzerland

Federal Code on Private International Law (CPIL)

Chapter 12: International Arbitration

1—167 Article 176—I. Scope of application; seat of the arbitral tribunal

    1. The provisions of this chapter shall apply to arbitrations if the seat of the arbitral tribunal is in Switzerland and if at least one of the parties at the time the arbitration agreement was concluded was neither domiciled nor habitually resident in Switzerland.

    2. The provisions of this chapter shall not apply if the parties have excluded its application in writing and agreed to the exclusive application of the cantonal rules of procedures concerning arbitration.

    3. The arbitrators shall determine the seat of the arbitral tribunal if the parties or the arbitration institution designated by them fail to do so.

1—168 Article 177—II. Arbitrability

    1. All pecuniary claims may be submitted to arbitration.

    2. If one party to an arbitration agreement is a State or an enterprise dominated by or an organization controlled by a State, it may invoke its own law to contest the arbitrability of a dispute or its capacity to be subject to an arbitration.

1—169 Article 178—III. Arbitration agreement

    1. As to form, the arbitration agreement shall be valid if it is made in writing, by telegram, telex, telecopier, or any other means of communication that establishes the terms of the agreement by a text. As to substance, the arbitration agreement shall be valid if it complies with the requirements of the law chosen by the parties or the law governing the object of

the dispute and, in particular, the law applicable to the principal contract, or with Swiss law.

2. The validity of an arbitration agreement may not be contested on the grounds that the principal contract is invalid or that the arbitration agreement concerns a dispute which has not yet arisen.

1—170　Article 179—IV. Arbitral tribunal

1. Appointment

1. The arbitrators shall be appointed, removed, or replaced in accordance with the agreement of the parties.

2. In the absence of such agreement, the judge at the seat of the arbitral tribunal may be called upon; he shall apply the provisions of cantonal law concerning the appointment, removal, or replacement of arbitrators by analogy.

3. If a judge is called upon to appoint an arbitrator, he must comply with this request unless a summary examination demonstrates that no arbitration agreement exists between the parties.

1—171　Article 180

2. Challenge of arbitrators

1. An arbitrator must be challenged:
    a. If he does not possess the qualification agreed upon by the parties;
    b. If there exist grounds for challenge in the rules of arbitration adopted by the parties; or
    c. If the circumstances permit legitimate doubt about his independence.

2. A party may challenge an arbitrator whom he nominated or in whose appointment he participated only on information discovered after the appointment. The arbitral tribunal and the other party must be informed immediately of the grounds for the challenge.

3. In the event of a dispute and if the parties have not agreed upon the procedures for challenge, the judge at the seat of the arbitral tribunal shall make final decision.

1—172   Article 181—V. Lis pendens

The arbitration proceeding shall be pending from the moment one of the parties files a claim before the sole arbitrator of the arbitrators designated in the arbitration agreement or, in the absence of such designation, if one of the parties institutes the procedure for the appointment of the arbitral tribunal.

1—173   Article 182—VI. Procedure

1. General rule

1. The parties may directly or by reference to rules of arbitration regulate the arbitral procedure; they may also subject the procedure to the procedural law of their choice.

2. If the parties have not regulated the procedure, it shall be fixed, as necessary, by the arbitral tribunal either directly or by reference to a law or rules of arbitration.

3. Irrespective of the procedure chosen, the arbitral tribunal shall accord equal treatment to the parties and their right to be heard in an adversarial proceeding.

1—174   Article 183

2. Provisional and protective measures

1. Unless the parties have agreed otherwise, the arbitral tribunal may enter provisional or protective measures at the request of one party.

2. If the party concerned does not comply voluntarily, the arbitral tribunal may request the assistance of the judge with jurisdiction who shall apply his own law.

3. The arbitral tribunal or the judge may make the entry of provisional or protective measures subject to the receipt of appropriate security.

1—175   Article 184

3. Taking of evidence

1. The arbitral tribunal shall take evidence.

2. If the assistance of the judicial or administrative authorities of the State is needed to take evidence, the arbitral tribunal or, with the consent of the arbitral tribunal, a party may

request the assistance of the judge at the seat of the arbitral tribunal who shall apply his own law.

1—176   Article 185

4. Further assistance by the judge

If further assistance of the judicial or administrative authorities is required, the judge at the seat of the arbitral tribunal shall have jurisdiction.

1—177   Article 186—VII. Jurisdiction

1. The arbitral tribunal shall rule on its own jurisdiction.
2. The objection of lack of jurisdiction must be raised prior to any defense on the merits.
3. In general, the arbitral tribunal shall rule on its own jurisdiction by means of an interlocutory decision.

1—178   Article 187—VIII. Decision on the merits

1. Applicable law

1. The arbitral tribunal shall rule according to the law chosen by the parties or, in the absence of such choice, according to the law with which the action is most closely connected.
2. The parties may authorize the arbitral tribunal to rule according to equity.

1—179   Article 188

2. Partial award

Unless the parties have agreed otherwise, the arbitral tribunal may render partial awards.

1—180   Article 189

3. Arbitral award

1. The arbitral award shall be rendered according to the procedure and in the form agreed upon by the parties.
2. In the absence of such agreement, the award shall be rendered by a majority or, in the ab-sence of such majority, by the

chairman alone. The award must be in writing, set forth the reasons on which it is based, and be dated and signed. The signature of the chairman is suffi-cient.

1—181 Article 190—IX. Finality, appeal

1. General rule

1. The award shall be final when communicated.
2. It can be challenged only:
    a. If a sole arbitrator was designated irregularly or the arbitral tribunal was constituted irregularly;
    b. If the arbitral tribunal erroneously held that it had or did not have jurisdiction;
    c. If the arbitral tribunal ruled on matters beyond the claims submitted to it or if it failed to rule on one of the claims;
    d. If the equality of the parties or their right to be heard in an adversarial proceeding was not respected;
    e. If the award is incompatible with Swiss public policy (ordre public).
3. An interlocutory award may only be challenged on the grounds stated in paragraph 2, letters a and b; the time limit for lodging an appeal shall commence when the interlocutory award is communicated.

1—182 Article 191

2. Court of appeal

1. An appeal may be taken only to the Swiss Federal Supreme Court. The procedure shall be subject to the provisions of the Federal Statute on the Organization of the Judiciary regarding appeals in constitutional matters.
2. The parties may agree, however, that instead of the Swiss Federal Supreme Court, the court at the seat of the arbitral tribunal shall issue a final ruling. The cantons shall designate a sole court for this purpose.

1—183 Article 192—X. Waiver of appeal

1. If neither party has a domicile, a place of habitual residence, or a place of business in Switzerland, they may, by an express declaration in the arbitration agreement or in a subsequent

written agreement, exclude all appeals against the award of the arbitral tribunal. They may also exclude an appeal only on one or several of the grounds enumerated in Article 190, paragraph 2.

2. If the parties have excluded all appeals against the award and enforcement of the awards is sought in Switzerland, the New York Convention of June 10, 1958 on the Recognition And Enforcement of Foreign Arbitral Awards shall apply by analogy.

1—184 Article 193—XI. Deposit and certificate of enforceability

1. Each party may deposit at its own expense a copy of the award with the Swiss court at the seat of the arbitral tribunal.

2. The Swiss court shall certify at the request of a party that the award is enforceable.

3. At the request of a party, the arbitral tribunal shall certify that the award was rendered inconformity with the provisions of this Code; such a certificate is equivalent to a deposit with the Court.

1—185 Article 194—XII. Foreign arbitral awards

The recognition and enforcement of foreign arbitral awards shall be governed by the New York Convention of June 10, 1958 on the Recognition and Enforcement of Foreign Arbitral Awards.

France

New Code of Civil Procedure

Title V
International Arbitration
(Decree of May 12, 1981)

1—186 Article 1492

Arbitration is international if it implicates international commercial interests.

1—187 Article 1493

The arbitration agreement may, directly or by reference to a set of arbitration rules, designate one or more arbitrators or provide the manner for their designation. If any difficulty arises in the constitution of the arbitral tribunal with respect to arbitration taking place in France, or in regard to which the parties provided have agreed that French procedural law should apply, either party may, in the absence of a clause to the contrary, apply to the President of the "Tribunal de Grande Instance de Paris" in the manner set forth in Article 1457.

1—188 Article 1494

The arbitration agreement may, directly or by reference to a set of arbitration rules, define the procedure to be followed in the arbitral proceedings; it may also subject them to a given procedural law.

If the agreement is silent, the arbitrator, either directly or by reference to a law or a set of arbitration rules, shall establish such rules of procedure as may be necessary.

1—189 Article 1495

Whenever international arbitration is subject to French law, the dispositions of Titles I, II, and III of the present Volume shall apply only in the absence of agreement between the parties, and subject to Articles 1493 and 1494.

1—190 Article 1496

The arbitrator shall decide the dispute according to the rules of law chosen by the parties; in the absence of such a choice, he shall decide according to rules he deems appropriate.

In all cases he shall take into account trade usages.

1—190a   Article 1497

The arbitrator shall decide as *amiable compositeur* if *the parties' agreement conferred* this task upon him.

1—191   Title VI

THE RECOGNITION, ENFORCEMENT, AND CHALLENGE OF ARBITRAL AWARDS RENDERED ABROAD OR IN INTERNATIONAL ARBITRATION.

Chapter 1: The Recognition and Enforcement of Arbitral Awards Rendered Abroad or in International Arbitration

1—192   Article 1498

Arbitral awards shall be recognized in France if their existence is proven by parties relying thereupon and if this recognition is not manifestly contrary to international public policy (*ordre public*).

Subject to the same conditions, such awards shall be judicially declared to have executory force in France.

1—193   Article 1499

The existence of an arbitral award must be established by the production of its original text together with the arbitration agreement, or by copies of said documents accompanied by proof of authenticity.

If said documents are not in the French language, the party shall produce a translation certified by a translator on the list of court-appointed experts.

1—194   Article 1500

The provisions of Article 1476 through 1479 are applicable.

Chapter II: Challenge of Arbitral Awards Rendered Abroad or in International Arbitration

1—195   Article 1501

A decision that refuses recognition or enforcement of an award may be appealed.

1—196 Article 1502

An appeal against a decision granting recognition or enforcement may be brought only in the following cases:

- 1st If there is no valid arbitration agreement or the arbitrator ruled on the basis of a void or expired agreement;
- 2nd If there are irregularities in the appointment of the arbitral tribunal or of the sole arbitrator, as the case may be;
- 3rd If the arbitrator exceeded the authority conferred upon him;
- 4th Whenever due process (literally: the principle of an adversary process) has not been respected;
- 5th If the recognition or enforcement are contrary to international public policy (*ordre public*).

1—197 Article 1503

The appeal defined in Articles 1501 and 1502 shall be made to the Court of Appeals of the jurisdiction of the judge having rendered the decision. It may be brought within one month of official notice of the judge's decision.

1—198 Article 1504

An arbitral award rendered in France an international arbitral proceedings is subject to an action to set aside on the grounds set forth in Article 1502.

An order to enforce such an award may not be challenged. However, the action to set aside comports *ipso facto*, within the limits of the terms of the action brought before the Court of Appeals, appeal from either the acceptance or refusal of the execution judge to make such an order.

1—199 Article 1505

Actions to set aside as defined in Article 1504 shall be brought before the Court of Appeals having jurisdiction in the place where the award was rendered. Such action may be heard as soon as the award has been rendered; it may no longer be heard if it has not been brought within the month following official notification of the order of execution of the award.

1—200 Article 1506

Execution of the arbitral award is suspended during the time limit for bringing the challenges defined in Articles 1501, 1502 and 1504. The bringing of a challenge action within the time limit also has a suspensive effect.

1—201   Article 1507

The provisions of Title IV of the present volume, with the exception of those of paragraph 1st and Article 1487 and of Article 1490, are not applicable to challenge actions.

Germany

Arbitration Law of 1998

Tenth Book of the Code of Civil Procedure Arbitration Procedure Sections 1025 to 1066

CHAPTER I: GENERAL PROVISIONS

1—202 Scope of application

Section 1025.—(1) The provisions of this Book apply if the place of arbitration as referred to in section 1043 subs. 1 is situated in Germany.

(2) The provisions of sections 1032, 1033 and 1050 also apply if the place of arbitration is situated outside Germany or has not yet been determined.

(3) If the place of arbitration has not yet been determined, the German courts are competent to perform the court functions specified in sections 1034, 1035, 1037 and 1038 if the respondent or the claimant has his place of business or habitual residence in Germany.

(4) Sections 1061 to 1065 apply to the recognition and enforcement of foreign arbitral awards.

1—203 Extent of court intervention

Section 1026.—In matters governed by sections 1025 to 1061, no court shall intervene except where so provided in this Book.

1—204 Loss of right to object

Section 1027.—A party who knows that any provision of this Book from which the parties may derogate or any agreed requirement under the arbitral procedure has not been complied with and yet proceeds with the arbitration without stating his objection to such non-compliance without undue delay or, if a time-limit is provided therefor, within such period of time, may not raise that objection later.

1—205 **Receipt of written communications in case of unknown whereabouts**

Section 1028.—(1) Unless otherwise agreed by the parties, if the whereabouts of a party or of a person entitled to receive communications on his behalf are not known, any written communication shall be deemed to have been received on the day on which it could have been received at the addressee's last-known mailing address, place of business or habitual residence after proper transmission by registered mail/return receipt requested or any other means which provides a record of the attempt to deliver it there.

(2) Subsection 1 does not apply to communications in court proceedings.

CHAPTER II: ARBITRATION AGREEMENT

1—206 **Definition**

Section 1029.—(1) "Arbitration agreement" is an agreement by the parties to submit to arbitration all or certain disputes which have arisen or which may arise between them in respect of a defined legal relationship, whether contractual or not.

(2) An arbitration agreement may be in the form of a separate agreement ("separate arbitration agreement") or in the form of a clause in a contract ("arbitration clause").

1—207 **Arbitrability**

Section 1030.—(1) Any claim involving an economic interest ("verm_gensrechtlicher Anspruch") can be the subject of an arbitration agreement. An arbitration agreement concerning claims not involving an economic interest shall have legal effect to the extent that the parties are entitled to conclude a settlement on the issue in dispute.

(2) An arbitration agreement relating to disputes on the existence of a lease of residential accommodation within Germany shall be null and void. This does not

apply to residential accommodation as specified in section 556a subs. 8 of the Civil Code.

(3) Statutory provisions outside this Book by virtue of which certain disputes may not be submitted to arbitration, or may be submitted to arbitration only under certain conditions, remain unaffected.

1—208   Form of arbitration agreement

Section 1031.—(1) The arbitration agreement shall be contained either in a document signed by the parties or in an exchange of letters, telecopies, telegrams or other means of telecommunication which provide a record of the agreement.

(2) The form requirement of subsection 1 shall be deemed to have been complied with if the arbitration agreement is contained in a document transmitted from one party to the other party or by a third party to both parties and—if no objection was raised in good time—the contents of such document are considered to be part of the contract in accordance with common usage.

(3) The reference in a contract complying with the form requirements of subsection 1 or 2 to a document containing an arbitration clause constitutes an arbitration agreement provided that the reference is such as to make that clause part of the contract.

(4) An arbitration agreement is also concluded by the issuance of a bill of lading, if the latter contains an express reference to an arbitration clause in a charter party.

(5) Arbitration agreements to which a consumer is a party must be contained in a document which has been personally signed by the parties. No agreements other than those referring to the arbitral proceedings may be contained in such a document; this shall not apply in the case of a notarial certification.

(6) Any non-compliance with the form requirements is cured by entering into argument on the substance of the dispute in the arbitral proceedings.

1—209 Arbitration agreement and substantive claim before court

Section 1032.—(1) A court before which an action is brought in a matter which is the subject of an arbitration agreement shall, if the respondent raises an objection prior to the beginning of the oral hearing on the substance of the dispute, reject the action as inadmissible unless the court finds that the arbitration agreement is null and void, inoperative or incapable of being performed.

(2) Prior to the constitution of the arbitral tribunal, an application may be made to the court to determine whether or not arbitration is admissible.

(3) Where an action or application referred to in subsection 1 or 2 has been brought, arbitral proceedings may nevertheless be commenced or continued, and an arbitral award may be made, while the issue is pending before the court.

1—210 Arbitration agreement and interim measures by court

Section 1033.—It is not incompatible with an arbitration agreement for a court to grant, before or during arbitral proceedings, an interim measure of protection relating to the subject-matter of the arbitration upon request of a party.

CHAPTER III: CONSTITUTION OF ARBITRAL TRIBUNAL

1—211 Composition of arbitral tribunal

Section 1034.—(1) The parties are free to determine the number of arbitrators. Failing such determination, the number of arbitrators shall be three.

(2) If the arbitration agreement grants preponderant rights to one party with regard to the composition of the arbitral tribunal which place the other party at a disadvantage, that other party may request the court to appoint the arbitrator or arbitrators in deviation from the nomination made, or from the agreed nomination procedure. The request must be submitted at the latest within two weeks of the party becoming aware of the constitution of the arbitral tribunal.

1—212 Appointment of arbitrators

Section 1035.—(1) The parties are free to agree on a procedure of appointing the arbitrator or arbitrators.

(2) Unless otherwise agreed by the parties, a party shall be bound by his appointment of an arbitrator as soon as the other party has received notice of the appointment.

(3) Failing an agreement between the parties on the appointment of the arbitrators, a sole arbitrator shall, if the parties are unable to agree on his appointment, be appointed, upon request of a party, by the court. In an arbitration with three arbitrators, each party shall appoint one arbitrator, and the two arbitrators thus appointed shall appoint the third arbitrator who shall act as chairman of the arbitral tribunal. If a party fails to appoint the arbitrator within one month of receipt of a request to do so from the other party, or if the two arbitrators fail to agree on the third arbitrator within one month of their appointment, the appointment shall be made, upon request of a party, by the court.

(4) Where, under an appointment procedure agreed upon by the parties, a party fails to act as required under such procedure, or if the parties, or two arbitrators, are unable to reach an agreement expected of them under such procedure, or a third party fails to perform any function entrusted to it under such procedure, any party may request the court to take the necessary measure, unless the agreement on the appointment procedure provides other means for securing the appointment.

(5) The court, in appointing an arbitrator, shall have due regard to any qualifications required of the arbitrator by the agreement of the parties and to such considerations as are likely to secure the appointment of an independent and impartial arbitrator. In the case of a sole or third arbitrator, the court shall take into account as well the advisability of appointing an arbitrator of a nationality other than those of the parties.

1—213   Challenge of an arbitrator

Section 1036.—(1) When a person is approached in connection with his possible appointment as an arbitrator, he shall disclose any circumstances likely to give rise to justifiable doubts as to his impartiality or independence. An arbitrator, from the time of his appointment and throughout the arbitral proceedings, shall without delay disclose any such circumstances to the parties unless they have already been informed of them by him.

(2) An arbitrator may be challenged only if circumstances exist that give rise to justifiable doubts as to his impartiality or independence, or if he does not possess qualifications agreed to by the parties. A party may challenge an arbitrator appointed by him, or in whose appointment he has participated, only for reasons of which he becomes aware after the appointment has been made.

1—214   Challenge procedure

Section 1037.—(1) The parties are free to agree on a procedure for challenging an arbitrator, subject to the provisions of subsection 3 of this section.

(2) Failing such agreement, a party who intends to challenge an arbitrator shall, within two weeks after becoming aware of the constitution of the arbitral tribunal or after becoming aware of any circumstance referred to in section 1036 subs. 2, send a written statement of the reasons for the challenge to the arbitral tribunal. Unless the challenged arbitrator withdraws from his office or the other party agrees to the challenge, the arbitral tribunal shall decide on the challenge.

(3) If a challenge under any procedure agreed upon by the parties or under the procedure of subsection 2 of this section is not successful, the challenging party may request, within one month after having received notice of the decision rejecting the challenge, the court to decide on the challenge; the parties may agree on a different time-limit. While such a request is pending, the arbitral tribunal, including the challenged arbitrator, may continue the arbitral proceedings and make an award.

1—215 Failure or impossibility to act

Section 1038.—(1) If an arbitrator becomes de jure or de facto unable to perform his functions or for other reasons fails to act without undue delay, his mandate terminates if he withdraws from his office or if the parties agree on the termination. If the arbitrator does not withdraw from his office or if the parties cannot agree on the termination, any party may request the court to decide on the termination of the mandate.

(2) If, under subsection 1 of this section or section 1037 subs. 2, an arbitrator withdraws from his office or a party agrees to the termination of the mandate of an arbitrator, this does not imply acceptance of the validity of any ground for withdrawal referred to in subsection 1 of this section or section 1036 subs. 2.

1—216 Appointment of substitute arbitrator

Section 1039.—(1) Where the mandate of an arbitrator terminates under section 1037 or 1038 or because of his withdrawal from office for any other reason or because of the revocation of his mandate by agreement of the parties, a substitute arbitrator shall be appointed according to the rules that were applicable to the appointment of the arbitrator being replaced.

(2) The parties are free to agree on another procedure.

CHAPTER IV: JURISDICTION OF ARBITRAL TRIBUNAL

1—217 Competence of arbitral tribunal to rule on its jurisdiction

Section 1040.—(1) The arbitral tribunal may rule on its own jurisdiction and in this connection on the existence or validity of the arbitration agreement. For that purpose, an arbitration clause which forms part of a contract shall be treated as an agreement independent of the other terms of the contract.

(2) A plea that the arbitral tribunal does not have jurisdiction shall be raised not later than the submission of the statement of defence. A party is not precluded

from raising such a plea by the fact that he has appointed, or participated in the appointment of, an arbitrator. A plea that the arbitral tribunal is exceeding the scope of its authority shall be raised as soon as the matter alleged to be beyond the scope of its authority is raised during the arbitral proceedings. The arbitral tribunal may, in either case, admit a later plea if it considers that the party has justified the delay.

(3) If the arbitral tribunal considers that it has jurisdiction, it rules on a plea referred to in subsection 2 of this section in general by means of a preliminary ruling. In this case, any party may request, within one month after having received written notice of that ruling, the court to decide the matter. While such a request is pending, the arbitral tribunal may continue the arbitral proceedings and make an award.

1—218 Interim measures of protection

Section 1041.—(1) Unless otherwise agreed by the parties, the arbitral tribunal may, at the request of a party, order such interim measures of protection as the arbitral tribunal may consider necessary in respect of the subject-matter of the dispute. The arbitral tribunal may require any party to provide appropriate security in connection with such measure.

(2) The court may, at the request of a party, permit enforcement of a measure referred to in subsection 1, unless application for a corresponding interim measure has already been made to a court. It may recast such an order if necessary for the purpose of enforcing the measure.

(3) The court may, upon request, repeal or amend the decision referred to in subsection 2.

(4) If a measure ordered under subsection 1 proves to have been unjustified from the outset, the party who obtained its enforcement is obliged to compensate the other party for damage resulting from the enforcement of such measure or from his providing security in order to avoid enforcement. This claim may be put forward in the pending arbitral proceedings.

Chapter V: Conduct of Arbitral Proceedings

1—219 General rules of procedure

Section 1042.—(1) The parties shall be treated with equality and each party shall be given a full opportunity of presenting his case.

(2) Counsel may not be excluded from acting as authorised representatives.

(3) Otherwise, subject to the mandatory provisions of this Book, the parties are free to determine the procedure themselves or by reference to a set of arbitration rules.

(4) Failing an agreement by the parties, and in the absence of provisions in this Book, the arbitral tribunal shall conduct the arbitration in such manner as it considers appropriate. The arbitral tribunal is empowered to determine the admissibility of taking evidence, take evidence and assess freely such evidence.

1—220 Place of arbitration

Section 1043.—(1) The parties are free to agree on the place of arbitration. Failing such agreement, the place of arbitration shall be determined by the arbitral tribunal having regard to the circumstances of the case, including the convenience of the parties.

(2) Notwithstanding the provisions of subsection 1 of this section, the arbitral tribunal may, unless otherwise agreed by the parties, meet at any place it considers appropriate for an oral hearing, for hearing witnesses, experts or the parties, for consultation among its members or for inspection of property or documents.

1—221 Commencement of arbitral proceedings

Section 1044.—Unless otherwise agreed by the parties, the arbitral proceedings in respect of a particular dispute commence on the date on which a request for that dispute to be referred to arbitration is received by the respondent The request shall state the names of the parties, the subject-matter of the dispute and contain a reference to the arbitration agreement

1—222 Language of proceedings

Section 1045.—(1) The parties are free to agree on the language or languages to be used in the arbitral proceedings. Failing such agreement, the arbitral tribunal shall determine the language or languages to be used in the proceedings. This agreement or determination, unless otherwise specified therein, shall apply to any written statement by a party, any hearing and any award, decision or other communication by the arbitral tribunal.

(2) The arbitral tribunal may order that any documentary evidence shall be accompanied by a translation into the language or languages agreed upon by the parties or determined by the arbitral tribunal.

1—223 Statements of claim and defence

Section 1046.—(1) Within the period of time agreed by the parties or determined by the arbitral tribunal, the claimant shall state his claim and the facts supporting the claim, and the respondent shall state his defence in respect of these particulars. The parties may submit with their statements all documents they consider to be relevant or may add a reference to other evidence they will submit.

(2) Unless otherwise agreed by the parties, either party may amend or supplement his claim or defence during the course of the arbitral proceedings, unless the arbitral tribunal considers it inappropriate to allow such amendment having regard to the delay in making it without sufficient justification.

(3) Subsections 1 and 2 apply mutatis mutandis to counter-claims.

1—224 Oral hearings and written proceedings

Section 1047.—(1) Subject to agreement by the parties, the arbitral tribunal shall decide whether to hold oral hearings or whether the proceedings shall be conducted on the basis of documents and other materials. Unless the parties have agreed that no hearings shall be held, the arbitral tribunal shall hold such hearings at an appropriate stage of the proceedings, if so requested by a party.

(2) The parties shall be given sufficient advance notice of any hearing and of any meeting of the arbitral tribunal for the purpose of taking evidence.

(3) All statements, documents or other information supplied to the arbitral tribunal by one party shall be communicated to the other party. Also, any expert report or evidentiary document on which the arbitral tribunal may rely in making its decision shall be communicated to both parties.

1—225 Default of a party

Section 1048.—(1) If the claimant fails to communicate his statement of claim in accordance with section 1046 subs. 1, the arbitral tribunal shall terminate the proceedings.

(2) If the respondent fails to communicate his statement of defence in accordance with section 1046 subs. 1, the arbitral tribunal shall continue the proceedings without treating such failure in itself as an admission of the claimant's allegations.

(3) If any party fails to appear at an oral hearing or to produce documentary evidence within a set time-limit, the arbitral tribunal may continue the proceedings and make the award on the evidence before it.

(4) Any default which has been justified to the tribunal's satisfaction will be disregarded. Apart from that, the parties may agree otherwise on the consequences of default.

1—226 Expert appointed by arbitral tribunal

Section 1049.—(1) Unless otherwise agreed by the parties, the arbitral tribunal may appoint one or more experts to report to it on specific issues to be determined by the arbitral tribunal. It may also require a party to give the expert any relevant information or to produce, or to provide access to, any relevant documents or property for his inspection.

(2) Unless otherwise agreed by the parties, if a party so requests or if the arbitral tribunal considers it necessary, the expert shall, after delivery of his written or oral report, participate in an oral hearing where the parties have the opportunity to put questions to him and to present expert witnesses in order to testify on the points at issue.

(3) Sections 1036 and 1037 subs. 1 and 2 apply mutatis mutandis to an expert appointed by the arbitral tribunal.

1—227 Court assistance in taking evidence and other judicial acts

Section 1050.—The arbitral tribunal or a party with the approval of the arbitral tribunal may request from a court assistance in taking evidence or performance of other judicial acts which the arbitral tribunal is not empowered to carry out. Unless it regards the application as inadmissible, the court shall execute the request according to its rules on taking evidence or other judicial acts. The arbitrators are entitled to participate in any judicial taking of evidence and to ask questions.

Chapter VI: Making of Award and Termination of Proceedings

1—228 Rules applicable to substance of dispute

Section 1051.—(1) The arbitral tribunal shall decide the dispute in accordance with such rules of law as are chosen by the parties as applicable to the substance of the dispute. Any designation of the law or legal system of a given State shall be construed, unless otherwise expressed, as directly referring to the substantive law of that State and not to its conflict of laws rules.

(2) Failing any designation by the parties, the arbitral tribunal shall apply the law of the State with which the subject-matter of the proceedings is most closely connected.

(3) The arbitral tribunal shall decide ex aequo et bono or as amiable compositeur only if the parties have expressly authorized it to do so. The parties may so authorize the arbitral tribunal up to the time of its decision.

(4) In all cases, the arbitral tribunal shall decide in accordance with the terms of the contract and shall take into account the usages of the trade applicable to the transaction.

1—229 Decision making by panel of arbitrators

Section 1052.—(1) In arbitral proceedings with more than one arbitrator, any decision of the arbitral tribunal shall be made, unless otherwise agreed by the parties, by a majority of all its members.

(2) If an arbitrator refuses to take part in the vote on a decision, the other arbitrators may take the decision without him, unless otherwise agreed by the parties. The parties shall be given advance notice of the intention to make an award without the arbitrator refusing to participate in the vote. In the case of other decisions, the parties shall subsequent to the decision be informed of the refusal to participate in the vote.

(3) Individual questions of procedure may be decided by a presiding arbitrator alone if so authorized by the parties or all members of the arbitral tribunal.

1—230 Settlement

Section 1053.—(1) If, during arbitral proceedings, the parties settle the dispute, the arbitral tribunal shall terminate the proceedings. If requested by the parties, it shall record the settlement in the form of an arbitral award on agreed terms, unless the contents are in violation of public policy (ordre public).

(2) An award on agreed terms shall be made in accordance with section 1054 and shall state that it is an award. Such an award has the same effect as any other award on the merits of the case.

(3) If notarial certification is required for a declaration to be effective, it will be substituted, in the case of an arbitral award on agreed terms, by recording the declaration of the parties in the award.

(4) An award on agreed terms may, upon agreement between the parties, also be declared enforceable by a notary whose notarial office is in the district of the court competent for the declaration of enforceability

according to section 1062 subs. 1, no. 2. The notary shall refuse the declaration of enforceability, if the requirements of subsection 1, sentence 2 are not complied with.

1—231 Form and contents of award

Section 1054.—(1) The award shall be made in writing and shall be signed by the arbitrator or arbitrators. In arbitral proceedings with more than one arbitrator, the signatures of the majority of all members of the arbitral tribunal shall suffice, provided that the reason for any omitted signature is stated.

(2) The award shall state the reasons upon which it is based, unless the parties have agreed that no reasons are to be given or the award is an award on agreed terms under section 1053.

(3) The award shall state its date and the place of arbitration as determined in accordance with section 1043 subs. 1. The award shall be deemed to have been made on that date and at that place. (4) A copy of the award signed by the arbitrators shall be delivered to each party.

1—232 Effect of arbitral award

Section 1055.—The arbitral award has the same effect between the parties as a final and binding court judgment.

1—233 Termination of proceedings

Section 1056.—(1) The arbitral proceedings are terminated by the final award or by an order of the arbitral tribunal in accordance with subsection 2 of this section.

(2) The arbitral tribunal shall issue an order for the termination of the arbitral proceedings when 1. the claimant: a) fails to state his claim according to section 1046 subs. 1 and section 1048 subs. 4 does not apply, or b) withdraws his claim, unless the respondent objects thereto and the arbitral tribunal recognizes a legitimate interest on his part in obtaining a final settlement of the dispute, or 2. the parties agree on the termination of the proceedings, or 3. the parties fail to pursue the arbitral proceedings in spite of being so

requested by the arbitral tribunal or when the continuation of the proceedings has for any other reason become impossible.

(3) The mandate of the arbitral tribunal terminates with the termination of the arbitral proceedings, subject to the provisions of sections 1057 subs. 2, 1058 and 1059 subs. 4.

1—234 Decision on costs

Section 1057.—(1) Unless the parties agree otherwise, the arbitral tribunal shall allocate, by means of an arbitral award, the costs of the arbitration as between the parties, including those incurred by the parties necessary for the proper pursuit of their claim or defence. It shall do so at its discretion and take into consideration the circumstances of the case, in particular the outcome of the proceedings.

(2) To the extent that the costs of the arbitral proceedings have been fixed, the arbitral tribunal shall also decide on the amount to be borne by each party. If the costs have not been fixed or if they can only be fixed once the arbitral proceedings have been terminated, the decision shall be taken by means of a separate award.

1—235 Correction and interpretation of award; additional award

Section 1058.—(1) Any party may request the arbitral tribunal 1. to correct in the award any errors in computation, any clerical or typographical errors or any errors of similar nature, 2. to give an interpretation of specific parts of the award, 3. to make an additional award as to claims presented in the arbitral proceedings but omitted from the award.

(2) Unless otherwise agreed by the parties, the request shall be made within one month of receipt of the award.

(3) The arbitral tribunal shall make the correction or give the interpretation within one month and make an additional award within two months.

(4) The arbitral tribunal may make a correction of the award on its own initiative.

(5) Section 1054 shall apply to a correction or interpretation of the award or to an additional award.

CHAPTER VII: RECOURSE AGAINST AWARD

1—236 Application for setting aside

Section 1059.—(1) Recourse to a court against an arbitral award may be made only by an application for setting aside in accordance with subsections 2 and 3 of this section.

(2) An arbitral award may be set aside only if: 1. the applicant shows sufficient cause that: a) a party to the arbitration agreement referred to in sections 1029 and 1031 was under some incapacity pursuant to the law applicable to him; or the said agreement is not valid under the law to which the parties have subjected it or, failing any indication thereon, under German law; or b) he was not given proper notice of the appointment of an arbitrator or of the arbitral proceedings or was otherwise unable to present his case; or c) the award deals with a dispute not contemplated by or not falling within the terms of the submission to arbitration, or contains decisions on matters beyond the scope of the submission to arbitration; provided that, if the decisions on matters submitted to arbitration can be separated from those not so submitted, only that part of the award which contains decisions on matters not submitted to arbitration may be set aside; or d) the composition of the arbitral tribunal or the arbitral procedure was not in accordance with a provision of this Book or with an admissible agreement of the parties and this presumably affected the award; or 2. the court finds that a) the subject-matter of the dispute is not capable of settlement by arbitration under German law; or b) recognition or enforcement of the award leads to a result which is in conflict with public policy (ordre public).

(3) Unless the parties have agreed otherwise, an application for setting aside to the court may not be made after three months have elapsed. The period of time shall commence on the date on which the party making the application had received the award. If a request had been made under section 1058, the time-

limit shall be extended by not more than one month from receipt of the decision on the request. No application for setting aside the award may be made once the award has been declared enforceable by a German court.

(4) The court, when asked to set aside an award, may, where appropriate, set aside the award and remit the case to the arbitral tribunal.

(5) Setting aside the arbitral award shall, in the absence of any indication to the contrary, result in the arbitration agreement becoming operative again in respect of the subject-matter of the dispute.

CHAPTER VIII: RECOGNITION AND ENFORCEMENT OF AWARDS

1—237 Domestic awards

Section 1060.—(1) Enforcement of the award takes place if it has been declared enforceable.

(2) An application for a declaration of enforceability shall be refused and the award set aside if one of the grounds for setting aside under section 1059 subs. 2 exists. Grounds for setting aside shall not be taken into account, if at the time when the application for a declaration of enforceability is served, an application for setting aside based on such grounds has been finally rejected. Grounds for setting aside under section 1059 subs. 2, no. 1 shall also not be taken into account if the time-limits set by section 1059 subs. 3 have expired without the party opposing the application having made an application for setting aside the award.

1—238 Foreign awards

Section 1061.—(1) Recognition and enforcement of foreign arbitral awards shall be granted in accordance with the Convention on the Recognition and Enforcement of Foreign Arbitral Awards of 10 June 1958 (Bundesgesetzblatt [BGBl.] 1961 Part II p. 121). The provisions of other treaties on the recognition and enforcement of arbitral awards shall remain unaffected.

(2) If the declaration of enforceability is to be refused, the court shall rule that the arbitral award is not to be recognized in Germany.

(3) If the award is set aside abroad after having been declared enforceable, application for setting aside the declaration of enforceability may be made.

CHAPTER IX: COURT PROCEEDINGS

1—239 **Competence**

Section 1062.—(1) The Higher Regional Court ("Oberlandesgericht") designated in the arbitration agreement or, failing such designation, the Higher Regional Court in whose district the place of arbitration is situated, is competent for decisions on applications relating to 1. the appointment of an arbitrator (sections 1034 and 1035), the challenge of an arbitrator (section 1037) or the termination of an arbitrator's mandate (section 1038); 2. the determination of the admissibility or inadmissibility of arbitration (section 1032) or the decision of an arbitral tribunal confirming its competence in a preliminary ruling (section 1040); 3. the enforcement, setting aside or amendment of an order for interim measures of protection by the arbitral tribunal (section 1041); 4. the setting aside (section 1059) or the declaration of enforceability of the award (section 1060 et seq.) or the setting aside of the declaration of enforceability (section 1061).

(2) If the place of arbitration in the cases referred to in subsection 1, no. 2, first alternative, nos. 3 and 4 is not in Germany, competence lies with the Higher Regional Court ("Oberlandesgericht") where the party opposing the application has his place of business or place of habitual residence, or where assets of that party or the property in dispute or affected by the measure is located, failing which the Berlin Higher Regional Court ("Kammergericht") shall be competent.

(3) In the cases referred to in section 1025 subs. 3, the Higher Regional Court ("Oberlandesgericht") in whose district the claimant or the respondent has his place of business or place of habitual residence is competent.

(4) For assistance in the taking of evidence and other judicial acts (section 1050), the Local Court ("Amtsgericht"), in whose district the judicial act is to be carried out, is competent.

(5) Where there are several Higher Regional Courts ("Oberlandesgerichte") in one Land, the Government of that Land may transfer by ordinance competence to one Higher Regional Court, or, where existent, to the highest Regional Court ("oberstes Landesgericht")1; the Land Government may transfer such authority to the Department of Justice of the Land concerned by ordinance. Several Länder may agree on cross-border competence of a single Higher Regional Court. 1At present existing only in Bavaria — "Bayerisches Obe rstes Landesgericht".

1—240   General provisions

Section 1063.—(1) The court shall decide by means of an order, which may be issued without an oral hearing. The party opposing the application shall be given an opportunity to comment before a decision is taken.

(2) The court shall order an oral hearing to be held, if the setting aside of the award has been requested or if, in an application for recognition or declaration of enforceability of the award, grounds for setting aside in terms of section 1059 subs. 2 are to be considered.

(3) The presiding judge of the civil court senate ("Zivilsenat") may issue, without prior hearing of the partyopposing the application, an order to the effect that, until a decision on the request has been reached, the applicant may pursue enforcement of the award or enforce the interim measure of protection of the arbitration court pursuant to section 1041. In the case of an award, enforcement of the award may not go beyond measures of protection. The party opposing the application may prevent enforcement by providing as security an amount corresponding to the amount that may be enforced by the applicant.

(4) As long as no oral hearing is ordered, applications and declarations may be put on record at the court registry.

1—241 Particularities regarding the enforcement of awards

Section 1064.—(1) At the time of the application for a declaration of enforceability of an arbitral award the award or a certified copy of the award shall be supplied. The certification may also be made by counsel authorised to represent the party in the judicial proceedings.

(2) The order declaring the award enforceable shall be declared provisionally enforceable.

(3) Unless otherwise provided in treaties, subsections 1 and 2 shall apply to foreign awards.

1—242 Legal remedies

Section 1065.—(1) A complaint on a point of law to the Federal Court of Justice ("Bundesgerichtshof") is available against the decisions mentioned under section 1062 subs. 1, nos. 2 and 4 if an appeal on points of law would have been available against them, had they been delivered as a final judgment. No recourse against other decisions in the proceedings specified in section 1062 subs. 1 may be made.

(2) The Federal Court of Justice may only examine whether the order is based on a violation of a treaty or of another statute. Section 546 subs. 1, sentence 3 and subs. 2, section 549 subs. 2, sections 550 to 554 b, 556, 558, 559, 561, 563, 573 subs. 1, section 575 and sections 707, 717 apply mutatis mutandis. Chapter X Arbitral tribunals not established by agreement.

1—243 Mutatis mutandis application of the provisions of the Tenth Book

Section 1066.—The provisions of this Book apply mutatis mutandis to arbitral tribunals established lawfully by disposition on death or other dispositions not based on an agreement.

RUSSIA

Law of the Russian Federation on International Commercial Arbitration

1—244   In force 14 August 1993

The present Law:

— is based on the recognition of the value of arbitration (third-party tribunal) as a widely used method of settling disputes arising in international trade, as well as on the recognition of the need for a comprehensive regulation of international commercial arbitration by means of legislation;

— takes into account the provisions on such arbitration contained in international treaties of the Russian Federation as well as in the Model Law adopted in 1985 by the United Nations Commission on International Trade Law and approved by the United Nations General Assembly with a view to its possible use by states in their legislation.

CHAPTER I: GENERAL PROVISIONS

1—245   Article 1—Scope of Application

1. The present Law applies to international commercial arbitration if the place of arbitration is in the territory of the Russian Federation. However, the provisions of Articles 8, 9, 35 and 36 apply also if the place of arbitration is abroad.

2. Pursuant to an agreement of the parties, the following may be referred to international commercial arbitration:

— disputes resulting from contractual and other civil law relationships arising in the course of foreign trade and other forms of international economic relations, provided that the place of business of at least one of the parties is situated abroad; as well as
— disputes arising between enterprises with foreign investment, international associations and organizations established in the territory of the Russian Federation; disputes between the participants of such entities; as well as disputes between such entities and other subjects of the Russian Federation law.

3. For the purposes of paragraph 2 of this article:

— if a party has more than one place of business, the place of business is that which has the closest relationship to the arbitration agreement

— if a party does not have a place of business, reference is to be made to his permanent residence.

4. The present Law does not affect any other law of the Russian Federation by virtue of which certain disputes may not be submitted to arbitration or may be submitted to arbitration only according to provisions other than those of the present Law.

5. If an international treaty of the Russian Federation establishes rules other than those which are contained in the Russian legislation relating to arbitration (third-party tribunal), the rules of the international treaty shall be applied.

1—246 Article 2—Definitions and Rules of Interpretation

For the purposes of the present Law:

—"arbitration" means any arbitration (third-party tribunal) whether conducted by a tribunal set up specifically for a given case or administered by a permanent arbitral institution, in particular the Court of International Commercial Arbitration or the Maritime Arbitration Commission at the Chamber of Commerce and Industry of the Russian Federation (Appendices I and II to the present Law);

— "third-party tribunal" means a sole arbitrator or a panel of arbitrators (third-party judges);

— "court" means a respective organ of the judicial system of a state;

— where a provision of the present Law, except article 28, leaves the parties free to determine a certain issue, such freedom includes the right of the parties to authorize a third party, including an institution, to make that determination;

— where a provision of the present Law refers to the fact that the parties have agreed or that they may agree or in any other way refers to an agreement of the parties, such agreement includes any arbitration rules referred to in that agreement;

— where a provision of the present Law, except Articles 25(1) and 32(2), refers to a claim, it also applies to a counter-claim, and where it refers to a defense, it also applies to a defence to such counter-claim.

1—247 Article 3—Receipt of Written Communications

    1. Unless otherwise agreed by the parties:

— any written communication is deemed to have been received if it is delivered to the addressee personally or if it is delivered at his place of business, permanent residence or mailing address; if none of these can be found after making a reasonable inquiry, a written communication is deemed to have been received if it is sent to the addressee's last-known place of business, permanent residence or mailing address by registered letter or any other means which provides a record of the attempt to deliver it;
— the communication is deemed to have been received on the day it is so delivered.

    2. The provisions of this Article do not apply to communications in court proceedings.

1—248 Article 4—Waiver of Right to Object

A party who knows that any provision of the present Law from which the parties may derogate or any requirement under the arbitration agreement has not been complied with and yet proceeds with the arbitration without stating his objection to such non-compliance without undue delay or, if a time-limit is provided therefor, within such period of time, shall be deemed to have waived his right to object.

1—249 Article 5—Extent of Court Intervention

In matters governed by the present Law, no court shall intervene except where so provided in the present Law.

1—250 Article 6—Authority for Certain Functions of Arbitration Assistance and Control

    1. The functions referred to in Articles 11(3), 11(4), 13(3) and 14 shall be performed by the President of the Chamber of Commerce and Industry of the Russian Federation.

    2. The functions referred to in Articles 16(3) and 34(2) shall be performed by the Supreme Court of a republic forming part of the Russian Federation, the territorial, regional or city

court, or the court of the autonomous region or autonomous area where the arbitration takes place.

Chapter II: Arbitration Agreement

1—251 **Article 7—Definition and Form of Arbitration Agreement**

1. Arbitration agreement is an agreement by the parties to submit to arbitration all or certain disputes which have arisen or which may arise between them in respect of a defined legal relationship, whether contractual or not. An arbitration agreement may be in the form of an arbitration clause in a contract or in the form of a separate agreement.

2. The arbitration agreement shall be in writing. An agreement is in writing if it is contained in a document signed by the parties or in an exchange of letters, telex, telegrams or other means of telecommunication which provide a record of the agreement, or in an exchange of statements of claim and defence in which the existence of an agreement is alleged by one party and not denied by another. The reference in a contract to a document containing an arbitration clause constitutes an arbitration agreement provided that the contract is in writing and the reference is such as to make that clause part of the contract.

1—252 **Article 8—Arbitration Agreement and Substantive Claim Before Court**

1. A court in which an action is brought in a matter which is the subject of an arbitration agreement shall, if any of the parties so requests not later than when submitting his first statement on the substance of the dispute, stay its proceedings and refer the parties to arbitration unless it finds that the agreement is null and void, inoperative or incapable of being performed.

2. Where an action referred to in paragraph 1 of this Article has been brought, arbitral proceedings may nevertheless be commenced or continued, and an award may be made, while the issue of jurisdiction is pending before the court.

1—253 Article 9—Arbitration Agreement and Interim Measures by Court

It is not incompatible with an arbitration agreement for a party to request, before or during arbitral proceedings, a court to order interim measures of protection and for a court to take a decision granting such measures.

CHAPTER III: COMPOSITION OF THIRD-PARTY TRIBUNAL

1—254 Article 10—Number of Arbitrators

1. The parties are free to determine the number of arbitrators.

2. If the parties have not determined such number, three arbitrators shall be appointed.

1—255 Article 11—Appointment of Arbitrators

1. No person shall be precluded by reason of his nationality from acting as an arbitrator, unless otherwise agreed by the parties.

2. The parties are free to agree on a procedure of appointing the arbitrator or arbitrators, subject to the provisions of paragraphs 4 and 5 of this article.

3. Failing such agreement,

— in an arbitration with three arbitrators, each party shall appoint one arbitrator, and the two arbitrators thus appointed shall appoint the third arbitrator; if a party fails to appoint the arbitrator within 30 days of receipt of a request to do so from the other party, or if the two arbitrators fail to agree on the third arbitrator within 30 days of their appointment, the appointment shall be made, upon request of a party, by the authority specified in article 6(1);
— in an arbitration with a sole arbitrator, if the parties are unable to agree on the arbitrator, he shall be appointed, upon request of a party, by the authority specified in article 6(1).

4. Where, under an appointment procedure agreed upon by the parties,

— a party fails to act as required under such procedure, or

— the parties, or two arbitrators, are unable to reach an agreement expected of them under such procedure; or
— a third party, including an institution, fails to perform any function entrusted to it under such procedure, any party may request the authority specified in article 6(1) to take the necessary measures, unless the agreement on the appointment procedure provides other means for securing the appointment.

5. A decision on any matter entrusted by paragraph 3 or 4 of this Article to the authority specified in article 6(1) shall be subject to no appeal. The authority, in appointing an arbitrator, shall have due regard to any qualifications required of the arbitrator by the agreement of the parties and to such considerations as are likely to secure the appointment of an independent and impartial arbitrator and, in the case of a sole or third arbitrator, shall take into account as well the advisability of appointing an arbitrator of a nationality other than those of the parties.

1—256 Article 12 — Grounds for Challenge of Arbitrator

1. When a person is approached in connection with his possible appointment as an arbitrator, he shall disclose any circumstances which may give rise to justifiable doubts as to his impartiality or independence. An arbitrator, from the time of his appointment and throughout the arbitral proceedings, shall without delay disclose any such circumstances to the parties, unless they have already been informed of them by him.

2. An arbitrator may be challenged only if circumstances exist that give rise to justifiable doubts as to his impartiality or independence, or if he does not possess qualifications required by the agreement of the parties. A party may challenge an arbitrator appointed by him, or in whose appointment he has participated, only for reasons of which he becomes aware after the appointment has been made.

1—257 Article 13 — Challenge Procedure

1. The parties are free to agree on a procedure for challenging an arbitrator, subject to the provisions of paragraph 3 of this article.

2. Failing such agreement, a party who intends to challenge an arbitrator shall, within 15 days after becoming aware of the

constitution of the arbitral tribunal or after becoming aware of any circumstances referred to in article 12(2), communicate the reasons for the challenge in writing to the arbitral tribunal. Unless the challenged arbitrator withdraws from his office or the other party agrees to the challenge, the arbitral tribunal shall decide on the challenge.

3. If a challenge under any procedure agreed upon by the parties or under the procedure of paragraph 2 of this Article is not successful, the challenging party may request, within 30 days after having received notice of the decision rejecting the challenge, the authority specified in article 6(1) to decide on the challenge; its decision shall be subject to no appeal. While such a request is pending, the arbitral tribunal, including the challenged arbitrator, may continue the arbitral proceedings and make an award.

1—258 **Article 14—Termination of Authority (Mandate) of Arbitrator**

1. If an arbitrator becomes de jure or de facto unable to perform his functions or for other reasons fails to act without undue delay, his authorization (mandate) terminates if he withdraws from his office or if the parties agree on the termination. Otherwise, if a controversy remains concerning any of these grounds, any party may request the authority specified in article 6(1) to decide on the termination of the mandate; its decision shall be subject to no appeal.

2. If, under this Article or article 13(2), an arbitrator withdraws from his office or a party agrees to the termination of the mandate of an arbitrator, this does not imply acceptance of the validity of any ground referred to in this Article or article 12(2).

1—259 **Article 15—Substitution of Arbitrator**

Where the mandate of an arbitrator terminates under article 13 or 14 or because of his withdrawal from office for any other reason or because of the revocation of his mandate by agreement of the parties or in any other case of termination of his mandate, a substitute arbitrator shall be appointed according to the rules that were applicable to the appointment of the arbitrator being replaced.

Chapter IV: Jurisdiction of Arbitral Tribunal

1—260 **Article 16—Competence of Arbitral Tribunal to Rule on its Jurisdiction**

1. The arbitral tribunal may rule on its own jurisdiction, including any objections with respect to the existence or validity of the arbitration agreement. For that purpose, an arbitration clause which forms part of a contract shall be treated as an agreement independent of the other terms of the contract. A decision by the arbitral tribunal that the contract is null and void shall not entail ipso jure the invalidity of the arbitration clause.

2. A plea that the arbitral tribunal does not have jurisdiction shall be raised not later than the submission of the statement of defence. A party is not precluded from raising such a plea by the fact that he has appointed, or participated in the appointment of, an arbitrator. A plea that the arbitral tribunal is exceeding the scope of its authority shall be raised as soon as the matter alleged to be beyond the scope of its authority is raised during the arbitral proceedings. The arbitral tribunal may, in either case, admit a later plea if it considers the delay justified.

3. The arbitral tribunal may rule on a plea referred to in paragraph 2 of this article either as a preliminary question or in an award on the merits. If the tribunal rules as a preliminary question that it has jurisdiction, any party may request, within 30 days after having received notice of that ruling, the court specified in article 6(2) to decide the matter; such a decision shall be subject to no appeal. While such a request is pending, the arbitral tribunal may continue the arbitral proceedings and make an award.

1—261 **Article 17—Power of Arbitral Tribunal to Order Interim Measures**

Unless otherwise agreed by the parties, the arbitral tribunal may, at the request of a party, order any party to take such interim measures of protection as the arbitral tribunal may consider necessary in respect of the subject-matter of the dispute. The arbitral tribunal may require any party to provide appropriate security in connection with such measures.

Chapter V: Conduct of Arbitral Proceedings

1—262   Article 18—Equal Treatment of Parties

The parties shall be treated with equality and each party shall be given a full opportunity of presenting his case.

1—263   Article 19—Determination of Rules of Procedure

1. Subject to the provisions of the present Law, the parties are free to agree on the procedure to be followed by the arbitral tribunal in conducting the proceedings.
2. Failing such agreement, the arbitral tribunal may, subject to the provisions of the present Law, conduct the arbitration in such manner as it considers appropriate. The powers conferred upon the arbitral tribunal include the power to determine the admissibility, relevance, materiality and weight of any evidence.

1—264   Article 20—Place of Arbitration

1. The parties are free to agree on the place of arbitration. Failing such agreement, the place of arbitration shall be determined by the arbitral tribunal having regard to the circumstances of the case, including the convenience of the parties.
2. Notwithstanding the provisions of paragraph 1 of this article, the arbitral tribunal may, unless otherwise agreed by the parties, meet at any other place it considers appropriate for consultation among the arbitrators, for hearing witnesses, experts or the parties, or for consultation of goods, other property or documents.

1—265   Article 21—Commencement of Arbitral Proceedings

Unless otherwise agreed by the parties, the arbitral proceedings in respect of a particular dispute commence on the date on which a request for that dispute to be referred to arbitration is received by the respondent.

1—266   Article 22—Language

1. The parties are free to agree on the language or languages to be used in the arbitral proceedings. Failing such agreement, the arbitral tribunal shall determine the language or languages

to be used in the proceedings. This agreement or determination, unless otherwise specified therein, shall apply to any written statement by a party, any hearing and any award, decision or other communication by the arbitral tribunal.

2. The arbitral tribunal may order that any documentary evidence shall be accompanied by a translation into the language or languages agreed upon by the parties or determined by the arbitral tribunal.

1—267   **Article 23—Statements of Claim and Defence**

1. Within the period of time agreed by the parties or determined by the arbitral tribunal, the claimant shall state the facts supporting his claim, the points at issue and the relief or remedy sought, and the respondent shall state his defence in respect of these particulars, unless the parties have otherwise agreed as to the required elements of such statements. The parties may submit with their statements all documents they consider to be relevant or may add a reference to the documents or other evidence they will submit.

2. Unless otherwise agreed by the parties, either party may amend or supplement his claim or defence during the course of the arbitral proceedings, unless the arbitral tribunal considers it inappropriate to allow such amendment having regard to the delay in making it.

1—268   **Article 24—Hearings and Written Proceedings**

1. Subject to any contrary agreement by the parties, the arbitral tribunal shall decide whether to hold oral hearings for the presentation of evidence or for oral argument, or whether the proceedings shall be conducted on the basis of documents and other materials. However, unless the parties have agreed that no hearings shall be held, the arbitral tribunal shall hold such hearings at an appropriate stage of the proceedings, if so requested by a party.

2. The parties shall be given sufficient advance notice of any hearing and of any meeting of the arbitral tribunal for the purposes of inspection of goods, other property or documents.

3. All statements, documents or other information supplied to the arbitral tribunal by one party shall be communicated to the other party. Also any expert report or evidentiary document on which the arbitral tribunal may rely in making its decision shall be communicated to the parties.

1—269 **Article 25—Failure to Submit Documents or to Appear at Hearing**

Unless otherwise agreed by the parties, if, without showing sufficient cause,

> — the claimant fails to communicate his statement of claim in accordance with article 23(1), the arbitral tribunal shall terminate the proceedings;
>
> — the respondent fails to communicate his statement of defence in accordance with article 23(1), the arbitral tribunal shall continue the proceedings without treating such failure in itself as an admission of the claimant's allegations;
>
> — any party fails to appear at a hearing or to produce documentary evidence, the arbitral tribunal may continue the proceedings and make the award on the evidence before it.

1—270 **Article 26—Expert Appointed by Arbitral Tribunal**

> 1. Unless otherwise agreed by the parties, the arbitral tribunal
>
>> — may appoint one or more experts to report to it on specific issues to be determined by the arbitral tribunal;
>> — may require a party to give the expert any relevant information or to produce, or to provide access to, any relevant documents, goods or other property for his inspection.
>
> 2. Unless otherwise agreed by the parties, if a party so requests or if the arbitral tribunal considers it necessary, the expert shall, after delivery of his written or oral report, participate in a hearing where the parties have the opportunity to put questions to him and to present expert witnesses in order to testify on the points at issue.

1—271 **Article 27—Court Assistance in Taking Evidence**

The arbitral tribunal or a party with the approval of the arbitral tribunal may request from a competent court of the Russian Federation assistance in taking evidence. The court may execute the request, being guided by its rules on taking evidence, including those on letters rogatory.

Chapter VI: Making of Award and Termination of Proceedings

1—272   Article 28—Rules Applicable to Substance of Dispute

1. The arbitral tribunal shall decide the dispute in accordance with such rules of law as are chosen by the parties as applicable to the substance of the dispute. Any designation of the law or legal system of a given State shall be construed as directly referring to the substantive law of that State and not to its conflict of laws rules.

2. Failing any designation by the parties, the arbitral tribunal shall apply the law determined by the conflict of laws rules which it considers applicable.

3. In all cases, the arbitral tribunal shall decide in accordance with the terms of the contract and shall take into account the usages of the trade applicable to the transaction.

1—273   Article 29—Decision Making by Panel of Arbitrators

In arbitral proceedings with more than one arbitrator, any decision of the arbitral tribunal shall be made, unless otherwise agreed by the parties, by a majority of all its members. However, questions of procedure may be decided by a presiding arbitrator, if so authorized by the parties or all members of the arbitral tribunal.

1—274   Article 30—Settlement

1. If, during arbitral proceedings, the parties settle the dispute, the arbitral tribunal shall terminate the proceedings and, if requested by the parties and not objected to by the arbitral tribunal, record the settlement in the form of an arbitral award on agreed terms.

2. An award on agreed terms shall be made in accordance with the provisions of article 31 and shall state that it is an award. Such an award has the same status and effect as any other award on the merits of the case.

1—275   Article 31—Form and Contents of Award

1. The award shall be made in writing and shall be signed by the arbitrator or arbitrators. In arbitral proceedings with more than one arbitrator, the signatures of the majority of all members of the arbitral tribunal shall suffice, provided that the reason for any omitted signature is stated.

2. The award shall state the reasons upon which it is based, a resolution regarding satisfaction or rejection of the claim, the amount of the arbitration fee and costs, and their apportioning.

3. The award shall state its date and the place of arbitration as determined in accordance with article 20(1). The award shall be deemed to have been made at that place.

4. After the award is made, a copy signed by the arbitrators in accordance with paragraph (1) of this Article shall be delivered to each party.

1—276 Article 32—Termination of Arbitral Proceedings

1. The arbitral proceedings are terminated by the final award or by an order of the arbitral tribunal in accordance with paragraph (2) of this article.

2. The arbitral tribunal shall issue an order for the termination of the arbitral proceedings when:

— the claimant withdraws his claim, unless the respondent objects thereto and the arbitral tribunal recognizes a legitimate interest on his part in obtaining a final settlement of the dispute;
— the parties agree on the termination of the proceedings;
— the arbitral tribunal finds that the continuation of the proceedings has for any other reason become unnecessary or impossible.

3. The mandate of the arbitral tribunal terminates with the termination of the arbitral proceedings, subject to the provisions of Articles 33 and 34(4).

1—277 Article 33—Correction and Interpretation of Award; Additional Award

1. Within 30 days of receipt of the award, unless another period of time has been agreed upon by the parties:

— any of the parties, with notice to the other party, may request the arbitral tribunal to correct in the award any errors in computation, any clerical or typographical errors or any errors of similar nature;
— if so agreed by the parties, a party, with notice to the other party, may request the arbitral tribunal to give an interpretation of a specific point or part of the award.

— if the arbitral tribunal considers the request to be justified, it shall make the correction or give the interpretation within 30 days of receipt of the request. Such interpretation shall form part of the award.

2. The arbitral tribunal may correct any error of the type referred to in the second subparagraph of paragraph 1 of this Article on its own initiative within 30 days of the date of the award.

3. Unless otherwise agreed by the parties, any of the parties, with notice to the other party, may request, within 30 days of receipt of the award, the arbitral tribunal to make an additional award as to claims presented in the arbitral proceedings but omitted from the award. If the arbitral tribunal considers the request to be justified, it shall make the additional award within 60 days.

4. The arbitral tribunal may extend, if necessary, the period of time within which it shall make a correction, interpretation or an additional award under paragraph 1 or 3 of this article.

5. The provisions of article 31 shall apply to a correction or interpretation of the award or to an additional award.

CHAPTER VII: RECOURSE AGAINST AWARD

1—278 **Article 34—Application for Setting Aside as Exclusive Recourse Against Arbitral Award**

1. Recourse to a court against an arbitral award may be made only by an application for setting aside in accordance with paragraphs 2 and 3 of this article.

2. An arbitral award may be set aside by the court specified in article 6(2) only if:

(1) the party making the application for setting aside furnishes proof that:

— a party to the arbitration agreement referred to in article 7 was under some incapacity, or the said agreement is not valid under the law to which the parties have subjected it or, failing any indication thereon, under the law of the Russian Federation; or
— he was not given proper notice of the appointment of an arbitrator or of the arbitral proceedings or was otherwise unable to present his case; or

— the award was made regarding a dispute not contemplated by or not falling within the terms of the submission to arbitration, or contains decisions on matters beyond the scope of the submission to arbitration, provided that, if the decisions on matters submitted to arbitration can be separated from those not so submitted, only that part of the award which contains decisions on matters not submitted to arbitration may be set aside; or

— the composition of the arbitral tribunal or the arbitral procedure was not in accordance with the agreement of the parties, unless such agreement was in conflict with a provision of this Law from which the parties cannot derogate, or, failing such agreement, was not in accordance with this Law; or

(2) the court finds that:

— the subject-matter of the dispute is not capable of settlement by arbitration under the law of the Russian Federation; or

— the award is in conflict with the public policy of the Russian Federation.

3. An application for setting aside may not be made after three months have elapsed from the date on which the party making that application had received the award and, if a request had been made under article 33, from the date on which that request had been disposed of by the arbitral tribunal.

4. The court, which has been asked to set aside an award, may, where appropriate and so requested by a party, suspend the setting aside proceedings for a period of time determined by it in order to give the arbitral tribunal an opportunity to resume the arbitral proceedings or to take such other action as in the arbitral tribunal's opinion will eliminate the grounds for setting aside.

CHAPTER VIII: RECOGNITION AND ENFORCEMENT OF AWARDS

1—279 Article 35—Recognition and Enforcement

1. An arbitral award, irrespective of the country in which it was made, shall be recognized as binding and, upon application in writing to the competent court, shall be enforced subject to the provisions of this Article and of article 36.

2. The party relying on an award or applying for its enforcement shall supply the duly authenticated original award or a duly certified copy thereof, and the original arbitration agreement referred to in article 7 or a duly certified copy thereof. If the award or agreement is made in a foreign language, the party shall supply a duly certified translation thereof into the Russian language.

1—280 **Article 36—Grounds for Refusing Recognition or Enforcement of Arbitral Award**

1. Recognition or enforcement of an arbitral award, irrespective of the country in which it was made, may be refused only:

   (1) at the request of the party against whom it is invoked, if that party furnishes to the competent court where recognition or enforcement is sought proof that:

   — a party to the arbitration agreement referred to in article 7 was under some incapacity; or the said agreement is not valid under the law to which the parties have subjected it or, failing any indication thereon, under the law of the country where the award was made; or
   — the party against whom the award was made was not given proper notice of the appointment of an arbitrator or of the arbitral proceedings or was otherwise unable to present his case; or
   — the award was made regarding a dispute not contemplated by or not falling within the terms of the submission to arbitration, or it contains decisions on matters beyond the scope of the submission to arbitration, provided that, if the decisions on matters submitted to arbitration can be separated from those not so submitted, that part of the award which contains decisions on matters submitted to arbitration may be recognized and enforced; or
   — the composition of the arbitral tribunal or the arbitral procedure was not in accordance with the agreement of the parties or, failing such agreement, was not in accordance with the law of the country where the arbitration took place; or
   — the award has not yet become binding on the parties or has been set aside or suspended by a court of the country in which, or under the law of which, that award was made; or

(2) if the court finds that:

— the subject-matter of the dispute is not capable of settlement by arbitration under the law of the Russian Federation; or
— the recognition or enforcement of the award would be contrary to the public policy of the Russian Federation.

2. If an application for setting aside or suspension of an award has been made to a court referred to in the fifth point of subparagraph 1 of paragraph 1 of this article, the Court where recognition or enforcement is sought may, if it considers it proper, adjourn its decision and may also, on the application of the party claiming recognition or enforcement of the award, order the other party to provide appropriate security.

C. Foreign Statutes: Non-European Jurisdictions

USA

Federal Arbitration Act 1925, as amended

CHAPTER 1: GENERAL PROVISIONS

1—281 **"Maritime transactions" and "commerce" defined; exceptions to operation of title**

Section 1.—"Maritime transaction", as herein defined, means charter parties, bills of lading of water carriers, agreements relating to wharfage, supplies furnished vessels or repairs to vessels, collisions, or any other matters in foreign commerce which, if the subject of controversy, would be embraced within admiralty jurisdiction; "commerce", as herein defined, means commerce among the several States or with foreign nations, or in any Territory of the United States or in the District of Columbia, or between any such Territory and another, or between any such Territory and any State or foreign nation, or between the District of Columbia and any State or Territory or foreign nation, but nothing herein contained shall apply to contracts of employment of seamen, railroad employees, or any other class of workers engaged in foreign or interstate commerce.

1—282 **Validity, irrevocability, and enforcement of agreements to arbitrate**

Section 2.—A written provision in any maritime transaction or a contract evidencing a transaction involving commerce to settle by arbitration a controversy thereafter arising out of such contract or transaction, or the refusal to perform the whole or any part thereof, or an agreement in writing to submit to arbitration an existing controversy arising out of such a contract, transaction, or refusal, shall be valid, irrevocable, and enforceable, save upon such grounds as exist at law or in equity for the revocation of any contract.

C. Foreign Statutes: Non-European Jurisdictions 139

1—283   Stay of proceedings where issue therein referable to arbitration

Section 3.—If any suit or proceeding be brought in any of the courts of the United States upon any issue referable to arbitration under an agreement in writing for such arbitration, the court in which such suit is pending, upon being satisfied that the issue involved in such suit or proceeding is referable to arbitration under such an agreement, shall on application of one of the parties stay the trial of the action until such arbitration has been had in accordance with the terms of the agreement, providing the applicant for the stay is not in default in proceeding with such arbitration.

1—284   Failure to arbitrate under agreement; petition to United States court having jurisdiction for order to compel arbitration; notice and service thereof; hearing and determination

Section 4.—A party aggrieved by the alleged failure, neglect, or refusal of another to arbitrate under a written agreement for arbitration may petition any United States district court which, save for such agreement, would have jurisdiction under Title 28, in a civil action or in admiralty of the subject matter of a suit arising out of the controversy between the parties, for an order directing that such arbitration proceed in the manner provided for in such agreement. Five days' notice in writing of such application shall be served upon the party in default. Service thereof shall be made in the manner provided by the Federal Rules of Civil Procedure. The court shall hear the parties, and upon being satisfied that the making of the agreement for arbitration or the failure to comply therewith is not in issue, the court shall make an order directing the parties to proceed to arbitration in accordance with the terms of the agreement. The hearing and proceedings, under such agreement, shall be within the district in which the petition for an order directing such arbitration is filed. If the making of the arbitration agreement or the failure, neglect, or refusal to perform the same be in issue, the court shall proceed summarily to the trial thereof. If no jury trial be demanded by the party alleged to be in default, or if the matter in dispute is within admiralty jurisdiction, the court shall hear and determine such issue. Where such an issue is raised, the party alleged to be in default may, except in cases of admiralty, on or before the return day of the notice of application, demand a jury trial of such issue, and upon such demand the court shall make an order referring the issue or issues to a jury in the manner provided by the Federal Rules of Civil Procedure, or may specially call a jury for that purpose. If the jury find that no agreement in writing for arbitration was made or that there is no default in proceeding thereunder, the proceeding shall be dismissed. If the jury find that an agreement for arbitration was made in writing and that there is a default in proceeding thereunder, the court shall make an order summarily directing the parties to proceed with the arbitration in accordance with the terms thereof.

1—285   Appointment of arbitrators or umpire

Section 5.—If in the agreement provision be made for a method of naming or appointing an arbitrator or arbitrators or an umpire, such method shall be followed; but if no method be provided therein, or if a method be provided and any party thereto shall fail to avail himself of such method, or if for any other reason there shall be a lapse in the naming of an arbitrator or arbitrators or umpire, or in filling a vacancy, then upon the application of either party to the controversy the court shall designate and appoint an arbitrator or arbitrators or umpire, as the case may require, who shall act under the said agreement with the same force and effect as if he or they had been specifically named therein; and unless otherwise provided in the agreement the arbitration shall be by a single arbitrator.

1—286   Application heard as motion

Section 6.— Any application to the court hereunder shall be made and heard in the manner provided by law for the making and hearing of motions, except as otherwise herein expressly provided.

1—287   Witnesses before arbitrators; fees; compelling attendance

Section 7.—The arbitrators selected either as prescribed in this title or otherwise, or a majority of them, may summon in writing any person to attend before them or any of them as a witness and in a proper case to bring with him or them any book, record, document, or paper which may be deemed material as evidence in the case. The fees for such attendance shall be the same as the fees of witnesses before masters of the United States courts. Said summons shall issue in the name of the arbitrator or arbitrators, or a majority of them, and shall be signed by the arbitrators, or a majority of them, and shall be directed to the said person and shall be served in the same manner as subpoenas to appear and testify before the court; if

C. Foreign Statutes: Non-European Jurisdictions   141

any person or persons so summoned to testify shall refuse or neglect to obey said summons, upon petition the United States district court for the district in which such arbitrators, or a majority of them, are sitting may compel the attendance of such person or persons before said arbitrator or arbitrators, or punish said person or persons for contempt in the same manner provided by law for securing the attendance of witnesses or their punishment for neglect or refusal to attend in the courts of the United States.

1—288   Proceedings begun by libel in admiralty and seizure of vessel or Property

Section 8.—If the basis of jurisdiction be a cause of action otherwise justiciable in admiralty, then, notwithstanding anything herein to the contrary, the party claiming to be aggrieved may begin his proceeding hereunder by seizure of the vessel or other property of the other party according to the usual course of admiralty proceedings, and the court shall then have jurisdiction to direct the parties to proceed with the arbitration and shall retain jurisdiction to enter its decree upon the award.

1—289   Award of arbitrators; confirmation; jurisdiction; procedure

Section 9.—If the parties in their agreement have agreed that a judgment of the court shall be entered upon the award made pursuant to the arbitration, and shall specify the court, then at any time within one year after the award is made any party to the arbitration may apply to the court so specified for an order confirming the award, and thereupon the court must grant such an order unless the award is vacated, modified, or corrected as prescribed in sections 10 and 11 of this title. If no court is specified in the agreement of the parties, then such application may be made to the United States court in and for the district within which such award was made. Notice of the application shall be served upon the adverse party, and thereupon the court shall have jurisdiction of such party as though he had appeared generally in the proceeding. If the adverse party is a resident of the district within which the award was made, such service shall be made upon the adverse party or his attorney as prescribed by law for service of notice of motion in an action in the same court. If the adverse party shall be a non resident, then the notice of the application shall be served by the marshal of any district within which the adverse party may be found in like manner as other process of the court.

1—290 Same; vacation; grounds; rehearing

Section 10.—(a) In either of the following cases the United States court in and for the district wherein the award was made may make an order vacating the award upon the application of any party to the arbitration

(1) where the award was procured by corruption, fraud, or undue means;
(2) where there was evident partiality or corruption in the arbitrators, or either of them;
(3) where the arbitrators were guilty of misconduct in refusing to postpone the hearing, upon sufficient cause shown, or in refusing to hear evidence pertinent and material to the controversy; or of any other misbehavior by which the rights of any party have been prejudiced; or
(4) Where the arbitrators exceeded their powers, or so imperfectly executed them that a mutual, final, and definite award upon the subject matter submitted was not made.

(b) If an award is vacated and the time within which the agreement required the award to be made has not expired, the court may, in its discretion, direct a rehearing by the arbitrators.

(c) The United States district court for the district wherein an award was made that was issued pursuant to section 580 of title 5 may make an order vacating the award upon the application of a person, other than a party to the arbitration, who is adversely affected or aggrieved by the award, if the use of arbitration or the award is clearly inconsistent with the factors set forth in section 572 of Title 5.

1—291 Same; modification or correction; grounds; order

Section 11.—In either of the following cases the United States court in and for the district wherein the award was made may make an order modifying or correcting the award upon the application of any party to the arbitration

(a) Where there was an evident material miscalculation of figures or an evident material mistake in the description of any person, thing, or property referred to in the award.

(b) Where the arbitrators have awarded upon a matter not submitted to them, unless it is a matter not affecting the merits of the decision upon the matter submitted.

(c) Where the award is imperfect in matter of form not affecting the merits of the controversy.

The order may modify and correct the award, so as to effect the intent thereof and promote justice between the parties.

1—292 **Notice of motions to vacate or modify; service; stay of proceedings**

Section 12.—Notice of a motion to vacate, modify, or correct an award must be served upon the adverse party or his attorney within three months after the award is filed or delivered. If the adverse party is a resident of the district within which the award was made, such service shall be made upon the adverse party or his attorney as prescribed by law for service of notice of motion in an action in the same court. If the adverse party shall be a nonresident then the notice of the application shall be served by the marshal of any district within which the adverse party may be found in like manner as other process of the court. For the purposes of the motion any judge who might make an order to stay the proceedings in an action brought in the same court may make an order, to be served with the notice of motion, staying the proceedings of the adverse party to enforce the award.

1—293 **Papers filed with order on motions; judgment; docketing; force and effect; enforcement**

Section 13.—The party moving for an order confirming, modifying, or correcting an award shall, at the time such order is filed with the clerk for the entry of judgment thereon, also file the following papers with the clerk:

(a) The agreement; the selection or appointment, if any, of an additional arbitrator or umpire; and each written extension of the time, if any, within which to make the award.

(b) The award.

(c) Each notice, affidavit, or other paper used upon an application to confirm, modify, or correct the award, and a copy of each order of the court upon such an application.

The judgment shall be docketed as if it was rendered in an action.

The judgment so entered shall have the same force and effect, in all respects, as, and be subject to all the provisions of law relating to, a judgment in an action; and it may be enforced as if it had been rendered in an action in the court in which it is entered.

1—294 Contracts not affected

Section 14.—This title shall not apply to contracts made prior to January 1, 1926.

1—295 Inapplicability of the Act of State doctrine

Section 15.—Enforcement of arbitral agreements, confirmation of arbitral awards, and execution upon judgments based on orders confirming such awards shall not be refused on the basis of the Act of State doctrine.

1—296 Appeals

Section 16.—(a) An appeal may be taken from

    (1) an order

        (A) refusing a stay of any action under section 3 of this title,

        (B) denying a petition under section 4 of this title to order arbitration to proceed,

        (C) denying an application under section 206 of this title to compel arbitration,

        (D) confirming or denying confirmation of an award or partial award, or

        (E) modifying, correcting, or vacating an award;

    (2) an interlocutory order granting, continuing, or modifying an injunction against an arbitration that is subject to this title; or

    (3) a final decision with respect to an arbitration that is subject to this title.

(b) Except as otherwise provided in section 1292 (b) of title 28, an appeal may not be taken from an interlocutory order,

    (1) granting a stay of any action under section 3 of this title;

    (2) directing arbitration to proceed under section 4 of this title;

C. Foreign Statutes: Non-European Jurisdictions 145

(3) compelling arbitration under section 206 of this title; or

(4) refusing to enjoin an arbitration that is subject to this title.

CHAPTER 2: CONVENTION ON THE RECOGNITION AND ENFORCEMENT OF FOREIGN ARBITRAL AWARDS

1—297 Enforcement of Convention

Section 201.—The Convention on the Recognition and Enforcement of Foreign Arbitral Awards of June 10, 1958, shall be enforced in United States courts in accordance with this chapter.

1—298 Agreement or award falling under the Convention

Section 202.—An arbitration agreement or arbitral award arising out of a legal relationship, whether contractual or not, which is considered as commercial, including a transaction, contract, or agreement described in section 2 of this title, falls under the Convention. An agreement or award arising out of such a relationship which is entirely between citizens of the United States shall be deemed not to fall under the Convention unless that relationship involves property located abroad, envisages performance or enforcement abroad, or has some other reasonable relation with one or more foreign states. For the purpose of this section a corporation is a citizen of the United States if it is incorporated or has its principal place of business in the United States.

1—299 Jurisdiction; amount in controversy

Section 203.—An action or proceeding falling under the Convention shall be deemed to arise under the laws and treaties of the United States. The district courts of the United States (including the courts enumerated in section 460 of Title 28) shall have original jurisdiction over such an action or proceeding, regardless of the amount in controversy.

1—300 Venue

Section 204.—An action or proceeding over which the district courts have jurisdiction pursuant to section 203 of this title may be brought in any such court in which save for the arbitration agreement an action or proceeding with respect to the controversy between the parties could be brought, or in such court for the district and division which embraces the place designated in the agreement as the place of arbitration if such place is within the United States.

1—301 Removal of cases from State courts

Section 205.—Where the subject matter of an action or proceeding pending in a State court relates to an arbitration agreement or award falling under the Convention, the defendant or the defendants may, at any time before the trial thereof, remove such action or proceeding to the district court of the United States for the district and division embracing the place where the action or proceeding is pending. The procedure for removal of causes otherwise provided by law shall apply, except that the ground for removal provided in this section need not appear on the face of the complaint but may be shown in the petition for removal. For the purposes of Chapter 1 of this title any action or proceeding removed under this section shall be deemed to have been brought in the district court to which it is removed.

1—302 Order to compel arbitration; appointment of arbitrators

Section 206.—A court having jurisdiction under this chapter may direct that arbitration be held in accordance with the agreement at any place therein provided for, whether that place is within or without the United States. Such court may also appoint arbitrators in accordance with the provisions of the agreement.

1—303 Award of arbitrators; confirmation; jurisdiction; proceeding

Section 207.—Within three years after an arbitral award falling under the Convention is made, any party to the arbitration may apply to any court having jurisdiction under this chapter for an order confirming the award as against any other party to the arbitration. The court shall confirm the award unless it finds one of the grounds for refusal or deferral of recognition or enforcement of the award specified in the said Convention.

1—304 Chapter 1; residual application

Section 208.—Chapter 1 applies to actions and proceedings brought under this chapter to the extent that chapter is not in conflict with this chapter or the Convention as ratified by the United States.

CHAPTER 3: INTER-AMERICAN CONVENTION ON INTERNATIONAL COMMERCIAL ARBITRATION

1—305   Enforcement of Convention

Section 301.—The Inter-American Convention on International Commercial Arbitration of January 30, 1975, shall be enforced in United States courts in accordance with this chapter.

1—306   Incorporation by reference

Section 302.—Sections 202, 203, 204, 205, and 207 of this title shall apply to this chapter as if specifically set forth herein, except that for the purposes of this chapter "the Convention" shall mean the Inter-American Convention.

1—307   Order to compel arbitration; appointment of arbitrators; locale

Section 303.—(a) A court having jurisdiction under this chapter may direct that arbitration be held in accordance with the agreement at any place therein provided for, whether that place is within or without the United States. The court may also appoint arbitrators in accordance with the provisions of the agreement.

(b) In the event the agreement does not make provision for the place of arbitration or the appointment of arbitrators, the court shall direct that the arbitration shall be held and the arbitrators be appointed in accordance with Article 3 of the Inter-American Convention.

1—308   Recognition and enforcement of foreign arbitral decisions and awards; reciprocity

Section 304.—Arbitral decisions or awards made in the territory of a foreign State shall, on the basis of reciprocity, be recognized and enforced under this chapter only if that State has ratified or acceded to the Inter-American Convention.

1—309 Relationship between the Inter-American Convention and the Convention on the Recognition and Enforcement of Foreign Arbitral Awards of June 10, 1958

Section 305.—When the requirements for application of both the Inter-American Convention and the Convention on the Recognition and Enforcement of Foreign Arbitral Awards of June 10, 1958, are met, determination as to which Convention applies shall, unless otherwise expressly agreed, be made as follows:

(1) If a majority of the parties to the arbitration agreement are citizens of a State or States that have ratified or acceded to the Inter-American Convention and are member States of the Organization of American States, the Inter-American Convention shall apply.

(2) In all other cases the Convention on the Recognition and Enforcement of Foreign Arbitral Awards of June 10, 1958, shall apply.

1—310 Applicable rules of Inter-American Commercial Arbitration Commission

Section 306.—(a) For the purposes of this chapter the rules of procedure of the Inter-American Commercial Arbitration Commission referred to in Article 3 of the Inter-American Convention shall, subject to subsection (b) of this section, be those rules as promulgated by the Commission on July 1, 1988.

(b) In the event the rules of procedure of the Inter-American Commercial Arbitration Commission are modified or amended in accordance with the procedures for amendment of the rules of that Commission, the Secretary of State, by regulation in accordance with section 553 of Title 5, consistent with the aims and purposes of this Convention, may prescribe that such modifications or amendments shall be effective for purposes of this chapter.

1—311 Chapter 1; residual application

Section 307.—Chapter 1 applies to actions and proceedings brought under this chapter to the extent chapter 1 is not in conflict with this chapter or the Inter-American Convention as ratified by the United States.

AUSTRALIA

International Arbitration Act 1974

1—312   Act No. 136 of 1974 as amended

This compilation was prepared on 19 October 2000 taking into account amendments up to Act No. 160 of 1991
The text of any of those amendments not in force on that date is appended in the Notes section
Prepared by the Office of Legislative Drafting, Attorney-General's Department, Canberra

AN ACT RELATING TO THE RECOGNITION AND ENFORCEMENT OF FOREIGN ARBITRAL AWARDS, AND THE CONDUCT OF INTERNATIONAL COMMERCIAL ARBITRATIONS, IN AUSTRALIA, AND FOR RELATED PURPOSES

PART I—PRELIMINARY

1—313   **1. Short title of Principal Act** [*see* Note 1]

This Act may be cited as the *International Arbitration Act 1974*.

1—314   **2. Commencement** [*see* Note 1]

(1) Sections 1, 2, 3 and 4 shall come into operation on the day on which this Act receives the Royal Assent.

(2) The remaining provisions of this Act shall come into operation on a date to be fixed by Proclamation, being a date not earlier than the date on which the Convention enters into force for Australia.

1—315   **2A. Territories**

This Act extends to all external Territories.

1—316   **2B. Crown to be bound**

This Act binds the Crown in right of the Commonwealth, of each of the States, of the Northern Territory and of Norfolk Island.

1—317   **2C. Carriage of goods by sea**

Nothing in this Act affects:

(a) the continued operation of section 9 of the Sea-Carriage of Goods Act 1924 under subsection 20(2) of the Carriage of Goods by Sea Act 1991; or

(b) the operation of section 11 or 16 of the Carriage of Goods by Sea Act 1991.

PART II—ENFORCEMENT OF FOREIGN AWARDS

1—318   **3. Interpretation**

(1) In this Part, unless the contrary intention appears:

agreement in writing has the same meaning as in the Convention.
arbitral award has the same meaning as in the Convention.
arbitration agreement means an agreement in writing of the kind referred to in sub-article 1 of Article II of the Convention.
Australia includes the Territories.
Convention means the Convention on the Recognition and Enforcement of Foreign Arbitral Awards adopted in 1958 by the United Nations Conference on International Commercial Arbitration at its twenty-fourth meeting, a copy of the English text of which is set out in Schedule 1.
Convention country means a country (other than Australia) that is a Contracting State within the meaning of the Convention.
court means any court in Australia, including a court of a State or Territory.
foreign award means an arbitral award made, in pursuance of an arbitration agreement, in a country other than Australia, being an arbitral award in relation to which the Convention applies.

(2) In this Part, where the context so admits, *enforcement*, in relation to a foreign award, includes the recognition of the award as binding for any purpose, and *enforce* and *enforced* have corresponding meanings.

(3) For the purposes of this Part, a body corporate shall be taken to be ordinarily resident in a country if, and only if, it is

incorporated or has its principal place of business in that country.

1—319   4. Accession to Convention

Approval is given to accession by Australia to the Convention without any declaration under sub-article 3 of Article I but with a declaration under Article X that the Convention shall extend to all the external Territories other than Papua New Guinea.

1—320   7. Enforcement of foreign arbitration agreements

(1) Where:
- (a) the procedure in relation to arbitration under an arbitration agreement is governed, whether by virtue of the express terms of the agreement or otherwise, by the law of a Convention country;
- (b) the procedure in relation to arbitration under an arbitration agreement is governed, whether by virtue of the express terms of the agreement or otherwise, by the law of a country not being Australia or a Convention country, and a party to the agreement is Australia or a State or a person who was, at the time when the agreement was made, domiciled or ordinarily resident in Australia;
- (c) a party to an arbitration agreement is the Government of a Convention country or of part of a Convention country or the Government of a territory of a Convention country, being a territory to which the Convention extends; or
- (d) a party to an arbitration agreement is a person who was, at the time when the agreement was made, domiciled or ordinarily resident in a country that is a Convention country;

this section applies to the agreement.

(2) Subject to this Part, where:
- (a) proceedings instituted by a party to an arbitration agreement to which this section applies against another party to the agreement are pending in a court; and
- (b) the proceedings involve the determination of a matter that, in pursuance of the agreement, is capable of settlement by arbitration;

on the application of a party to the agreement, the court shall, by order, upon such conditions (if any) as it thinks fit, stay the proceedings or so much of the proceedings as involves the determination of that matter, as the case may be, and refer the parties to arbitration in respect of that matter.

(3) Where a court makes an order under subsection (2), it may, for the purpose of preserving the rights of the parties, make such interim or supplementary orders as it thinks fit in relation to any property that is the subject of the matter to which the first-mentioned order relates.

(4) For the purposes of subsections (2) and (3), a reference to a party includes a reference to a person claiming through or under a party.

(5) A court shall not make an order under subsection (2) if the court finds that the arbitration agreement is null and void, inoperative or incapable of being performed.

1—321 **8. Recognition of foreign awards**

(1) Subject to this Part, a foreign award is binding by virtue of this Act for all purposes on the parties to the arbitration agreement in pursuance of which it was made.

(2) Subject to this Part, a foreign award may be enforced in a court of a State or Territory as if the award had been made in that State or Territory in accordance with the law of that State or Territory.

(4) Where:

(a) at any time, a person seeks the enforcement of a foreign award by virtue of this Part; and
(b) the country in which the award was made is not, at that time, a Convention country;

subsections (1) and (2) do not have effect in relation to the award unless that person is, at that time, domiciled or ordinarily resident in Australia or in a Convention country.

(5) Subject to subsection (6), in any proceedings in which the enforcement of a foreign award by virtue of this Part is sought, the court may, at the request of the party against whom it is invoked, refuse to enforce the award if that party proves to the satisfaction of the court that:

(a) that party, being a party to the arbitration agreement in pursuance of which the award was made, was, under the law applicable to him, under some incapacity at the time when the agreement was made;

C. Foreign Statutes: Non-European Jurisdictions 153

    (b) the arbitration agreement is not valid under the law expressed in the agreement to be applicable to it or, where no law is so expressed to be applicable, under the law of the country where the award was made;

    (c) that party was not given proper notice of the appointment of the arbitrator or of the arbitration proceedings or was otherwise unable to present his case in the arbitration proceedings;

    (d) the award deals with a difference not contemplated by, or not falling within the terms of, the submission to arbitration, or contains a decision on a matter beyond the scope of the submission to arbitration;

    (e) the composition of the arbitral authority or the arbitral procedure was not in accordance with the agreement of the parties or, failing such agreement, was not in accordance with the law of the country where the arbitration took place; or

    (f) the award has not yet become binding on the parties to the arbitration agreement or has been set aside or suspended by a competent authority of the country in which, or under the law of which, the award was made.

(6) Where an award to which paragraph (5)(d) applies contains decisions on matters submitted to arbitration and those decisions can be separated from decisions on matters not so submitted, that part of the award which contains decisions on matters so submitted may be enforced.

(7) In any proceedings in which the enforcement of a foreign award by virtue of this Part is sought, the court may refuse to enforce the award if it finds that:

    (a) the subject matter of the difference between the parties to the award is not capable of settlement by arbitration under the laws in force in the State or Territory in which the court is sitting; or

    (b) to enforce the award would be contrary to public policy.

(8) Where, in any proceedings in which the enforcement of a foreign award by virtue of this Part is sought, the court is satisfied that an application for the setting aside or suspension of the award has been made to a competent authority of the country in which, or under the law of which, the award was made, the court may, if it considers it proper to do so, adjourn the proceedings, or so much of the proceedings as relates to the award, as the case may be, and may also, on the application of the party claiming enforcement of the award, order the other party to give suitable security.

1—322 **9. Evidence of awards and arbitration agreements**

(1) In any proceedings in which a person seeks the enforcement of a foreign award by virtue of this Part, he shall produce to the court:

(a) the duly authenticated original award or a duly certified copy; and

(b) the original arbitration agreement under which the award purports to have been made or a duly certified copy.

(2) For the purposes of subsection (1), an award shall be deemed to have been duly authenticated, and a copy of an award or agreement shall be deemed to have been duly certified, if:

(a) it purports to have been authenticated or certified, as the case may be, by the arbitrator or, where the arbitrator is a tribunal, by an officer of that tribunal, and it has not been shown to the court that it was not in fact so authenticated or certified; or

(b) it has been otherwise authenticated or certified to the satisfaction of the court.

(3) If a document or part of a document produced under subsection (1) is written in a language other than English, there shall be produced with the document a translation, in the English language, of the document or that part, as the case may be, certified to be a correct translation.

(4) For the purposes of subsection (3), a translation shall be certified by a diplomatic or consular agent in Australia of the country in which the award was made or otherwise to the satisfaction of the court.

(5) A document produced to a court in accordance with this section is, upon mere production, receivable by the court as *prima facie* evidence of the matters to which it relates.

1—323 **10. Evidence relating to Convention**

(1) For the purposes of this Part, a certificate purporting to be signed by the Secretary to the Department of Foreign Affairs and stating that a country specified in the certificate is, or was at a time so specified, a Convention country is, upon mere production, receivable in any proceedings as *prima facie* evidence of that fact.

(2) For the purposes of this Part, a copy of the *Gazette* containing a Proclamation fixing a date under subsection 2(2) is,

upon mere production, receivable in any proceedings as *prima facie* evidence of:

(a) the fact that Australia has acceded to the Convention in accordance with section 4; and
(b) the fact that the Convention entered into force for Australia on or before the date so fixed.

1—324   **10A. Delegation by Secretary to the Department of Foreign Affairs and Trade**

(1) The Secretary may, either generally or as otherwise provided by the instrument of delegation, in writing, delegate to the person occupying a specified office in the Department of Foreign Affairs and Trade all or any of the Secretary's powers under subsection 10(1).

(2) A power delegated under subsection (1) shall, when exercised by the delegate, be deemed to have been exercised by the Secretary.

(3) The delegate is, in the exercise of a power delegated under subsection (1), subject to the directions of the Secretary.

(4) The delegation of a power under subsection (1) does not prevent the exercise of the power by the Secretary.

(5) In this section, *Secretary* means the Secretary to the Department of Foreign Affairs and Trade.

1—325   **12. Effect of this Part on other laws**

(1) This Part applies to the exclusion of any provisions made by a law of a State or Territory with respect to the recognition of arbitration agreements and the enforcement of foreign awards, being provisions that operate in whole or in part by reference to the Convention.

(2) Except as provided in subsection (1), nothing in this Part affects the right of any person to the enforcement of a foreign award otherwise than in pursuance of this Act.

1—325/1   **13. Judiciary Act**

A matter arising under this Part, including a question of interpretation of the Convention for the purposes of this Act, shall, for the purposes of section 38 of the *Judiciary Act 1903–1973*, be deemed not to be a matter arising directly under a treaty.

1—325/2   **14. Application of Part**

The application of this Part extends to agreements and awards made before the date fixed under subsection 2(2), including agreements and awards made before the day referred to in subsection 2(1).

PART III—INTERNATIONAL COMMERCIAL ARBITRATION

Division 1—Preliminary

1—325/3   **15. Interpretation**

(1) In this Part:

Model Law means the UNCITRAL Model Law on International Commercial Arbitration adopted by the United Nations Commission on International Trade Law on 21 June 1985, the English text of which is set out in Schedule 2.

(2) Except so far as the contrary intention appears, a word or expression that is used both in this Part and in the Model Law (whether or not a particular meaning is given to it by the Model Law) has, in this Part, the same meaning as it has in the Model Law.

Division 2—Model Law

1—325/4   **16. Model Law to have force of law**

(1) Subject to this Part, the Model Law has the force of law in Australia.

(2) In the Model Law:

State means Australia (including the external Territories) and any foreign country.
this State means Australia (including the external Territories).

1—325/5   **17. Interpretation of Model Law—use of extrinsic material**

(1) For the purposes of interpreting the Model Law, reference may be made to the documents of:

(a) the United Nations Commission on International Trade Law; and
(b) its working group for the preparation of the Model Law;

relating to the Model Law.

(2) Subsection (1) does not affect the application of section 15AB of the *Acts Interpretation Act 1901* for the purposes of interpreting this Part.

1—325/6   **18. Courts specified for purposes of Article 6 of Model Law**

The following courts shall be taken to have been specified in Article 6 of the Model Law as courts competent to perform the functions referred to in that article:

(a) if the place of arbitration is, or is to be, in a State—the Supreme Court of that State;

(b) if the place of arbitration is, or is to be, in a Territory:
   (i) the Supreme Court of that Territory; or
   (ii) if there is no Supreme Court established in that Territory—the Supreme Court of the State or Territory that has jurisdiction in relation to that Territory.

1—325/7   **19. Articles 34 and 36 of Model Law—public policy**

Without limiting the generality of subparagraphs 34(2)(b)(ii) and 36(1)(b)(ii) of the Model Law, it is hereby declared, for the avoidance of any doubt, that, for the purposes of those subparagraphs, an award is in conflict with the public policy of Australia if:

(a) the making of the award was induced or affected by fraud or corruption; or

(b) a breach of the rules of natural justice occurred in connection with the making of the award.

1—325/8   **20. Chapter VIII of Model Law not to apply in certain cases**

Where, but for this section, both Chapter VIII of the Model Law and Part II of this Act would apply in relation to an award, Chapter VIII of the Model Law does not apply in relation to the award.

1—325/9   21. Settlement of dispute otherwise than in accordance with Model Law

If the parties to an arbitration agreement have (whether in the agreement or in any other document in writing) agreed that any dispute that has arisen or may arise between them is to be settled otherwise than in accordance with the Model Law, the Model Law does not apply in relation to the settlement of that dispute.

Division 3—Optional provisions

1—325/10   22. Application of optional provisions

If the parties to an arbitration agreement have (whether in the agreement or in any other document in writing) agreed that the other provisions, or any of the other provisions, of this Division are to apply in relation to the settlement of any dispute (being a dispute that is to be settled in accordance with the Model Law) that has arisen or may arise between them, those provisions apply in relation to the settlement of that dispute.

1—325/11   23. Orders under Article 17 of the Model Law

Chapter VIII of the Model Law applies to orders by an arbitral tribunal under Article 17 of the Model Law requiring a party:

(a) to take an interim measure of protection; or

(b) to provide security in connection with such a measure;

as if any reference in that chapter to an arbitral award or an award were a reference to such an order.

1—325/12   24. Consolidation of arbitral proceedings

(1) A party to arbitral proceedings before an arbitral tribunal may apply to the tribunal for an order under this section in relation to those proceedings and other arbitral proceedings (whether before that tribunal or another tribunal or other tribunals) on the ground that:

(a) a common question of law or fact arises in all those proceedings;

(b) the rights to relief claimed in all those proceedings are in respect of, or arise out of, the same transaction or series of transactions; or

(c) for some other reason specified in the application, it is desirable that an order be made under this section.

(2) The following orders may be made under this section in relation to 2 or more arbitral proceedings:

(a) that the proceedings be consolidated on terms specified in the order;
(b) that the proceedings be heard at the same time or in a sequence specified in the order;
(c) that any of the proceedings be stayed pending the determination of any other of the proceedings.

(3) Where an application has been made under subsection (1) in relation to 2 or more arbitral proceedings (in this section called the *related proceedings*), the following provisions have effect.

(4) If all the related proceedings are being heard by the same tribunal, the tribunal may make such order under this section as it thinks fit in relation to those proceedings and, if such an order is made, the proceedings shall be dealt with in accordance with the order.

(5) If 2 or more arbitral tribunals are hearing the related proceedings:

(a) the tribunal that received the application shall communicate the substance of the application to the other tribunals concerned; and
(b) the tribunals shall, as soon as practicable, deliberate jointly on the application.

(6) Where the tribunals agree, after deliberation on the application, that a particular order under this section should be made in relation to the related proceedings:

(a) the tribunals shall jointly make the order;
(b) the related proceedings shall be dealt with in accordance with the order; and
(c) if the order is that the related proceedings be consolidated—the arbitrator or arbitrators for the purposes of the consolidated proceedings shall be appointed, in accordance with Articles 10 and 11 of the Model Law, from the members of the tribunals.

(7) If the tribunals are unable to make an order under subsection (6), the related proceedings shall proceed as if no application has been made under subsection (1).

(8) This section does not prevent the parties to related proceedings from agreeing to consolidate them and taking such steps as are necessary to effect that consolidation.

1—325/13   25. Interest up to making of award

(1) Unless the parties to an arbitration agreement have (whether in the agreement or in any other document in writing) otherwise agreed, where an arbitral tribunal determines to make an award for the payment of money (whether on a claim for a liquidated or an unliquidated amount), the tribunal may, subject to subsection (2), include in the sum for which the award is made interest, at such reasonable rate as the tribunal determines on the whole or any part of the money, for the whole or any part of the period between the date on which the cause of action arose and the date on which the award is made.

(2) Subsection (1) does not:

(a) authorise the awarding of interest upon interest;
(b) apply in relation to any amount upon which interest is payable as of right whether by virtue of an agreement or otherwise; or
(c) affect the damages recoverable for the dishonour of a bill of exchange.

1—325/14   26. Interest on debt under award

Unless the parties to an arbitration agreement have (whether in the agreement or in any other document in writing) otherwise agreed, where an arbitral tribunal makes an award for the payment of money, the tribunal may direct that interest, at such reasonable rate as the tribunal determines, is payable, from the day of the making of the award or such later day as the tribunal specifies, on so much of the money as is from time to time unpaid and any interest that so accrues shall be deemed to form part of the award.

1—325/14A   27. Costs

(1) Unless the parties to an arbitration agreement have (whether in the agreement or in any other document in writing) otherwise agreed, the costs of an arbitration (including the fees and expenses of the arbitrator or arbitrators) shall be in the discretion of the arbitral tribunal.

(2) An arbitral tribunal may in making an award:

(a) direct to whom, by whom, and in what manner, the whole or any part of the costs that it awards shall be paid;
(b) tax or settle the amount of costs to be so paid or any part of those costs; and

(c) award costs to be taxed or settled as between party and party or as between solicitor and client.

(3) Any costs of an arbitration (other than the fees or expenses of an arbitrator) that are directed to be paid by an award are, to the extent that they have not been taxed or settled by the arbitral tribunal, taxable in the Court having jurisdiction under Article 34 of the Model Law to hear applications for setting aside the award.

(4) If no provision is made by an award with respect to the costs of the arbitration, a party to the arbitration agreement may, within 14 days after receiving the award, apply to the arbitral tribunal for directions as to the payment of those costs, and thereupon the tribunal shall, after hearing any party who wishes to be heard, amend the award by adding to it such directions as the tribunal thinks proper with respect to the payment of the costs of the arbitration.

Division 4—Miscellaneous

1—325/15   28. Liability of arbitrator

An arbitrator is not liable for negligence in respect of anything done or omitted to be done in the capacity of arbitrator, but is liable for fraud in respect of anything done or omitted to be done in that capacity.

1—325/16   29. Representation in proceedings

(1) Where, in accordance with the Model Law, with the agreement of the parties or at the request of a party, as the case may be, the arbitral tribunal holds oral hearings for the presentation of evidence or for oral argument, or conducts proceedings on the basis of documents or other materials, the following provisions shall, without prejudice to the Model Law, apply.

(2) A party may appear in person before an arbitral tribunal and may be represented:
   (a) by himself or herself;
   (b) by a duly qualified legal practitioner from any legal jurisdiction of that party's choice; or
   (c) by any other person of that party's choice.

(3) A legal practitioner or a person, referred to in paragraphs (2)(b) or (c) respectively, while acting on behalf of a party to

an arbitral proceeding to which Part III applies, including appearing before an arbitral tribunal, shall not thereby be taken to have breached any law regulating admission to, or the practice of, the profession of the law within the legal jurisdiction in which the arbitral proceedings are conducted.

(4) Where, subject to the agreement of the parties, an arbitral tribunal conducts proceedings on the basis of documents and other materials, such documents and materials may be prepared and submitted by any legal practitioner or person who would, under subsection (2), be entitled to appear before the tribunal, and, in such a case, subsection (3) shall apply with the same force and effect to such a legal practitioner or person.

1—325/17   30. Application of Part

This Part does not apply in relation to an international commercial arbitration between parties to an arbitration agreement that was concluded before the commencement of this Part unless the parties have (whether in the agreement or in any other document in writing) otherwise agreed.

PART IV—APPLICATION OF THE CONVENTION ON THE SETTLEMENT OF INVESTMENT DISPUTES BETWEEN STATES AND NATIONALS OF OTHER STATES

Division 1—Preliminary

1—325/18   31. Interpretation

(1) In this Part:

award includes:

(a) an interpretation of an award under Article 50; and
(b) a revision of an award under Article 51; and
(c) an annulment of an award under Article 52.

Department means the Department of the Commonwealth primarily responsible for matters relating to foreign affairs.

Investment Convention means the Convention on the Settlement of Investment Disputes between States and Nationals of Other States signed by Australia on 24 March 1975, the English text of which is set out in Schedule 3.

Secretary means the Secretary to the Department.

(2) Except so far as the contrary intention appears, a word or expression used in this Part and in the Investment Convention (whether or not a particular meaning is given to it in the Investment Convention) has, in this Part, the same meaning as it has in the Investment Convention.

(3) A reference in this Part to a numbered Article is a reference to the Article so numbered in the Investment Convention.

Division 2—Investment Convention

1—325/19   32. Application of Investment Convention to Australia

Subject to this Part, Chapters II to VII (inclusive) of the Investment Convention have the force of law in Australia.

1—325/19A   33. Award is binding

(1) An award is binding on a party to the investment dispute to which the award relates.

(2) An award is not subject to any appeal or to any other remedy, otherwise than in accordance with the Investment Convention.

1—325/20   34. Investment Convention awards to prevail over other laws

Other laws relating to the recognition and enforcement of arbitral awards, including the provisions of Parts II and III, do not apply to:

(a) a dispute within the jurisdiction of the Centre; or

(b) an award under this Part.

1—325/21   35. Recognition of awards

(1) The Supreme Court of each State and Territory is designated for the purposes of Article 54.

(2) An award may be enforced in the Supreme Court of a State or Territory as if the award had been made in that State or Territory in accordance with the law of the State or Territory.

Division 3—Miscellaneous

1—325/22 36. Evidence relating to Investment Convention

(1) A certificate purporting to be signed by the Secretary and stating that a country specified in the certificate is, or was at a time so specified, a Contracting State is, upon mere production, receivable in any proceedings as *prima facie* evidence of that fact.

(2) The Secretary may, by signed instrument, delegate the power to sign a certificate under subsection (1) to the holder of a specified office in the Department.

1—325/23 37. Representation in proceedings

(1) A party appearing in conciliation or arbitration proceedings may appear in person and may be represented:

(a) by himself or herself; or
(b) by a duly qualified legal practitioner from any legal jurisdiction of the partyîs choice; or
(c) by any other person of the partyîs choice.

(2) A legal practitioner or a person referred to in paragraph (1)(b) or (c) respectively, while acting on behalf of a party to conciliation or arbitration proceedings, is not thereby to be taken to have breached any law regulating admission to, or the practice of, the profession of the law within the legal jurisdiction in which the proceedings are being conducted.

(3) Where conciliation or arbitration proceedings are conducted on the basis of documents and other materials, the documents and materials may be prepared and submitted by any legal practitioner or person who would, under subsection (1), be entitled to appear in those proceedings, and, in such a case, subsection (2) applies with the same force and effect to such a legal practitioner or person.

1—325/24 38. Judiciary Act

A matter arising under this Part, including a question of interpretation of the Investment Convention for the purposes of this Part, is not taken to be a matter arising directly under a treaty for the purposes of section 38 of the *Judiciary Act 1903*.

SCHEDULE 1—UNITED NATIONS CONFERENCE ON INTERNATIONAL COMMERCIAL ARBITRATION CONVENTION ON THE RECOGNITION AND ENFORCEMENT OF FOREIGN ARBITRAL AWARDS

Section 3

1—325/24A   Article I

1. This Convention shall apply to the recognition and enforcement of arbitral awards made in the territory of a State other than the State where the recognition and enforcement of such awards are sought, and arising out of differences between persons, whether physical or legal. It shall also apply to arbitral awards not considered as domestic awards in the State where their recognition and enforcement are sought.

2. The term "arbitral awards" shall include not only awards made by arbitrators appointed for each case but also those made by permanent arbitral bodies to which the parties have submitted.

3. When signing, ratifying or acceding to this Convention, or notifying extensions under article X hereof, any State may on the basis of reciprocity declare that it will apply the Convention to the recognition and enforcement of awards made only in the territory of another Contracting State. It may also declare that it will apply the Convention only to differences arising out of legal relationships, whether contractual or not, which are considered as commercial under the national law of the State making such declaration.

1—325/25   Article II

1. Each Contracting State shall recognize an agreement in writing under which the parties undertake to submit to arbitration all or any differences which have arisen or which may arise between them in respect of a defined legal relationship, whether contractual or not, concerning a subject matter capable of settlement by arbitration.

2. The term "agreement in writing" shall include an arbitral clause in a contract or an arbitration agreement, signed by the parties or contained in an exchange of letters or telegrams.

3. The court of a Contracting State, when seized of an action in a matter in respect of which the parties have made an

agreement within the meaning of this article, shall, at the request of one of the parties, refer the parties to arbitration, unless it finds that the said agreement is null and void, inoperative or incapable of being performed.

1—325/26   Article III

Each Contracting State shall recognize arbitral awards as binding and enforce them in accordance with the rules of procedure of the territory where the award is relied upon, under the conditions laid down in the following articles. There shall not be imposed substantially more onerous conditions or higher fees or charges on the recognition or enforcement of arbitral awards to which this Convention applies than are imposed on the recognition or enforcement of domestic arbitral awards.

1—325/27   Article IV

1. To obtain the recognition and enforcement mentioned in the preceding article, the party applying for recognition and enforcement shall, at the time of the application, supply:

    (a) The duly authenticated original award or a duly certified copy thereof;
    (b) The original agreement referred to in article II or a duly certified copy thereof.

2. If the said award or agreement is not made in an official language of the country in which the award is relied upon, the party applying for recognition and enforcement of the award shall produce a translation of these documents into such language. The translation shall be certified by an official or sworn translator or by a diplomatic or consular agent.

1—325/28   Article V

1. Recognition and enforcement of the award may be refused, at the request of the party against whom it is invoked, only if that party furnishes to the competent authority where the recognition and enforcement is sought, proof that:

    (a) The parties to the agreement referred to in article II were, under the law applicable to them, under some incapacity, or the said agreement is not valid under the law to which the parties have subjected it or, failing any indication thereon, under the law of the country where the award was made; or
    (b) The party against whom the award is invoked was not

given proper notice of the appointment of the arbitrator or of the arbitration proceedings or was otherwise unable to present his case; or

(c) The award deals with a difference not contemplated by or not falling within the terms of the submission to arbitration, or it contains decisions on matters beyond the scope of the submission to arbitration, provided that, if the decisions on matters submitted to arbitration can be separated from those not so submitted, that part of the award which contains decisions on matters submitted to arbitration may be recognized and enforced; or

(d) The composition of the arbitral authority or the arbitral procedure was not in accordance with the agreement of the parties, or, failing such agreement, was not in accordance with the law of the country where the arbitration took place; or

(e) The award has not yet become binding on the parties, or has been set aside or suspended by a competent authority of the country in which, or under the law of which, that award was made.

2. Recognition and enforcement of an arbitral award may also be refused if the competent authority in the country where recognition and enforcement is sought finds that:

(a) The subject matter of the difference is not capable of settlement by arbitration under the law of that country; or

(b) The recognition or enforcement of the award would be contrary to the public policy of that country.

1—325/29   Article VI

If an application for the setting aside or suspension of the award has been made to a competent authority referred to in article V (1) (e), the authority before which the award is sought to be relied upon may, if it considers it proper, adjourn the decision on the enforcement of the award and may also, on the application of the party claiming enforcement of the award, order the other party to give suitable security.

1—325/30   Article VII

1. The provisions of the present Convention shall not affect the validity of multilateral or bilateral agreements concerning the recognition and enforcement of arbitral awards entered into by the Contracting States nor deprive any interested party of any right he may have to avail himself of an arbitral award in the manner and to the extent allowed by the law or the

treaties of the country where such award is sought to be relied upon.

2. The Geneva Protocol on Arbitration Clauses of 1923 and the Geneva Convention on the Execution of Foreign Arbitral Awards of 1927 shall cease to have effect between Contracting States on their becoming bound and to the extent that they become bound, by this Convention.

1—325/31   **Article VIII**

1. This Convention shall be open until 31 December 1958 for signature on behalf of any Member of the United Nations and also on behalf of any other State which is or hereafter becomes a member of any specialized agency of the United Nations, or which is or hereafter becomes a party to the Statute of the International Court of Justice, or any other State to which an invitation has been addressed by the General Assembly of the United Nations.

2. This Convention shall be ratified and the instrument of ratification shall be deposited with the Secretary-General of the United Nations.

1—325/32   **Article IX**

1. This Convention shall be open for accession to all States referred to in article VIII.

2. Accession shall be effected by the deposit of an instrument of accession with the Secretary-General of the United Nations.

1—325/33   **Article X**

1. Any State may, at the time of signature, ratification or acccssion, declare that this Convention shall extend to all or any of the territories for the international relations of which it is responsible. Such a declaration shall take effect when the Convention enters into force for the State concerned.

2. At any time thereafter any such extensions shall be made by notification addressed to the Secretary-General of the United Nations and shall take effect as from the ninetieth day after the day of receipt by the Secretary-General of the United Nations of this notification, or as from the date of entry into force of the Convention for the State concerned, whichever is the later.

3. With respect to those territories to which this Convention is not extended at the time of signature, ratification or accession, each State concerned shall consider the possibility of taking the necessary steps in order to extend the application of this Convention to such territories, subject, where necessary for constitutional reasons, to the consent of the Governments of such territories.

1—325/34   Article XI

In the case of a federal or non-unitary State, the following provisions shall apply:

(a) With respect to those articles of this Convention that come within the legislative jurisdiction of the federal authority, the obligations of the federal Government shall to this extent be the same as those of Contracting States which are not federal States;

(b) With respect to those articles of this Convention that come within the legislative jurisdiction of constituent states or provinces which are not, under the constitutional system of the federation, bound to take legislative action, the federal Government shall bring such articles with a favourable recommendation to the notice of the appropriate authorities of constituent states or provinces at the earliest possible moment;

(c) A federal State party to this Convention shall, at the request of any other Contracting State transmitted through the Secretary-General of the United Nations, supply a statement of the law and practice of the federation and its constituent units in regard to any particular provision of this Convention, showing the extent to which effect has been given to that provision by legislative or other action.

1—325/35   Article XII

1. This Convention shall come into force on the ninetieth day following the date of deposit of the third instrument of ratification or accession.

2. For each State ratifying or acceding to this Convention after the deposit of the third instrument of ratification or accession, this Convention shall enter into force on the ninetieth day after deposit by such State of its instrument of ratification or accession.

1—325/36   Article XIII

    1. Any Contracting State may denounce this Convention by a written notification to the Secretary-General of the United Nations. Denunciation shall take effect one year after the date of receipt of the notification by the Secretary-General.

    2. Any State which has made a declaration or notification under article X may, at any time thereafter, by notification to the Secretary-General of the United Nations, declare that this Convention shall cease to extend to the territory concerned one year after the date of the receipt of the notification by the Secretary-General.

    3. This Convention shall continue to be applicable to arbitral awards in respect of which recognition or enforcement proceedings have been instituted before the denunciation takes effect.

1—325/37   Article XIV

A Contracting State shall not be entitled to avail itself of the present Convention against other Contracting States except to the extent that it is itself bound to apply the Convention.

1—325/38   Article XV

The Secretary-General of the United Nations shall notify the States contemplated in article VIII of the following:

    (a) Signatures and ratifications in accordance with article VIII;

    (b) Accessions in accordance with article IX;

    (c) Declarations and notifications under articles I, X and XI;

    (d) The date upon which this Convention enters into force in accordance with article XII;

    (e) Denunciations and notifications in accordance with article XIII.

1—325/39   Article XVI

    1. This Convention, of which the Chinese, English, French, Russian and Spanish texts shall be equally authentic, shall be deposited in the archives of the United Nations.

    2. The Secretary-General of the United Nations shall transmit a certified copy of this Convention to the States contemplated in article VIII.

SCHEDULE 2—UNCITRAL MODEL LAW ON INTERNATIONAL COMMERCIAL ARBITRATION (AS ADOPTED BY THE UNITED NATIONS COMMISSION ON INTERNATIONAL TRADE LAW ON 21 JUNE 1985)

Subsection 15 (1)

Chapter I: General Provisions

1—325/40   Article 1—Scope of application*

(1) This Law applies to international commercial** arbitration, subject to any agreement in force between this State and any other State or States.

(2) The provisions of this Law, except articles 8, 9, 35 and 36, apply only if the place of arbitration is in the territory of this State.

(3) An arbitration is international if:

  (a) the parties to an arbitration agreement have, at the time of the conclusion of that agreement, their places of business in different States; or
  (b) one of the following places is situated outside the State in which the parties have their places of business:

   (i) the place of arbitration if determined in, or pursuant to, the arbitration agreement;
   (ii) any place where a substantial part of the obligations of the commercial relationship is to be performed or the place with which the subject-matter of the dispute is most closely connected; or

  (c) the parties have expressly agreed that the subject-matter of the arbitration agreement relates to more than one country.

---

* Article headings are for reference purposes only and are not to be used for purposes of interpretation.
** The term "commercial" should be given a wide interpretation so as to cover matters arising from all relationships of a commercial nature, whether contractual or not. Relationships of a commercial nature include, but are not limited to, the following transactions: any trade transaction for the supply or exchange of goods or services; distribution agreement; commercial representation or agency; factoring; leasing; construction of works; consulting; engineering; licensing; investment; financing; banking; insurance; exploitation agreement or concession; joint venture and other forms of industrial or business co-operation; carriage of goods or passengers by air, sea, rail or road.

(4) For the purposes of paragraph (3) of this article:

    (a) if a party has more than one place of business, the place of business is that which has the closest relationship to the arbitration agreement;

    (b) if a party does not have a place of business, reference is to be made to his habitual residence.

(5) This Law shall not affect any other law of this State by virtue of which certain disputes may not be submitted to arbitration or may be submitted to arbitration only according to provisions other than those of this Law.

1—325/41 Article 2—Definitions and rules of interpretation

For the purposes of this Law:

    (a) "arbitration" means any arbitration whether or not administered by a permanent arbitral institution;

    (b) "arbitral tribunal" means a sole arbitrator or a panel of arbitrators;

    (c) "court" means a body or organ of the judicial system of a State;

    (d) where a provision of this Law, except article 28, leaves the parties free to determine a certain issue, such freedom includes the right of the parties to authorize a third party, including an institution, to make that determination;

    (e) where a provision of this Law refers to the fact that the parties have agreed or that they may agree or in any other way refers to an agreement of the parties, such agreement includes any arbitration rules referred to in that agreement;

    (f) where a provision of this Law, other than in articles 25 (a) and 32 (2) (a), refers to a claim, it also applies to a counter-claim, and where it refers to a defence, it also applies to a defence to such counter-claim.

1—325/42 Article 3—Receipt of written communications

(1) Unless otherwise agreed by the parties:

    (a) any written communication is deemed to have been received if it is delivered to the addressee personally or if it is delivered at his place of business, habitual residence or mailing address; if none of these can be found after making a reasonable inquiry, a written communication is deemed to have been received if it is sent to the addressee's last-known place of business, habitual residence or mailing address by registered letter or any other means which provides a record of the attempt to deliver it;

(b) the communication is deemed to have been received on the day it is so delivered.

(2) The provisions of this article do not apply to communications in court proceedings.

1—325/43   Article 4—Waiver of right to object

A party who knows that any provision of this Law from which the parties may derogate or any requirement under the arbitration agreement has not been complied with and yet proceeds with the arbitration without stating his objection to such non-compliance without undue delay or, if a time-limit is provided therefor, within such period of time, shall be deemed to have waived his right to object.

1—325/44   Article 5—Extent of court intervention

In matters governed by this Law, no court shall intervene except where so provided in this Law.

1—325/45   Article 6—Court or other authority for certain functions of arbitration assistance and supervision

The functions referred to in articles 11 (3), 11 (4), 13 (3), 14, 16 (3) and 34 (2) shall be performed by . . . [Each State enacting this model law specifies the court, courts or, where referred to therein, other authority competent to perform these functions.]

CHAPTER II: ARBITRATION AGREEMENT

1—325/46   Article 7—Definition and form of arbitration agreement

(1) "Arbitration agreement" is an agreement by the parties to submit to arbitration all or certain disputes which have arisen or which may arise between them in respect of a defined legal relationship, whether contractual or not. An arbitration agreement may be in the form of an arbitration clause in a contract or in the form of a separate agreement.

(2) The arbitration agreement shall be in writing. An agreement is in writing if it is contained in a document signed by the parties

or in an exchange of letters, telex, telegrams or other means of telecommunication which provide a record of the agreement, or in an exchange of statements of claim and defence in which the existence of an agreement is alleged by one party and not denied by another. The reference in a contract to a document containing an arbitration clause constitutes an arbitration agreement provided that the contract is in writing and the reference is such as to make that clause part of the contract.

1—325/47   Article 8—Arbitration agreement and substantive claim before court

(1) A court before which an action is brought in a matter which is the subject of an arbitration agreement shall, if a party so requests not later than when submitting his first statement on the substance of the dispute, refer the parties to arbitration unless it finds that the agreement is null and void, inoperative or incapable of being performed.

(2) Where an action referred to in paragraph (1) of this article has been brought, arbitral proceedings may nevertheless be commenced or continued, and an award may be made, while the issue is pending before the court.

1—325/48   Article 9—Arbitration agreement and interim measures by court

It is not incompatible with an arbitration agreement for a party to request, before or during arbitral proceedings, from a court an interim measure of protection and for a court to grant such measure.

Chapter III: Composition of Arbitral Tribunal

1—325/49   Article 10—Number of arbitrators

(1) The parties are free to determine the number of arbitrators.

(2) Failing such determination, the number of arbitrators shall be three.

1—325/50   Article 11—Appointment of arbitrators

(1) No person shall be precluded by reason of his nationality from acting as an arbitrator, unless otherwise agreed by the parties.

(2) The parties are free to agree on a procedure of appointing the arbitrator or arbitrators, subject to the provisions of paragraphs (4) and (5) of this article.

(3) Failing such agreement,

    (a) in an arbitration with three arbitrators, each party shall appoint one arbitrator, and the two arbitrators thus appointed shall appoint the third arbitrator; if a party fails to appoint the arbitrator within thirty days of receipt of a request to do so from the other party, or if the two arbitrators fail to agree on the third arbitrator within thirty days of their appointment, the appointment shall be made, upon request of a party, by the court or other authority specified in article 6;

    (b) in an arbitration with a sole arbitrator, if the parties are unable to agree on the arbitrator, he shall be appointed, upon request of a party, by the court or other authority specified in article 6.

(4) Where, under an appointment procedure agreed upon by the parties,

    (a) a party fails to act as required under such procedure, or
    (b) the parties, or two arbitrators, are unable to reach an agreement expected of them under such procedure, or
    (c) a third party, including an institution, fails to perform any function entrusted to it under such procedure,

any party may request the court or other authority specified in article 6 to take the necessary measure, unless the agreement on the appointment procedure provides other means for securing the appointment.

(5) A decision on a matter entrusted by paragraph (3) or (4) of this article to the court or other authority specified in article 6 shall be subject to no appeal. The court or other authority, in appointing an arbitrator, shall have due regard to any qualifications required of the arbitrator by the agreement of the parties and to such considerations as are likely to secure the appointment of an independent and impartial arbitrator and, in the case of a sole or third arbitrator, shall take into account as well the advisability of appointing an arbitrator of a nationality other than those of the parties.

1—325/51   Article 12—Grounds for challenge

(1) When a person is approached in connection with his possible appointment as an arbitrator, he shall disclose any

circumstances likely to give rise to justifiable doubts as to his impartiality or independence. An arbitrator, from the time of his appointment and throughout the arbitral proceedings, shall without delay disclose any such circumstances to the parties unless they have already been informed of them by him.

(2) An arbitrator may be challenged only if circumstances exist that give rise to justifiable doubts as to his impartiality or independence, or if he does not possess qualifications agreed to by the parties. A party may challenge an arbitrator appointed by him, or in whose appointment he has participated, only for reasons of which he becomes aware after the appointment has been made.

1—325/52   Article 13—Challenge procedure

(1) The parties are free to agree on a procedure for challenging an arbitrator, subject to the provisions of paragraph (3) of this article.

(2) Failing such agreement, a party who intends to challenge an arbitrator shall, within fifteen days after becoming aware of the constitution of the arbitral tribunal or after becoming aware of any circumstance referred to in article 12 (2), send a written statement of the reasons for the challenge to the arbitral tribunal. Unless the challenged arbitrator withdraws from his office or the other party agrees to the challenge, the arbitral tribunal shall decide on the challenge.

(3) If a challenge under any procedure agreed upon by the parties or under the procedure of paragraph (2) of this article is not successful, the challenging party may request, within thirty days after having received notice of the decision rejecting the challenge, the court or other authority specified in article 6 to decide on the challenge, which decision shall be subject to no appeal; while such a request is pending, the arbitral tribunal, including the challenged arbitrator, may continue the arbitral proceedings and make an award.

1—325/53   Article 14—Failure or impossibility to act

(1) If an arbitrator becomes *de jure* or *de facto* unable to perform his functions or for other reasons fails to act without undue delay, his mandate terminates if he withdraws from his office or if the parties agree on the termination. Otherwise, if a controversy remains concerning any of these grounds, any party may request the court or other authority specified in article 6

to decide on the termination of the mandate, which decision shall be subject to no appeal.

(2) If, under this article or article 13 (2), an arbitrator withdraws from his office or a party agrees to the termination of the mandate of an arbitrator, this does not imply acceptance of the validity of any ground referred to in this article or article 12 (2).

1—325/54   Article 15—Appointment of substitute arbitrator

Where the mandate of an arbitrator terminates under article 13 or 14 or because of his withdrawal from office for any other reason or because of the revocation of his mandate by agreement of the parties or in any other case of termination of his mandate, a substitute arbitrator shall be appointed according to the rules that were applicable to the appointment of the arbitrator being replaced.

CHAPTER IV: JURISDICTION OF ARBITRAL TRIBUNAL

1—325/55   Article 16—Competence of arbitral tribunal to rule on its jurisdiction

(1) The arbitral tribunal may rule on its own jurisdiction, including any objections with respect to the existence or validity of the arbitration agreement. For that purpose, an arbitration clause which forms part of a contract shall be treated as an agreement independent of the other terms of the contract. A decision by the arbitral tribunal that the contract is null and void shall not entail *ipso jure* the invalidity of the arbitration clause.

(2) A plea that the arbitral tribunal does not have jurisdiction shall be raised not later than the submission of the statement of defence. A party is not precluded from raising such a plea by the fact that he has appointed, or participated in the appointment of, an arbitrator. A plea that the arbitral tribunal is exceeding the scope of its authority shall be raised as soon as the matter alleged to be beyond the scope of its authority is raised during the arbitral proceedings. The arbitral tribunal may, in either case, admit a later plea if it considers the delay justified.

(3) The arbitral tribunal may rule on a plea referred to in paragraph (2) of this article either as a preliminary question or in an award on the merits. If the arbitral tribunal rules as a

preliminary question that it has jurisdiction, any party may request, within thirty days after having received notice of that ruling, the court specified in article 6 to decide the matter, which decision shall be subject to no appeal; while such a request is pending, the arbitral tribunal may continue the arbitral proceedings and make an award.

1—325/56   Article 17—Power of arbitral tribunal to order interim measures

Unless otherwise agreed by the parties, the arbitral tribunal may, at the request of a party, order any party to take such interim measure of protection as the arbitral tribunal may consider necessary in respect of the subject-matter of the dispute. The arbitral tribunal may require any party to provide appropriate security in connection with such measure.

CHAPTER V: CONDUCT OF ARBITRAL PROCEEDINGS

1—325/57   Article 18—Equal treatment of parties

The parties shall be treated with equality and each party shall be given a full opportunity of presenting his case.

1—325/57   Article 19—Determination of rules of procedure

(1) Subject to the provisions of this Law, the parties are free to agree on the procedure to be followed by the arbitral tribunal in conducting the proceedings.

(2) Failing such agreement, the arbitral tribunal may, subject to the provisions of this Law, conduct the arbitration in such manner as it considers appropriate. The power conferred upon the arbitral tribunal includes the power to determine the admissibility, relevance, materiality and weight of any evidence.

1—325/58   Article 20—Place of arbitration

(1) The parties are free to agree on the place of arbitration. Failing such agreement, the place of arbitration shall be determined by the arbitral tribunal having regard to the circumstances of the case, including the convenience of the parties.

(2) Notwithstanding the provisions of paragraph (1) of this article, the arbitral tribunal may, unless otherwise agreed by the parties, meet at any place it considers appropriate for

consultation among its members, for hearing witnesses, experts or the parties, or for inspection of goods, other property or documents.

1—325/59   Article 21—Commencement of arbitral proceedings

Unless otherwise agreed by the parties, the arbitral proceedings in respect of a particular dispute commence on the date on which a request for that dispute to be referred to arbitration is received by the respondent.

1—325/60   Article 22—Language

(1) The parties are free to agree on the language or languages to be used in the arbitral proceedings. Failing such agreement, the arbitral tribunal shall determine the language or languages to be used in the proceedings. This agreement or determination, unless otherwise specified therein, shall apply to any written statement by a party, any hearing and any award, decision or other communication by the arbitral tribunal.

(2) The arbitral tribunal may order that any documentary evidence shall be accompanied by a translation into the language or languages agreed upon by the parties or determined by the arbitral tribunal.

1—325/61   Article 23—Statements of claim and defence

(1) Within the period of time agreed by the parties or determined by the arbitral tribunal, the claimant shall state the facts supporting his claim, the points at issue and the relief or remedy sought, and the respondent shall state his defence in respect of these particulars, unless the parties have otherwise agreed as to the required elements of such statements. The parties may submit with their statements all documents they consider to be relevant or may add a reference to the documents or other evidence they will submit.

(2) Unless otherwise agreed by the parties, either party may amend or supplement his claim or defence during the course of the arbitral proceedings, unless the arbitral tribunal considers it inappropriate to allow such amendment having regard to the delay in making it.

1—325/62   Article 24—Hearings and written proceedings

(1) Subject to any contrary agreement by the parties, the arbitral tribunal shall decide whether to hold oral hearings for the

presentation of evidence or for oral argument, or whether the proceedings shall be conducted on the basis of documents and other materials. However, unless the parties have agreed that no hearings shall be held, the arbitral tribunal shall hold such hearings at an appropriate stage of the proceedings, if so requested by a party.

(2) The parties shall be given sufficient advance notice of any hearing and of any meeting of the arbitral tribunal for the purposes of inspection of goods, other property or documents.

(3) All statements, documents or other information supplied to the arbitral tribunal by one party shall be communicated to the other party. Also any expert report or evidentiary document on which the arbitral tribunal may rely in making its decision shall be communicated to the parties.

1—325/63   Article 25—Default of a party

Unless otherwise agreed by the parties, if, without showing sufficient cause,

(a) the claimant fails to communicate his statement of claim in accordance with article 23 (1), the arbitral tribunal shall terminate the proceedings;

(b) the respondent fails to communicate his statement of defence in accordance with article 23 (1), the arbitral tribunal shall continue the proceedings without treating such failure in itself as an admission of the claimant's allegations;

(c) any party fails to appear at a hearing or to produce documentary evidence, the arbitral tribunal may continue the proceedings and make the award on the evidence before it.

1—325/64   Article 26—Expert appointed by arbitral tribunal

(1) Unless otherwise agreed by the parties, the arbitral tribunal

   (a) may appoint one or more experts to report to it on specific issues to be determined by the arbitral tribunal;
   (b) may require a party to give the expert any relevant information or to produce, or to provide access to, any relevant documents, goods or other property for his inspection.

(2) Unless otherwise agreed by the parties, if a party so requests or if the arbitral tribunal considers it necessary, the expert shall, after delivery of his written or oral report, participate

C. Foreign Statutes: Non-European Jurisdictions

in a hearing where the parties have the opportunity to put questions to him and to present expert witnesses in order to testify on the points at issue.

1—325/65   Article 27—Court assistance in taking evidence

The arbitral tribunal or a party with the approval of the arbitral tribunal may request from a competent court of this State assistance in taking evidence. The court may execute the request within its competence and according to its rules on taking evidence.

Chapter VI: Making of Award and Termination of Proceedings

1—325/66   Article 28—Rules applicable to substance of dispute

(1) The arbitral tribunal shall decide the dispute in accordance with such rules of law as are chosen by the parties as applicable to the substance of the dispute. Any designation of the law or legal system of a given State shall be construed, unless otherwise expressed, as directly referring to the substantive law of that State and not to its conflict of laws rules.

(2) Failing any designation by the parties, the arbitral tribunal shall apply the law determined by the conflict of laws rules which it considers applicable.

(3) The arbitral tribunal shall decide *ex aequo et bono* or as *amiable compositeur* only if the parties have expressly authorized it to do so.

(4) In all cases, the arbitral tribunal shall decide in accordance with the terms of the contract and shall take into account the usages of the trade applicable to the transaction.

1—325/67   Article 29—Decision-making by panel of arbitrators

In arbitral proceedings with more than one arbitrator, any decision of the arbitral tribunal shall be made, unless otherwise agreed by the parties, by a majority of all its members. However, questions of procedure may be decided by a presiding arbitrator, if so authorized by the parties or all members of the arbitral tribunal.

1—325/68   Article 30—Settlement

(1) If, during arbitral proceedings, the parties settle the dispute, the arbitral tribunal shall terminate the proceedings and, if

requested by the parties and not objected to by the arbitral tribunal, record the settlement in the form of an arbitral award on agreed terms.

(2) An award on agreed terms shall be made in accordance with the provisions of article 31 and shall state that it is an award. Such an award has the same status and effect as any other award on the merits of the case.

1—325/69   Article 31—Form and contents of award

(1) The award shall be made in writing and shall be signed by the arbitrator or arbitrators. In arbitral proceedings with more than one arbitrator, the signatures of the majority of all members of the arbitral tribunal shall suffice, provided that the reason for any omitted signature is stated.

(2) The award shall state the reasons upon which it is based, unless the parties have agreed that no reasons are to be given or the award is an award on agreed terms under article 30.

(3) The award shall state its date and the place of arbitration as determined in accordance with article 20 (1). The award shall be deemed to have been made at that place.

(4) After the award is made, a copy signed by the arbitrators in accordance with paragraph (1) of this article shall be delivered to each party.

1—325/70   Article 32—Termination of proceedings

(1) The arbitral proceedings are terminated by the final award or by an order of the arbitral tribunal in accordance with paragraph (2) of this article.

(2) The arbitral tribunal shall issue an order for the termination of the arbitral proceedings when:

(a) the claimant withdraws his claim, unless the respondent objects thereto and the arbitral tribunal recognizes a legitimate interest on his part in obtaining a final settlement of the dispute;
(b) the parties agree on the termination of the proceedings;
(c) the arbitral tribunal finds that the continuation of the proceedings has for any other reason become unnecessary or impossible.

(3) The mandate of the arbitral tribunal terminates with the termination of the arbitral proceedings, subject to the provisions of articles 33 and 34 (4).

1—325/71   **Article 33—Correction and interpretation of award; additional award**

(1) Within thirty days of receipt of the award, unless another period of time has been agreed upon by the parties:

   (a) a party, with notice to the other party, may request the arbitral tribunal to correct in the award any errors in computation, any clerical or typographical errors or any errors of similar nature;
   (b) if so agreed by the parties, a party, with notice to the other party, may request the arbitral tribunal to give an interpretation of a specific point or part of the award.

   If the arbitral tribunal considers the request to be justified, it shall make the correction or give the interpretation within thirty days of receipt of the request. The interpretation shall form part of the award.

(2) The arbitral tribunal may correct any error of the type referred to in paragraph (1) (a) of this article on its own initiative within thirty days of the date of the award.

(3) Unless otherwise agreed by the parties, a party, with notice to the other party, may request, within thirty days of receipt of the award, the arbitral tribunal to make an additional award as to claims presented in the arbitral proceedings but omitted from the award. If the arbitral tribunal considers the request to be justified, it shall make the additional award within sixty days.

(4) The arbitral tribunal may extend, if necessary, the period of time within which it shall make a correction, interpretation or an additional award under paragraph (1) or (3) of this article.

(5) The provisions of article 31 shall apply to a correction or interpretation of the award or to an additional award.

CHAPTER VII: RECOURSE AGAINST AWARD

1—325/72   **Article 34—Application for setting aside as exclusive recourse against arbitral award**

(1) Recourse to a court against an arbitral award may be made only by an application for setting aside in accordance with paragraphs (2) and (3) of this article.

(2) An arbitral award may be set aside by the court specified in article 6 only if:

(a) the party making the application furnishes proof that:

(i) a party to the arbitration agreement referred to in article 7 was under some incapacity; or the said agreement is not valid under the law to which the parties have subjected it or, failing any indication thereon, under the law of this State; or

(ii) the party making the application was not given proper notice of the appointment of an arbitrator or of the arbitral proceedings or was otherwise unable to present his case; or

(iii) the award deals with a dispute not contemplated by or not falling within the terms of the submission to arbitration, or contains decisions on matters beyond the scope of the submission to arbitration, provided that, if the decisions on matters submitted to arbitration can be separated from those not so submitted, only that part of the award which contains decisions on matters not submitted to arbitration may be set aside; or

(iv) the composition of the arbitral tribunal or the arbitral procedure was not in accordance with the agreement of the parties, unless such agreement was in conflict with a provision of this Law from which the parties cannot derogate, or, failing such agreement, was not in accordance with this Law; or

(b) the court finds that:

(i) the subject-matter of the dispute is not capable of settlement by arbitration under the law of this State; or

(ii) the award is in conflict with the public policy of this State.

(3) An application for setting aside may not be made after three months have elapsed from the date on which the party making that application had received the award or, if a request had been made under article 33, from the date on which that request had been disposed of by the arbitral tribunal.

(4) The court, when asked to set aside an award, may, where appropriate and so requested by a party, suspend the setting aside proceedings for a period of time determined by it in order to give the arbitral tribunal an opportunity to resume

the arbitral proceedings or to take such other action as in the arbitral tribunal's opinion will eliminate the grounds for setting aside.

Chapter VIII: Recognition and Enforcement of Awards

1—325/73   Article 35—Recognition and enforcement

(1) An arbitral award, irrespective of the country in which it was made, shall be recognized as binding and, upon application in writing to the competent court, shall be enforced subject to the provisions of this article and of article 36.

(2) The party relying on an award or applying for its enforcement shall supply the duly authenticated original award or a duly certified copy thereof, and the original arbitration agreement referred to in article 7 or a duly certified copy thereof. If the award or agreement is not made in an official language of this State, the party shall supply a duly certified translation thereof into such language.***

1—325/74   Article 36—Grounds for refusing recognition or enforcement

(1) Recognition or enforcement of an arbitral award, irrespective of the country in which it was made, may be refused only:

(a) at the request of the party against whom it is invoked, if that party furnishes to the competent court where recognition or enforcement is sought proof that:

(i) a party to the arbitration agreement referred to in article 7 was under some incapacity; or the said agreement is not valid under the law to which the parties have subjected it or, failing any indication thereon, under the law of the country where the award was made; or

(ii) the party against whom the award is invoked was not given proper notice of the appointment of an arbitrator or of the arbitral proceedings or was otherwise unable to present his case; or

(iii) the award deals with a dispute not contemplated by

*** The conditions set forth in this paragraph are intended to set maximum standards. It would, thus, not be contrary to the harmonization to be achieved by the model law if a State retained even less onerous conditions.

or not falling within the terms of the submission to arbitration, or it contains decisions on matters beyond the scope of the submission to arbitration, provided that, if the decisions on matters submitted to arbitration can be separated from those not so submitted, that part of the award which contains decisions on matters submitted to arbitration may be recognized and enforced; or

(iv) the composition of the arbitral tribunal or the arbitral procedure was not in accordance with the agreement of the parties or, failing such agreement, was not in accordance with the law of the country where the arbitration took place; or

(v) the award has not yet become binding on the parties or has been set aside or suspended by a court of the country in which, or under the law of which, that award was made; or

(b) if the court finds that:

(i) the subject-matter of the dispute is not capable of settlement by arbitration under the law of this State; or

(ii) the recognition or enforcement of the award would be contrary to the public policy of this State.

(2) If an application for setting aside or suspension of an award has been made to a court referred to in paragraph (1) (a) (v) of this article, the court where recognition or enforcement is sought may, if it considers it proper, adjourn its decision and may also, on the application of the party claiming recognition or enforcement of the award, order the other party to provide appropriate security.

SCHEDULE 3—CONVENTION ON THE SETTLEMENT OF INVESTMENT DISPUTES BETWEEN STATES AND NATIONALS OF OTHER STATES

Subsection 31 (1)

1—325/75 Preamble

The Contracting States

Considering the need for international cooperation for economic development, and the role of private international investment therein;

Bearing in mind the possibility that from time to time disputes may arise in connection with such investment between Contracting States and nationals of other Contracting States;

Recognizing that while such disputes would usually be subject to national legal processes, international methods of settlement may be appropriate in certain cases;

Attaching particular importance to the availability of facilities for international conciliation or arbitration to which Contracting States and nationals of other Contracting States may submit such disputes if they so desire;

Desiring to establish such facilities under the auspices of the International Bank for Reconstruction and Development;

Recognizing that mutual consent by the parties to submit such disputes to conciliation or to arbitration through such facilities constitutes a binding agreement which requires in particular that due consideration be given to any recommendation of conciliators, and that any arbitral award be complied with; and

Declaring that no Contracting State shall by the mere fact of its ratification, acceptance or approval of this Convention and without its consent be deemed to be under any obligation to submit any particular dispute to conciliation or arbitration,

Have agreed as follows:

CHAPTER I: INTERNATIONAL CENTRE FOR SETTLEMENT OF INVESTMENT DISPUTES

Section 1: Establishment and Organization

1—325/76   Article 1

(1) There is hereby established the International Centre for Settlement of Investment Disputes (hereinafter called the Centre).

(2) The purpose of the Centre shall be to provide facilities for conciliation and arbitration of investment disputes between Contracting States and nationals of other Contracting States in accordance with the provisions of this Convention.

Article 2

The seat of the Centre shall be at the principal office of the International Bank for Reconstruction and Development (hereinafter called the Bank). The seat may be moved to another place by decision of the Administrative Council adopted by a majority of two-thirds of its members.

Article 3

The Centre shall have an Administrative Council and a Secretariat and shall maintain a Panel of Conciliators and a Panel of Arbitrators.

Section 2: The Administrative Council

1—325/77 Article 4

(1) The Administrative Council shall be composed of one representative of each Contracting State. An alternate may act as representative in case of his principalîs absence from a meeting or inability to act.

(2) In the absence of a contrary designation, each governor and alternate governor of the Bank appointed by a Contracting State shall be *ex officio* its representative and its alternate respectively.

Article 5

The President of the Bank shall be *ex officio* Chairman of the Administrative Council (hereinafter called the Chairman) but shall have no vote. During his absence or inability to act and during any vacancy in the office of President of the Bank, the person for the time being acting as President shall act as Chairman of the Administrative Council.

Article 6

(1) Without prejudice to the powers and functions vested in it by other provisions of this Convention, the Administrative Council shall

(a) adopt the administrative and financial regulations of the Centre;
(b) adopt the rules of procedure for the institution of conciliation and arbitration proceedings;
(c) adopt the rules of procedure for conciliation and arbi-

tration proceedings (hereinafter called the Conciliation Rules and the Arbitration Rules);
(d) approve arrangements with the Bank for the use of the Bank's administrative facilities and services;
(e) determine the conditions of service of the Secretary-General and of any Deputy Secretary-General;
(f) adopt the annual budget of revenues and expenditures of the Centre;
(g) approve the annual report on the operation of the Centre.

The decisions referred to in sub-paragraphs (a), (b), (c) and (f) above shall be adopted by a majority of two-thirds of the members of the Administrative Council.

(2) The Administrative Council may appoint such committees as it considers necessary.

(3) The Administrative Council shall also exercise such other powers and perform such other functions as it shall determine to be necessary for the implementation of the provisions of this Convention.

Article 7

(1) The Administrative Council shall hold an annual meeting and such other meetings as may be determined by the Council, or convened by the Chairman, or convened by the Secretary-General at the request of not less than five members of the Council.

(2) Each member of the Administrative Council shall have one vote and, except as otherwise herein provided, all matters before the Council shall be decided by a majority of the votes cast.

(3) A quorum for any meeting of the Administrative Council shall be a majority of its members.

(4) The Administrative Council may establish, by a majority of two-thirds of its members, a procedure whereby the Chairman may seek a vote of the Council without convening a meeting of the Council. The vote shall be considered valid only if the majority of the members of the Council cast their votes within the time limit fixed by the said procedure.

Article 8

Members of the Administrative Council and the Chairman shall serve without remuneration from the Centre.

Section 3: The Secretariat

1—325/78   Article 9

The Secretariat shall consist of a Secretary-General, one or more Deputy Secretaries-General and staff.

Article 10

(1) The Secretary-General and any Deputy Secretary-General shall be elected by the Administrative Council by a majority of two-thirds of its members upon the nomination of the Chairman for a term of service not exceeding six years and shall be eligible for re-election. After consulting the members of the Administrative Council, the Chairman shall propose one or more candidates for each such office.

(2) The offices of Secretary-General and Deputy Secretary-General shall be incompatible with the exercise of any political function. Neither the Secretary-General nor any Deputy Secretary-General may hold any other employment or engage in any other occupation except with the approval of the Administrative Council.

(3) During the Secretary-General's absence or inability to act, and during any vacancy of the office of Secretary-General, the Deputy Secretary-General shall act as Secretary-General. If there shall be more than one Deputy Secretary-General, the Administrative Council shall determine in advance the order in which they shall act as Secretary-General.

Article 11

The Secretary-General shall be the legal representative and the principal officer of the Centre and shall be responsible for its administration, including the appointment of staff, in accordance with the provisions of this Convention and the rules adopted by the Administrative Council. He shall perform the function of registrar and shall have the power to authenticate arbitral awards rendered pursuant to this Convention, and to certify copies thereof.

Section 4: The Panels

1—325/79   Article 12

The Panel of Conciliators and the Panel of Arbitrators shall each consist of qualified persons, designated as hereinafter provided, who are willing to serve thereon.

Article 13

(1) Each Contracting State may designate to each Panel four persons who may but need not be its nationals.

(2) The Chairman may designate ten persons to each Panel. The persons so designated to a Panel shall each have a different nationality.

Article 14

(1) Persons designated to serve on the Panels shall be persons of high moral character and recognized competence in the fields of law, commerce, industry or finance, who may be relied upon to exercise independent judgment. Competence in the field of law shall be of particular importance in the case of persons on the Panel of Arbitrators.

(2) The Chairman, in designating persons to serve on the Panels, shall in addition pay due regard to the importance of assuring representation on the Panels of the principal legal systems of the world and of the main forms of economic activity.

Article 15

(1) Panel members shall serve for renewable periods of six years.

(2) In case of death or resignation of a member of a Panel, the authority which designated the member shall have the right to designate another person to serve for the remainder of that memberîs term.

(3) Panel members shall continue in office until their successors have been designated.

Article 16

(1) A person may serve on both Panels.

(2) If a person shall have been designated to serve on the same Panel by more than one Contracting State, or by one or more Contracting States and the Chairman, he shall be deemed to have been designated by the authority which first designated him or, if one such authority is the State of which he is a national, by that State.

(3) All designations shall be notified to the Secretary-General and shall take effect from the date on which the notification is received.

Section 5: Financing the Centre

1—325/80 Article 17

If the expenditure of the Centre cannot be met out of charges for the use of its facilities, or out of other receipts, the excess shall be borne by Contracting States which are members of the Bank in proportion to their respective subscriptions to the capital stock of the Bank, and by Contracting States which are not members of the Bank in accordance with rules adopted by the Administrative Council.

Section 6: Status, Immunities and Privileges

1—325/81 Article 18

The Centre shall have full international legal personality. The legal capacity of the Centre shall include the capacity

(a) to contract;

(b) to acquire and dispose of movable and immovable property;

(c) to institute legal proceedings.

Article 19

To enable the Centre to fulfil its functions, it shall enjoy in the territories of each Contracting State the immunities and privileges set forth in this Section.

Article 20

The Centre, its property and assets shall enjoy immunity from all legal process, except when the Centre waives this immunity.

Article 21

The Chairman, the members of the Administrative Council, persons acting as conciliators or arbitrators or members of a Committee appointed pursuant to paragraph (3) of Article 52, and the officers and employees of the Secretariat

(a) shall enjoy immunity from legal process with respect to acts performed by them in the exercise of their functions, except when the Centre waives this immunity;

(b) not being local nationals, shall enjoy the same immunities from immigration restrictions, alien registration requirements and national service obligations, the same facilities as regards exchange restrictions and the same treatment in respect of travelling facilities as are accorded by Contracting States to the representatives, officials and employees of comparable rank of other Contracting States.

Article 22

The provisions of Article 21 shall apply to persons appearing in proceedings under this Convention as parties, agents, counsel, advocates, witnesses or experts; provided, however, that sub-paragraph (b) thereof shall apply only in connection with their travel to and from, and their stay at, the place where the proceedings are held.

Article 23

(1) The archives of the Centre shall be inviolable, wherever they may be.

(2) With regard to its official communications, the Centre shall be accorded by each Contracting State treatment not less favourable than that accorded to other international organizations.

Article 24

(1) The Centre, its assets, property and income, and its operations and transactions authorized by this Convention shall be exempt from all taxation and customs duties. The Centre shall also be exempt from liability for the collection or payment of any taxes or customs duties.

(2) Except in the case of local nationals, no tax shall be levied on or in respect of expense allowances paid by the Centre to the Chairman or members of the Administrative Council, or on or in respect of salaries, expense allowances or other emoluments paid by the Centre to officials or employees of the Secretariat.

(3) No tax shall be levied on or in respect of fees or expense allowances received by persons acting as conciliators, or arbitrators, or members of a Committee appointed pursuant to paragraph (3) of Article 52, in proceedings under this Convention, if the sole jurisdictional basis for such tax is the location of the Centre or the place where such proceedings

are conducted or the place where such fees or allowances are paid.

CHAPTER II: JURISDICTION OF THE CENTRE

1—325/82   Article 25

(1) The jurisdiction of the Centre shall extend to any legal dispute arising directly out of an investment, between a Contracting State (or any constituent subdivision or agency of a Contracting State designated to the Centre by that State) and a national of another Contracting State, which the parties to the dispute consent in writing to submit to the Centre. When the parties have given their consent, no party may withdraw its consent unilaterally.

(2) "National of another Contracting State" means:

(a) any natural person who had the nationality of a Contracting State other than the State party to the dispute on the date on which the parties consented to submit such dispute to conciliation or arbitration as well as on the date on which the request was registered pursuant to paragraph (3) of Article 28 or paragraph (3) of Article 36, but does not include any person who on either date also had the nationality of the Contracting State party to the dispute; and

(b) any juridical person which had the nationality of a Contracting State other than the State party to the dispute on the date on which the parties consented to submit such dispute to conciliation or arbitration and any juridical person which had the nationality of the Contracting State party to the dispute on that date and which, because of foreign control, the parties have agreed should be treated as a national of another Contracting State for the purposes of this Convention.

(3) Consent by a constituent subdivision or agency of a Contracting State shall require the approval of that State unless that State notifies the Centre that no such approval is required.

(4) Any Contracting State may, at the time of ratification, acceptance or approval of this Convention or at any time thereafter, notify the Centre of the class or classes of disputes which it would or would not consider submitting to the juris-

diction of the Centre. The Secretary-General shall forthwith transmit such notification to all Contracting States. Such notification shall not constitute the consent required by paragraph (1).

Article 26

Consent of the parties to arbitration under this Convention shall, unless otherwise stated, be deemed consent to such arbitration to the exclusion of any other remedy. A Contracting State may require the exhaustion of local administrative or judicial remedies as a condition of its consent to arbitration under this Convention.

Article 27

(1) No Contracting State shall give diplomatic protection, or bring an international claim, in respect of a dispute which one of its nationals and another Contracting State shall have consented to submit or shall have submitted to arbitration under this Convention, unless such other Contracting State shall have failed to abide by and comply with the award rendered in such dispute.

(2) Diplomatic protection, for the purposes of paragraph (1), shall not include informal diplomatic exchanges for the sole purpose of facilitating a settlement of the dispute.

CHAPTER III: CONCILIATION

Section 1: Request for Conciliation

1—325/83   Article 28

(1) Any Contracting State or any national of a Contracting State wishing to institute conciliation proceedings shall address a request to that effect in writing to the Secretary-General who shall send a copy of the request to the other party.

(2) The request shall contain information concerning the issues in dispute, the identity of the parties and their consent to conciliation in accordance with the rules of procedure for the institution of conciliation and arbitration proceedings.

(3) The Secretary-General shall register the request unless he finds, on the basis of the information contained in the

request, that the dispute is manifestly outside the jurisdiction of the Centre. He shall forthwith notify the parties of registration or refusal to register.

Section 2: Constitution of the Conciliation Commission

1—325/84   Article 29

(1) The Conciliation Commission (hereinafter called the Commission) shall be constituted as soon as possible after registration of a request pursuant to Article 28.

(2) (a) The Commission shall consist of a sole conciliator or any uneven number of conciliators appointed as the parties shall agree.
   (b) Where the parties do not agree upon the number of conciliators and the method of their appointment, the Commission shall consist of three conciliators, one conciliator appointed by each party and the third, who shall be the president of the Commission, appointed by agreement of the parties.

Article 30

If the Commission shall not have been constituted within 90 days after notice of registration of the request has been dispatched by the Secretary-General in accordance with paragraph (3) of Article 28, or such other period as the parties may agree, the Chairman shall, at the request of either party and after consulting both parties as far as possible, appoint the conciliator or conciliators not yet appointed.

Article 31

(1) Conciliators may be appointed from outside the Panel of Conciliators, except in the case of appointments by the Chairman pursuant to Article 30.

(2) Conciliators appointed from outside the Panel of Conciliators shall possess the qualities stated in paragraph (1) of Article 14.

Section 3: Conciliation Proceedings

1—325/85   Article 32

(1) The Commission shall be the judge of its own competence.

(2) Any objection by a party to the dispute that that dispute is not within the jurisdiction of the Centre, or for other reasons is not within the competence of the Commission, shall be considered by the Commission which shall determine whether to deal with it as a preliminary question or to join it to the merits of the dispute.

Article 33

Any conciliation proceeding shall be conducted in accordance with the provisions of this Section and, except as the parties otherwise agree, in accordance with the Conciliation Rules in effect on the date on which the parties consented to conciliation. If any question of procedure arises which is not covered by this Section or the Conciliation Rules or any rules agreed by the parties, the Commission shall decide the question.

Article 34

(1) It shall be the duty of the Commission to clarify the issues in dispute between the parties and to endeavour to bring about agreement between them upon mutually acceptable terms. To that end, the Commission may at any stage of the proceedings and from time to time recommend terms of settlement to the parties. The parties shall cooperate in good faith with the Commission in order to enable the Commission to carry out its functions, and shall give their most serious consideration to its recommendations.

(2) If the parties reach agreement, the Commission shall draw up a report noting the issues in dispute and recording that the parties have reached agreement. If, at any stage of the proceedings, it appears to the Commission that there is no likelihood of agreement between the parties, it shall close the proceedings and shall draw up a report noting the submission of the dispute and recording the failure of the parties to reach agreement. If one party fails to appear or participate in the proceedings, the Commission shall close the proceedings and shall draw up a report noting that partyîs failure to appear or participate.

Article 35

Except as the parties to the dispute shall otherwise agree, neither party to a conciliation proceeding shall be entitled in any other proceeding, whether before arbitrators or in a court of law or otherwise, to invoke or rely on any views expressed or statements or admissions or offers of settlement made by the other party in the conciliation proceedings, or the report or any recommendations made by the Commission.

Chapter IV: Arbitration

Section 1: Request for Arbitration

1—325/86   Article 36

(1) Any Contracting State or any national of a Contracting State wishing to institute arbitration proceedings shall address a request to that effect in writing to the Secretary-General who shall send a copy of the request to the other party.

(2) The request shall contain information concerning the issues in dispute, the identity of the parties and their consent to arbitration in accordance with the rules of procedure for the institution of conciliation and arbitration proceedings.

(3) The Secretary-General shall register the request unless he finds, on the basis of the information contained in the request, that the dispute is manifestly outside the jurisdiction of the Centre. He shall forthwith notify the parties of registration or refusal to register.

Section 2: Constitution of the Tribunal

1—325/87   Article 37

(1) The Arbitral Tribunal (hereinafter called the Tribunal) shall be constituted as soon as possible after registration of a request pursuant to Article 36.

(2) (a) The Tribunal shall consist of a sole arbitrator or any uneven number of arbitrators appointed as the parties shall agree.

  (b) Where the parties do not agree upon the number of arbitrators and the method of their appointment, the Tribunal shall consist of three arbitrators, one arbitrator appointed by each party and the third, who shall be the president of the Tribunal, appointed by agreement of the parties.

Article 38

If the Tribunal shall not have been constituted within 90 days after notice of registration of the request has been dispatched by the Secretary-General in accordance with paragraph (3) of Article 36, or such other period as the parties may agree, the Chairman shall, at the request of either party and after consulting both parties as far as possible, appoint the arbitrator or arbitrators not yet appointed. Arbitrators appointed by the Chairman pursuant to this Article shall not be nationals of the Contracting State party to the dispute or of the Contracting State whose national is a party to the dispute.

Article 39

The majority of the arbitrators shall be nationals of States other than the Contracting State party to the dispute and the Contracting State whose national is a party to the dispute; provided, however, that the foregoing provisions of this Article shall not apply if the sole arbitrator or each individual member of the Tribunal has been appointed by agreement of the parties.

Article 40

(1) Arbitrators may be appointed from outside the Panel of Arbitrators, except in the case of appointments by the Chairman pursuant to Article 38.

(2) Arbitrators appointed from outside the Panel of Arbitrators shall possess the qualities stated in paragraph (1) of Article 14.

Section 3: Powers and Functions of the Tribunal

1—325/87 Article 41

(1) The Tribunal shall be the judge of its own competence.

(2) Any objection by a party to the dispute that that dispute is not within the jurisdiction of the Centre, or for other reasons is not within the competence of the Tribunal, shall be considered by the Tribunal which shall determine whether to deal with it as a preliminary question or to join it to the merits of the dispute.

Article 42

(1) The Tribunal shall decide a dispute in accordance with such rules of law as may be agreed by the parties. In the absence

of such agreement, the Tribunal shall apply the law of the Contracting State party to the dispute (including its rules on the conflict of laws) and such rules of international law as may be applicable.

(2) The Tribunal may not bring in a finding of *non liquet* on the ground of silence or obscurity of the law.

(3) The provisions of paragraphs (1) and (2) shall not prejudice the power of the Tribunal to decide a dispute *ex aequo et bono* if the parties so agree.

Article 43

Except as the parties otherwise agree, the Tribunal may, if it deems it necessary at any stage of the proceedings,

(a) call upon the parties to produce documents or other evidence, and

(b) visit the scene connected with the dispute, and conduct such inquiries there as it may deem appropriate.

Article 44

Any arbitration proceeding shall be conducted in accordance with the provisions of this Section and, except as the parties otherwise agree, in accordance with the Arbitration Rules in effect on the date on which the parties consented to arbitration. If any question of procedure arises which is not covered by this Section or the Arbitration Rules or any rules agreed by the parties, the Tribunal shall decide the question.

Article 45

(1) Failure of a party to appear or to present his case shall not be deemed an admission of the other partyîs assertions.

(2) If a party fails to appear or to present his case at any stage of the proceedings the other party may request the Tribunal to deal with the questions submitted to it and to render an award. Before rendering an award, the Tribunal shall notify, and grant a period of grace to, the party failing to appear or to present its case, unless it is satisfied that that party does not intend to do so.

Article 46

Except as the parties otherwise agree, the Tribunal shall, if requested by a party, determine any incidental or additional claims or counter-claims arising directly out of the subject-matter of the dispute provided that they are within the scope of the consent of the parties and are otherwise within the jurisdiction of the Centre.

Article 47

Except as the parties otherwise agree, the Tribunal may, if it considers that the circumstances so require, recommend any provisional measures which should be taken to preserve the respective rights of either party.

Section 4: The Award

1—325/88   Article 48

(1) The Tribunal shall decide questions by a majority of the votes of all its members.

(2) The award of the Tribunal shall be in writing and shall be signed by the members of the Tribunal who voted for it.

(3) The award shall deal with every question submitted to the Tribunal, and shall state the reasons upon which it is based.

(4) Any member of the Tribunal may attach his individual opinion to the award, whether he dissents from the majority or not, or a statement of his dissent.

(5) The Centre shall not publish the award without the consent of the parties.

Article 49

(1) The Secretary-General shall promptly dispatch certified copies of the award to the parties. The award shall be deemed to have been rendered on the date on which the certified copies were dispatched.

(2) The Tribunal upon the request of a party made within 45 days after the date on which the award was rendered may after notice to the other party decide any question which it had omitted to decide in the award, and shall rectify any clerical, arithmetical or similar error in the award. Its decision shall become part of the award and shall be notified to the parties in the same manner as the award. The periods of time provided for under paragraph (2) of Article 51 and paragraph (2) of Article 52 shall run from the date on which the decision was rendered.

Section 5: Interpretation, Revision and Annulment of the Award

1—325/89   Article 50

(1) If any dispute shall arise between the parties as to the meaning or scope of an award, either party may request interpretation of the award by an application in writing addressed to the Secretary-General.

(2) The request shall, if possible, be submitted to the Tribunal which rendered the award. If this shall not be possible, a new Tribunal shall be constituted in accordance with Section 2 of this Chapter. The Tribunal may, if it considers that the circumstances so require, stay enforcement of the award pending its decision.

Article 51

(1) Either party may request revision of the award by an application in writing addressed to the Secretary-General on the ground of discovery of some fact of such a nature as decisively to affect the award, provided that when the award was rendered that fact was unknown to the Tribunal and to the applicant and that the applicant's ignorance of that fact was not due to negligence.

(2) The application shall be made within 90 days after the discovery of such fact and in any event within three years after the date on which the award was rendered.

(3) The request shall, if possible, be submitted to the Tribunal which rendered the award. If this shall not be possible, a new Tribunal shall be constituted in accordance with Section 2 of this Chapter.

(4) The Tribunal may, if it considers that the circumstances so require, stay enforcement of the award pending its decision. If the applicant requests a stay of enforcement of the award in his application, enforcement shall be stayed provisionally until the Tribunal rules on such request.

Article 52

(1) Either party may request annulment of the award by an application in writing addressed to the Secretary-General on one or more of the following grounds:

(a) that the Tribunal was not properly constituted;
(b) that the Tribunal has manifestly exceeded its powers;

(c) that there was corruption on the part of a member of the Tribunal;
(d) that there has been a serious departure from a fundamental rule of procedure; or
(e) that the award has failed to state the reasons on which it is based.

(2) The application shall be made within 120 days after the date on which the award was rendered except that when annulment is requested on the ground of corruption such application shall be made within 120 days after discovery of the corruption and in any event within three years after the date on which the award was rendered.

(3) On receipt of the request the Chairman shall forthwith appoint from the Panel of Arbitrators an *ad hoc* Committee of three persons. None of the members of the Committee shall have been a member of the Tribunal which rendered the award, shall be of the same nationality as any such member, shall be a national of the State party to the dispute or of the State whose national is a party to the dispute, shall have been designated to the Panel of Arbitrators by either of those States, or shall have acted as a conciliator in the same dispute. The Committee shall have the authority to annul the award or any part thereof on any of the grounds set forth in paragraph (1).

(4) The provisions of Articles 41–45, 48, 49, 53 and 54, and of Chapters VI and VII shall apply *mutatis mutandis* to proceedings before the Committee.

(5) The Committee may, if it considers that the circumstances so require, stay enforcement of the award pending its decision. If the applicant requests a stay of enforcement of the award in his application, enforcement shall be stayed provisionally until the Committee rules on such request.

(6) If the award is annulled the dispute shall, at the request of either party, be submitted to a new Tribunal constituted in accordance with Section 2 of this Chapter.

Section 6: Recognition and Enforcement of the Award

1—325/90   Article 53

(1) The award shall be binding on the parties and shall not be subject to any appeal or to any other remedy except those

provided for in this Convention. Each party shall abide by and comply with the terms of the award except to the extent that enforcement shall have been stayed pursuant to the relevant provisions of this Convention.

(2) For the purposes of this Section, "award" shall include any decision interpreting, revising or annulling such award pursuant to Articles 50, 51 or 52.

Article 54

(1) Each Contracting State shall recognize an award rendered pursuant to this Convention as binding and enforce the pecuniary obligations imposed by that award within its territories as if it were a final judgment of a court in that State. A Contracting State with a federal constitution may enforce such an award in or through its federal courts and may provide that such courts shall treat the award as if it were a final judgment of the courts of a constituent state.

(2) A party seeking recognition or enforcement in the territories of a Contracting State shall furnish to a competent court or other authority which such State shall have designated for this purpose a copy of the award certified by the Secretary-General. Each Contracting State shall notify the Secretary-General of the designation of the competent court or other authority for this purpose and of any subsequent change in such designation.

(3) Execution of the award shall be governed by the laws concerning the execution of judgments in force in the State in whose territories such execution is sought.

Article 55

Nothing in Article 54 shall be construed as derogating from the law in force in any Contracting State relating to immunity of that State or of any foreign State from execution.

CHAPTER V: REPLACEMENT AND DISQUALIFICATION OF CONCILIATORS AND ARBITRATORS

1—325/91   **Article 56**

(1) After a Commission or a Tribunal has been constituted and proceedings have begun, its composition shall remain

unchanged; provided, however, that if a conciliator or an arbitrator should die, become incapacitated, or resign, the resulting vacancy shall be filled in accordance with the provisions of Section 2 of Chapter III or Section 2 of Chapter IV.

(2) A member of a Commission or Tribunal shall continue to serve in that capacity notwithstanding that he shall have ceased to be a member of the Panel.

(3) If a conciliator or arbitrator appointed by a party shall have resigned without the consent of the Commission or Tribunal of which he was a member, the Chairman shall appoint a person from the appropriate Panel to fill the resulting vacancy.

Article 57

A party may propose to a Commission or Tribunal the disqualification of any of its members on account of any fact indicating a manifest lack of the qualities required by paragraph (1) of Article 14. A party to arbitration proceedings may, in addition, propose the disqualification of an arbitrator on the ground that he was ineligible for appointment to the Tribunal under Section 2 of Chapter IV.

Article 58

The decision on any proposal to disqualify a conciliator or arbitrator shall be taken by the other members of the Commission or Tribunal as the case may be, provided that where those members are equally divided, or in the case of a proposal to disqualify a sole conciliator or arbitrator, or a majority of the conciliators or arbitrators, the Chairman shall take that decision. If it is decided that the proposal is well-founded the conciliator or arbitrator to whom the decision relates shall be replaced in accordance with the provisions of Section 2 of Chapter III or Section 2 of Chapter IV.

CHAPTER VI: COST OF PROCEEDINGS

1—325/92   Article 59

The charges payable by the parties for the use of the facilities of the Centre shall be determined by the Secretary-General in accordance with the regulations adopted by the Administrative Council.

Article 60

(1) Each Commission and each Tribunal shall determine the fees and expenses of its members within limits established from time to time by the Administrative Council and after consultation with the Secretary-General.

(2) Nothing in paragraph (1) of this Article shall preclude the parties from agreeing in advance with the Commission or Tribunal concerned upon the fees and expenses of its members.

Article 61

(1) In the case of conciliation proceedings the fees and expenses of members of the Commission as well as the charges for the use of the facilities of the Centre, shall be borne equally by the parties. Each party shall bear any other expenses it incurs in connection with the proceedings.

(2) In the case of arbitration proceedings the Tribunal shall, except as the parties otherwise agree, assess the expenses incurred by the parties in connection with the proceedings, and shall decide how and by whom those expenses, the fees and expenses of the members of the Tribunal and the charges for the use of the facilities of the Centre shall be paid. Such decision shall form part of the award.

CHAPTER VII: PLACE OF PROCEEDINGS

1—325/93   **Article 62**

Conciliation and arbitration proceedings shall be held at the seat of the Centre except as hereinafter provided.

Article 63

Conciliation and arbitration proceedings may be held, if the parties so agree,

(a) at the seat of the Permanent Court of Arbitration or of any other appropriate institution, whether private or public, with which the Centre may make arrangements for that purpose; or

(b) at any other place approved by the Commission or Tribunal after consultation with the Secretary-General.

CHAPTER VIII: DISPUTES BETWEEN CONTRACTING STATES

1—325/94   Article 64

Any dispute arising between Contracting States concerning the interpretation or application of this Convention which is not settled by negotiation shall be referred to the International Court of Justice by the application of any party to such dispute, unless the States concerned agree to another method of settlement.

CHAPTER IX: AMENDMENT

1—325/95   Article 65

Any Contracting State may propose amendment of this Convention. The text of a proposed amendment shall be communicated to the Secretary-General not less than 90 days prior to the meeting of the Administrative Council at which such amendment is to be considered and shall forthwith be transmitted by him to all the members of the Administrative Council.

Article 66

(1) If the Administrative Council shall so decide by a majority of two-thirds of its members, the proposed amendment shall be circulated to all Contracting States for ratification, acceptance or approval. Each amendment shall enter into force 30 days after dispatch by the depositary of this Convention of a notification to Contracting States that all Contracting States have ratified, accepted or approved the amendment.

(2) No amendment shall affect the rights and obligations under this Convention of any Contracting State or of any of its constituent subdivisions or agencies, or of any national of such State arising out of consent to the jurisdiction of the Centre given before the date of entry into force of the amendment.

CHAPTER X: FINAL PROVISIONS

1—325/96   Article 67

This Convention shall be open for signature on behalf of States members of the Bank. It shall also be open for signature on behalf of any other State which is a party to the Statute of the International Court of Justice and which the Administrative Council, by a vote of two-thirds of its members, shall have invited to sign the Convention.

Article 68

(1) This Convention shall be subject to ratification, acceptance or approval by the signatory States in accordance with their respective constitutional procedures.

(2) This Convention shall enter into force 30 days after the date of deposit of the twentieth instrument of ratification, acceptance or approval. It shall enter into force for each State which subsequently deposits its instrument of ratification, acceptance or approval 30 days after the date of such deposit.

Article 69

Each Contracting State shall take such legislative or other measures as may be necessary for making the provisions of this Convention effective in its territories.

Article 70

This Convention shall apply to all territories for whose international relations a Contracting State is responsible, except those which are excluded by such State by written notice to the depositary of this Convention either at the time of ratification, acceptance or approval or subsequently.

Article 71

Any Contracting State may denounce this Convention by written notice to the depositary of this Convention. The denunciation shall take effect six months after receipt of such notice.

Article 72

Notice by a Contracting State pursuant to Articles 70 or 71 shall not affect the rights or obligations under this Convention of that State or of any of its constituent subdivisions or agencies or of any national of that State arising out of consent to the jurisdiction of the Centre given by one of them before such notice was received by the depositary.

Article 73

Instruments of ratification, acceptance or approval of this Convention and of amendments thereto shall be deposited with the Bank which shall act as the depositary of this Convention. The depositary shall transmit certified copies of this Convention to States members of the Bank and to any other State invited to sign the Convention.

Article 74

The depositary shall register this Convention with the Secretariat of the United Nations in accordance with Article 102 of the Charter of the United Nations and the Regulations thereunder adopted by the General Assembly.

Article 75

The depositary shall notify all signatory States of the following:

(a) signatures in accordance with Article 67;

(b) deposits of instruments of ratification, acceptance and approval in accordance with Article 73;

(c) the date on which this Convention enters into force in accordance with Article 68;

(d) exclusions from territorial application pursuant to Article 70;

(e) the date on which any amendment of this Convention enters into force in accordance with Article 66; and

(f) denunciations in accordance with Article 71.

DONE at Washington in the English, French and Spanish languages, all three texts being equally authentic, in a single copy which shall remain deposited in the archives of the International Bank for Reconstruction and Development, which has indicated by its signature below its agreement to fulfil the functions with which it is charged under this Convention.

1—325/97   Notes to the International Arbitration Act 1974

Note 1

The *International Arbitration Act 1974* as shown in this compilation comprises Act No. 136, 1974 amended as indicated in the Tables below.

Table of Acts

Act	Number and year	Date of Assent	Date of commencement	Application, saving or transitional provisions
Arbitration (Foreign Awards and Agreements) Act 1974	136, 1974	9 Dec 1974	Ss. 1–4: Royal Assent Remainder: 24 June 1975 (see *Gazette* 1975, No. G24, p. 2)	
Jurisdiction of Courts (Miscellaneous Amendments) Act 1979	19, 1979	28 Mar 1979	Parts II–XVII (ss. 3–123): 15 May 1979 (see *Gazette* 1979, No. S86) Remainder: Royal Assent	S. 124
Statute Law (Miscellaneous Provisions) Act 1987	141, 1987	18 Dec 1987	S. 3: Royal Assent (a)	S. 5(1)
International Arbitration Amendment Act 1989	25, 1989	15 May 1989	12 June 1989	—
ICSID Implementation Act 1990	107, 1990	18 Dec 1990	Parts 2 and 3 (ss. 3–8): 1 June 1991 (see s. 2(2) and *Gazette* 1991, No. S98) Remainder: Royal Assent	—
Carriage of Goods by Sea Act 1991	160, 1991	31 Oct 1991	S. 21: Royal Assent (b)	—

(a) The *International Arbitration Act 1974* was amended by section 3 only of the *Statute Law (Miscellaneous Provisions) Act 1987*, subsection 2(1) of which provides as follows:

   (1) Subject to this section, this Act shall come into operation on the day on which it receives the Royal Assent.

(b) The *International Arbitration Act 1974* was amended by section 21 only of the *Carriage of Goods by Sea Act 1991*, subsection 2(1) of which provides as follows:

   (1) Subject to subsection (2), this Act commences on the day on which it receives the Royal Assent.

1—325/98   Table of Amendments

ad. = added or inserted   am. = amended   rep. = repealed   rs. = repealed and substituted

Provision affected	How affected
Title	rs. No. 25, 1989
Heading to Part I	ad. No. 25, 1989
S. 1	am. No. 25, 1989
Ss. 2A, 2B	ad. No. 25, 1989
S. 2C	ad. No. 25, 1989
	rs. No. 160, 1991
Heading to Part II	ad. No. 25, 1989
S. 3	am. No. 25, 1989
Ss. 5, 6	rep. No. 25, 1989
S. 7	am. No. 25, 1989
S. 8	am. No. 19, 1979; No. 25, 1989
Ss. 9, 10	am. No. 25, 1989
S. 10A	ad. No. 141, 1987
S. 11	rep. No. 25, 1989
Ss. 12–14	am. No. 25, 1989
Part III (ss. 15–30)	ad. No. 25, 1989
Ss. 15–30	ad. No. 25, 1989
Part IV (ss. 31–38)	ad. No. 107, 1990
Ss. 31–38	ad. No. 107, 1990
Heading to Schedule	rep. No. 25, 1989
Heading to Schedule 1	ad. No. 25, 1989
Schedule 2	ad. No. 25, 1989
Schedule 3	ad. No. 107, 1990

China

Arbitration Law, 1994

(Adopted at the Ninth Meeting of the Standing Committee of the Eighth National Peoples Congress on August 31, 1994)

Chapter I: General Principles

1—326   Article 1

This law is formulated with a view to ensuring fair and timely arbitration of disputes over economic matters, safeguarding the legitimate rights and interests of the litigants and guaranteeing the sound development of the socialist market economy.

1—327   Article 2

Disputes over contracts or other disputes involving property between civil subjects with equal status, that is, between citizens, legal persons, and other organizations, are subject to arbitration.

1—328   Article 3

Disputes over the following matters are not subject to arbitration:

(1) disputes over marriage, adoption, custody, support and inheritance;

(2) administrative disputes that by law should be handled by administrative organs.

1—329   Article 4

Where the litigants choose to settle their dispute through arbitration, they should reach an arbitration agreement of their own accord. When, in the absence of an arbitration agreement, a litigant applies for arbitration, the arbitration commission shall not accept it.

1—330   Article 5

Where the litigants have an arbitration agreement and one litigant brings a suit in the people's court, the people's court shall not accept it. However, exception is to be made when the arbitration agreement is invalid.

1—331   Article 6

The arbitration commission shall be chosen by the litigants by agreement. Arbitration is not subject to jurisdiction by level or territorial jurisdiction.

1—332   Article 7

Arbitration shall be carried out on the basis of act and in accordance with law to settle disputes in a fair and rational manner.

1—333   Article 8

Arbitration shall be done independently, free of interference and from administrative organs, mass organizations or individuals.

1—334   Article 9

The system of one ruling only is practised in arbitration. Where, after a ruling is made, a litigant files another application for arbitration or brings a lawsuit in the people's court over the same dispute, the arbitration commission or the people's court shall not accept it.

Where a court repeals a ruling or orders it not to be executed in accordance with law, the litigants may refile an application for arbitration of the dispute pursuant with a new arbitration agreement reached between the parties or bring a suit in the people's court.

CHAPTER II: THE ARBITRATION COMMISSION AND ARBITRATION ASSOCIATION

1—335   Article 10

The arbitration commission may be set up in municipalities directly under the central government or in cities where the provincial or autonomous regional people's government is seated. It may also be set up in other cities that are divided into districts. It is not to be set up at all levels of administrative divisions.

The people's government in the cities specified in the preceding paragraph shall organize relevant departments and the chambers of commerce to form the arbitration commission in a unified way. When an arbitration commission is set up, it shall register with the judicial and administrative departments of the province, autonomous region or municipalities directly under the central government.

1—336   Article 11

The arbitration commission shall have the following qualifications:

(1) its own name, domicile and articles of association;

(2) the required property;

(3) members that make up the commission; and

(4) arbitration officers retained by it.

The articles of association of the arbitration commission shall be formulated pursuant to this law.

1—337   Article 12

The arbitration commission shall consist of one director, two to four deputy directors and seven to 11 commission members.

The director, deputy directors, and members of the arbitration commission shall be held by legal, economic or trade experts and persons with working experience. Legal, economic or trade experts shall make up at least two- thirds of the arbitration commission.

1—338   Article 13

The arbitration commission shall appoint fair-minded and respectable persons as arbitration officers.

Arbitration officers shall have one of the following qualifications:

(1) have eight years of arbitration experience;

(2) have worked as a lawyer for eight years;

(3) have served as a judge for eight years;

(4) have studied law or engaged in educational work and have a senior professional title; or

(5) have legal knowledge, worked in the fields of economics or trade, and have a senior professional title or equivalent professional expertise.

The arbitration commission shall compile the panel of arbitrators by their specialities.

1—339   Article 14

Arbitration commissions are independent from administrative organs; they are not subordinate to administrative organs. There is no affiliation among arbitration commissions themselves.

1—340   Article 15

The China Arbitration Association is a social organization as a legal person. The arbitration commissions are members of the China Arbitration Association. The articles of association of the China Arbitration Association shall be formulated by its national membership meeting.

The China Arbitration Association is an organization for enforcing self-discipline among the arbitration commissions that, pursuant to its articles of association, oversees violations of discipline by the arbitration commissions and their members and the administration officers.

The China Arbitration Association shall formulate arbitration rules in accordance with the relevant provisions of this law and the Law of Civil Procedure.

CHAPTER III: ARBITRATION AGREEMENT

1—341   Article 16

An arbitration agreement refers to an arbitration clause provided in the contract or other written agreements requesting arbitration concluded prior or subsequent to the occurrence of disputes.

An arbitration agreement shall have the following contents:

(1) an expressed intent to request arbitration;

(2) items for arbitration; and

(3) the chosen arbitration commission

1—342   Article 17

An arbitration agreement shall be invalid in any of the following circumstances:

(1) the items for arbitration agreed upon are beyond the scope of arbitration as prescribed by law;

(2) a party to the arbitration agreement is a person having no capacity or with limited capacity for civil conduct; or

(3) the arbitration agreement is imposed by one party on the other party by means of coercion.

1—343   Article 18

Where an arbitration agreement does not specify or clearly specify the items for arbitration or an arbitration commission, the litigants may reach a supplementary agreement. Where they fail to reach a supplementary agreement, the arbitration agreement shall be deemed invalid.

1—344   Article 19

An arbitration agreement stands on its own. Modification, rescission, termination of the contract or its being declared invalid does not affect the arbitration agreement's validity.

The arbitration tribunal has the power to confirm the validity of the contract.

1—345   Article 20

Where a litigant takes exception to the validity of the arbitration agreement, he may request that the arbitration commission make a decision or that the people's court make a judgment.

Where one litigant requests that the arbitration commission make a decision while the other litigant requests that the people's court make a judgment, the people's court shall make a judgment.

Where a litigant takes exception to the validity of the arbitration agreement, he shall raise a challenge before the arbitration tribunal starts the first hearing of the case.

CHAPTER IV: ARBITRATION PROCEDURE

Section 1: Application and Acceptance

1—346   Article 21

The litigants requesting arbitration shall meet the following requirements:

(1) there shall be an arbitration agreement;

(2) there shall be a specific appeal request, facts and reasons for the appeal; and

(3) the case shall be within the jurisdictional power of the arbitration commission.

1—347   Article 22

The litigants shall submit to the arbitration commission the arbitration agreement and application for arbitration and copies.

1—348   Article 23

The application for arbitration shall carry the following items:

(1) the names, sex, age, profession, work units and addresses of the litigants; the names and addresses of the legal person or other organization concerned; and the names and professions of the legal representative and other principal persons in charge.

(2) arbitration requested and the facts and reasons on which the request is based; and

(3) evidence and its sources; the names and addresses of witnesses.

1—349   Article 24

When the arbitration commission has received the application, it shall accept it and so notify the litigants within five days if it deems the application meets the requirements; with respect to cases that do not meet the requirements, it shall notify the litigants in writing that the cases may not be accepted and heard along with an explanation.

1—350   Article 25

After accepting the arbitration application, the arbitration commission shall, within the period prescribed in the arbitration rules, deliver the arbitration rules and the names of the arbitration panel to the applicant; and it shall also deliver a copy of the application as well as the rules and the panel to the adverse litigant.

After receiving the copy of the arbitration application, the adverse litigant shall furnish a defense to the arbitration commission within the period prescribed in the arbitration rules. After receiving the defense, the arbitration commission shall, within the period prescribed in the arbitration rules, deliver a copy of the defense to the applicant. The absence of a defense on the part of the adverse litigant does not affect the arbitration process.

1—351   Article 26

Where an arbitration agreement has already been reached and one litigant has filed a suit with the people's court but failed to state the agreement, the people's court shall reject the case it has accepted when the other litigant had submitted the arbitration agreement prior to the opening of the first court session, except when the arbitration agreement is invalid. Failure of the adverse litigant to express objection before the first court session is considered to be a waiving of the agreement and the people's court shall proceed in examining the case.

1—352 Article 27

The applicant may renounce or change the arbitration request. The adverse litigant may acknowledge or rebut the arbitration request and has the right to submit a counter-request.

1—353 Article 28

Either litigant may request protection of his property when he believes the arbitration cannot be carried out or will be carried out with difficulty owing to the other litigant's conduct or other causes.

When one litigant requests protection of his property, the arbitration commission shall submit the request to the people's court in accordance with the relevant regulations in the Law of Civil Procedure.

When the application is faulty, the applicant shall compensate the adverse litigant for the losses incurred from the protection of property.

1—354 Article 29

Either litigant or his legal representative may request a lawyer or an agent to represent him at the arbitration. When he does so, he shall submit a power of attorney to the arbitration commission.

Section 2: The Formation of an Arbitration Tribunal

1—355 Article 30

An arbitration tribunal may be composed of three arbitrators or only one. A tribunal which is composed of three arbitrators shall have a president arbitration officer.

1—356 Article 31

Where the litigants agree that an arbitration tribunal be composed of three arbitrators, each of them shall elect his own arbitrator, or request the arbitration commission director to designate an arbitrator for him. The third arbitrator shall be selected by the litigants, or by the arbitration commission director at their request. The third arbitrator shall serve as the presiding arbitration officer.

1—357   Article 32

In the event the litigants fail to reach an agreement on the form of an arbitration tribunal, or fail to select their arbitrators within the period prescribed in the arbitration rules, the arbitration commission director shall make the decision for them.

1—358   Article 33

After an arbitration tribunal has been formed, the arbitration commission shall notify the litigants, in writing, about the formation or the tribunal.

1—359   Article 34

An arbitrator shall withdraw from serving in the tribunal when his case is one of the following, and the litigants also have the right to present a withdrawal request:

> (1) where he is one of the litigants in the arbitration, or he is a close relative of any one litigant, or a relative of the attorney;
>
> (2) where he has a vital interest in the arbitration;
>
> (3) where he is related to the litigants, or their attorneys, in other respects in the case and the relationship may affect an impartial arbitration; or
>
> (4) where he has had private meetings with the litigants or with their attorneys, or when he has accepted the invitation of the litigants or their attorneys, to dine, or accepted their gifts.

1—360   Article 35

Where one litigant submits a withdrawal request, he shall state the reasons, and the reasons shall be submitted prior to the opening of the first court session. When a cause of the withdrawal is not known until the first court session has been held, the cause may be submitted prior the closure of the last court session.

1—361   Article 36

The arbitration commission director shall decide whether an arbitrator should withdraw; when the arbitration commission director serves as an arbitrator, other members or the arbitration commission shall make the decision collectively.

1—362   Article 37

When an arbitrator cannot perform his duties owing to withdrawal or other causes, a new arbitrator shall be elected or designated to take his place in accordance with this law.

After a new arbitrator has been elected or designated as a result of the withdrawal of another arbitrator, the litigants may request that the ongoing arbitration process be started anew, and the arbitration process tribunal shall decide whether or not to approve the request. The arbitration tribunal may also decide on its own whether the ongoing arbitration process should be started anew.

1—363   Article 38

Where an arbitrator has situation (4) under Article 34, and the case is serious, or where an arbitrator has situation (6) under Article 58, he shall be liable for legal responsibilities according to the law and the arbitration commission shall remove his name from the panel.

Section 3: Hearing and Ruling

1—364   Article 39

The arbitration shall be held as a tribunal. Where the litigants agree to have an open session, arbitrations may be held openly, except for cases, which involve state secrets.

1—365   Article 40

Arbitrations do not proceed openly. Where the litigants agree to have an open session, arbitrations may be held openly, except for cases which involve state secrets.

1—366   Article 41

The arbitration commission shall notify both litigants of the date of the tribunal session within the period prescribed in the arbitration rules. Within the period prescribed in the arbitration rules, litigants may request a postponement of the session if any of them has a legitimate reason. The arbitration tribunal shall decide whether the session should be postponed.

1—367   Article 42

The applicant shall be considered to have withdrawn his arbitration request if he, after being notified, fails to attend the tribunal session without a legitimate reason, or if he leaves the tribunal during the session without the tribunal's approval.

If the adverse litigant, after being notified, fails to attend the tribunal session without a legitimate reason; or if he leaves the tribunal session without the arbitration tribunal's approval, a ruling can be made by default.

1—368   Article 43

Litigants shall provide evidence to support their respective stands.

The arbitration tribunal may collect on its own account evidence it deems essential.

1—369   Article 44

When the arbitration tribunal maintains that a certain specialized issue must be appraised, it may also designate an appraising department to have the appraisal made.

In accordance with the request submitted by the litigants or the arbitration tribunal, the appraisal department shall send a appraiser to attend the tribunal session. With the tribunal's approval, the litigants may question the appraiser.

1—370   Article 45

The evidence shall be exhibited at the tribunal session. Litigants may cross- examine one another.

1—371   Article 46

If the evidence is perishable or if the evidence may be hard to obtain in the future, the litigants may request that the evidence be preserved. Where the litigants request preservation of the evidence, the arbitration commission shall submit the request to the grass-roots people's court of the location where the evidence is obtained.

1—372   Article 47

Either litigant has the right to debate during the arbitration process. When the debate ends, the presiding arbitration officer, or an arbitrator acting alone, shall solicit the litigants' final views.

1—373   Article 48

The arbitration tribunal shall record the session in writing. The litigants, or other arbitration participants, have the right to request corrections when they think the records of their statements are incomplete or faulty. If corrections are denied, their requests shall be stated in the record.

The written records shall be signed, or sealed, by the arbitrators, the recorders, the litigants and other arbitration participants.

1—374   Article 49

The litigants may reach a settlement by themselves after they have requested arbitration. If a settlement agreement has been reached, the litigants may request that the arbitration tribunal make a written ruling on the basis of the settlement, and they may also retract their arbitration request.

1—375   Article 50

If any litigant wants to retract the withdrawal request after a settlement agreement has been reached, they may request arbitration in accordance with the arbitration agreement.

1—376   Article 51

The arbitration tribunal may carry out mediation prior to making a ruling. The arbitration tribunal shall mediate when the litigants agree to mediation. If the mediation fails, a ruling should be made promptly.

If an agreement has been reached through mediation, the arbitration tribunal shall draw up a written mediation, which has the same legal effect a ruling letter.

1—377   Article 52

The written mediation shall state the arbitration request and the litigants' agreement. The written mediation, after it has been signed by the arbitrators and sealed by the arbitration commission, shall be delivered to the litigants.

The written mediation becomes legally valid after it has been signed and accepted by the litigants.

If one litigant backs out prior to the signing of the written mediation, the arbitration tribunal shall make a ruling promptly.

1—378   Article 53

The ruling shall be made on the basis of the views expressed by the majority of arbitrators. The different views of the minority of arbitrators may be stated in the record. When the arbitration tribunal fails to come up with a majority view, a ruling shall be made according to the view of the presiding arbitration officer.

1—379 Article 54

The written arbitration shall state the arbitration request, facts of the dispute, the reasons for the ruling, the result of the ruling, the arbitration expenses that have to be borne and the date of the arbitration. The written arbitration may omit the facts of dispute and the reasons for the ruling if the litigants so desire. The written mediation shall be signed by the arbitrators and sealed by the arbitration commission. The signatures of the arbitrators who hold different views are optional.

1—380 Article 55

When arbitrating a dispute, the arbitration tribunal may make a ruling on the part of dispute for which facts have been ascertained.

1—381 Article 56

The arbitration tribunal shall correct any terminological or calculation error in the written arbitration, or any ruling decision left out in the written arbitration. The litigants may request that the arbitration tribunal make corrections within 30 days after receiving the written ruling.

1—382 Article 57

The legal effects of the ruling letter begin on the day it is written.

CHAPTER V: REQUEST TO REPEAL A RULING

1—383 Article 58

If one litigant produces evidence to prove a ruling has one of the following, he may request that the intermediate people's court of the place where the arbitration commission is located repeal the ruling:

   (1) where there is no arbitration agreement;

   (2) where the dispute to be arbitrated is not within the scope of the arbitration agreement, or one which the arbitration commission has no authority to arbitrate;

   (3) where the formation of the arbitration tribunal or the arbitration process has violated legal procedure;

   (4) where the evidence on which the arbitration is based is counterfeited;

(5) where one litigant has concealed evidence that could affect an impartial ruling; or

(6) where arbitrators have solicited or accepted bribes, practised favouritism and bent the law while arbitrating a case or making a ruling.

The people's court shall repeal the ruling if a collegial panel formed by the people's court has examined the arbitration and ascertained that it has one of the situations mentioned above.

1—384   Article 59

When one party requests a repeal of the ruling, he shall do so within six months after receiving the ruling letter.

1—385   Article 60

The people's court shall decide whether to approve or reject the request to repeal the ruling within two months after accepting the request.

1—386   Article 61

After accepting the request to repeal the ruling, if the people's court maintains that the arbitration tribunal still should arbitrate the dispute, it shall notify the arbitration tribunal to rearbitrate the dispute within a specified period and it shall also rule to terminate the repeal procedure. If the arbitration tribunal refuses to rearbitrate the dispute, the people's court shall rule that the repeal procedure be reinstated.

CHAPTER VI: EXECUTION

1—387   Article 62

Litigants shall abide by the ruling. When one litigant fails to abide by the ruling, the other litigant may, in accordance with provisions in the Law of Civil Procedure, request the people's court execute the ruling, and the people's court that accepts the request shall execute the ruling.

1—388   Article 63

When the adverse litigant produces evidence proving that the ruling is one the situations stated in Section 2 of Article 217 of the Law of Civil Procedure, and the evidence has been ascertained by the collegial panel formed by the people's court, the ruling shall not be executed.

1—389   Article 64

When one litigant requests that the ruling be executed and the other litigant requests that the ruling be repealed, the people's court shall rule that the execution be terminated.

When the people's court judges that a ruling be repealed, the execution of the ruling shall be terminated. When the request to repeal the ruling has been rejected, the people's court shall judge that the ruling be executed again.

Chapter VII: Special Provisions for Arbitrations Involving Foreign Concerns

1—390   Article 65

Provisions in this chapter are applicable in the arbitration of economic, trade, transport and maritime disputes which involve foreign concerns. Other relevant provisions in this law shall be applied where there is no applicable provision in this chapter.

1—391   Article 66

A commission for arbitrations involving foreign concerns may be set up in the China International Chamber of Commerce.

This arbitration commission may be composed of one director, several deputy directors and several members.

The director, deputy directors and members may be hired by the China International Chamber of Commerce.

1—392   Article 67

This arbitration commission may hire its arbitrators from among foreign nationals who are specialized in laws, economic affairs and trade, and science and technology.

1—393   Article 68

When a litigant requests preservation of evidence in an arbitration which involves foreign concerns, the commission for arbitration involving foreign concerns shall refer the litigant's request to the intermediate people's court in the place where the evidence is located.

1—394   Article 69

The arbitration tribunal which handles arbitrations involving foreign concerns may record the proceedings of the tribunal session, or the main points of the session. The record of the main points shall be signed or sealed by the litigants and other arbitration participants.

1—395   Article 70

When one litigant produces evidence proving the ruling made by the commission for arbitration involving foreign concerns falls within one of the situations prescribed in Section 1 of Article 260 of the Law of Civil Procedure, the people's court shall repeal and the ruling after the evidence has been ascertained by the collegial panel organized by the people's court.

1—396   Article 71

When the adverse litigant produces evidence proving that a foreign affairs arbitration ruling falls within one of the situations stated in Section 1 of Article 260 of the Law of Civil Procedure, the people's court shall judge that the ruling not be executed after it has been examined and ascertained by a collegial panel organized by the court.

1—397   Article 72

If one litigant requests execution of the legally effective ruling made by the commission for arbitration involving foreign concerns, and the adverse litigant's property is not within the PRC, the litigant shall directly request acknowledgement and enforcement from the foreign court which has the jurisdiction over the property.

1—398   Article 73

The China International Chamber of Commerce may draw up the regulations for arbitrations involving foreign concerns on the basis of this law and the Law of Civil Procedure.

Chapter VIII: Supplementary Articles

1—399   Article 74

Where the law has provisions governing the validity period of an arbitration, the provisions shall be applied. If the law has no such provisions, the provisions for the validity period of lawsuits shall be used.

1—400   Article 75

Before the China Arbitration Association draws up the arbitration regulations, the arbitration commission shall draw up interim arbitration regulations on the basis of this law and the Law of Civil Procedure.

1—401   Article 76

Litigants shall pay arbitration fees according to regulations.
  Measures for collecting arbitration fees shall be reported to the price control authorities for approval.

1—402   Article 77

Separate regulations shall be drawn up for arbitration of labour disputes and disputes over agricultural contracts drawn up by collective agricultural economic organizations.

1—403   Article 78

When arbitration-related provisions drawn up before the implementation of this law contravene the provisions in this law, this law shall prevail.

1—404   Article 79

Arbitration institutions established by cities and other cities divided into districts—where the seats of people's governments of municipalities under the central government's direct jurisdiction, provinces and autonomous regions are located—prior to the implementation of this law shall be reorganized according to this law; and the operation of those which are not reorganized shall be terminated one year from the day this law goes into effect.
  The operation of other arbitration institutions which are established before this law goes into effect and which are not in line with this law shall be terminated when this law goes into effect.

1—405   Article 80

This law goes into effect on September 1, 1995.

Egypt

Law No. 27 for 1994 promulgating the Law concerning Arbitration in Civil and Commercial Matters[1]

1—406   In the Name of the People,
The President of the Republic,
The People's Assembly has adopted the following law and we have promulgated it.

1—407   Article (1)

The provisions of the annexed Law shall apply to any arbitration pending at the time of its entry into force or which commences thereafter, even if it is based on an arbitral agreement concluded before the entry into force of this Law.

1—408   Article (2)

The Minister of Justice shall issue the Decrees required for the execution of this Law, and shall establish the lists of arbitrators from which selections could be made pursuant to the provisions of Article (17) thereof.

1—409   Article (3)

Articles from 501 to 513 of Law No. 13/1968 promulgating the Code of Civil and Commercial Procedures are hereby repealed, as well as any provision contrary to the provisions of this Law.

1—410   Article (4)

This Law shall be stamped in the Official Gazette and shall enter into force one month from the day following the date of its publication.[2]

This Law shall be stamped with the Seal of State and enforced as one of its Laws.

Issued at the Presidency on 18 April, 1994.

Hosni Mubarak, President of the Republic

Law Concerning Arbitration in Civil and Commercial Matters

PART I—GENERAL PROVISIONS

1—411   Article (1)

Without prejudice to the provisions of international conventions applicable in the Arab Republic of Egypt, the provisions of the present Law shall apply to all arbitrations between public law or private law persons, whatever the nature of the legal relationship around which the dispute revolves, when such an arbitration is conducted in Egypt or when an international commercial arbitration is conducted abroad and its parties agree to submit it to the provisions of this Law.

1—412   Article (2)

An arbitration is commercial within the scope of this Law when the dispute arises over a legal relationship of an economic nature, whether contractual or non-contractual. This comprises for example the supply of commodities or services, commercial agencies, construction and engineering or technical know-how contracts, the granting of industrial, touristic and other licenses, technology transfer, investment and development contracts, banking, insurance and transport operations, and operations relating to the exploration and extraction of natural wealth, energy supply, laying of gas or oil pipelines, building of roads and tunnels, reclamation of agricultural land, protection of the environment and establishment of nuclear reactors.

1—413   Article (3)

Within the context of this Law, the arbitration is international whenever its subject matter is a dispute related to international commerce in any of the following cases:

First: If the principal places of business of the two parties to the arbitration are situated in two different States at the time of the conclusion of the arbitration agreement. If either party to the arbitration has more than one place of business, due consideration shall be given to the place of business which has the closest relationship with the arbitration agreement. If either party to the arbitration does not have a business establishment, then the place of its habitual residence shall be relied upon.

Second: If the parties to the arbitration have agreed to resort to a permanent arbitral organization or to an arbitration center having its headquarters in the Arab Republic of Egypt or abroad.

Third: If the subject matter of the dispute falling within the scope of the arbitral agreement is linked to more than one State.

Fourth: If the principal places of business of the two parties to the arbitration are situated in the same State at the time of the conclusion of the arbitration agreement, but one of the following places is located outside said State:

> (a) the place of arbitration as determined in the arbitration agreement or pursuant to the methods provided therein for determining it;
>
> (b) the place where a substantial part of the obligations emerging from the commercial relationship between the parties shall be performed;
>
> (c) the place with which the subject matter of the dispute is most closely linked.

1—414 Article (4)

> 1. For the purpose of the present Law, the term "arbitration" relates to the voluntary arbitration agreed upon by the two parties to the dispute according to their own free will, whether or not the chosen body to which the arbitral mission is entrusted by agreement of the two parties is a permanent arbitral organization or center.
>
> 2. The term "arbitral panel" denotes the panel composed of one or more arbitrators for the purpose of adjudicating the dispute referred to arbitration. As to the term, "court", it means the court belonging to the judicial system of the State.
>
> 3. The expression "the two parties to the arbitration" when used in this Law shall denote the parties to the arbitration, whatever their number may be.

1—415 Article (5)

In the cases where this Law permits the two parties to the arbitration to select the procedures which must be followed in a given matter, this also includes their right to allow third parties to make such selection.

In this respect, any arbitration organization or center in the Arab Republic of Egypt or abroad shall be deemed a third party.

1—416 Article (6)

Whenever the parties to the arbitration agree to subject the legal relationship between them to the provisions of a standard contract, or international convention or any other document, then the provisions of such document must apply, including the provisions related to arbitration provided for therein.

C. Foreign Statutes: Non-European Jurisdictions 231

1—417 Article (7)

1. Unless otherwise provided in a special agreement between the two parties to the arbitration, any letter or written communication shall be delivered to the addressee personally or at his place of business, his habitual residence or mailing address, known to both parties, defined in the arbitration agreement or in the document which contains the relationship subject to the arbitration.

2. In case that none of these addresses can be identified after making the required inquiries, communication to the addresses is deemed to have been received if it is sent in the form of a registered letter to the addressee's last known place of business, habitual residence or mailing address.

3. The provisions of this article shall not apply to communications concerning judicial procedures before the courts.

1—418 Article (8)

If either party to a dispute proceeds with the arbitration proceedings in spite of its knowledge that there has been a violation which occurred regarding a certain requirement under the arbitration agreement or a non-compliance with a non-mandatory provision of the present Law, and if the party does not state its objection to such violation or non-compliance within the period agreed upon and does not raise an objection or within a reasonable period in the absence of agreement, such inaction shall be deemed to constitute a waiver of the party's right to object.

1—419 Article (9)

1. Competence to review the arbitral matters referred to by the present Law to the Egyptian judiciary lies within the court having original jurisdiction over the dispute. However, in the case of international commercial arbitration, whether conducted in Egypt or abroad, competence lies within the Cairo Court of Appeal unless the parties agree on the competence of another appellate court in Egypt.

2. The court having competence in accordance with the preceding paragraph shall continue to exercise exclusive jurisdiction until completion of all arbitration procedures.

Part II—The Arbitration Agreement

1—420   Article (10)

1. The arbitration agreement is the agreement by which the two parties agree to submit to arbitration in order to resolve all or part of the disputes which arose or which may arise between them in connection with a defined legal relationship, contractual or non-contractual.

2. The arbitration agreement may be concluded before the dispute has arisen either in the form of a separate agreement or as a clause in a given Contract concerning all or part of the disputes which may arise between the two parties. In the latter case, the subject matter of the dispute has to be determined in the Request for Arbitration referred to in para (1) of article 30 hereof. The arbitration agreement may also be concluded after the dispute has arisen, even if an action has already been brought before a judicial court, and in such case, the agreement must indicate the issues subject to arbitration, otherwise it will be null and void.

3. Any reference in the Contract to a document containing an arbitral clause shall be considered an arbitration agreement, provided that such reference clearly considers such clause an integral part of the Contract.

1—421   Article (11)

Arbitration agreements may only be concluded by natural or juridical persons having the capacity to dispose of their rights.

Arbitration is not permitted in matters which can not be subject to compromise.

1—422   Article (12)

The arbitration agreement must be in writing, otherwise it shall be null and void.

An agreement is in writing if it is contained in a document signed by both parties or contained in an exchange of letters, telegrams or other means of written communication.

1—423   Article (13)

1. The court before which an action is brought concerning a disputed matter which is subject to an arbitration agreement

shall hold this action inadmissible provided that the defendant raises this objection before submitting any demand or defence on the merits of the case.

2. The fact that the judicial action referred to in the preceding paragraph is brought shall not prevent the arbitral proceedings from being commenced or continued, or the making of the arbitral award.

1—424 Article (14)

Upon request of either party to the arbitration, the court referred to in Article (9) may order the taking of an interim or conservatory measure, whether before the commencement of the arbitral proceedings or during said proceedings.

PART III—THE ARBITRAL PANEL

1—425 Article (15)

1. The arbitral panel consists, by agreement between the parties, of one or more arbitrators. In the absence of such agreement on the number of arbitrators, the number shall be three.

2. If there is more than one arbitrator, the panel must consist of an odd number, otherwise the arbitration shall be null and void.

1—426 Article (16)

1. The arbitrator cannot be a minor, under guardianship, have been deprived of his civil rights by reason of judgment against him for a felony or misdemeanor contrary to honesty or due to a declaration of his bankruptcy; unless he has been restored to his status.

2. The arbitrator is not required to be of a given gender or nationality, unless otherwise agreed upon between the two parties or provided for by Law.

3. The arbitrator's acceptance of his mission shall be in writing. When accepting, he must disclose any circumstances which cast doubts on his independence or impartiality.

1—427 Article (17)

1. The two parties to the arbitration may agree on the choice of the arbitrators, and on the method and period of time for effecting their choice. In the absence of such agreement, the following steps shall be followed:

    (a) In case the arbitral panel consists of a sole arbitrator, the court referred to in Article (9) of the present Law shall undertake the appointment of the arbitrator upon request from either party.

    (b) In case the arbitral panel consists of three arbitrators, each party shall select one arbitrator and the two arbitrators shall then choose the third. If either party fails to appoint his arbitrator within thirty days from the date of receiving a request to that effect from the other party, or if the two appointed arbitrators fail to agree on the third arbitrator within the thirty days following the date of the latest appointment between the two, the court referred to in Article (9) of the present Law shall undertake the appointment upon request of either party. The arbitrator chosen by the two arbitrators or appointed by the court shall chair the arbitral panel. The above provisions shall apply to the case when the arbitral panel consists of more than three arbitrators.

2. If either party violates the agreed procedures for the choice of arbitrators, or if the two appointed arbitrators fail to agree on a matter on which their agreement is required, or if a third party does not perform an act entrusted to him in this regard, then the court referred to in Article (9) of the present Law shall carry out the required procedure or the act needed upon the request of either party, unless the agreement provides for another method of accomplishing such procedure or act.

3. In the choice of the arbitrator, the court shall observe the conditions required by the present Law and those agreed upon by the parties, and shall render its decision on said choice expeditiously. Without prejudice to the provisions of Articles (18) and (19) of the present Law, such decision can not be subject to any possible recourse.

1—428 Article (18)

1. An arbitrator may not be challenged except if circumstances emerge that give rise to serious doubts on his impartiality or independence.

2. Neither party to the arbitration may challenge the arbitrator appointed by it or in whose appointment it has participated, except for some reason that became known only after making such appointment.

1—429 Article (19)

1. The challenge request shall be submitted in writing to the arbitral panel, indicating the reasons or the challenge, within fifteen days following the date when the challenging party became aware of the Panel's constitution or of the circumstances which justify the challenge. If the challenged arbitrator does not step down, the arbitral panel shall decide on the request.

2. A challenge request shall not be accepted from a party who had previously submitted a request challenging the same arbitrator in the same arbitration.

3. The challenging party may lodge a recourse against the decision refusing his request, within thirty days of receiving notice thereof, before the court referred to in Article (9) of the present Law, and the court's judgment shall not be subject to any possible recourse.

4. Neither the submission of the challenging request nor the recourse against the decision of the arbitral panel rejecting such request shall entail the suspension of the arbitral proceedings. However, if the arbitrator is recused, whether by a decision of the arbitral panel or by the court reviewing the challenge, this shall entail considering null and void the arbitral proceedings already conducted, including the arbitral award.

1—430 Article (20)

If the arbitrator is unable to perform his mission, fails to perform his task or interrupts the performance thereof in a manner which causes undue delay in the arbitral proceedings, and if he does not withdraw and the parties have not agreed to revoke him, then the court referred to in Article (9) of the present Law may order the termination of his mission upon request of either party

1—431 Article (21)

If the arbitrator's function is terminated through challenge, revocation, withdrawal or for any other reason, a substitute arbitrator' shall be appointed to replace him in accordance with the same procedural rules applicable to the appointment of the arbitrator whose function has been terminated.

1—432 Article (22)

1. The arbitral panel is competent to rule on the objections related to its lack of jurisdiction, including objections based on claiming the non-existence of an arbitration agreement, its extinction, nullity of said agreement, or that it does not cover the subject matter in dispute.

2. Those pleas must be invoked at a date not later than that of submitting the respondent's statement of defence referred to in para 2 of Article (30) of the present Law. The appointment or participation in the appointment of an arbitrator by one of the two parties to the arbitration shall not preclude such party from its right to raise any of these pleas. As to the plea that the arbitration agreement does not cover the disputed issues, it must be invoked immediately, otherwise the right to invoke it shall be precluded. In all cases, the arbitral panel may accept the plea invoked after the prescribed time limit if it considers that the delay was due to a justified reason.

3. The arbitral panel may either rule on the pleas referred to in para (1) of this Article as a preliminary question before ruling on the merits or adjoin them to the merits in order to be ruled upon together. If the arbitral panel rules to dismiss a plea, such motion may not be invoked except through the institution of a recourse for the annulment of the arbitral award disposing of the whole dispute pursuant to Article (53) of the present Law.

1—433 Article (23)

The arbitration clause shall be treated as an independent agreement separate from the other contractual conditions. The nullity, resiliation or termination of the Contract shall not affect the arbitration clause, provided that such clause is valid per se.

1—434 Article (24)

1. Both parties to the arbitration may agree to confer upon the arbitral panel the power to order, upon request of either party, interim or conservatory measures deemed necessary according to the nature of the dispute and to require any party to provide adequate security to cover the costs of the measure ordered.

2. If the party against whom the order was issued fails to execute it, the arbitral panel upon the request of the other party, may authorize the latter to undertake the procedures necessary for the execution of the order, without prejudice to the right of said party to apply to the president of the court referred to in Article (9) of the present Law for rendering an execution order.

PART IV—CONDUCT OF THE ARBITRAL PROCEEDINGS

1—435   Article (25)

The two parties to the arbitration are entitled to agree on the procedures to be followed by the arbitral panel, including the right to submit the arbitral proceedings to the rules prevailing under the auspices of any arbitral organization or center in the Arab Republic of Egypt or abroad. In the absence of such agreement, the arbitral panel may, without prejudice to the provisions of the present Law, adopt the arbitration procedures it deems suitable.

1—436   Article (26)

The two parties to arbitration shall be treated to an equal footing, and each shall be accorded a balanced and full opportunity to present its case.

1—437   Article (27)

The arbitral proceedings shall commence on the date on which the defendant receives the request for arbitration from the claimant, unless the two parties agree on another date.

1—438   Article (28)

The two parties to the arbitration are entitled to agree on the place of arbitration in Egypt or abroad. In the absence of such agreement, the arbitral panel shall determine the place of arbitration taking into consideration the circumstance of the case and the convenience of the place to the parties. This shall be without prejudice to the power of the arbitral panel to convene in any place it considers appropriate to undertake any of the arbitral proceedings, such as hearing the parties to the dispute, witnesses and experts, reviewing documents, inspecting goods or other property, conducting deliberations among its members or for any other reason.

1—439 Article (29)

1. The arbitration shall be conducted in Arabic, unless another language or languages are agreed upon by the two parties or determined by the arbitral panel. The agreement or determination in question shall apply to all written statements and briefs, to the oral hearings as well as to all awards and decisions rendered or communications addressed by the arbitral panel, unless specified otherwise by the agreement of the two parties or by determination of the arbitral panel.

2. The arbitral panel may order that all or part of the written documents submitted in the case, be accompanied by a translation to the language or languages used in the arbitration. In the case of multiplicity of such languages, the arbitral panel may limit the translation to some languages to the exclusion of others.

1—440 Article (30)

1. Within the period of time agreed upon between the two parties or determined by the arbitral panel, the claimant shall send to the defendant and to each of the arbitrators a written statement of its case that includes its name, address, the defendant's name and address, explanation of the facts, of the case, determination of the points at issue in the dispute, the relief or remedy requested as well as all other elements which are required to be mentioned in such statement by agreement between the two parties.

2. Within the period of time agreed by the parties or determined by the arbitral panel, the defendant shall send to the claimant and to each of the arbitrators a written Statement of Defence in reply to the Statement of the claimant's case. He may include in such Statement any incidental claims related to the subject matter of the dispute or to invoke a right arising thereunder in view of raising a plea for set-off. He may do so even at a later stage of the proceedings, if the arbitral panel deems that the circumstances justify the delay.

3. Both the claimant and the defendant are authorized to enclose with the Statement of Claim or with the Statement of Defence, as the case may be, copies of the documents supporting the position of the concerned party, and may refer to all or some of the documents and evidence it intends to submit. This does not prejudice the right of the arbitral panel, at any stage of the proceedings, to request the submission of

the originals of the documents or materials invoked by either party to support its case.

1—441 Article (31)

A copy of all briefs, statements, documents or other materials submitted to the arbitral panel by one of the parties shall be sent to the other party. Similarly, copies of whatever may be submitted to the arbitral panel such as expert reports, evidentiary documents or other elements of proof shall be sent to both parties.

1—442 Article (32)

Either party may amend or supplement its submissions or supporting arguments during the course of the arbitral proceedings, unless the arbitral panel considers it inappropriate in view of avoiding to delay adjudicating the case.

1—443 Article (33)

1. The arbitral panel may hold oral hearings, in order to enable each party to explain the merits of the case and to present its arguments as well as evidence. It may also decide that the proceedings shall be conducted exclusively on the basis of the submitted briefs and written documents, unless the two parties agree otherwise.

2. The two parties to the arbitration must be notified of the dates fixed for the hearings or the meetings which the arbitral panel decides to hold, sufficiently in advance of the scheduled date as determined by the panel according to circumstances.

3. Summary minutes of each meeting held by the arbitral panel shall be recorded in a *procès-verbal*, and a copy thereof shall be delivered to each of the two parties, unless they both agree otherwise.

4. The hearing of witnesses and experts shall be conducted without taking an oath.

1—444 Article (34)

1. If the claimant fails without a justifiable excuse to submit the written Statement of Claim pursuant to para 1 of Article (30) of the present Law, the arbitral panel shall order the termination of the arbitral proceedings, unless the two parties have agreed otherwise.

2. In the defendant fails to submit its statement of defence pursuant to para 2 of Article (30) of the present Law, the arbitral panel shall continue the arbitral proceedings without considering such failure as admission by the defendant of the claimant's case, unless the two parties have agreed otherwise.

1—445   Article (35)

If either party fails to attend any of the meetings or to submit the documents required from it, the arbitral panel may continue the arbitral proceedings and render its award on the dispute based upon the elements of evidence in its possession.

1—446   Article (36)

1. The arbitral panel may appoint one or more experts to submit on certain specific issues determined by the arbitral panel a written report or an oral report to be included in the *procès-verbal* of the meeting. A copy of the terms of reference regarding the mission entrusted to the expert shall be sent to each party.

2. Each party shall provide the expert with all relevant information concerning the dispute, to enable him to have access to and inspect what the expert requires as documents, goods or other property related to the dispute. The arbitral panel shall decide on any controversy arising in this respect between the expert and one of the parties.

3. The arbitral panel shall send to each party a copy of the expert's report immediately after its submission, granting each party the opportunity to express its opinion thereon. Each of the two parties is entitled to review and examine the documents upon which the expert relied in his report.

4. The arbitral panel may decide, after the submission of the expert's report, whether on its own initiative or upon request of a party to the arbitration, to hold a meeting to hear the expert and to provide for both parties the opportunity to hear him and to question him about what is contained in his report. One or more expert witness in order to give testimony on the issues raised in the report of the expert appointed by the arbitral panel, unless otherwise agreed upon between the two parties to the arbitration.

1—447   Article (37)

The President of the court referred to in Article (9) of the present Law is competent, upon the request of the arbitral panel, to order the following:

   a) Condemning any of the witnesses who refrains from attending or declines replying, by inflicting the sanction, prescribed in Articles 78 and 80 of the Law of Evidence in Civil and Commercial matters.

   b) Ordering a rogatory commission.

1—448   Article (38)

The proceedings before the arbitral panel shall be suspended upon accordance of any of the grounds for suspension and according to the conditions related thereto as provided for in the Code of Civil and Commercial Procedures. The effects of the suspension shall be those prescribed in the said Code.

PART V—THE ARBITRAL AWARD AND THE CLOSING OF THE PROCEDURES

1—449   Article (39)

   1. The arbitral panel shall apply to the substance of the dispute the rules agreed upon by the two parties. If they agree on the applicability of the law of a given State, only the substantive rules thereof shall be applicable to the exclusion of the rules pertaining to the conflict of laws, unless the parties have agreed otherwise.

   2. If the two parties have not agreed on the legal rules applicable to the substance of the dispute, the arbitral panel shall apply the substantive rules of the Law it considers most closely connected to the dispute.

   3. The arbitral panel must, when adjudicating the merits of the dispute, observe the terms of the contract in dispute and the current trade customs prevailing in that type of transaction.

   4. The arbitral panel may, if it has been expressly empowered to act as an "amiable compositeur" by agreement between the two parties to the arbitration, adjudicate the merits of the dispute in conformity with the rules of justice and fairness (*ex aequo et bono*), without being restricted by the legal provisions.

1—450   Article (40)

The award of an arbitral panel consisting of more than one arbitrator shall be rendered by the majority after deliberations conducted in the manner determined by the arbitral panel, unless the two parties to the arbitration agree otherwise.

1—451   Article (41)

If the two parties agree, during the arbitral proceedings, on a settlement that terminates the dispute, they may request that the terms of the settlement be recorded by the arbitral panel, in the form of an arbitral award or agreed terms which terminate the proceedings. Such award shall have the same effect with regard to enforcement as all other arbitral awards.

1—452   Article (42)

The arbitral panel may make interim or partial awards before rendering its final arbitral award which terminates the entire dispute.

1—453   Article (43)

1. The arbitral award shall be made in writing and signed by the arbitrators. If the arbitral panel consists of more than one arbitrator, the signatures of the majority of the arbitrators shall suffice, provided that the award states the reasons for which the minority did not sign.

2. The arbitral award must include the reasons upon which it is based, unless the two parties to arbitration have agreed otherwise or the Law applicable to the arbitral proceedings does not require the award to be supported by reasons.

3. The arbitral award must include the names and addresses of the parties, the names, addresses, nationalities and capacities of the arbitrators, a copy of the arbitration agreement, a summary of the parties' requests, submissions, documents, the dispositive part of the award, date and place of making, as well as the reasons whenever their inclusion is required.

1—454   Article (44)

1. The arbitral panel shall deliver to each of the two parties a copy of the arbitral award signed by the arbitrators who approved it within thirty days from the date of its making.

2. No publication of the award or parts thereof shall be authorized except with the approval of both parties to the arbitration.

1—455 Article (45)

1. The arbitral panel has to render the award terminating the dispute within the period agreed upon by the two parties. In the absence of such agreement, the award must be rendered within twelve months from the date of commencement of the arbitral proceedings. In all cases, the arbitral panel may decide to extend the deadline, provided that the period of extension shall not exceed six months, unless the two parties agree on a longer period.

2. If the arbitral award is not rendered within the period referred to in the preceding paragraph, either of the two parties to arbitration may request the president of the court referred to in Article (9) of the present Law to issue an order either extending the time limit or terminating the arbitral proceedings. In the latter case, either party may bring the dispute to the court having initial jurisdiction to adjudicate the case.

1—456 Article (46)

If, in the course of the arbitral proceedings, a matter falling outside the scope of the arbitral panel's jurisdiction is raised, or if a document submitted to it is challenged for forgery, or if criminal proceedings are undertaken regarding the alleged forgery or for any other criminal act, the arbitral panel may decide to proceed with the subject matter of the dispute without any reliance on the incidental matter raised or on the document alleged to be a forgery or on the other criminal act. Otherwise, the arbitral panel shall suspend the proceedings until a final judgement is rendered in this respect. Such measure shall entail suspension of the period of the making of the arbitral award.

1—457 Article (47)

The party in whose favour the arbitral award has been rendered must deposit, at the Secretariat of the court referred to in Article (9) of the present Law, the original award or a copy thereof in the language in which it was rendered, or an Arabic translation thereof authenticated by a competent organism if it was rendered in a foreign language.

The court's secretary shall evidence such deposit in a *procès-verbal*, and each of the two parties to arbitration may request obtaining a copy of the said *procès-verbal*.

1—458   Article (48)

1. The arbitral proceedings are terminated either by the making of the award ending the dispute or by a court decision ordering the closing of the arbitral proceedings pursuant to para (2) of Article 45, of the present Law. The arbitral proceedings can also be terminated by a decision of the arbitral panel in the following cases:

   (a) If the two parties agree to terminate the arbitration.
   (b) If the claimant withdraws its claim, unless the arbitral panel decides, upon request of the defendant, that the latter has a legitimate interest in continuing the arbitral proceedings until the dispute is settled by a final award.
   (c) If for any other reason the arbitral panel considers that the continuation of the proceedings has become unnecessary or impossible.

2. Without prejudice to the provisions of Articles (49), (50) and (51) of the present Law, the mandate of the arbitral panel ends with the termination of arbitral proceedings.

1—459   Article (49)

1. Either party to the arbitration may request the arbitral panel, within the thirty days following the reception of the arbitral award, to give an interpretation clarifying an ambiguity that appears in the dispotive part of the award. The party requesting clarification must notify the other party of the request before presenting it to the arbitral panel.

2. The interpretation shall be made in writing within the thirty days following the receipt of the request for clarification by the arbitral panel. The panel may extend that period by another thirty days if it considers such extension necessary.

3. The interpretation decision made by the arbitral panel shall form an integral part complementing of the arbitral award which it clarifies and shall be provided the same treatment.

1—460   Article (50)

1. The arbitral panel shall undertake to correct any exclusively material errors in its award, whether typographical or in computation. Such corrections shall be undertaken by the arbitral panel on its own initiative or upon request from either party. The arbitral panel shall make the correction without holding any hearing within the thirty days following

the making of the award or the deposition of the request for correction as the case may be, and it may extend this period by another thirty days if it considers this to be necessary.

2. The correction decision shall be rendered in writing by the arbitral panel and notified to the two parties within thirty days from the date of its making. If the arbitral panel abuses its powers of correction, the nullity of its decision may be subject to recourse by means of an action for nullity in conformity with the provisions of Articles 53 and 54 of the present law.

1—461   Article (51)

1. Either party to the arbitration may, even after the expiration of the arbitration period, request the arbitral panel, within the thirty days following the reception of the arbitral award, to make an additional award as to claims presented in the arbitral proceedings but omitted in the award. Such request must be notified to the other party before submission to the arbitral panel.

2. The arbitral panel shall make its decision within sixty days from submission of the request, and it may extend this period for a further thirty days if it considers this to be necessary.

PART VI—NULLITY OF THE ARBITRAL AWARD

1—462   Article (52)

1. Arbitral awards rendered in accordance with the provisions of the present Law may not be challenged by any of the means of recourse provided for in the Code of Civil and Commercial Procedures.

2. An action for the nullity of the arbitration award may be instituted in accordance with the provisions of the following two articles.

1—463   Article (53)

1. An action for the nullity of the arbitral award cannot be admitted except for the following causes:

  (a) If there is no arbitration agreement, if it was void, voidable or its duration had elapsed;

(b) If either party to the arbitration agreement was at the time of the conclusion of the arbitration agreement fully or partially incapacitated according to the law governing its legal capacity;

(c) If either party to arbitration was unable to submit its defence as a result of not being duly notified of the appointment of an arbitrator, of the arbitral proceedings, or for any other reason beyond its control;

(d) If the arbitral award excluded the application of the Law agreed upon by the parties to govern the subject matter in dispute;

(e) If the composition of the arbitral panel or the appointment of the arbitrators had been undertaken in violation of the Law or contrary to the parties' agreement.

(f) If the arbitral award dealt with matters not failing within the scope of the arbitration agreement or exceeding the limits of this agreement. However, in the case when matters falling within the scope of the arbitration can be separated from the part of the award which contains matters not included Within the scope of the arbitration, the nullity affects exclusively the latter parts only;

(g) If the arbitral award itself or the arbitration procedures affecting the award contain a legal violation that causes nullity.

2. The court adjudicating the action for nullity, shall *ipso jure* annul the arbitral award if it contains violation of the public order in the Arab Republic of Egypt.

1—464 Article (54)

1. The action for nullity of the arbitral award must be brought within the ninety days following the date the notification of the arbitral award to the party against whom it was rendered.

    The admissibility of the action for annulment shall not be prevented by the applicant's renouncement of its right to raise it prior to the making of the arbitral award.

2. Jurisdiction with regard to an action for the nullity of awards rendered in international commercial arbitrations lies with the court referred to in Article (9) of the present Law. In cases not related to international commercial arbitration, jurisdiction lies with the court of appeal having competence over the tribunal that would have been initially competent to adjudicate the dispute.

PART VII—RECOGNITION AND ENFORCEMENT OF ARBITRAL AWARDS

1—465 Article (55)

Arbitral awards rendered in accordance with the provisions of the present Law have the authority of the *res judicata* and shall be enforceable in conformity with the provisions of the present Law.

1—466 Article (56)

Jurisdiction to issue an enforcement order of arbitral awards lies with the President of the court referred to in Article (9) of the present Law or with the member of said court who has been mandated for this purpose by delegation from said President. The application for enforcement of the arbitral award shall be accompanied by the following:

1. The original award or a signed copy thereof.

2. A copy of the arbitration agreement.

3. An Arabic translation of the award, certified by a competent organism, in case the award was not rendered in Arabic.

4. A copy of the *procès-verbal* attesting the deposit of the award pursuant to Article (47) of the present Law.

1—467 Article (57)

The filing of an action for nullity does not suspend the enforcement of the arbitral award. Nevertheless, the court may order said suspension if the applicant requests it in his application and such request is based upon serious grounds. The court shall rule on the request for suspension of the enforcement within sixty days from the date of the first hearing fixed in relation thereto. If suspension is ordered, the court may require providing a given security or monetary guarantee. When the court orders a suspension of enforcement, it must rule on the action for nullity within six months from the date when the suspension order was rendered.

1—468 Article (58)

1. Application for the enforcement of an arbitral award shall not be admissible before the expiration of the period during which the action for nullity should be filed in the court registry.

2. The application to obtain leave for enforcement of the arbitral award according to the present Law shall not be granted except after having ascertained the following:

(a) That it does not contradict a judgment previously rendered by the Egyptian Courts on the subject matter in dispute;

(b) That it does not violate the public policy in the Arab Republic of Egypt; and

(c) That it was properly notified to the party against whom it was rendered.

3. The order granting leave for enforcement is not subject to any recourse. However, the order refusing to grant enforcement may be subject to a petition lodged, within thirty days from the date thereof, before the competent court referred to in Article 9 of the present Law.

NOTES

(1) Translated from the Arabic Official Text under the auspices of the "Association for Arab and African Arbitrators" having its headquarters in Cairo.

(2) Published in the Official Gazette No. 16, bis, on 21st of April 1994

D. Uniform and Model Laws

UNCITRAL Model Law on International Commercial Arbitration

CONTENTS

Chapter I. General provisions

Article.

1. Scope of application
2. Definitions and rules of interpretation
3. Receipt of written communications
4. Waiver of right to object
5. Extent of court intervention
6. Court or other authority for certain functions of arbitration assistance and supervision

Chapter II. Arbitration agreement

7. Definition and form of arbitration agreement
8. Arbitration and substantive claim before court
9. Arbitration agreement and interim measures by court

Chapter III. Composition of arbitral tribunal

10. Number of arbitrators
11. Appointment of arbitrators
12. Grounds for challenge
13. Challenge procedure
14. Failure or impossibility to act
15. Appointment of substitute arbitrator

Chapter IV. Jurisdiction of arbitral tribunal

16. Competence of arbitral tribunal to rule on its jurisdiction
17. Power of arbitral tribunal to order interim measures

Chapter V. Conduct of arbitral proceedings

18. Equal treatment of parties
19. Determination of rules of procedure
20. Place of arbitration
21. Commencement of arbitral proceedings
22. Language
23. Statements of claim and defence
24. Hearings and written proceedings
25. Default of a party
26. Expert appointed by arbitral tribunal
27. Court assistance in taking evidence

Chapter VI. Making of award and termination of proceedings

28. Rules applicable to substance of dispute
29. Decision making by panel of arbitrators
30. Settlement
31. Form and contents of award
32. Termination of proceedings
33. Correction and interpretation of award; additional award

Chapter VII. Recourse against award

34. Application for setting aside as exclusive recourse against arbitral award

Chapter VIII. Recognition and enforcement of awards

35. Recognition and enforcement
36. Grounds for refusing recognition or enforcement

UNCITRAL Model Law on International Commercial Arbitration

1—469 UNCITRAL Model Law on International Commercial Arbitration (1985) (as adopted by the United Nations Commission on International Trade Law on 21 June 1985)

Chapter I: General Provisions

1—470 Article 1—Scope of application

1. This Law applies to international commercial arbitration, subject to any agreement in force between this State and any other State or States.

2. The provisions of this Law, except articles 8, 9, 35 and 36, apply only if the place of arbitration is in the territory of this State.

3. An arbitration is international if:

   (a) the parties to an arbitration agreement have, at the time of the conclusion of that agreement, their places of business in different States; or
   (b) one of the following places is situated outside the State in which the parties have their places of business:

   (i) the place of arbitration if determined in, or pursuant to, the arbitration agreement;
   (ii) any place where a substantial part of the obligations of the commercial relationship is to be performed or the place with which the subject-matter of the dispute is most closely connected; or

   (c) the parties have expressly agreed that the subject-matter of the arbitration agreement relates to more than one country.

4. For the purposes of paragraph (3) of this article:

   (a) if a party has more than one place of business, the place of business is that which has the closest relationship to the arbitration agreement;
   (b) if a party does not have a place of business, reference is to be made to his habitual residence.

5. This Law shall not affect any other law of this State by virtue of which certain disputes may not be submitted to arbitration

or may be submitted to arbitration only according to provisions other than those of this Law.

1—471   Article 2—Definitions and rules of interpretation

For the purposes of this Law:

(a) "arbitration" means any arbitration whether or not administered by a permanent arbitral institution;

(b) "arbitral tribunal" means a sole arbitrator or a panel of arbitrators;

(c) "court" means a body or organ of the judicial system of a State;

(d) where a provision of this Law, except article 28, leaves the parties free to determine a certain issue, such freedom includes the right of the parties to authorize a third party, including an institution, to make that determination;

(e) where a provision of this Law refers to the fact that the parties have agreed or that they may agree or in any other way refers to an agreement of the parties; such agreement includes any arbitration rules referred to in that agreement;

(f) where a provision of this Law, other than in articles 25 (a) and 32

(2) (a), refers to a claim, it also applies to a counter-claim, and where it refers to a defence, it also applies to a defence to such counter-claim.

1—472   Article 3—Receipt of written communications

1. Unless otherwise agreed by the parties:

    (a) any written communication is deemed to have been received if it is delivered to the addressee personally or if it is delivered at his place of business, habitual residence or mailing address; if none of these can be found after making a reasonable inquiry, a written communication is deemed to have been received if it is sent to the addressee's last-known place of business, habitual residence or mailing address by registered letter or any other means which provides a record of the attempt to deliver it;

    (b) the communication is deemed to have been received on the day it is so delivered.

2. The provisions of this article do not apply to communications in court proceedings.

1—473 Article 4—Waiver of right to object

A party who knows that any provision of this Law from which the parties may derogate or any requirement under the arbitration agreement has not been complied with and yet proceeds with the arbitration without stating his objection to such non-compliance without undue delay or, if a time-limit is provided therefor, within such period of time, shall be deemed to have waived his right to object.

1—474 Article 5—Extent of court intervention

In matters governed by this Law, no court shall intervene except where so provided in this Law.

1—475 Article 6—Court or other authority for certain functions of arbitration assistance and supervision

The functions referred to in articles 11(3), 11(4), 13(3),14,16 (3) and 34 (2) shall be performed by . . . [Each State enacting this model law specifies the court, courts or, where referred to therein, other authority competent to perform these functions.]

CHAPTER II: ARBITRATION AGREEMENT

1—476 Article 7—Definition and form of arbitration agreement

1. "Arbitration agreement" is an agreement by the parties to submit to arbitration all or certain disputes which have arisen or which may arise between them in respect of a defined legal relationship, whether contractual or not. An arbitration agreement may be in the form of an arbitration clause in a contract or in the form of a separate agreement.

2. The arbitration agreement shall be in writing. An agreement is in writing if it is contained in a document signed by the parties or in an exchange of letters, telex, telegrams or other means of telecommunication which provide a record of the agreement, or in an exchange of statements of claim and defence in which the existence of an agreement is alleged by one party and not denied by another. The reference in a contract to a document containing an arbitration clause constitutes an arbitration agreement provided that the contract is in writing and the reference is such as to make that clause part of the contract.

1—477   **Article 8—Arbitration agreement and substantive claim before court**

1. A court before which an action is brought in a matter which is the subject of an arbitration agreement shall, if a party so requests not later than when submitting his first statement on the substance of the dispute, refer the parties to arbitration unless it finds that the agreement is real and void, inoperative or incapable of being performed.

2. Where an action referred to in paragraph (1) of this article has been brought, arbitral proceedings may nevertheless be commenced or continued, and an award may be made, while the issue is pending before the court.

1—478   **Article 9—Arbitration agreement and interim measures by court**

It is not incompatible with an arbitration agreement for a party to request, before or during arbitral proceedings, from a court an interim measure of protection and for a court to grant such measure.

CHAPTER III: COMPOSITION OF ARBITRAL TRIBUNAL

1—479   **Article 10—Number of arbitrators**

1. The parties are free to determine the number of arbitrators.

2. Failing such determination, the number of arbitrators shall be three.

1—480   **Article 11—Appointment of arbitrators**

1. No person shall be precluded by reason of his nationality from acting as an arbitrator, unless otherwise agreed by the parties.

2. The parties are free to agree on a procedure of appointing the arbitrator or arbitrators, subject to the provisions of paragraphs (4) and (5) of this article.

3. Failing such agreement,

   (a) in an arbitration with three arbitrators, each party shall appoint one arbitrator, and the two arbitrators thus appointed shall appoint the third arbitrator; if a party fails to appoint the arbitrator within thirty days of receipt of a request to do so from the other party, or if the two arbitrators fail to agree on the third arbitrator within thirty days of their appointment, the appointment shall be made, upon request of a party, by the court or other authority specified in article 6;

(b) in an arbitration with a sole arbitrator, if the parties are unable to agree on the arbitrator, he shall be appointed, upon request of a party, by the court or other authority specified in article 6.

4. Where, under an appointment procedure agreed upon by the parties,

(a) a party fails to act as required under such procedure, or
(b) the parties, or two arbitrators, are unable to reach an agreement expected of them under such procedure, or
(c) a third party, including an institution, fails to perform any function entrusted to it under such procedure, any party may request the court or other authority specified in article

5. to take the necessary measure, unless the agreement on the appointment procedure provides other means for securing the appointment.

6. A decision on a matter entrusted by paragraph (3) and (4) of this article to the court or other authority specified in article 6 shall be subject to no appeal. The court or other authority, in appointing an arbitrator, shall have due regard to any qualifications required of the arbitrator by the agreement of the parties and to such considerations as are likely to secure the appointment of an independent and impartial arbitrator and, in the case of a sole or third arbitrator, shall take into account as well the advisability of appointing an arbitrator of a nationality other than those of the parties.

1—481 Article 12—Grounds for challenge

1. When a person is approached in connection with his possible appointment as an arbitrator, he shall disclose any circumstances likely to give rise to justifiable doubts as to his impartiality or independence. An arbitrator, from the time of his appointment and throughout the arbitral proceedings, shall without delay disclose any such circumstances to the parties unless they have already been informed of them by him.

2. An arbitrator may be challenged only if circumstances exist that give rise to justifiable doubts as to his impartiality or independence, or if he does not possess qualifications agreed to by the parties. A party may challenge an arbitrator appointed by him, or in whose appointment he has participated, only for reasons of which he becomes aware after the appointment has been made.

1—482   Article 13—Challenge procedure

1. The parties are free to agree on a procedure for challenging an arbitrator, subject to the provisions of paragraph (3) of this article.

2. Failing such agreement, a party which intends to challenge an arbitrator shall, within fifteen days after becoming aware of the constitution of the arbitral tribunal or after becoming aware of any circumstance referred to in article 12(2), send a written statement of the reasons for the challenge to the arbitral tribunal. Unless the challenged arbitrator withdraws from his office or the other party agrees to the challenge, the arbitral tribunal shall decide on the challenge.

3. If a challenge under any procedure agreed upon by the parties or under the procedure of paragraph (2) of this article is not successful, the challenging party may request, within thirty days after having received notice of the decision rejecting the challenge, the court or other authority specified in article 6 to decide on the challenge, which decision shall be subject to no appeal; while such a request is pending, the arbitral tribunal, including the challenged arbitrator, may continue the arbitral proceedings and make an award.

1—483   Article 14—Failure or impossibility to act

1. If an arbitrator becomes de jure or de facto unable to perform his functions or for other reasons fails to act without undue delay, his mandate terminates if he withdraws from his office or if the parties agree on the termination. Otherwise, if a controversy remains concerning any of these grounds, any party may request the court or other authority specified in article 6 to decide on the termination of the mandate, which decision shall be subject to no appeal.

2. If, under this article or article 13 (2), an arbitrator withdraws from his office or a party agrees to the termination of the mandate of an arbitrator, this does not imply acceptance of

the validity of any ground referred to in this article or article 12 (2).

1—484 Article 15—Appointment of substitute arbitrator

Where the mandate of an arbitrator terminates under article 13 or 14 or because of his withdrawal from office for any other reason or because of the revocation of his mandate by agreement of the parties or in any other case of termination of his mandate, a substitute arbitrator shall be appointed according to the rules that were applicable to the appointment of the arbitrator being replaced.

CHAPTER IV: JURISDICTION OF ARBITRAL TRIBUNAL

1—485 Article 16—Competence of arbitral tribunal to rule on its jurisdiction

1. The arbitral tribunal may rule on its own jurisdiction, including any objections with respect to the existence or validity of the arbitration agreement. For that purpose, an arbitration clause which forms part of a contract shall be treated as an agreement independent of the other terms of the contract. A decision by the arbitral tribunal that the contract is null and void shall not entail ipso jure the invalidity of the arbitration clause.

2. A plea that the arbitral tribunal does not have jurisdiction shall be raised not later than the submission of the statement of defence. A party is not precluded from raising such a plea by the fact that he has appointed, or participated in the appointment of, an arbitrator. A plea that the arbitral tribunal is exceeding the scope of its authority shall be raised as soon as the matter alleged to be beyond the scope of its authority is raised during the arbitral proceedings. The arbitral tribunal may, in either case, admit a later plea if it considers the delay justified.

3. The arbitral tribunal may rule on a plea referred to in paragraph (2) of this article either as a preliminary question or in an award on the merits. If the arbitral tribunal rules as a preliminary question that it has jurisdiction, any party may request, within thirty days after having received notice of that ruling, the court specified in article 6 to decide the matter, which decision shall be subject to no appeal; while such a request is pending, the arbitral tribunal may continue the arbitral proceedings and make an award.

1—486 **Article 17—Power of arbitral tribunal to order interim measures**

Unless otherwise agreed by the parties, the arbitral tribunal may, at the request of a party, order any party to take such interim measure of protection as the arbitral tribunal may consider necessary in respect of the subject-matter of the dispute. The arbitral tribunal may require any party to provide appropriate security in connection with such measure.

CHAPTER V: CONDUCT OF ARBITRAL PROCEEDINGS

1—487 **Article 18—Equal treatment of parties**

The parties shall be treated with equality and each party shall be given a full opportunity of presenting his case.

1—488 **Article 19—Determination of rules of procedure**

1. Subject to the provisions of this Law, the parties are free to agree on the procedure to be followed by the arbitral tribunal in conducting the proceedings.

2. Failing such agreement, the arbitral tribunal may, subject to the provisions of this Law, conduct the arbitration in such manner as it considers appropriate. The power conferred upon the arbitral tribunal includes the power to determine the admissibility, relevance, materiality and weight of any evidence.

1—489 **Article 20—Place of arbitration**

1. The parties are free to agree on the place of arbitration. Failing such agreement, the place of arbitration shall be determined by the arbitral tribunal having regard to the circumstances of the case, including the convenience of the parties.

2. Notwithstanding the provisions of paragraph (1) of this article, the arbitral tribunal may, unless otherwise agreed by the parties, meet at any place it considers appropriate for consultation among its members, for hearing witnesses, experts or the parties, or for inspection of goods, other property or documents.

1—490   Article 21—Commencement of arbitral proceedings

Unless otherwise agreed by the parties, the arbitral proceedings in respect of a particular dispute commence on the date on which a request for that dispute to be referred to arbitration is received by the respondent.

1—491   Article 22—Language

1. The parties are free to agree on the language or languages to be used in the arbitral proceedings. Failing such agreement, the arbitral tribunal shall determine the language or languages to be used in the proceedings. This agreement or determination, unless otherwise specified therein, shall apply to any written statement by a party, any hearing and any award, decision or other communication by the arbitral tribunal.

2. The arbitral tribunal may order that any documentary evidence shall be accompanied by a translation into the language or languages agreed upon by the parties or determined by the arbitral tribunal.

1—492   Article 23—Statements of claim and defence

1. Within the period of time agreed by the parties or determined by the arbitral tribunal, the claimant shall state the facts supporting his claim, the points at issue and the relief or remedy sought, and the respondent shall state his defence in respect of these particulars, unless the parties have otherwise agreed as to the required elements of such statements. The parties may submit with their statements all documents they consider to be relevant or may add a reference to the documents or other evidence they will submit.

2. Unless otherwise agreed by the parties, either party may amend or supplement his claim or defence during the course of the arbitral proceedings, unless the arbitral tribunal considers it inappropriate to allow such amendment having regard to the delay in making it.

1—493   Article 24—Hearings and written proceedings

1. Subject to any contrary agreement by the parties, the arbitral tribunal shall decide whether to hold oral hearings for the presentation of evidence or for oral argument, or whether the proceedings shall be conducted on the basis of documents

and other materials. However, unless the parties have agreed that no hearings shall be held, the arbitral tribunal shall hold such hearings at an appropriate stage of the proceedings, if so requested by a party.

2. The parties shall be given sufficient advance notice of any hearing and of any meeting of the arbitral tribunal for the purposes of inspection of goods, other property or documents.

3. All statements, documents or other information supplied to the arbitral tribunal by one party shall be communicated to the other party. Also any expert report or evidentiary document on which the arbitral tribunal may rely in making its decision shall be communicated to the parties.

1—494 Article 25—Default of a party

Unless otherwise agreed by the parties, if, without showing sufficient cause,

(a) the claimant fails to communicate his statement of claim in accordance with article 23 (1), the arbitral tribunal shall terminate the proceedings;

(b) the respondent fails to communicate his statement of defence in accordance with article 23 (1), the arbitral tribunal shall continue the proceedings without treating such failure in itself as an admission of the claimant's allegations;

(c) any party fails to appear at a hearing or to produce documentary evidence, the arbitral tribunal may continue the proceedings and make the award on the evidence before it.

1—495 Article 26—Expert appointed by arbitral tribunal

1. Unless otherwise agreed by the parties, the arbitral tribunal

   (a) may appoint one or more experts to report to it on specific issues to be determined by the arbitral tribunal;
   (b) may require a party to give the expert any relevant information or to produce, or to provide access to, any relevant documents, goods or other property for his inspection.

2. Unless otherwise agreed by the parties, if a party so requests or if the arbitral tribunal considers it necessary, the expert shall, after delivery of his written or oral report, participate

in a hearing where the parties have the opportunity to put questions to him and to present expert witnesses in order to testify on the points at issue.

1—496   Article 27—Court assistance in taking evidence

The arbitral tribunal or a party with the approval of the arbitral tribunal may request from a competent court of this State assistance in taking evidence. The court may execute the request within its competence and according to its rules on taking evidence.

CHAPTER VI: MAKING OF AWARD AND TERMINATION OF PROCEEDINGS

1—497   Article 28—Rules applicable to substance of dispute

1. The arbitral tribunal shall decide the dispute in accordance with such rules of law as are chosen by the parties as applicable to the substance of the dispute. Any designation of the law or legal system of a given State shall be construed, unless otherwise expressed, as directly referring to the substantive law of that State and not to its conflict of laws rules.

2. Failing any designation by the parties, the arbitral tribunal shall apply the law determined by the conflict of laws rules which it considers applicable.

3. The arbitral tribunal shall decide ex aequo et bono or as amiable compositeur only if the parties have expressly authorized it to do so.

4. In all cases, the arbitral tribunal shall decide in accordance with the terms of the contract and shall take into account the usages of the trade applicable to the transaction.

1—498   Article 29—Decision-making by panel of arbitrators

In arbitral proceedings with more than one arbitrator, any decision of the arbitral tribunal shall be made, unless otherwise agreed by the parties, by a majority of all its members. However, questions of procedure may be decided by a presiding arbitrator, if so authorized by the parties or all members of the arbitral tribunal.

1—499   Article 30—Settlement

1. If, during arbitral proceedings, the parties settle the dispute, the arbitral tribunal shall terminate the proceedings and, if

requested by the parties and not objected to by the arbitral tribunal, record the settlement in the form of an arbitral award on agreed terms.

2. An award on agreed terms shall be made in accordance with the provisions of article 31 and shall state that it is an award. Such an award has the same status and effect as any other award on the merits of the case.

1—500   Article 31—Form and contents of award

1. The award shall be made in writing and shall be signed by the arbitrator or arbitrators. In arbitrator proceedings with more than one arbitrator, the signatures of the majority of all members of the arbitral tribunal shall suffice, provided that the reason for any omitted signature is stated.

2. The award shall state the reasons upon which it is based, unless the parties have agreed that no reasons are to be given or the award is an award on agreed terms under article 30.

3. The award shall state its date and the place of arbitration as determined in accordance with article 20 (1). The award shall be deemed to have been made at that place.

4. After the award is made, a copy signed by the arbitrators in accordance with paragraph (1) of this article shall be delivered to each party.

1—501   Article 32—Termination of proceedings

1. The arbitral proceedings are terminated by the final award or by an order of the arbitral tribunal in accordance with paragraph (2) of this article.

2. The arbitral tribunal shall issue an order for the termination of the arbitral proceedings when:

   (a) the claimant withdraws his claim, unless the respondent objects thereto and the arbitral tribunal recognizes a legitimate interest on his part in obtaining a final settlement of the dispute;
   (b) the parties agree on the termination of the proceedings;
   (c) the arbitral tribunal finds that the continuation of the proceedings has for any other reason become unnecessary or impossible.

3. The mandate of the arbitral tribunal terminates with the termination of the arbitral proceedings, subject to the provisions of articles 33 and 34 (4).

1—502 **Article 33—Correction of interpretation of award; additional award**

1. Within thirty days of receipt of the award, unless another period of time has been agreed upon by the parties:

   (a) a party, with notice to the other party, may request the arbitral tribunal to correct in the award any errord in computation, any clerical or typographical errors or any errors of similar nature;

   (b) if so agreed by the parties, a party, with notice to the other party, may request the arbitral tribunal to give an interpretation of a specific point or part of the award. If the arbitral tribunal considers the request to be justified, it shall make the correction or give the interpretation within thirty days of receipt of the request. The interpretation shall form part of the award.

2. The arbitral tribunal may correct any error of the type referred to in paragraph (1) (a) of this article on its own initiative within thirty days of the day of the award.

3. Unless otherwise agreed by the parties, a party, with notice to the other party, may request, within thirty days of receipt of the award, the arbitral tribunal to make an additional award as to claims presented in the arbitral proceedings but omitted from the award. If the arbitral tribunal considers the request to be justified, it shall make the additional award within sixty days.

4. The arbitral tribunal may extend, if necessary, the period of time within which it shall make a correction, interpretation or an additional award under paragraph (1) or (3) of this article.

5. The provisions of article 31 shall apply to a correction or interpretation of the award or to an additional award.

CHAPTER VII: RECOURSE AGAINST AWARD

1—503 **Article 34—Application for setting aside as exclusive recourse against arbitral award**

1. Recourse to a court against an arbitral award may be made only by an application for setting aside in accordance with paragraphs (2) and (3) of this article.

2. An arbitral award may be set aside by the court specified in article 6 only if:

(a) the party making the application furnishes proof that:

(i) a party to the arbitration agreement referred to in article 7 was under some incapacity; or the said agreement is not valid under the law to which the parties have subjected it or, failing any indication thereon, under the law of this State; or

(ii) the party making the application was not given proper notice of the appointment of an arbitrator or of the arbitral proceedings or was otherwise unable to present his case; or

(iii) the award deals with a dispute not contemplated by or not falling within the terms of the submission to arbitration, or contains decisions on matters beyond the scope of the submission to arbitration, provided that, if the decisions on matters submitted to arbitration can be separated from those not so submitted, only that part of the award which contains decisions on matters not submitted to arbitration may be set aside; or

(iv) the composition of the arbitral tribunal or the arbitral procedure was not in accordance with the agreement of the parties, unless such agreement was in conflict with a provision of this Law from which the parties cannot derogate, or, failing such agreement, was not in accordance with this Law; or

(b) the court finds that:

(i) the subject-matter of the dispute is not capable of settlement by arbitration under the law of this State; or

(ii) the award is in conflict with the public policy of this State.

3. An application for setting aside may not be made after three months have elapsed from the date on which the party making that application had received that award or, if a request had been made under article 33, from the date on which that request had been disposed of by the arbitral tribunal.

4. The court, when asked to set aside an award, may, where appropriate and so requested by a party, suspend the setting aside proceedings for a period of time determined by it in order to give the arbitral tribunal an opportunity to resume the arbitral proceedings or to take such other action as in the

arbitral tribunal's opinion will eliminate the grounds for setting aside.

CHAPTER VIII: RECOGNITION AND ENFORCEMENT OF AWARDS

1—504   Article 35—Recognition and enforcement

1. An arbitral award, irrespective of the country in which it was made, shall be recognized as binding and, upon application in writing to the competent court, shall be enforced subject to the provisions of this article and of article 36.

2. The party relying on an award or applying for its enforcement shall supply the duly authenticated original award or a duly certified copy thereof, and the original arbitration agreement referred to in article 7 or a duly certified copy thereof. If the award or agreement is not made in an official language of this State, the party shall supply a duly certified translation thereof into such language.

1—505   Article 36—Grounds for refusing recognition or enforcement

1. Recognition or enforcement of an arbitral award, irrespective of the country in which it was made, may be refused only:

   (a) at the request of the party against whom it is invoked, if that party furnishes to the competent court where recognition or enforcement is sought proof that:

   (i) a party to the arbitration agreement referred to in article 7 was under some incapacity; or the said agreement is not valid under the law to which the parties have subjected it or, failing any indication thereon, under the law of the country where the award was made; or

   (ii) the party against whom the award is invoked was not given proper notice of the appointment of an arbitrator or of the arbitrator proceedings or was otherwise unable to present his case; or

   (iii) the award deals with a dispute not contemplated by or not falling within the terms of the submission to arbitration, or it contains decisions on matters beyond the scope of the submission to arbitration, provided that, if the decisions on matters submitted to arbitration can be separated from those not so submitted, that part of the award which contains decisions on matters submitted to arbitration may be recognized and enforced; or

(iv) the composition of the arbitral tribunal or the arbitral procedure was not in accordance with the agreement of the parties or, failing such agreement, was not in accordance with the law of the country where the arbitration took place; or

(v) the award has not yet become binding on the parties or has been set aside or suspended by a court of the country in which, or under the law of which, that award was made; or

(b) if the court finds that:

(i) the subject-matter of the dispute is not capable of settlement by arbitration under the law of this State; or

(ii) the recognition or enforcement of the award would be contrary to the public policy of this State.

2. If an application for setting aside or suspension of an award has been made to a court referred to in paragraph (1) (a) (v) of this article, the court where recognition or enforcement is sought may, if it considers it proper, adjourn its decision and may also, on the application of the party claiming recognition or enforcement of the award, order the other party to provide appropriate security.

UNCITRAL Model Law on International Commercial Conciliation (2003)

1—506 Article 1—Scope of application and definitions

(1) This Law applies to international commercial conciliation. (A. B.)

(2) For the purposes of this Law, "conciliator" means a sole conciliator ortwo or more conciliators, as the case may be.

(3) For the purposes of this Law, "conciliation" means a process, whetherreferred to by the expression conciliation, mediation or an expression of similarimport, whereby parties request a third person or persons ("the conciliator") to assistthem in their attempt to reach an amicable settlement of their dispute arising out ofor relating to a contractual or other legal relationship. The conciliator does not havethe authority to impose upon the parties a solution to the dispute.

(4) A conciliation is international if:

   (a) The parties to an agreement to conciliate have, at the time of the conclusion of that agreement, their places of business in different States; or
   (b) The State in which the parties have their places of business is different from either:

      (i) The State in which a substantial part of the obligations of the commercialrelationship is to be performed; or
      (ii) The State with which the subject matter of the dispute is most closely connected.

(5) For the purposes of this article:

   (a) If a party has more than one place of business, the place of business is that which has the closest relationship to the agreement to conciliate;
   (b) If a party does not have a place of business, reference is to be made to the party's habitual residence.

(6) This Law also applies to a commercial conciliation when the partiesagree that the conciliation is international or agree to the applicability of this Law.

(7) The parties are free to agree to exclude the applicability of this Law.

(8) Subject to the provisions of paragraph (9) of this article, this Law applies irrespective of the basis upon which the conciliation is carried out, includingagreement between the parties whether reached before or after a dispute has arisen, an obligation established by law, or a direction or suggestion of a court, arbitral tribunal or competent governmental entity.

(9) This Law does not apply to:

(a) Cases where a judge or an arbitrator, in the course of judicial or arbitralproceedings, attempts to facilitate a settlement; and

(b) [. . .].

1—507 Article 2—Interpretation

(1) In the interpretation of this Law, regard is to be had to its international origin and to the need to promote uniformity in its application and the observance of good faith.

(2) Questions concerning matters governed by this Law which are not expressly settled in it are to be settled in conformity with the general principles on which this Law is based.

1—508 Article 3—Variation by agreement

Except for the provisions of article 2 and article 6, paragraph (3), the parties may agree to exclude or vary any of the provisions of this Law.

1—509 Article 4—Commencement of conciliation proceedings (C)

(1) Conciliation proceedings in respect of a dispute that has arisen commence on the day on which the parties to that dispute agree to engage in conciliation proceedings.

(2) If a party that invited another party to conciliate does not receive an acceptance of the invitation within thirty days from the day on which the invitation was sent, or within such other period of time as specified in the invitation, the party may elect to treat this as a rejection of the invitation to conciliate.

1—510 Article 5—Number and appointment of conciliators

(1) There shall be one conciliator, unless the parties agree that there shall be two or more conciliators.

(3) The parties shall endeavour to reach agreement on a conciliator or conciliators, unless a different procedure for their appointment has been agreed upon.

(4) Parties may seek the assistance of an institution or person in connection with the appointment of conciliators. In particular:

    (a) A party may request such an institution or person to recommend suitable persons to act as conciliator; or

    (b) The parties may agree that the appointment of one or more conciliators be made directly by such an institution or person.

(5) In recommending or appointing individuals to act as conciliator, the institution or person shall have regard to such considerations as are likely to secure the appointment of an independent and impartial conciliator and, where appropriate, shall take into account the advisability of appointing a conciliator of a nationality other than the nationalities of the parties.

(6) When a person is approached in connection with his or her possible appointment as conciliator, he or she shall disclose any circumstances likely to give rise to justifiable doubts as to his or her impartiality or independence. A conciliator, from the time of his or her appointment and throughout the conciliation proceedings, shall without delay disclose any such circumstances to the parties unless they have already been informed of them by him or her.

1—511   **Article 6—Conduct of conciliation**

(1) The parties are free to agree, by reference to a set of rules or otherwise, on the manner in which the conciliation is to be conducted.

(2) Failing agreement on the manner in which the conciliation is to be conducted, the conciliator may conduct the conciliation proceedings in such a manner as the conciliator considers appropriate, taking into account the circumstances of the case, any wishes that the parties may express and the need for a speedy settlement of the dispute.

(3) In any case, in conducting the proceedings, the conciliator shall seek to maintain fair treatment of the parties and, in so doing, shall take into account the circumstances of the case.

(4) The conciliator may, at any stage of the conciliation proceedings, make proposals for a settlement of the dispute.

1—512 Article 7—Communication between conciliator and parties

The conciliator may meet or communicate with the parties together or with each of them separately.

1—513 Article 8—Disclosure of information

When the conciliator receives information concerning the dispute from a party, the conciliator may disclose the substance of that information to any other party to the conciliation. However, when a party gives any information to the conciliator, subject to a specific condition that it be kept confidential, that information shall not be disclosed to any other party to the conciliation.

1—514 Article 9—Confidentiality

Unless otherwise agreed by the parties, all information relating to the conciliation proceedings shall be kept confidential, except where disclosure is required under the law or for the purposes of implementation or enforcement of a settlement agreement.

1—515 Article 10—Admissibility of evidence in other proceedings

(1) A party to the conciliation proceedings, the conciliator and any third person, including those involved in the administration of the conciliation proceedings, shall not in arbitral, judicial or similar proceedings rely on, introduce as evidence or give testimony or evidence regarding any of the following:

(a) An invitation by a party to engage in conciliation proceedings or the fact that a party was willing to participate in conciliation proceedings;
(b) Views expressed or suggestions made by a party in the conciliation in respect of a possible settlement of the dispute;
(c) Statements or admissions made by a party in the course of the conciliation proceedings;
(d) Proposals made by the conciliator;
(e) The fact that a party had indicated its willingness to accept a proposal for settlement made by the conciliator;
(f) A document prepared solely for purposes of the conciliation proceedings.

(2) Paragraph (1) of this article applies irrespective of the form of the information or evidence referred to therein.

(3) The disclosure of the information referred to in paragraph (1) of this article shall not be ordered by an arbitral tribunal, court or other competent governmental authority and, if such information is offered as evidence in contravention of paragraph (1) of this article, that evidence shall be treated as inadmissible. Nevertheless, such information may be disclosed or admitted in evidence to the extent required under the law or for the purposes of implementation or enforcement of a settlement agreement.

(4) The provisions of paragraphs (1), (2) and (3) of this article apply whether or not the arbitral, judicial or similar proceedings relate to the dispute that is or was the subject matter of the conciliation proceedings.

(5) Subject to the limitations of paragraph (1) of this article, evidence that is otherwise admissible in arbitral or judicial or similar proceedings does not become inadmissible as a consequence of having been used in a conciliation.

1—516   Article 11—Termination of conciliation proceedings

The conciliation proceedings are terminated:

(a) By the conclusion of a settlement agreement by the parties, on the date of the agreement;

(b) By a declaration of the conciliator, after consultation with the parties, to the effect that further efforts at conciliation are no longer justified, on the date of the declaration;

(c) By a declaration of the parties addressed to the conciliator to the effect that the conciliation proceedings are terminated, on the date of the declaration; or

(d) By a declaration of a party to the other party or parties and the conciliator, if appointed, to the effect that the conciliation proceedings are terminated, on the date of the declaration.

1—517   Article 12—Conciliator acting as arbitrator

Unless otherwise agreed by the parties, the conciliator shall not act as an arbitrator in respect of a dispute that was or is the subject of the conciliation proceedings or in respect of another dispute that has arisen from the same contract or legal relationship or any related contract or legal relationship.

1—518 Article 13—Resort to arbitral or judicial proceedings

Where the parties have agreed to conciliate and have expressly undertaken not to initiate during a specified period of time or until a specified event has occurred arbitral or judicial proceedings with respect to an existing or future dispute, such an undertaking shall be given effect by the arbitral tribunal or the court until the terms of the undertaking have been complied with, except to the extent necessary for a party, in its opinion, to preserve its rights. Initiation of such proceedings is not of itself to be regarded as a waiver of the agreement to conciliate or as a termination of the conciliation proceedings.

1—519 Article 14—Enforceability of settlement agreement 9(D)

If the parties conclude an agreement settling a dispute, that settlement agreement is binding and enforceable ... [*the enacting State may insert a description of the method of enforcing settlement agreements or refer to provisions governing such enforcement*].

NOTES

(A) States wishing to enact this Model Law to apply to domestic as well as internationalconciliation may wish to consider the following changes to the text:
— Delete the word "international" in paragraph (1) of article 1; and
— Delete paragraphs (4), (5) and (6) of article 1.
(B) The term "commercial" should be given a wide interpretation so as to cover matters arisingfrom all relationships of a commercial nature, whether contractual or not. Relationships of acommercial nature include, but are not limited to, the following transactions: any trade transaction for the supply or exchange of goods or services; distribution agreement;commercial representation or agency; factoring; leasing; construction of works; consulting; engineering; licensing; investment; financing; banking; insurance; exploitation agreement or concession; joint venture and other forms of industrial or business cooperation; carriage of goods or passengers by air, sea, rail or road.
(C) The following text is suggested for States that might wish to adopt a provision on the suspension of the limitation period:
Article X. Suspension of limitation period
(1) When the conciliation proceedings commence, the running of the limitation period regarding the claim that is the subject matter of the conciliation is suspended.

(2) Where the conciliation proceedings have terminated without a settlement agreement, the limitation period resumes running from the time the conciliation ended without a settlement agreement.
(D) When implementing the procedure for enforcement of settlement agreements, an enacting State may consider the possibility of such a procedure being mandatory.

European Convention Providing a Uniform Law on Arbitration

1—520 The member States of the Council of Europe, signatory hereto,

Considering that the aim of the Council of Europe is to achieve greater unity among its members, in particular by the adoption of common rules in the legal field;

Convinced that the unification of national laws would make for a more effective settlement of private law disputes by arbitration and would facilitate commercial relations between the member countries of the Council of Europe;

Considering it desirable to adopt to this end a uniform law on arbitration in civil and commercial matters,

Have agreed as follows:

1—521 Article 1

1. Each Contracting Party undertakes to incorporate in its law, within six months of the date of entry into force of this Convention in respect of that Party, the provisions of the uniform law contained in Annex I to this Convention.

2. Each Contracting Party has the right, in its law to supplement the uniform law by provisions designed to regulate questions for which no solutions are provided, on condition that such provisions are not incompatible with the uniform law.

3. Each Contracting Party has the right to provide in its law, in respect of specific matters, that disputes may not be referred to arbitration or may be submitted to arbitration according to rules other than those laid down in the uniform law.

4. Each Contracting Party has the right to declare, at the time of signature of this Convention or at the time of deposit of its instrument of ratification, acceptance or accession, that it will apply the uniform law only to disputes arising out of legal relationships which are considered as commercial under its national law.

1—522 Article 2

Each Contracting Party undertakes not to maintain or introduce into its law provisions excluding aliens from being arbitrators.

1—523   Article 3

Each Contracting Party shall, for the purposes of the provisions of the uniform, law define "judicial authority", "competent authority" and, if need be, "registry of the court".

1—524   Article 4

Each Contracting Party retains the right to determine the conditions to be fulfilled by persons who may represent or assist the parties before the arbitral tribunal and, to that end, to amend the provisions of paragraph 4 of Article 16 of the uniform law.

1—525   Article 5

Each Contracting Party may:

> 1. regard notification within the meaning of paragraph 1 of Article 28 of the uniform law as implying either notification as provided for in paragraph 1 of Article 23 of the uniform law, or service, and, in particular, service by one party on another party;
>
> 2. regard notification under paragraphs 1 and 3 of Article 30 of the uniform law as implying either notification by the authority which has opposed the enforcement formula to the award or service, and, in particular, service by one party on another party.

The Contracting Party may, if need be, replace the words "give notice to", "notified" and "notification" by the appropriate technical terms.

It shall inform the Secretary General of the Council of Europe of its choice.

1—526   Article 6

Each Contracting Party may provide that the enforcement formula within the meaning of paragraph 1 of Article 29, Article 30 and paragraph 1 of Article 31 of the uniform law shall consist of an authorisation to enforce or of any other legal process which, under its law, enables an award to be enforced.

1—527   Article 7

Each Contracting Party shall have the right, in its law, to make provision for and to regulate the provisional enforcement of arbitral awards which are still appealable before arbitrators.

1—528   Article 8

> 1. Each Contracting Party may, when signing this Convention or depositing its instrument of ratification, acceptance or accession, declare that it avails itself of one or more of the reservations set forth in Annex II to this Convention. No other reservation shall be admissible.
>
> 2. Each Contracting Party may, at any time, by means of a notification addressed to the Secretary General of the Council of Europe, withdraw, wholly or in part, a reservation made by it under the preceding paragraph; the notification shall take effect on the date of its receipt.

1—529   Article 9

The provisions of the present Convention shall not affect the application of bilateral or multilateral conventions on arbitration which have been or may be concluded. This is subject to the right available to a Contracting Party under Annex III to the present Convention.

1—530   Article 10

> 1. Each Contracting Party shall communicate to the Secretary General of the Council of Europe the texts which, in implementation of this Convention, will govern arbitration after the entry into force of the Convention in respect of that Party.
>
> 2. The Secretary General shall transmit these texts to the other member States of the Council of Europe and to any State acceding to this Convention.

1—531   Article 11

> 1. This Convention shall be open to signature by the member States of the Council of Europe. It shall be subject to ratification or acceptance. Instruments of ratification or acceptance shall be deposited with the Secretary General of the Council of Europe.
>
> 2. This Convention shall enter into force three months after the date of the deposit of the third instrument of ratification or acceptance.
>
> 3. In respect of a signatory State ratifying or accepting subsequently the Convention shall come into force three months after the date of the deposit of its instrument of ratification or acceptance.

D. Uniform and Model Laws 277

1—532   Article 12

> 1. After the entry into force of this Convention, the Committee of Ministers of the Council of Europe may invite any non-member State to accede thereto.
>
> 2. Such accession shall be effected by depositing with the Secretary General of the Council of Europe an instrument of accession, which shall take effect three months after the date of its deposit.

1—533   Article 13

> 1. Any Contracting Party may, at the time of signature or when depositing its instrument of ratification, acceptance or accession, specify the territory or territories to which this Convention shall apply.
>
> 2. Any Contracting Party may, when depositing its instrument of ratification, acceptance or accession or at any later date, by declaration addressed to the Secretary General of the Council of Europe, extend this Convention to any other territory or territories specified in the declaration and for whose international relations it is responsible or on whose behalf it is authorised to give undertakings.
>
> 3. Any declaration made in pursuance of the preceding paragraph may, in respect of any territory mentioned in such declaration, be withdrawn according to the procedure laid down in Article 14 of this Convention.

1—534   Article 14

> 1. This Convention shall remain in force indefinitely.
>
> 2. Any Contracting Party may, in so far as it is concerned, denounce this Convention by means of a notification addressed to the Secretary General of the Council of Europe.
>
> 3. Such denunciation shall take effect six months after the date of receipt by the Secretary General of such notification.

1—535   Article 15

The Secretary General of the Council of Europe shall notify the member States of the Council and any State which has acceded to this Convention of:

a) any signature;

b) any deposit of an instrument of ratification, acceptance or accession;

c) any date of entry into force of this Convention in accordance with the provisions of Articles 11 and 12;

d) any reservation made in pursuance of the provisions of paragraph 1 of Article 8;

e) the withdrawal of any reservation made in pursuance of the provisions of paragraph 2 of Article 8;

f) any communication received in pursuance of the provisions of Articles 5 and 10;

g) any declaration received in pursuance of the provisions of Article 13;

h) any notification received in pursuance of the provisions of Article 14 and the date on which the denunciation takes effect;

i) any declaration or notification received in pursuance of the provisions of Annex III.

In witness whereof the undersigned, being duly authorised thereto, have signed this Protocol.

Done at Strasbourg, this 20th day of January 1966, in English and in French, both texts being equally authoritative, in a single copy which shall remain deposited in the archives of the Council of Europe. The Secretary General shall transmit certified copies to each of the signatory governments.

Annex I

Uniform Law

1—536   Article 1

Any dispute which has arisen or may arise out of a specific legal relationship and in respect of which it is permissible to compromise may be the subject of an arbitration agreement.

1—537   Article 2

1. An arbitration agreement shall be constituted by an instrument in writing signed by the parties or by other documents

binding on the parties and showing their intention to have recourse to arbitration.

2. If, in an arbitration agreement, the parties have referred to a particular arbitration procedure, that procedure shall be deemed to be included in the agreement.

1—538   Article 3

An arbitration agreement shall not be valid if it gives one of the parties thereto a privileged position with regard to the appointment of the arbitrator or arbitrators.

1—539   Article 4

1. The judicial authority seized of a dispute which is the subject of an arbitration agreement shall, at the request of either party, declare that it has no jurisdiction, unless, in so far as concerns the dispute, the agreement is not valid or has terminated.

2. An application to the judicial authority for preservation or interim measures shall not be incompatible with an arbitration agreement and shall not imply a renunciation of the agreement.

1—540   Article 5

1. The arbitral tribunal shall be composed of an uneven number of arbitrators. There may be a sole arbitrator.

2. If the arbitration agreement provides for an even number of arbitrators an additional arbitrator shall be appointed.

3. If the parties have not settled the number of arbitrators in the arbitration agreement and do not agree on the number, the arbitral tribunal shall be composed of three arbitrators.

1—541   Article 6

The parties may, either in the arbitration agreement or subsequently thereto, appoint the sole arbitrator or the arbitrators or entrust the appointment to a third person. If the parties have not appointed the arbitrators and have not agreed on a method of appointment, each party shall, when the dispute arises, appoint an arbitrator or an equal number of arbitrators, as the case may be.

1—542   Article 7

1. The party who intends bringing a dispute before an arbitral tribunal shall give notice to the other party. The notice shall refer to the arbitration agreement and specify the subject-matter of the dispute, unless the arbitration agreement already does so.

2. If there is more than one arbitrator, and if the parties are entitled to appoint them, the notice shall specify the arbitrator or arbitrators appointed by the party invoking the arbitration agreement; the other party shall be invited, in the notice, to appoint the arbitrator or arbitrators whom he is entitled to appoint.

3. If a third person has been entrusted with the appointment of a sole arbitrator or of arbitrators and has not done so, he also shall be given notice in accordance with paragraph 1 and invited to make the appointment.

4. The appointment of an arbitrator may not be withdrawn after notification of the appointment.

1—543   Article 8

1. If the party or third person to whom notice has been given in accordance with Article 7 has not, within a period of one month from the notice, appointed the arbitrator or arbitrators whom the party or third person is entitled to appoint, the judicial authority shall make the nomination at the request of either party.

2. If the parties have agreed that there shall be a sole arbitrator and they have not appointed him by mutual consent within a period of one month from the notice under Article 7, the judicial authority shall make the nomination at the request of either party.

1—544   Article 9

1. Where the arbitrators appointed or nominated in accordance with the foregoing provisions are even in number, they shall nominate another arbitrator to be president of the arbitral tribunal. If they do not agree and if the parties have not provided otherwise, the judicial authority shall make the necessary nomination at the request of either party. The judicial authority may be seized after the expiration of a period of one month from the acceptance of his office by the last arbitrator or as soon as the failure to agree is established.

2. Where the arbitrators appointed are uneven in number they shall nominate one of themselves to be president of the arbitral tribunal, unless the parties have agreed on another method of appointment. If the arbitrators do not agree, the judicial authority seized under paragraph 1 shall make the necessary nomination.

1—545   Article 10

1. If an arbitrator dies or cannot for a reason of law or of fact perform his office, or if he refuses to accept it or does not carry it out, or if his office is terminated by mutual agreement of the parties, he shall be replaced in accordance with the rules governing his appointment or nomination. However, if the arbitrator or arbitrators are named in the arbitration agreement, the agreement shall terminate *ipso jure*.

2. A disagreement arising out of any case envisaged in paragraph 1 shall be brought before the judicial authority on the application of one of the parties. If the judicial authority decides that there are grounds for replacing the arbitrator, it shall nominate his successor, taking into account the intention of the parties, as appearing from the arbitration agreement.

3. The parties may derogate from the provisions of this article.

1—546   Article 11

Unless the parties have agreed otherwise, neither the arbitration agreement nor the office of arbitrator shall be terminated by the death of one of the parties.

1—547   Article 12

1. Arbitrators may be challenged on the same grounds as judges.

2. A party may not challenge an arbitrator appointed by him except on a ground of which the party becomes aware after the appointment.

1—548   Article 13

1. The challenge shall, as soon as the challenger becomes aware of the ground of challenge, be brought to the notice of the arbitrators and, where applicable, of the third person who

has, in pursuance of the arbitration agreement, appointed the arbitrator challenged. The arbitrators shall thereupon suspend further proceedings.

2. If, within a period of ten days of the notice of the challenge being given to him, the arbitrator challenged has not resigned, the arbitral tribunal shall so notify the challenger. The challenger shall, on pain of being barred, bring the matter before the judicial authority within a period of ten days from receiving such notification. Otherwise, the proceedings before the arbitrators shall be resumed *ipso jure*.

3. If the arbitrator resigns or if the challenge is upheld by the judicial authority, the arbitrator shall be replaced in accordance with the rules governing his appointment or nomination. However, if he has been named in the arbitration agreement, the agreement shall terminate *ipso jure*. The parties may derogate from the provisions of this paragraph.

1—549 **Article 14**

1. The parties may in the arbitration agreement exclude certain categories of persons from being arbitrators.

2. If such an exclusion has been disregarded with respect to the composition of the arbitral tribunal, the irregularity shall be invoked in accordance with the provisions of Article 13.

1—550 **Article 15**

1. Without prejudice to the provisions of Article 16, the parties may decide on the rules of the arbitral procedure and on the place of arbitration. If the parties do not indicate their intention before the first arbitrator has accepted his office, the decision shall be a matter for the arbitrators.

2. The president of the arbitral tribunal shall regulate the hearings and conduct the proceedings.

1—551 **Article 16**

1. The arbitral tribunal shall give each party an opportunity of substantiating his claims and of presenting his case.

2. The arbitral tribunal shall make an award after oral proceedings. The parties may validly be summoned by registered letter, unless they have agreed upon any other method of summons. The parties may appear in person.

3. The procedure shall be in writing where the parties have so provided or in so far as they have waived oral proceedings.

4. Each party shall have the right to be represented by an advocate or by a duly accredited representative. Each party may be assisted by any person of his choice.

1—552   Article 17

If, without legitimate cause, a party properly summoned does not appear or does not present his case within the period fixed, the arbitral tribunal may, unless the other party requests an adjournment, investigate the matter in dispute and make an award.

1—553   Article 18

1. The arbitral tribunal may rule in respect of its own jurisdiction and, for this purpose, may examine the validity of the arbitration agreement.

2. A ruling that the contract is invalid shall not entail *ipso jure* the nullity of the arbitration agreement contained in it.

3. The arbitral tribunal's ruling that it has jurisdiction may not be contested before the judicial authority except at the same time as the award on the main issue and by the same procedure. The judicial authority may at the request of one of the parties decide whether a ruling that the arbitral tribunal has no jurisdiction is well founded.

4. The appointment of an arbitrator by a party shall not deprive that party of his rights to challenge the jurisdiction of the arbitral tribunal.

1—554   Article 19

1. The parties may, up to the time of acceptance of office by the first arbitrator, settle the period within which the award is to be made or provide for a method according to which the period is to be settled.

2. If the parties have not prescribed a period or a method of prescribing a period, if the arbitral tribunal delays in making the award and if a period of six months has elapsed from the date on which all the arbitrators accepted office in respect of the dispute submitted to arbitration, the judicial authority may, at the request of one of the parties, stipulate a period for the arbitral tribunal.

3. The office of arbitrator shall terminate if the award is not made within the relevant period unless that period is extended by agreement between the parties.

4. Where arbitrators are named in the arbitration agreement and the award is not made within the relevant period, the arbitration agreement shall terminate *ipso jure*, unless the parties have agreed otherwise.

1—555   Article 20

Except where otherwise stipulated, an arbitral tribunal may make a final award in the form of one or more awards.

1—556   Article 21

Except where otherwise stipulated, arbitrators shall make their awards in accordance with the rules of law.

1—557   Article 22

1. An award shall be made after a deliberation in which all the arbitrators shall take part. The award shall be made by an absolute majority of votes, unless the parties have agreed on another majority.

2. The parties may also agree that, when a majority cannot be obtained, the president of the arbitral tribunal shall have a casting vote.

3. Except where otherwise stipulated, if the arbitrators are to award a sum of money, and a majority cannot be obtained for any particular sum, the votes for the highest sum shall be counted as votes for the next highest sum until a majority is obtained.

4. An award shall be set down in writing and signed by the arbitrators. If one or more of the arbitrators are unable or unwilling to sign, the fact shall be recorded in the award. However, the award shall bear a number of signatures which is at least equal to a majority of the arbitrators.

5. An award shall, in addition to the operative part, contain the following particulars:

   a) the names and permanent addresses of the arbitrators;
   b) the names and permanent addresses of the parties;
   c) the subject-matter of the dispute;
   d) the date on which the award was made;

e) the place of arbitration and the place where the award was made.

6. The reasons for an award shall be stated.

1—558   Article 23

1. The president of the arbitral tribunal shall give notice to each party of the award by sending him a copy thereof, signed in accordance with paragraph 4 of Article 22.

2. The president of the arbitral tribunal shall deposit the original of the award with the registry of the court having jurisdiction; he shall inform the parties of the deposit.

1—559   Article 24

Unless the award is contrary to *ordre public* or the dispute was not capable of settlement by arbitration, an arbitral award has the authority of *res judicata* when it has been notified in accordance with paragraph 1 of Article 23 and may no longer be contested before arbitrators.

1—560   Article 25

1. An arbitral award may be contested before a judicial authority only by way of an application to set aside and may be set aside only in the cases mentioned in this article.

2. An arbitral award may be set aside:
   a) if it is contrary to *ordre public*;
   b) if the dispute was not capable of settlement by arbitration;
   c) if there is no valid arbitration agreement;
   d) if the arbitral tribunal has exceeded its jurisdiction or its powers;
   e) if the arbitral tribunal has omitted to make an award in respect of one or more points of the dispute and if the points omitted cannot be separated from the points in respect of which an award has been made;
   f) if the award was made by an arbitral tribunal irregularly constituted;
   g) if the parties have not been given an opportunity of substantiating their claims and presenting their case, or if there has been disregard of any other obligatory rule of the arbitral procedure, in so far as such disregard has had an influence on the arbitral award;

- h) if the formalities prescribed in paragraph 4 of Article 22 have not been fulfilled;
- i) if the reasons for the award have not been stated;
- j) if the award contains conflicting provisions.

3. An award may also be set aside:
   - a) if it was obtained by fraud;
   - b) if it is based on evidence that has been declared false by a judicial decision having the force of *res judicata* or on evidence recognised as false;
   - c) if, after it was made, there has been discovered a document or other piece of evidence which would have had a decisive influence on the award and which was withheld through the act of the other party.

4. A case mentioned in sub-paragraph c, d or f of paragraph 2 shall be deemed not to constitute a ground for setting aside an award where the party availing himself of it had knowledge of it during the arbitration proceedings and did not invoke it at the time.

5. Grounds for the challenge and exclusion of arbitrators provided for under Articles 12 and 14 shall not constitute grounds for setting aside within the meaning of paragraph 2.f of this article, even when they become known only after the award is made.

1—561 Article 26

If there are grounds for setting aside any part of an award, that part shall be set aside only if it can be separated from the other parts of the award.

1—562 Article 27

1. The grounds for setting aside an arbitral award shall, on pain of being barred, be put forward by the party concerned in one and the same proceedings, except, however, in the case of a ground for setting aside provided for in paragraph 3 of Article 25 where the ground is not known until later.

2. An application to set aside an award shall be admissible only where the award may no longer be contested before arbitrators.

1—563 Article 28

1. An application to set aside an award, based on one of the grounds provided for in paragraph 2.c to j of Article 25 shall,

on pain or being barred, be made within a period of three months from the date on which the award was notified. However, that period shall begin to run only from the date on which the award is no longer capable of contestation before arbitrators.

2. The defendant in an application to set aside an award may apply, in the same proceedings, for the award to be set aside, even if the period laid down in paragraph 1 has expired.

3. An application to set aside an award, based on one of the grounds provided for in paragraph 3 of Article 25, shall be made within a period of three months from either the date of the discovery of the fraud, document or other piece of evidence, or the date on which the evidence was declared false or recognised as false, provided that a period of five years from the date on which the award was notified in accordance with paragraph 1 of Article 23 has not expired.

4. The judicial authority seized of an application to set aside an award shall examine *proprio motu* whether the award is contrary to *ordre public* and whether the dispute was capable of settlement by arbitration.

1—564 Article 29

1. An arbitral award may be enforced only when it can no longer be contested before arbitrators and when an enforcement formula has been apposed to it by the competent authority on the application of the interested party.

2. The competent authority shall refuse the application if the award or its enforcement is contrary to *ordre public* or if the dispute was not capable of settlement by arbitration.

3. A decision refusing the application is appealable.

1—565 Article 30

1. A decision apposing an enforcement formula to an award shall be notified. The decision is appealable within a period of one month from the date on which the decision is notified.

2. A party exercising this right of appeal who seeks to secure the setting aside of the award without having previously made application for this shall, on pain of being barred, make his application in the same proceedings and within the period prescribed in paragraph 1. A party who, while not exercising the right of appeal provided for in paragraph 1, seeks to

secure the setting aside of an award shall, on pain of being barred, make his application for setting aside within the period prescribed in paragraph 1. The application for setting aside envisaged in the present paragraph shall be admissible only if the period prescribed in Article 28 has not expired.

3. The provisions of paragraph 2 of this article shall apply to the grounds for setting aside an award provided for in paragraph 3 of Article 25 only if such grounds were known at the time of notification of the decision apposing the enforcement formula to the award.

4. Without prejudice to the provisions of paragraph 4 of Article 25, a party exercising the right of appeal provided for in paragraph 1 of this article may apply for the setting aside of the award if there is no valid arbitration agreement, even if the period prescribed in Article 28 has expired.

5. In the case either of an appeal against the decision apposing an enforcement formula to an award or of an application for an award to be set aside, the judicial authority may, at the request of one of the parties, order the enforcement of the award to be stayed.

6. A decision apposing an enforcement formula to an award shall be without effect to the extent that the arbitral award has been set aside.

1—566 Article 31

1. Where, before an arbitral tribunal, a compromise has been entered into between the parties in order to put an end to a dispute of which the tribunal is seized, that compromise may be recorded in an instrument prepared by the arbitral tribunal and signed by the arbitrators as well as by the parties. The instrument shall be subject to the provisions of paragraph 2 of Article 23. The instrument may, on the application of the interested party, have an enforcement formula apposed to it by the competent authority.

2. The competent authority shall refuse the application if the compromise or its enforcement is contrary to *ordre public* or if the dispute was not capable of settlement by arbitration.

3. The decision of the competent authority is appealable.

Annex II

1—567 Any Contracting Party may declare that it reserves the right:

a) to derogate from the provisions of paragraph 1 of Article 2 of the uniform law, particularly in respect of disputes between defined categories of persons;

b) not to introduce into its law the provisions of paragraph 2 of Article 2 of the uniform law, or to regulate differently the case where the parties have referred to a particular arbitration procedure;

c) to provide in its law that the additional arbitrator provided for in paragraph 2 of Article 5 of the uniform law shall be appointed or nominated only in the case of a tie in voting;

d) to provide in its law that, in the cases mentioned in paragraph 1 of Article 10 and in paragraph 4 of Article 19 of the uniform law, the arbitration agreement shall, where the arbitrator or arbitrators are named therein, terminate *ipso jure* only in so far as concerns the dispute submitted to arbitration.

e) not to introduce into its law paragraph 2 of Article 18 of the uniform law or to regulate differently the effects which a ruling that a contract is void may have on the arbitration agreement;

f) to derogate from the provisions of paragraph 5 of Article 25 and, if need be, from those of paragraphs 2 and 3 of Article 13 and of paragraph 2 of Article 14 of the uniform law in so far as, under those provisions, the grounds of challenge or of irregularity in the composition of the arbitral tribunal may not constitute grounds for setting aside the award but must be invoked before the judicial authority during the arbitration proceedings;

g) to provide that it is only after a dispute has arisen that the parties may, in pursuance of Article 21 of the uniform law, exempt the arbitrators from deciding in accordance with the rules of law;

h) not to introduce into its law paragraph 2 of Article 22 of the uniform law, or to regulate differently the case where a majority of votes cannot be obtained;

i) not to introduce into its law the provisions of paragraph 6 of Article 22 and of paragraph 2.i of Article 25 of the uniform law or to derogate from those provisions;

j) to derogate from the provisions of paragraph 2 of Article 23 of the uniform law;

k) to amend or not to introduce into its law the provisions of Article 24 of the uniform law;

l) to derogate from paragraph 3.c of Article 25 of the uniform law and, if need be, to replace in paragraph 3 of Article 28 the words "document or other piece of evidence" by different expressions;

m) to restrict in its law the application of paragraph 4 of Article 25 of the uniform law to the case where the arbitral tribunal has been irregularly constituted by reason of being composed of an even number of arbitrators;

n) to derogate from the provisions of Article 30 of the uniform law;

o) not to introduce into its law Article 31 of the uniform law.

Annex III

1—568   1. Each Contracting Party may, at the time of signature of the present Convention or when depositing its instrument of ratification, acceptance or accession, declare that, in case of conflict between the provisions of the uniform law contained in Annex I and those of other international conventions, which it may specify, it will apply the provisions of the uniform law to arbitrations between physical or legal persons having, when concluding the arbitration agreement, their habitual place of residence or their seat in the territories of different States which are Parties to the present Convention and which have made a like declaration.

Each Contracting Party may make the declaration after the entry into force of the present Convention in respect of that Party, in which case the declaration will take effect six months after notification thereof has been addressed to the Secretary General of the Council of Europe.

2. A declaration made in pursuance of the preceding paragraph may be withdrawn at any time by notification addressed to the Secretary General of the Council of Europe. The withdrawal shall take effect six months after the notification.

OHADA Uniform Act on Arbitration 1999

Chapter I: Scope of Application

1—569   Article 1

This Uniform Act shall apply to any arbitration when the seat of the Arbitral Tribunal is in one of the Member States.

1—570   Article 2

Any natural person or corporate body may recourse to arbitration on rights of which he has free disposal. States and other territorial public bodies as well as public establishments may equally be parties to an arbitration without having the possibility to invoke their own law to contest the arbitrability of the claim, their authority to sign arbitration agreements or the validity of the arbitration agreement.

1—571   Article 3

The arbitration agreement shall be in writing, or by any other means permitting it to be evidenced, notably, by reference made to a document stipulating it.

1—572   Article 4

The arbitration agreement is independent of the main contract.
Its validity shall not be affected by the nullity of this contract and it is assessed according to the intention of both parties, without necessary reference to a state law. The parties can always mutually agree to resort to an arbitration agreement, even when a hearing has already been initiated before another court.

Chapter II: Constitution of the Arbitral Tribunal

1—573   Article 5

Arbitrators shall be appointed, dismissed or replaced in accordance with the agreement of the parties. Where there is no such arbitration agreement, or where the agreement is not sufficient:

a) in an arbitration with three arbitrators, each party shall appoint one arbitrator and the two arbitrators thus appointed shall appoint the third arbitrator; if a party fails to appoint the arbitrator within thirty days of receipt of a request to do so from the other party, or if the two arbitrators fail to agree on the third arbitrator within thirty days of their appointment, the appointment shall be made upon request of a party, by the competent judge in the Member State.

b) in an arbitration with a sole arbitrator, if the parties are unable to agree on the arbitrator, he shall be appointed, upon request of a party, by the competent judge in the Member State.

1—574   Article 6

The function of an arbitrator may only be performed by a natural person. The arbitrator must enjoy fully his civic rights, must remain independent and impartial vis-à-vis the parties.

1—575   Article 7

The arbitrator who accepts to perform his function shall communicate his acceptance to the parties by any means in writing. If the arbitrator knows of any circumstances about himself for which he may be challenged, he shall disclose them to the parties and may only accept his function with the unanimous agreement, in writing, of other parties.

In case of dispute, and if the parties have not determined the procedure for challenging an arbitrator, the competent judge in the Member State shall decide on the challenge. His decision shall not be subject to any appeal.

Any reasons for challenging an arbitrator must be disclosed without delay by the party who intends to challenge the arbitrator.

The challenge of an arbitrator shall only be admissible for reasons which became known after his appointment has been made.

1—576   Article 8

The arbitral Tribunal shall be composed of a sole arbitrator or a panel of three arbitrators. Where the parties designate the arbitrators in even numbers, the arbitral Tribunal shall be completed by one arbitrator, chosen either in accordance with the agreement of the parties, or, in the absence of such agreement, by the arbitrators appointed or, where they are unable to agree on the arbitrator, by the competent court in the Member State.

The same is true in case of challenge, incapacity, death, resignation or revocation of an arbitrator.

Chapter III: The Arbitral Hearing

1—577 Article 9

The parties shall be treated with equality and each party shall be given a full opportunity to present its case.

1—578 Article 10

Except where the parties expressly exclude the application of certain provisions of the arbitration rules of an institution, submission to this arbitration institution shall bind them to apply the arbitration rules of such institution.

The arbitral hearing is linked as soon as one of the parties seizes one or all the arbitrators in accordance with the arbitration agreement, or, failing such appointment, as soon as one of the parties initiates the procedure for the constitution of the arbitral tribunal.

1—579 Article 11

The arbitral tribunal shall rule on its own jurisdiction including any questions with respect to the existence or validity of the arbitration agreement. A plea for lack of the arbitral tribunal's jurisdiction shall be raised not later than the time of submission of the statement of defence on the substance except where the facts on which they are based were discovered later. The arbitral tribunal may rule on its own jurisdiction in the award on the substance or in a partial award subject to recourse for nullity.

1—580 Article 12

If the arbitration agreement does not determine a time limit, the assignment of the arbitrators may not exceed six months as from the date when the last of them accepted the assignment.

The legal or agreed time limit may be extended either by agreement of the parties, or at the request of one of them or of the arbitral tribunal, by the competent judge in the Member State.

1—581 Article 13

When a dispute of which an arbitral tribunal bas been seized by virtue of an arbitration agreement is brought before a state court, the said Court shall, if one of the parties makes a request to this effect, declare having jurisdiction. If the arbitral tribunal bas not yet been seized of the matter, the state court shall equally declare itself incompetent unless the arbitration agreement is manifestly void. In any case, the state court cannot automatically declare its incompetence.

However the existence of an arbitration agreement shall not be an obstacle to the fact that on the application of one party, a court, in case of emergency and with reasons given, or when a measure shall have to be enforced in a non-member State of OHBLA, order interim measures as long as the measures do not require an examination of the claim on the substance, for which only the arbitral Tribunal is competent.

1—582   Article 14

The parties may directly or by reference to arbitration rules, determine the arbitration procedure; they may also subject this procedure to a procedural law of their choice.

Where there is no such agreement, the arbitral Tribunal may conduct the arbitration as it considers appropriate. To support their claims, the parties shall have to allege and adduce evidence to establish their claims. The arbitrators may invite the parties to furnish them with factual explanations, and to present to them by any means legally admissible, evidence which they believe will provide a solution to the claim. Any explanations or documents invoked or produced by the parties and retained as evidence must have been the subject of an adversary procedure.

They cannot base their ruling on evidence they established on their own without having invited the parties to present their remarks. If the aid of judicial authorities is necessary for the production of evidence, the arbitral Tribunal may automatically or on application, request the assistance of the competent judge in the

Member State. A party who, knowingly, abstains from stating without undue delay an irregularity and pursues the arbitration, is deemed to have waived his right to object to it.

Unless agreed otherwise, the arbitrator shall equally be empowered to rule on all points of law concerning the verification of writing and fraud.

1—583   Article 15

The arbitrators shall decide the dispute in accordance with the rules of law chosen by the parties or, in the absence of such a choice, according to those chosen by them as the most appropriate taking into account, where necessary, the international trade usages.

They may also decide as amiable compositeur when the parties have authorized them to do so.

1—584   Article 16

The arbitration proceedings end by the expiration of the time limit for arbitration, except where there is an extension of time agreed by the parties or ordered.

It may equally be terminated in case of acknowledgement of claim, withdrawal of claim, agreement by the parties to terminate proceedings or final award.

1—585   Article 17

The arbitral Tribunal shall determine the date on which the dispute shall be deliberated upon.

After this date, no other claim may be raised. No remarks may be presented, neither can any piece of evidence be produced except on the express request, in writing, of the arbitral tribunal.

1—586   Article 18

The deliberations of the arbitral tribunal shall be secret.

Chapter IV: The Arbitral Award

1—587   Article 19

The arbitration award is made following the procedure and form agreed upon by the parties.

Where there is no such agreement, the award shall be made by majority vote when the tribunal is composed of three arbitrators.

1—588   Article 20

The arbitration award shall contain:

- the full name of the arbitrator or arbitrators
- the date of the award:
- the seat of the arbitral Tribunal:
- the full names and company name of the parties, as well as their residence or registered office;
- where necessary, the full names of advocates or any person having represented or assisted the parties.
- the statement of the respective claims of the parties, their arguments as well as the stages of the procedure.

Reasons upon which the award is based shall be given.

1—589   Article 21

The award shall be signed by the arbitrator or arbitrators.

However, where a minority of them refuses to sign the award, mention shall be made of such refusal and the award shall have the same effect as if it had been signed by all the arbitrators.

1—590   Article 22

The award shall discharge the arbitrator of the dispute.

The arbitrator shall nevertheless have the power to interpret the award or to redress clerical errors and omissions affecting the award.

Where be bas omitted to rule on part of the claim, be may do it by an additional award.

In one case or the other mentioned above, the request must be made within 30 days from the date of notification of the award. The Tribunal shall have a period of 45 days to give a ruling.

If the arbitral Tribunal can no longer be reconvened, the competent judge in the in the member State shall give such ruling.

1—591   Article 23

As soon as the award is made, the dispute so settled is res judicata.

1—592   Article 24

The arbitrators may grant provisional enforcement of the award where the provisional enforcement has been requested, or may reject the request, with reasons given.

CHAPTER V: RECOURSE AGAINST THE ARBITRAL AWARD

1—593   Article 25

The award is not subject to any opposition, appeal or judgment setting it aside.

It may be subject to a petition for nullity, which must be lodged with the competent judge in the Member State.

The decision of the competent judge in the Member State can only be set aside by the Common Court of Justice and Arbitration.

The award may be subject to opposition before the arbitral Tribunal by any third party, be he a natural person or corporate body, who had not been called, and when the award is damaging to his rights.

It may also be the object of an application for revision before the arbitral Tribunal by reason of the discovery of a fact capable of having a decisive influence and which, before the making of the award, was unknown to both the arbitral Tribunal and the party applying for revision.

1—594   Article 26

Recourse for nullity is only admissible in the following cases:

- if the arbitral Tribunal has ruled without an arbitration agreement or on an agreement which is void or bas expired
- if the arbitral Tribunal was irregularly composed or the sole arbitrator was irregularly appointed;
- if the arbitral Tribunal has settled without conforming to the assignment it has been conferred;
- if the principle of adversary procedure has not been observed;
- if the arbitral Tribunal bas violated an international public policy rule of the States, signatories of the Treaty.
- if no reasons are given for the award.

1—595   Article 27

The petition for nullity is admissible as soon as the award is made; it ceases to be admissible if it bas not been made within one month of notification of the award furnished with an exequatur.

1—596   Article 28

Except where the provisional enforcement of the award bas been ordered by the arbitral Tribunal, the exercise of the recourse for nullity shall stay execution of the award until such time that the competent judge in the member State makes a ruling.

The judge shall also have jurisdiction to rule on a dispute concerning provisional enforcement.

1—597   Article 29

In case of annulment of the award, the earliest party, if he so wishes, shall initiate another arbitration proceedings in accordance with this uniform Act.

CHAPTER VI: RECOGNITION AND ENFORCEMENT OF ARBITRAL AWARDS

1—598   Article 30

The award can only be subject to compulsory enforcement by virtue of an exequatur awarded by the competent judge in the member State.

1—599   Article 31

Recognition and exequatur of the award presupposes the fact that the party wishing to rely on it shall establish the existence of the award.

The existence of the award is established by the production of the original award accompanied by the arbitration agreement or copies of these documents satisfying the conditions required for their authenticity.

Where the documents are not written in French, the party shall have to produce a translation certified by a translator registered on the list of experts established by competent courts.

The recognition and exequatur shall be refused where the award is manifestly contrary to international public policy of the Member States.

1—600   Article 32

The ruling refusing the exequatur of the award can only be set aside by the Common Court of Justice and Arbitration.

The ruling granting the exequatur is not subject to any recourse.

However a petition for nullity of the award shall, as matter of law, and within the limits of the seizing of the competent judge of the member state, mean recourse against the ruling allowing exequatur by the court.

1—601   Article 33

The rejection of the petition for nullity shall, as a matter of law, mean validation of the award as well as the ruling granting the exequatur.

1—602   Article 34

Awards made on the basis of rules different from those provided by this Uniform Act shall be recognized as binding within the member States under the conditions provided by International agreements possibly applicable and. failing which, under the same conditions as those provided in this Uniform Act.

Chapter VII: Final Provisions

1—603   Article 35

This Uniform Act shall be the law governing any arbitration in the member States.

This Act is only applicable to arbitration proceedings, arising after its entry into force.

1—604   Article 36

This Uniform Act shall be published in the Official Gazette of OHBLA and of the ContractingStates.

It shall enter into force in accordance with the provisions of article 9 of the Treaty relative to the Harmonization of Business Law in Africa.

Chapter 2

International Arbitration Conventions

A. World-wide Multilateral Conventions

United Nations Convention on the Recognition and Enforcement of Foreign Arbitral Awards

(NEW YORK, 10 JUNE 1958)

2—001 Article I

1. This Convention shall apply to the recognition and enforcement of arbitral awards made in the territory of a State other than the State where the recognition and enforcement of such awards are sought, and arising out of differences between persons, whether physical or legal. It shall also apply to arbitral awards not considered as domestic awards in the State where their recognition and enforcement are sought.

2. The term "arbitral awards" shall include not only awards made by arbitrators appointed for each case but also those made by permanent arbitral bodies to which the parties have submitted.

3. When signing, ratifying or acceding to this Convention, or notifying extension under article X hereof, any State may on the basis of reciprocity declare that it will apply the Convention to the recognition and enforcement of awards made only in the territory of another Contracting State. It may also declare that it will apply the Convention only to differences arising out of legal relationships, whether contractual or not, which are considered as commercial under the national law of the State making such declaration.

2—002   Article II

1. Each Contracting State shall recognize an agreement in writing under which the parties undertake to submit to arbitration all or any differences which have arisen or which may arise between them in respect of a defined legal relationship, whether contractual or not, concerning a subject matter capable of settlement by arbitration.

2. The term "agreement in writing" shall include an arbitral clause in a contract or an arbitration agreement, signed by the parties or contained in an exchange of letters or telegrams.

3. The court of a Contracting State, when seized of an action in a matter in respect of which the parties have made an agreement within the meaning of this article, shall, at the request of one of the parties, refer the parties to arbitration, unless it finds that the said agreement is null and void, inoperative or incapable of being performed.

2—003   Article III

Each Contracting State shall recognize arbitral awards as binding and enforce them in accordance with the rules of procedure of the territory where the award is relied upon, under the conditions laid down in the following articles. There shall not be imposed substantially more onerous conditions or higher fees or charges on the recognition or enforcement of arbitral awards to which this Convention applies than are imposed on the recognition or enforcement of domestic arbitral awards.

2—004   Article IV

1. To obtain the recognition and enforcement mentioned in the preceding article, the party applying for recognition and enforcement shall, at the time of the application, supply:

    (a) The duly authenticated original award or a duly certified copy thereof;
    (b) The original agreement referred to in article II or a duly certified copy thereof.

2. If the said award or agreement is not made in an official language of the country in which the award is relied upon, the party applying for recognition and enforcement of the award shall produce a translation of these documents into such language. The translation shall be certified by an official or sworn translator or by a diplomatic or consular agent.

2—005   Article V

1. Recognition and enforcement of the award may be refused, at the request of the party against whom it is invoked, only if that party furnishes to the competent authority where the recognition and enforcement is sought, proof that:

    (a) The parties to the agreement referred to in article II were, under the law applicable to them, under some incapacity, or the said agreement is not valid under the law to which the parties have subjected it or, failing any indication thereon, under the law of the country where the award was made; or
    (b) The party against whom the award is invoked was not given proper notice of the appointment of the arbitrator or of the arbitration proceedings or was otherwise unable to present his case; or
    (c) The award deals with a difference not contemplated by or not falling within the terms of the submission to arbitration, or it contains decisions on matters beyond the scope of the submission to arbitration, provided that, if the decisions on matters submitted to arbitration can be separated from those not so submitted, that part of the award which contains decisions on matters submitted to arbitration may be recognized and enforced; or
    (d) The composition of the arbitral authority or the arbitral procedure was not in accordance with the agreement of the parties, or, failing such agreement, was not in accordance with the law of the country where the arbitration took place; or
    (e) The award has not yet become binding, on the parties, or has been set aside or suspended by a competent authority of the country in which, or under the law of which, that award was made.

2. Recognition and enforcement of an arbitral award may also be refused if the competent authority in the country where recognition and enforcement is sought finds that:

    (a) The subject matter of the difference is not capable of settlement by arbitration under the law of that country; or
    (b) The recognition or enforcement of the award would be contrary to the public policy of that country.

2—006   Article VI

If an application for the setting, aside or suspension of the award has been made to a competent authority referred to in article V (1) (e), the authority before which the award is sought to be relied upon may, if it considers it proper, adjourn the decision on the enforcement of the award and may also, on the application of the party claiming enforcement of the award, order the other party to give suitable security.

2—207   Article VII

1. The provisions of the present Convention shall not affect the validity of multilateral or bilateral agreements concerning the recognition and enforcement of arbitral awards entered into by the Contracting States nor deprive any interested party of any right he may have to avail himself of an arbitral award in the manner and to the extent allowed by the law or the treaties of the country where such award is sought to be relied upon.

2. The Geneva Protocol on Arbitration Clauses of 1923 and the Geneva Convention on the Execution of Foreign Arbitral Awards of 1927 shall cease to have effect between Contracting States on their becoming bound and to the extent that they become bound, by this Convention.

2—208   Article VIII

1. This Convention shall be open until 31 December 1958 for signature on behalf of any Member of the United Nations and also on behalf of any other State which is or hereafter becomes a member of any specialized agency of the United Nations, or which is or hereafter becomes a party to the Statute of the International Court of Justice, or any other State to which an invitation has been addressed by the General Assembly of the United Nations.

2. This Convention shall be ratified and the instrument of ratification shall be deposited with the Secretary-General of the United Nations.

2—209   Article IX

1. This Convention shall be open for accession to all States referred to in article VIII.

2. Accession shall be effected by the deposit of an instrument of accession with the Secretary-General of the United Nations.

2—210   Article X

1. Any State may, at the time of signature, ratification or accession, declare that this Convention shall extend to all or any of the territories for the international relations of which it is responsible. Such a declaration shall take effect when the Convention enters into force for the State concerned.

2. At any time thereafter any such extension shall be made by notification addressed to the Secretary-General of the United Nations and shall take effect as from the ninetieth day after the day of receipt by the Secretary-General of the United Nations of this notification, or as from the date of entry into force of the Convention for the State concerned, whichever is the later.

3. With respect to those territories to which this Convention is not extended at the time of signature, ratification or accession, each State concerned shall consider the possibility of taking the necessary steps in order to extend the application of this Convention to such territories, subject, where necessary for constitutional reasons, to the consent of the Governments of such territories.

2—011   Article XI

In the case of a federal or non-unitary State, the following provisions shall apply:

(a) With respect to those articles of this Convention that come within the legislative jurisdiction of the federal authority, the obligations of the federal Government shall to this extent be the same as those of Contracting States which are not federal States;

(b) With respect to those articles of this Convention that come within the legislative jurisdiction of constituent states or provinces which are not, under the constitutional system of the federation, bound to take legislative action, the federal Government shall bring such articles with a favourable recommendation to the notice of the appropriate authorities of constituent states or provinces at the earliest possible moment;

(c) A federal State Party to this Convention shall, at the request of any other Contracting State transmitted through the Secretary-General of the United Nations, supply a statement of the law and practice of the federation and its constituent units in regard to any particular provision of this Convention, showing the extent to which effect has been given to that provision by legislative or other action.

2—012   Article XII

1. This Convention shall come into force on the ninetieth day following the date of deposit of the third instrument of ratification or accession.

2. For each State ratifying or acceding to this Convention after the deposit of the third instrument of ratification or accession, this Convention shall enter into force on the ninetieth day after deposit by such State of its instrument of ratification or accession.

2—013   Article XIII

1. Any Contracting State may denounce this Convention by a written notification to the Secretary-General of the United Nations. Denunciation shall take effect one year after the date of receipt of the notification by the Secretary-General.

2. Any State which has made a declaration or notification under article X may, at any time thereafter, by notification to the Secretary-General of the United Nations, declare that this Convention shall cease to extend to the territory concerned one year after the date of the receipt of the notification by the Secretary-General.

3. This Convention shall continue to be applicable to arbitral awards in respect of which recognition or enforcement proceedings have been instituted before the denunciation takes effect.

2—014   Article XIV

A Contracting State shall not be entitled to avail itself of the present Convention against other Contracting States except to the extent that it is itself bound to apply the Convention.

2—015   Article XV

The Secretary-General of the United Nations shall notify the States contemplated in article VIII of the following:

(a) Signatures and ratifications in accordance with article VIII;

(b) Accessions in accordance with article IX;

(c) Declarations and notifications under articles I, X and XI;

(d) The date upon which this Convention enters into force in accordance with article XII;

(e) Denunciations and notifications in accordance with article XIII.

2—016   Article XVI

1. This Convention, of which the Chinese, English, French, Russian and Spanish texts shall be equally authentic, shall be deposited in the archives of the United Nations.

2. The Secretary-General of the United Nations shall transmit a certified copy of this Convention to the States contemplated in article VIII.

NOTES

1. The Convention went into force on 7 June 1959.

ICSID — Convention on the Settlement of Investment Disputes Between States and Nationals of Other States

CONTENTS

PREAMBLE

CHAPTER I: International Centre for Settlement of Investment Disputes

Section.

1. Establishment and Organization
2. The Administrative Council
3. The Secretariat
4. The Panels
5. Financing the Centre
6. Status, Immunities and Privileges

CHAPTER II: Jurisdiction of the Centre

CHAPTER III: Conciliation

1. Request for Conciliation
2. Constitution of the Conciliation Commission
3. Conciliation Proceedings

CHAPTER IV: Arbitration

1. Request for Arbitration
2. Constitution of the Tribunal
3. Powers and Functions of the Tribunal
4. The Award
5. Interpretation, Revision and Annulment of the Award
6. Recognition and Enforcement of the Award

CHAPTER V: Replacement and Disqualification of Conciliators and Arbitrators

CHAPTER VI: Cost of Proceedings

CHAPTER VII: Place of Proceedings

CHAPTER VIII: Disputes Between Contracting States

CHAPTER IX: Amendment

CHAPTER X: Final Provisions

ICSID — Convention on the Settlement of Investment Disputes Between States and Nationals of Other States

WASHINGTON 1965

Submitted to Governments by the Executive Directors of the International Bank for Reconstruction and Development, Submitted: March 18, 1965, Washington
Entered into Force: October 14, 1966

2—017 Preamble

The Contracting States
Considering the need for international cooperation for economic development, and the role of private international investment therein;

> Bearing in mind the possibility that from time to time disputes may arise in connection with such investment between Contracting States and nationals of other Contracting States;

> Recognizing that while such disputes would usually be subject to national legal processes, international methods of settlement may be appropriate in certain cases;

> Attaching particular importance to the availability of facilities for international conciliation or arbitration to which Contracting States and nationals of other Contracting States may submit such disputes if they so desire;

> Desiring to establish such facilities under the auspices of the International Bank for Reconstruction and Development; Recognizing that mutual consent by the parties to submit such disputes to conciliation or to arbitration through such facilities constitutes a binding agreement which requires in particular that due consideration be given to any recommendation of conciliators, and that any arbitral award be complied with; and

> Declaring that no Contracting State shall by the mere fact of its ratification, acceptance or approval of this Convention and without its consent be deemed to be under any obligation to submit any particular dispute to conciliation or arbitration,

> Have agreed as follows:

Chapter I: International Centre for Settlement of Investment Disputes

Section 1: Establishment and Organization

2—018   Article 1

    1. There is hereby established the International Centre for Settlement of Investment Disputes (hereinafter called the Centre).

    2. The purpose of the Centre shall be to provide facilities for conciliation and arbitration of investment disputes between Contracting States and nationals of other Contracting States in accordance with the provisions of this Convention.

2—019   Article 2

The seat of the Centre shall be at the principal office for the International Bank for Reconstruction and Development (hereinafter called the Bank). The seat may be moved to another place by decision of the Administrative Council adopted by a majority of two-thirds of its members.

2—020   Article 3

The Centre shall have an Administrative Council and a Secretariat and shall maintain a Panel of Conciliators and a Panel of Arbitrators.

Section 2: The Administrative Council

2—021   Article 4

The Administrative Council shall be composed of one representative of each Contracting State. An alternate may act as representative in case of his principal's absence from a meeting or inability to act.

In the absence of a contrary designation, each governor and alternate of the Bank appointed by a Contracting State shall be ex officio its representative and its alternate respectively.

2—022   Article 5

The President of the Bank shall be ex officio Chairman of the Administrative Council (hereinafter called the Chairman) but shall have no vote. During his absence or inability to act and during any vacancy in the office of President of the Bank, the person for the time being acting as President shall act as Chairman of the Administrative Council.

2—023   Article 6

1. Without prejudice to the powers and functions vested in it by other provisions of this Convention, the Administrative Council shall

   (a) adopt the administrative and Financial regulations of the Centre;
   (b) adopt the rules of procedure for the institution of conciliation and arbitration proceedings;
   (c) adopt the rules of procedure for conciliation and arbitration proceedings (hereinafter called the Conciliation Rules and the Arbitration Rules);
   (d) approve arrangements with the Bank for the use of the Bank's administrative facilities and services;
   (e) determine the conditions of service of the Secretary-General and of any Deputy Secretary-General;
   (f) adopt the annual budget of revenues and expenditures of the Centre;
   (g) approve the annual report on the operation of the Centre. The decisions referred to in sub-paragraphs (a), (b), (c) and (0 above shall be adopted by a majority of two-thirds of the members of the Administrative Council.

2. The Administrative Council may appoint such committees as it considers necessary.

3. The Administrative Council shall also exercise such other powers and perform such other functions as it shall determine to be necessary for the implementation of the provisions of the Convention.

2—024   Article 7

1. The Administrative Council shall hold an annual meeting and such other meetings as may be determined by the Council, or convened by the Chairman, or convened by the Secretary-General at the request of not less than five members of the Council.

2. Each member of the Administrative Council shall have one vote and, except as otherwise herein provided, all matters before the Council shall be decided by a majority of the votes cast.

3. A quorum for any meeting of the Administrative Council shall be a majority of its members.

4. The Administrative Council may establish, by a majority of two-thirds of its members, a procedure whereby the Chairman may seek a vote of the Council without convening a meeting of the Council. The vote shall be considered valid only if the majority of the members of the Council cast their votes within the time limit fixed by the said procedure.

2—025   Article 8

Members of the Administrative Council and the Chairman shall serve without remuneration from the Centre.

Section 3: The Secretariat

2—026   Article 9

The Secretariat shall consist of a Secretary-General, one or more Deputy Secretaries-General and staff.

2—027   Article 10

1. The Secretary-General and any Deputy Secretary-General shall be elected by the Administrative Council by a majority of two-thirds of its members upon the nomination of the Chairman for a term of service not exceeding six years and shall be eligible for re-election. After consulting the members of the Administrative Council, the Chairman shall propose one or more candidates for each such office.

2. The offices of Secretary-General and Deputy Secretary-General shall be incompatible with the exercise of any political function. Neither the Secretary-General nor any Deputy Secretary-General may hold any other employment or engage in any other occupation except with the approval of the Administrative Council.

3. During the Secretary-General's absence or inability to act, and during any vacancy of the office of Secretary-General, the Deputy Secretary-General shall act as Secretary-General. If there shall be more than one Deputy Secretary-General, the Administrative Council shall determine in advance the order in which they shall act as Secretary-General.

2—028   Article 11

The Secretary-General shall be the legal representative and the principal officer of the Centre and shall be responsible for its administration, including the appointment of staff, in accordance with the provisions of this Convention and the rules adopted by the Administrative Council. He shall perform the function of registrar and shall have the power to authenticate arbitral awards rendered pursuant to this Convention, and to certify copies thereof.

Section 4: The Panels

2—029   Article 12

The Panel of Conciliators and the Panel of Arbitrators shall each consist of qualified persons, designated as hereinafter provided, who are willing to serve thereon.

2—030   Article 13

> 1. Each Contracting State may designate to each Panel four persons who may but need not be its nationals.
>
> 2. The Chairman may designate ten persons to each Panel: The persons so designated to a Panel shall each have a, different nationality.

2—031   Article 14

> 1. Persons designated to serve on the Panels shall be persons of high moral character and recognized competence in the Fields of law, commerce, industry or finance, who may be relied upon to exercise independent judgement. Competence in the Field of law shall be of particular importance in the case of persons on the Panel or Arbitrators.
>
> 2. The Chairman, in designating persons to serve on the Panels, shall in addition pay due regard to the importance of assuring representation on the Panels of the principal legal systems of the world and of the main forms of economic activity.

2—032   Article 15

> 1. Panel members shall serve for renewable periods of six years.

2. In case of death or resignation of a member of a Panel, the authority which designated the member shall have the right to designate another person to serve for the remainder of that member's term.

3. Panel members shall continue in office until their successors have been designated.

2—033   Article 16

1. A person may serve on both Panels.

2. If a person shall have been designated to serve on the same Panel by more than one Contracting State, or by one or more Contracting States and the Chairman, he shall be deemed to have been designated by the authority which First designated him or, if one such authority is the State or which he is a national, by that State.

3. All designations shall be notified to the Secretary-General and shall take effect from the date on which the notification is received.

Section 5: Financing the Centre

2—034   Article 17

If the expenditure of the Centre cannot be met out of charges for the use of its facilities, or out of other receipts, the excess shall be borne by Contracting States which are members of the Bank in proportion to their respective subscriptions to the capital stock of the Bank, and by Contracting States which are not members of the Bank in accordance with rules adopted by the Administrative Council.

Section 6: Status, Immunities and Privileges

2—035   Article 18

The Centre shall have full international legal personality. The legal capacity of the Centre shall include the capacity

(a) to contract;

(b) to acquire and dispose of movable and immovable property;

(c) to institute legal proceedings

2—036 Article 19

To enable the Centre to fulfil its functions, it shall enjoy in the territories of each Contracting State the immunities and privileges set forth in this Section.

2—037 Article 20

The Centre, its property and assets shall enjoy immunity from all legal process, except when the Centre waives this immunity.

2—038 Article 21

The Chairman, the members of the Administrative Council, persons acting as conciliators or arbitrators or members of a Committee appointed pursuant to paragraph (3) of Article 52, and the officers and employees of the Secretariat.

> (a) shall enjoy immunity from legal process with respect to acts performed by them in the exercise of their functions, except when the Centre waives this immunity;
>
> (b) not being local nationals, shall enjoy the same immunities from immigration restrictions, alien registration requirements and national service obligations, the same facilities as regards exchange restrictions and the same treatment in respect of travelling facilities as are accorded by Contracting States to the representatives, officials and employees of comparable rank of other Contracting States.

2—039 Article 22

The provisions of Article 21 shall apply to persons appearing in proceedings under this Convention as parties, agents, counsel, advocates, witnesses or experts; provided, however, that sub-paragraph (b) thereof shall apply only in connection with their travel to and from, and their stay at, the place where the proceedings are held.

2—040 Article 23

> 1. The archives of the Centre shall be inviolable, wherever they may be.
>
> 2. With regard to its official communications, the Centre shall be accorded by each Contracting State treatment not less favorable than that accorded to other international organizations.

2—041   Article 24

1. The Centre, its assets, property and income, and its operations and transactions authorized by this Convention shall be exempt from all taxation and customs duties. The Centre shall also be exempt from liability for the collection or payment of any taxes or customs duties.

2. Except in the case of local nationals, no tax shall be levied on or in respect of expense allowances paid by the Centre to the Chairman or members of the Administrative Council, or on or in respect of salaries, expense allowances or other emoluments paid by the Centre to officials or employees of the Secretariat.

3. No tax shall be levied on or in respect of fees or expense allowances received by persons acting as conciliators, or arbitrators, or members of a Committee appointed pursuant to paragraph (3) of Article 52, in proceedings under this Convention, if the sole jurisdictional basis for such tax is the location of the Centre or the place where such proceedings are conducted or the place where such fees or allowances are paid.

Chapter II: Jurisdiction of the Centre

2—042   Article 25

1. The jurisdiction of the Centre shall extend to any legal dispute arising directly out of an investment, between a Contracting State (or any constituent subdivision or agency of a Contracting State designated to the Centre by that State) and a national of another Contracting State, which the parties to the dispute consent in writing to submit to the Centre. When the parties have given their consent, no party may withdraw its consent unilaterally.

2. "National of another Contracting State" means:

   (a) any natural person who had the nationality of a Contracting State other than the State party to the dispute on the date on which the parties consented to submit such dispute to conciliation or arbitration as well as on the date on which the request was registered pursuant to paragraph (3) of Article 28 or paragraph (3) of Article 36, but does not include any person who on either date also had the nationality of the Contracting State party to the dispute; and

(b) any juridical person which had the nationality of a Contracting State other than the State party to the dispute on the date on which the parties consented to submit such dispute to conciliation or arbitration and any juridical person which had the nationality of the Contracting State party to the dispute on that date and which, because of foreign control, the parties have agreed should be treated as a national of another Contracting State for the purposes of this Convention.

3. Consent by a constituent subdivision or agency of a Contracting State shall require the approval of that State unless that State notifies the Centre that no such approval is required.

4. Any Contracting State may, at the time of ratification, acceptance or approval of this Convention or at any time thereafter, notify the Centre of the class or classes of disputes which it would or would not consider submitting to the jurisdiction of the Centre. The Secretary-General shall forthwith transmit such notification to all Contracting States. Such notification shall not constitute the consent required by paragraph (1).

2—043   Article 26

Consent of the parties to arbitration under this Convention shall, unless otherwise stated, be deemed consent to such arbitration to the exclusion of any other remedy. A Contracting State may require the exhaustion of local administrative or judicial remedies as a condition of its consent to arbitration under this Convention.

2—044   Article 27

1. No Contracting State shall give diplomatic protection, or bring an international claim, in respect of a dispute which one of its nationals and another Contracting State shall have consented to submit or shall have submitted to arbitration under this Convention, unless such other Contracting State shall have failed to abide by and comply with the award rendered in such dispute.

2. Diplomatic protection, for the purposes of paragraph (1), shall not include informal diplomatic exchanges for the sole purpose of facilitating a settlement of the dispute.

Chapter III: Conciliation

Section 1: Request for Conciliation

2—045   Article 28

1. Any Contracting State or any national of a Contracting State wishing to institute conciliation proceedings shall address a request to that effect in writing to the Secretary-General who shall send a copy of the request to the other party.

2. The request shall contain information concerning the issues in dispute, the identity of the parties and their consent to conciliation in accordance with the rules of procedure for the institution of conciliation and arbitration proceedings.

3. The Secretary-General shall register the request unless he finds, on the basis of the information contained in the request, that the dispute is manifestly outside the jurisdiction of the Centre. He shall forthwith notify the parties of registration or refusal to register.

Section 2: Constitution of the Conciliation Commission

2—046   Article 29

1. The Conciliation Commission (hereinafter called the Commission) shall be constituted as soon as possible after registration of a request pursuant to Article 28.

2. (a) The Commission shall consist of a sole conciliator or any uneven number of conciliators appointed as the parties shall agree.

   (b) Where the parties do not agree upon the number of conciliators and the method of their appointment, the Commission shall consist of three conciliators, one conciliator appointed by each party and the third, who shall be the president of the Commission, appointed by agreement of the parties.

2—047   Article 30

If the Commission shall not have been constituted within 90 days after notice of registration of the request has been dispatched by the

Secretary-General in accordance with paragraph (3) of Article 28, or such other period as the parties may agree, the Chairman shall, at the request of either party and after consulting both parties as far as possible, appoint the conciliator or conciliators not yet appointed.

2—048   Article 31

1. Conciliators may be appointed from outside the Panel of Conciliators, except in the case of appointments by the Chairman pursuant to Article 30.

2. Conciliators appointed from outside the Panel of Conciliators shall possess the qualities stated in paragraph (1) of Article 14.

Section 3: Conciliation Proceedings

2—049   Article 32

1. The Commission shall be the judge of its own competence.

2. Any objection by a party to the dispute that the dispute is not within the jurisdiction of the Centre, or for other reasons is not within the competence of the Commission, shall be considered by the Commission which shall determine whether to deal with it as a preliminary question or to join it to the merits of the dispute.

2—050   Article 33

Any conciliation proceeding shall be conducted in accordance with the provisions of this Section and, except as parties otherwise agree, in accordance with the Conciliation Rules in effect on the date on which the parties consented to conciliation. If any question of procedure arises which is not covered by this Section or the Conciliation Rules or any rules agreed by the parties, the Commission shall decide the question.

2—051   Article 34

1. It shall be the duty of the Commission to clarify the issues in dispute between the parties and to endeavour to bring about agreement between them upon mutually acceptable terms. To that end, the Commission may at any stage of the proceedings and from time to time recommend terms of settlement to the parties. The parties shall cooperate in good faith with the Commission in order to enable the Commission to carry out

its functions, and shall give their most serious consideration to its recommendations.

2. If the parties reach agreement, the Commission shall draw up a report noting the issues in dispute and recording that the parties have reached agreement. If, at any stage of the proceedings, it appears to the Commission that there is no likelihood of agreement between the parties, it shall close the proceedings and shall draw up a report noting the submission of the dispute and recording the failure of the parties to reach agreement. If one party fails to appear or participate in the proceedings, the Commission shall close the proceedings and shall draw up a report noting that party's failure to appear or participate.

2—052   Article 35

Except as the parties to the dispute shall otherwise agree, neither party to a conciliation proceeding shall be entitled in any other proceeding, whether before arbitrators or in a court of law or otherwise, to invoke or rely on any views expressed or statements or admissions or offers of settlement made by the other party in the conciliation proceedings, or the report or any recommendations made by the Commission.

CHAPTER IV: ARBITRATION

Section 1: Request for Arbitration

2—053   Article 36

1. Any Contracting State or any national of a Contracting State wishing to institute arbitration proceedings shall address a request to that effect in writing to the Secretary-General who shall send a copy of the request to the other party

2. The request shall contain information concerning the issues in dispute, the identity of the parties and their consent to arbitration in accordance with the rules of procedure for the institution of conciliation and arbitration proceedings.

3. The Secretary-General shall register the request unless he finds, on the basis of the information contained in the request, that the dispute is manifestly outside the jurisdiction of the Centre. He shall forthwith notify the parties of registration or refusal to register.

Section 2: Constitution of the Tribunal

2—054   Article 37

1. The Arbitral Tribunal (hereinafter called the Tribunal) shall be constituted as soon as possible after registration of a request pursuant to Article 36.

2. (a) The Tribunal shall consist of a sole arbitrator or any uneven number of arbitrators appointed as the parties shall agree.

   (b) Where the parties do not agree upon the number of arbitrators and the method of their appointment, the Tribunal shall consist of three arbitrators, one arbitrator appointed by each party and the third, who shall be the president of the Tribunal, appointed by agreement of the parties.

2—055   Article 38

If the Tribunal shall not have been constituted within 90 days after notice of registration of the request has been dispatched by the Secretary-General in accordance with paragraph (3) of Article 36, or such other period as the parties may agree, the Chairman shall, at the request of either party and after consulting both parties as far as possible, appoint the arbitrator or arbitrators not yet appointed. Arbitrators appointed by the Chairman pursuant to this Article shall not be nationals of the Contracting State party to the dispute or of the Contracting State whose national is a party to the dispute.

2—056   Article 39

The majority of the arbitrators shall be nationals of States other than the Contracting State party to the dispute and the Contracting State whose national is a party to the dispute; provided, however, that the foregoing provisions of this Article shall not apply if the sole arbitrator or each individual member of the Tribunal has been appointed by agreement of the parties.

2—057   Article 40

1. Arbitrators may be appointed from outside the Panel of Arbitrators, except in the case of appointments by the Chairman pursuant to Article 38.

2. Arbitrators appointed from outside the Panel of Arbitrators shall possess the qualities stated in paragraph (1) of Article 14.

Section 3: Powers and Functions of the Tribunal

2—058   Article 41

1. The Tribunal shall be the judge of its own competence.

2. Any objection by a party to the dispute that that dispute is not within the jurisdiction of the Centre, or for other reasons is not within the competence of the Tribunal, shall be considered by the Tribunal which shall determine whether to deal with it as a preliminary question or to join it to the merits of the dispute.

2—059   Article 42

1. The Tribunal shall decide a dispute in accordance with such rules of law as may be agreed by the parties. In the absence of such agreement, the Tribunal shall apply the law of the Contracting State party to the dispute (including its rules on the conflict of laws) and such rules of international law as may be applicable.

2. The Tribunal may not bring in a Finding of non liquet on the ground of silence or obscurity of the law.

3. The provisions of paragraphs (1) and (2) shall not prejudice the power of the Tribunal to decide a dispute ex aequo et bono if the parties so agree.

2—060   Article 43

Except as the parties otherwise agree, the Tribunal may, if it deems it necessary at any stage of the proceedings;

(a) call upon the parties to produce documents or other evidence, and

(b) visit the scene connected with the dispute, and conduct such inquiries there as it may deem appropriate.

2—061   Article 44

Any arbitration proceeding shall be conducted in accordance with the provisions of this Section and, except as the parties otherwise agree, in accordance with the Arbitration Rules in effect on the date on which the parties consented to arbitration. If any question of procedure arises which is not covered by this Section or the Arbitration Rules or any rules agreed by the parties, the Tribunal shall decide the question.

2—062   Article 45

1. Failure of a party to appear or to present his case shall not be deemed an admission of the other party's assertions.

2. If a party fails to appear or to present his case at any stage of the proceedings the other party may request the Tribunal to deal with the questions submitted to it and to render an award. Before rendering an award, the Tribunal shall notify, and grant a period of grace to, the party failing to appear or to present its case, unless it is satisfied that that party does not intend to do so.

2—063   Article 46

Except as the parties otherwise agree, the Tribunal shall, if requested by a party, determine any incidental or additional claims or counter-claims arising directly out of the subject-matter of the dispute provided that they are within the scope of the consent of the parties and are otherwise within the jurisdiction of the Centre.

2—064   Article 47

Except as the parties otherwise agree, the Tribunal may, if it considers that the circumstances so require, recommend any provisional measures which should be taken to preserve the respective rights of either party.

Section 4: The Award

2—065   Article 48

1. The Tribunal shall decide questions by a majority of the votes of all its members.

2. The award of the Tribunal shall be in writing and shall be signed by the members of the Tribunal who voted for it.

3. The award shall deal with every question submitted to the Tribunal, and shall state the reasons upon which it is based.

4. Any member of the Tribunal may attach his individual opinion to the award, whether he dissents from the majority or not, or a statement of his dissent.

5. The Centre shall not publish the award without the consent of the parties.

2—066   Article 49

1. The Secretary-General shall promptly dispatch certified copies of the award to the parties. The award shall be deemed to have been rendered on the date on which the certified copies were dispatched.

2. The Tribunal upon the request of a party made within 45 days after the date on which the award was rendered may after notice to the other party decide any question which it had omitted to decide in the award, and shall rectify any clerical, arithmetical or similar error in the award. Its decision shall become part of the award and shall be notified to the parties in the same manner as the award. The periods of time provided for under paragraph (2) of Article 51 and paragraph (2) of Article 52 shall run from the date on which the decision was rendered.

Section 5: Interpretation, Revision and Annulment of the Award

2—067   Article 50

1. If any dispute shall arise between the parties as to the meaning or scope of an award, either party may request interpretation of the award by an application in writing addressed to the Secretary-General.

2. The request shall, if possible, be submitted to the Tribunal which rendered the award. If this shall not be possible, a new Tribunal shall be constituted in accordance with Section 2 of this Chapter. The Tribunal may, if it considers that the circumstances so require, stay enforcement of the award pending its decision.

2—068   Article 51

1. Either party may request revision of the award by an application in writing addressed to the Secretary-General on the ground of discovery of some fact of such a nature as decisively to affect the award, provided that when the award was rendered that fact was unknown to the Tribunal and to the applicant and that the applicant's ignorance of that fact was not due to negligence.

2. The application shall be made within 90 days after the discovery of such fact and in any event within three years after the date on which the award was rendered.

3. The request shall, if possible, be submitted to the Tribunal which rendered the award. If this shall not be possible, a new Tribunal shall be constituted in accordance with Section 2 of this Chapter.

4. The Tribunal may, if it considers that the circumstances so require, stay enforcement of the award pending its decision. If the applicant requests a stay of enforcement of the award in his application, enforcement shall be stayed provisionally until the Tribunal rules on such request.

2—069   Article 52

1. Either party may request annulment of the award by an application in writing addressed to the Secretary-General on one or more of the following grounds:

    (a) that the Tribunal was not properly constituted;
    (b) that the Tribunal has manifestly exceeded its powers;
    (c) that there was corruption on the part of a member of the Tribunal;
    (d) that there has been a serious departure from a fundamental rule of procedure; or
    (e) that the award has failed to state the reasons on which it is based.

2. The application shall be made within 120 days after the date on which the award was rendered except that when annulment is requested on the ground of corruption such application shall be made within 120 days after discovery of the corruption and in any event within three years after the date on which the award was rendered.

3. On receipt of the request the Chairman shall forthwith appoint from the Panel of Arbitrators an ad hoc Committee of three persons. None of the members of the Committee shall have been a member of the Tribunal which rendered the award, shall be of the same nationality as any such member, shall be a national of the State party to the dispute or of the State whose national is a party to the dispute, shall have been designated to the Panel of Arbitrators by either of those States, or shall have acted as a conciliator in the same dispute. The Committee shall have the authority to annul the award or any part thereof on any of the grounds set forth in paragraph (1).

4. The provisions of Articles 41–45, 48, 49, 53 and 54, and of Chapters VI and VII shall apply mutatis mutandis to proceedings before the Committee.

5. The Committee may, if it considers that the circumstances so require, stay enforcement of the award pending its decision. If the applicant requests a stay of enforcement of the award in his application, enforcement shall be stayed provisionally until the Committee rules on such request.

6. If the award is annulled the dispute shall, at the request of either party, be submitted to a new Tribunal constituted in accordance with Section 2 of this Chapter.

Section 6: Recognition and Enforcement of the Award

2—070   Article 53

1. The award shall be binding on the parties and shall not be subject to any appeal or to any other remedy except those provided for in this Convention. Each party shall abide by and comply with the terms of the award except to the extent that enforcement shall have been stayed pursuant to the relevant provisions of this Convention.

2. For the purposes of this Section, "award" shall include any decision interpreting, revising or annulling such award pursuant to Articles 50, 51 or 52.

2—071   Article 54

1. Each Contracting State shall recognize an award rendered pursuant to this Convention as binding and enforce the

pecuniary obligations imposed by that award within its territories as if it were a final judgment of a court in that State. A Contracting State with a federal constitution may enforce such an award in or through its federal courts and may provide that such courts shall treat the award as if it were a final judgement of the courts of a constituent state.

2. A party seeking recognition or enforcement in the territories of a Contracting State shall furnish to a competent court or other authority which such State shall have designated for this purpose a copy of the award certified by the Secretary-General. Each Contracting State shall notify the Secretary-General of the designation of the competent court or other authority for this purpose and of any subsequent change in such designation.

3. Execution of the award shall be governed by the laws concerning the execution of judgments in force in the State in whose territories such execution is sought.

2—072 Article 55

Nothing in Article 54 shall be construed as derogating from the law in force in any Contracting State relating to immunity of that State or of any foreign State from execution.

CHAPTER V: REPLACEMENT AND DISQUALIFICATION OF CONCILIATORS AND ARBITRATORS

2—073 Article 56

1. After a Commission or a Tribunal has been constituted and proceedings have begun, its composition shall remain unchanged; provided, however, that if a conciliator or an arbitrator should die, become incapacitated, or resign, the resulting vacancy shall be filled in accordance with the provisions of Section 2 of Chapter III or Section 2 of Chapter IV.

2. A member of a Commission or Tribunal shall continue to serve in that capacity notwithstanding that he shall have ceased to be a member of the Panel.

3. If a conciliator or arbitrator appointed by a party shall have resigned without the consent of the Commission or Tribunal of which he was a member, the Chairman shall appoint a person from the appropriate Panel to fill the resulting vacancy.

2—074 Article 57

A party may propose to a Commission or Tribunal the disqualification of any of its members on account of any fact indicating a manifest lack of the qualities required by paragraph (1) of Article 14. A party to arbitration proceedings may, in addition, propose the disqualification of an arbitrator on the ground that he was ineligible for appointment to the Tribunal under Section 2 of Chapter IV.

2—075 Article 58

The decision on any proposal to disqualify a conciliator or arbitrator shall be taken by the other members of the Commission or Tribunal as the case may be, provided that where those members are equally divided, or in the case of a proposal to disqualify a sole conciliator or arbitrator, or a majority of the conciliators or arbitrators, the Chairman shall take that decision. If it is decided that the proposal well-founded the conciliator or arbitrator to whom the decision relates shall be replaced in accordance with the provisions of Section 2 of Chapter III or Section 2 of Chapter IV.

CHAPTER VI: COST OF PROCEEDINGS

2—076 Article 59

The charges payable by the parties for the use of the facilities of the Centre shall be determined by the Secretary-General in accordance with the regulations adopted by the Administrative Council.

2—077 Article 60

1. Each Commission and each Tribunal shall determine the fees and expenses of its members within limits established from time to time by the Administrative Council and after consultation with the Secretary-General.

2. Nothing in paragraph (1) of this Article shall preclude the parties from agreeing in advance with the Commission or Tribunal concerned upon the fees and expenses of its members.

2—078 Article 61

1. In the case of conciliation proceedings the fees and expenses of members of the Commission as well as the charges for the use of the facilities of the Centre, shall be borne equally by

the parties. Each party shall bear any other expenses it incurs in connection with the proceedings.

2. In the case of arbitration proceedings the Tribunal shall, except as the parties otherwise agree, assess the expenses incurred by the parties in connection with the proceedings, and shall decide how and by whom those expenses, the fees and expenses of the members of the Tribunal and the charges for the use of the facilities of the Centre shall be paid. Such decision shall form part of the award.

Chapter VII: Place of Proceedings

2—079   Article 62

Conciliation and arbitration proceedings shall be held at the seat of the Centre except as hereinafter provided.

2—080   Article 63

Conciliation and arbitration proceedings may be held, if the parties so agree,

(a) at the seat of the Permanent Court of Arbitration or of any other appropriate institution, whether private or public, with which the Centre may make arrangements for that purpose; or

(b) at any other place approved by the Commission or Tribunal after consultation with the Secretary-General.

Chapter VIII: Disputes between Contracting States

2—081   Article 64

Any dispute arising between Contracting States concerning the interpretation or application of this Convention which is not settled by negotiation shall be referred to the International Court of Justice by the application of any party to such dispute, unless the States concerned agree to another method of settlement.

CHAPTER IX: AMENDMENT

2—082   Article 65

Any Contracting State may propose amendment of this Convention. The text of a proposed amendment shall be communicated to the Secretary-General not less than 90 days prior to the meeting of the Administrative Council at which such amendment is to be considered and shall forthwith be transmitted by him to all the members of the Administrative Council.

2—083   Article 66

If the Administrative Council shall so decide by a majority of two-thirds of its members, the proposed amendment shall be Circulated to all Contracting States for ratification, acceptance or approval. Each amendment shall enter into force 30 days after dispatch by the depository of the Convention of a notification to Contracting States that all Contracting States have ratified, accepted or approved the amendment.

CHAPTER X: FINAL PROVISIONS

2—084   Article 67

This Convention shall be open for signature on behalf of States members of the Bank. It shall also be open for signature on behalf of any other State which is a party to the Statute of the International Court of Justice and which the Administrative Council, by a vote of two-thirds of its members, shall have invited to sign the Convention.

2—085   Article 68

1. This Convention shall be subject to ratification, acceptance or approval by the signatory States in accordance with their respective constitutional procedures.

2. This Convention shall enter into force 30 days after the date of deposit of the twentieth instrument of ratification, acceptance or approval. It shall enter into force for each State which subsequently deposits its instrument of ratification, acceptance or approval 30 days after the date of such deposit.

2—086   Article 69

Each Contracting State shall take such legislative or other measures as may be necessary for making the provisions of this Convention effective in its territories.

2—087   Article 70

This Convention shall apply to all territories for whose international relations a Contracting State is responsible, except those which are excluded by such State by written notice to the depository of this Convention either at the time of ratification, acceptance or approval or subsequently.

2—088   Article 71

Any Contracting State may denounce this Convention by written notice to the depositary of this Convention. The denunciation shall take effect six months after receipt of such notice.

2—089   Article 72

Notice by Contracting State pursuant to Articles 70 or 71 shall not affect the rights or obligations under this Convention of that State or of any of its constituent subdivisions or agencies or of any national of that State arising out of consent to the jurisdiction of the Centre given by one of them before such notice was received by the depositary.

2—090   Article 73

Instruments of ratification, acceptance or approval of this Convention and of amendments thereto shall be deposited with the Bank which shall act as the depositary of this Convention. The depositary shall transmit certified copies of this Convention to States members of the Bank and to any other State invited to sign the Convention.

2—091   Article 74 [Article 75]

The depositary shall notify all signatory States of the following:

   (a) signatures in accordance with Article 67;

   (b) deposits of instruments of ratification, acceptance and approval in accordance with Article 73;

   (c) the date on which this Convention enters into force in accordance with Article 68;

(d) exclusions from territorial application pursuant to Article 70;

(e) the date on which any amendment of this Convention enters into force in accordance with Article 66; and

(f) denunciations in accordance with Article 71.

DONE at Washington, in the English, French and Spanish languages, all three texts being equally authentic, in a single copy which shall remain deposited in the archives of the International Bank for Reconstruction and Development, which has indicated by its signature below its agreement to fulfil the functions with which it is charged under this Convention.

WTO—Understanding on Rules and Procedures Governing the Settlement of Disputes

Contents

Article.

1. Coverage and Application
2. Administration
3. General Provisions
4. Consultations
5. Good Offices, Conciliation and Mediation
6. Establishment of Panels
7. Terms of Reference of Panels
8. Composition of Panels
9. Procedures for Multiple Complainants
10. Third Parties
11. Function of Panels
12. Panel Procedures
13. Right to Seek Information
14. Confidentiality
15. Interim Review Stage
16. Adoption of Panel Reports
17. Appellate Review
    Standing Appellate Body
    Procedures for Appellate Review
    Adoption of Appellate Body Reports
18. Communications with the Panel or Appellate Body
19. Panel and Appellate Body Recommendations
20. Time-frame for DSB Decisions
21. Surveillance of Implementation of Recommendations and Rulings
22. Compensation and the Suspension of Concessions
23. Strengthening of the Multilateral System

24. Special Procedures Involving Least-Developed Country Members

25. Arbitration

26.
   1. Non-Violation Complaints of the Type Described in Paragraph 1(b) of Article XXIII of GATT 1994
   2. Complaints of the Type Described in Paragraph 1(c) of Article XXIII of GATT 1994

27. Responsibilities of the Secretariat

Appendix.
   1 Agreements Covered by the Understanding
   2 Special or Additional Rules and Procedures Contained in the Covered Agreements
   Agreement Rules and Procedures
   3. Working Procedures
   4 Expert Review Groups

WTO—Understanding on Rules and Procedures Governing the Settlement of Disputes

2—092 Article 1—Coverage and Application

1. The rules and procedures of this Understanding shall apply to disputes brought pursuant to the consultation and dispute settlement provisions of the agreements listed in Appendix 1 to this Understanding (referred to in this Understanding as the "covered agreements"). The rules and procedures of this Understanding shall also apply to consultations and the settlement of disputes between Members concerning their rights and obligations under the provisions of the Agreement Establishing the World Trade Organization (referred to in this Understanding as the "WTO Agreement") and of this Understanding taken in isolation or in combination with any other covered agreement.

2. The rules and procedures of this Understanding shall apply subject to such special or additional rules and procedures on dispute settlement contained in the covered agreements as are identified in Appendix 2 to this Understanding. To the extent that there is a difference between the rules and procedures of this Understanding and the special or additional rules and procedures set forth in Appendix 2, the special or additional rules and procedures in Appendix 2 shall prevail. In disputes involving rules and procedures under more than one covered agreement, if there is a conflict between special or additional rules and procedures of such agreements under review, and where the parties to the dispute cannot agree on rules and procedures within 20 days of the establishment of the panel, the Chairman of the Dispute Settlement Body provided for in paragraph 1 of Article 2 (referred to in this Understanding as the "DSB"), in consultation with the parties to the dispute, shall determine the rules and procedures to be followed within 10 days after a request by either Member. The Chairman shall be guided by the principle that special or additional rules and procedures should be used where possible, and the rules and procedures set out in this Understanding should be used to the extent necessary to avoid conflict.

2—093   Article 2—Administration

1. The Dispute Settlement Body is hereby established to administer these rules and procedures and, except as otherwise provided in a covered agreement, the consultation and dispute settlement provisions of the covered agreements. Accordingly, the DSB shall have the authority to establish panels, adopt panel and Appellate Body reports, maintain surveillance of implementation of rulings and recommendations, and authorize suspension of concessions and other obligations under the covered agreements. With respect to disputes arising under a covered agreement which is a Plurilateral Trade Agreement, the term "Member" as used herein shall refer only to those Members that are parties to the relevant Plurilateral Trade Agreement. Where the DSB administers the dispute settlement provisions of a Plurilateral Trade Agreement, only those Members that are parties to that Agreement may participate in decisions or actions taken by the DSB with respect to that dispute.

2. The DSB shall inform the relevant WTO Councils and Committees of any developments in disputes related to provisions of the respective covered agreements.

3. The DSB shall meet as often as necessary to carry out its functions within the time-frames provided in this Understanding.

4. Where the rules and procedures of this Understanding provide for the DSB to take a decision, it shall do so by consensus.(1)

2—094   Article 3—General Provisions

1. Members affirm their adherence to the principles for the management of disputes heretofore applied under Articles XXII and XXIII of GATT 1947, and the rules and procedures as further elaborated and modified herein.

2. The dispute settlement system of the WTO is a central element in providing security and predictability to the multilateral trading system. The Members recognize that it serves to preserve the rights and obligations of Members under the covered agreements, and to clarify the existing provisions of those agreements in accordance with customary rules of interpretation of public international law. Recommendations and rulings of the DSB cannot add to or diminish the rights and obligations provided in the covered agreements.

3. The prompt settlement of situations in which a Member considers that any benefits accruing to it directly or indirectly under the covered agreements are being impaired by measures taken by another Member is essential to the effective functioning of the WTO and the maintenance of a proper balance between the rights and obligations of Members.

4. Recommendations or rulings made by the DSB shall be aimed at achieving a satisfactory settlement of the matter in accordance with the rights and obligations under this Understanding and under the covered agreements.

5. All solutions to matters formally raised under the consultation and dispute settlement provisions of the covered agreements, including arbitration awards, shall be consistent with those agreements and shall not nullify or impair benefits accruing to any Member under those agreements, nor impede the attainment of any objective of those agreements.

6. Mutually agreed solutions to matters formally raised under the consultation and dispute settlement provisions of the covered agreements shall be notified to the DSB and the relevant Councils and Committees, where any Member may raise any point relating thereto.

7. Before bringing a case, a Member shall exercise its judgement as to whether action under these procedures would be fruitful. The aim of the dispute settlement mechanism is to secure a positive solution to a dispute. A solution mutually acceptable to the parties to a dispute and consistent with the covered agreements is clearly to be preferred. In the absence of a mutually agreed solution, the first objective of the dispute settlement mechanism is usually to secure the withdrawal of the measures concerned if these are found to be inconsistent with the provisions of any of the covered agreements. The provision of compensation should be resorted to only if the immediate withdrawal of the measure is impracticable and as a temporary measure pending the withdrawal of the measure which is inconsistent with a covered agreement. The last resort which this Understanding provides to the Member invoking the dispute settlement procedures is the possibility of suspending the application of concessions or other obligations under the covered agreements on a discriminatory basis vis-à-vis the other Member, subject to authorization by the DSB of such measures.

8. In cases where there is an infringement of the obligations assumed under a covered agreement, the action is considered prima facie to constitute a case of nullification or impair-

ment. This means that there is normally a presumption that a breach of the rules has an adverse impact on other Members parties to that covered agreement, and in such cases, it shall be up to the Member against whom the complaint has been brought to rebut the charge.

9. The provisions of this Understanding are without prejudice to the rights of Members to seek authoritative interpretation of provisions of a covered agreement through decision-making under the WTO Agreement or a covered agreement which is a Plurilateral Trade Agreement.

10. It is understood that requests for conciliation and the use of the dispute settlement procedures should not be intended or considered as contentious acts and that, if a dispute arises, all Members will engage in these procedures in good faith in an effort to resolve the dispute. It is also understood that complaints and counter-complaints in regard to distinct matters should not be linked.

11. This Understanding shall be applied only with respect to new requests for consultations under the consultation provisions of the covered agreements made on or after the date of entry into force of the WTO Agreement. With respect to disputes for which the request for consultations was made under GATT 1947 or under any other predecessor agreement to the covered agreements before the date of entry into force of the WTO Agreement, the relevant dispute settlement rules and procedures in effect immediately prior to the date of entry into force of the WTO Agreement shall continue to apply.(2)

12. Notwithstanding paragraph 11, if a complaint based on any of the covered agreements is brought by a developing country Member against a developed country Member, the complaining party shall have the right to invoke, as an alternative to the provisions contained in Articles 4, 5, 6 and 12 of this Understanding, the corresponding provisions of the Decision of 5 April 1966 (BISD 14S/18), except that where the Panel considers that the time-frame provided for in paragraph 7 of that Decision is insufficient to provide its report and with the agreement of the complaining party, that time-frame may be extended. To the extent that there is a difference between the rules and procedures of Articles 4, 5, 6 and 12 and the corresponding rules and procedures of the Decision, the latter shall prevail.

2—095   **Article 4—Consultations**

1. Members affirm their resolve to strengthen and improve the effectiveness of the consultation procedures employed by Members.

2. Each Member undertakes to accord sympathetic consideration to and afford adequate opportunity for consultation regarding any representations made by another Member concerning measures affecting the operation of any covered agreement taken within the territory of the former.(3)

3. If a request for consultations is made pursuant to a covered agreement, the Member to which the request is made shall, unless otherwise mutually agreed, reply to the request within 10 days after the date of its receipt and shall enter into consultations in good faith within a period of no more than 30 days after the date of receipt of the request, with a view to reaching a mutually satisfactory solution. If the Member does not respond within 10 days after the date of receipt of the request, or does not enter into consultations within a period of no more than 30 days, or a period otherwise mutually agreed, after the date of receipt of the request, then the Member that requested the holding of consultations may proceed directly to request the establishment of a panel.

4. All such requests for consultations shall be notified to the DSB and the relevant Councils and Committees by the Member which requests consultations. Any request for consultations shall be submitted in writing and shall give the reasons for the request, including identification of the measures at issue and an indication of the legal basis for the complaint.

5. In the course of consultations in accordance with the provisions of a covered agreement, before resorting to further action under this Understanding, Members should attempt to obtain satisfactory adjustment of the matter.

6. Consultations shall be confidential, and without prejudice to the rights of any Member in any further proceedings.

7. If the consultations fail to settle a dispute within 60 days after the date of receipt of the request for consultations, the complaining party may request the establishment of a panel. The complaining party may request a panel during the 60-day period if the consulting parties jointly consider that consultations have failed to settle the dispute.

8. In cases of urgency, including those which concern perishable goods, Members shall enter into consultations within a period of no more than 10 days after the date of receipt of the request. If the consultations have failed to settle the dispute within a period of 20 days after the date of receipt of the request, the complaining party may request the establishment of a panel.

9. In cases of urgency, including those which concern perishable goods, the parties to the dispute, panels and the Appellate Body shall make every effort to accelerate the proceedings to the greatest extent possible.

10. During consultations Members should give special attention to the particular problems and interests of developing country Members.

11. Whenever a Member other than the consulting Members considers that it has a substantial trade interest in consultations being held pursuant to paragraph 1 of Article XXII of GATT 1994, paragraph 1 of Article XXII of GATS, or the corresponding provisions in other covered agreements(4), such Member may notify the consulting Members and the DSB, within 10 days after the date of the circulation of the request for consultations under said Article, of its desire to be joined in the consultations. Such Member shall be joined in the consultations, provided that the Member to which the request for consultations was addressed agrees that the claim of substantial interest is well-founded. In that event they shall so inform the DSB. If the request to be joined in the consultations is not accepted, the applicant Member shall be free to request consultations under paragraph 1 of Article XXII or paragraph 1 of Article XXIII of GATT 1994, paragraph 1 of Article XXII or paragraph 1 of Article XXIII of GATS, or the corresponding provisions in other covered agreements.

2—096   Article 5—Good Offices, Conciliation and Mediation

1. Good offices, conciliation and mediation are procedures that are undertaken voluntarily if the parties to the dispute so agree.

2. Proceedings involving good offices, conciliation and mediation, and in particular positions taken by the parties to the dispute during these proceedings, shall be confidential, and without prejudice to the rights of either party in any further proceedings under these procedures.

3. Good offices, conciliation or mediation may be requested at any time by any party to a dispute. They may begin at any time and be terminated at any time. Once procedures for good offices, conciliation or mediation are terminated, a complaining party may then proceed with a request for the establishment of a panel.

4. When good offices, conciliation or mediation are entered into within 60 days after the date of receipt of a request for consultations, the complaining party must allow a period of 60 days after the date of receipt of the request for consultations before requesting the establishment of a panel. The complaining party may request the establishment of a panel during the 60-day period if the parties to the dispute jointly consider that the good offices, conciliation or mediation process has failed to settle the dispute.

5. If the parties to a dispute agree, procedures for good offices, conciliation or mediation may continue while the panel process proceeds.

6. The Director-General may, acting in an ex officio capacity, offer good offices, conciliation or mediation with the view to assisting Members to settle a dispute.

2—097 Article 6—Establishment of Panels

1. If the complaining party so requests, a panel shall be established at the latest at the DSB meeting following that at which the request first appears as an item on the DSB's agenda, unless at that meeting the DSB decides by consensus not to establish a panel.(5)

2. The request for the establishment of a panel shall be made in writing. It shall indicate whether consultations were held, identify the specific measures at issue and provide a brief summary of the legal basis of the complaint sufficient to present the problem clearly. In case the applicant requests the establishment of a panel with other than standard terms of reference, the written request shall include the proposed text of special terms of reference.

Article 7—Terms of Reference of Panels

1. Panels shall have the following terms of reference unless the parties to the dispute agree otherwise within 20 days from the establishment of the panel:

"To examine, in the light of the relevant provisions in (name of the covered agreement(s) cited by the parties to the dispute), the matter referred to the DSB by (name of party) in document . . . and to make such findings as will assist the DSB in making the recommendations or in giving the rulings provided for in that/those agreement(s)."

2. Panels shall address the relevant provisions in any covered agreement or agreements cited by the parties to the dispute.

3. In establishing a panel, the DSB may authorize its Chairman to draw up the terms of reference of the panel in consultation with the parties to the dispute, subject to the provisions of paragraph 1. The terms of reference thus drawn up shall be circulated to all Members. If other than standard terms of reference are agreed upon, any Member may raise any point relating thereto in the DSB.

2—099   Article 8—Composition of Panels

1. Panels shall be composed of well-qualified governmental and/or non-governmental individuals, including persons who have served on or presented a case to a panel, served as a representative of a Member or of a contracting party to GATT 1947 or as a representative to the Council or Committee of any covered agreement or its predecessor agreement, or in the Secretariat, taught or published on international trade law or policy, or served as a senior trade policy official of a Member.

2. Panel members should be selected with a view to ensuring the independence of the members, a sufficiently diverse background and a wide spectrum of experience.

3. Citizens of Members whose governments (6) are parties to the dispute or third parties as defined in paragraph 2 of Article 10 shall not serve on a panel concerned with that dispute, unless the parties to the dispute agree otherwise.

4. To assist in the selection of panelists, the Secretariat shall maintain an indicative list of governmental and non-governmental individuals possessing the qualifications outlined in paragraph 1, from which panelists may be drawn as appropriate. That list shall include the roster of non-governmental panelists established on 30 November 1984 (BISD 31S/9), and other rosters and indicative lists established under any of the covered agreements, and shall retain the names of persons on those rosters and indicative lists at the time of entry into force of the WTO Agreement. Members may

periodically suggest names of governmental and non-governmental individuals for inclusion on the indicative list, providing relevant information on their knowledge of international trade and of the sectors or subject matter of the covered agreements, and those names shall be added to the list upon approval by the DSB. For each of the individuals on the list, the list shall indicate specific areas of experience or expertise of the individuals in the sectors or subject matter of the covered agreements.

5. Panels shall be composed of three panelists unless the parties to the dispute agree, within 10 days from the establishment of the panel, to a panel composed of five panelists. Members shall be informed promptly of the composition of the panel.

6. The Secretariat shall propose nominations for the panel to the parties to the dispute. The parties to the dispute shall not oppose nominations except for compelling reasons.

7. If there is no agreement on the panelists within 20 days after the date of the establishment of a panel, at the request of either party, the Director-General, in consultation with the Chairman of the DSB and the Chairman of the relevant Council or Committee, shall determine the composition of the panel by appointing the panelists whom the Director-General considers most appropriate in accordance with any relevant special or additional rules or procedures of the covered agreement or covered agreements which are at issue in the dispute, after consulting with the parties to the dispute. The Chairman of the DSB shall inform the Members of the composition of the panel thus formed no later than 10 days after the date the Chairman receives such a request.

8. Members shall undertake, as a general rule, to permit their officials to serve as panelists.

9. Panelists shall serve in their individual capacities and not as government representatives, nor as representatives of any organization. Members shall therefore not give them instructions nor seek to influence them as individuals with regard to matters before a panel.

10. When a dispute is between a developing country Member and a developed country Member the panel shall, if the developing country Member so requests, include at least one panelist from a developing country Member.

11. Panelists' expenses, including travel and subsistence allowance, shall be met from the WTO budget in accordance with

criteria to be adopted by the General Council, based on recommendations of the Committee on Budget, Finance and Administration.

2—100 Article 9—Procedures for Multiple Complainants

1. Where more than one Member requests the establishment of a panel related to the same matter, a single panel may be established to examine these complaints taking into account the rights of all Members concerned. A single panel should be established to examine such complaints whenever feasible.

2. The single panel shall organize its examination and present its findings to the DSB in such a manner that the rights which the parties to the dispute would have enjoyed had separate panels examined the complaints are in no way impaired. If one of the parties to the dispute so requests, the panel shall submit separate reports on the dispute concerned. The written submissions by each of the complainants shall be made available to the other complainants, and each complainant shall have the right to be present when any one of the other complainants presents its views to the panel.

3. If more than one panel is established to examine the complaints related to the same matter, to the greatest extent possible the same persons shall serve as panelists on each of the separate panels and the timetable for the panel process in such disputes shall be harmonized.

2—101 Article 10—Third Parties

1. The interests of the parties to a dispute and those of other Members under a covered agreement at issue in the dispute shall be fully taken into account during the panel process.

2. Any Member having a substantial interest in a matter before a panel and having notified its interest to the DSB (referred to in this Understanding as a "third party") shall have an opportunity to be heard by the panel and to make written submissions to the panel. These submissions shall also be given to the parties to the dispute and shall be reflected in the panel report.

3. Third parties shall receive the submissions of the parties to the dispute to the first meeting of the panel.

4. If a third party considers that a measure already the subject of a panel proceeding nullifies or impairs benefits accruing to

it under any covered agreement, that Member may have recourse to normal dispute settlement procedures under this Understanding. Such a dispute shall be referred to the original panel wherever possible.

2—102 Article 11—Function of Panels

The function of panels is to assist the DSB in discharging its responsibilities under this Understanding and the covered agreements. Accordingly, a panel should make an objective assessment of the matter before it, including an objective assessment of the facts of the case and the applicability of and conformity with the relevant covered agreements, and make such other findings as will assist the DSB in making the recommendations or in giving the rulings provided for in the covered agreements. Panels should consult regularly with the parties to the dispute and give them adequate opportunity to develop a mutually satisfactory solution.

2—103 Article 12—Panel Procedures

1. Panels shall follow the Working Procedures in Appendix 3 unless the panel decides otherwise after consulting the parties to the dispute.

2. Panel procedures should provide sufficient flexibility so as to ensure high-quality panel reports, while not unduly delaying the panel process.

3. After consulting the parties to the dispute, the panelists shall, as soon as practicable and whenever possible within one week after the composition and terms of reference of the panel have been agreed upon, fix the timetable for the panel process, taking into account the provisions of paragraph 9 of Article 4, if relevant.

4. In determining the timetable for the panel process, the panel shall provide sufficient time for the parties to the dispute to prepare their submissions.

5. Panels should set precise deadlines for written submissions by the parties and the parties should respect those deadlines.

6. Each party to the dispute shall deposit its written submissions with the Secretariat for immediate transmission to the panel and to the other party or parties to the dispute. The complaining party shall submit its first submission in advance of the responding party's first submission unless the panel decides, in fixing the timetable referred to in paragraph 3 and after consultations with the parties to the dispute, that the parties should submit their first submissions simultane-

ously. When there are sequential arrangements for the deposit of first submissions, the panel shall establish a firm time-period for receipt of the responding party's submission. Any subsequent written submissions shall be submitted simultaneously.

7. Where the parties to the dispute have failed to develop a mutually satisfactory solution, the panel shall submit its findings in the form of a written report to the DSB. In such cases, the report of a panel shall set out the findings of fact, the applicability of relevant provisions and the basic rationale behind any findings and recommendations that it makes. Where a settlement of the matter among the parties to the dispute has been found, the report of the panel shall be confined to a brief description of the case and to reporting that a solution has been reached.

8. In order to make the procedures more efficient, the period in which the panel shall conduct its examination, from the date that the composition and terms of reference of the panel have been agreed upon until the date the final report is issued to the parties to the dispute, shall, as a general rule, not exceed six months. In cases of urgency, including those relating to perishable goods, the panel shall aim to issue its report to the parties to the dispute within three months.

9. When the panel considers that it cannot issue its report within six months, or within three months in cases of urgency, it shall inform the DSB in writing of the reasons for the delay together with an estimate of the period within which it will issue its report. In no case should the period from the establishment of the panel to the circulation of the report to the Members exceed nine months.

10. In the context of consultations involving a measure taken by a developing country Member, the parties may agree to extend the periods established in paragraphs 7 and 8 of Article 4. If, after the relevant period has elapsed, the consulting parties cannot agree that the consultations have concluded, the Chairman of the DSB shall decide, after consultation with the parties, whether to extend the relevant period and, if so, for how long. In addition, in examining a complaint against a developing country Member, the panel shall accord sufficient time for the developing country Member to prepare and present its argumentation. The provisions of paragraph 1 of Article 20 and paragraph 4 of Article 21 are not affected by any action pursuant to this paragraph.

11. Where one or more of the parties is a developing country Member, the panel's report shall explicitly indicate the form in which account has been taken of relevant provisions on differential and more-favourable treatment for developing country Members that form part of the covered agreements which have been raised by the developing country Member in the course of the dispute settlement procedures.

12. The panel may suspend its work at any time at the request of the complaining party for a period not to exceed 12 months. In the event of such a suspension, the time-frames set out in paragraphs 8 and 9 of this Article, paragraph 1 of Article 20, and paragraph 4 of Article 21 shall be extended by the amount of time that the work was suspended. If the work of the panel has been suspended for more than 12 months, the authority for establishment of the panel shall lapse.

2—104   Article 13—Right to Seek Information

1. Each panel shall have the right to seek information and technical advice from any individual or body which it deems appropriate. However, before a panel seeks such information or advice from any individual or body within the jurisdiction of a Member it shall inform the authorities of that Member. A Member should respond promptly and fully to any request by a panel for such information as the panel considers necessary and appropriate. Confidential information which is provided shall not be revealed without formal authorization from the individual, body, or authorities of the Member providing the information.

2. Panels may seek information from any relevant source and may consult experts to obtain their opinion on certain aspects of the matter. With respect to a factual issue concerning a scientific or other technical matter raised by a party to a dispute, a panel may request an advisory report in writing from an expert review group. Rules for the establishment of such a group and its procedures are set forth in Appendix 4.

2—105   Article 14—Confidentiality

1. Panel deliberations shall be confidential.
2. The reports of panels shall be drafted without the presence of the parties to the dispute in the light of the information provided and the statements made.

3. Opinions expressed in the panel report by individual panelists shall be anonymous.

2—106 Article 15—Interim Review Stage

1. Following the consideration of rebuttal submissions and oral arguments, the panel shall issue the descriptive (factual and argument) sections of its draft report to the parties to the dispute. Within a period of time set by the panel, the parties shall submit their comments in writing.

2. Following the expiration of the set period of time for receipt of comments from the parties to the dispute, the panel shall issue an interim report to the parties, including both the descriptive sections and the panel's findings and conclusions. Within a period of time set by the panel, a party may submit a written request for the panel to review precise aspects of the interim report prior to circulation of the final report to the Members. At the request of a party, the panel shall hold a further meeting with the parties on the issues identified in the written comments. If no comments are received from any party within the comment period, the interim report shall be considered the final panel report and circulated promptly to the Members.

3. The findings of the final panel report shall include a discussion of the arguments made at the interim review stage. The interim review stage shall be conducted within the time-period set out in paragraph 8 of Article 12.

2—107 Article 16—Adoption of Panel Reports

1. In order to provide sufficient time for the Members to consider panel reports, the reports shall not be considered for adoption by the DSB until 20 days after the date they have been circulated to the Members.

2. Members having objections to a panel report shall give written reasons to explain their objections for circulation at least 10 days prior to the DSB meeting at which the panel report will be considered.

3. The parties to a dispute shall have the right to participate fully in the consideration of the panel report by the DSB, and their views shall be fully recorded.

4. Within 60 days after the date of circulation of a panel report to the Members, the report shall be adopted at a DSB meeting

(7) unless a party to the dispute formally notifies the DSB of its decision to appeal or the DSB decides by consensus not to adopt the report. If a party has notified its decision to appeal, the report by the panel shall not be considered for adoption by the DSB until after completion of the appeal. This adoption procedure is without prejudice to the right of Members to express their views on a panel report.

2—108 Article 17—Appellate Review

Standing Appellate Body

1. A standing Appellate Body shall be established by the DSB. The Appellate Body shall hear appeals from panel cases. It shall be composed of seven persons, three of whom shall serve on any one case. Persons serving on the Appellate Body shall serve in rotation. Such rotation shall be determined in the working procedures of the Appellate Body.

2. The DSB shall appoint persons to serve on the Appellate Body for a four-year term, and each person may be reappointed once. However, the terms of three of the seven persons appointed immediately after the entry into force of the WTO Agreement shall expire at the end of two years, to be determined by lot. Vacancies shall be filled as they arise. A person appointed to replace a person whose term of office has not expired shall hold office for the remainder of the predecessor's term.

3. The Appellate Body shall comprise persons of recognized authority, with demonstrated expertise in law, international trade and the subject matter of the covered agreements generally. They shall be unaffiliated with any government. The Appellate Body membership shall be broadly representative of membership in the WTO. All persons serving on the Appellate Body shall be available at all times and on short notice, and shall stay abreast of dispute settlement activities and other relevant activities of the WTO. They shall not participate in the consideration of any disputes that would create a direct or indirect conflict of interest.

4. Only parties to the dispute, not third parties, may appeal a panel report. Third parties which have notified the DSB of a substantial interest in the matter pursuant to paragraph 2 of Article 10 may make written submissions to, and be given an opportunity to be heard by, the Appellate Body.

5. As a general rule, the proceedings shall not exceed 60 days from the date a party to the dispute formally notifies its decision to appeal to the date the Appellate Body circulates its report. In fixing its timetable the Appellate Body shall take into account the provisions of paragraph 9 of Article 4, if relevant. When the Appellate Body considers that it cannot provide its report within 60 days, it shall inform the DSB in writing of the reasons for the delay together with an estimate of the period within which it will submit its report. In no case shall the proceedings exceed 90 days.

6. An appeal shall be limited to issues of law covered in the panel report and legal interpretations developed by the panel.

7. The Appellate Body shall be provided with appropriate administrative and legal support as it requires.

8. The expenses of persons serving on the Appellate Body, including travel and subsistence allowance, shall be met from the WTO budget in accordance with criteria to be adopted by the General Council, based on recommendations of the Committee on Budget, Finance and Administration.

Procedures for Appellate Review

9. Working procedures shall be drawn up by the Appellate Body in consultation with the Chairman of the DSB and the Director-General, and communicated to the Members for their information.

10. The proceedings of the Appellate Body shall be confidential. The reports of the Appellate Body shall be drafted without the presence of the parties to the dispute and in the light of the information provided and the statements made.

11. Opinions expressed in the Appellate Body report by individuals serving on the Appellate Body shall be anonymous.

12. The Appellate Body shall address each of the issues raised in accordance with paragraph 6 during the appellate proceeding.

13. The Appellate Body may uphold, modify or reverse the legal findings and conclusions of the panel.

Adoption of Appellate Body Reports

14. An Appellate Body report shall be adopted by the DSB and unconditionally accepted by the parties to the dispute unless the DSB decides by consensus not to adopt the Appellate Body report within 30 days following its circulation to the

Members.(8) This adoption procedure is without prejudice to the right of Members to express their views on an Appellate Body report.

2—109   Article 18—Communications with the Panel or Appellate Body

1. There shall be no ex parte communications with the panel or Appellate Body concerning matters under consideration by the panel or Appellate Body.

2. Written submissions to the panel or the Appellate Body shall be treated as confidential, but shall be made available to the parties to the dispute. Nothing in this Understanding shall preclude a party to a dispute from disclosing statements of its own positions to the public. Members shall treat as confidential information submitted by another Member to the panel or the Appellate Body which that Member has designated as confidential. A party to a dispute shall also, upon request of a Member, provide a non-confidential summary of the information contained in its written submissions that could be disclosed to the public.

2—110   Article 19—Panel and Appellate Body Recommendations

1. Where a panel or the Appellate Body concludes that a measure is inconsistent with a covered agreement, it shall recommend that the Member concerned(9) bring the measure into conformity with that agreement.(10) In addition to its recommendations, the panel or Appellate Body may suggest ways in which the Member concerned could implement the recommendations.

2. In accordance with paragraph 2 of Article 3, in their findings and recommendations, the panel and Appellate Body cannot add to or diminish the rights and obligations provided in the covered agreements.

2—111   Article 20—Time-frame for DSB Decisions

Unless otherwise agreed to by the parties to the dispute, the period from the date of establishment of the panel by the DSB until the date the DSB considers the panel or appellate report for adoption shall as a general rule not exceed nine months where the panel report is not appealed or 12 months where the report is appealed. Where either the panel or the Appellate Body has acted, pursuant to paragraph 9 of Article 12 or paragraph 5 of Article 17, to extend the time for providing its report, the additional time taken shall be added to the above periods.

2—112 Article 21—Surveillance of Implementation of Recommendations and Rulings

1. Prompt compliance with recommendations or rulings of the DSB is essential in order to ensure effective resolution of disputes to the benefit of all Members.

2. Particular attention should be paid to matters affecting the interests of developing country Members with respect to measures which have been subject to dispute settlement.

3. At a DSB meeting held within 30 days(11) after the date of adoption of the panel or Appellate Body report, the Member concerned shall inform the DSB of its intentions in respect of implementation of the recommendations and rulings of the DSB. If it is impracticable to comply immediately with the recommendations and rulings, the Member concerned shall have a reasonable period of time in which to do so. The reasonable period of time shall be:

   (a) the period of time proposed by the Member concerned, provided that such period is approved by the DSB; or, in the absence of such approval,
   (b) a period of time mutually agreed by the parties to the dispute within 45 days after the date of adoption of the recommendations and rulings; or, in the absence of such agreement,
   (c) a period of time determined through binding arbitration within 90 days after the date of adoption of the recommendations and rulings.(12) In such arbitration, a guideline for the arbitrator(13) should be that the reasonable period of time to implement panel or Appellate Body recommendations should not exceed 15 months from the date of adoption of a panel or Appellate Body report. However, that time may be shorter or longer, depending upon the particular circumstances.

4. Except where the panel or the Appellate Body has extended, pursuant to paragraph 9 of Article 12 or paragraph 5 of Article 17, the time of providing its report, the period from the date of establishment of the panel by the DSB until the date of determination of the reasonable period of time shall not exceed 15 months unless the parties to the dispute agree otherwise. Where either the panel or the Appellate Body has

acted to extend the time of providing its report, the additional time taken shall be added to the 15-month period; provided that unless the parties to the dispute agree that there are exceptional circumstances, the total time shall not exceed 18 months.

5. Where there is disagreement as to the existence or consistency with a covered agreement of measures taken to comply with the recommendations and rulings such dispute shall be decided through recourse to these dispute settlement procedures, including wherever possible resort to the original panel. The panel shall circulate its report within 90 days after the date of referral of the matter to it. When the panel considers that it cannot provide its report within this time frame, it shall inform the DSB in writing of the reasons for the delay together with an estimate of the period within which it will submit its report.

6. The DSB shall keep under surveillance the implementation of adopted recommendations or rulings. The issue of implementation of the recommendations or rulings may be raised at the DSB by any Member at any time following their adoption. Unless the DSB decides otherwise, the issue of implementation of the recommendations or rulings shall be placed on the agenda of the DSB meeting after six months following the date of establishment of the reasonable period of time pursuant to paragraph 3 and shall remain on the DSB's agenda until the issue is resolved. At least 10 days prior to each such DSB meeting, the Member concerned shall provide the DSB with a status report in writing of its progress in the implementation of the recommendations or rulings.

7. If the matter is one which has been raised by a developing country Member, the DSB shall consider what further action it might take which would be appropriate to the circumstances.

8. If the case is one brought by a developing country Member, in considering what appropriate action might be taken, the DSB shall take into account not only the trade coverage of measures complained of, but also their impact on the economy of developing country Members concerned.

2—113 Article 22—Compensation and the Suspension of Concessions

1. Compensation and the suspension of concessions or other obligations are temporary measures available in the event that the recommendations and rulings are not implemented within

a reasonable period of time. However, neither compensation nor the suspension of concessions or other obligations is preferred to full implementation of a recommendation to bring a measure into conformity with the covered agreements. Compensation is voluntary and, if granted, shall be consistent with the covered agreements.

2. If the Member concerned fails to bring the measure found to be inconsistent with a covered agreement into compliance therewith or otherwise comply with the recommendations and rulings within the reasonable period of time determined pursuant to paragraph 3 of Article 21, such Member shall, if so requested, and no later than the expiry of the reasonable period of time, enter into negotiations with any party having invoked the dispute settlement procedures, with a view to developing mutually acceptable compensation. If no satisfactory compensation has been agreed within 20 days after the date of expiry of the reasonable period of time, any party having invoked the dispute settlement procedures may request authorization from the DSB to suspend the application to the Member concerned of concessions or other obligations under the covered agreements.

3. In considering what concessions or other obligations to suspend, the complaining party shall apply the following principles and procedures:

   (a) the general principle is that the complaining party should first seek to suspend concessions or other obligations with respect to the same sector(s) as that in which the panel or Appellate Body has found a violation or other nullification or impairment;

   (b) if that party considers that it is not practicable or effective to suspend concessions or other obligations with respect to the same sector(s), it may seek to suspend concessions or other obligations in other sectors under the same agreement;

   (c) if that party considers that it is not practicable or effective to suspend concessions or other obligations with respect to other sectors under the same agreement, and that the circumstances are serious enough, it may seek to suspend concessions or other obligations under another covered agreement;

   (d) in applying the above principles, that party shall take into account:

      (i) the trade in the sector or under the agreement under which the panel or Appellate Body has found

a violation or other nullification or impairment, and the importance of such trade to that party;
(ii) the broader economic elements related to the nullification or impairment and the broader economic consequences of the suspension of concessions or other obligations;

(e) if that party decides to request authorization to suspend concessions or other obligations pursuant to subparagraphs (b) or (c), it shall state the reasons therefor in its request. At the same time as the request is forwarded to the DSB, it also shall be forwarded to the relevant Councils and also, in the case of a request pursuant to subparagraph (b), the relevant sectoral bodies;

(f) for purposes of this paragraph, "sector" means:

(i) with respect to goods, all goods;
(ii) with respect to services, a principal sector as identified in the current "Services Sectoral Classification List" which identifies such sectors;(14)
(iii) with respect to trade-related intellectual property rights, each of the categories of intellectual property rights covered in Section 1, or Section 2, or Section 3, or Section 4, or Section 5, or Section 6, or Section 7 of Part II, or the obligations under Part III, or Part IV of the Agreement on TRIPS;

(g) for purposes of this paragraph, "agreement" means:

(i) with respect to goods, the agreements listed in Annex 1A of the WTO Agreement, taken as a whole as well as the Plurilateral Trade Agreements in so far as the relevant parties to the dispute are parties to these agreements;
(ii) with respect to services, the GATS;
(iii) with respect to intellectual property rights, the Agreement on TRIPS.

4. The level of the suspension of concessions or other obligations authorized by the DSB shall be equivalent to the level of the nullification or impairment.

5. The DSB shall not authorize suspension of concessions or other obligations if a covered agreement prohibits such suspension.

6. When the situation described in paragraph 2 occurs, the DSB, upon request, shall grant authorization to suspend concessions or other obligations within 30 days of the expiry of the

reasonable period of time unless the DSB decides by consensus to reject the request. However, if the Member concerned objects to the level of suspension proposed, or claims that the principles and procedures set forth in paragraph 3 have not been followed where a complaining party has requested authorization to suspend concessions or other obligations pursuant to paragraph 3(b) or (c), the matter shall be referred to arbitration. Such arbitration shall be carried out by the original panel, if members are available, or by an arbitrator(15) appointed by the Director-General and shall be completed within 60 days after the date of expiry of the reasonable period of time. Concessions or other obligations shall not be suspended during the course of the arbitration.

7. The arbitrator(16) acting pursuant to paragraph 6 shall not examine the nature of the concessions or other obligations to be suspended but shall determine whether the level of such suspension is equivalent to the level of nullification or impairment. The arbitrator may also determine if the proposed suspension of concessions or other obligations is allowed under the covered agreement. However, if the matter referred to arbitration includes a claim that the principles and procedures set forth in paragraph 3 have not been followed, the arbitrator shall examine that claim. In the event the arbitrator determines that those principles and procedures have not been followed, the complaining party shall apply them consistent with paragraph 3. The parties shall accept the arbitrator's decision as final and the parties concerned shall not seek a second arbitration. The DSB shall be informed promptly of the decision of the arbitrator and shall upon request, grant authorization to suspend concessions or other obligations where the request is consistent with the decision of the arbitrator, unless the DSB decides by consensus to reject the request.

8. The suspension of concessions or other obligations shall be temporary and shall only be applied until such time as the measure found to be inconsistent with a covered agreement has been removed, or the Member that must implement recommendations or rulings provides a solution to the nullification or impairment of benefits, or a mutually satisfactory solution is reached. In accordance with paragraph 6 of Article 21, the DSB shall continue to keep under surveillance the implementation of adopted recommendations or rulings, including those cases where compensation has been provided or concessions or other obligations have been suspended but the recommendations to bring a measure into conformity with the covered agreements have not been implemented.

9. The dispute settlement provisions of the covered agreements may be invoked in respect of measures affecting their observance taken by regional or local governments or authorities within the territory of a Member. When the DSB has ruled that a provision of a covered agreement has not been observed, the responsible Member shall take such reasonable measures as may be available to it to ensure its observance. The provisions of the covered agreements and this Understanding relating to compensation and suspension of concessions or other obligations apply in cases where it has not been possible to secure such observance.(17)

2—114 Article 23—Strengthening of the Multilateral System

1. When Members seek the redress of a violation of obligations or other nullification or impairment of benefits under the covered agreements or an impediment to the attainment of any objective of the covered agreements, they shall have recourse to, and abide by, the rules and procedures of this Understanding.

2. In such cases, Members shall:

   (a) not make a determination to the effect that a violation has occurred, that benefits have been nullified or impaired or that the attainment of any objective of the covered agreements has been impeded, except through recourse to dispute settlement in accordance with the rules and procedures of this Understanding, and shall make any such determination consistent with the findings contained in the panel or Appellate Body report adopted by the DSB or an arbitration award rendered under this Understanding;

   (b) follow the procedures set forth in Article 21 to determine the reasonable period of time for the Member concerned to implement the recommendations and rulings; and

   (c) follow the procedures set forth in Article 22 to determine the level of suspension of concessions or other obligations and obtain DSB authorization in accordance with those procedures before suspending concessions or other obligations under the covered agreements in response to the failure of the Member concerned to implement the recommendations and rulings within that reasonable period of time.

2—115 Article 24—Special Procedures Involving Least-Developed Country Members

1. At all stages of the determination of the causes of a dispute and of dispute settlement procedures involving a least--developed country Member, particular consideration shall be given to the special situation of least-developed country Members. In this regard, Members shall exercise due restraint in raising matters under these procedures involving a least-developed country Member. If nullification or impairment is found to result from a measure taken by a least-developed country Member, complaining parties shall exercise due restraint in asking for compensation or seeking authorization to suspend the application of concessions or other obligations pursuant to these procedures.

2. In dispute settlement cases involving a least-developed country Member, where a satisfactory solution has not been found in the course of consultations the Director-General or the Chairman of the DSB shall, upon request by a least-developed country Member offer their good offices, conciliation and mediation with a view to assisting the parties to settle the dispute, before a request for a panel is made. The Director-General or the Chairman of the DSB, in providing the above assistance, may consult any source which either deems appropriate.

2—116 Article 25—Arbitration

1. Expeditious arbitration within the WTO as an alternative means of dispute settlement can facilitate the solution of certain disputes that concern issues that are clearly defined by both parties.

2. Except as otherwise provided in this Understanding, resort to arbitration shall be subject to mutual agreement of the parties which shall agree on the procedures to be followed. Agreements to resort to arbitration shall be notified to all Members sufficiently in advance of the actual commencement of the arbitration process.

3. Other Members may become party to an arbitration proceeding only upon the agreement of the parties which have agreed to have recourse to arbitration. The parties to the proceeding shall agree to abide by the arbitration award. Arbitration awards shall be notified to the DSB and the Council or Committee of any relevant agreement where any Member may raise any point relating thereto.

4. Articles 21 and 22 of this Understanding shall apply mutatis mutandis to arbitration awards.

2—117 Article 26

1. Non-Violation Complaints of the Type Described in Paragraph 1(b) of Article XXIII of GATT 1994

Where the provisions of paragraph 1(b) of Article XXIII of GATT 1994 are applicable to a covered agreement, a panel or the Appellate Body may only make rulings and recommendations where a party to the dispute considers that any benefit accruing to it directly or indirectly under the relevant covered agreement is being nullified or impaired or the attainment of any objective of that Agreement is being impeded as a result of the application by a Member of any measure, whether or not it conflicts with the provisions of that Agreement. Where and to the extent that such party considers and a panel or the Appellate Body determines that a case concerns a measure that does not conflict with the provisions of a covered agreement to which the provisions of paragraph 1(b) of Article XXIII of GATT 1994 are applicable, the procedures in this Understanding shall apply, subject to the following:

(a) the complaining party shall present a detailed justification in support of any complaint relating to a measure which does not conflict with the relevant covered agreement;

(b) where a measure has been found to nullify or impair benefits under, or impede the attainment of objectives, of the relevant covered agreement without violation thereof, there is no obligation to withdraw the measure. However, in such cases, the panel or the Appellate Body shall recommend that the Member concerned make a mutually satisfactory adjustment;

(c) notwithstanding the provisions of Article 21, the arbitration provided for in paragraph 3 of Article 21, upon request of either party, may include a determination of the level of benefits which have been nullified or impaired, and may also suggest ways and means of reaching a mutually satisfactory adjustment; such suggestions shall not be binding upon the parties to the dispute;

(d) notwithstanding the provisions of paragraph 1 of Article 22, compensation may be part of a mutually satisfactory adjustment as final settlement of the dispute.

2. Complaints of the Type Described in Paragraph 1(c) of Article XXIII of GATT 1994

Where the provisions of paragraph 1(c) of Article XXIII of GATT 1994 are applicable to a covered agreement, a panel may only make rulings and recommendations where a party considers that any benefit accruing to it directly or indirectly under the relevant covered agreement is being nullified or impaired or the attainment of any objective of that Agreement is being impeded as a result of the existence of any situation other than those to which the provisions of paragraphs 1(a) and 1(b) of Article XXIII of GATT 1994 are applicable. Where and to the extent that such party considers and a panel determines that the matter is covered by this paragraph, the procedures of this Understanding shall apply only up to and including the point in the proceedings where the panel report has been circulated to the Members. The dispute settlement rules and procedures contained in the Decision of 12 April 1989 (BISD 36S/61–67) shall apply to consideration for adoption, and surveillance and implementation of recommendations and rulings. The following shall also apply:

(a) the complaining party shall present a detailed justification in support of any argument made with respect to issues covered under this paragraph;
(b) in cases involving matters covered by this paragraph, if a panel finds that cases also involve dispute settlement matters other than those covered by this paragraph, the panel shall circulate a report to the DSB addressing any such matters and a separate report on matters falling under this paragraph.

2—118 Article 27—Responsibilities of the Secretariat

1. The Secretariat shall have the responsibility of assisting panels, especially on the legal, historical and procedural aspects of the matters dealt with, and of providing secretarial and technical support.

2. While the Secretariat assists Members in respect of dispute settlement at their request, there may also be a need to provide additional legal advice and assistance in respect of dispute settlement to developing country Members. To this end, the Secretariat shall make available a qualified legal expert from the WTO technical cooperation services to any developing country Member which so requests. This expert shall assist the developing country Member in a manner ensuring the continued impartiality of the Secretariat.

3. The Secretariat shall conduct special training courses for interested Members concerning these dispute settlement procedures and practices so as to enable Members' experts to be better informed in this regard.

2—119 **Appendix 1—Agreements Covered by the Understanding**

(A) Agreement Establishing the World Trade Organization

(B) Multilateral Trade Agreements

Annex 1A: Multilateral Agreements on Trade in Goods

Annex 1B: General Agreement on Trade in Services

Annex 1C: Agreement on Trade-Related Aspects of Intellectual Property Rights

Annex 2: Understanding on Rules and Procedures Governing the Settlement of Disputes

(C) Plurilateral Trade Agreements

Annex 4: Agreement on Trade in Civil Aircraft

Agreement on Government Procurement

International Dairy Agreement

International Bovine Meat Agreement

The applicability of this Understanding to the Plurilateral Trade

Agreements shall be subject to the adoption of a decision by the parties to each agreement setting out the terms for the application of the Understanding to the individual agreement, including any special or additional rules or procedures for inclusion in Appendix 2, as notified to the DSB.

2—120 **Appendix 2—Special or Additional Rules and Procedures Contained in the Covered Agreements**

Agreement Rules and Procedures

Agreement on the Application of Sanitary and Phytosanitary Measures 11.2

Agreement on Textiles and Clothing 2.14, 2.21, 4.4, 5.2, 5.4, 5.6, 6.9, 6.10, 6.11, 8.1 through 8.12

Agreement on Technical Barriers to Trade 14.2 through 14.4, Annex 2

Agreement on Implementation of Article VI of GATT 199417.4 through 17.7

Agreement on Implementation of Article VII of GATT 199419.3 through 19.5, Annex II.2(f), 3, 9, 21

Agreement on Subsidies and Countervailing Measures4.2 through 4.12, 6.6, 7.2 through 7.10, 8.5, footnote 35, 24.4, 27.7, Annex V

General Agreement on Trade in ServicesXXII:3, XXIII:3

Annex on Financial Services4

Annex on Air Transport Services4

Decision on Certain Dispute Settlement

Procedures for the GATS 1 through 5

The list of rules and procedures in this Appendix includes provisions where only a part of the provision may be relevant in this context.Any special or additional rules or procedures in the Plurilateral Trade Agreements as determined by the competent bodies of each agreement and as notified to the DSB.

2—121 Appendix 3—Working Procedures

1. In its proceedings the panel shall follow the relevant provisions of this Understanding. In addition, the following working procedures shall apply.

2. The panel shall meet in closed session. The parties to the dispute, and interested parties, shall be present at the meetings only when invited by the panel to appear before it.

3. The deliberations of the panel and the documents submitted to it shall be kept confidential. Nothing in this Understanding shall preclude a party to a dispute from disclosing statements of its own positions to the public. Members shall treat as confidential information submitted by another Member to the panel which that Member has designated as confidential. Where a party to a dispute submits a confidential version of its written submissions to the panel, it shall also, upon request of a Member, provide a non-confidential summary of the information contained in its submissions that could be disclosed to the public.

4. Before the first substantive meeting of the panel with the parties, the parties to the dispute shall transmit to the panel

written submissions in which they present the facts of the case and their arguments.

5. At its first substantive meeting with the parties, the panel shall ask the party which has brought the complaint to present its case. Subsequently, and still at the same meeting, the party against which the complaint has been brought shall be asked to present its point of view.

6. All third parties which have notified their interest in the dispute to the DSB shall be invited in writing to present their views during a session of the first substantive meeting of the panel set aside for that purpose. All such third parties may be present during the entirety of this session.

7. Formal rebuttals shall be made at a second substantive meeting of the panel. The party complained against shall have the right to take the floor first to be followed by the complaining party. The parties shall submit, prior to that meeting, written rebuttals to the panel.

8. The panel may at any time put questions to the parties and ask them for explanations either in the course of a meeting with the parties or in writing.

9. The parties to the dispute and any third party invited to present its views in accordance with Article 10 shall make available to the panel a written version of their oral statements.

10. In the interest of full transparency, the presentations, rebuttals and statements referred to in paragraphs 5 to 9 shall be made in the presence of the parties. Moreover, each party's written submissions, including any comments on the descriptive part of the report and responses to questions put by the panel, shall be made available to the other party or parties.

11. Any additional procedures specific to the panel.

12. Proposed timetable for panel work:

    (a) Receipt of first written submissions of the parties:

    (1) complaining Party: 3–6 weeks
    (2) Party complained against: 2–3 weeks

    (b) Date, time and place of first substantive meeting with the parties; third party session: 1–2 weeks
    (c) Receipt of written rebuttals of the parties: 2–3 weeks
    (d) Date, time and place of second substantive meeting with the parties: 1–2 weeks
    (e) Issuance of descriptive part of the report to the parties: 2–4 weeks

(f) Receipt of comments by the parties on the descriptive part of the report: 2 weeks
(g) Issuance of the interim report, including the findings and conclusions, to the parties: 2–4 weeks
(h) Deadline for party to request review of part(s) of report: 1 week
(i) Period of review by panel, including possible additional meeting with parties: 2 weeks
(j) Issuance of final report to parties to dispute: 2 weeks
(k) Circulation of the final report to the Members: 3 weeks

The above calendar may be changed in the light of unforeseen developments. Additional meetings with the parties shall be scheduled if required.

2—122 Appendix 4—Expert Review Groups

The following rules and procedures shall apply to expert review groups established in accordance with the provisions of paragraph 2 of Article 13.

1. Expert review groups are under the panel's authority. Their terms of reference and detailed working procedures shall be decided by the panel, and they shall report to the panel.

2. Participation in expert review groups shall be restricted to persons of professional standing and experience in the field in question.

3. Citizens of parties to the dispute shall not serve on an expert review group without the joint agreement of the parties to the dispute, except in exceptional circumstances when the panel considers that the need for specialized scientific expertise cannot be fulfilled otherwise. Government officials of parties to the dispute shall not serve on an expert review group. Members of expert review groups shall serve in their individual capacities and not as government representatives, nor as representatives of any organization. Governments or organizations shall therefore not give them instructions with regard to matters before an expert review group.

4. Expert review groups may consult and seek information and technical advice from any source they deem appropriate. Before an expert review group seeks such information or advice from a source within the jurisdiction of a Member, it shall inform the government of that Member. Any Member shall respond promptly and fully to any request by an expert review group for such information as the expert review group considers necessary and appropriate.

5. The parties to a dispute shall have access to all relevant information provided to an expert review group, unless it is of a confidential nature. Confidential information provided to the expert review group shall not be released without formal authorization from the government, organization or person providing the information. Where such information is requested from the expert review group but release of such information by the expert review group is not authorized, a non-confidential summary of the information will be provided by the government, organization or person supplying the information.

6. The expert review group shall submit a draft report to the parties to the dispute with a view to obtaining their comments, and taking them into account, as appropriate, in the final report, which shall also be issued to the parties to the dispute when it is submitted to the panel. The final report of the expert review group shall be advisory only.

NOTES

1. The DSB shall be deemed to have decided by consensus on a matter submitted for its consideration, if no Member, present at the meeting of the DSB when the decision is taken, formally objects to the proposed decision.

2. This paragraph shall also be applied to disputes on which panel reports have not been adopted or fully implemented.

3. Where the provisions of any other covered agreement concerning measures taken by regional or local governments or authorities within the territory of a Member contain provisions different from the provisions of this paragraph, the provisions of such other covered agreement shall prevail.

4. The corresponding consultation provisions in the covered agreements are listed hereunder: Agreement on Agriculture, Article 19; Agreement on the Application of Sanitary and Phytosanitary Measures, paragraph 1 of Article 11; Agreement on Textiles and Clothing, paragraph 4 of Article 8; Agreement on Technical Barriers to Trade, paragraph 1 of Article 14; Agreement on Trade-Related Investment Measures, Article 8; Agreement on Implementation of Article VI of GATT 1994, paragraph 2 of Article 17; Agreement on Implementation of Article VII of GATT 1994, paragraph 2 of Article 19; Agreement on Preshipment Inspection, Article 7; Agreement on Rules of Origin, Article 7; Agreement on Import Licensing Procedures, Article 6; Agreement on Subsidies and Countervailing Measures, Article 30; Agreement on Safeguards, Article 14; Agreement on Trade-Related Aspects of Intellectual Property Rights, Article 64.1; and any corre-

sponding consultation provisions in Plurilateral Trade Agreements as determined by the competent bodies of each Agreement and as notified to the DSB.

5. If the complaining party so requests, a meeting of the DSB shall be convened for this purpose within 15 days of the request, provided that at least 10 days' advance notice of the meeting is given.

6. In the case where customs unions or common markets are parties to a dispute, this provision applies to citizens of all member countries of the customs unions or common markets.

7. If a meeting of the DSB is not scheduled within this period at a time that enables the requirements of paragraphs 1 and 4 of Article 16 to be met, a meeting of the DSB shall be held for this purpose.

8. If a meeting of the DSB is not scheduled during this period, such a meeting of the DSB shall be held for this purpose.

9. The "Member concerned" is the party to the dispute to which the panel or Appellate Body recommendations are directed.

10. With respect to recommendations in cases not involving a violation of GATT 1994 or any other covered agreement, see Article 26.

11. If a meeting of the DSB is not scheduled during this period, such a meeting of the DSB shall be held for this purpose.

12. If the parties cannot agree on an arbitrator within ten days after referring the matter to arbitration, the arbitrator shall be appointed by the Director-General within ten days, after consulting the parties.

13. The expression "arbitrator" shall be interpreted as referring either to an individual or a group.

14. The list in document MTN.GNS/W/120 identifies eleven sectors.

15. The expression "arbitrator" shall be interpreted as referring either to an individual or a group.

16. The expression "arbitrator" shall be interpreted as referring either to an individual or a group or to the members of the original panel when serving in the capacity of arbitrator.

17. Where the provisions of any covered agreement concerning measures taken by regional or local governments or authorities within the territory of a Member contain provisions different from the provisions of this paragraph, the provisions of such covered agreement shall prevail.

B. REGIONAL MULTILATERAL CONVENTIONS

European Convention on International Commercial Arbitration

GENEVA, APRIL 21, 1961

United Nations, Treaty Series, vol. 484, p. 364 No.7041 (1963–1964)

2—123 Preamble

The undersigned, duly authorized, convened under the auspices of the Economic Commission for Europe of the United Nations.

Having noted that on 10th June 1958 at the United Nations Conference on International Commercial Arbitration has been signed in New York a Convention on the Recognition and Enforcement of Foreign Arbitral Awards, desirous of promoting the development of European trade by, as far as possible, removing certain difficulties that may impede the organization and operation of international commercial arbitration in relations between physical or legal persons of different European countries, have agreed on the following provisions:

2—124 Article I—Scope of the Convention

1. This Convention shall apply:

   (a) to arbitration agreements concluded for the purpose of settling disputes arising from international trade between physical or legal persons having, when concluding the agreement, their habitual place of residence or their seat in different Contracting States;

   (b) to arbitral procedures and awards based on agreements referred to in paragraph 1(a) above.

2. For the purpose of this Convention,

   (a) the term: "arbitration agreement" shall mean either an arbitral clause in a contract or an arbitration agreement, the contract or arbitration agreement being signed by the parties, or contained in an exchange of letters, telegrams, or in a communication by teleprinter and, in relations between States whose laws do not require that an arbitration agreement be made in writing, any arbitration agreement concluded in the form authorized by these laws;

   (b) the term "arbitration" shall mean not only settlement by arbitrators appointed for each case (ad hoc arbitration) but also by permanent arbitral institutions;

(c) the term "seat" shall mean the place of the situation of the establishment that has made the arbitration agreement.

2—125 **Article II—Right of Legal Persons of Public Law to Resort to Arbitration**

1. In cases referred to in Article I, paragraph 1, of this Convention, legal persons considered by the law which is applicable to them as "legal persons of public law" have the right to conclude valid arbitration agreements.

2. On signing, ratifying or acceding to this Convention any State shall be entitled to declare that it limits the above faculty to such conditions as may be stated in its declaration.

2—126 **Article III—Right of Foreign Nationals to be Designated as Arbitrators**

In arbitration covered by this Convention, foreign nationals may be designated as arbitrators.

2—127 **Article IV—Organization of the Arbitration**

1. The parties to an arbitration agreement shall be free to submit their disputes:
    (a) to a permanent arbitral institution; in this case, the arbitration proceedings shall be held in conformity with the rules of the said institution;
    (b) to an ad hoc arbitral procedure; in this case, they shall be free inter alia
       (i) to appoint arbitrators or to establish means for their appointment in the event of an actual dispute;
       (ii) to determine the place of arbitration; and
       (iii) to lay down the procedure to be followed by the arbitrators.

2. Where the parties have agreed to submit any disputes to an ad hoc arbitration, and where within thirty days of the notification of the request for arbitration to the respondent one of the parties fails to appoint his arbitrator, the latter shall, unless otherwise provided, be appointed at the request of the other party by the President of the competent Chamber of Commerce of the country of the defaulting party's habitual place of residence or seat at the time of the introduction of the request for arbitration. This paragraph shall also apply to

the replacement of the arbitrator(s) appointed by one of the parties or by the President of the Chamber of Commerce above referred to.

3. Where the parties have agreed to submit any disputes to an ad hoc arbitration by one or more arbitrators and the arbitration agreement contains no indication regarding the organization of the arbitration, as mentioned in paragraph 1 of this Article, the necessary steps shall be taken by the arbitrator(s) already appointed, unless the parties are able to agree thereon and without prejudice to the case referred to in paragraph 2 above. Where the parties cannot agree on the appointment of the sole arbitrator or where the arbitrators appointed cannot agree on the measures to be taken, the claimant shall apply for the necessary action, where the place of arbitration has been agreed upon by the parties, at his option to the President of the Chamber of Commerce of the place of arbitration agreed upon or to the President of the competent Chamber of Commerce of the respondent's habitual place of residence or seat at the time of the introduction of the request for arbitration. Where such a place has not been agreed upon, the claimant shall be entitled at his option to apply for the necessary action either to the President of the competent Chamber of Commerce of the country of the respondent's habitual place of residence or seat at the time of the introduction of the request for arbitration, or to the Special Committee whose composition and procedure are specified in the Annex to this Convention. Where the claimant fails to exercise the rights given to him under this paragraph the respondent or the arbitrator(s) shall be entitled to do so.

4. When seized of a request the President or the Special Committee shall be entitled as need be:

   (a) to appoint the sole arbitrator, presiding arbitrator, umpire, or referee;
   (b) to replace the arbitrator(s) appointed under any procedure other than that referred to in paragraph 2 above;
   (c) to determine the place of arbitration, provided that the arbitrator(s) may fix another place of arbitration;
   (d) to establish directly or by reference to the rules and statutes of a permanent arbitral institution the rules of procedure to be followed by the arbitrator(s), provided that the arbitrators have not established these rules themselves in the absence of any agreement thereon between the parties.

5. Where the parties have agreed to submit their disputes to a permanent arbitral institution without determining the institution in question and cannot agree thereon, the claimant may request the determination of such institution in conformity with the procedure referred to in paragraph 3 above.

6. Where the arbitration agreement does not specify the mode of arbitration (arbitration by a permanent arbitral institution or an ad hoc arbitration) to which the parties have agreed to submit their dispute, and where the parties cannot agree thereon, the claimant shall be entitled to have recourse in this case to the procedure referred to in paragraph 3 to determine the question. The President of the competent Chamber of Commerce or the Special Committee, shall be entitled either to refer the parties to a permanent arbitral institution or to request the parties to appoint their arbitrator within such time-limits as the President of the competent Chamber of Commerce or the Special Committee may have fixed and to agree within such time-limits on the necessary measures for the functioning of the arbitration. In the latter case, the provisions of paragraphs 2, 3 and 4 of this Article shall apply.

7. Where within a period of sixty days from the moment when he was requested to fulfil one of the functions set out in paragraphs 2, 3, 4, 5 and 6 of this Article, the President of the Chamber of Commerce designated by virtue of these paragraphs has not fulfilled one of these functions, the party requesting shall be entitled to ask the Special Committee to do so.

2—128 Article V—Plea as to Arbitral Jurisdiction

1. The party which intends to raise a plea as to the arbitrator's jurisdiction based on the fact that the arbitration agreement was either non-existent or null and void or had lapsed shall do so during the arbitration proceedings, not later than the delivery of its statement of claim or defence relating to the substance of the dispute; those based on the fact that an arbitrator has exceeded his terms of reference shall be raised during the arbitration proceedings as soon as the question on which the arbitrator is alleged to have no jurisdiction is raised during the arbitral procedure. Where the delay in raising the plea is due to a cause which the arbitrator deems justified, the arbitrator shall declare the plea admissible.

2. Pleas to the jurisdiction referred to in paragraph 1 above that have not been raised during the time-limits there referred to, may not be entered either during a subsequent stage of the arbitral proceedings where they are pleas left to the sole discretion of the parties under the law applicable by the arbitrator, or during subsequent court proceedings concerning the substance or the enforcement of the award where such pleas are left to the discretion of the parties under the rule of conflict of the court seized of the substance of the dispute or the enforcement of the award. The arbitrator's decision on the delay in raising the plea, will, however, be subject to judicial control.

3. Subject to any subsequent judicial control provided for under the lex fori , the arbitrator whose jurisdiction is called in question shall be entitled to proceed with the arbitration, to rule on his own jurisdiction and to decide upon the existence or the validity of the arbitration agreement or of the contract of which the agreement forms part.

2—129 Article VI—Jurisdiction of Courts of Law

1. A plea as to the jurisdiction of the court made before the court seized by either party to the arbitration agreement, on the basis of the fact that an arbitration agreement exists shall, under penalty of estoppel, be presented by the respondent before or at the same time as the presentation of his substantial defence, depending upon whether the law of the court seized regards this plea as one of procedure or of substance.

2. In taking a decision concerning the existence or the validity of an arbitration agreement, courts of Contracting States shall examine the validity of such agreement with reference to the capacity of the parties, under the law applicable to them, and with reference to other questions.

(a) under the law to which the parties have subjected their arbitration agreement;
(b) failing any indication thereon, under the law of the country in which the award is to be made;
(c) failing any indication as to the law to which the parties have subjected the agreement, and where at the time when the question is raised in court the country in which the award is to be made cannot be determined, under the competent law by virtue of the rules of conflict of the court seized of the dispute.

The courts may also refuse recognition of the arbitration agreement if under the law of their country the dispute is not capable of settlement by arbitration.

3. Where either party to an arbitration agreement has initiated arbitration proceedings before any resort is had to a court, courts of Contracting States subsequently asked to deal with the same subject-matter between the same parties or with the question whether the arbitration agreement was non-existent or null and void or had lapsed, shall stay their ruling on the arbitrator's jurisdiction until the arbitral award is made, unless they have good and substantial reasons to the contrary.

4. A request for interim measures or measures of conservation addressed to a judicial authority shall not be deemed incompatible with the arbitration agreement, or regarded as a submission of the substance of the case to the court.

2—130   Article VII—Applicable Law

1. The parties shall be free to determine, by agreement, the law to be applied by the arbitrators to the substance of the dispute. Failing any indication by the parties as to the applicable law, the arbitrators shall apply the proper law under the rule of conflict that the arbitrators deem applicable. In both cases the arbitrators shall take account of the terms of the contract and trade usages.

2. The arbitrators shall act as amiables compositeurs if the parties so decide and if they may do so under the law applicable to the arbitration.

2—131   Article VIII—Reasons for the Award

The parties shall be presumed to have agreed that reasons shall be given for the award unless they

(a) either expressly declare that reasons shall not be given; or

(b) have assented to an arbitral procedure under which it is not customary to give reasons for awards, provided that in this case neither party requests before the end of the hearing, or if there has not been a hearing then before the making of the award, that reasons be given.

2—132   Article IX—Setting Aside of the Arbitral Award

1. The setting aside in a Contracting State of an arbitral award covered by this Convention shall only constitute a ground for the refusal of recognition or enforcement in another Contracting State where such setting aside took place in a State in which, or under the law of which, the award has been made and for one of the following reasons:

    (a) the parties to the arbitration agreement were under the law applicable to them, under some incapacity or the said agreement is not valid under the law to which the parties have subjected it or, failing any indication thereon, under the law of the country where the award was made, or
    (b) the party requesting the setting aside of the award was not given proper notice of the appointment of the arbitrator or of the arbitration proceedings or was otherwise unable to present his case; or
    (c) the award deals with a difference not contemplated by or not falling within the terms of the submission to arbitration, or it contains decisions on matters beyond the scope of the submission to arbitration, provided that, if the decisions on matters submitted to arbitration can be separated from those not so submitted, that part of the award which contains decisions on matters submitted to arbitration need not be set aside;
    (d) the composition of the arbitral authority or the arbitral procedure was not in accordance with the agreement of the parties, or failing such agreement, with the provisions of Article IV of this Convention.

2. In relations between Contracting States that are also parties to the New York Convention on the Recognition and Enforcement of Foreign Arbitral Awards of 10th June 1958, paragraph 1 of this Article limits the application of Article V (1) (e) of the New York Convention solely to the cases of setting aside set out under paragraph 1 above.

2—133   Article X—Final Clauses

1. This Convention is open for signature or accession by countries members of the Economic Commission for Europe and countries admitted to the Commission in a consultative capacity under paragraph 8 of the Commission's terms of reference.

2. Such countries as may participate in certain activities of the Economic Commission for Europe in accordance with paragraph 11 of the Commission's terms of reference may become Contracting Parties to this Convention by acceding thereto after its entry into force.

3. The Convention shall be open for signature until 31 December 1961 inclusive. Thereafter, it shall be open for accession.

4. This Convention shall be ratified.

5. Ratification or accession shall be effected by the deposit of an instrument with the Secretary-General of the United Nations.

6. When signing, ratifying or acceding to this Convention, the Contracting Parties shall communicate to the Secretary-General of the United Nations a list of the Chambers of Commerce or other institutions in their country who will exercise the functions conferred by virtue of Article IV of this Convention on Presidents of the competent Chambers of Commerce.

7. The provisions of the present Convention shall not affect the validity of multi-lateral or bilateral agreements concerning arbitration entered into by Contracting States.

8. This Convention shall come into force on the ninetieth day after five of the countries referred to in paragraph 1 above have deposited their instruments of ratification or accession. For any country ratifying or acceding to it later this Convention shall enter into force on the ninetieth day after the said country has deposited its instrument of ratification or accession.

9. Any Contracting Party may denounce this Convention by so notifying the Secretary-General of the United Nations. Denunciation shall take effect twelve months after the date of receipt by the Secretary-General of the notification of denunciation.

10. If, after the entry into force of this Convention, the number of Contracting Parties is reduced, as a result of denunciations, to less than five, the Convention shall cease to be in force from the date on which the last of such denunciations takes effect.

11. The Secretary-General of the United Nations shall notify the countries referred to in paragraph 1, and the countries which have become Contracting Parties under paragraph 2 above, of

(a) declarations made under Article II, paragraph 2;
(b) ratifications and accessions under paragraphs 1 and 2 above;
(c) communications received in pursuance of paragraph 6 above;
(d) the dates of entry into force of this Convention in accordance with paragraph 8 above;
(e) denunciations under paragraph 9 above;
(f) the termination of this Convention in accordance with paragraph 10 above.

12. After 31 December 1961, the original of this Convention shall be deposited with the Secretary-General of the United Nations, who shall transmit certified true copies to each of the countries mentioned in paragraphs 1 and 2 above.

IN WITNESS THEREOF the undersigned, being duly authorized thereto, have signed this Convention.

DONE at Geneva, this twenty-first day of April, one thousand nine hundred and sixty-one, in a single copy in the English, French and Russian languages, each text being equally authentic.

Annex Composition and Procedure of the Special Committee Referred to in Article IV of the Convention

2—134 1. The Special Committee referred to in Article IV of the Convention shall consist of two regular members and a Chairman. One of the regular members shall be elected by the Chambers of Commerce or other institutions designated, under Article X, paragraph 6, of the Convention, by States in which at the time when the Convention is open to signature national Committees of the International Chamber of Commerce exist, and which at the time of the election are parties to the Convention. The other member shall be elected by the Chambers of Commerce or other institutions designated, under Article X, paragraph 6, of the Convention, by States in which at the time when the Convention is open to signature no National Committees of the International Chamber of Commerce exist and which at the time of the election are parties to the Convention.

2. The persons who are to act as Chairman of the Special Committee pursuant to paragraph 7 of this Annex shall also be elected in like manner by the Chambers of Commerce or other institutions referred to in paragraph 1 of this Annex.

3. The Chambers of Commerce or other institutions referred to in paragraph 1 of this Annex shall elect alternates at the same time and in the same manner as they elect the Chairman and other regular members, in case of the temporary inability of the Chairman or regular members to act. In the event of the permanent inability to act or of the resignation of a Chairman or of a regular member, then the alternate elected to replace him shall become, as the case may be, the Chairman or regular member, and the group of Chambers of Commerce or other institutions which had elected the alternate who has become Chairman or regular member shall elect another alternate.

4. The first elections to the Committee shall be held within ninety days from the date of the deposit of the fifth instrument of ratification or accession. Chambers of Commerce and other institutions designated by Signatory States who are not yet parties to the Convention shall also be entitled to take part in these elections. If however it should not be possible to hold elections within the prescribed period, the entry into force of paragraphs 3 to 7 of Article IV of the Convention shall be postponed until elections are held as provided for above.

5. Subject to the provisions of paragraph 7 below, the members of the Special Committee shall be elected for a term of four years. New elections shall be held within the first six months of the fourth year following the previous elections. Nevertheless, if a new procedure for the election of the members of the Special Committee has not produced results, the members previously elected shall continue to exercise their functions until the election of new members.

6. The results of the elections of the members of the Special Committee shall be communicated to the Secretary-General of the United Nations who shall notify the States referred to in Article X, paragraph 1, of the Convention and the States which have become Contracting Parties under Article X, paragraph 2. The Secretary-General shall likewise notify the said States of any postponement and of the entry into force of paragraphs 3 and 7 of Article IV of the Convention in pursuance of paragraph 4 of this Annex.

7. The persons elected to the office of Chairman shall exercise their functions in rotation, each during a period of two years. The question which of these two persons shall act as chairman during the first two-year period after entry into force of

the Convention shall be decided by the drawing of lots. The office of Chairman shall thereafter be vested, for each successive two year period, in the person elected Chairman by the group of countries other than that by which the Chairman exercising his functions during the immediately preceding two-year period was elected.

8. The reference to the Special Committee of one of the requests referred to in paragraphs 3 to 7 of the aforesaid Article IV shall be addressed to the Executive Secretary of the Economic Commission for Europe. The Executive Secretary shall in the first instance lay the request before the member of the Special Committee elected by the group of countries other than that by which the Chairman holding office at the time of the introduction of the request was elected. The proposal of the member applied to in the first instance shall be communicated by the Executive Secretary to the other member of the Committee and, if that other member agrees to this proposal, it shall be deemed to be the Committee's ruling and shall be communicated as such by the Executive Secretary to the person who made the request.

9. If the two members of the Special Committee applied to by the Executive Secretary are unable to agree on a ruling by correspondence, the Executive Secretary of the Economic Commission for Europe shall convene a meeting of the said Committee at Geneva in an attempt to secure a unanimous decision of unanimity, the Committee's decision shall be given by a majority vote and shall be communicated by the Executive Secretary to the person who made the request.

10. The expenses connected with the Special Committee's action shall be advanced by the person requesting such action but shall be considered as costs in the cause.

Inter-American Convention on International Commercial Arbitration

PANAMA, JANUARY 30, 1975

2—135   The Governments of the Member States of the Organization of American States, desirous of concluding a convention on international commercial arbitration, have agreed as follows:

2—136   Article 1

An agreement in which the parties undertake to submit to arbitral decision any differences that may arise or have arisen between them with respect to a commercial transaction is valid. The agreement shall be set forth in an instrument signed by the parties, or in the form of an exchange of letters, telegrams, or telex communications.

2—137   Article 2

Arbitrators shall be appointed in the manner agreed upon by the parties. Their appointment may be delegated to a third party, whether a natural or juridical person. Arbitrators may be nationals or foreigners.

2—138   Article 3

In the absence of an express agreement between the parties, the arbitration shall be conducted in accordance with the rules of procedure of the Inter-American Commercial Arbitration Commission.

2—139   Article 4

An arbitral decision or award that is not appealable under the applicable law or procedural rules shall have the force of a final judicial judgment. Its execution or recognition may be ordered in the same manner as that of decisions handed down by national or foreign ordinary courts, in accordance with the procedural laws of the country where it is to be executed and the provisions of international treaties.

2—140   Article 5

> 1. The recognition and execution of the decision may be refused, at the request of the party against which it is made, only if such party is able to prove to the competent authority of the State in which recognition and execution are requested:

(a) That the parties to the agreement were subject to some incapacity under the applicable law or that the agreement is not valid under the law to which the parties have submitted it, or, if such law is not specified under the law of the State in which the decision was made; or

(b) That the party against which the arbitral decision has been made was not duly notified of the appointment of the arbitrator or of the arbitration procedure to be followed, or was unable, for any other reason, to present his defense; or

(c) That the decision concerns a dispute not envisaged in the agreement between the parties to submit to arbitration; nevertheless, if the provisions of the decision that refer to issues submitted to arbitration can be separated from those not submitted to arbitration, the former may be recognized and executed; or

(d) That the constitution of the arbitral tribunal or the arbitration procedure has not been carried out in accordance with the terms of the agreement signed by the parties or, in the absence of such agreement, that the constitution of the arbitral tribunal or the arbitration procedure has not been carried out in accordance with the law of the State where the arbitration took place; or

(e) That the decision is not yet binding on the parties or has been annulled or suspended by a competent authority of the State in which, or according to the law of which, the decision has been made.

2. The recognition and execution of an arbitral decision may also be refused if the competent authority of the State in which the recognition and execution is requested finds:

(a) That the subject of the dispute cannot be settled by arbitration under the law of that State; or

(b) That the recognition or execution of the decision would be contrary to the public policy ("ordre public") of that State.

2—141 Article 6

If the competent authority mentioned in Article 5.1.e has been requested to annul or suspend the arbitral decision, the authority before which such decision is invoked may, if it deems it appropriate, postpone a decision on the execution of the arbitral decision and, at the request of the party requesting execution, may also instruct the other party to provide appropriate guaranties.

2—142   Article 7

This Convention shall be open for signature by the Member States of the Organization of American States.

2—143   Article 8

This Convention is subject to ratification. The instruments of ratification shall be deposited with the General Secretariat of the Organization of American States.

2—144   Article 9

This Convention shall remain open for accession by any other State. The instruments of accession shall be deposited with the General Secretariat of the Organization of American States.

2—145   Article 10

This Convention shall enter into force on the thirtieth day following the date of deposit of the second instrument of ratification. For each State ratifying or acceding to the Convention after the deposit of the second instrument of ratification, the Convention shall enter into force on the thirtieth day after deposit by such State of its instrument of ratification or accession.

2—146   Article 11

If a State Party has two or more territorial units in which different systems of law apply in relation to the matters dealt with in this Convention, it may, at the time of signature, ratification or accession, declare that this Convention shall extend to all its territorial units or only to one or more of them.

Such declaration may be modified by subsequent declarations, which shall expressly indicate the territorial unit or units to which the Convention applies. Such subsequent declarations shall be transmitted to the General Secretariat of the Organization of American States, and shall become effective thirty days after the date of their receipt.

2—147   Article 12

This Convention shall remain in force indefinitely, but any of the States Parties may denounce it. The instrument of denunciation shall be deposited with the General Secretariat of the Organization of American States. After one year from the date of deposit of the instrument of denunciation, the Convention shall no longer be in effect for the denouncing State, but shall remain in effect for the other States Parties.

2—148   Article 13

The original instrument of this Convention, the English, French, Portuguese and Spanish texts of which are equally authentic, shall be deposited with the General Secretariat of the Organization of American States. The Secretariat shall notify the Member States of the Organization of American States and the States that have acceded to the Convention of the signatures, deposits of instruments of ratification, accession, and denunciation as well as of reservations, if any. It shall also transmit the declarations referred to in Article 11 of this Convention.

IN WITNESS WHEREOF the undersigned Plenipotentiaries, being duly authorized thereto by their respective Governments, have signed this Convention.

DONE AT PANAMA CITY, Republic of Panama, this thirtieth day of January one thousand nine hundred and seventy-five.

Arab Convention on Commercial Arbitration

AMMAN, APRIL 14, 1987

2—149 The governments of the following States: The Hashemite Kingdom of Jordan, The Tunisian Republic, The Algerian Democratic and People's Republic, The Republic of Djibuti, The Republic of Sudan, The Arab Republic of Syria, The Iraqi Republic, Palestinia, The Lebanese Republic, The Libyan People's Socialist Arab Jamahiriya, The Kingdom of Morocco, The Islamic Republic of Mauritania, The Arab Republic of Yemen, The People's Democratic Republic of Yemen.

Convinced of the need to conceive unified Arab rules on commercial arbitrations which would find their place amongst the international and regional arbitration rules;

Wishing to obtain a fair balance in the matters of solution of disputes which might arise out of international commercial contracts as well as wishing to find fair solutions to these disputes;

And on the basis of the objectives of the Council of Arab Ministers of Justice with the purpose of a unification of Arab legislations and their adaption to modern evolution;

Have agreed the following:

CHAPTER 1: GENERAL PROVISIONS

2—150 Article 1

The terms used in this Convention shall have the following meaning:

(a) "The Convention" means the Arab Convention on Commercial Arbitration.

(b) "The Contracting State" means a State acceding to this Convention.

(c) "The Council" means the Council of Arab Ministers of Justice.

(d) "The Secretary General" means the Secretary General of the Council of Arab Ministers of Justice.

(e) "The Centre" means the Arab Centre for Commercial Arbitration.

(f) "The Board of Directors" means the Board of Directors of the Arab Centre for Commercial Arbitration.

(g) "The Bureau" means the Bureau of the Centre.

(h) "The Director of authentifications" means the Director appointed for the authentifications of the Centre.

(i) "The Agreement to Arbitrate" means the written agreement by which the parties agreed to resort to arbitration before or after the dispute arose.

(j) "The Roster" means the roster of the names of arbitrators.

2—151   Article 2

This Convention applies to commercial disputes between natural or juristic persons of any nationality, linked by commercial transactions with one of the contracting States or one of its nationals, or which have their main headquarters in one of these States.

2—152   Article 3

1. Reference to arbitration can be made by one of the two following means: The first is to insert an arbitration clause in contracts entered into between the concerned parties, and the second is to establish an arbitration agreement once the dispute has arisen.

2. The following standard clause should be inserted into contracts where one wishes to refer to arbitration: "All disputes arising out of this Contract shall be settled by the Arab Centre for Commercial Arbitration in compliance with the provisions of the Arab Convention on Commercial Arbitration."

CHAPTER 2: THE ARAB CENTRE FOR COMMERCIAL ARBITRATION

2—153   Article 4

By virtue of this Convention, a permanent organization called Arab Centre for Commercial Arbitration is created. It shall be an independent juristic person which is administratively and financially linked to the Secretariat General of the Council of Arab Ministers of Justice.

The Secretary General appoints the officials of this Centre in compliance with the provisions of the statutes of the Council and its implementation rules.

2—154 Article 5

> 1. The Centre shall have a Board of Directors made up of Arab personalities experienced in matters of law and arbitration and who are appointed by each of the contracting States for a period of three years, renewable.
>
> 2. The Board of Directors chooses amongst its members a president for the Centre and two Vice-Presidents elected for a period of three years, renewable. The President thus elected shall also be the chairman of the Board of Directors.
>
> 3. The Chairman of the Board of Directors and the two Vice-Presidents shall devote all their time to the Centre.
>
> 4. The Centre shall dispose of a Bureau made up of the Chairman and the two Vice-Presidents.

2—155 Article 6

> 1. The Board of Directors shall meet each year in an ordinary session but it can may also meet in extraordinary sessions if necessary. The internal rules of the Centre determine the date of these sessions and the manner in which they are held.
>
> 2. The quorum is deemed to have been met when the majority of the members of the Board of Directors are present. The decisions are taken by a majority of two-thirds of those present.
>
> 3. The meeting of the Board of Directors are directed by the chairman who must also convene them.

2—156 Article 7

The Board of Directors has the following functions:

> 1. To make sure of the execution of the provisions of this Convention.
>
> 2. To establish internal rules for the Centre.
>
> 3. To examine the annual report on the activities of the Centre and to refer them to the Council for approval.
>
> 4. To establish the roster of arbitrators.
>
> 5. To exercise the other functions foreseen in this Convention.
>
> 6. To establish a list of fees and expenses.

2—157 Article 8

The Bureau organizes commercial arbitration, fixes its bases, drafts model agreements to arbitrate in international commerce, establishes rules for commercial transactions, summarizes the principles on which awards were based and classifies, prints and edits them.

2—158 Article 9

The Chairman of the Board of Directors of the Centre is also its legal representative.

2—159 Article 10

1. The Convention of the League of the Arab States on the privileges and immunities is applicable to the Centre and to all persons appointed as members of the arbitral tribunal, as well as to the parties to the dispute and their Counsels and Lawyers as well as to witnesses and experts within the limits of what is necessary for a good performance of their mission.

2. The provisions relating to documents and archives of the Council are applicable to the documents and archives of the Centre.

2—160 Article 11

The Council determines the fees of the Chairman, the two Vice-Presidents of the Centre and the members of the Board of Directors.

2—161 Article 12

The seat of the Centre is that of the Secretariat General of the Council in Rabat, capital of the Kingdom of Morocco.

2—162 Article 13

1. The Secretary General of the Council appoints a director for the authentifications, chosen amongst persons holding a law degree ("licence en droit") and who have experience in this matter.

2. This Director works under the supervision of the President of the Centre.

3. He gives an official character to the arbitral awards and certifies each copy. He also takes all official measures foreseen in this Convention and which need execution of its provisions.

Chapter 3: The Srbitral Tribunal

2—163   Article 14

1. The Board of Directors shall establish each year a roster of arbitrators chosen amongst lawyers or jurists or persons having a large experience and knowledge of commerce, industry and finances and of good reputations and morals.

2. Before performing their mission, the arbitrators must take an oath before the President of the Centre or his deputy. This oath shall be as follows:

"I swear before God almighty that I shall judge fairly and that I shall respect the law applicable and that I shall exercise my mission with fidelity, fairness and impartiality."

2—164   Article 15

1. The arbitral tribunal shall be made up of three members, but the parties may agree on a sole arbitrator.

2. Without prejudice of Article 33 of this Convention, the mission of arbitrators is only terminated once they have settled the dispute subject to the arbitration.

Chapter 4: The Arbitral Proceedings

2—165   Article 16

The claimant must:

1. present to the Chairman of the Centre a claim containing:

    (a) its names, first name, qualifications, nationality and address;
    (b) the names, first name, qualifications and nationality of the defendant;
    (c) a summary of the dispute and the facts relating thereto;
    (d) its claims;
    (e) the name of the proposed arbitrator.

2. Join to its claim the agreement to arbitrate and all documents and evidence relating to the dispute.

3. The request for arbitration is only accepted after payment of the dues.

2—166   Article 17

1. As of receipt of the request, the chairman of the Centre acknowledges receipt thereof and notifies a copy of this to the defendant.

2. The defendant must, within thirty days following this notification, present its defence and counterclaims, if any, as well as the name of the arbitrator which it had chosen. To this must be added all documents of which this party disposes. Upon its request, the Bureau may grant it an additional time-period not exceeding thirty days.

2—167   Article 18

1. If the claimant does not appoint its arbitrator in its request, the Bureau itself appoints the arbitrator chosen on the roster within a week following registration of the request.

2. If the defendant does not appoint its arbitrator within the thirty days foreseen in the above article, the Bureau appoints him itself from the roster.

3. The chairman of the Centre invites the parties to agree on a chairman of the arbitral tribunal chosen upon the roster once the two other arbitrators have been appointed provided that such appointment of the chairman shall be made within thirty days following the date at which the parties have been invited to do so. If the parties cannot agree on this choice the Bureau itself appoints the Chairman from the roster.

4. The arbitrators appointed by the Bureau may not be nationals of one of the parties.

5. If one of the parties objects against the validity of the appointment of an arbitrator, the Bureau settles this dispute by a final decision which must be taken urgently.

6. If one of the arbitrators dies or is unable to perform his mission because of an event of force majeure, another arbitrator is appointed in his place according to the same manner that was used for the appointment of the first arbitrator.

7. The arbitrator may not resign after having started his mission. If serious grounds appear which hinder him from following up his mission, he may resign after approval of the Bureau of the Centre.

2—168   Article 19

> 1. Each party may challenge one of the arbitrators provided the grounds for such challenge are mentioned in the request for challenge.
>
> 2. The Bureau settles the request for challenge within seven days following the date at which this request was received.
>
> 3. If the request for challenge is accepted, a new arbitrator is appointed according to the same manner than the challenged arbitrator. The latter as well as the parties are notified of the Bureau's decision as of its making.

2—169   Article 20

Once the arbitral tribunal has been set up, the chairman of the Centre transmits the file to it so that it starts to perform its mission.

2—170   Article 21

> 1. The arbitral tribunal shall settle the dispute in compliance with the contract entered into between the parties and the provisions of the law on which they might expressly or tacitly have agreed, else with the law which has the closest relation with the subject matter of the dispute provided that the well-established rules of international commercial usages are respected.
>
> 2. The arbitral tribunal must settle the case ex aequo, et bono if the parties expressly so agree.

2—171   Article 22

The arbitration takes place at the seat of the Centre unless the parties have agreed that it shall take place in another country approved by the arbitral tribunal after consultation of the Bureau.

2—172   Article 23

> 1. The language of the proceedings, pleadings and the award is arabic.
>
> 2. The arbitral tribunal may decide to hear parties, witnesses and experts who do not speak arabic by resorting to a translator after having him take an oath.

3. The arbitral tribunal may authorize that pleadings and evidence as well as all submissions be made in languages other than arabic provided that they be translated into arabic.

2—173   Article 24

A plea for a lack of jurisdiction as well as other pleas must be raised before the first hearing. The arbitral tribunal must settle these points before going into the substance of the dispute and its decision in this respect is final.

2—174   Article 25

The arbitral tribunal may, at any stage during the proceedings, request the parties to produce other documents and evidence. It may also inspect places and make any investigations it deems necessary.

2—175   Article 26

At any time after the closure of the hearing and before the award is made, the arbitral tribunal may, by its own motion or upon request of one of the parties, decide to re-open the hearings for serious grounds.

2—176   Article 27

Arbitration under the provisions of this Convention shall have the effect to forbid reference of the dispute to the courts of law as well as a recourse against the award before these courts.

2—177   Article 28

1. If one of the parties refrains from appearing without valid grounds during any stage of the proceedings, the proceedings shall take place in its absence.

2. If a party does not appear and does not submit any defence before the arbitral tribunal, this shall not be considered as an acknowledgment (by such party) of the truth of the other party's allegations.

2—178   Article 29

Upon request of any of the parties, the arbitral tribunal may take any interim measure of protection it deems necessary.

2—179   Article 30

A party who is aware of a breach of any of the provisions or conditions of this Convention and continues the arbitration without objecting against this shall be deemed to have waived its right to put this forward.

CHAPTER 5: THE AWARD

2—180   Article 31

1. Once the hearing is closed, the arbitral tribunal shall meet to deliberate and make the award.

2. The award is made by mutual agreement or by a majority within six months following the date of transmission of the file to the arbitral tribunal.

3. Upon request of the arbitral tribunal, the Bureau may extend the above-mentioned time.

4. If the Bureau is not convinced by the reasons put forward by the arbitral tribunal to request an extension of time, the Bureau fixes a time in which the arbitral tribunal must make its award and once this time has expired, the mission of the arbitral tribunal shall be terminated.

5. If the arbitrators cannot agree, the award is made according to the opinion of the Chairman and it is signed by the latter but this must be mentioned in the award.

6. A dissenting arbitrator may mention his dissenting opinion on a separate page which is joined to the award.

2—181   Article 32

1. The award must give the reasons on which it is based and it must mention the names of the arbitrators and of the parties, the date and place where it was made, a general summary of the facts, the claims of the parties, the summary of their arguments, the reply of the arbitral tribunal which is given to these and the award must mention which party must pay the expenses in whole or in part.

2. Within the three months following the making of the award, the Director of Authentification sends a copy of it to each party by registered letter with acknowledgment of receipt.

2—182   Article 33

>   1. If there is a material error in the award, the arbitral tribunal, either by its own motion or upon written request of one of the parties, may correct this error after having notified this request to the other party and provided that this request is made within fifteen days following the date at which the written award was received.
>   2. The decision to correct a material error is made on the award itself and is deemed to be an integral part thereof. Both parties must be notified of the decision to correct.

2—183   Article 34

>   1. Each party may, by a request sent to the Chairman of the Centre, request that the award be set aside in one of the following cases:
>   (a) if it is obvious that the arbitral tribunal exceeded the scope of its functions;
>   (b) if a judgment established a new fact which could substantially influence the award, provided, however, that the ignorance of these facts was not due to the lack of diligence of the party which requests the setting aside;
>   (c) if one of the arbitrators was under undue influence and if this had an effect on the award.
>   2. The request for setting aside must be presented within sixty days following the date of receipt of the award. However, if this request is based on one of the two grounds mentioned in paragraphs (b) and (c) above, it must be presented within sixty days following the date at which these facts were discovered. In all cases, the request of setting aside cannot be accepted after expiry of one year following the date of making the award.
>   3. The Bureau appoints a Commission made up of a chairman and two members chosen upon the roster which studies the request and settles it quickly. However, this Commission cannot analyze grounds other than those mentioned in the request for setting aside.
>   4. (sic) The Commission may not contain among its members one of the arbitrators who made the award or an arbitrator who has the same nationality as one of the parties to the dispute.
>   5. The Commission may set aside totally or in part the decision if the ground on which the request for setting aside was made is justified.

6. The Commission may provisionally suspend enforcement of the award until the request for challenge had been dealt with.

2—184 Article 35

The Supreme Court of each contracting State must give leave to enforce to awards of the arbitral tribunal. Leave may only be refused if this award is contrary to public order.

2—185 Article 36—Transitory provisions

By exception to the provisions of paragraph 2 of Article 5 and the provisions of Articles 11 and 13 of this Convention, the Secretariat General of the Council shall be the Chairman of the Bureau and shall appoint two vice-presidents chosen amongst the officials of the Secretariat General of the Council. He also chooses the Director of Authentifications amongst the officials of the Secretariat General holding at least a law degree ("licence en droit") until the Centre has sufficient financial capacity to cover its expenses.

Chapter 6: Final Provisions

2—186 Article 37

This Convention is subject to approval, acceptance and ratification of the signatory parties. The instruments of approval, acceptance and ratification shall be deposited with the Secretariat General of the League of Arab States within thirty days following the date of approval, acceptance and ratification. The Secretariat General must notify the other member States of the deposit of these instruments and its date, as well as the Secretariat General of the Council and the Presidence of the Centre.

2—187 Article 38

Each concerned authority in each signatory country shall take the necessary national measures for the execution of this Convention.

2—188 Article 39

This Convention shall come into force thirty days after the seventh deposit of the instrument of approval, acceptance or ratification.

2—189   Article 40

1. Each State of the League of Arab States, who has not signed this Convention may accede thereto by addressing a request to this effect to the Secretariat General of the League.

2. A State wishing to accede to the Convention is held to be bound by this Convention due to the sole fact that he has deposited the instrument of approval, acceptance or ratification and 30 days after the date of this deposit.

2—190   Article 41

No party may make any reservation implying explicitly or tacitly a contradiction with the provisions of this Convention or contrary to its purpose.

2—191   Article 42

1. Any contracting or acceding party may withdraw from this Convention by presenting a written reasoned request which it must send to the Secretary General of the League of Arab States.

2. This withdrawal will only be effective one whole year after the date of sending of this request.

… B. REGIONAL MULTILATERAL CONVENTIONS

North American Free Trade Agreement
Washington D.C., 1992

Ottawa, Mexico Df

CHAPTER ELEVEN

Subchapter A — Investment

Subchapter B — Settlement of Disputes Between a Party and an Investor of Another Party

2—192   Article 1115 — Purpose

This Subchapter establishes a mechanism for the settlement of investment disputes that assures both equal treatment among investors of the Parties in accordance with the principle of international reciprocity and due process before an impartial tribunal.

2—193   Article 1116 — Claim by an Investor of a Party on Behalf of Itself

1. An investor of a Party may submit to arbitration under this Subchapter a claim that another Party has breached:

    (a) a provision of Subchapter A; or
    (b) Article 1502(3)(a) (Monopolies and State Enterprises) or Article 1503(2) (State Enterprises) where the alleged breach pertains to the obligations of Subchapter A, and that the investor has incurred loss or damage by reason of, or arising out of, that breach.

2. An investor may not make a claim if more than three years have elapsed from the date on which the investor first acquired, or should have first acquired, knowledge of the alleged breach and knowledge that the investor has incurred loss or damage.

2—194   **Article 1117—Claim by an Investor of a Party on Behalf of an Enterprise**

1. An investor of a Party, on behalf of an enterprise of another Party that is a juridical person that the investor owns or controls directly or indirectly, may submit to arbitration under this Subchapter a claim that the other Party has breached:
   (a) a provision of Subchapter A; or
   (b) Article 1502 (3)(a) (Monopolies and State Enterprises) or Article 1503(2) (State Enterprises) where the alleged breach pertains to the obligations of Subchapter A; and that the enterprise has incurred loss or damage by reason of, or arising out of, that breach.

2. An investor may not make a claim on behalf of an enterprise described in paragraph 1 if more than three years have elapsed from the date on which the enterprise first acquired, or should have first acquired, knowledge of the alleged breach and knowledge that the enterprise has incurred loss or damage.

3. Where an investor makes a claim under this Article and the investor or a non-controlling investor in the enterprise makes a claim under Article 1116 arising out of the same events which gave rise to the claim under this Article, and two or more of the claims are submitted to arbitration under Article 1120, the claims should be heard together by a Tribunal established pursuant to Article 1125, unless the Tribunal finds that the interests of a disputing party would be prejudiced thereby.

4. An investment may not make a claim under this Subchapter.

2—195   **Article 1118—Settlement of a Claim Through Consultation and Negotiation**

The disputing parties should first attempt to settle a claim through consultation or negotiation.

2—196   **Article 1119: Notice of Intent to Submit a Claim to Arbitration**

The disputing investor shall give to the disputing Party written notice of its intention to submit a claim to arbitration at least 90 days before the claim is submitted, which notice shall specify:

(a) the name and address of the disputing investor;

(b) the provisions of this Agreement alleged to have been breached and any other relevant provisions;
(c) the issues and the factual basis for the claim; and
(d) the relief sought and the approximate amount of damages claimed.

2—197 **Article 1120—Submission of a Claim to Arbitration**

1. Except as provided in Annex 1120.1, and provided that six months have elapsed since the events giving rise to a claim, a disputing investor may submit the claim to arbitration under:

    (a) the ICSID Convention, provided that both the disputing Party and the Party of the investor are parties to the Convention;
    (b) the Additional Facility Rules of ICSID, provided that either the disputing Party or the Party of the investor, but not both, is a party to the ICSID Convention; or
    (c) the UNCITRAL Arbitration Rules.

2. The applicable arbitration rules shall govern the arbitration except to the extent modified by this Subchapter.

2—198 **Article 1121—Conditions Precedent to Submission of a Claim to Arbitration**

1. A disputing investor may submit a claim under Article 1116 to arbitration only if:

    (a) the investor consents to arbitration in accordance with the provisions of this Subchapter; and
    (b) both the investor and an enterprise of another Party that is a juridical person that the investor owns or controls directly or indirectly, waive their right to initiate or continue before any administrative tribunal or court under the domestic law of any Party any proceedings with respect to the measure of the disputing Party that is alleged to be a breach of Subchapter A of this Chapter, Article 1502(3)(a) (Monopolies and State Enterprises) or Article 1503(2) (State Enterprises), except for proceedings for injunctive, declaratory or other extraordinary relief, not involving the payment of damages, before an administrative tribunal or court under the domestic law of the disputing Party.

2. A disputing investor may submit a claim under Article 1117 to arbitration only if both the investor and the enterprise:

(a) consent to arbitration in accordance with the provisions of this Subchapter; and

(b) waive their right to initiate or continue before any administrative tribunal or court under the domestic law of any Party any proceedings with respect to the measure of the disputing Party that is alleged to be a breach of Subchapter A of this Chapter, Article 1502(3)(a) (Monopolies and State Enterprises) or Article 1503(2) (State Enterprises), except for proceedings for injunctive, declaratory or other extraordinary relief, not involving the payment of damages, before an administrative tribunal or court under the domestic law of the disputing Party.

3. A consent and waiver required by this Article shall be in writing, shall be given to the disputing Party, and shall be included in the submission of a claim to arbitration.

2—199   **Article 1122—Consent to Arbitration**

1. Each Party consents to the submission of a claim to arbitration in accordance with the provisions of this Subchapter.

2. The consent given by paragraph 1 and the submission by a disputing investor of a claim to arbitration in accordance with the provisions of this Subchapter shall satisfy the requirement of:

   (a) Chapter II of the ICSID Convention (Jurisdiction of the Center) and the Additional Facility Rules for written consent of the parties;
   (b) Article II of the New York Convention for an agreement in writing; and
   (c) Article I of the Inter-American Convention for an agreement.

2—200   **Article 1123—Number of Arbitrators and Method of Appointment**

Subject to Article 1125, and unless the disputing parties agree otherwise, the Tribunal shall consist of three arbitrators. One arbitrator shall be appointed by each of the disputing parties. The third, who shall be the presiding arbitrator, shall be appointed by agreement of the disputing parties.

2—201 **Article 1124—Constitution of Tribunal When a Party Fails to Appoint an Arbitrator or the Disputing Parties Are Unable to Agree on a Presiding Arbitrator**

1. The Secretary-General of ICSID shall serve as appointing authority for an arbitration under this Subchapter.

2. If a Tribunal has not been constituted within 90 days from the date that a claim is submitted to arbitration, the Secretary-General, at the request of either disputing party:

    (a) shall appoint the arbitrator or arbitrators not yet appointed in his discretion, except for the presiding arbitrator; and
    (b) shall appoint the presiding arbitrator in accordance with paragraph 3.

3. The Secretary-General shall appoint the presiding arbitrator from the list of presiding arbitrators described in paragraph 4. In the event that no such presiding arbitrator is available to serve, the Secretary-General shall appoint a presiding arbitrator who is not a national of any of the Parties from the ICSID Panel of Arbitrators.

4. As of the date of entry into force of this Agreement, the Parties shall have jointly designated, without regard to nationality, 45 presiding arbitrators meeting the qualifications of the rules referred to in Article 1120 and experienced in international law and investment.

5. Subject to paragraph 8, where a disputing investor submits a claim to arbitration under the ICSID Convention or the Additional Facility Rules, each Party agrees:

    (a) to the appointment by the investor of a national of the Party of the investor as an arbitrator; and
    (b) to the appointment by the Secretary-General of a national of the Party of the investor as an arbitrator or as a presiding arbitrator.

6. Subject to paragraph 8, a disputing investor described in Article 1116 may submit a claim to arbitration, or continue a claim, under the ICSID Convention or the Additional Facility Rules, only on the following conditions:

    (a) where the disputing Party appoints a national of the disputing Party as an arbitrator, the investor agrees in writing to the appointment; and
    (b) where the Secretary-General appoints a national of the disputing Party as an arbitrator or as a presiding arbitrator, the investor agrees in writing to the appointment.

7. Subject to paragraph 8, a disputing investor described in Article 1117(1) may submit a claim to arbitration, or continue a claim, under the ICSID Convention or the Additional Facility Rules, only on the following conditions:

(a) where the disputing Party appoints a national of the disputing Party as an arbitrator, the investor and the enterprise agree in writing to the appointment; and

(b) where the Secretary-General appoints a national of the disputing Party as an arbitrator or as a presiding arbitrator, the investor and the enterprise agree in writing to the appointment.

8. A disputing party:

(a) in the case of a claim submitted to arbitration under the ICSID Convention, may propose, under Article 57 of the Convention, the disqualification of a member of the Tribunal on account of any fact indicating a manifest lack of the qualities required by paragraph 1 of Article 14 of the Convention; and

(b) in the case of a claim submitted to arbitration under the Additional Facility Rules, may propose, under Article 14 of the Rules, the disqualification of a member of the Tribunal on account of any fact indicating a manifest lack of the qualities required by Article 9 of the Rules.

2—202   Article 1125—Consolidation

1. A Tribunal established under this Article shall be established under the UNCITRAL Arbitration Rules, and shall conduct its proceedings in accordance with those Rules, except as modified by this Subchapter.

2. Where a Tribunal established under this Article is satisfied that claims have been submitted to arbitration under Article 1120 that have a question of law or fact in common, the Tribunal may, in the interests of fair and efficient resolution of the claims, and after hearing the disputing parties, order that the Tribunal:

(a) shall assume jurisdiction over, and hear and determine together, all or part of the claims; or

(b) shall assume jurisdiction over, and hear and determine one or more of the claims, the determination of which it believes would assist in the resolution of the others.

3. A disputing party that seeks an order under paragraph 2 shall request the Secretary-General of ICSID to establish a Tribunal and shall specify in the request:

(a) the name of the disputing Party or disputing parties against which the order is sought;
(b) the nature of the order sought; and
(c) the grounds on which the order is sought.

4. The disputing party shall give to the disputing Party or disputing parties against which the order is sought a copy of the request.

5. Within 60 days of receipt of the request, the Secretary-General of ICSID shall establish a Tribunal consisting of three arbitrators. The Secretary-General shall appoint the presiding arbitrator from the roster described in paragraph 4 of Article 1124. In the event that no such presiding arbitrator is available to serve, the Secretary-General shall appoint a presiding arbitrator, who is not a national of any of the Parties, from the ICSID Panel of Arbitrators. The Secretary-General shall appoint the two other members from the roster described in paragraph 4 of Article 1124, and to the extent not available from that roster, from the ICSID Panel of Arbitrators, and to the extent not available from that panel, in the discretion of the Secretary-General. One member shall be a national of the disputing Party and one member shall be a national of the Party of the disputing investors.

6. Where a Tribunal has been established under this Article, a disputing party that has not been named in a request made under paragraph 3 may make a written request to the Tribunal that it be included in an order made under paragraph 2, and shall specify in the request:

(a) the party's name and address;
(b) the nature of the order sought; and
(c) the grounds on which the order is sought.

7. A disputing party described in paragraph 6 shall give a copy of its request to the parties named in a request made under paragraph 3.

8. A Tribunal established under Article 1120 shall not have jurisdiction to decide a claim, or a part of a claim, over which a Tribunal established under this Article has assumed jurisdiction.

9. A disputing Party shall give to the Secretariat of the Commission, within 15 days of receipt by the disputing Party, a copy of:

(a) a request for arbitration made under paragraph 1 of Article 36 of the ICSID Convention;

(b) a notice for arbitration made under Article 2 of the Additional Facility Rules; or

(c) a notice of arbitration given under the UNCITRAL Arbitration Rules.

10. A disputing Party shall give to the Secretariat of the Commission a copy of a request made under paragraph 3 of this Article:

(a) within 15 days of receipt of the request, in the case of a request made by a disputing investor;

(b) within 15 days of making the request, in the case of a request made by the disputing Party.

11. A disputing Party shall give to the Secretariat of the Commission a copy of a request made under paragraph 6 of this Article within 15 days of receipt of the request.

12. The Secretariat of the Commission shall maintain a public register consisting of the documents referred to in paragraphs 9, 10 and 11.

2—203   Article 1126—Notice

A disputing Party shall deliver to the other Parties:

(a) written notice of a claim that has been submitted to arbitration within 30 days from the date that the claim is submitted; and

(b) copies of all pleading filed in the arbitration.

2—204   Article 1127—Participation by a Party

On written notice to the disputing parties, a Party may make submissions to a Tribunal on a question of interpretation of this Agreement.

2—205   Article 1128—Documents

A Party shall be entitled to receive from the disputing Party at the cost of the requesting Party:

(a) a copy of the evidence that has been tendered to the Tribunal; and

(b) a copy of the written argument of the disputing parties.

2—206 Article 1129—Place of Arbitration

Unless the disputing parties agree otherwise, a Tribunal shall hold an arbitration in the territory of a Party which is a party to the New York Convention, selected in accordance with:

  (a) the Additional Facility Rules if the arbitration is under those rules or the ICSID Arbitration Rules; or

  (b) the UNCITRAL Arbitration Rules if the arbitration is under those rules.

2—207 Article 1130—Governing Law

A Tribunal established under this Subchapter shall decide the issues in dispute in accordance with this Agreement and applicable rules of international law.

2—208 Article 1131—Interpretation of Annexes

  1. Where a disputing Party asserts as a defense that the measure alleged to be a breach of this Chapter is within the scope of an exception set forth in Annex I, Annex II, Annex III or Annex IV, on request of the disputing Party, the Tribunal shall request the interpretation of the Commission on this question. The Commission shall have 60 days to submit its interpretation in writing to the Tribunal.

  2. If the Commission submits to the Tribunal an agreed interpretation, the interpretation shall be binding on the Tribunal. If the Commission fails to submit an agreed interpretation or fails to submit an agreed interpretation within such 60 day period, the Tribunal shall decide the issue of interpretation of the exception.

2—209 Article 1132—Report from an Expert

Without prejudice to the appointment of other kinds of experts where authorized by the applicable arbitration rules, a Tribunal, at the request of a disputing party or, unless the disputing parties disapprove, on its own initiative, may appoint one or more experts to report to it in writing on any factual issue concerning environmental, health, safety or other scientific matters raised by a disputing party in a proceeding, subject to such terms and conditions as the disputing parties may agree.

2—210   Article 1133—Interim Measures of Protection

A Tribunal may take such measures as it deems necessary to preserve the respective rights of the disputing parties, or to ensure that the Tribunal's jurisdiction is made fully effective. Such measures may include, but are not limited to, orders to preserve evidence in the possession or control of a disputing party, or to protect the Tribunal's jurisdiction. An interim measure of protection may not include an order of attachment or an order to enjoin the application of the measure alleged to be the breach of Subchapter A of this Chapter, Article 1502(3)(a) (Monopolies and State Enterprises) or Article 1503(2) (State Enterprises). For purposes of this paragraph, an order includes a recommendation.

2—211   Article 1134—Final Award

1. Where a Tribunal makes a final award against a Party, the Tribunal may award only:

   (a) monetary damages, and any applicable interest; or
   (b) restitution of property, in which case the award shall provide that the disputing Party may pay monetary damages, and any applicable interest, in lieu of restitution.

2. Subject to paragraph 1, where a claim is made under paragraph 1 of Article 1117:

   (a) an award of restitution of property shall provide that restitution be made to the enterprise;
   (b) an award of monetary damages, and any applicable interest, shall provide that the sum be paid to the enterprise; and
   (c) the award shall provide that it is made without prejudice to any right that any person may have in the relief under applicable domestic law.

3. A Tribunal may not order a Party to pay punitive damages.

2—212   Article 1135—Finality and Enforcement of Award

1. An award made by a Tribunal is binding on the disputing parties but shall have no binding force except between the disputing parties and in respect of the particular case.

2. Subject to paragraph 3, a disputing party shall abide by and comply with an award without delay.

3. A disputing party may not seek enforcement of a final award until:

(a) in the case of a final award made under the ICSID Convention:

   (i) 120 days have elapsed from the date the award was rendered and no disputing party has requested revision or annulment of the award, or

   (ii) revision or annulment proceedings have been completed, and

(b) in the case of a final award under the Additional Facility Rules of ICSID or the UNCITRAL Arbitration Rules:

   (i) 3 months have elapsed from the date the award was rendered and no disputing party has commenced a proceeding to revise, set aside or annul the award, or

   (ii) a court has dismissed or allowed an application to revise, set aside or annul the award and there is no further appeal.

5. Each Party undertakes to provide for the enforcement in its territory of an award.

6. If a Party fails to abide by or comply with the terms of a final award under this Subchapter, the Commission provided for in Chapter Twenty (Institutional Arrangements and Dispute Settlement Procedures) shall, upon delivery of a request by any other Party whose investor was party to the investment dispute, establish a panel under Article 2008(1). The requesting Party may seek in such proceedings:

   (a) a determination that the failure to abide by and comply-with the terms of the final award is inconsistent with the obligations of this Agreement; and

   (b) a recommendation that the defaulting Party abide by or comply with the terms of the final award.

7. A disputing investor may seek enforcement of an arbitration award under the ICSID Convention, the New York Convention or the Inter-American Convention regardless of whether proceedings have been taken under paragraph 6.

8. A claim that is submitted to arbitration shall be considered to arise out of a commercial relationship or transaction for purposes of Article I of the New York Convention and Article I of the Inter-American Convention.

2—213 Article 1136—General

1. Time when a Claim is Submitted to Arbitration: A claim is submitted to arbitration under this Subchapter when:
   (a) the notice of registration of the request to institute arbitration proceedings has been dispatched by the Secretary-General of ICSID in accordance with paragraph 3 of Article 36 of the ICSID Convention;
   (b) the certificate of registration of the notice for arbitration has been dispatched by the Secretary-General of ICSID in accordance with Article 4 of Schedule C of the Additional Facility Rules; or
   (c) the notice of arbitration given under the UNCITRAL Arbitration Rules is received by the disputing Party.

2. Receipts under Insurance or Guarantee Contracts: In an arbitration under this Subchapter, a Party shall not assert, as a defense, counterclaim, right of set off or otherwise, that the investor concerned has received or will receive, pursuant to an insurance or guarantee contract, indemnification or other compensation for all or part of its alleged damages.

2—214 Article 1137—Exclusions

1. Without prejudice to the applicability or non-applicability of the dispute settlement provisions of this Subchapter or of Chapter Twenty (Institutional Arrangements and Dispute Settlement Procedures) to other actions taken by a Party pursuant to Article 2102 (National Security), a decision by a Party to prohibit or restrict the acquisition of an investment in its territory by an investor of another Party, or its investment, pursuant to that Article shall not be subject to such provisions.

2. The dispute settlement provisions of this Subchapter and of Chapter Twenty shall not apply to the matters described in Annex 1137.2.

2—215 Article 1138—Definitions

For purposes of this Chapter:

disputing Party means a Party against which a claim is made under Subchapter B;

disputing party means the disputing investor or the disputing Party;

disputing parties means the disputing investor and the disputing Party;

enterprise means an "enterprise" as defined in Article 201, except that it shall also include a branch;

enterprise of a Party means an enterprise constituted or organized under the laws and regulations of a Party, and a branch;

equity or debt securities includes voting and non-voting shares, bonds, convertible debentures, stock options and warrants;

G7 Currency means the currency of Canada, Germany, France, Italy, Japan, the United States or the United Kingdom of Great Britain and Northern Ireland;

ICSID Convention means the Convention on the Settlement of Investment Disputes between States and Nationals of other States done at Washington, March 18, 1965;

ICSID means the International Centre for Settlement of Investment Disputes;

Inter-American Convention means the Inter-American Convention on International Commercial Arbitration, done at Panama, January 30,1975;

investment means:

(a) an enterprise;
(b) an equity security of an enterprise;
(c) a debt security of an enterprise

    (i) that is an affiliate of the investor, or
    (ii) where the original maturity of the debt security is at least three years, but does not include a debt security, regardless of original maturity, of a state enterprise;

(d) a loan to an enterprise,

    (i) that is an affiliate of the investor, or
    (ii) where the original maturity of the loan is at least three years, but does not include a loan, regardless of original maturity, to a state enterprise;

(e) an interest in an enterprise that entitles the owner to share in the income or profits;
(f) an interest in an enterprise that entitles the owner to share in the assets on dissolution, other than a debt

security or a loan excluded from sub-paragraph (c) or (d);

(g) real estate or other property (tangible and intangible) acquired in the expectation or used for the purpose of economic benefit or other business purposes;

(h) interests arising from the commitment of capital or other resources in the territory of a Party to economic activity in such territory, such as under:

   (i) contracts involving the presence of an investor's property in the territory of the Party (including turnkey or construction contracts, or concessions), or

   (ii) contracts where the remuneration depends substantially on the production, revenues or profits of an enterprise.

But investment does not mean,

(i) claims to money that arise solely from:

   (i) commercial contracts for the sale of goods or services by a national or enterprise in the territory of one Party to an enterprise in the territory of another Party, or

   (ii) the extension of credit in connection with a commercial transaction, such as trade financing, other than a loan covered by sub-paragraph (d), or

(j) any other claims to money,

which do not involve the kinds of interests set out in sub-paragraphs (a) through (h);

investment of an investor of a Party means an investment owned or controlled directly or indirectly by an investor of such Party;

investor of a Party means a Party or state enterprise thereof, or a national or an enterprise of such Party, that seeks to make, makes or has made an investment;

investor of a non-Party means an investor other than an investor of a Party, that makes, seeks to make or has made an investment;

New York Convention means the United Nations Convention on the Recognition and Enforcement of Foreign Arbitral Awards, done at New York, June 10, 1958;

Tribunal means an arbitration tribunal established under Article 1120 or 1125; and

UNCITRAL Arbitration rules means the arbitration rules of the United Nations Commission on International Trade Law, approved by the United Nations General Assembly on December 15, 1976.

Annex 1120.1

2—216 Submission of Claims to Arbitration

1. An investor of another Party may not allege that Mexico has breached:

   (a) a provision of Subchapter A; or
   (b) Article 1502(3)(a) (Monopolies and State Enterprises) or Article 1503(2) (State Enterprises) where the alleged breach pertains to the obligations of Subchapter A,

   both in an arbitration under this Subchapter and in proceedings before a Mexican court or administrative tribunal.

2. Where an enterprise of Mexico that is a juridical personthat an investor of another Party owns or controls directly or indirectly alleges in proceedings before a Mexican court or administrative tribunal that Mexico has breached:

   (a) a provision of Subchapter A; or
   (b) Article 1502(3)(a) (Monopolies and State Enterprises) or Article 1503(2) (State Enterprises) where the alleged breach pertains to the obligations of Subchapter A,
   the investor may not allege the breach in an arbitration under this Subchapter.

Annex 1137.2

2—217 Exclusions from Dispute Settlement

CANADA

A decision by Canada following a review under the Investment Canada Act, with respect to whether or not to permit an acquisition that is subject to review, shall not be subject to the dispute settlement provisions of Subchapter B or of Chapter Twenty (Institutional Arrangements and Dispute Settlement Procedures).

MEXICO

A decision by the National Commission on Foreign Investment ("Comisicion Nacional de Inversiones Extranjeras") following a review pursuant to Annex I, page I-M-7, with respect to whether or not to permit an acquisition that is subject to review, shall not be subject to the dispute settlement provisions of Subchapter B or of Chapter Twenty (Institutional Arrangements and Dispute Settlement Procedures).

CHAPTER 3

International Arbitration Procedural and Ethical Rules

A. CODE OF ETHICS FOR ARBITRATORS IN INTERNATIONAL ARBITRATION

American Arbitration Association's Code Of Ethics For Arbitrators In Commercial Disputes

3—001 The Code of Ethics for Arbitrators in Commercial Disputes was prepared in 1977 by a joint committee consisting of a special committee of the American Arbitration Association and a special committee of the American Bar Association. It has been approved and recommended by both organizations.

3—002 Preamble

The use of commercial arbitration to resolve a wide variety of disputes has grown extensively and forms a significant part of the system of justice on which our society relies for fair determination of legal rights. Persons who act as commercial arbitrators therefore undertake serious responsibilities to the public as well as to the parties. Those responsibilities include important ethical obligations.

Few cases of unethical behavior by commercial arbitrators have arisen. Nevertheless, the American Bar Association and the American Arbitration Association believe that it is in the public interest to set forth generally accepted standards of ethical conduct for guidance of arbitrators and parties in commercial disputes. By establishing this code, the sponsors hope to contribute to the maintenance of high standards and continued confidence in the process of arbitration.

There are many different types of commercial arbitration. Some cases are conducted under arbitration rules established by various organizations and trade associations, while others are conducted without such rules. Although most cases are arbitrated pursuant to voluntary agreement of the parties, certain types of dispute are submitted to arbitration by reason of particular laws. This code is intended to apply to all such proceedings in which disputes or claims are submitted for decision to one or more arbitrators appointed in a manner provided by an agreement of the parties, by applicable arbitration rules, or by law. In all such cases, the persons who have the power to decide should observe fundamental standards of ethical conduct. In this code all such persons are called "arbitrators" although, in some types of case, they might be called "umpires" or have some other title.

Various aspects of the conduct of arbitrators, including some matters covered by this code, may be governed by agreements of the parties, by arbitration rules to which the parties have agreed, or by applicable law. this code does not take the place of or supersede such agreements, rules, or laws and does not establish new or additional grounds for judicial review of arbitration awards.

While this code is intended to provide ethical guidelines in many types of arbitration, it does not form a part of the arbitration rules of the American Arbitration Association or of any other organization, nor is it intended to apply to mediation or conciliation. Labor arbitration is governed by the Code of Professional Responsibility for Arbitrators of Labor-Management Disputes, not by this code.

Arbitrators, like judges, have the power to decide cases. However, unlike full-time judges, arbitrators are usually engaged in other occupations before, during, and after the time that they serve as arbitrators. Often, arbitrators are purposely chosen from the same trade or industry as the parties in order to bring special knowledge to the task of deciding. This code recognizes these fundamental differences between arbitrators and judges.

In some types of arbitration, there are three or more arbitrators. In such cases, it is sometimes the practice for each party, acting alone, to appoint one arbitrator and for the other arbitrators to be designated by those two, by the parties, or by an independent institution or individual. The sponsors of this code believe that it is preferable for parties to agree that all arbitrators should comply with the same ethical standards. However, it is recognized that there is a long-established practice in some types of arbitration for the arbitrators who are appointed by one party, acting alone, to be governed by special ethical considerations. Those special considerations are set forth in the last section of the code, headed "Ethical Considerations Relating to Arbitrators Appointed by One Party."

Although this code is sponsored by the American Arbitration Association and the American Bar Association, its use is not limited to arbitrations administered by the AAA or to cases in which the arbitrators are lawyers. Rather, it is presented as a public service to provide guidance in all types of commercial arbitration.

Canon I: An Arbitrator Should Uphold the Integrity and Fairness of the Arbitration Process

3—003 A. Fair and just processes for resolving disputes are indispensable in our society. Commercial arbitration is an important method for deciding many types of disputes. In order for commercial arbitration to be effective, there must be broad public confidence in the integrity and fairness of the process. Therefore, an arbitrator has a responsibility not only to the parties but also to the process of arbitration itself, and must observe high standards of conduct so that the integrity and fairness of the process will be preserved. Accordingly, an arbitrator should recognize a responsibility to the public, to the parties whose rights will be decided, and to all other participants in the proceeding. The provisions of this code should be construed and applied to further these objectives.

B. It is inconsistent with the integrity of the arbitration process for persons to solicit appointment for themselves. However, a person may indicate a general willingness to serve as an arbitrator.

C. Persons should accept appointment as arbitrators only if they believe that they can be available to conduct the arbitration promptly.

D. After accepting appointment and while serving as an arbitrator, a person should avoid entering into any financial, business, professional, family or social relationship, or acquiring any financial or personal interest, which is likely to affect impartiality or which might reasonably create the appearance of partiality or bias. For a reasonable period of time after the decision of a case, persons who have served as arbitrators should avoid entering into any such relationship, or acquiring any such interest, in circumstances which might reasonably create the appearance that they had been influenced in the arbitration by the anticipation or expectation of the relationship or interest.

E. Arbitrators should conduct themselves in a way that is fair to all parties and should not be swayed by outside pressure, by public clamor, by fear of criticism or by self-interest.

F. When an arbitrator's authority is derived from an agreement of the parties, the arbitrator should neither exceed that authority nor do less than is required to exercise that authority completely. Where the agreement of the parties sets forth procedures to be followed in conducting the arbitration or refers to rules to be followed, it is the obligation of the arbitrator to comply with such procedures or rules.

G. An arbitrator should make all reasonable efforts to prevent delaying tactics, harassment of parties or other participants, or other abuse or disruption of the arbitration process.

H. The ethical obligations of an arbitrator begin upon acceptance of the appointment and continue throughout all stages of the proceeding. In addition, wherever specifically set forth in this code, certain ethical obligations begin as soon as a person is requested to serve as an arbitrator and certain ethical obligations continue even after the decision in the case has been given to the parties.

CANON II: AN ARBITRATOR SHOULD DISCLOSE ANY INTEREST OR RELATIONSHIP LIKELY TO AFFECT IMPARTIALITY OR WHICH MIGHT CREATE AN APPEARANCE OF PARTIALITY OR BIAS

3—004 Introductory Note

This code reflects the prevailing principle that arbitrators should disclose the existence of interests or relationships that are likely to affect their impartiality or that might reasonably create an appearance that they are biased against one party or favorable to another. These provisions of the code are intended to be applied realistically so that the burden of detailed disclosure does not become so great that it is impractical for persons in the business world to be arbitrators, thereby depriving parties of the services of those who might be best informed and qualified to decide particular types of case.

This code does not limit the freedom of parties to agree on whomever they choose as an arbitrator. When parties, with knowledge of a person's interests and relationships, nevertheless desire that individual to serve as an arbitrator, that person may properly serve.

3—005 Disclosure

A. Persons who are requested to serve as arbitrators should, before accepting, disclose

1. any direct or indirect financial or personal interest in the outcome of the arbitration;
2. any existing or past financial, business, professional, family or social relationships which are likely to affect

impartiality or which might reasonably create an appearance of partiality or bias. Persons requested to serve as arbitrators should disclose any such relationships which they personally have with any party or its lawyer, or with any individual whom they have been told will be a witness. They should also disclose any such relationships involving members of their families or their current employers, partners or business associates.

B. Persons who are requested to accept appointment as arbitrators should make a reasonable effort to inform themselves of any interests or relationships described in the preceding paragraph A.

C. The obligation to disclose interests or relationships described in the preceding paragraph A is a continuing duty which requires a person who accepts appointment as an arbitrator to disclose, at any stage of the arbitration, any such interests or relationships which may arise, or which are recalled or discovered.

D. Disclosure should be made to all parties unless other procedures for disclosure are provided in the rules or practices of an institution which is administering the arbitration. Where more than one arbitrator has been appointed, each should inform the others of the interests and relationships which have been disclosed.

E. In the event that an arbitrator is requested by all parties to withdraw, the arbitrator should do so. In the event that an arbitrator is requested to withdraw by less than all of the parties because of alleged partiality or bias, the arbitrator should withdraw unless either of the following circumstances exists.

1. If an agreement of the parties, or arbitration rules agreed to by the parties, establishes procedures for determining challenges to arbitrators, then those procedures should be followed; or,
2. if the arbitrator, after carefully considering the matter, determines that the reason for the challenge is not substantial, and that he or she can nevertheless act and decide the case impartially and fairly, and that withdrawal would cause unfair delay or expense to another party or would be contrary to the ends of justice.

CANON III: AN ARBITRATOR IN COMMUNICATING WITH THE PARTIES SHOULD AVOID IMPROPRIETY OR THE APPEARANCE OF IMPROPRIETY

3—006 A. If an agreement of the parties or applicable arbitration rules referred to in that agreement, establishes the manner or content of communications between the arbitrator and the parties, the arbitrator should follow those procedures notwithstanding any contrary provision of the following paragraphs B and C.

B. Unless otherwise provided in applicable arbitration rules or in an agreement of the parties, arbitrators should not discuss a case with any party in the absence of each other party, except in any of the following circumstances.

1. Discussions may be had with a party concerning such matters as setting the time and place of hearings or making other arrangements for the conduct of the proceedings. However, the arbitrator should promptly inform each other party of the discussion and should not make any final determination concerning the matter discussed before giving each absent party an opportunity to express its views.
2. If a party fails to be present at a hearing after having beengiven due notice, the arbitrator may discuss the case with any party who is present.
3. If all parties request or consent to it, such discussion may take place.

C. Unless otherwise provided in applicable arbitration rules or in an agreement of the parties, whenever an arbitrator communicates in writing with one party, the arbitrator should at the same time send a copy of the communication to each other party. Whenever the arbitrator receives any written communication concerning the case from one party which has not already been sent to each other party, the arbitrator should do so.

CANON IV: AN ARBITRATOR SHOULD CONDUCT THE PROCEEDINGS FAIRLY AND DILIGENTLY

3—007 A. An arbitrator should conduct the proceedings in an even handed manner and treat all parties with equality and fairness at all stages of the proceedings.

A. Code of Ethics for Arbitrators

B. An arbitrator should perform duties diligently and conclude the case as promptly as the circumstances reasonably permit.

C. An arbitrator should be patient and courteous to the parties, to their lawyers and to the witnesses and should encourage similar conduct by all participants in the proceedings.

D. Unless otherwise agreed by the parties or provided in arbitration rules agreed to by the parties, an arbitrator should accord to all parties the right to appear in person and to be heard after due notice of the time and place of hearing.

E. An arbitrator should not deny any party the opportunity to be represented by counsel.

F. If a party fails to appear after due notice, an arbitrator should proceed with the arbitration when authorized to do so by the agreement of the parties, the rules agreed to by the parties or by law. However, an arbitrator should do so only after receiving assurance that notice has been given to the absent party.

G. When an arbitrator determines that more information than has been presented by the parties is required to decide the case, it is not improper for the arbitrator to ask questions, call witnesses, and request documents or other evidence.

H. It is not improper for an arbitrator to suggest to the parties that they discuss the possibility of settlement of the case. However, an arbitrator should not be present or otherwise participate in the settlement discussions unless requested to do so by all parties. An arbitrator should not exert pressure on any party to settle.

I. Nothing in this code is intended to prevent a person from acting as a mediator or conciliator of a dispute in which he or she has been appointed as arbitrator, if requested to do so by all parties or where authorized or required to do so by applicable laws or rules.

J. When there is more than one arbitrator, the arbitrators should afford each other the full opportunity to participate in all aspects of the proceedings.

CANON V: AN ARBITRATOR SHOULD MAKE DECISIONS IN A JUST, INDEPENDENT AND DELIBERATE MANNER

3—008 A. An arbitrator should, after careful deliberation, decide all issues submitted for determination. An arbitrator should decide no other issues.

B. An arbitrator should decide all matters justly, exercising independent judgment, and should not permit outside pressure to affect the decision.

C. An arbitrator should not delegate the duty to decide to any other person.

D. In the event that all parties agree upon a settlement of issues in dispute and request an arbitrator to embody that agreement in an award, an arbitrator may do so, but is not required to do so unless satisfied with the propriety of the terms of settlement. Whenever an arbitrator embodies a settlement by the parties in an award, the arbitrator should state in the award that it is based on an agreement of the parties.

CANON VI: AN ARBITRATOR SHOULD BE FAITHFUL TO THE RELATIONSHIP OF TRUST AND CONFIDENTIALITY INHERENT IN THAT OFFICE

3—009 A. An arbitrator is in a relationship of trust to the parties and should not, at any time, use confidential information acquired during the arbitration proceeding to gain personal advantage or advantage for others, or to affect adversely the interest of another.

B. Unless otherwise agreed by the parties, or required by applicable rules or law, an arbitrator should keep confidential all matters relating to the arbitration proceedings and decision.

C. It is not proper at any time for an arbitrator to inform anyone of the decision in advance of the time it is given to all parties. In a case in which there is more than one arbitrator, it is not proper at any time for an arbitrator to inform anyone concerning the deliberations of the arbitrators. After an arbitration award has been made, it is not proper for an arbitrator to assist in post-arbitral proceedings, except as is required by law.

D. In many types of arbitration it is customary practice for the arbitrators to serve without pay. However, in some types of cases it is customary for arbitrators to receive compensation for their services and reimbursement for their expenses. In cases in which any such payments are to be made, all persons who are requested to serve, or who are serving as arbitrators, should be governed by the same high standards of integrity and fairness as apply to their other activities in the case. Accordingly, such persons should scrupulously avoid bargaining with parties over the amount of payments or engaging in any communications concerning payments which would create an appearance of coercion or other impropriety. In the absence of governing provisions in the agreement of the parties or in rules agreed to by the parties or in applicable law, certain practices, relating to payments are generally recognized as being preferable in order to preserve the integrity and fairness of the arbitration process. These practices include the following.

1. It is preferable that before the arbitrator finally accepts appointment the basis of payment be established and that all parties be informed thereof in writing.
2. In cases conducted under the rules or administration of an institution that is available to assist in making arrangements for payments, the payments should be arranged by the institution to avoid the necessity for communication by the arbitrators directly with the parties concerning the subject.
3. In cases where no institution is available to assist in making arrangement for payments, it is preferable that any discussions with arbitrators concerning payments should take place in the presence of all parties.

CANON VII: ETHICAL CONSIDERATIONS RELATING TO ARBITRATORS APPOINTED BY ONE PARTY

3—010 **Introductory Note**

In some types of arbitration in which there are three arbitrators, it is customary for each party, acting alone, to appoint one arbitrator. The third arbitrator is then appointed by agreement either of the parties or of the two arbitrators, or, failing such agreement, by an independent institution or individual. In some of these types of arbitration, all three arbitrators are customarily considered to be neutral and are expected to observe the same standards of ethical conduct. However, there are also many types of tripartite arbitration in which it has been the practice that the two arbitrators appointed by the parties are not considered to be neutral and are expected to observe many but not all of the same ethical standards as the neutral third arbitrator. For the purposes of this code, an arbitrator appointed by one party who is not expected to observe all of the same standards as the third arbitrator is called a "non neutral arbitrator." This Canon VII describes the ethical obligations that non neutral party-appointed arbitrators should observe and those that are not applicable to them.

In all arbitrations in which there are two or more party-appointed arbitrators, it is important for everyone concerned to know from the start whether the party-appointed arbitrators are expected to be neutrals or non neutrals. In such arbitrations, the two party-appointed arbitrators should be considered non neutrals unless both parties inform the arbitrators that all three arbitrators are to be neutral or unless the contract, the applicable arbitration rules, or any governing law requires that all three arbitrators be neutral.

It should be noted that, in cases conducted outside the United States, the applicable law might require that all arbitrators be neutral. Accordingly, in such cases, the governing law should be considered before applying any of the following provisions relating to non neutral party-appointed arbitrators.

3—011   A. Obligations under Canon I

Non neutral party-appointed arbitrators should observe all of the obligations of Canon I to uphold the integrity and fairness of the arbitration process, subject only to the following provisions.

1. Non neutral arbitrators may be predisposed toward the party who appointed them but in all other respects are obligated to act in good faith and with integrity and fairness. For example, non neutral arbitrators should not engage in delaying tactics or harassment of any party or witness and should not knowingly make untrue or misleading statements to the other arbitrators.

2. The provisions of Canon I.D relating to relationships and interests are not applicable to non neutral arbitrators.

3—012   B. Obligations under Canon II

Non neutral party-appointed arbitrators should disclose to all parties, and to the other arbitrators, all interests and relationships which Canon II requires be disclosed. Disclosure as required by Canon II is for the benefit not only of the party who appointed the non neutral arbitrator, but also for the benefit of the other parties and arbitrators so that they may know of any bias which may exist or appear to exist. However, this obligation is subject to the following provisions.

1. Disclosure by non neutral arbitrators should be sufficient to describe the general nature and scope of any interest or relationship, but need not include as detailed information as is expected from persons appointed as neutral arbitrators.

2. Non neutral arbitrators are not obliged to with draw if requested to do so by the party who did not appoint them, notwithstanding the provisions of Canon II.E.

3—013   C. Obligations under Canon III

Non neutral party-appointed arbitrators should observe all of the obligations of Canon III concerning communications with the parties, subject only to the following provisions.

1. In an arbitration in which the two party-appointed arbitrators are expected to appoint the third arbitrator, non neutral arbitrators may consult with the party who appointed them concerning the acceptability of persons under consideration for appointment as the third arbitrator.

2. Non neutral arbitrators may communicate with the party whoappointed them concerning any other aspect of the case, provided theyfirst inform the other arbitrators and the parties that they intend todo so. If such communication occurred prior to the time the person wasappointed as arbitrator, or prior to the first hearing or other meetingof the parties with the arbitrators, the non neutral arbitrator should,at the first hearing or meeting, disclose the fact that such communication has taken place. In complying with the provisions of this paragraph, it is sufficient that there be disclosure of the fact that such communication has occurred without disclosing the content of the communication. It is also sufficient to disclose at any time the intention to follow the procedure of having such communications in the future and there is no requirement thereafter that there be disclosure before each separate occasion on which such a communication occurs.

3. When non neutral arbitrators communicate in writing with the party who appointed them concerning any matter as to which communication is permitted under this code, they are not required to send copies of any such written communication to any other party or arbitrator.

3—014   D. Obligations under Canon IV

Non neutral party-appointed arbitrators should observe all of the obligations of Canon IV to conduct the proceedings fairly and diligently.

3—015   E. Obligations under Canon V

Non neutral party-appointed arbitrators should observe all of the obligations of Canon V concerning making decisions, subject only to the following provision.

> 1. Non neutral arbitrators are permitted to be predisposed toward deciding in favor of the party who appointed them.

3—016   F. Obligations under Canon VI

Non neutral party-appointed arbitrators should observe all of the obligations of Canon VI to be faithful to the relationship of trust inherent in the office of arbitrator, subject only to the following provision.

> 1. Non neutral arbitrators are not subject to the provisions of Canon VI.D with respect to any payments by the party who appointed them.

IBA Guidelines on Conflicts of Interest in International Arbitration

Approved on 22 May 2004 by the Council of the
International Bar Association

3—017 Introduction

Problems of conflicts of interest increasingly challenge international arbitration. Arbitrators are often unsure about what facts need to be disclosed, and they make different choices about disclosures than other arbitrators in the same situation. The growth of international business and the manner in which it is conducted, including interlocking corporate relationships and larger international law firms, have caused more disclosures and have created more difficult conflict of interest issues to determine. Reluctant parties have more opportunities to use challenges of arbitrators to delay arbitrations or to deny the opposing party the arbitrator of its choice. Disclosure of any relationship, no matter how minor or serious, has too often led to objections, challenge and withdrawal or removal of the arbitrator.

Thus, parties, arbitrators, institutions and courts face complex decisions about what to disclose and what standards are to apply. In addition, institutions and courts face difficult decisions if an objection or a challenge is made after disclosure. There is a tension between, on the one hadn, the parties' right to disclosure of situations that may reasonably call into question an arbitrator's impartiality or independence and their right to a fair hearing and, on the other hand, the parties' righ tot select arbitrators of their choosing. Even though laws and arbitrations rules provide some standards, there is a lack of detail in their guidance and of uniformity in their application. As a result, quite often members of the international arbitration community apply different standards in making decisions concerning disclosure, objections and challenges.

It is in the interest of everyone in the international arbitration community that international arbitration proceedings not be hindered by these growing conflicts of interest issues. The Committee on Arbitration and ADR of the International Bar Association appointed a Working Group of 19 experts[1] in international arbitration from 14 countries to study, with the intent of helping this decision-making process, national laws, judicial decisions, arbitration rules and practical considerations and applications regarding impartiality and independence and disclosure in international arbitration. The Working Group has determined that existing standards lack sufficient clarity and uniformity in their application. It has therefore prepared these Guidelines, which set forth some General Standards and Explanatory Notes on the Standards. Moreover, the Working Group believes that greater consistency and few unnecessary challenges and arbitrator withdrawals and removals could be achieved by providing lists of specific situations that, in the view of the Working Group, do or do not warrant disclosure or disqualification of an arbitrator. Such lists – designated Red, Orange and Green (the "Application Lists") – appear at the end of these Guidelines.

The Guidelines reflect the Working Group's understanding of the best current international practice firmly rooted in the principles expressed in the General Standards. The Working Group has based the General Standards and the Application List upon statutes and case law in jurisdiction and upon the judgment and experience of members of the Working Group and others involved in international commercial arbitration. The Working Group has attempted to balance the various interests of parties, representatives, arbitrators and arbitration institutions, all of whom have a responsibility for ensuring the integrity, reputation and efficiency of international commerical arbitration. In particular, the Working Group has sought and considered the views of many leading arbitration institutions, as well as corporate counsel and other persons involved in international arbitration. The Working Group also published drafts of the Guidelines and sought comments at two annual meetings of the International Bar Association and other meetings of arbitrators. While the comments received by the Working Group varied, and included some points of criticisms, the arbitration community generally supported and encouraged these efforts to help reduce the growing problems of conflicts and interests. The Working Group has studied all the comments received and has adopted many of the proposals that it has received. The Working Group is very grateful indeed for the serious considerations given to its proposals by so many insitutions and individuals all over the globe and for the comments and proposals received.

Originally, the Working Group developed the Guidelines for international commercial arbitration. However, in the light of comments received, it realized that the Guidelines should equally apply to other types of arbitration, such as investment arbitrations (insofar as these may not be considered as commercial arbitrations).[2]

These Guidelines are not legal provisions and do not override any applicable national law or arbitral rules chosen by the paries. However, the Working Group hopes that these Guidelines will find general acceptance within the international abritration community (as was the case with the IBA Rules on the Talking of Evidence in International Commercial Arbitration) and that they thus will help parties , practitioners, arbitrators, institutions and the courts in their decision-making process on these very important questions of impartiality, independence, disclosure, objections and challenges made in that connection. The Working Group trusts that the Guidelines will be applied with robust common sense and without pedantic and unduly formalistic interpretation. The Working Group is also publishing a Background and History, which describes the studies made by the Working Group and may be helpful in interpreting the Guidelines.

The IBA and the Working Group view these Guidelines as a beginning, tather than an end, of the process. The Application Lists cover many of the varied situations that commonly arise in practice, but they do no purport to be comprehensive, nor could they be. Nevertheless, the Working Group is confident that the Application Lists provide better concrete guidance that the General Standards (and certainly more than existing standards). The IBA and the Working Group seek comments on the actual use of the Guidelines, and they plan to supplement, revise and refine the Guidelines based on that practical experience.

In 1897, the IBA published Rules of Ethics for International Arbitrators. Those Rules cover more topics than these Guidelines, and they remain in effect as to subjects that are not discussed in the Guidelines. The Guidelines supersede the Rules of Ethics as to the matters treated here.

PART I—GENERAL STANDARDS REGARDING IMPARTIALITY, INDEPENDENCE AND DISCLOSURE

3—018 (1) *General Principle*

Every arbitrator shall be impartial and independent of the parties at the time of accepting an appointment to serve and shall remain so during the entire arbitration proceeding until the final award has been rendered or the proceeding has otherwise finally terminated.

Explanation to General Standard 1:

The Working Group is guided by the fundamental principle in international arbitration that each arbitrator must be impartial and independent of the parties at the time he or she accepts an appointment to acts as arbitrator and must remain so during the entire course of the arbitrator proceedings. The Working Group considered whether this obligation should extend even during the period that the award may be challenged but has decided against this. The Working Group takes the veiw that the arbitrator's duty ends when the Arbitral Tribunal has rendered the final award or the proceedings have otherwise been finally terminated (e.g., because of a settlement). If, after setting aside or other proceedings, the dispute is referred back to the same arbitrator, a fresh round of disclosure may be necessary.

(2) *Conflicts of Interest*

(a) An arbitrator shall decline to accept an appointment or, if the arbitration has already been commenced, refuse to continue to act as an arbitrator if he or she has any doubts as to his or her ability to be impartial or independent.

(b) The same principle applies if facts or circumstances exist, or have arisen since the appointment, that, from a reasonable third person's point of view having knowledge of the relevant facts, given rise to justifiable doubts as to the arbitrator's impartiality or independence, unless the parties have accepted the arbitrator in accordance with the requirements set out in General Standard (4).

(c) Doubts are justifiable if a reasonable and informed third party would reach the conclusion that there was a likelihood that the arbitrator may be influenced by factors other than the merits of the case as presented by the parties in reaching his or her decision.

(d) Justifiable doubts necessarily exist as to the arbitrator's impartiality or independence if there is an identity between a party and the arbitrator, if the arbitrator is a legal representative of a legal entity that is a party in the arbitration, or if the arbitrator has a significant financial or personal interest in the matter at stake.

Explanation to General Standard 2:

(a) It is the main ethical guiding principle of every arbitrator that actual bias from the arbitrator's own point of view must lead to that arbitrator declining his or her appointment. This standard should apply regardless of the stage of the proceedings. This principle is so self-evident that many national laws do not explicitly say so. See e.g. Article 12, UNCITRAL Model Law. The Working Group, however, has included it in the General Standards because explicit expression in these Guidelines helps to avoid confusion and to create confidence in procedures before arbitral tribunals. In addition, the Working Group believed that the broad standard of "any doubts as to any ability to be impartial and independent" should lead to the arbitrator declining the appointment.

(b) In order for standards to be aplied as consistently as possible, the Working Group believes that the test for disqualification should be an objective one. The Working Group uses the word "impartiality or independence" derived from the broadly adopted Article 12 of the

UNCITRAL Model Law, and the use of an appearance test, based on justifiable doubts as to the impartiality or independence of the arbitrator, as provided in Article 12(2) of the UNCITRAL Model Law, to be applied objectively (a "reasonable third person test"). As described in the Explanation to General Standard 3(d), this standard should apply regardless of the stage of the proceedings.

(c) Most laws and rules that apply the standard of justifiable doubts do not further define that standard. The Working Group believes that this General Standard provides some context for making this determination.

(d) The Working Group supports the view that no one is allowed to be his or her own judge; i.e. there cannot be identity between an arbitrator and a party. The Working Group believes that situation cannot be waived by the parties. The same principle should apply to persons who are legal representatives of a legal entity that is a party in the arbitration, like board members, or who have a significant economic interest in the matter at stake. Because of the importance of this principle, this non-waivable situation is made a General Standard, and examples are provided in the non-waivable Red List.

The General Standard purposely uses the terms "identity" and "legal representatives." In the light of comments received, the Working Group considered whether these terms should be extended or further defined, but decided against doing so. It realizes that there are situations in which an employee of a party or a civil servant can be in a position similar, if not identical, to the position of an official legal representative. The Working Group decided that is should suffice to state the principle.

3—019 (3) *Disclosure by the Arbitrator*

(a) If facts or circumstances exist that may, in the eyes of the parties, give rise to doubts as to the arbitrator's impartiality or independence, the arbitrator shall disclose such facts or circumstances to the parties, the arbitration institution or other appointing authority (if any, and if so required by the applicable institutional rules) and to the co-arbitrators, if any, prior to accepting his or her appointment or, if thereafter, as soon as he or she learns about them.

(b) It follows from General Standards 1 and 2(a) that an arbitrator who has made a disclosure considers himself

or herself to be impartial and independent of the parties despite the disclosed facts and therefore capable of performing his or her duties as arbitrator. Otherwise, he or she would have declined the nomination or appointment at the outset or resigned.
(c) Any doubt as to whether an arbitrator should disclose certain facts or circumstances should be resolved in favour of disclosure.
(d) When considering whether or not facts or circumstances exist that should be disclosed, the arbitrator shall not take into account whether the arbitration proceeding is at the beginning or at a later stage.

Explanation to General Standard 3:

(a) General Standard 2(b) above sets out an objective test for disqualification or an arbitrator. However, because ov varying considerations with respect to disclosure, the proper standard of disclosure may be different. A purely objective test for disclosure exists in the majority of the jurisdictions analyzed and in the UNCITRAL Model Law. Nevertheless, the Working Group recognizes that the parties have an interest in being fully informed about any circumstances that may be relevant in their view. Because of the strongly held views of many arbitration institutions (as reflected in their rules and as stated to the Working Group) that the disclosure test should reflect the perspectives of the parties, the Working Group in principle accepted, after much debate, a subjective approach for disclosure. The Working Group has adapted the language of Article 7(2) of the ICC Rules for this standard.

However, the Working Group believes that this principle should not be applied without limitations. Because some situations should never elad to disqualification under the objective test, such situations need not be disclosed, regardless of the parties' perspective. These limitations to the subjective test are reflected in the Green List, which lists some situations in which disclosure is not required.

Similarly, the Working Group emphasizes that the two tests (objective test for disqualification and subjective test for disclosure) are clearly distinct from each other, and that a disclosure shall not automatically lead to disqualification, as reflected in General Standard 3(b).

In determining what facts should be disclosed, an arbitrator should take into account all circumstances known to him or her, including to the extent known the culture and the customs of the country of which the parties are domiciled or nationals.

(b) Disclosure is not an admission of a conflict of interest. An arbitrator who has made a disclosure to the parties considers himself or herself to be impartial and independent of the parties, despite the disclosed facts, or else he or she would have declined the nomination or resigned. An arbitrator making disclosure thus feels capable of performing his or her duties. It is the purpose of disclosure to allow the parties to judge whether or not they agree with the evaluation of the arbitrator and, if they so wish, to explore the situation further. The Working Group hopes that the promulgation of this General Standard will eliminate the misunderstanding that disclosure demonstrates doubts sufficient to disqualify the arbitrator. Instead, any challenge should be successful only if an objective test, as set forth above, is met.

(c) Unnecessary disclosure sometimes raises an incorrect implication in the minds of the parties that the disclosed circumstances would affect his or her impartiality or independence. Excessive disclosures thus unnecessarily undermine the parties' confidence in the process. Nevertheless, after some debate, the Working Group believes it is important to provide expressly in the General Standards that in case of doubt the arbitrator should disclose. If the arbitrator feels that he or she should disclose but that professional secrecy rules or other rules of practice prevent such disclosure, he or she should not accept the appointment or should resign.

(d) The Working Group has concluded that disclosure or disqualification (as set out in General Standard 2) should not depend on the particular stage of the arbitration. In order to determine whether the arbitrator should disclose, decline the appointment or refuse to continue to act or whether a challenge by a party should be successful, the facts and circumstances alone are relevant and not the current stage of the procedure or the consequences of the withdrawal. As a practical matter, institutions make a distinction between the commencement of an arbitration proceeding and a later stage. Also, courts tend to apply different standard. Nevertheless, the Working Group believes it important to clarify that no distinction should be made regarding the stage of the arbitral procedure. While there are practical concerns if an arbitrator must withdraw after an arbitration has commenced, a distinction based on the stage of arbitration would be inconsistent with the General Standards.

(4) *Waiver by the Parties*

(a) If, within 30 days after the receipt of any disclosure by the arbitrator or after a party learns of facts or circumstances that could constitute a potential conflict of interest for an arbitrator, a party does not raise an express objection with regard to that arbitrator, subject to paragraphs (b) and (c) of this General Standard, the party is deemed to have waived any potential conflict of interest by the arbitrator based on such facts or circumstances and may not raise any objection to such facts or circumstances at a later stage.

(b) However, if facts or circumstances exist as described in General Standard 2(d), any waiver by a party or any agreement by the parties to have such a person serve as an arbitrator shall be regarded as invalid.

(c) A person should not serve as an arbitrator when a conflict of interst, such as those exemplified in the waivable Red List, exists. Nevertheless, such a person may accept appointment as arbitrator or continue to act as an arbitrator, if the following conditions are met:

(i) All parties, all arbitrators and the arbitration institution or other appointing authority (if any) must have full knowledge of the conflict of interest; and

(ii) All parties must expressly agree that such person may serve as arbitrator despite the conflict of interest.

(d) An arbitrator may assist the parties in reaching a settlement of the dispute at any stage of the proceedings. However, before doing so, the arbitrator should receive an express agreement by the parties that acting in such a manner shall not disqualify the arbitrator from continuing to serve as arbitrator. Such express agreement shall be considered to be an effective waiver of any potential conflict of interest that may arise from the arbitrator's participation in such process or from information that the arbitrator may learn in the process. If the assistance by the arbitrator does not lead to final settlement of the case, the parties remain bound by their waiver. However, consistent with General Standard 2(a) and notwithstanding such agreement, the arbitrator shall resign if, as a consequence of his or her involvement in the settlement process, the arbitrator develops doubts as to his or her ability to remain impartial or independent in the future course of the arbitration proceedings.

Explanation to General Standard 4:

(a) The Working Group suggests a requirement of an explicit objection by the parties within a certain time limit. In the view of the Working Group, this time limit should also apply to a party who refuses to be involved.
(b) This General Standard is included to make General Standard 4(a) consistent with the non-waivable provisions of General Standard 2(d). Examples of such circumstances are described in the non-waivable Red List.
(c) In a serious conflict of interest, such as those that are described by way of example in the waivable Red List, the parties may nevertheless wish to use such a person as an arbitrator. Here, party autonomy and the desire to have only impartial and independent arbitrators must be balanced. The Working Group believes persons with such a serious conflict of interests may seve as arbitrators only if the parties make fully informed, explicit waivers.
(d) The concept of the Aribtral Tribunal assisting the parties in reaching a settlement of their dispute in the course of the arbitration proceedings is well established in some jurisdictions but not in others. Informed consent by the parties to such a proess prior to its beginning should be regarded as effective waiver of a potential conflict of interest. Express consent is generally sufficient, as opposed to a consent made in writing which in certain jurisdictions requires a signature. In practice, the requirement of an express waiver allows such consent to be made in the minutes or transcript of a hearing. In addition, in order to avoid parties using an arbitrator as a mediator as a means of disqualifying the arbitrator, the General Standard makes clear that the waiver should remain effective if the mediation is unsuccessful. Thus, parties assume the risk of what the arbitrator may learn in the settlement process. In giving their express consent, the parties should realize the consequences of the arbitrator assisting the parties in a settlement process and agree on regulating this special position further where appropriate.

3—020 (5) *Scope*

These Guidelines apply equally to tribunal chairs, sole arbitrators an party-appointed arbitrators. These Guidelines do not apply to non-neutral arbitrators, who do not have an obligation to be independent and impartial, as may be permitted by some arbitration rules or national laws.

Explanation to General Standard 5:

Because each member of an Arbitral Tribunal has an obligation to be impartal and independent, the General Standards should not distinguish among sole arbitrators, party-appointed arbitrators and tribunal chairs. With regard to secretaries of Arbitral Tribunals, the Working Group takes the view that it is the responsibility of the arbitrator to ensure that the secretary is and remains impartial and independent.

Some arbitration rules and domestic laws permit party-appointed arbirtrators to be non-neutral. When an arbitrator is serving in such a role, these Guidelines should not apply to him or her, since their purpose is to protect impartiality and independence.

(6) *Relationships*

(a) When considering the relevance of facts or circumstances to determine whether a potential conflict of interest exists or whether disclosure should be made, the activities of an arbitrator's law firm, if any, should be reasonably considered in each individual case. Therefore, the fact that the activities of the arbitrator's firm involve on of the parties shall not automatically constitute a source of such conflict or a reason for disclosure.

(b) Similarly, if one of the parties is a legal entity which is a member of a group with which the arbitrator's firm has an involvement, such facts or circumstances should be reasonably considered in each case. Therefore, this fact alone shall not automatically constitute a source of a conflict of interest or a reason for disclosure.

(c) If one of the parties is a legal entity, the managers, directors and members of a supervisory board of such legal entity and any person having a similar controlling influence on the legal entity shall be considered to be the equivalent of the legal entity.

Explanation to General Standard 6:

(a) The growing size of law firms should be taken into account as part of today's reality in international arbitration. There is a need to balance the interests of a party to use the arbitrator of its choice and the importance of maintaining confidence in the impartiality and independence of international arbitration. In the opinion of the

Working Group, the arbitrator must in principle be considered as identical to his or her law firm, but nevertheless the activities of the arbitrator's firm should not automatically constitute a conflict of interest. The relevance of such activities, such as the nature, timing and scope of the work by the law firm, should be reasonably considered in each individual case. The Working Group uses the term "involvement" rather than "acting for" because a law firm's relevant connections with a party may include activities other than representation on a legal matter.

(b) When a party to an arbitration is a member of a group of companies, special questions regarding conflict of interset arise. As in the prior paragraph, the Working Group believes that because individual corporate structure arrangements vary so widely an automatic rule is not appropriate. Instead, the particular circumstances of an affiliation with another entity within the same group of companies should be reasonably considered in each individual case.

(c) The party in International arbitration is usually a legal entity. Therefore, this General Standard clarifies which individuals should be considered effectively to be that party.

(7) *Duty of Arbitrator and Parties*

(a) A party shall inform an arbitrator, the Arbitral Tribunal, the other parties and the arbitration or other appointing authority (if any) about any direct or indirect relationship between it (or another company of the same group of companies) and the arbitrator. The party shall do so on its own initiative before the beginning of the proceeding or as soon as it becomes aware of such relationship.

(b) In order to comply with General Standard 7(a), a party shall provide any information already available to it and shall perform a reasonable search of publicly available information.

(c) An arbitrator is under a duty to make reasonable enquiries to investigate any potential conflict of interest, as well as any facts or circumstances that may cause his or her impartiality or independence to be questioned. Failure to disclose a potential conflict is not excused by lack of knowledge if the arbitrator makes no reasonable attempt to investigate.

Explanation of General Standard 7:

To reduce the risk of abuse by unmeritorious challenge of an arbitrator's impartiality or independence, it is necessary that the parties disclose any relevant relationship with the arbitrator. In addition, any party or potential party to an arbitration is, at the outset, required to make a reasonable effort to ascertain and to disclose publicly available information that, applying the general standard, might affect the arbitrator's impartiality and independence. It is the arbitrator or putative arbitrator's obligation to make similar enquiries and to disclose any information that may cause his or her impartiality or independence to be called into question.

PART II—EXPLANATORY NOTES CONCERNING THE GENERAL STANDARDS

3—021   1. The Working Group believes that if the Guidelines are to have important practical influence, they should reflect situations that are likely to occur in today's arbitration practice. The Guidelines should provide specific guidance to arbitrator's parties, institutions and courts as to what situations do or do not constitute conflicts of interest or should be disclosed.

For this purpose, the members of the Working Group analyzed their respctive case law and categorized situations that can occur in the following Application Lists. These lists obviously cannot contain every situations, but they provide guidance in many circumstances, and the Working Group has sought to make them as comprehensive as possible. In all cases, the General Standards should control.

2. The Red List consists of two parts: "a non-waivable Red List" (see General Standards 2(c) and 4(b)) and "a waivable Red List" (see General Standard 4(c)). These lists are non-exhaustive enumeration of specific situations which, depending on the facts of a given case, give rise to justifiable doubts as to the arbitrator's impartiality and independence, *i.e.*, in these circumstances an objective conflict of interest exists from the point of view of a reasonable third person having knowledge of the relevant facts (*see* General Standard 2(b)). The non-waivable Red List includes situations deriving from the overriding principle that no person can be his or her own judge. Therefore, disclosure of such a situation cannot cure the conflict. The waivable Red List encompasses situations

described in the Orange List, these situations should be considered waivable only if and when the parties, being aware of the conflict of interest situation, nevertheless expressly state their willingness to have such a person act as arbitrator, as set forth in General Standard 4(c).

3. The Orange List is a non-exhaustive enumeration of specific situations which (depending on the facts of a given case) in the eyes of the parties may give rise to justifiable doubts as to the arbitrator's impartiality or independence. The Orange List thus reflects situations that would fall under General Standard 3(a), so that the arbitrator has a duty to disclose such situations. In all these situations, the parties are deemed to have accepted the arbitrator if, after disclosure, no timely objection is made. (General Standard 4(a)).

3—022 4. It should be stressed that, as stated above, such disclosure should not automatically result in a disqualification of the arbitrator; no presumption regarding disqualification should arise from a disclosure. The purpose of the disclosure is to inform the parties of a situation that they may wish to explore further in order determine whether objectively—*i.e.*, from a reasonable third person's point of view having knowledge of the relevant facts—there is a justifiable doubt as to the arbitrator's impartiality or independence. If the conclusion is that there is no justifiable doubt, the arbitrator can act. He or she can also act if there is no timely objection by the parties or, in situations covered by the waivable Red List, a specific acceptance by the parties in accordance with General Standard 4(c). Of course, it a party challenges the appointment of the arbitrator, he or she can nevertheless act if the authority that has to rule on the challenge decides that the challenge does not meet the objective test for disqualification.

5. In addition, a later challenge based on the fact that an arbitrator did not disclos such facts or circumstances should not result automatically in either non-appointment, later disqualification or a successful challenge to any award. In the view of the Working Group, non-disclosure cannot make an arbitrator partial or lacking independence; only the facts or circumstances that he or she did not disclose can do so.

6. The Green List contains a non-exhaustive enumeration of specific situations where no appearance of, and no actual, conflict of interest exists from the relevant objective point of view. Thus, the arbitrator has no duty to disclos situations falling withing the Green List. In the opinion of the Working Group, as already expressed in the Explanation to General

Standard 3(a), there should be a limit to disclosure, based on reasonableness; in some situations, an objective test should prevail over the purely subjective test of "the eyes of the parties."

7. Situations falling outside the time limit used in some of the Orange List situations should generally be considered as falling in the Green list, even though they are not specifically stated. An arbitrator may nevertheless wish to make disclosure if, under the General Standards, he or she believes it to be appropriate. While there has been much debate with respect to the time limits used in the Lists, the Working Group had concluded that the limits indicated are appropriate and provide guidance where none exists now. For example, the three-year period in Orange List 3.1 may be too long in certain circumstances and too short in others, but the Working Group believes that the period is an appropriate general criterion, subject to the special circumstances of any cause.

8. The borderline between the situations is often thin. It can be debated whether a certain situation should be on one List of instead of another. Also, the Lists contain, for various situations, open norms like "significant". The Working Group has extensivvely and repeatedly discussed both of these issues, in the light of comments received. It believes that the decisions reflected in the Lists reflect international principles to the best extent possible and that further definition of the norms, which should be interpreted reasonably in light of the facts and circumstances in each case, would be counter-productive.

9. There has been much debate as to whether there should be a Green List at all and also, with respect to the Red List, whether the situations on the Non-Waivable Red List should be waivable in light of party autonomy. With respect to the first question, the Working Group has maintained its decision that the subjective test for disclosure should not be the absolute criterion but that some objective thesholds should be added. With respect to the second question, the conclusion of the Working Group has that the party autonomy, in this respect, has its limits.

3—023 **1. Non-Waivable Red List**

1. There is an identity between a party and the arbitrator, or the arbitrator is a legal representative of an entity that is a party in the arbitration.

2. The arbitrator is a manager, director or member of the supervisory board, or has a similar controlling influence in one of the parties.
3. The aritrator has a significant financial interest in one of the parties or the outcome of the case.
4. The arbitrator regularly advises the appointing party of an affiliate of the appointing party, and the arbitrator or his or her firm derives a significant financial outcome therefrom.

3—024 **2. Waivable Red List**

1. Relationship of the arbitrator to the dispute
   (a) The arbitrator has given legal advice or provided an expert opinion on the dispute to a party or an affiliate of one of the parties.
   (b) The arbitrator has previous involvement in the case.
2. Arbitrator's direct or indirect interest in the dispute
   (a) The arbitrator holds shares, either directl or indirectly, in one of the parties or an affiliate of one of the parties that is privately held.
   (b) A close family member[3] of the arbitrator has a significant financial interest in the outcome of the dispute.
   (c) The arbitrator or a close family member of the arbitraor has a close relationship with a third party who may be liable to recourse on the part of the unsuccessful party in the dispute.

3—025 3. Arbtrator's relationship with the parties or counsel
   (a) The arbitrator currently represents or advises one of the parties or an affiliate of one of the parties.
   (b) The arbitrator currently represents the lawyer or law firm actings as counsel for one of the parties.
   (c) The arbitrator is a lawyer in the same law firm as the counsel to one of the parties.
   (d) The arbitrator is a manager, director or member of the supervisory board, or has a similar controlling influence, in an affiliate[4] of one of the parties if the affiliate is directly involved in the matters in dispute in the arbitration.
   (e) The aribtrator's law firm had a previous but terminated involvement in the case without the arbitrator being involved himself or herself.
   (f) The arbitrator's law firm currently has a significant commerical relationship with one of the parties or an affiliate of one of the parties.
   (g) The arbitrator regularly advises the appointing party or an affiliate of the appointing party, but neither the

arbitrator nor his or her firm derives a significant financial income therefrom.
(h) The arbitrator has a close family relationship with one of the parties or with a manager, director or member of the supervisory board or any person having a similar controlling influence in one of the parties or an affiliate of one of the parties or with a counsel representing a party.
(i) A close family member of the arbitrator has a significant financial interest in one of the parties or an affiliate of one of the parties.

3—026   3. Orange List

1. Previous services for one of the parties or other involvement of the case
   (a) The arbitrator has within the past three years served as counsel for one of the parties or an affiliate of one of the parties or has previously advised or been consulted by the party or an affiliate of the party making the appointment in an unrelated matter, but the arbitrator and the party or the affiliate of the party have no ongoing relationship.
   (b) The arbitrator has within the past three years served as counsel against one of the parties or an affiliate of one of the parties in an unrelated matter.
   (c) The arbitrator has within the past three years been appointed as arbitrator on two or more occasions by one of the parties or an affiliate of one of the parties.[5]
   (d) The arbitrator's law firm has within the past three years acted for one of the parties or an affiliate of one of the parties in an unrelated matter without the involvement of the arbitrator.
   (e) The arbitrator currently serves, or has served within the past three years, as arbitrator in another arbitration on a related issue involving one of the parties or an affiliate of one of the parties.
2. Current services for one of the parties
   (a) The arbitrator's law firm is currently rendering services to one of the parties or to an affiliate of one of the parties without creating a significant commercial relationship and without the involvement of the arbitrator.
   (b) A law firm that shares revenues or fees with the arbitrator's law firm renders services to one of the parties or an affiliate of one of the parties before the arbitral tribunal.

(c) The arbitrator or his or her firm represents a party or an affiliate to the arbitration on a regular basis but is not involved in the current dispute.
3. Relationship between an arbitrator and another arbitrator or counsel.
   (a) The arbitrator and another arbitrator are lawyers in the same law firm.
   (b) The arbitrator and another arbitrator or the counsel for one of the parties are members of the same barristers' chambers.[6]
   (c) The arbitrator was within the past three years a partner of, or otherwise affiliated with, another arbitrator or any of the counsel in the same arbitration.
   (d) A lawyer in the arbitrator's law firm is an arbitrator in another dispute involving the same party or parties or an affiliate of one of the parties.
   (e) A close family member of the arbitrator is a partner or employee of the law firm representing one of the parties, but is not assissting with the dispute.
   (f) A close personal friendship exists between an arbitrator and a counsel of one party, as demonstrated by the fact that the arbitrator and the counsel regularly spend considerable time together unrelated to professional work commitments or the activities of professional associations or social organizations.
   (g) The arbitrator has within the past three years received more than three appointments by the same counsel or the same law firm.

3—027
4. Relationship between arbitrator and party and others involved in the arbitration
   (a) The arbitrator's law firm is currently acting adverse to one of the parties or an affiliate of one of the parties.
   (b) The arbitrator has been associated within the past three years with a party or an affiliate of one of the parties in a professional capacity, such as a former employee or partner.
   (c) A close personal friendship exists between an arbirator and a manager or director or a member of the supervisory board or any person having a similar controlling influence in one of the parties or an affiliate of one of the parties or a witness or expert, as demonstrated by the fact that the arbitrator and such director, manager, other person, witness withness or expert regularly spend considerable time together unrelated to professional work commitments or the activities of professional associations or social organizations.

(d) If the arbitrator is a former judge, he or she has within the path three years herad a significant case involving one of the parties.
5. Other circumstances
   (a) The arbitrator holds shares, either directly or indirectly, which by reason of number or denomination constitute a material holding in one of the parties or an affiliate of one of the parties that is publicly listed.
   (b) The arbitrator has publicly advocated a specific position regarding the case that is being arbitrated, whether in a published paper or speech or otherwise.
   (c) The arbitrator holds one position in an arbitration institution with appointing authority over the dispute.
   (d) The arbitrator is a manager, director or member of the supervisory board, or has a similar controlling influence, in an affiliate of one of the parties, where the affiliate is not directly involved in the matters in dispute in the arbitration.

3—028 **4. Green List**

1. Previously expressed legally opinions
   (a) The arbitrator has previously published a general opinion (such as in a law review article or public lecture) concerning an issue which also arises in the arbitration (but this opinion is not focused on the case that is being arbitrated).
2. Previous services against one party
   (a) The arbitrator's law firm has acted against one of the parties or an affiliate of one of the parties in an unrelated matter without the involvement of the arbitrator.
3. Current services for one of the parties
   (a) A firm in association or in alliance with the arbitrator's law firm, but which does not share fees or other revenues with the arbitrator's law firm, renders services to one of the parties of an affiliate of one of the parties in an unrelated matter.
4. Contacts with another arbitrator or with counsel for one of the parties
   (a) The arbitrator has a relationship with another or with the counsel for one of the parties through membership in the same professional association or social organization.

(b) The arbitrator and counsel or one of the parties or another arbitrator have previously served together as arbitrators or as co-counsel.
 5. Contacts between the arbitrator and one of the parties
  (a) The arbitrator has held an initial contact with the appointing party or an affiliate of the appointing party (or the respective counsels) prior to appointment, if this contact is limited to the arbitrator's availability and qualifications to serve or to the names of possible candidates for a chairperson and did not address the merits or procedural aspects of the dispute.
  (b) The arbitrator holds an insignificant amount of shares in one of the parties or an affiliate of one of the parties, which is publicly listed.
  (c) The arbitrator and a manager, director or member of the supervisory board, or any person having a similar controlling influence, in one of the parties or an affiliate of one of the parties, have worked together as joint experts or in another professional capacity, including as arbitrators in the same case.

A flow chart is attached to these Guidelines for easy reference to the application of the Lists. However, it should be stressed that there is only a schematic reflection of the very complex reality. Always, the specific circumstances of the case prevail. [Not reproduced]

NOTES

1 The members of the Working Group are: (1) Henri Alvarez, Canada; (2) John Beechey, England; (3) Jim Carter, United States; (4) Emmanuel Gaillard, France; (5) Emilio Gonzales de Castilla, Mexico; (6) Bernard Hanotiau, Belgium; (7) Michael Hwang, Singapore; (8) Albert Jan van den Ber, Belgium; (9) Doug Jones, Australia; (10) Gabrielle Kaufmann-Kohler, Switzerland; (11) Arthur Marriott, England; (12) Tore Wiwen Nilsson, Sweden; (13) Hilmar Raeschke-Kessler, Germany; (14) David W. Rivkin, United States; (15) Klaus Sachs, Germany; (16) Nathalie Voser, Switzerland (Rapporteur); (17) David Williams, New Zealand; (18) Des Williams, South Africa; (19) Otto de Witt Wijnen, The Netherlands (Chair).

2 Similarly, the Working Group is of the opinion that these Guidelines should apply by analogy to civil servants and government officers who are appointed as arbitrators by States or State entities that are parties to arbitration proceedings.

3 Throughout the Application Lists, the term "close family member" refers to a spouse, sibling, child, parent or life partner.

4 Throughout the Applicication Lists, the term "affiliate" encompasses all companies in one group of companies including the parent company.

5 It may be the practice in certain specific kinds of arbitration, such as maritime or commodities arbitration, to draw arbitrators from a small, specialized pool. If in such fields it is the custom and practice for parties frequently to appoint the same arbitrator in different cases, no disclosure of this fact is required where all parties in the arbitration should be familiar with such custom and practice.

6 Issues concerning special considerations involving barristers in England are discussed in the Background Information issued by the Working Group.

B. Rules of Procedure

UNCITRAL Notes on Organizing Arbitral Proceedings

Introduction

3—029 **Purpose of the Notes**

1. The purpose of the Notes is to assist arbitration practitioners by listing and briefly describing questions on which appropriately timed decisions on organizing arbitral proceedings may be useful. The text, prepared with a particular view to international arbitrations, may be used whether or not the arbitration is administered by an arbitral institution.

3—030 **Non-binding character of the Notes**

2. No legal requirement binding on the arbitrators or the parties is imposed by the Notes. The arbitral tribunal remains free to use the Notes as it sees fit and is not required to give reasons for disregarding them.

3. The Notes are not suitable to be used as arbitration rules, since they do not establish any obligation of the arbitral tribunal or the parties to act in a particular way. Accordingly, the use of the Notes cannot imply any modification of the arbitration rules that the parties may have agreed upon.

3—031 **Discretion in conduct of proceedings and usefulness of timely decisions on organizing proceedings**

4. Laws governing the arbitral procedure and arbitration rules that parties may agree upon typically allow the arbitral tribunal broad discretion and flexibility in the conduct of arbitral proceedings. This is useful in that it enables the arbitral tribunal to take decisions on the organization of proceedings that take into account the circumstances of the case, the expectations of the parties and of the members of the arbitral tribunal, and the need for a just and cost-efficient resolution of the dispute. A prominent example of such rules are the UNCITRAL Arbitration Rules, which provide in article

15(1): "Subject to these Rules, the arbitral tribunal may conduct the arbitration in such manner as it considers appropriate, provided that the parties are treated with equality and that at any stage of the proceedings each party is given a full opportunity of presenting his case."

5. Such discretion may make it desirable for the arbitral tribunal to give the parties a timely indication as to the organization of the proceedings and the manner in which the tribunal intends to proceed. This is particularly desirable in international arbitrations, where the participants may be accustomed to differing styles of conducting arbitrations. Without such guidance, a party may find aspects of the proceedings unpredictable and difficult to prepare for. That may lead to misunderstandings, delays and increased costs.

3—032 **Multi-party arbitration**

6. These Notes are intended for use not only in arbitrations with two parties but also in arbitrations with three or more parties. Use of the Notes in multi-party arbitration is referred to below in paragraphs 86–88 (item 18).

3—033 **Process of making decisions on organizing arbitral proceedings**

7. Decisions by the arbitral tribunal on organizing arbitral proceedings may be taken with or without previous consultations with the parties. The method chosen depends on whether, in view of the type of the question to be decided, the arbitral tribunal considers that consultations are not necessary or that hearing the views of the parties would be beneficial for increasing the predictability of the proceedings or improving the procedural atmosphere.

8. The consultations, whether they involve only the arbitrators or also the parties, can be held in one or more meetings, or can be carried out by correspondence or telecommunications such as telefax or conference telephone calls or other electronic means. Meetings may be held at the venue of arbitration or at some other appropriate location.

9. In some arbitrations a special meeting may be devoted exclusively to such procedural consultations; alternatively, the consultations may be held in conjunction with a hearing on the substance of the dispute. Practices differ as to whether

such special meetings should be held and how they should be organized. Special procedural meetings of the arbitrators and the parties separate from hearings are in practice referred to by expressions such as "preliminary meeting", "pre-hearing conference", "preparatory conference", "pre-hearing review", or terms of similar meaning. The terms used partly depend on the stage of the proceedings at which the meeting is taking place.

3—034 **List of matters for possible consideration in organizing arbitral proceedings**

10. The Notes provide a list, followed by annotations, of matters on which the arbitral tribunal may wish to formulate decisions on organizing arbitral proceedings.

11. Given that procedural styles and practices in arbitration vary widely, that the purpose of the Notes is not to promote any practice as best practice, and that the Notes are designed for universal use, it is not attempted in the Notes to describe in detail different arbitral practices or express a preference for any of them.

12. The list, while not exhaustive, covers a broad range of situations that may arise in an arbitration. In many arbitrations, however, only a limited number of the matters mentioned in the list need to be considered. It also depends on the circumstances of the case at which stage or stages of the proceedings it would be useful to consider matters concerning the organization of the proceedings. Generally, in order not to create opportunities for unnecessary discussions and delay, it is advisable not to raise a matter prematurely, i.e. before it is clear that a decision is needed.

13. When the Notes are used, it should be borne in mind that the discretion of the arbitral tribunal in organizing the proceedings may be limited by arbitration rules, by other provisions agreed to by the parties and by the law applicable to the arbitral procedure. When an arbitration is administered by an arbitral institution, various matters discussed in the Notes may be covered by the rules and practices of that institution.

LIST OF MATTERS FOR POSSIBLE CONSIDERATION IN ORGANIZING ARBITRAL PROCEEDINGS

3—035 1. Set of arbitration rules: paras. 14—16

If the parties have not agreed on a set of arbitration rules, would they wish to do so: paras. 14—16

2. Language of proceedings 17–20

   (a) Possible need for translation of documents, in full or in part 18
   (b) Possible need for interpretation of oral presentations 19
   (c) Cost of translation and interpretation 20

3. Place of arbitration 21–23

   (a) Determination of the place of arbitration, if not already agreed upon by the parties 21–22
   (b) Possibility of meetings outside the place of arbitration 23

4. Administrative services that may be needed for the arbitral tribunal to carry out its functions 24–27

5. Deposits in respect of costs 28–30

   (a) Amount to be deposited 28
   (b) Management of deposits 29
   (c) Supplementary deposits 30

6. Confidentiality of information relating to the arbitration; possible agreement thereon 31–32

7. Routing of written communications among the parties and the arbitrators 33–34

8. Telefax and other electronic means of sending documents 35–37

   (a) Telefax 35
   (b) Other electronic means (e.g. electronic mail and magnetic or optical disk) 36–37

9. Arrangements for the exchange of written submissions 38–41

   (a) Scheduling of written submissions 39–40
   (b) Consecutive or simultaneous submissions 41

10. Practical details concerning written submissions and evidence (e.g. method of submission, copies, numbering, references) 42

11. Defining points at issue; order of deciding issues; defining relief or remedy sought 43–46

    (a) Should a list of points at issue be prepared 43
    (b) In which order should the points at issue be decided 44–45
    (c) Is there a need to define more precisely the relief or remedy sought 46

12. Possible settlement negotiations and their effect on scheduling proceedings 47

13. Documentary evidence 48–54

    (a) Time-limits for submission of documentary evidence intended to be submitted by the parties; consequences of late submission 48–49
    (b) Whether the arbitral tribunal intends to require a party to produce documentary evidence 50–51
    (c) Should assertions about the origin and receipt of documents and about the correctness of photocopies be assumed as accurate 52
    (d) Are the parties willing to submit jointly a single set of documentary evidence 53
    (e) Should voluminous and complicated documentary evidence be presented through summaries, tabulations, charts, extracts or samples 54

14. Physical evidence other than documents 55–58

    (a) What arrangements should be made if physical evidence will be submitted 56
    (b) What arrangements should be made if an on-site inspection is necessary 57–58

15. Witnesses 59–68

    (a) Advance notice about a witness whom a party intends to present; written witnesses' statements 60–62
    (b) Manner of taking oral evidence of witnesses 63–65

        (i) Order in which questions will be asked and the manner in which the hearing of witnesses will be conducted 63
        (ii) Whether oral testimony will be given under oath or affirmation and, if so, in what form an oath or affirmation should be made 64

(iii) May witnesses be in the hearing room when they are not testifying 65

(c) The order in which the witnesses will be called 66
(d) Interviewing witnesses prior to their appearance at a hearing 67
(e) Hearing representatives of a party 68

16. Experts and expert witnesses 69–73

    (a) Expert appointed by the arbitral tribunal 70–72

        (i) The expert's terms of reference 71
        (ii) The opportunity of the parties to comment on the expert's report, including by presenting expert testimony 72

    (b) Expert opinion presented by a party (expert witness) 73

17. Hearings 74–85

    (a) Decision whether to hold hearings 74–75
    (b) Whether one period of hearings should be held or separate periods of hearings 76
    (c) Setting dates for hearings 77
    (d) Whether there should be a limit on the aggregate amount of time each party will have for oral arguments and questioning witnesses 78–79
    (e) The order in which the parties will present their arguments and evidence 80
    (f) Length of hearings 81
    (g) Arrangements for a record of the hearings 82–83
    (h) Whether and when the parties are permitted to submit notes summarizing their oral arguments 84–85

18. Multi-party arbitration 86–88

19. Possible requirements concerning filing or delivering the award 89–90 Who should take steps to fulfil any requirement 90

ANNOTATIONS

3—036 **1. Set of arbitration rules**

If the parties have not agreed on a set of arbitration rules, would they wish to do so

14. Sometimes parties who have not included in their arbitration agreement a stipulation that a set of arbitration rules will

govern their arbitral proceedings might wish to do so after the arbitration has begun. If that occurs, the UNCITRAL Arbitration Rules may be used either without modification or with such modifications as the parties might wish to agree upon. In the alternative, the parties might wish to adopt the rules of an arbitral institution; in that case, it may be necessary to secure the agreement of that institution and to stipulate the terms under which the arbitration could be carried out in accordance with the rules of that institution.

15. However, caution is advised as consideration of a set of arbitration rules might delay the proceedings or give rise to unnecessary controversy.

16. It should be noted that agreement on arbitration rules is not a necessity and that, if the parties do not agree on a set of arbitration rules, the arbitral tribunal has the power to continue the proceedings and determine how the case will be conducted.

3—037   **2. Language of proceedings**

17. Many rules and laws on arbitral procedure empower the arbitral tribunal to determine the language or languages to be used in the proceedings, if the parties have not reached an agreement thereon.

3—038   **(a) Possible need for translation of documents, in full or in part**

18. Some documents annexed to the statements of claim and defence or submitted later may not be in the language of the proceedings. Bearing in mind the needs of the proceedings and economy, it may be considered whether the arbitral tribunal should order that any of those documents or parts thereof should be accompanied by a translation into the language of the proceedings.

3—039   **(b) Possible need for interpretation of oral presentations**

19. If interpretation will be necessary during oral hearings, it is advisable to consider whether the interpretation will be simultaneous or consecutive and whether the arrangements should be the responsibility of a party or the arbitral tribunal. In an arbitration administered by an institution, interpretation as well as translation services are often arranged by the arbitral institution.

3—040 (c) Cost of translation and interpretation

20. In taking decisions about translation or interpretation, it is advisable to decide whether any or all of the costs are to be paid directly by a party or whether they will be paid out of the deposits and apportioned between the parties along with the other arbitration costs.

3—041 3. Place of arbitration

(a) **Determination of the place of arbitration, if not already agreed upon by the parties**

21. Arbitration rules usually allow the parties to agree on the place of arbitration, subject to the requirement of some arbitral institutions that arbitrations under their rules be conducted at a particular place, usually the location of the institution. If the place has not been so agreed upon, the rules governing the arbitration typically provide that it is in the power of the arbitral tribunal or the institution administering the arbitration to determine the place. If the arbitral tribunal is to make that determination, it may wish to hear the views of the parties before doing so.

22. Various factual and legal factors influence the choice of the place of arbitration, and their relative importance varies from case to case. Among the more prominent factors are:

   (a) suitability of the law on arbitral procedure of the place of arbitration;
   (b) whether there is a multilateral or bilateral treaty on enforcement of arbitral awards between the State where the arbitration takes place and the State or States where the award may have to be enforced;
   (c) convenience of the parties and the arbitrators, including the travel distances;
   (d) availability and cost of support services needed; and
   (e) location of the subject-matter in dispute and proximity of evidence.

3—042 (b) **Possibility of meetings outside the place of arbitration**

23. Many sets of arbitration rules and laws on arbitral procedure expressly allow the arbitral tribunal to hold meetings elsewhere than at the place of arbitration. For example, under the UNCITRAL Model Law on International Commercial Arbitration "the arbitral tribunal may, unless otherwise

B. RULES OF PROCEDURE

agreed by the parties, meet at any place it considers appropriate for consultation among its members, for hearing witnesses, experts or the parties, or for inspection of goods, other property or documents" (article 20(2)). The purpose of this discretion is to permit arbitral proceedings to be carried out in a manner that is most efficient and economical.

3—043   **4. Administrative services that may be needed for the arbitral tribunal to carry out its functions**

24. Various administrative services (e.g. hearing rooms or secretarial services) may need to be procured for the arbitral tribunal to be able to carry out its functions. When the arbitration is administered by an arbitral institution, the institution will usually provide all or a good part of the required administrative support to the arbitral tribunal. When an arbitration administered by an arbitral institution takes place away from the seat of the institution, the institution may be able to arrange for administrative services to be obtained from another source, often an arbitral institution; some arbitral institutions have entered into cooperation agreements with a view to providing mutual assistance in servicing arbitral proceedings.

25. When the case is not administered by an institution, or the involvement of the institution does not include providing administrative support, usually the administrative arrangements for the proceedings will be made by the arbitral tribunal or the presiding arbitrator; it may also be acceptable to leave some of the arrangements to the parties, or to one of the parties subject to agreement of the other party or parties. Even in such cases, a convenient source of administrative support might be found in arbitral institutions, which often offer their facilities to arbitrations not governed by the rules of the institution. Otherwise, some services could be procured from entities such as chambers of commerce, hotels or specialized firms providing secretarial or other support services.

26. Administrative services might be secured by engaging a secretary of the arbitral tribunal (also referred to as registrar, clerk, administrator or rapporteur), who carries out the tasks under the direction of the arbitral tribunal. Some arbitral institutions routinely assign such persons to the cases administered by them. In arbitrations not administered by an institution or where the arbitral institution does not appoint a secretary, some arbitrators frequently engage such persons, at

least in certain types of cases, whereas many others normally conduct the proceedings without them.

27. To the extent the tasks of the secretary are purely organizational (e.g. obtaining meeting rooms and providing or coordinating secretarial services), this is usually not controversial. Differences in views, however, may arise if the tasks include legal research and other professional assistance to the arbitral tribunal (e.g. collecting case law or published commentaries on legal issues defined by the arbitral tribunal, preparing summaries from case law and publications, and sometimes also preparing drafts of procedural decisions or drafts of certain parts of the award, in particular those concerning the facts of the case). Views or expectations may differ especially where a task of the secretary is similar to professional functions of the arbitrators. Such a role of the secretary is in the view of some commentators inappropriate or is appropriate only under certain conditions, such as that the parties agree thereto. However, it is typically recognized that it is important to ensure that the secretary does not perform any decision-making function of the arbitral tribunal.

3—044   5. Deposits in respect of costs

(a) **Amount to be deposited**

28. In an arbitration administered by an institution, the institution often sets, on the basis of an estimate of the costs of the proceedings, the amount to be deposited as an advance for the costs of the arbitration. In other cases it is customary for the arbitral tribunal to make such an estimate and request a deposit. The estimate typically includes travel and other expenses by the arbitrators, expenditures for administrative assistance required by the arbitral tribunal, costs of any expert advice required by the arbitral tribunal, and the fees for the arbitrators. Many arbitration rules have provisions on this matter, including on whether the deposit should be made by the two parties (or all parties in a multi-party case) or only by the claimant.

3—045   (b) **Management of deposits**

29. When the arbitration is administered by an institution, the institution's services may include managing and accounting for the deposited money. Where that is not the case, it might be useful to clarify matters such as the type and location of

the account in which the money will be kept and how the deposits will be managed.

3—046   (c) Supplementary deposits

30. If during the course of proceedings it emerges that the costs will be higher than anticipated, supplementary deposits may be required (e.g. because the arbitral tribunal decides pursuant to the arbitration rules to appoint an expert).

3—047   6. Confidentiality of information relating to the arbitration; possible agreement thereon

31. It is widely viewed that confidentiality is one of the advantageous and helpful features of arbitration. Nevertheless, there is no uniform answer in national laws as to the extent to which the participants in an arbitration are under the duty to observe the confidentiality of information relating to the case. Moreover, parties that have agreed on arbitration rules or other provisions that do not expressly address the issue of confidentiality cannot assume that all jurisdictions would recognize an implied commitment to confidentiality. Furthermore, the participants in an arbitration might not have the same understanding as regards the extent of confidentiality that is expected. Therefore, the arbitral tribunal might wish to discuss that with the parties and, if considered appropriate, record any agreed principles on the duty of confidentiality.

32. An agreement on confidentiality might cover, for example, one or more of the following matters: the material or information that is to be kept confidential (e.g. pieces of evidence, written and oral arguments, the fact that the arbitration is taking place, identity of the arbitrators, content of the award); measures for maintaining confidentiality of such information and hearings; whether any special procedures should be employed for maintaining the confidentiality of information transmitted by electronic means (e.g. because communication equipment is shared by several users, or because electronic mail over public networks is considered not sufficiently protected against unauthorized access); circumstances in which confidential information may be disclosed in part or in whole (e.g. in the context of disclosures of information in the public domain, or if required by law or a regulatory body).

3—048   **7. Routing of written communications among the parties and the arbitrators**

33. To the extent the question how documents and other written communications should be routed among the parties and the arbitrators is not settled by the agreed rules, or, if an institution administers the case, by the practices of the institution, it is useful for the arbitral tribunal to clarify the question suitably early so as to avoid misunderstandings and delays.

34. Among various possible patterns of routing, one example is that a party transmits the appropriate number of copies to the arbitral tribunal, or to the arbitral institution, if one is involved, which then forwards them as appropriate. Another example is that a party is to send copies simultaneously to the arbitrators and the other party or parties. Documents and other written communications directed by the arbitral tribunal or the presiding arbitrator to one or more parties may also follow a determined pattern, such as through the arbitral institution or by direct transmission. For some communications, in particular those on organizational matters (e.g. dates for hearings), more direct routes of communication may be agreed, even if, for example, the arbitral institution acts as an intermediary for documents such as the statements of claim and defence, evidence or written arguments.

3—049   **8. Telefax and other electronic means of sending documents**

(a) **Telefax**

35. Telefax, which offers many advantages over traditional means of communication, is widely used in arbitral proceedings. Nevertheless, should it be thought that, because of the characteristics of the equipment used, it would be preferable not to rely only on a telefacsimile of a document, special arrangements may be considered, such as that a particular piece of written evidence should be mailed or otherwise physically delivered, or that certain telefax messages should be confirmed by mailing or otherwise delivering documents whose facsimile were transmitted by electronic means. When a document should not be sent by telefax, it may, however, be appropriate, in order to avoid an unnecessarily rigid procedure, for the arbitral tribunal to retain discretion to accept an advance copy of a document by telefax for the purposes of meeting a deadline, provided that the document itself is received within a reasonable time thereafter.

3—050 (b) Other electronic means (e.g. electronic mail and magnetic or optical disk)

36. It might be agreed that documents, or some of them, will be exchanged not only in paper-based form, but in addition also in an electronic form other than telefax (e.g. as electronic mail, or on a magnetic or optical disk), or only in electronic form. Since the use of electronic means depends on the aptitude of the persons involved and the availability of equipment and computer programs, agreement is necessary for such means to be used. If both paper-based and electronic means are to be used, it is advisable to decide which one is controlling and, if there is a time-limit for submitting a document, which act constitutes submission.

37. When the exchange of documents in electronic form is planned, it is useful, in order to avoid technical difficulties, to agree on matters such as: data carriers (e.g. electronic mail or computer disks) and their technical characteristics; computer programs to be used in preparing the electronic records; instructions for transforming the electronic records into human-readable form; keeping of logs and back-up records of communications sent and received; information in human-readable form that should accompany the disks (e.g. the names of the originator and recipient, computer program, titles of the electronic files and the back-up methods used); procedures when a message is lost or the communication system otherwise fails; and identification of persons who can be contacted if a problem occurs.

3—051 9. Arrangements for the exchange of written submissions

38. After the parties have initially stated their claims and defences, they may wish, or the arbitral tribunal might request them, to present further written submissions so as to prepare for the hearings or to provide the basis for a decision without hearings. In such submissions, the parties, for example, present or comment on allegations and evidence, cite or explain law, or make or react to proposals. In practice such submissions are referred to variously as, for example, statement, memorial, counter-memorial, brief, counter-brief, reply, réplique, duplique, rebuttal or rejoinder; the terminology is a matter of linguistic usage and the scope or sequence of the submission.

3—052   (a) Scheduling of written submissions

39. It is advisable that the arbitral tribunal set time-limits for written submissions. In enforcing the time-limits, the arbitral tribunal may wish, on the one hand, to make sure that the case is not unduly protracted and, on the other hand, to reserve a degree of discretion and allow late submissions if appropriate under the circumstances. In some cases the arbitral tribunal might prefer not to plan the written submissions in advance, thus leaving such matters, including time-limits, to be decided in light of the developments in the proceedings. In other cases, the arbitral tribunal may wish to determine, when scheduling the first written submissions, the number of subsequent submissions.

40. Practices differ as to whether, after the hearings have been held, written submissions are still acceptable. While some arbitral tribunals consider post-hearing submissions unacceptable, others might request or allow them on a particular issue. Some arbitral tribunals follow the procedure according to which the parties are not requested to present written evidence and legal arguments to the arbitral tribunal before the hearings; in such a case, the arbitral tribunal may regard it as appropriate that written submissions be made after the hearings.

3—053   (b) Consecutive or simultaneous submissions

41. Written submissions on an issue may be made consecutively, i.e. the party who receives a submission is given a period of time to react with its counter-submission. Another possibility is to request each party to make the submission within the same time period to the arbitral tribunal or the institution administering the case; the received submissions are then forwarded simultaneously to the respective other party or parties. The approach used may depend on the type of issues to be commented upon and the time in which the views should be clarified. With consecutive submissions, it may take longer than with simultaneous ones to obtain views of the parties on a given issue. Consecutive submissions, however, allow the reacting party to comment on all points raised by the other party or parties, which simultaneous submissions do not; thus, simultaneous submissions might possibly necessitate further submissions.

3—054 10. **Practical details concerning written submissions and evidence (eg method of submission, copies, numbering, references)**

42. Depending on the volume and kind of documents to be handled, it might be considered whether practical arrangements on details such as the following would be helpful:

> Whether the submissions will be made as paper documents or by electronic means, or both (see paragraphs 35–37);
> The number of copies in which each document is to be submitted;
> A system for numbering documents and items of evidence, and a method for marking them, including by tabs;
> The form of references to documents (e.g. by the heading and the number assigned to the document or its date);
> Paragraph numbering in written submissions, in order to facilitate precise references to parts of a text;
> When translations are to be submitted as paper documents, whether the translations are to be contained in the same volume as the original texts or included in separate volumes.

3—054a 11. **Defining points at issue; order of deciding issues; defining relief or remedy sought**

(a) **Should a list of points at issue be prepared**

43. In considering the parties' allegations and arguments, the arbitral tribunal may come to the conclusion that it would be useful for it or for the parties to prepare, for analytical purposes and for ease of discussion, a list of the points at issue, as opposed to those that are undisputed. If the arbitral tribunal determines that the advantages of working on the basis of such a list outweigh the disadvantages, it chooses the appropriate stage of the proceedings for preparing a list, bearing in mind also that subsequent developments in the proceedings may require a revision of the points at issue. Such an identification of points at issue might help to concentrate on the essential matters, to reduce the number of points at issue by agreement of the parties, and to select the best and most economical process for resolving the dispute. However, possible disadvantages of preparing such a list include delay, adverse effect on the flexibility of the proceedings, or unnecessary disagreements about whether the arbitral tribunal has

decided all issues submitted to it or whether the award contains decisions on matters beyond the scope of the submission to arbitration. The terms of reference required under some arbitration rules, or in agreements of parties, may serve the same purpose as the above-described list of points at issue.

3—055 **(b) In which order should the points at issue be decided**

44. While it is often appropriate to deal with all the points at issue collectively, the arbitral tribunal might decide to take them up during the proceedings in a particular order. The order may be due to a point being preliminary relative to another (e.g. a decision on the jurisdiction of the arbitral tribunal is preliminary to consideration of substantive issues, or the issue of responsibility for a breach of contract is preliminary to the issue of the resulting damages). A particular order may be decided also when the breach of various contracts is in dispute or when damages arising from various events are claimed.

45. If the arbitral tribunal has adopted a particular order of deciding points at issue, it might consider it appropriate to issue a decision on one of the points earlier than on the other ones. This might be done, for example, when a discrete part of a claim is ready for decision while the other parts still require extensive consideration, or when it is expected that after deciding certain issues the parties might be more inclined to settle the remaining ones. Such earlier decisions are referred to by expressions such as "partial", "interlocutory" or "interim" awards or decisions, depending on the type of issue dealt with and on whether the decision is final with respect to the issue it resolves. Questions that might be the subject of such decisions are, for example, jurisdiction of the arbitral tribunal, interim measures of protection, or the liability of a party.

3—056 **(c) Is there a need to define more precisely the relief or remedy sought**

46. If the arbitral tribunal considers that the relief or remedy sought is insufficiently definite, it may wish to explain to the parties the degree of definiteness with which their claims should be formulated. Such an explanation may be useful since criteria are not uniform as to how specific the claimant must be in formulating a relief or remedy.

3—057 **12. Possible settlement negotiations and their effect on scheduling proceedings**

47. Attitudes differ as to whether it is appropriate for the arbitral tribunal to bring up the possibility of settlement. Given the divergence of practices in this regard, the arbitral tribunal should only suggest settlement negotiations with caution. However, it may be opportune for the arbitral tribunal to schedule the proceedings in a way that might facilitate the continuation or initiation of settlement negotiations.

3—058 **13. Documentary evidence**

(a) Time-limits for submission of documentary evidence intended to be submitted by the parties; consequences of late submission

48. Often the written submissions of the parties contain sufficient information for the arbitral tribunal to fix the time-limit for submitting evidence. Otherwise, in order to set realistic time periods, the arbitral tribunal may wish to consult with the parties about the time that they would reasonably need.

49. The arbitral tribunal may wish to clarify that evidence submitted late will as a rule not be accepted. It may wish not to preclude itself from accepting a late submission of evidence if the party shows sufficient cause for the delay.

3—058a **(b) Whether the arbitral tribunal intends to require a party to produce documentary evidence**

50. Procedures and practices differ widely as to the conditions under which the arbitral tribunal may require a party to produce documents. Therefore, the arbitral tribunal might consider it useful, when the agreed arbitration rules do not provide specific conditions, to clarify to the parties the manner in which it intends to proceed.

51. The arbitral tribunal may wish to establish time-limits for the production of documents. The parties might be reminded that, if the requested party duly invited to produce documentary evidence fails to do so within the established period of time, without showing sufficient cause for such failure, the arbitral tribunal is free to draw its conclusions from the failure and may make the award on the evidence before it.

3—059 (c) Should assertions about the origin and receipt of documents and about the correctness of photocopies be assumed as accurate

52. It may be helpful for the arbitral tribunal to inform the parties that it intends to conduct the proceedings on the basis that, unless a party raises an objection to any of the following conclusions within a specified period of time:

(a) a document is accepted as having originated from the source indicated in the document;

(b) a copy of a dispatched communication (e.g. letter, telex, telefax or other electronic message) is accepted without further proof as having been received by the addressee; and

(c) a copy is accepted as correct. A statement by the arbitral tribunal to that effect can simplify the introduction of documentary evidence and discourage unfounded and dilatory objections, at a late stage of the proceedings, to the probative value of documents. It is advisable to provide that the time-limit for objections will not be enforced if the arbitral tribunal considers the delay justified.

3—060 (d) Are the parties willing to submit jointly a single set of documentary evidence

53. The parties may consider submitting jointly a single set of documentary evidence whose authenticity is not disputed. The purpose would be to avoid duplicate submissions and unnecessary discussions concerning the authenticity of documents, without prejudicing the position of the parties concerning the content of the documents. Additional documents may be inserted later if the parties agree. When a single set of documents would be too voluminous to be easily manageable, it might be practical to select a number of frequently used documents and establish a set of "working" documents. A convenient arrangement of documents in the set may be according to chronological order or subject-matter. It is useful to keep a table of contents of the documents, for example, by their short headings and dates, and to provide that the parties will refer to documents by those headings and dates.

3—061 (e) Should voluminous and complicated documentary evidence be presented through summaries, tabulations, charts, extracts or samples

54. When documentary evidence is voluminous and complicated, it may save time and costs if such evidence is presented by a

report of a person competent in the relevant field (e.g. public accountant or consulting engineer). The report may present the information in the form of summaries, tabulations, charts, extracts or samples. Such presentation of evidence should be combined with arrangements that give the interested party the opportunity to review the underlying data and the methodology of preparing the report.

3—062   **14. Physical evidence other than documents**

55. In some arbitrations the arbitral tribunal is called upon to assess physical evidence other than documents, for example, by inspecting samples of goods, viewing a video recording or observing the functioning of a machine.

3—063   **(a) What arrangements should be made if physical evidence will be submitted**

56. If physical evidence will be submitted, the arbitral tribunal may wish to fix the time schedule for presenting the evidence, make arrangements for the other party or parties to have a suitable opportunity to prepare itself for the presentation of the evidence, and possibly take measures for safekeeping the items of evidence.

3—064   **(b) What arrangements should be made if an on-site inspection is necessary**

57. If an on-site inspection of property or goods will take place, the arbitral tribunal may consider matters such as timing, meeting places, other arrangements to provide the opportunity for all parties to be present, and the need to avoid communications between arbitrators and a party about points at issue without the presence of the other party or parties.

58. The site to be inspected is often under the control of one of the parties, which typically means that employees or representatives of that party will be present to give guidance and explanations. It should be borne in mind that statements of those representatives or employees made during an on-site inspection, as contrasted with statements those persons might make as witnesses in a hearing, should not be treated as evidence in the proceedings.

15. Witnesses

3—065

59. While laws and rules on arbitral procedure typically leave broad freedom concerning the manner of taking evidence of witnesses, practices on procedural points are varied. In order to facilitate the preparations of the parties for the hearings, the arbitral tribunal may consider it appropriate to clarify, in advance of the hearings, some or all of the following issues.

3—066 **(a) Advance notice about a witness whom a party intends to present; written witnesses' statements**

60. To the extent the applicable arbitration rules do not deal with the matter, the arbitral tribunal may wish to require that each party give advance notice to the arbitral tribunal and the other party or parties of any witness it intends to present. As to the content of the notice, the following is an example of what might be required, in addition to the names and addresses of the witnesses:

(a) the subject upon which the witnesses will testify;
(b) the language in which the witnesses will testify; and
(c) the nature of the relationship with any of the parties, qualifications and experience of the witnesses if and to the extent these are relevant to the dispute or the testimony, and how the witnesses learned about the facts on which they will testify. However, it may not be necessary to require such a notice, in particular if the thrust of the testimony can be clearly ascertained from the party's allegations.

61. Some practitioners favour the procedure according to which the party presenting witness evidence submits a signed witness's statement containing testimony itself. It should be noted, however, that such practice, which implies interviewing the witness by the party presenting the testimony, is not known in all parts of the world and, moreover, that some practitioners disapprove of it on the ground that such contacts between the party and the witness may compromise the credibility of the testimony and are therefore improper (see paragraph 67). Notwithstanding these reservations, signed witness's testimony has advantages in that it may expedite the proceedings by making it easier for the other party or parties to prepare for the hearings or for the parties to identify uncontested matters. However, those advantages might be outweighed by the time and expense involved in obtaining the written testimony.

62. If a signed witness's statement should be made under oath or similar affirmation of truthfulness, it may be necessary to clarify by whom the oath or affirmation should be administered and whether any formal authentication will be required by the arbitral tribunal.

3—067 **(b) Manner of taking oral evidence of witnesses**

(i) Order in which questions will be asked and the manner in which the hearing of witnesses will be conducted.

63. To the extent that the applicable rules do not provide an answer, it may be useful for the arbitral tribunal to clarify how witnesses will be heard. One of the various possibilities is that a witness is first questioned by the arbitral tribunal, whereupon questions are asked by the parties, first by the party who called the witness. Another possibility is for the witness to be questioned by the party presenting the witness and then by the other party or parties, while the arbitral tribunal might pose questions during the questioning or after the parties on points that in the tribunal's view have not been sufficiently clarified. Differences exist also as to the degree of control the arbitral tribunal exercises over the hearing of witnesses. For example, some arbitrators prefer to permit the parties to pose questions freely and directly to the witness, but may disallow a question if a party objects; other arbitrators tend to exercise more control and may disallow a question on their initiative or even require that questions from the parties be asked through the arbitral tribunal.

(ii) Whether oral testimony will be given under oath or affirmation and, if so, in what form an oath or affirmation should be made.

64. Practices and laws differ as to whether or not oral testimony is to be given under oath or affirmation. In some legal systems, the arbitrators are empowered to put witnesses on oath, but it is usually in their discretion whether they want to do so. In other systems, oral testimony under oath is either unknown or may even be considered improper as only an official such as a judge or notary may have the authority to administer oaths.

(iii) May witnesses be in the hearing room when they are not testifying.

65. Some arbitrators favour the procedure that, except if the circumstances suggest otherwise, the presence of a

witness in the hearing room is limited to the time the witness is testifying; the purpose is to prevent the witness from being influenced by what is said in the hearing room, or to prevent that the presence of the witness would influence another witness. Other arbitrators consider that the presence of a witness during the testimony of other witnesses may be beneficial in that possible contradictions may be readily clarified or that their presence may act as a deterrent against untrue statements. Other possible approaches may be that witnesses are not present in the hearing room before their testimony, but stay in the room after they have testified, or that the arbitral tribunal decides the question for each witness individually depending on what the arbitral tribunal considers most appropriate. The arbitral tribunal may leave the procedure to be decided during the hearings, or may give guidance on the question in advance of the hearings.

3—068 **(c) The order in which the witnesses will be called**

66. When several witnesses are to be heard and longer testimony is expected, it is likely to reduce costs if the order in which they will be called is known in advance and their presence can be scheduled accordingly. Each party might be invited to suggest the order in which it intends to present the witnesses, while it would be up to the arbitral tribunal to approve the scheduling and to make departures from it.

3—069 **(d) Interviewing witnesses prior to their appearance at a hearing**

67. In some legal systems, parties or their representatives are permitted to interview witnesses, prior to their appearance at the hearing, as to such matters as their recollection of the relevant events, their experience, qualifications or relation with a participant in the proceedings. In those legal systems such contacts are usually not permitted once the witness's oral testimony has begun. In other systems such contacts with witnesses are considered improper. In order to avoid misunderstandings, the arbitral tribunal may consider it useful to clarify what kind of contacts a party is permitted to have with a witness in the preparations for the hearings.

3—070 **(e) Hearing representatives of a party**

68. According to some legal systems, certain persons affiliated with a party may only be heard as representatives of the party

but not as witnesses. In such a case, it may be necessary to consider ground rules for determining which persons may not testify as witnesses (e.g. certain executives, employees or agents) and for hearing statements of those persons and for questioning them.

3—071   16. Experts and expert witnesses

69. Many arbitration rules and laws on arbitral procedure address the participation of experts in arbitral proceedings. A frequent solution is that the arbitral tribunal has the power to appoint an expert to report on issues determined by the tribunal; in addition, the parties may be permitted to present expert witnesses on points at issue. In other cases, it is for the parties to present expert testimony, and it is not expected that the arbitral tribunal will appoint an expert.

3—072   (a) Expert appointed by the arbitral tribunal

70. If the arbitral tribunal is empowered to appoint an expert, one possible approach is for the tribunal to proceed directly to selecting the expert. Another possibility is to consult the parties as to who should be the expert; this may be done, for example, without mentioning a candidate, by presenting to the parties a list of candidates, soliciting proposals from the parties, or by discussing with the parties the "profile" of the expert the arbitral tribunal intends to appoint, i.e. the qualifications, experience and abilities of the expert.

(i) The expert's terms of reference

71. The purpose of the expert's terms of reference is to indicate the questions on which the expert is to provide clarification, to avoid opinions on points that are not for the expert to assess and to commit the expert to a time schedule. While the discretion to appoint an expert normally includes the determination of the expert's terms of reference, the arbitral tribunal may decide to consult the parties before finalizing the terms. It might also be useful to determine details about how the expert will receive from the parties any relevant information or have access to any relevant documents, goods or other property, so as to enable the expert to prepare the report. In order to facilitate the evaluation of the expert's report, it is advisable to require the expert to include in the report information on the method used in arriving at the conclusions

and the evidence and information used in preparing the report.

(ii) The opportunity of the parties to comment on the expert's report, including by presenting expert testimony

72. Arbitration rules that contain provisions on experts usually also have provisions on the right of a party to comment on the report of the expert appointed by the arbitral tribunal. If no such provisions apply or more specific procedures than those prescribed are deemed necessary, the arbitral tribunal may, in light of those provisions, consider it opportune to determine, for example, the time period for presenting written comments of the parties, or, if hearings are to be held for the purpose of hearing the expert, the procedures for interrogating the expert by the parties or for the participation of any expert witnesses presented by the parties.

3—073 **(b) Expert opinion presented by a party (expert witness)**

73. If a party presents an expert opinion, the arbitral tribunal might consider requiring, for example, that the opinion be in writing, that the expert should be available to answer questions at hearings, and that, if a party will present an expert witness at a hearing, advance notice must be given or that the written opinion must be presented in advance, as in the case of other witnesses (see paragraphs 60–62).

3—074 **17. Hearings**

(a) Decision whether to hold hearings

74. Laws on arbitral procedure and arbitration rules often have provisions as to the cases in which oral hearings must be held and as to when the arbitral tribunal has discretion to decide whether to hold hearings.

75. If it is up to the arbitral tribunal to decide whether to hold hearings, the decision is likely to be influenced by factors such as, on the one hand, that it is usually quicker and easier to clarify points at issue pursuant to a direct confrontation of arguments than on the basis of correspondence and, on the other hand, the travel and other cost of holding hearings, and that the need of finding acceptable dates for the hearings might delay the proceedings. The arbitral tribunal may wish to consult the parties on this matter.

3—075 **(b) Whether one period of hearings should be held or separate periods of hearings**

76. Attitudes vary as to whether hearings should be held in a single period of hearings or in separate periods, especially when more than a few days are needed to complete the hearings. According to some arbitrators, the entire hearings should normally be held in a single period, even if the hearings are to last for more than a week. Other arbitrators in such cases tend to schedule separate periods of hearings. In some cases issues to be decided are separated, and separate hearings set for those issues, with the aim that oral presentation on those issues will be completed within the allotted time. Among the advantages of one period of hearings are that it involves less travel costs, memory will not fade, and it is unlikely that people representing a party will change. On the other hand, the longer the hearings, the more difficult it may be to find early dates acceptable to all participants. Furthermore, separate periods of hearings may be easier to schedule, the subsequent hearings may be tailored to the development of the case, and the period between the hearings leaves time for analysing the records and negotiations between the parties aimed at narrowing the points at issue by agreement.

3—076 **(c) Setting dates for hearings**

77. Typically, firm dates will be fixed for hearings. Exceptionally, the arbitral tribunal may initially wish to set only "target dates" as opposed to definitive dates. This may be done at a stage of the proceedings when not all information necessary to schedule hearings is yet available, with the understanding that the target dates will either be confirmed or rescheduled within a reasonably short period. Such provisional planning can be useful to participants who are generally not available on short notice.

3—077 **(d) Whether there should be a limit on the aggregate amount of time each party will have for oral arguments and questioning witnesses**

78. Some arbitrators consider it useful to limit the aggregate amount of time each party has for any of the following:

(a) making oral statements;
(b) questioning its witnesses; and
(c) questioning the witnesses of the other party or parties. In

general, the same aggregate amount of time is considered appropriate for each party, unless the arbitral tribunal considers that a different allocation is justified. Before deciding, the arbitral tribunal may wish to consult the parties as to how much time they think they will need.

79. Such planning of time, provided it is realistic, fair and subject to judiciously firm control by the arbitral tribunal, will make it easier for the parties to plan the presentation of the various items of evidence and arguments, reduce the likelihood of running out of time towards the end of the hearings and avoid that one party would unfairly use up a disproportionate amount of time.

3—078 **(e) The order in which the parties will present their arguments and evidence**

80. Arbitration rules typically give broad latitude to the arbitral tribunal to determine the order of presentations at the hearings. Within that latitude, practices differ, for example, as to whether opening or closing statements are heard and their level of detail; the sequence in which the claimant and the respondent present their opening statements, arguments, witnesses and other evidence; and whether the respondent or the claimant has the last word. In view of such differences, or when no arbitration rules apply, it may foster efficiency of the proceedings if the arbitral tribunal clarifies to the parties, in advance of the hearings, the manner in which it will conduct the hearings, at least in broad lines.

3—079 **(f) Length of hearings**

81. The length of a hearing primarily depends on the complexity of the issues to be argued and the amount of witness evidence to be presented. The length also depends on the procedural style used in the arbitration. Some practitioners prefer to have written evidence and written arguments presented before the hearings, which thus can focus on the issues that have not been sufficiently clarified. Those practitioners generally tend to plan shorter hearings than those practitioners who prefer that most if not all evidence and arguments are presented to the arbitral tribunal orally and in full detail. In order to facilitate the parties' preparations and avoid misunderstandings, the arbitral tribunal may wish to clarify to the parties, in advance of the hearings, the intended use of time and style of work at the hearings.

B. Rules of Procedure

3—080   (g) Arrangements for a record of the hearings

82. The arbitral tribunal should decide, possibly after consulting with the parties, on the method of preparing a record of oral statements and testimony during hearings. Among different possibilities, one method is that the members of the arbitral tribunal take personal notes. Another is that the presiding arbitrator during the hearing dictates to a typist a summary of oral statements and testimony. A further method, possible when a secretary of the arbitral tribunal has been appointed, may be to leave to that person the preparation of a summary record. A useful, though costly, method is for professional stenographers to prepare verbatim transcripts, often within the next day or a similarly short time period. A written record may be combined with tape-recording, so as to enable reference to the tape in case of a disagreement over the written record.

83. If transcripts are to be produced, it may be considered how the persons who made the statements will be given an opportunity to check the transcripts. For example, it may be determined that the changes to the record would be approved by the parties or, failing their agreement, would be referred for decision to the arbitral tribunal.

3—081   (h) Whether and when the parties are permitted to submit notes summarizing their oral arguments

84. Some legal counsel are accustomed to giving notes summarizing their oral arguments to the arbitral tribunal and to the other party or parties. If such notes are presented, this is usually done during the hearings or shortly thereafter; in some cases, the notes are sent before the hearing. In order to avoid surprise, foster equal treatment of the parties and facilitate preparations for the hearings, advance clarification is advisable as to whether submitting such notes is acceptable and the time for doing so.

85. In closing the hearings, the arbitral tribunal will normally assume that no further proof is to be offered or submission to be made. Therefore, if notes are to be presented to be read after the closure of the hearings, the arbitral tribunal may find it worthwhile to stress that the notes should be limited to summarizing what was said orally and in particular should not refer to new evidence or new argument.

3—082   18. Multi-party arbitration

86. When a single arbitration involves more than two parties (multi-party arbitration), considerations regarding the need to organize arbitral proceedings, and matters that may be considered in that connection, are generally not different from two-party arbitrations. A possible difference may be that, because of the need to deal with more than two parties, multi-party proceedings can be more complicated to manage than bilateral proceedings. The Notes, notwithstanding a possible greater complexity of multi-party arbitration, can be used in multi-party as well as in two-party proceedings.

87. The areas of possibly increased complexity in multi-party arbitration are, for example, the flow of communications among the parties and the arbitral tribunal (see paragraphs 33, 34 and 38–41); if points at issue are to be decided at different points in time, the order of deciding them (paragraphs 44–45); the manner in which the parties will participate in hearing witnesses (paragraph 63); the appointment of experts and the participation of the parties in considering their reports (paragraphs 70–72); the scheduling of hearings (paragraph 76); the order in which the parties will present their arguments and evidence at hearings (paragraph 80).

88. The Notes, which are limited to pointing out matters that may be considered in organizing arbitral proceedings in general, do not cover the drafting of the arbitration agreement or the constitution of the arbitral tribunal, both issues that give rise to special questions in multi-party arbitration as compared to two-party arbitration.

3—083   19. Possible requirements concerning filing or delivering the award

89. Some national laws require that arbitral awards be filed or registered with a court or similar authority, or that they be delivered in a particular manner or through a particular authority. Those laws differ with respect to, for example, the type of award to which the requirement applies (e.g. to all awards or only to awards not rendered under the auspices of an arbitral institution); time periods for filing, registering or delivering the award (in some cases those time periods may be rather short); or consequences for failing to comply with the requirement (which might be, for example, invalidity of the award or inability to enforce it in a particular manner). Who should take steps to fulfil any requirement.

90. If such a requirement exists, it is useful, some time before the award is to be issued, to plan who should take the necessary steps to meet the requirement and how the costs are to be borne.

UNCITRAL Arbitration Rules

3—084 RESOLUTION 31/98 ADOPTED BY THE GENERAL ASSEMBLY ON 15 DECEMBER 1976 31/98. Arbitration Rules of the United Nations Commission on International Trade Law

The General Assembly,

Recognizing the value of arbitration as a method of settling disputes arising in the context of international commercial relations,

Being convinced that the establishment of rules for ad hoc arbitration that are acceptable in countries with different legal, social and economic systems would significantly contribute to the development of harmonious international economic relations,

Bearing in mind that the Arbitration Rules of the United Nations Commission on International Trade Law have been prepared after extensive consultation with arbitral institutions and centres of international commercial arbitration,

Noting that the Arbitration Rules were adopted by the United Nations Commission on International Trade Law at its ninth session 1/ after due deliberation,

1. Recommends the use of the Arbitration Rules of the United Nations Commission on International Trade Law in the settlement of disputes arising in the context of international commercial relations, particularly by reference to the Arbitration Rules in commercial contracts;

2. Requests the Secretary-General to arrange for the widest possible distribution of the Arbitration Rules.

Section I: Introductory rules

Scope of application

3—085 Article 1

1. Where the parties to a contract have agreed in writing[A] that disputes in relation to that contract shall be referred to arbitration under the UNCITRAL Arbitration Rules, then such disputes shall be settled in accordance with these Rules subject to such modification as the parties may agree in writing.

2. These Rules shall govern the arbitration except that where any of these Rules is in conflict with a provision of the law

applicable to the arbitration from which the parties cannot derogate, that provision shall prevail.

Notice, calculation of periods of time

3—086 **Article 2**

1. For the purposes of these Rules, any notice, including a notification, communication or proposal, is deemed to have been received if it is physically delivered to the addressee or if it is delivered at his habitual residence, place of business or mailing address, or, if none of these can be found after making reasonable inquiry, then at the addressee's last-known residence or place of business. Notice shall be deemed to have been received on the day it is so delivered.

2. For the purposes of calculating a period of time under these Rules, such period shall begin to run on the day following the day when a notice, notification, communication or proposal is received. If the last day of such period is an official holiday or a non-business day at the residence or place of business of the addressee, the period is extended until the first business day which follows. Official holidays or non-business days occurring during the running of the period of time are included in calculating the period.

Notice of arbitration

3—087 **Article 3**

1. The party initiating recourse to arbitration (hereinafter called the "claimant") shall give to the other party (hereinafter called the "respondent") a notice of arbitration.

2. Arbitral proceedings shall be deemed to commence on the date on which the notice of arbitration is received by the respondent.

3. The notice of arbitration shall include the following:

   (a) A demand that the dispute be referred to arbitration;
   (b) The names and addresses of the parties;
   (c) A reference to the arbitration clause or the separate arbitration agreement that is invoked;
   (d) A reference to the contract out of or in relation to which the dispute arises;
   (e) The general nature of the claim and an indication of the amount involved, if any;
   (f) The relief or remedy sought;

(g) A proposal as to the number of arbitrators (i.e. one or three), if the parties have not previously agreed thereon.

4. The notice of arbitration may also include:

(a) The proposals for the appointments of a sole arbitrator and an appointing authority referred to in article 6, paragraph 1;
(b) The notification of the appointment of an arbitrator referred to in article 7;
(c) The statement of claim referred to in article 18.

Representation and assistance

3—088 Article 4

The parties may be represented or assisted by persons of their choice. The names and addresses of such persons must be communicated in writing to the other party; such communication must specify whether the appointment is being made for purposes of representation or assistance.

Section II: Composition of the arbitral tribunal

Number of arbitrators

3—089 Article 5

If the parties have not previously agreed on the number of arbitrators (i.e. one or three), and if within fifteen days after the receipt by the respondent of the notice of arbitration the parties have not agreed that there shall be only one arbitrator, three arbitrators shall be appointed.

Appointment of arbitrators

3—090 Article 6

1. If a sole arbitrator is to be appointed, either party may propose to the other:

(a) The names of one or more persons, one of whom would serve as the sole arbitrator; and
(b) If no appointing authority has been agreed upon by the parties, the name or names of one or more institutions or persons, one of whom would serve as appointing authority.

2. If within thirty days after receipt by a party of a proposal made in accordance with paragraph 1 the parties have not reached agreement on the choice of a sole arbitrator, the sole arbitrator shall be appointed by the appointing authority agreed upon by the parties. If no appointing authority has been agreed upon by the parties, or if the appointing authority agreed upon refuses to act or fails to appoint the arbitrator within sixty days of the receipt of a party's request therefor, either party may request the Secretary-General of the Permanent Court of Arbitration at The Hague to designate an appointing authority.

3. The appointing authority shall, at the request of one of the parties, appoint the sole arbitrator as promptly as possible. In making the appointment the appointing authority shall use the following list-procedure, unless both parties agree that the list-procedure should not be used or unless the appointing authority determines in its discretion that the use of the list-procedure is not appropriate for the case:

   (a) At the request of one of the parties the appointing authority shall communicate to both parties an identical list containing at least three names;
   (b) Within fifteen days after the receipt of this list, each party may return the list to the appointing authority after having deleted the name or names to which he objects and numbered the remaining names on the list in the order of his preference;
   (c) After the expiration of the above period of time the appointing authority shall appoint the sole arbitrator from among the names approved on the lists returned to it and in accordance with the order of preference indicated by the parties;
   (d) If for any reason the appointment cannot be made according to this procedure, the appointing authority may exercise its discretion in appointing the sole arbitrator.

4. In making the appointment, the appointing authority shall have regard to such considerations as are likely to secure the appointment of an independent and impartial arbitrator and shall take into account as well the advisability of appointing an arbitrator of a nationality other than the nationalities of the parties.

3—091 Article 7

1. If three arbitrators are to be appointed, each party shall appoint one arbitrator. The two arbitrators thus appointed shall choose the third arbitrator who will act as the presiding arbitrator of the tribunal.

2. If within thirty days after the receipt of a party's notification of the appointment of an arbitrator the other party has not notified the first party of the arbitrator he has appointed:

   (a) The first party may request the appointing authority previously designated by the parties to appoint the second arbitrator; or
   (b) If no such authority has been previously designated by the parties, or if the appointing authority previously designated refuses to act or fails to appoint the arbitrator within thirty days after receipt of a party's request therefor, the first party may request the Secretary-General of the Permanent Court of Arbitration at The Hague to designate the appointing authority. The first party may then request the appointing authority so designated to appoint the second arbitrator. In either case, the appointing authority may exercise its discretion in appointing the arbitrator.

3. If within thirty days after the appointment of the second arbitrator the two arbitrators have not agreed on the choice of the presiding arbitrator, the presiding arbitrator shall be appointed by an appointing authority in the same way as a sole arbitrator would be appointed under article 6.

3—092 Article 8

1. When an appointing authority is requested to appoint an arbitrator pursuant to article 6 or article 7, the party which makes the request shall send to the appointing authority a copy of the notice of arbitration, a copy of the contract out of or in relation to which the dispute has arisen and a copy of the arbitration agreement if it is not contained in the contract. The appointing authority may require from either party such information as it deems necessary to fulfil its function.

2. Where the names of one or more persons are proposed for appointment as arbitrators, their full names, addresses and nationalities shall be indicated, together with a description of their qualifications.

Challenge of arbitrators

3—093   **Article 9**

A prospective arbitrator shall disclose to those who approach him in connexion with his possible appointment any circumstances likely to give rise to justifiable doubts as to his impartiality or independence. An arbitrator, once appointed or chosen, shall disclose such circumstances to the parties unless they have already been informed by him of these circumstances.

3—094   **Article 10**

1. Any arbitrator may be challenged if circumstances exist that give rise to justifiable doubts as to the arbitrators impartiality or independence.

2. A party may challenge the arbitrator appointed by him only for reasons of which he becomes aware after the appointment has been made.

3—095   **Article 11**

1. A party who intends to challenge an arbitrator shall send notice of his challenge within fifteen days after the appointment of the challenged arbitrator has been notified to the challenging party or within fifteen days after the circumstances mentioned in articles 9 and 10 became known to that party.

2. The challenge shall be notified to the other party, to the arbitrator who is challenged and to the other members of the arbitral tribunal. The notification shall be in writing and shall state the reasons for the challenge.

3. When an arbitrator has been challenged by one party, the other party may agree to the challenge. The arbitrator may also, after the challenge, withdraw from his office. In neither case does this imply acceptance of the validity of the grounds for the challenge. In both cases the procedure provided in article 6 or 7 shall be used in full for the appointment of the substitute arbitrator, even if during the process of appointing the challenged arbitrator a party had failed to exercise his right to appoint or to participate in the appointment.

3—096   **Article 12**

1. If the other party does not agree to the challenge and the challenged arbitrator does not withdraw, the decision on the challenge will be made:

(a) When the initial appointment was made by an appointing authority, by that authority;
(b) When the initial appointment was not made by an appointing authority, but an appointing authority has been previously designated, by that authority;
(c) In all other cases, by the appointing authority to be designated in accordance with the procedure for designating an appointing authority as provided for in article 6.

2. If the appointing authority sustains the challenge, a substitute arbitrator shall be appointed or chosen pursuant to the procedure applicable to the appointment or choice of an arbitrator as provided in articles 6 to 9 except that, when this procedure would call for the designation of an appointing authority, the appointment of the arbitrator shall be made by the appointing authority which decided on the challenge.

Replacement of an arbitrator

3—097 Article 13

1. In the event of the death or resignation of an arbitrator during the course of the arbitral proceedings, a substitute arbitrator shall be appointed or chosen pursuant to the procedure provided for in articles 6 to 9 that was applicable to the appointment or choice of the arbitrator being replaced.

2. In the event that an arbitrator fails to act or in the event of the de jure or de facto impossibility of his performing his functions, the procedure in respect of the challenge and replacement of an arbitrator as provided in the preceding articles shall apply.

Repetition of hearings in the event of the replacement of an arbitrator

3—098 Article 14

If under articles 11 to 13 the sole or presiding arbitrator is replaced, any hearings held previously shall be repeated; if any other arbitrator is replaced, such prior hearings may be repeated at the discretion of the arbitral tribunal.

Section III: Arbitral proceedings

General provisions

3—099 **Article 15**

1. Subject to these Rules, the arbitral tribunal may conduct the arbitration in such manner as it considers appropriate, provided that the parties are treated with equality and that at any stage of the proceedings each party is given a full opportunity of presenting his case.

2. If either party so requests at any stage of the proceedings, the arbitral tribunal shall hold hearings for the presentation of evidence by witnesses, including expert witnesses, or for oral argument. In the absence of such a request, the arbitral tribunal shall decide whether to hold such hearings or whether the proceedings shall be conducted on the basis of documents and other materials.

3. All documents or information supplied to the arbitral tribunal by one party shall at the same time be communicated by that party to the other party.

Place of arbitration

3—100 **Article 16**

1. Unless the parties have agreed upon the place where the arbitration is to be held, such place shall be determined by the arbitral tribunal, having regard to the circumstances of the arbitration.

2. The arbitral tribunal may determine the locale of the arbitration within the country agreed upon by the parties. It may hear witnesses and hold meetings for consultation among its members at any place it deems appropriate, having regard to the circumstances of the arbitration.

3. The arbitral tribunal may meet at any place it deems appropriate for the inspection of goods, other property or documents. The parties shall be given sufficient notice to enable them to be present at such inspection.

4. The award shall be made at the place of arbitration.

Language

3—101 **Article 17**

1. Subject to an agreement by the parties, the arbitral tribunal shall, promptly after its appointment, determine the language or languages to be used in the proceedings. This determination shall apply to the statement of claim, the statement of defence, and any further written statements and, if oral hearings take place, to the language or languages to be used in such hearings.

2. The arbitral tribunal may order that any documents annexed to the statement of claim or statement of defence, and any supplementary documents or exhibits submitted in the course of the proceedings, delivered in their original language, shall be accompanied by a translation into the language or languages agreed upon by the parties or determined by the arbitral tribunal.

Statement of claim

3—102 **Article 18**

1. Unless the statement of claim was contained in the notice of arbitration, within a period of time to be determined by the arbitral tribunal, the claimant shall communicate his statement of claim in writing to the respondent and to each of the arbitrators. A copy of the contract, and of the arbitration agreement if not contained in the contract, shall be annexed thereto.

2. The statement of claim shall include the following particulars:

    (a) The names and addresses of the parties;
    (b) A statement of the facts supporting the claim;
    (c) The points at issue;
    (d) The relief or remedy sought.

    The claimant may annex to his statement of claim all documents he deems relevant or may add a reference to the documents or other evidence he will submit.

Statement of defence

3—103 **Article 19**

1. Within a period of time to be determined by the arbitral tribunal, the respondent shall communicate his statement of

defence in writing to the claimant and to each of the arbitrators.

2. The statement of defence shall reply to the particulars (b), (c) and (d) of the statement of claim (article 18, para. 2). The respondent may annex to his statement the documents on which he relies for his defence or may add a reference to the documents or other evidence he will submit.

3. In his statement of defence, or at a later stage in the arbitral proceedings if the arbitral tribunal decides that the delay was justified under the circumstances, the respondent may make a counter-claim arising out of the same contract or rely on a claim arising out of the same contract for the purpose of a set-off.

4. The provisions of article 18, paragraph 2, shall apply to a counter-claim and a claim relied on for the purpose of a set-off.

Amendments to the claim or defence

3—104   Article 20

During the course of the arbitral proceedings either party may amend or supplement his claim or defence unless the arbitral tribunal considers it inappropriate to allow such amendment having regard to the delay in making it or prejudice to the other party or any other circumstances. However, a claim may not be amended in such a manner that the amended claim falls outside the scope of the arbitration clause or separate arbitration agreement.

Pleas as to the jurisdiction of the arbitral tribunal

3—105   Article 21

1. The arbitral tribunal shall have the power to rule on objections that it has no jurisdiction, including any objections with respect to the existence or validity of the arbitration clause or of the separate arbitration agreement.

2. The arbitral tribunal shall have the power to determine the existence or the validity of the contract of which an arbitration clause forms a part. For the purposes of article 21, an arbitration clause which forms part of a contract and which provides for arbitration under these Rules shall be treated as an agreement independent of the other terms of the contract. A decision by the arbitral tribunal that the contract

is null and void shall not entail ipso jure the invalidity of the arbitration clause.

3. A plea that the arbitral tribunal does not have jurisdiction shall be raised not later than in the statement of defence or, with respect to a counter-claim, in the reply to the counter-claim.

4. In general, the arbitral tribunal should rule on a plea concerning its jurisdiction as a preliminary question. However, the arbitral tribunal may proceed with the arbitration and rule on such a plea in their final award.

Further written statements

3—106   Article 22

The arbitral tribunal shall decide which further written statements, in addition to the statement of claim and the statement of defence, shall be required from the parties or may be presented by them and shall fix the periods of time for communicating such statements.

Periods of time

3—107   Article 23

The periods of time fixed by the arbitral tribunal for the communication of written statements (including the statement of claim and statement of defence) should not exceed forty-five days. However, the arbitral tribunal may extend the time-limits if it concludes that an extension is justified.

Evidence and hearings

3—108   Article 24

1. Each party shall have the burden of proving the facts relied on to support his claim or defence.

2. The arbitral tribunal may, if it considers it appropriate, require a party to deliver to the tribunal and to the other party, within such a period of time as the arbitral tribunal shall decide, a summary of the documents and other evidence which that party intends to present in support of the facts in issue set out in his statement of claim or statement of defence.

3. At any time during the arbitral proceedings the arbitral tribunal may require the parties to produce documents, exhib-

its or other evidence within such a period of time as the tribunal shall determine.

3—109 Article 25

1. In the event of an oral hearing, the arbitral tribunal shall give the parties adequate advance notice of the date, time and place thereof.

2. If witnesses are to be heard, at least fifteen days before the hearing each party shall communicate to the arbitral tribunal and to the other party the names and addresses of the witnesses he intends to present, the subject upon and the languages in which such witnesses will give their testimony.

3. The arbitral tribunal shall make arrangements for the translation of oral statements made at a hearing and for a record of the hearing if either is deemed necessary by the tribunal under the circumstances of the case, or if the parties have agreed thereto and have communicated such agreement to the tribunal at least fifteen days before the hearing.

4. Hearings shall be held in camera unless the parties agree otherwise. The arbitral tribunal may require the retirement of any witness or witnesses during the testimony of other witnesses. The arbitral tribunal is free to determine the manner in which witnesses are examined.

5. Evidence of witnesses may also be presented in the form of written statements signed by them.

6. The arbitral tribunal shall determine the admissibility, relevance, materiality and weight of the evidence offered.

Interim measures of protection

3—110 Article 26

1. At the request of either party, the arbitral tribunal may take any interim measures it deems necessary in respect of the subject-matter of the dispute, including measures for the conservation of the goods forming the subject-matter in dispute, such as ordering their deposit with a third person or the sale of perishable goods.

2. Such interim measures may be established in the form of an interim award. The arbitral tribunal shall be entitled to require security for the costs of such measures.

3. A request for interim measures addressed by any party to a judicial authority shall not be deemed incompatible with the agreement to arbitrate, or as a waiver of that agreement.

Experts

3—111   Article 27

1. The arbitral tribunal may appoint one or more experts to report to it, in writing, on specific issues to be determined by the tribunal. A copy of the expert's terms of reference, established by the arbitral tribunal, shall be communicated to the parties.

2. The parties shall give the expert any relevant information or produce for his inspection any relevant documents or goods that he may require of them. Any dispute between a party and such expert as to the relevance of the required information or production shall be referred to the arbitral tribunal for decision.

3. Upon receipt of the expert's report, the arbitral tribunal shall communicate a copy of the report to the parties who shall be given the opportunity to express, in writing, their opinion on the report. A party shall be entitled to examine any document on which the expert has relied in his report.

4. At the request of either party the expert, after delivery of the report, may be heard at a hearing where the parties shall have the opportunity to be present and to interrogate the expert. At this hearing either party may present expert witnesses in order to testify on the points at issue. The provisions of article 25 shall be applicable to such proceedings.

Default

3—112   Article 28

1. If, within the period of time fixed by the arbitral tribunal, the claimant has failed to communicate his claim without showing sufficient cause for such failure, the arbitral tribunal shall issue an order for the termination of the arbitral proceedings. If, within the period of time fixed by the arbitral tribunal, the respondent has failed to communicate his statement of defence without showing sufficient cause for such failure, the arbitral tribunal shall order that the proceedings continue.

2. If one of the parties, duly notified under these Rules, fails to appear at a hearing, without showing sufficient cause for such failure, the arbitral tribunal may proceed with the arbitration.

3. If one of the parties, duly invited to produce documentary evidence, fails to do so within the established period of time, without showing sufficient cause for such failure, the arbitral tribunal may make the award on the evidence before it.

Closure of hearings

3—113   Article 29

1. The arbitral tribunal may inquire of the parties if they have any further proof to offer or witnesses to be heard or submissions to make and, if there are none, it may declare the hearings closed.

2. The arbitral tribunal may, if it considers it necessary owing to exceptional circumstances, decide, on its own motion or upon application of a party, to reopen the hearings at any time before the award is made.

Waiver of rules

3—114   Article 30

A party who knows that any provision of, or requirement under, these Rules has not been complied with and yet proceeds with the arbitration without promptly stating his objection to such non-compliance, shall be deemed to have waived his right to object.

Section IV: The award

Decisions

3—115   Article 31

1. When there are three arbitrators, any award or other decision of the arbitral tribunal shall be made by a majority of the arbitrators.

2. In the case of questions of procedure, when there is no majority or when the arbitral tribunal so authorizes, the presiding arbitrator may decide on his own, subject to revision, if any, by the arbitral tribunal.

Form and effect of the award

3—116 Article 32

1. In addition to making a final award, the arbitral tribunal shall be entitled to make interim, interlocutory, or partial awards.

2. The award shall be made in writing and shall be final and binding on the parties. The parties undertake to carry out the award without delay.

3. The arbitral tribunal shall state the reasons upon which the award is based, unless the parties have agreed that no reasons are to be given.

4. An award shall be signed by the arbitrators and it shall contain the date on which and the place where the award was made. Where there are three arbitrators and one of them fails to sign, the award shall state the reason for the absence of the signature.

5. The award may be made public only with the consent of both parties.

6. Copies of the award signed by the arbitrators shall be communicated to the parties by the arbitral tribunal.

7. If the arbitration law of the country where the award is made requires that the award be filed or registered by the arbitral tribunal, the tribunal shall comply with this requirement within the period of time required by law.

Applicable law, amiable composition

3—117 Article 33

1. The arbitral tribunal shall apply the law designated by the parties as applicable to the substance of the dispute. Failing such designation by the parties, the arbitral tribunal shall apply the law determined by the conflict of laws rules which it considers applicable.

2. The arbitral tribunal shall decide as amiable compositeur or ex aequo et bono only if the parties have expressly authorized the arbitral tribunal to do so and if the law applicable to the arbitral procedure permits such arbitration.

3. In all cases, the arbitral tribunal shall decide in accordance with the terms of the contract and shall take into account the usages of the trade applicable to the transaction.

Settlement or the grounds for termination

3—118   Article 34

1. If, before the award is made, the parties agree on a settlement of the dispute, the arbitral tribunal shall either issue an order for the termination of the arbitral proceedings or, if requested by both parties and accepted by the tribunal, record the settlement in the form of an arbitral award on agreed terms. The arbitral tribunal is not obliged to give reasons for such an award.

2. If, before the award is made, the continuation of the arbitral proceedings becomes unnecessary or impossible for any reason not mentioned in paragraph 1, the arbitral tribunal shall inform the parties of its intention to issue an order for the termination of the proceedings. The arbitral tribunal shall have the power to issue such an order unless a party raises justifiable grounds for objection.

3. Copies of the order for termination of the arbitral proceedings or of the arbitral award on agreed terms, signed by the arbitrators, shall be communicated by the arbitral tribunal to the parties. Where an arbitral award on agreed terms is made, the provisions of article 32, paragraphs 2 and 4 to 7, shall apply.

Interpretation of the award

3—119   Article 35

1. Within thirty days after the receipt of the award, either party, with notice to the other party, may request that the arbitral tribunal give an interpretation of the award.

2. The interpretation shall be given in writing within forty-five days after the receipt of the request. The interpretation shall form part of the award and the provisions of article 32, paragraphs 2 to 7, shall apply.

Correction of the award

3—120   Article 36

1. Within thirty days after the receipt of the award, either party, with notice to the other party, may request the arbitral

tribunal to correct in the award any errors in computation, any clerical or typographical errors, or any errors of similar nature. The arbitral tribunal may within thirty days after the communication of the award make such corrections on its own initiative.

2. Such corrections shall be in writing, and the provisions of article 32, paragraphs 2 to 7, shall apply.

Additional award

3—121   Article 37

1. Within thirty days after the receipt of the award, either party, with notice to the other party, may request the arbitral tribunal to make an additional award as to claims presented in the arbitral proceedings but omitted from the award.

2. If the arbitral tribunal considers the request for an additional award to be justified and considers that the omission can be rectified without any further hearings or evidence, it shall complete its award within sixty days after the receipt of the request.

3. When an additional award is made, the provisions of article 32, paragraphs 2 to 7, shall apply.

Costs

3—122   Article 38

The arbitral tribunal shall fix the costs of arbitration in its award. The term "costs" includes only:

(a) The fees of the arbitral tribunal to be stated separately as to each arbitrator and to be fixed by the tribunal itself in accordance with article 39;

(b) The travel and other expenses incurred by the arbitrators;

(c) The costs of expert advice and of other assistance required by the arbitral tribunal;

(d) The travel and other expenses of witnesses to the extent such expenses are approved by the arbitral tribunal;

(e) The costs for legal representation and assistance of the successful party if such costs were claimed during the arbitral proceedings, and only to the extent that the arbitral tribunal determines that the amount of such costs is reasonable;

(f) Any fees and expenses of the appointing authority as well as the expenses of the Secretary-General of the Permanent Court of Arbitration at The Hague.

3—123   Article 39

1. The fees of the arbitral tribunal shall be reasonable in amount, taking into account the amount in dispute, the complexity of the subject-matter, the time spent by the arbitrators and any other relevant circumstances of the case.

2. If an appointing authority has been agreed upon by the parties or designated by the Secretary-General of the Permanent Court of Arbitration at The Hague, and if that authority has issued a schedule of fees for arbitrators in international cases which it administers, the arbitral tribunal in fixing its fees shall take that schedule of fees into account to the extent that it considers appropriate in the circumstances of the case.

3. If such appointing authority has not issued a schedule of fees for arbitrators in international cases, any party may at any time request the appointing authority to furnish a statement setting forth the basis for establishing fees which is customarily followed in international cases in which the authority appoints arbitrators. If the appointing authority consents to provide such a statement, the arbitral tribunal in fixing its fees shall take such information into account to the extent that it considers appropriate in the circumstances of the case.

4. In cases referred to in paragraphs 2 and 3, when a party so requests and the appointing authority consents to perform the function, the arbitral tribunal shall fix its fees only after consultation with the appointing authority which may make any comment it deems appropriate to the arbitral tribunal concerning the fees.

3—124   Article 40

1. Except as provided in paragraph 2, the costs of arbitration shall in principle be borne by the unsuccessful party. However, the arbitral tribunal may apportion each of such costs between the parties if it determines that apportionment is reasonable, taking into account the circumstances of the case.

2. With respect to the costs of legal representation and assistance referred to in article 38, paragraph (e), the arbitral

tribunal, taking into account the circumstances of the case, shall be free to determine which party shall bear such costs or may apportion such costs between the parties if it determines that apportionment is reasonable.

3. When the arbitral tribunal issues an order for the termination of the arbitral proceedings or makes an award on agreed terms, it shall fix the costs of arbitration referred to in article 38 and article 39, paragraph 1, in the text of that order or award.

4. No additional fees may be charged by an arbitral tribunal for interpretation or correction or completion of its award under articles 35 to 37.

Deposit of the costs

3—125 Article 41

1. The arbitral tribunal, on its establishment, may request each party to deposit an equal amount as an advance for the costs referred to in article 38, paragraphs (a), (b) and (c).

2. During the course of the arbitral proceedings the arbitral tribunal may request supplementary deposits from the parties.

3. If an appointing authority has been agreed upon by the parties or designated by the Secretary-General of the Permanent Court of Arbitration at The Hague, and when a party so requests and the appointing authority consents to perform the function, the arbitral tribunal shall fix the amounts of any deposits or supplementary deposits only after consultation with the appointing authority which may make any comments to the arbitral tribunal which it deems appropriate concerning the amount of such deposits and supplementary deposits.

4. If the required deposits are not paid in full within thirty days after the receipt of the request, the arbitral tribunal shall so inform the parties in order that one or another of them may make the required payment. If such payment is not made, the arbitral tribunal may order the suspension or termination of the arbitral proceedings.

5. After the award has been made, the arbitral tribunal shall render an accounting to the parties of the deposits received and return any unexpended balance to the parties.

NOTES

(A) MODEL ARBITRATION CLAUSE

Any dispute, controversy or claim arising out of or relating to this contract, or the breach, termination or invalidity thereof, shall be settled by arbitration in accordance with the UNCITRAL Arbitration Rules as at present in force.

Note—Parties may wish to consider adding:

(a) The appointing authority shall be . . . (name of institution or person);
(b) The number of arbitrators shall be . . . (one or three);
(c) The place of arbitration shall be . . . (town or country);
(d) The language(s) to be used in the arbitral proceedings shall be . . .

IBA Rules on the Taking of Evidence in International Commercial Arbitration

Adopted by a resolution of the IBA Council 1 June 1999
IBA Rules on the Taking of Evidence in International Commercial Arbitration

3—126 Preamble

1. These IBA Rules on the Taking of Evidence in International Commercial Arbitration (the IBA Rules of Evidence) are intended to govern in an efficient and economical manner the taking of evidence in international commercial arbitrations, particularly those between Parties from different legal traditions. They are designed to supplement the legal provisions and the institutional or ad hoc rules according to which the Parties are conducting their arbitration.

2. Parties and Arbitral Tribunals may adopt the IBA Rules of Evidence, in whole or in part, to govern arbitration proceedings, or they may vary them or use them as guidelines in developing their own procedures. The Rules are not intended to limit the flexibility that is inherent in, and an advantage of, international arbitration, and Parties and Arbitral Tribunals are free to adapt them to the particular circumstances of each arbitration.

3. Each Arbitral Tribunal is encouraged to identify to the Parties, as soon as it considers it to be appropriate, the issues that it may regard as relevant and material to the outcome of the case, including issues where a preliminary determination may be appropriate.

4. The taking of evidence shall be conducted on the principle that each Party shall be entitled to know, reasonably in advance of any Evidentiary Hearing, the evidence on which the other Parties rely.

3—127 Article 1—Definitions

In the IBA Rules of Evidence:

Arbitral Tribunal means a sole arbitrator or a panel of arbitrators validly deciding by majority or otherwise;

Claimant means the Party or Parties who commenced the arbitration and any Party who, through joinder or otherwise, becomes aligned with such Party or Parties;

Document means a writing of any kind, whether recorded on paper, electronic means, audio or visual recordings or any other mechanical or electronic means of storing or recording information;

Evidentiary Hearing means any hearing, whether or notheld on consecutive days, at which the Arbitral Tribunal receives oral evidence;

Expert Report means a written statement by a Tribunal-Appointed Expert or a Party-Appointed Expert submitted pursuant to the IBA Rules of Evidence;

General Rules mean the institutional or ad hoc rules according to which the Parties are conducting their arbitration;

Party means a party to the arbitration;

Party-Appointed Expert means an expert witness presented by a Party;

Request to Produce means a request by a Party for a procedural order by which the Arbitral Tribunal would direct another Party to produce documents;

Respondent means the Party or Parties against whom the Claimant made its claim, and any Party who, through joinder or otherwise, becomes aligned with such Party or Parties, and includes a Respondent making a counterclaim;

Tribunal-Appointed Expert means a person Or organization appointed by the Arbitral Tribunal in order to report to it on specific issues determined by the Arbitral Tribunal.3

3—128 Article 2—Scope of Application

1. Whenever the Parties have agreed or the Arbitral Tribunal has determined to apply the IBA Rules of Evidence, the Rules shall govern the taking of evidence, except to the extent that any specific provision of them may be found to be in conflict with any mandatory provision of law determined to be applicable to the case by the Parties or by the Arbitral Tribunal.

2. In case of conflict between any provisions of the IBA Rules of Evidence and the General Rules, the Arbitral Tribunal shall apply the IBA Rules of Evidence in the manner that it determines best in order to accomplish the purposes of both

the General Rules and the IBA Rules of Evidence, unless the Parties agree to the contrary.

3. In the event of any dispute regarding the meaning of the IBA Rules of Evidence, the Arbitral Tribunal shall interpret them according to their purpose and in the manner most appropriate for the particulararbitration.4. Insofar as the IBA Rules of Evidence and the General Rules are silent on any matter concerning the taking of evidence and the Parties have not agreed otherwise, the Arbitral Tribunal may conduct the taking of evidence as it deems appropriate, in accordance with the general principles of the IBA Rules of Evidence.

3—129 Article 3—Documents

1. Within the time ordered by the Arbitral Tribunal, each Party shall submit to the Arbitral Tribunal and to the other Parties all documents available to it on which it relies, including public documents and those in the public domain, except for any documents that have already been submitted by another Party.

2. Within the time ordered by the Arbitral Tribunal, any Party may submit to the Arbitral Tribunal a Request to Produce.

3. A Request to Produce shall contain:

    (a) (i) a description of a requested document sufficient to identify it, or

    (ii) a description insufficient detail (including subject matter) of a narrow and specific requested category of documents that are reasonably believed to exist;

    (b) a description of how the documents requested are relevant and material to the outcome of the case; and

    (c) a statement that the documents requested are not in the possession, custody or control of there questing Party, and of the reason why that Party assumes the documents requested to be in the possession, custody or control of the other Party.

4. Within the time ordered by the Arbitral Tribunal, the Party to whom the Request to Produce is addressed shall produce to the Arbitral Tribunal and to the other Parties all the documents requested in its possession, custody or control as to which no objection is made.

5. If the Party to whom the Request to Produce is addressed has objections to some or all of the documents requested, it shall state them in writing to the Arbitral Tribunal within the time

ordered by the Arbitral Tribunal. The reasons for such objections shall be any of those set forth in Article 9.2.

6. The Arbitral Tribunal shall, in consultation with the Parties and in timely fashion, consider the Request to Produce and the objections. The Arbitral Tribunal may order the Party to whom such Request is addressed to produce to the Arbitral Tribunal and to the other Parties those requested documents in its possession, custody or control as to which the Arbitral Tribunal determines that (i) the issues that the requesting Party wishes to prove are relevant and material to the outcome of the case, and (ii) none of the reasons for objection set forth in Article 9.2 apply.

7. In exceptional circumstances, if the propriety of an objection can only be determined by review of the document, the Arbitral Tribunal may determine that it should not review the document. In that event, the Arbitral Tribunal may, after consultation with the Parties, appoint an independent and impartial expert, bound to confidentiality, to review any such document and to report on the objection. To the extent that the objection is upheld by the Arbitral Tribunal, the expert shall not disclose to the Arbitral Tribunal and to the other Parties the contents of the document reviewed.

8. If a Party wishes to obtain the production of documents from a person or organization who is not a Party to the arbitration and from whom the Party cannot obtain the documents on its own, the Party may, within the time ordered by the Arbitral Tribunal, ask it to take whatever steps are legally available to obtain the requested documents. The Party shall identify the documents in sufficient detail and state why such documents are relevant and material to the outcome of the case. The Arbitral Tribunal shall decide on this request and shall take the necessary steps if in its discretion it determines that the documents would be relevant and material.

9. The Arbitral Tribunal, at any time before the arbitration is concluded, may request a Party to produce to the Arbitral Tribunal and to the other Parties any documents that it believes to be relevant and material to the outcome of the case. A Party may object to such a request based on any of the reasons set forth in Article 9.2. If a Party raises such an objection, the Arbitral Tribunal shall Decide whether to order the production of such documents based upon the considerations set forth in Article 3.6 and, if the Arbitral Tribunal considers it appropriate, through the use of the procedures set forth in Article 3.7.

10. Within the time ordered by the Arbitral Tribunal, the Parties may submit to the Arbitral Tribunal and to the other Parties any additional documents which they believe have become relevant and material as a consequence of the issues raised in documents, Witness Statements or Expert Reports submitted or produced by another Party or in other submissions of the Parties.

11. If copies are submitted or produced, they must conform fully to the originals. At the request of the Arbitral Tribunal, any original must be presented for inspection.

12. All documents produced by a Party pursuant to the IBA Rules of Evidence (or by a non-Party pursuant to Article 3.8) shall be kept confidential by the Arbitral Tribunal and by the other Parties, and they shall be used only in connection with the arbitration. The Arbitral Tribunal may issue orders to set forth the terms of this confidentiality. This requirement is without prejudice to all other obligations of confidentiality in arbitration.

3—130   Article 4—Witnesses of Fact

1. Within the time ordered by the Arbitral Tribunal, each Party shall identify the witnesses on whose testimony it relies and the subject matter of that testimony.

2. Any person may present evidence as a witness, including a Party or a Party's officer, employee or other representative.

3. It shall not be improper for a Party, its officers, employees, legal advisors or other representatives to interview its witnesses or potential witnesses.

4. The Arbitral Tribunal may order each Party to submit within a specified time to the Arbitral Tribunal and to the other Parties a written statement by each witness on whose testimony it relies, except for those witnesses whose testimony is sought pursuant to Article 4.10 (the Witness Statement).If Evidentiary Hearings are organized on separate issues (such as liability and damages), the Arbitral Tribunal or the Parties by agreement may schedule the submission of Witness Statements separately For each Evidentiary Hearing.

5. Each Witness Statement shall contain:

    (a) the full name and address of the witness, his or her present and past relationship (if any) with any of the

Parties, and a description of his or her background, qualifications, training and experience, if such a description may be relevant and material to the dispute or to the contents of the statement;

(b) a full and detailed description of the facts, and the source of the witness's information as to those facts, sufficient to serve as that witness's evidence in the matter in dispute;

   (a) an affirmation of the truth of the statement; and
   (b) the signature of the witness and its date and place.

6. If Witness Statements are submitted, any Party may, within the time ordered by the Arbitral Tribunal, submit to the Arbitral Tribunal and to the other Parties revised or additional Witness Statements, including statements from persons not previously named as witnesses, so long as any such revisions or additions only respond to matters contained in another Party's Witness Statement or Expert Report and such matters have not been previously presented in the arbitration.

7. Each witness who has submitted a Witness Statement shall appear for testimony at an Evidentiary Hearing, unless the Parties agree otherwise.

8. If a witness who has submitted a Witness Statement does not appear without a valid reason for testimony at an Evidentiary Hearing, except by agreement of the Parties, the Arbitral Tribunal shall disregard that Witness Statement unless, in exceptional circumstances, the Arbitral Tribunal determines otherwise.

9. If the Parties agree that a witness who has Submitted a Witness Statement does not need to appear for testimony at an Evidentiary Hearing, such an agreement shall not be considered to reflect An agreement as to the correctness of the content of the Witness Statement.

10. If a Party wishes to present evidence from a person who will not appear voluntarily at its request, the Party may, within the time ordered by the Arbitral Tribunal, ask it to take whatever steps are legally available to obtain the testimony of that person. The Party shall identify the intended witness, shall describe the subjects on which the witness's testimony is sought and shall state why such subjects are relevant and material to the outcome of the case. The Arbitral Tribunal shall decide on this request and shall take the necessary steps if in its discretion it determines that the testimony of that witness would be relevant and material.

11. The Arbitral Tribunal may, at any time before the arbitration is concluded, order any Party to provide, or to use its best efforts to provide, the appearance for testimony at an Evidentiary Hearing of any person, including one whose testimony has not yet been offered.

3—131   Article 5—Party-Appointed Experts

1. A Party may rely on a Party-Appointed Expert as a means of evidence on specific issues. Within the time ordered by the Arbitral Tribunal, a Party-Appointed Expert shall submit an Expert Report.

2. The Expert Report shall contain:
   (a) the full name and address of the Party-Appointed Expert, his or her present and past relationship (if any) with any of the Parties, and a description of his or her background, qualifications, training and experience;
   (b) a statement of the facts on which he or she is basing his or her expert opinions and conclusions;
   (c) his or her expert opinions and conclusions, including a description of the method, evidence and information used in arriving at the conclusions;
   (d) an affirmation of the truth of the Expert Report; and
   (e) the signature of the Party-Appointed Expert and its date and place.

3. The Arbitral Tribunal in its discretion may order that any Party-Appointed Experts who have submitted Expert Reports on the same or Related issues meet and confer on such issues. At such meeting, the Party-Appointed Experts shall attempt to reach agreement on those issues as to which they had differences of opinion in their Expert Reports, and they shall record in writing any such issues on which they reach agreement.

4. Each Party-Appointed Expert shall appear for testimony at an Evidentiary Hearing, unless the Parties agree otherwise and the Arbitral Tribunal accepts this agreement.

5. If a Party-Appointed Expert does not appear without a valid reason for testimony at an Evidentiary Hearing, except by agreement of the Parties accepted by the Arbitral Tribunal, the Arbitral Tribunal shall disregard his or her Expert Report unless, in exceptional circumstances, the Arbitral Tribunal determines otherwise.

6. If the Parties agree that a Party-Appointed Expert does not need to appear for testimony at an Evidentiary Hearing, such

an agreement shall not be considered to reflect an agreement as to the correctness of the content of the Expert Report.

3—132 Article 6—Tribunal-Appointed Experts

1. The Arbitral Tribunal, after having consulted with the Parties, may appoint one or more independent Tribunal-Appointed Experts to report to it on specific issues designated by the Arbitral Tribunal. The Arbitral Tribunal shall establish the terms of reference for any Tribunal-Appointed Expert report after having consulted with the Parties. A copy of the final terms of reference shall be sent by the Arbitral Tribunal to the Parties.

2. The Tribunal-Appointed Expert shall, before accepting appointment, submit to the Arbitral Tribunal and to the Parties a statement of his or her independence from the Parties and the Arbitral Tribunal. Within the time ordered by the Arbitral Tribunal, the Parties shall inform The Arbitral Tribunal whether they have any objections to the Tribunal-Appointed Expert's independence. The Arbitral Tribunal shall decide promptly whether to accept any such objection.

3. Subject to the provisions of Article 9.2, the Tribunal-Appointed Expert may request a Party to provide any relevant and material information or to provide access to any relevant documents, goods, samples, property or site for inspection. The authority of a Tribunal-Appointed Expert to request such information or access shall be the same as the authority of the Arbitral Tribunal. The Parties and their representatives shall have the right to receive any such information and to attend any such inspection. Any disagreement between a Tribunal-Appointed Expert and a Party as to the relevance, materiality or appropriateness of such a request shall be decided by the Arbitral Tribunal, in the manner provided in Articles 3.5 through 3.7. The Tribunal-Appointed Expert shall record in the report any non-compliance by a Party with an appropriate request or decision by the Arbitral Tribunal and shall describe its effects on the determination of the specific issue.

4. The Tribunal-Appointed Expert shall report in writing to the Arbitral Tribunal. The Tribunal-Appointed Expert shall describe in the report the method, evidence and information used in Arriving at the conclusions.

5. The Arbitral Tribunal shall send a copy of Such Expert Report to the Parties. The Parties may examine any docu-

ment that the Tribunal-Appointed Expert has examined and any correspondence between the Arbitral Tribunal and the Tribunal-Appointed Expert. Within the time ordered by the Arbitral Tribunal, any Party shall have the opportunity to respond to the report in a submission by the Party or through an Expert Report by a Party-Appointed Expert. The Arbitral Tribunal shall send the submission or Expert Report to the Tribunal-Appointed Expert and to the other Parties.

6. At the request of a Party or of the Arbitral Tribunal, the Tribunal-Appointed Expert shall be present at an Evidentiary Hearing. The Arbitral Tribunal may question the Tribunal-Appointed Expert, and he or she may be questioned by the Parties or by any Party-Appointed Expert on issues raised in the Parties' submissions or in the Expert Reports made by the Party-Appointed Experts pursuant to Article 6.5.

7. Any Expert Report made by a Tribunal-Appointed Expert and its conclusions shall be assessed by the Arbitral Tribunal with due regard to all circum-stances of the case.

8. The fees and expenses of a Tribunal-Appointed Expert, to be funded in a manner determined by the Arbitral Tribunal, shall form part of the costs of the arbitration.

3—133 **Article 7**

On Site Inspection Subject to the provisions of Article 9.2, the Arbitral Tribunal may, at the request of a Party or on its own motion, inspect or require the inspection by a Tribunal-Appointed Expert of any site, property, machinery or any other goods or process, or documents, as it deems appropriate. The Arbitral Tribunal shall, in consultation with the Parties, determine the timing and arrangement for the inspection. The Parties and their representatives shall have the right to attend any such inspection.

3—134 **Article 8—Evidentiary Hearing**

1. The Arbitral Tribunal shall at all times have complete control over the Evidentiary Hearing. The Arbitral Tribunal may limit or exclude any question to, answer by or appearance of a witness (which term includes, for the purposes of this Article, witnesses of fact and any Experts), if it considers such question, answer or appearance to be irrelevant, immaterial, burdensome, duplicative or covered by a reason for objection set forth in Article9.2. Questions to a witness during direct and re-direct testimony may not be unreasonably leading.

2. The Claimant shall ordinarily first present the testimony of its witnesses, followed by the Respondent presenting testimony of its witnesses, and then by the presentation by Claimant of rebuttal witnesses, if any. Following direct testimony, any other Party may question such witness, in an order to be determined by the Arbitral Tribunal. The Party who initially presented the witness shall subsequently have the opportunity to ask additional questions on the matters raised in the other Parties' questioning. The Arbitral Tribunal, upon request of a Party or on its own motion, may vary this order of proceeding, including the arrangement of testimony by particular issues or in such a manner that witnesses presented by different Parties be questioned at the same time and in confrontation with each other. The Arbitral Tribunal may ask questions to a witness at any time.

3. Any witness providing testimony shall first affirm, in a manner determined appropriate by the Arbitral Tribunal, that he or she is telling the truth. If the witness has submitted a Witness Statement or an Expert Report, the witness shall confirm it. The Parties may agree or the Arbitral Tribunal may order that the Witness Statement or Expert Report shall serve as that witness's direct testimony.

4. Subject to the provisions of Article 9.2, the Arbitral Tribunal may request any person to give oral or written evidence on any issue that the Arbitral Tribunal considers to be relevant and material. Any witness called and questioned by the Arbitral Tribunal may also be questioned by the Parties.

3—135 **Article 9—Admissibility and Assessment of Evidence**

1. The Arbitral Tribunal shall determine the admissibility, relevance, materiality and weight of evidence.

2. The Arbitral Tribunal shall, at the request of a Party or on its own motion, exclude from evidence or production any document, statement, oral testimony or inspection for any of the following reasons:

    (a) lack of sufficient relevance or materiality;
    (b) legal impediment or privilege under the legal or ethical rules determined by the Arbitral Tribunal to be applicable;
    (c) unreasonable burden to produce the requested evidence;
    (d) loss or destruction of the document that has been reasonably shown to have occurred;

(e) grounds of commercial or technical confidentiality that the Arbitral Tribunal determines to be compelling;

(f) grounds of special political or institutional sensitivity (including evidence that has been classified as secret by a government or a public international institution) that the Arbitral Tribunal determines to be compelling; or

(g) considerations of fairness or equality of the Parties that the Arbitral Tribunal determines to be compelling.

3. The Arbitral Tribunal may, where appropriate, make necessary arrangements to permit evidence to be considered subject to suitable confidentiality protection.

4. If a Party fails without satisfactory explanation to produce any document requested in a Request to Produce to which it has not objected in due time or fails to produce any document ordered to be produced by the Arbitral Tribunal, the Arbitral Tribunal may infer that such document would be adverse to the interests of that Party.

5. If a Party fails without satisfactory explanation to make available any other relevant evidence, including testimony, sought by one Party to which he Party to whom the request was addressed has not objected in due time or fails to make available any evidence, including testimony, ordered by the Arbitral Tribunal to be produced, the Arbitral Tribunal may infer that such evidence would be adverse to the interests of that Party.

CHAPTER 4

International Contractual Instruments

A. TRANSNATIONAL CONTRACT PRINCIPLES

UNIDROIT Principles of International Commercial Contracts 1994

CONTENTS

PREAMBLE—PURPOSE OF THE PRINCIPLES

CHAPTER 1: General Provisions

Article.
- 1.1 Freedom of Contract
- 1.2 No form required
- 1.3 Binding character of contract
- 1.4 Mandatory rules
- 1.5 Exclusion or modification by the parties
- 1.6 Interpretation and supplementation of the Principles
- 1.7 Good faith and fair dealing
- 1.8 Usages and practices
- 1.9 Notice
- 1.10 Definitions

CHAPTER 2: Formation

- 2.1 Manner of formation
- 2.2 Definition of offer

2.3 Withdrawal of offer

2.4 Revocation of offer

2.5 Rejection of offer

2.6 Mode of acceptance

2.7 Time of acceptance

2.8 Acceptance within a fixed period of time

2.9 Late acceptance. Delay in transmission

2.10 Withdrawal of acceptance

2.11 Modified acceptance

2.12 Writings in confirmation

2.13 Conclusion of contract dependent on agreement on specific matters or in a specific form

2.14 Contract with terms deliberately left open

2.15 Negotiations in bad faith

2.16 Duty of confidentiality

2.17 Merger clause

2.18 Written modification clause

2.19 Contracting under standard terms

2.20 Surprising terms

2.21 Conflict between standard terms and non-standard terms

2.22 Battle of forms

CHAPTER 3: Validity

3.1 Matters not covered

3.2 Validity of mere agreement

3.3 Initial impossibility

3.4 Definition of mistake

3.5 Relevant Mistake

3.6 Error in expression or transmission

3.7 Remedies for non-performance

3.8 Fraud

3.9 Threat

3.10 Gross disparity

3.11 Third persons

3.12 Confirmation

3.13 Loss of right to avoid

3.14 Notice of avoidance

3.15 Time limits

3.16 Partial avoidance

3.17 Retroactive effect of avoidance

3.18 Damages

3.19 Mandatory character of the provision

3.20 Unilateral declarations

CHAPTER 4: Interpretation

4.1 Intention of the parties

4.2 Interpretation of statements and other conduct

4.3 Relevant Circumstances

4.4 Reference to contract or statement as a whole

4.5 All terms to be given effect

4.6 Contra proferentem rule

4.7 Linguistic discrepancies

4.8 Supplying an omitted term

CHAPTER 5: Content

5.1 Express and implied obligations

5.2 Implied obligations

5.3 Co-operation between the parties

5.4 Duty to achieve a specific result. Duty of best efforts

5.5 Determination of kind of duty involved

5.6 Determination of quality of performance

5.7 Price determination

5.8 Contract for an indefinite period

CHAPTER 6: Performance

Section 1: Performance in general

- 6.1.1 Time of performance
- 6.1.2 Performance at one time or in instalments
- 6.1.3 Partial Performance
- 6.1.4 Order of performance
- 6.1.5 Earlier performance
- 6.1.6 Place of performance
- 6.1.7 Payment by cheque or other instrument
- 6.1.8 Payment by funds transfer
- 6.1.9 Currency of payment
- 6.1.10 Currency not expressed
- 6.1.11 Costs of performance
- 6.1.12 Imputation of payments
- 6.1.13 Imputation of non-monetary obligations
- 6.1.14 Application for public permission
- 6.1.15 Procedure in applying for permission
- 6.1.16 Permission neither granted nor refused
- 6.1.17 Permission refused

Section 2: Hardship

- 6.2.1 Contract to be observed
- 6.2.2 Definition of hardship
- 6.2.3 Effects of hardship

CHAPTER 7: Non-Performance

Section 1: Non-performance in general

- 7.1.1 Non-performance defined
- 7.1.2 Interference by the other party
- 7.1.3 Withholding performance
- 7.1.4 Cure by non-performing party
- 7.1.5 Additional period for performance

7.1.6 Exemption clauses

7.1.7 Force majeure

Section 2: Right to performance

7.2.1 Performance of monetary obligation

7.2.2 Performance of non-monetary obligation

7.2.3 Repair and replacement of defective performance

7.2.4 Judicial penalty

7.2.5 Change of remedy

Section 3: Termination

7.3.1 Right to terminate the contract

7.3.2 Notice of termination

7.3.3 Anticipatory non-performance

7.3.4 Adequate assurance of due performance

7.3.5 Effects of termination in general

7.3.6 Restitution

Section 4: Damages

7.4.1 Right to damages

7.4.2 Full compensation

7.4.3 Certainty of harm

7.4.4 Foreseeability of harm

7.4.5 Proof of harm in case of replacement transaction

7.4.6 Proof of harm by current price

7.4.7 Harm due in part to aggrieved party

7.4.8 Mitigation of harm

7.4.9 Interest for failure to pay money

7.4.10 Interest on damages

7.4.11 Manner of monetary redress

7.4.12 Currency in which to access damages

7.4.13 Agreed payment for non-performance

UNIDROIT Principles for International Commercial Contracts, 1994

4—001   Preamble—Purpose of the Principles

These Principles set forth general rules for international commercial contracts.

They shall be applied when the parties have agreed that their contract be governed by them.

They may be applied when the parties have agreed that their contracts be governed by general principles of law, the lex mercatoria or the like.

They may provide a solution to an issue raised when it proves impossible to establish the relevant rule of applicable law.

They may be used to interpret or supplement international uniform law instruments.

They may serve as a model for national and international legislators.

Chapter 1: General Provisions

4—002   Article 1.1—Freedom of Contract

The parties are free to enter into a contract and determine its content.

4—003   Article 1.2—No Form Required

Nothing in these Principles requires a contract to be concluded in or evidenced by writing. It may be proved by any means, including witnesses.

4—003a   Article 1.3—Binding Character of Contract

A contract validly entered into is binding upon the parties. It can only be modified or terminated in accordance with its terms or by agreement or as otherwise provided in these Principles.

4—004   Article 1.4—Mandatory Rules

Nothing in these Principles shall restrict the application of mandatory rules, whether of national, international or supranational origin, which are applicable in accordance with the relevant rules of private international law.

4—005 **Article 1.5—Exclusion or Modification by the Parties**

The parties may exclude the application of these Principles or derogate from or vary the effect of any of their provisions, except as otherwise provided in the Principles.

4—006 **Article 1.6—Interpretation and supplementation of the Principles**

(1) In the interpretation of these Principles, regard is to be had to their international character and to their purposes including the need to promote uniformity in their application.

(2) Issues within the scope of these Principles but not expressly settled by them are as far as possible to be settled in accordance with their underlying general principles.

4—007 **Article 1.7—Good Faith and Fair Dealing**

(1) Each party must act in accordance with good faith and fair dealing in international trade.

(2) The parties may not exclude or limit this duty.

4—008 **Article 1.8—Usages and Practices**

(1) The parties are bound by any usage to which they have agreed and by any practices which they have established between themselves.

(2) The parties are bound by a usage that is widely known to and regularly observed in international trade by parties in the particular trade concerned except where the application of such usage would be unreasonable.

4—009 **Article 1.9—Notice**

(1) Where notice is required it may be given by any means appropriate to the circumstances.

(2) A notice is effective when it reaches the person to whom it is given.

(3) For the purpose of paragraph (2) a notice "reaches" a person when given to that person orally or delivered at that person's place of business or mailing address.

(4) For the purpose of this article "notice" includes a declaration, demand, request or any other communication of intention.

4—010   Article 1.10—Definitions

In these Principles

>—"court" includes an arbitral tribunal;

>—where a party has more than one place of business the relevant "place of business" is that which has the closest relationship to the contract and its performance, having regard to the circumstances known to or contemplated by the parties at any time before or at the conclusion of the contract;

>—"obligor" refers to the party who is to perform an obligation and "obligee" refers to the party who is entitled to performance of that obligation.

>—"writing" means any mode of communication that preserves a record of the information contained therein and is capable of being reproduced in tangible form.

CHAPTER 2: FORMATION

4—011   Article 2.1—Manner of Formation

A contract may be concluded either by the acceptance of an offer or by conduct of the parties that is sufficient to show agreement.

4—012   Article 2.2—Definition of Offer

A proposal for concluding a contract constitutes an offer if it is sufficiently definite and indicates the intention of the offeror to be bound in case of acceptance.

4—013   Article 2.3—Withdrawal of Offer

> (1) An offer becomes effective when it reaches the offeree.
>
> (2) An offer, even if it is irrevocable, may be withdrawn if the withdrawal reaches the offeree before or at the same time as the offer.

4—014   Article 2.4—Revocation of Offer

> (1) Until a contract is concluded an offer may be revoked if the revocation reaches the offeree before it has dispatched an acceptance.

(2) However, an offer cannot be revoked

    (a) if it indicates, whether by stating a fixed time for acceptance or otherwise, that it is irrevocable; or

    (b) if it was reasonable for the offeree to rely on the offer as being irrevocable and the offeree has acted in reliance on the offer.

4—015   **Article 2.5—Rejection of Offer**

An offer is terminated when a rejection reaches the offeror.

4—016   **Article 2.6—Mode of Acceptance**

(1) A statement made by or other conduct of the offeree indicating assent to an offer is an acceptance. Silence or inactivity does not in itself amount to acceptance.

(2) An acceptance of an offer becomes effective when the indication of assent reaches the offeror.

(3) However, if, by virtue of the offer or as a result of practices which the parties have established between themselves or of usage, the offeree may indicate assent by performing an act without notice to the offeror, the acceptance is effective when the act is performed.

4—017   **Article 2.7—Time of Acceptance**

An offer must be accepted within the time the offeror has fixed or, if no time is fixed, within a reasonable time having regard to the circumstances, including the rapidity of the means of communication employed by the offeror. An oral offer must be accepted immediately unless the circumstances indicate otherwise.

4—018   **Article 2.8—Acceptance Within a Fixed Period of Time**

(1) A period of time for acceptance fixed by the offeror in a telegram or a letter begins to run from the moment the telegram is handed in for dispatch or from the date shown on the letter or, if no such date is shown, from the date shown on the envelope. A period of time for acceptance fixed by the offeror by means of instantaneous communication begins to run from the moment that offer reaches the offeree.

(2) Official holidays or non-business days occurring during the period for acceptance are included in calculating the period.

However, if a notice of acceptance cannot be delivered at the address of the offeror on the last day of the period because that day falls on an official holiday or a non-business day at the place of business of the offeror, the period is extended until the first business day which follows.

4—019 Article 2.9—Late Acceptance Delay in Transmission

(1) A late acceptance is nevertheless effective as an acceptance if without undue delay the offeror so informs the offeree or gives notice to that effect.

(2) If a letter or other writing containing a late acceptance shows that it has been sent in such circumstances that if its transmission had been normal it would have reached the offeror in due time, the late acceptance is effective as an acceptance, unless without undue delay, the offeror informs the offeree that it considers the offer as having lapsed.

4—020 Article 2.10—Withdrawal of Acceptance

An acceptance may be withdrawn if the withdrawal reaches the offeror before or at the same time as the acceptance would have become effective.

4—021 Article 2.11—Modified Acceptance

(1) A reply to an offer which purports to be an acceptance but contains additions, limitations or other modifications is a rejection of the offer and constitutes a counter-offer.

(2) However, a reply to an offer which purports to be an acceptance but contains additional or different terms which do not materially alter the terms of the offer constitutes an acceptance, unless the offeror without undue delay, objects to the discrepancy. If the offeror does not object, the terms of the contract are the terms of the offer with the modifications contained in the acceptance.

4—022 Article 2.12—Writings in Confirmation

If a writing which is sent within a reasonable time after the conclusion of the contract and which purports to be a confirmation of the contract contains additional or different terms, such terms become part of the contract, unless they materially alter the contract or the recipient, without undue delay, objects to the discrepancy.

4—023   Article 2.13—Conclusion of Contract Dependent on Agreement on Specific Matters or in a Specific Form

Where in the course of negotiations one of the parties insists that the contract is not concluded until there is agreement on specific matters or in a specific form, no contract is concluded before agreement is reached on those matters or in that form

4—024   Article 2.14—Contract with Terms Deliberately Left Open

(1) If the parties intend to conclude a contract, the fact that they intentionally leave a term to be agreed upon in further negotiations or to be determined by a third person does not prevent a contract from coming into existence.

(2) The existence of the contract is not affected by the fact that subsequently

(a) the parties reach no agreement on the terms; or
(b) the third person does not determine the term, provided that there is an alternative means of rendering the term definite that is reasonable in the circumstances, having regard to the intention of the parties.

4—025   Article 2.15—Negotiations in Bad Faith

(1) A party is free to negotiate and is not liable for failure to reach an agreement.

(2) However, a party who negotiates or breaks off negotiations in bad faith is liable for the losses caused to the other party.

(3) It is bad faith, in particular, for a party to enter into or continue negotiations when intending not to reach an agreement with the other party.

4—026   Article 2.16—Duty of Confidentiality

Where information is given as confidential by one party in the course of negotiations, the other party is under a duty not to disclose that information or to use it improperly for its own purposes, whether or not a contract is subsequently concluded. Where appropriate, the remedy for breach of that duty may include compensation based on the benefit received by the other party.

4—027   Article 2.17—Merger Clause

A contract in writing which contains a clause indicating that the writing completely embodies the terms on which the parties have agreed cannot be contradicted or supplemented by evidence of prior statements or agreements. However, such statements or agreements may be used to interpret the writing.

4—028   Article 2.18—Written Modification Clauses

A contract in writing which contains a clause requiring any modification or termination by agreement to be in writing may not be otherwise modified or terminated. However, a party may be precluded by its conduct from asserting such a clause to the extent that the other party has acted in reliance on that conduct.

4—029   Article 2.19—Contracting Under Standard Terms

(1) Where one party or both parties use standard terms in concluding a contract, the general rules of formation apply, subject to Articles 2.20—2.22.

(2) Standard terms are provisions which are prepared in advance for general and repeated use by one party and which are actually used without negotiation with the other party.

4—030   Article 2.20—Surprising Terms

(1) No term contained in standard terms which is of such a character that the other party could not reasonably have expected it, is effective unless it has been expressly accepted by that party.

(2) In determining whether a term is of such a character regard is to be had to its content, language and presentation.

4—031   Article 2.21—Conflict Between Standard Terms and Non-Standard Terms

In case of conflict between a standard term which is not a standard term the latter prevails.

4—032   Article 2.22—Battle of Forms

Where both parties use standard terms and reach agreement except on those terms, a contract is concluded on the basis of the agreed terms and of any standard terms which are common in substance unless one party clearly indicates in advance, or later and without undue delay informs the other party, that it does not intend to be bound by such a contract.

Chapter 3: Validity

4—033   Article 3.1—Matters Not Covered

These Principles do not deal with invalidity arising from:

     (a) lack of capacity;

     (b) lack of authority;

     (c) immorality or illegality.

4—034   Article 3.2—Validity of Mere Agreement

A contract is concluded, modified or terminated by the mere agreement of the parties, without any further requirements.

4—035   Article 3.3—Initial Impossibility

     (1) The mere fact that at the time of the conclusion of the contract the performance of the obligation assumed was impossible does not affect the validity of the contract.

     (2) The mere fact that at the time of the conclusion of the contract a party was not entitled to dispose of the assets to which the contract relates does not affect the validity of the contract.

4—036   Article 3.4—Definition of Mistake

Mistake is an erroneous assumption relating to facts or to law existing when the contract was concluded.

4—037   Article 3.5—Relevant Mistake

     (1) A party may only avoid the contract for mistake if, when the contract was concluded, the mistake was of such importance that a reasonable person in the same situation as the party would not have concluded it at all if the true state of affairs had been known, and

          (a) the other party made the same mistake, or caused the mistake, or knew or ought to have known of the mistake

and it was contrary to reasonable commercial standards of fair dealing to leave the mistaken party in error; or
(b) the other party had not at the time of avoidance acted in reliance on the contract

(2) However, a party may not avoid the contract if
(a) it was grossly negligent in committing the mistake; or
(b) the mistake relates to a matter in regard to which the risk of mistake was assumed or, having regard to the circumstances, should be borne by the mistaken party.

4—038   Article 3.6—Error in Expression or Transmission

An error occurring in the expression or transmission of a declaration is considered to be a mistake of the person from whom the declaration emanated.

4—039   Article 3.7—Remedies for Non-Performance

A party is not entitled to avoid the contract on the ground of mistake if the circumstances on which that party relies afford, or could have afforded, a remedy for non-performance.

4—040   Article 3.8—Fraud

A party may avoid the contract when it has been led to conclude the contract by the other party's fraudulent representation, including language or practices, or fraudulent non-disclosure of circumstances which, according to reasonable commercial standards of fair dealing, the latter party should have disclosed.

4—041   Article 3.9—Threat

A party may avoid the contract when it has been led to conclude the contract by the other party's unjustified threat which, having regard to the circumstances, is so imminent and serious as to leave the first party no reasonable alternative. In particular, a threat is unjustified if the act or omission with which a party has been threatened is wrongful in itself, or is wrong to use it as a means to obtain the conclusion of the contract.

4—042   Article 3.10—Gross Disparity

(1) A party may avoid the contract or an individual term of it if, at the time of the conclusion of the contract, the contract

term unjustifiably gave the other party an excessive advantage. Regard is to be had, among other factors, to

(a) the fact that the other party has taken unfair advantage of the first party's dependence, economic distress or urgent needs, or of its improvidence, ignorance, inexperience or lack of bargaining skill; and
(b) the nature and purpose of the contract.

(2) Upon the request of the party entitled to avoidance, a court may adapt the contract or term in order to make it accord with reasonable commercial standards of fair dealing.

(3) A court may also adapt the contract or term upon the request of the party receiving notice of avoidance, provided that that party informs the other party of its request promptly after receiving such notice and before the other party has acted in reliance on it. The provisions of Article 3.13(2) apply accordingly.

4—043   Article 3.11—Third Persons

(1) Where fraud, threat, gross disparity or a party's mistake is imputable to, or is known or ought to be known by, a third person for whose acts the other party is responsible, the contract may be avoided under the same conditions as if the behaviour or knowledge had been that of the party itself.

(2) Where fraud, threat or gross disparity is imputable to a third person for whose acts the other party is not responsible, the contract may be avoided if that party knew or ought to have known of the fraud, threat or disparity, or has not at the time of avoidance acted in reliance on the contract.

4—044   Article 3.12—Confirmation

If the party entitled to avoid the contract expressly or impliedly confirms the contract after the period of time for giving notice of avoidance has begun to run, avoidance of contract is excluded.

4—045   Article 3.13—Loss of Right to Avoid

(1) If a party is entitled to avoid the contract for mistake but the other party declares itself willing to perform or performs the contract as it was understood by the party entitled to avoidance, the contract is considered to have been concluded as the latter party understood it. The other party must make such a

declaration or render such performance promptly after having been informed of the manner in which the party entitled to avoidance had understood the contract and before that party has acted in reliance on a notice of avoidance.

(2) After such a declaration or performance the right to avoidance is lost and any earlier notice of avoidance is ineffective.

4—046   Article 3.14—Notice of Avoidance

The right of a party to avoid the contract is exercised by notice to the other party.

4—047   Article 3.15—Time Limits

(1) Notice of avoidance shall be given within a reasonable time, having regard to the circumstances, after the avoiding party knew or could not have been unaware of the relevant facts or became capable of acting freely.

(2) Where an individual term of the contract may be avoided by a party under Article 3.10, the period of time for giving notice of avoidance begins to run when that term is asserted by the other party.

4—048   Article 3.16—Partial Avoidance

Where a ground of avoidance affects only individual terms of the contract, the effect of avoidance is limited to those terms unless, having regard to the circumstances, it is unreasonable to uphold the remaining contract.

4—049   Article 3.17—Retroactive Effect of Avoidance

(1) Avoidance takes effect retroactively.

(2) On avoidance either party may claim restitution of whatever is supplied under the contract or the part of it avoided, provided that it concurrently makes restitution of whatever it has received under the contract or the part of it avoided or, if it cannot make restitution in kind, it makes an allowance for what it has received.

4—050   Article 3.18—Damages

Irrespective of whether or not the contract has been avoided, the party who knew or ought to have known of the ground for avoidance is liable for damages so as to put the other party in the same position in which it would have been if it had not concluded the contract.

4—051   Article 3.19—Mandatory Character of the Provisions

The provisions of this Chapter are mandatory, except insofar as they relate to the binding force of mere agreement, initial impossibility or mistake.

4—052   Article 3.20—Unilateral Declarations

The provisions of this Chapter apply with appropriate adaptations to any communication of intention addressed by one party to the other.

Chapter 4: Interpretation

4—053   Article 4.1—Intention of the Parties

   (1) A contract shall be interpreted according to the common intention of the parties.

   (2) If such an intention cannot be established, the contract shall be interpreted according to the meaning that reasonable persons of the same kind as the parties would give to it in the same circumstances.

4—054   Article 4.2—Interpretation of Statements and Other Conduct

   (1) The statements and other conduct of a party shall be interpreted according to that party's intention if the other party knew or could not have been unaware of that intention.

   (2) If the preceding paragraph is not applicable, such statements and other conduct shall be interpreted according to the meaning that a reasonable person of the same kind as the other party would give to it in the same circumstances.

4—055   Article 4.3—Relevant Circumstances

In applying Articles 4.1 and 4.2, regard shall be had to all the circumstances, including

(a) preliminary negotiations between the parties;

(b) practices which the parties have established between themselves;

(c) the conduct of the parties subsequent to the conclusion of the contract;

(d) the nature and purpose of the contract;

(e) the meaning commonly given to terms and expressions in the trade concerned;

(f) usages.

4—056   Article 4.4—Reference to Contract or Statement as a Whole

Terms and expressions shall be interpreted in the light of the whole contract or statement in which they appear.

4—057   Article 4.5—All Terms to be Given Effect

Contract terms shall be interpreted so as to give effect to all the terms rather than to deprive some of them of effect.

4—058   Article 4.6—Contra Proferentem Rule

If contract terms supplied by one party are unclear, an interpretation against that party is preferred.

4—059   Article 4.7—Linguistic Discrepancies

Where a contract is drawn up in two or more language versions which are equally authoritative there is, in case of discrepancy between the versions, a preference for the interpretation according to a version in which the contract was originally drawn up.

4—060   Article 4.8—Supplying an Omitted Term

(1) Where the parties to a contract have not agreed with respect to a term which is important for a determination of their rights and duties, a term which is appropriate in the circumstances shall be supplied.

(2) In determining what is an appropriate term regard shall be had, among other factors to

(a) the intention of the parties;
(b) the nature and purpose of the contract;

(c) good faith and fair dealing;
(d) reasonableness.

Chapter 5: Content

4—061   Article 5.1—Express and Implied Obligations

The contractual obligations of the parties may be express or implied.

4—062   Article 5.2—Implied Obligations

Implied obligations stem from

(a) the nature and purpose of the contract;

(b) practices established between the parties and usages;

(c) good faith and fair dealing;

(d) reasonableness.

4—063   Article 5.3—Co-operation between the Parties

Each party shall co-operate with the other party when such co-operation may reasonably be expected for the performance of that party's obligations.

4—064   Article 5.4—Duty to Achieve a Specific Result Duty of Best Efforts

(1) To the extent that an obligation of a party involves a duty to achieve a specific result, that party is bound to achieve that result.

(2) To the extent that an obligation of a party involves a duty of best efforts in the performance of an activity, that party is bound to make such efforts as would be made by a reasonable person of the same kind in the same circumstances.

4—065   Article 5.5—Determination of Kind of Duty Involved

In determining the extent to which an obligation of a party involves a duty of best efforts in the performance of an activity or duty to achieve a specific result, regard shall be had, among other factors, to

(a) the way in which the obligation is expressed in the contract;

(b) the contractual price and other terms of the contract;

(c) the degree of risk normally involved in achieving the expected result;

(d) the ability of the other party to influence the performance of the obligation.

4—066 Article 5.6—Determination of Quality of Performance

Where the quality of performance is neither fixed by, nor determinable from, the contract a party is bound to render a performance of a quality that is reasonable and not less than average in the circumstances.

4—067 Article 5.7—Price Determination

(1) Where a contract does not fix or make provision for determining the price, the parties are considered, in the absence of any indication to the contrary, to have made reference to the price generally charged at the time of the conclusion of the contract for such performance in comparable circumstances in the trade concerned or, if no such price is available, to a reasonable price.

(2) Where the price is to be determined by one party and that determination is manifestly unreasonable, a reasonable price shall be substituted notwithstanding any contract term to the contrary.

(3) Where the price is to be fixed by a third person, and that person cannot or will not do so, the price shall be a reasonable price.

(4) Where the price is to be fixed by reference to factors which do not exist or have ceased to exist or to be accessible, the nearest equivalent factor shall be treated as a substitute.

4—068 Article 5.8—Contract for an Indefinite Period

A contract for an indefinite period may be ended by either party by giving notice a reasonable time in advance.

Chapter 6: Performance

Section 1: Performance in General

4—069 Article 6.1.1—Time of Performance

A party must perform its obligations:

(a) if a time is fixed by or determinable from the contract, at that time;

(b) if a period of time is fixed by or determinable from the contract, at any time within that period unless circumstances indicate that the other party is to choose a time;

(c) in any other case, within a reasonable time after the conclusion of the contract.

4—070 Article 6.1.2—Performance at one Time or in Instalments

In cases under Article 6.1(b) or (c), a party must perform its obligations at one time if that performance can be rendered at one time ad the circumstances do not indicate otherwise.

4—071 Article 6.1.3—Partial Performance

(1) The obligee may reject an offer to perform in part at the time performance is due, whether or not such offer is coupled with an assurance as to the balance of the performance, unless the obligee has no legitimate interest in so doing.

(2) Additional expenses caused to the obligee by partial performance are to be borne by the obligor without prejudice to any other remedy.

4—072 Article 6.1.4—Order of Performance

(1) To the extent that the performances of the parties can be rendered simultaneously, the parties are bound to render them simultaneously unless the circumstances indicate otherwise.

(2) To the extent that the performance of only one party requires a period of time, that party is bound to render its performance first, unless the circumstances indicate otherwise.

4—073   **Article 6.1.5—Earlier Performance**

(1) The obligee may reject an earlier performance unless it has no legitimate interest in so doing.

(2) Acceptability by a party of an earlier performance does not affect the time for the performance of its own obligations if that time has been fixed irrespective of the performance of the other party's obligations.

(3) Additional expenses caused to the obligee by earlier performance are to be borne by the obligor, without prejudice to any other remedy.

4—074   **Article 6.1.6—Place of Performance**

(1) If the place of performance is neither fixed by, nor determinable from the contract, a party is to perform:

(a) a monetary obligation, at the obligee's place of business;
(b) any other obligation, at its own place of business.

(2) A party must bear any increase in the expenses incidental to performance which is caused by a change in its place of business subsequent to the conclusion of the contract.

4—075   **Article 6.1.7—Payment by Cheque or other Instrument**

(1) Payment may be made in any form used in the ordinary course of business at the place for payment.

(2) However, an obligee who accepts, either by virtue of paragraph (1) or voluntarily, a cheque, any other order to pay or a promise to pay, is presumed to do so only on condition that it will be honoured.

4—076   **Article 6.1.8—Payment by Funds Transfer**

(1) Unless the obligee has indicated a particular account, payment may be made by a transfer to any of the financial institutions in which the obligee has made it known that it has an account.

(2) In case of payment by a transfer of the obligation of the obligor is discharged when the transfer to the obligee's financial institution becomes effective.

4—077   Article 6.1.9—Currency of Payment

(1) If a monetary obligation is expressed in a currency other than that of the place of payment, it may be paid by the obligor in the currency of the place for payment unless

(a) the currency is freely convertible; or
(b) the parties have agreed that payment should be made only in the currency in which the monetary obligation is expressed.

(2) If it is impossible for the obligor to make payment in the currency in which the monetary obligation is expressed, the obligee may require payment in the currency of the place for payment, even in the case referred to in paragraph (1)(b).

(3) Payment in the currency of the place for payment is to be made according to the applicable rate of exchange prevailing there when payment is due.

(4) However, if the obligor has not paid at the time when payment is due, the obligee may require payment according to the applicable rate of exchange prevailing either when payment is due or at the time of actual payment.

4—078   Article 6.1.10—Currency Not Expressed

Where a monetary obligation is not expressed in a particular currency, payment must be made in the currency of the place where payment is to be made.

4—079   Article 6.1.11—Costs of Performance

Each party shall bear the costs of performance of its obligations.

4—080   Article 6.1.12—Imputation of Payments

(1) An obligor owing several monetary obligations to the same obligee may specify at the time of payment the debt to which it intends the payment to be applied. However, the payment discharges first any expenses, then interest due and finally the principal.

(2) If the obligor makes no such specification, the obligee may, within a reasonable time after payment, declare to the obligor the obligation to which it imputes the payment, provided that the obligation is due and undisputed.

(3) In the absence of imputation under paragraphs (1) or (2), payment is imputed to that obligation which satisfies one of the following criteria and in the order indicated:

    (a) an obligation which is due or which is the first to fall due;
    (b) the obligation for which the obligee has least security;
    (c) the obligation which is the most burdensome for the obligor;
    (d) the obligation which has arisen first.

    If none of the preceding criteria applies, payment is imputed to all the obligations proportionally.

4—081   **Article 6.1.13—Imputation of Non-Monetary Obligations**

Article 6.1.12 applies with appropriate adaptations to the imputation of performance of non-monetary obligations.

4—082   **Article 6.1.14—Application for Public Permission**

Where the law of a State requires a public permission affecting the validity of the contract or its performance and neither that law nor the circumstances indicate otherwise

    (a) if only one party has its place of business in that State, that party shall take the measures necessary to obtain the permission;

    (b) in any other case the party whose performance requires permission shall take the necessary measures.

4—083   **Article 6.1.15—Procedure in Applying for Permission**

(1) The party required to take the measures necessary to obtain the permission shall do so without undue delay and shall bear any expenses incurred.

(2) That party shall whenever appropriate give the other party notice of the grant or refusal of such permission without undue delay.

4—084   **Article 6.1.16—Permission Neither Granted Nor Refused**

(1) If, notwithstanding the fact that the party responsible has taken all measures required, permission is neither granted nor refused within an agreed period or, where no period has

been agreed, within a reasonable time from the conclusion of the contract, either party is entitled to terminate the contract.

(2) Where the permission affects some terms only, paragraph (1) does not apply if, having regard to the circumstances, it is reasonable to uphold the remaining contract even if the permission is refused.

4—085   Article 6.1.17—Permission Refused

(1) The refusal of a permission affecting the validity of the contract renders the contract void. If the refusal affects the validity of some terms only, only such terms are void if, having regard to the circumstances, it is reasonable to uphold the remaining contract.

(2) Where the refusal of a permission renders the performance of the contract impossible in whole or in part, the rules on non-performance apply.

Section 2: Hardship

4—086   Article 6.2.1—Contract to be Observed

Where the performance of a contract becomes more onerous for one of the parties, that party is nevertheless bound to perform its obligations subject to the following provisions on hardship.

4—087   Article 6.2.2—Definition of Hardship

There is hardship where the occurrence of events fundamentally alters the equilibrium of the contract either because the cost of a party's performance has increased or because the value of the performance a party receives has diminished, and

(a) the events occur or become known to the disadvantaged party after the conclusion of the contract;

(b) the events could not reasonably have been taken into account by the disadvantaged party at the time of the conclusion of the contract;

(c) the events are beyond the control of the disadvantaged party; and

(d) the risk of the events was not assumed by the disadvantaged party.

4—088   Article 6.2.3—Effects of Hardship

(1) In case of hardship the disadvantaged party is entitled to request renegotiations. The request shall be made without undue delay and shall indicate the grounds on which it is based.

(2) The request for renegotiation does not itself entitle the disadvantaged party to withhold performance.

(3) Upon failure to reach agreement within a reasonable time either party may resort to the court.

(4) If the court finds hardship it may, if reasonable,

   (a) terminate the contract at a date and on terms to be fixed; or
   (b) adapt the contract with a view to restoring its equilibrium.

CHAPTER 7: NON-PERFORMANCE

Section 1: Non-Performance in General

4—089   Article 7.1.1—Non-Performance Defined

Non-performance is failure by a party to perform any of its obligations under the contract, including defective performance or late performance.

4—090   Article 7.1.2—Interference by the Other Party

A party may not rely on the non-performance of the other party to the extent that such non-performance was caused by the first party's act or omission or by another event as to which the first party bears the risk.

4—091   Article 7.1.3—Withholding Performance

(1) Where the parties are to perform simultaneously, either party may withhold performance until the other party tenders performance.

(2) Where the parties are to perform consecutively, the party that is to perform later may withhold its performance until the first party has performed.

4—092   Article 7.1.4—Cure by Non-Performing Party

(1) The non-performing party may, at its own expense, cure any non-performance, provided that

   (a) without undue delay, it gives notice indicating the proposed manner and timing of the cure;
   (b) cure is appropriate in the circumstances;
   (c) the aggrieved party has no legitimate interest in refusing cure; and
   (d) cure is effected promptly.

(2) The right to cure is not precluded by notice of termination.

(3) Upon effective notice of cure, rights of the aggrieved party that are inconsistent with the nonperforming party's performances are suspended until the time for cure has expired.

(4) The aggrieved party may withhold performance pending cure.

(5) Notwithstanding cure, the aggrieved party retains the right to claim damages for delay as well as for any harm caused or not prevented by the cure.

4—093   Article 7.1.5—Additional Period for Performance

(1) In a case of non-performance the aggrieved party may by notice to the other party allow an additional period of time for performance.

(2) During the additional period the aggrieved party may withhold performance of its own reciprocal obligations and may claim damages but may not resort to any other remedy. If it receives notice from the other party that the latter will not perform within that period, or if upon expiry of that period due performance has not been made, the aggrieved party may resort to any of the remedies that may be available under this Chapter.

(3) Where in a case of delay in performance which is not fundamental the aggrieved party has given notice allowing an additional period of time of reasonable length, it may terminate the contract at the end of that period. If the additional period allowed is not of reasonable length it shall be extended to a reasonable length. The aggrieved party may in its notice provide that if the other party fails to perform within the period allowed by the notice the contract shall automatically terminate.

(4) Paragraph (3) does not apply where the obligation which has not been performed is only a minor part of the contractual obligation of the non-performing party.

4—094   Article 7.1.6 — Exemption Clauses

A clause which limits or excludes one party's liability for non-performance or which permits one party to tender performance substantially different from what the other party reasonably expected may not be invoked if it would be grossly unfair to do so, having regard to the purpose of the contract.

4—095   Article 7.1.7 — Force Majeure

(1) Non-performance by a party is excused if that party proves that the non-performance was due to an impediment beyond its control and that it could not reasonably be expected to have taken the impediment into account at the time of the conclusion of the contract or to have avoided or overcome it or its consequences.

(2) When the impediment is only temporary, the excuse shall have effect for such period as is reasonable having regard to the effect of the impediment on performance of the contract.

(3) The party who fails to perform must give notice to the other party of the impediment and its effect on its ability to perform. If the notice is not received by the other party within a reasonable time after the party who fails to perform knew or ought to have known of the impediment, it is liable for damages resulting from such non-receipt.

(4) Nothing in this article prevents a party from exercising a right to terminate the contract or to withhold performance or request interest on money due.

Section 2: Right to Performance

4—096   Article 7.2.1 — Performance of monetary Obligation

Where a party who is obliged to pay money does not do so, the other may require payment.

4—097   Article 7.2.2—Performance of Non-Monetary Obligation

Where a party who owes an obligation other than one to pay money does not perform, the other party may require performance, unless

    (a) performance is impossible in law or fact;

    (b) performance or, where relevant, enforcement is unreasonably burdensome or expensive;

    (c) the party entitled to performance may reasonably obtain performance from another source;

    (d) performance is of an exclusively personal character; or

    (e) the party entitled to performance does not require performance within a reasonable time after it has, or ought to have, become aware of the non-performance.

4—098   Article 7.2.3—Repair and Replacement of Defective Performance

The right to performance includes in appropriate cases the right to require repair, replacement, or other cure of defective performance. The provisions of Articles 7.2.1 and 7.2.2 apply accordingly.

4—099   Article 7.2.4—Judicial Penalty

    (1) Where the court orders a party to perform, it may also direct that this party pay a penalty if it does not comply with the order.

    (2) The penalty shall be paid to the aggrieved party unless mandatory provisions of the law of the forum provide otherwise. Payment of the penalty to the aggrieved party does not exclude any claim for damages.

4—100   Article 7.2.5—Change of Remedy

    (1) An aggrieved party who has required performance of a non-monetary obligation and who has not received performance within a period fixed or otherwise within a reasonable period of time may invoke any other remedy.

    (2) Where the decision of a court for performance of a non-monetary obligation cannot be enforced, the aggrieved party may invoke any other remedy.

Section 3: Termination

4—101 Article 7.3.1—Right to Terminate the Contract

(1) A party may terminate the contract where the failure of the other party to perform an obligation under the contract amounts to a fundamental performance.

(2) In determining whether a failure to perform an obligation amounts to a fundamental nonperformance regard shall be had, in particular, to whether

  (a) the non-performance substantially deprives the aggrieved party of what it was entitled to expect under the contract unless the other party did not foresee and could not reasonably have foreseen such result;
  (b) strict compliance with the obligation which has not been performed is of essence under the contract;
  (c) the non-performance is intentional or reckless;
  (d) the non-performance gives the aggrieved party reason to believe that it cannot rely on the other party's future performance;
  (e) the non-performing party will suffer disproportionate loss as a result of the preparation or performance if the contract is terminated.

(3) In the case of delay the aggrieved party may also terminate the contract if the other party fails to perform before the time allowed under Article 7.1.5 has expired.

4—102 Article 7.3.2—Notice of Termination

(1) The right of a party to terminate the contract is exercised by notice to the other party.

(2) If performance has been offered late or otherwise does not conform to the contract the aggrieved party will lose its right to terminate the contract unless it gives notice to the other party within a reasonable time after it has or ought to have become aware of the non-conforming performance.

4—103 Article 7.3.3—Anticipatory Non-Performance

Where prior to the date for performance by one of the parties it is clear that there will be a fundamental non-performance by that party, the other party may terminate the contract.

4—104   Article 7.3.4—Adequate Assurance of Due Performance

A party who reasonably believes that there will be a fundamental non-performance by the other party may demand adequate assurance of due performance and may meanwhile withhold its own performance. Where this assurance is not provided within a reasonable time the party demanding it may terminate the contract.

4—105   Article 7.3.5—Effects of Termination in General

(1) Termination of the contract releases both parties from their obligation to effect and to receive future performance.

(2) Termination does not preclude a claim for damages for non-performance.

(3) Termination does not affect any provision in the contract for the settlement of disputes or any other term of the contract which is to operate even after termination.

4—106   Article 7.3.6—Restitution

(1) On termination of contract either party may claim restitution of whatever it has supplied, provided that such party concurrently makes restitution of whatever it has received. If restitution in kind is not possible or appropriate allowance should be made in money whenever reasonable.

(2) However, if performance of the contract has extended over a period of time and the contract is divisible, such restitution can only be claimed for the period after termination has taken effect.

Section 4: Damages

4—107   Article 7.4.1—Right to Damages

Any non-performance gives the aggrieved party a right to damages either exclusively or in conjunction with any other remedies except where the non-performance is excused under these Principles.

4—108   Article 7.4.2—Full Compensation

(1) The aggrieved party is entitled to full compensation for harm sustained as a result of the nonperformance. Such harm includes both any loss which it suffered and any gain of

which it was deprived, taking into account any gain to the aggrieved party resulting from its avoidance of cost or harm.

(2) Such harm may be non-pecuniary and includes, for instance, physical suffering or emotional distress.

4—109   Article 7.4.3—Certainty of Harm

(1) Compensation is due only for harm, including future harm, that is established with a reasonable degree of certainty.

(2) Compensation may be due for the loss of a chance in proportion to the stability of its occurrence.

(3) Where the amount of damages cannot be established with a sufficient degree of certainty, the assessment is at the discretion of the court.

4—110   Article 7.4.4—Foreseeability of Harm

The non-performing party is liable only for harm which it foresaw or could reasonably have foreseen at the time of the conclusion of the contract as bcing likcly to result from its non-performance.

4—111   Article 7.4.5—Proof of Harm in case of Replacement Transaction

Where the aggrieved party has terminated the contract and has made a replacement transaction within a reasonable time and in a reasonable manner it may recover the difference between the contract price and the price of the replacement transaction as well as damages for any further harm.

4—112   Article 7.4.6—Proof of Harm by Current Price

(1) Where the aggrieved party has terminated the contract and has not made a replacement transaction but there is a current price for the performance contracted for, it may recover the difference between the contract price and the price current at the time the contract is terminated as well as damages for any further harm.

(2) Current price is the price generally charged for goods delivered or services rendered in comparable circumstances at the place where the contract should have been performed or, if the re is no current price at that place, the current price at such other place that appears reasonable to take as a reference.

4—113 Article 7.4.7—Harm Due in Part to Aggrieved Party

Where the harm is due in part to an act or omission of the aggrieved party or to another event as to which that party bears the risk, the amount of damages shall be reduced to the extent that these factors have contributed to the harm, having regard to the conduct of the parties.

4—114 Article 7.4.8—Mitigation of Harm

(1) The non-performing party is not liable for harm suffered by the aggrieved party to the extent that the harm could have been reduced by the latter party's taking reasonable steps.

(2) The aggrieved party is entitled to recover any expenses reasonably incurred in attempting to reduce the harm.

4—115 Article 7.4.9—Interest for Failure to Pay Money

(1) I a party does not pay a sum of money when it falls due the aggrieved party is entitled to interest upon that sum from the time when payment is due to the time of payment whether or not the nonpayment is excused.

(2) The rate of interest shall be the average bank short-term lending rate to prime borrowers prevailing for the currency of payment at the place for payment, or where no such rate exists at that place, then the same rate in the State of the currency of payment. In the absence of such a rate at either place the rate of interest shall l be the appropriate rate fixed by the law of the State of the currency of payment.

(3) The aggrieved party is entitled to additional damages if the non-payment caused it a greater harm.

4—116 Article 7.4.10—Interest on Damages

Unless otherwise agreed, interest on damages for non-performance of non-monetary obligations accrues as from the time of non-performance.

4—117 Article 7.4.11—Manner of Monetary Redress

(1) Damages are to be paid in a lump sum. However, they may be payable in instalments where the nature of the harm makes this appropriate.

(2) Damages to be paid in instalments may be indexed.

4—117 Article 7.4.12—Currency in which to Access Damages

Damages are to be assessed either in the currency in which the monetary obligation was expressed or in the currency in which the harm was suffered, whichever is more appropriate.

4—119 Article 7.4.13—Agreed Payment for Non-Performance

(1) Where the contract provides that a party who does not perform is to pay a specified sum to the aggrieved party for such non-performance, the aggrieved party is entitled to that sum irrespective of its actual harm.

(2) However, notwithstanding any agreement to the contrary the specified sum may be reduced to a reasonable amount where it is grossly excessive in relation to the harm resulting from the nonperformance and to the other circumstances.

Principles of European Contract Law

CONTENTS

CHAPTER 1: General Provisions

Section 1: Scope of the Principles

Article

    1.101 Application of the Principles

    1.102 Freedom of Contract

    1.103 Mandatory Law

    1.104 Application to Questions of Consent

    1.105 Usages and Practices

    1.106 Interpretation and Supplementation

Section 2: General Duties

    1.201 Good Faith and Fair Dealing

    1.202 Duty to Co-operate

Section 3: Terminology and Other Provisions

    1.301 Meaning of Terms

    1.302 Reasonableness

    1.303 Notice

    1.304 Computation of Time

    1.305 Imputed Knowledge and Intention

CHAPTER 2: Formation

Section 1 : General Provisions

    2.101 Conditions for the Conclusion of a Contract

    2.102 Intention

    2.103 Sufficient Agreement

    2.104 Terms Not Individually Negotiated

    2.105 Merger Clause

2.106 Written Modification Only

2.107 Promises Binding without Acceptance

Section 2 : Offer and Acceptance

2.201 Offer

2.202 Revocation of an Offer

2.203 Rejection

2.204 Acceptance

2.205 Time of Conclusion of the Contract

2.206 Time Limit for Acceptance

2.207 Late Acceptance

2.208 Modified Acceptance

2.209 Conflicting General Conditions

2.210 Professional's Written Confirmation

2.211 Contracts not Concluded through Offer and Acceptance

Section 3: Liability for negotiations

2.301 Negotiations Contrary to Good Faith

2.302 Breach of Confidentiality

CHAPTER 3: Authority of Agents

Section 1: General Provisions

3.101 Scope of the Chapter

3.102 Categories of Representation

Section 2 : Direct Representation

3.201 Express, Implied and Apparent Authority

3.202 Agent acting in Exercise of its Authority

3.203 Unidentified Principal

3.204 Agent acting without or outside its Authority

3.205 Conflict of Interest

3.206 Subagency

3.207 Ratification by Principal

3.208 Third Party's Right with Respect to Confirmation of Authority

3.209 Duration of Authority

Section 3: Indirect Representation

3.301 Intermediaries not acting in the name of a Principal

3.302 Intermediary's Insolvency or Fundamental Non-performance to Principal

3.303 Intermediary's Insolvency or Fundamental Non-performance to Third Party

3.304 Requirement of Notice

CHAPTER 4: Validity

4.101 Matters not Covered

4.102 Initial Impossibility

4.104 Inaccuracy in Communication

4.105 Adaptation of Contract

4.106 Incorrect Information

4.107 Fraud

4.108 Threats

4.109 Excessive Benefit or Unfair Advantage

4.110 Unfair Terms not Individually Negotiated

4.111 Third Persons

4.112 Notice of Avoidance

4.113 Time Limits

4.114 Confirmation

4.115 Effect of Avoidance

4.116 Partial Avoidance

4.117 Damages

4.118 Exclusion or Restriction of Remedies

4.119 Remedies for Non-performance

CHAPTER 5: Interpretation

5.101 General Rules of Interpretation

5.102 Relevant Circumstances

5.103 Contra Proferentem Rule

5.104 Preference to Negotiated Terms

5.105 Reference to Contract as a Whole

5.106 Terms to Be Given Effect

5.107 Linguistic Discrepancies

CHAPTER 6: Contents and Effects

6.101 Statements giving rise to Contractual Obligations

6.102 Implied Terms

6.103 Simulation

6.104 Determination of Price

6.105 Unilateral Determination by a Party

6.106 Determination by a Third Person

6.107 Reference to a Non Existent Factor

6.108 Quality of Performance

6.109 Contract for an Indefinite Period

6.110 Stipulation in Favour of a Third Party

6.111 Change of Circumstances

CHAPTER 7: Performance

7.101 Place of Performance

7.102 Time of Performance

7.103 Early Performance

7.104 Order of Performance

7.105 Alternative Performance

7.106 Performance by a Third Person

7.107 Form of Payment

7.108 Currency of Payment

7.109 Appropriation of Performance

7.110 Property Not Accepted

7.111 Money not Accepted

7.112 Costs of Performance

CHAPTER 8: Non-Performance and Remedies in General

8.101 Remedies Available

8.102 Cumulation of Remedies

8.103 Fundamental Non-Performance

8.104 Cure by Non-Performing Party

8.105 Assurance of Performance

8.106 Notice Fixing Additional Period for Performance

8.107 Performance Entrusted to Another

8.108 Excuse Due to an Impediment

8.109 Clause Excluding or Restricting Remedies

CHAPTER 9: Particular Remedies for Non-Performance

Section 1: Right to Performance

9.101 Monetary Obligations

9.102 Non-monetary Obligations

9.103 Damages Not Precluded

Section 2: Withholding Performance

9.201 Right to Withhold Performance

Section 3: Termination Of The Contract

9.301 Right to Terminate the Contract

9.302 Contract to be Performed in Parts

9.303 Notice of Termination

9.304 Anticipatory Non-Performance

9.305 Effects of Termination in General

9.306 Property Reduced in Value

9.307 Recovery of Money Paid

9.308 Recovery of Property

9.309 Recovery for Performance that Cannot be Returned

Section 4: Price Reduction

9.401 Right to Reduce Price

Section 5: Damages and Interest

9.501 Right to Damages

9.502 General Measure of Damages

9.503 Foreseeability

9.504 Loss Attributable to Aggrieved Party

9.505 Reduction of Loss

9.506 Substitute Transaction

9.507 Current Price

9.508 Delay in Payment of Money

9.509 Agreed Payment for Non-performance

CHAPTER 10: Plurality of Parties

Section 1: Plurality of debtors

10.101 Solidary, Separate and Communal Obligations

10.102 When Solidary Obligations Arise

10.103 Liability under Separate Obligations

10.104 Communal Obligations. Special Rule when Money claimed for Non-performance

10.105 Apportionment between Solidary Debtors

10.106 Recourse between Solidary Debtors

10.107 Performance, Set-off and Merger in Solidary Obligations

10.108 Release or Settlement in Solidary Obligations

10.109 Effect of Judgment in Solidary Obligations

10.110 Prescription in Solidary Obligations

10.111 Opposability of other Defences in Solidary Obligations

Section 2 : Plurality of creditors

10.201 Solidary, Separate and Communal Claims

10.202 Apportionment of Separate Claims

10.203 Difficulties of executing a Communal Claim

10.204 Apportionment of Solidary Claims

10.205 Regime of Solidary Claims

CHAPTER 11: Assignment of Claims

Section 1: General Principles

11.101 Scope of Chapter

11.102 Contractual Claims Generally Assignable

11.103 Partial Assignment

11.104 Form of Assignment

Section 2: Effects of Assignment As Between Assignor and Assignee

11.201 Rights Transferred to Assignee

11.202 When Assignment Takes Effect

11.203 Preservation of Assignee's Rights Against Assignor

11.204 Undertakings by Assignor

Section 3: Effects of Assignment As Between Assignee and Debtor

11.301 Contractual Prohibition of Assignment

11.302 Other Ineffective Assignments

11.303 Effect on Debtor's Obligation

11.304 Protection Of Debtor

11.305 Competing Demands

11.306 Place of Performance

11.307 Defences and Rights of Set-Off

11.308 Unauthorised Modification not Binding on Assignee

Section 4: Order of Priority between Assignee and Competing Claimants

11.401 Priorities

CHAPTER 12: Substitution of New Debtor: Transfer of Contract

Section 1: Substitution of New Debtor

12.101 Substitution. General rules

12.102 Effects of Substitution on Defences and Securities

Section 2: Transfer of Contract

12.201 Transfer of Contract

CHAPTER 13: Set-Off

13.101 Requirements for Set-Off

13.102 Unascertained Claims

13.103 Foreign Currency Set-Off

13.104 Notice of Set-Off

13.105 Plurality of Claims and Obligations

13.106 Effect of Set-Off

13.107 Exclusion of Right of Set-Off

CHAPTER 14: Prescription

Section 1: General Provision

14.101 Claims subject to Prescription

Section 2: Periods of Prescription and their Commencement

14.201 General Period

14.202 Period for a Claim Established by Legal Proceedings

14.203 Commencement

Section 3: Extension of Period

14.301 Suspension in Case of Ignorance

14.302 Suspension in Case of Judicial and Other Proceedings

14.303 Suspension in Case of Impediment beyond Creditor's Control

14.304 Postponement of Expiry in Case of Negotiations

14.305 Postponement of Expiry in Case of Incapacity

14.306 Postponement of Expiry: Deceased's Estate

14.307 Maximum Length of Period

Section 4: Renewal of Periods

14.401 Renewal by Acknowledgement

14.402 Renewal by Attempted Execution

Section 5: Effects of Prescription

14.501 General Effect

14.502 Effect on Ancillary Claims

14.503 Effect on Set-Off

Section 6: Modification by Agreement

14.601 Agreements Concerning Prescription

CHAPTER 15: Illegality

15.101 Contracts Contrary to Fundamental Principles

15.102 Contracts Infringing Mandatory Rules

15.103 Partial Ineffectiveness

15.104 Restitution

15.105 Damages

CHAPTER 16: Conditions

16.101 Types of Condition

16.102 Interference with Conditions

16.103 Effect of Conditions

CHAPTER 17: Capitalisation of Interest

17.101 When Interest to be Added to Capital

The Principles of European Contract Law

Prepared by the Commission on European Contract Law

As revised in 1999 and supplemented in 2002

CHAPTER 1: GENERAL PROVISIONS

Section 1: Scope of the Principles

4—120   **Article 1.101—Application of the Principles**

(1) These Principles are intended to be applied as general rules of contract law in the European Union.

(2) These Principles will apply when the parties have agreed to incorporate them into their contract or that their contract is to be governed by them.

(3) These Principles may be applied when the parties:

(a) have agreed that their contract is to be governed by "general principles of law", the "lex mercatoria" or the like; or
(b) have not chosen any system or rules of law to govern their contract.

(4) These Principles may provide a solution to the issue raised where the system or rules of law applicable do not do so.

4—121   **Article 1.102—Freedom of Contract**

(1) Parties are free to enter into a contract and to determine its contents, subject to the requirements of good faith and fair dealing, and the mandatory rules established by these Principles.

(2) The parties may exclude the application of any of the Principles or derogate from or vary their effects, except as otherwise provided by these Principles.

4—122   **Article 1.103—Mandatory Law**

(1) Where the law therwise applicable so allows, the parties may choose to have their contract governed by the Principles,

with the effect that national mandatory rules are not applicable.

(2) Effect should nevertheless be given to those mandatory rules of national, supranational and international law which, according to the relevant rules of private international law, are applicable irrespective of the law governing the contract.

4—123   Article 1.104—Application to Questions of Consent

(1) The existence and validity of the agreement of the parties to adopt or incorporate these Principles shall be determined by these Principles.

(2) Nevertheless, a party may rely upon the law of the country in which it has its habitual residence to establish that it did not consent if it appears from the circumstances that it would not be reasonable to determine the effect of the party's conduct in accordance with these Principles.

4—124   Article 1.105—Usages and Practices

(1) The parties are bound by any usage to which they have agreed and by any practice they have established between themselves.

(2) The parties are bound by a usage which would be considered generally applicable by persons in the same situation as the parties, except where the application of such usage would be unreasonable.

4—125   Article 1.106—Interpretation and Supplementation

(1) These Principles should be interpreted and developed in accordance with their purposes. In particular, regard should be had to the need to promote good faith and fair dealing, certainty in contractual relationships and uniformity of application.

(2) Issues within the scope of these Principles but not expressly settled by them are so far as possible to be settled in accordance with the ideas underlying the Principles. Failing this, the legal system applicable by virtue of the rules of private international law is to be applied.

4—126 **Article 1.107—Application of the Principles by Way of Analogy**

These Principles apply with appropriate modifications to agreements to modify or end a contract, to unilateral promises and other statements and conduct indicating intention.

Section 2: General Duties

4—127 **Article 1.201—Good Faith and Fair Dealing**

(1) Each party must act in accordance with good faith and fair dealing.

(2) The parties may not exclude or limit this duty.

4—128 **Article 1.202—Duty to Co-operate**

Each party owes to the other a duty to co-operate in order to give full effect to the contract.

Section 3: Terminology and Other Provisions

4—129 **Article 1.301—Meaning of Terms**

In these Principles, except where the context otherwise requires:

(1) 'act' includes omission;

(2) 'court' includes arbitral tribunal;

(3) an 'intentional' act includes an act done recklessly;

(4) 'non-performance' denotes any failure to perform an obligation under the contract, whether or not excused, and includes delayed performance, defective performance and failure to co-operate in order to give full effect to the contract.

(5) a matter is 'material' if it is one which a reasonable person in the same situation as one party ought to have known would influence the other party in its decision whether to contract on the proposed terms or to contract at all;

(6) 'written' statements include communications made by telegram, telex, telefax and electronic mail and other means of communication capable of providing a readable record of the statement on both sides

4—130   Article 1.302—Reasonableness

Under these Principles reasonableness is to be judged by what persons acting in good faith and in the same situation as the parties would consider to be reasonable. In particular, in assessing what is reasonable the nature and purpose of the contract, the circumstances of the case, and the usages and practices of the trades or professions involved should be taken into account.

4—131   Article 1.303—Notice

    (1) Any notice may be given by any means, whether in writing or otherwise, appropriate to the circumstances.

    (2) Subject to paragraphs (4) and (5), any notice becomes effective when it reaches the addressee.

    (3) A notice reaches the addressee when it is delivered to it or to its place of business or mailing address, or, if it does not have a place of business or mailing address, to its habitual residence

    (4) If one party gives notice to the other because of the other's non-performance or because such non-performance is reasonably anticipated by the first party, and the notice is properly dispatched or given, a delay or inaccuracy in the transmission of the notice or its failure to arrive does not prevent it from having effect. The notice shall have effect from the time at which it would have arrived in normal circumstances.

    (5) A notice has no effect if a withdrawal of it reaches the addressee before or at the same time as the notice.

    (6) In this Article, 'notice' includes the communication of a promise, statement, offer, acceptance, demand, request or other declaration.

4—132   Article 1.304—Computation of Time

    (1) A period of time set by a party in a written document for the addressee to reply or take other action begins to run from the date stated as the date of the document. If no date is shown, the period begins to run from the moment the document reaches the addressee.

    (2) Official holidays and official non-working days occurring during the period are included in calculating the period.

However, if the last day of the period is an official holiday or official non-working day at the address of the addressee, or at the place where a prescribed act is to be performed, the period is extended until the first following working day in that place.

(3) Periods of time expressed in days, weeks, months or years shall begin at 00.00 on the next day and shall end at 24.00 on the last day of the period; but any reply that has to reach the party who set the period must arrive, or other act which is to be done must be completed, by the normal close of business in the relevant place on the last day of the period.

4—133   Article 1.305—Imputed Knowledge and Intention

If any person who with a party's assent was involved in making a contract, or who was entrusted with performance by a party or performed with its assent:

(a) knew or foresaw a fact, or ought to have known or foreseen it; or

(b) acted intentionally or with gross negligence, or not in accordance with good faith and fair dealing,

this knowledge, foresight or behaviour is imputed to the party itself.

CHAPTER 2: FORMATION

Section 1: General Provisions

4—134   Article 2.101—Conditions for the Conclusion of a Contract

(1) A contract is concluded if:
   (a) the parties intend to be legally bound, and
   (b) they reach a sufficient agreement without any further requirement.

(2) A contract need not be concluded or evidenced in writing nor is it subject to any other requirement as to form. The contract may be proved by any means, including witnesses.

4—135   Article 2.102—Intention

The intention of a party to be legally bound by contract is to be determined from the party's statements or conduct as they were reasonably understood by the other party.

4—136   Article 2.103—Sufficient Agreement

(1) There is sufficient agreement if the terms:

  (a) have been sufficiently defined by the parties so that the contract can be enforced, or
  (b) can be determined under these Principles.

(2) However, if one of the parties refuses to conclude a contract unless the parties have agreed on some specific matter, there is no contract unless agreement on that matter has been reached.

4—137   Article 2.104—Terms Not Individually Negotiated

(1) Contract terms which have not been individually negotiated may be invoked against a party who did not know of them only if the party invoking them took reasonable steps to bring them to the other party's attention before or when the contract was concluded.

(2) Terms are not brought appropriately to a party's attention by a mere reference to them in a contract document, even if that party signs the document.

4—138   Article 2.105—Merger Clause

(1) If a written contract contains an individually negotiated clause stating that the writing embodies all the terms of the contract (a merger clause), any prior statements, undertakings or agreements which are not embodied in the writing do not form part of the contract.

(2) If the merger clause is not individually negotiated it will only establish a presumption that the parties intended that their prior statements, undertakings or agreements were not to form part of the contract. This rule may not be excluded or restricted.

(3) The parties' prior statements may be used to interpret the contract. This rule may not be excluded or restricted except by an individually negotiated clause.

(4) A party may by its statements or conduct be precluded from asserting a merger clause to the extent that the other party has reasonably relied on them.

4—139   Article 2.106—Written Modification Only

(1) A clause in a written contract requiring any modification or ending by agreement to be made in writing establishes only a presumption that an agreement to modify or end the contract is not intended to be legally binding unless it is in writing.

(2) A party may by its statements or conduct be precluded from asserting such a clause to the extent that the other party has reasonably relied on them.

4—140   Article 2.107—Promises Binding without Acceptance

A promise which is intended to be legally binding without acceptance is binding.

Section 2: Offer and Acceptance

4—141   Article 2.201—Offer

(1) A proposal amounts to an offer if:
   (a) it is intended to result in a contract if the other party accepts it, and
   (b) it contains sufficiently definite terms to form a contract.

(2) An offer may be made to one or more specific persons or to the public.

(3) A proposal to supply goods or services at stated prices made by a professional supplier in a public advertisement or a catalogue, or by a display of goods, is presumed to be an offer to sell or supply at that price until the stock of goods, or the supplier's capacity to supply the service, is exhausted.

4—142   Article 2.202—Revocation of an Offer

(1) An offer may be revoked if the revocation reaches the offeree before it has dispatched its acceptance or, in cases of acceptance by conduct, before the contract has been concluded under Article 2.205(2) or (3).

(2) An offer made to the public can be revoked by the same means as were used to make the offer.

(3) However, a revocation of an offer is ineffective if:
(a) the offer indicates that it is irrevocable; or
(b) it states a fixed time for its acceptance; or
(c) it was reasonable for the offeree to rely on the offer as being irrevocable and the offeree has acted in reliance on the offer.

4—143   Article 2.203—Rejection

When a rejection of an offer reaches the offeror, the offer lapses..

4—144   Article 2.204—Acceptance

(1) Any form of statement or conduct by the offeree is an acceptance if it indicates assent to the offer.

(2) Silence or inactivity does not in itself amount to acceptance.

4—145   Article 2.205—Time of Conclusion of the Contract

(1) If an acceptance has been dispatched by the offeree the contract is concluded when the acceptance reaches the offeror.

(2) In case of acceptance by conduct, the contract is concluded when notice of the conduct reaches the offeror.

(3) If by virtue of the offer, of practices which the parties have established between themselves, or of a usage, the offeree may accept the offer by performing an act without notice to the offeror, the contract is concluded when the performance of the act begins.

4—146   Article 2.206—Time Limit for Acceptance

(1) In order to be effective, acceptance of an offer must reach the offeror within the time fixed by it.

(2) If no time has been fixed by the offeror acceptance must reach it within a reasonable time.

(3) In the case of an acceptance by an act of performance under art. 2.205 (3), that act must be performed within the time for acceptance fixed by the offeror or, if no such time is fixed, within a reasonable time.

4—147   Article 2.207—Late Acceptance

(1) A late acceptance is nonetheless effective as an acceptance if without delay the offeror informs the offeree that he treats it as such.

(2) If a letter or other writing containing a late acceptance shows that it has been sent in such circumstances that if its transmission had been normal it would have reached the offeror in due time, the late acceptance is effective as an acceptance unless, without delay, the offeror informs the offeree that it considers its offer as having lapsed.

4—148   Article 2.208—Modified Acceptance

(1) A reply by the offeree which states or implies additional or different terms which would materially alter the terms of the offer is a rejection and a new offer.

(2) A reply which gives a definite assent to an offer operates as an acceptance even if it states or implies additional or different terms, provided these do not materially alter the terms of the offer. The additional or different terms then become part of the contract.

(3) However, such a reply will be treated as a rejection of the offer if:

   (a) the offer expressly limits acceptance to the terms of the offer; or
   (b) the offeror objects to the additional or different terms without delay; or
   (c) the offeree makes its acceptance conditional upon the offeror's assent to the additional or different terms, and the assent does not reach the offeree within a reasonable time.

4—149   Article 2.209—Conflicting General Conditions

(1) If the parties have reached agreement except that the offer and acceptance refer to conflicting general conditions of contract, a contract is nonetheless formed. The general conditions form part of the contract to the extent that they are common in substance.

(2) However, no contract is formed if one party:

   (a) has indicated in advance, explicitly, and not by way of general conditions, that it does not intend to be bound by a contract on the basis of paragraph (1); or

(b) without delay, informs the other party that it does not intend to be bound by such contract.

(3) General conditions of contract are terms which have been formulated in advance for an indefinite number of contracts of a certain nature, and which have not been individually negotiated between the parties.

4—150   Article 2.210—Professional's Written Confirmation

If professionals have concluded a contract but have not embodied it in a final document, and one without delay sends the other a writing which purports to be a confirmation of the contract but which contains additional or different terms, such terms will become part of the contract unless:

(a) the terms materially alter the terms of the contract, or

(b) the addressee objects to them without delay.

4—151   Article 2.211—Contracts not Concluded through Offer and Acceptance

The rules in this section apply with appropriate adaptations even though the process of conclusion of a contract cannot be analysed into offer and acceptance.

Section 3: Liability for negotiations

4—152   Article 2.301—Negotiations Contrary to Good Faith

(1) A party is free to negotiate and is not liable for failure to reach an agreement.

(2) However, a party who has negotiated or broken off negotiations contrary to good faith and fair dealing is liable for the losses caused to the other party.

(3) It is contrary to good faith and fair dealing, in particular, for a party to enter into or continue negotiations with no real intention of reaching an agreement with the other party.

4—153   Article 2.302—Breach of Confidentiality

If confidential information is given by one party in the course of negotiations, the other party is under a duty not to disclose that information or use it for its own purposes whether or not a contract is subsequently concluded. The remedy for breach of this duty may include compensation for loss suffered and restitution of the benefit received by the other party.

CHAPTER 3: AUTHORITY OF AGENTS

Section 1: General Provisions

4—154   Article 3.101—Scope of the Chapter

(1) This Chapter governs the authority of an agent or other intermediary to bind its principal in relation to a contract with a third party.

(2) This Chapter does not govern an agent's authority bestowed by law or the authority of an agent appointed by a public or judicial authority.

(3) This Chapter does not govern the internal relationship between the agent or intermediary and its principal.

4—155   Article 3.102—Categories of Representation

(1) Where an agent acts in the name of a principal, the rules on direct representation apply (Section 2). It is irrelevant whether the principal's identity is revealed at the time the agent acts or is to be revealed later.

(2) Where an intermediary acts on instructions and on behalf of, but not in the name of, a principal, or where the third party neither knows nor has reason to know that the intermediary acts as an agent, the rules on indirect representation apply (Section 3).

Section 2: Direct Representation

4—156   Article 3.201—Express, Implied and Apparent Authority

(1) The principal's grant of authority to an agent to act in its name may be express or may be implied from the circumstances.

(2) The agent has authority to perform all acts necessary in the circumstances to achieve the purposes for which the authority was granted.

A person is to be treated as having granted authority to an apparent agent if the person's statements or conduct induce the third party reasonably and in good faith to believe that the apparent agent has been granted authority for the act performed by it.

4—157   Article 3.202—Agent acting in Exercise of its Authority

Where an agent is acting within its authority as defined by article 3.201, its acts bind the principal and the third party directly to each other. The agent itself is not bound to the third party.

4—158   Article 3.203—Unidentified Principal

If an agent enters into a contract in the name of a principal whose identity is to be revealed later, but fails to reveal that identity within a reasonable time after a request by the third party, the agent itself is bound by the contract.

4—159   Article 3.204—Agent acting without or outside its Authority

(1) Where a person acting as an agent acts without authority or outside the scope of its authority, its acts are not binding upon the principal and the third party.

(2) Failing ratification by the principal according to article 3.207, the agent is liable to pay the third party such damages as will place the third party in the same position as if the agent had acted with authority. This does not apply if the third party knew or could not have been unaware of the agent's lack of authority.

4—160   Article 3.205—Conflict of Interest

(1) If a contract concluded by an agent involves the agent in a conflict of interest of which the third party knew or could not have been unaware, the principal may avoid the contract according to the provisions of articles 4.112 to 4.116.

(2) There is presumed to be a conflict of interest where:

(a) the agent also acted as agent for the third party; or
(b) the contract was with itself in its personal capacity.

(3) However, the principal may not avoid the contract:

(a) if it had consented to, or could not have been unaware of, the agent's so acting; or

(b) if the agent had disclosed the conflict of interest to it and it had not objected within a reasonable time.

4—161   Article 3.206—Subagency

An agent has implied authority to appoint a subagent to carry out tasks which are not of a personal character and which it is not reasonable to expect the agent to carry out itself. The rules of this Section apply to the subagency; acts of the subagent which are within its and the agent's authority bind the principal and the third party directly to each other.

4—162   Article 3.207—Ratification by Principal

(1) Where a person acting as an agent acts without authority or outside its authority, the principal may ratify the agent's acts.

(2) Upon ratification, the agent's acts are considered as having been authorised, without prejudice to the rights of other persons.

4—163   Article 3.208—Third Party's Right with Respect to Confirmation of Authority

Where the statements or conduct of the principal gave the third party reason to believe that an act performed by the agent was authorised, but the third party is in doubt about the authorisation, it may send a written confirmation to the principal or request ratification from it. If the principal does not object or answer the request without delay, the agent's act is treated as having been authorised.

4—164   Article 3.209—Duration of Authority

(1) An agent's authority continues until the third party knows or ought to know that:
   (a) the agent's authority has been brought to an end by the principal, the agent, or both; or
   (b) the acts for which the authority had been granted have been completed, or the time for which it had been granted has expired; or
   (c) the agent has become insolvent or, where a natural person, has died or become incapacitated; or
   (d) the principal has become insolvent.

(2) The third party is considered to know that the agent's authority has been brought to an end under paragraph(1) (a) above if this has been communicated or publicised in the same

manner in which the authority was originally communicated or publicised.

(3) However, the agent remains authorised for a reasonable time to perform those acts which are necessary to protect the interests of the principal or its successors.

Section 3: Indirect Representation

4—165 **Article 3.301—Intermediaries not acting in the name of a Principal**

(1) Where an intermediary acts:

(a) on instructions and on behalf, but not in the name, of a principal, or
(b) on instructions from a principal but the third party does not know and has no reason to know this, the intermediary and the third party are bound to each other.

(2) The principal and the third party are bound to each other only under the conditions set out in Articles 3.302 to 3.304.

4—166 **Article 3.302—Intermediary's Insolvency or Fundamental Non-performance to Principal**

If the intermediary becomes insolvent, or if it commits a fundamental non-performance towards the principal, or if prior to the time for performance it is clear that there will be a fundamental non-performance:

(a) on the principal's demand, the intermediary shall communicate the name and address of the third party to the principal; and

(b) the principal may exercise against the third party the rights acquired on the principal's behalf by the intermediary, subject to any defences which the third party may set up against the intermediary.

4—167 **Article 3.303—Intermediary's Insolvency or Fundamental Non-performance to Third Party**

If the intermediary becomes insolvent, or if it commits a fundamental non-performance towards the third party, or if prior to the time for performance it is clear that there will be a fundamental non-performance:

(a) on the third party's demand, the intermediary shall communicate the name and address of the principal to the third party; and

(b) the third party may exercise against the principal the rights which the third party has against the intermediary, subject to any defences which the intermediary may set up against the third party and those which the principal may set up against the intermediary.

4—168   Article 3.304—Requirement of Notice

The rights under Articles 3.302 and 3.303 may be exercised only if notice of intention to exercise them is given to the intermediary and to the third party or principal, respectively. Upon receipt of the notice, the third party or the principal is no longer entitled to render performance to the intermediary.

Chapter 4: Validity

4—169   Article 4.101—Matters not Covered

This chapter does not deal with invalidity arising from illegality, immorality or lack of capacity.

4—170   Article 4.102—Initial Impossibility

A contract is not invalid merely because at the time it was concluded performance of the obligation assumed was impossible, or because a party was not entitled to dispose of the assets to which the contract relates.

4—171   Article 4.103—Fundamental Mistake as to Facts or Law

(1) A party may avoid a contract for mistake of fact or law existing when the contract was concluded if:

(a) (i) the mistake was caused by information given by the other party; or

(ii) the other party knew or ought to have known of the mistake and it was contrary to good faith and fair dealing to leave the mistaken party in error; or

(iii) the other party made the same mistake, and

(b) the other party knew or ought to have known that the mistaken party, had it known the truth, would not have entered the contract or would have done so only on fundamentally different terms.

(2) However a party may not avoid the contract if:
(a) in the circumstances its mistake was inexcusable, or
(b) the risk of the mistake was assumed, or in the circumstances should be borne, by it.

4—172   Article 4.104—Inaccuracy in Communication

An inaccuracy in the expression or transmission of a statement is to be treated as a mistake of the person who made or sent the statement and Article 4.103 applies.

4—173   Article 4.105—Adaptation of Contract

(1) If a party is entitled to avoid the contract for mistake but the other party indicates that it is willing to perform, or actually does perform, the contract as it was understood by the party entitled to avoid it, the contract is to be treated as if it had been concluded as the that party understood it. The other party must indicate its willingness to perform, or render such performance, promptly after being informed of the manner in which the party entitled to avoid it understood the contract and before that party acts in reliance on any notice of avoidance.

(2) After such indication or performance the right to avoid is lost and any earlier notice of avoidance is ineffective.

(3) Where both parties have made the same mistake, the court may at the request of either party bring the contract into accordance with what might reasonably have been agreed had the mistake not occurred.

4—174   Article 4.106—Incorrect Information

A party who has concluded a contract relying on incorrect information given it by the other party may recover damages in accordance with Article 4.117(2) and (3) even if the information does not give rise to a fundamental mistake under Article 4.103, unless the party who gave the information had reason to believe that the information was correct.

4—175   Article 4.107—Fraud

(1) A party may avoid a contract when it has been led to conclude it by the other party's fraudulent representation,

whether by words or conduct, or fraudulent non-disclosure of any information which in accordance with good faith and fair dealing it should have disclosed.

(2) A party's representation or non-disclosure is fraudulent if it was intended to deceive.

(3) In determining whether good faith and fair dealing required that a party disclose particular information, regard should be had to all the circumstances, including:

(a) whether the party had special expertise;
(b) the cost to it of acquiring the relevant information;
(c) whether the other party could reasonably acquire the information for itself; and
(d) the apparent importance of the information to the other party.

4—176   Article 4.108—Threats

A party may avoid a contract when it has been led to conclude it by the other party's imminent and serious threat of an act:

(a) which is wrongful in itself, or
(b) which it is wrongful to use as a means to obtain the conclusion of the contract, unless in the circumstances the first party had a reasonable alternative.

4—177   Article 4.109—Excessive Benefit or Unfair Advantage

(1) A party may avoid a contract if, at the time of the conclusion of the contract:

(a) it was dependent on or had a relationship of trust with the other party, was in economic distress or had urgent needs, was improvident, ignorant, inexperienced or lacking in bargaining skill, and
(b) the other party knew or ought to have known of this and, given the circumstances and purpose of the contract, took advantage of the first party's situation in a way which was grossly unfair or took an excessive benefit.

(2) Upon the request of the party entitled to avoidance, a court may if it is appropriate adapt the contract in order to bring it into accordance with what might have been agreed had the requirements of good faith and fair dealing been followed.

(3) A court may similarly adapt the contract upon the request of a party receiving notice of avoidance for excessive benefit or unfair advantage, provided that this party informs the party who gave the notice promptly after receiving it and before that party has acted in reliance on it.

4—178 **Article 4.110—Unfair Terms not Individually Negotiated**

(1) A party may avoid a term which has not been individually negotiated if, contrary to the requirements of good faith and fair dealing, it causes a significant imbalance in the parties' rights and obligations arising under the contract to the detriment of that party, taking into account the nature of the performance to be rendered under the contract, all the other terms of the contract and the circumstances at the time the contract was concluded.

(2) This Article does not apply to:
   (a) a term which defines the main subject matter of the contract, provided the term is in plain and intelligible language; or to
   (b) the adequacy in value of one party's obligations compared to the value of the obligations of the other party.

4—179 **Article 4.111—Third Persons**

(1) Where a third person for whose acts a party is responsible, or who with a party's assent is involved in the making of a contract:
   (a) causes a mistake by giving information, or knows of or ought to have known of a mistake,
   (b) gives incorrect information,
   (c) commits fraud,
   (d) makes a threat, or
   (e) takes excessive benefit or unfair advantage, remedies under this Chapter will be available under the same conditions as if the behaviour or knowledge had been that of the party itself.
   (a) gives incorrect information,
   (b) commits fraud,
   (c) makes a threat, or
   (d) takes excessive benefit or unfair advantage, remedies under this Chapter will be available if the party knew or ought to have known of the relevant facts, or at the time of avoidance it has not acted in reliance on the contract.

4—180   Article 4.112—Notice of Avoidance

Avoidance must be by notice to the other party.

4—181   Article 4.113—Time Limits

> (1) Notice of avoidance must be given within a reasonable time, with due regard to the circumstances, after the avoiding party knew or ought to have known of the relevant facts or became capable of acting freely.
>
> (2) However, a party may avoid an individual term under Article 4.110 if it gives notice of avoidance within a reasonable time after the other party has invoked the term.

4—182   Article 4.114—Confirmation

If the party who is entitled to avoid a contract confirms it, expressly or impliedly, after it knows of the ground for avoidance, or becomes capable of acting freely, avoidance of the contract is excluded.

4—183   Article 4.115—Effect of Avoidance

On avoidance either party may claim restitution of whatever it has supplied under the contract, provided it makes concurrent restitution of whatever it has received. If restitution cannot be made in kind for any reason, a reasonable sum must be paid for what has been received.

4—184   Article 4.116—Partial Avoidance

If a ground of avoidance affects only particular terms of a contract, the effect of an avoidance is limited to those terms unless, giving due consideration to all the circumstances of the case, it is unreasonable to uphold the remaining contract.

4—185   Article 4.117—Damages

> (1) A party who avoids a contract under this Chapter may recover from the other party damages so as to put the avoiding party as nearly as possible into the same position as if it had not concluded the contract, provided that the other party knew or ought to have known of the mistake, fraud, threat or taking of excessive benefit or unfair advantage.
>
> (2) If a party has the right to avoid a contract under this Chapter, but does not exercise its right or has lost its right under the

provisions of Articles 4.113 or 4.114, it may recover, subject to paragraph (1), damages limited to the loss caused to it by the mistake, fraud, threat or taking of excessive benefit or unfair advantage. The same measure of damages shall apply when the party was misled by incorrect information in the sense of Article 4.106.

(3) In other respects, the damages shall be in accordance with the relevant provisions of Chapter 9, Section 5, with appropriate adaptations.

4—186 Article 4.118—Exclusion or Restriction of Remedies

(1) Remedies for fraud, threats and excessive benefit or unfair advantage-taking, and the right to avoid an unfair term which has not been individually negotiated, cannot be excluded or restricted.

(2) Remedies for mistake and incorrect information may be excluded or restricted unless the exclusion or restriction is contrary to good faith and fair dealing.

4—187 Article 4.119—Remedies for Non-performance

A party who is entitled to a remedy under this Chapter in circumstances which afford that party a remedy for non-performance may pursue either remedy.

CHAPTER 5: INTERPRETATION

4—188 Article 5.101—General Rules of Interpretation

(1) A contract is to be interpreted according to the common intention of the parties even if this differs from the literal meaning of the words.

(2) If it is established that one party intended the contract to have a particular meaning, and at the time of the conclusion of the contract the other party could not have been unaware of the first party's intention, the contract is to be interpreted in the way intended by the first party.

(3) If an intention cannot be established according to (1) or (2), the contract is to be interpreted according to the meaning that reasonable persons of the same kind as the parties would give to it in the same circumstances.

4—189   Article 5.102—Relevant Circumstances

In interpreting the contract, regard shall be had, in particular, to:

- (a) the circumstances in which it was concluded, including the preliminary negotiations;
- (b) the conduct of the parties, even subsequent to the conclusion of the contract;
- (c) the nature and purpose of the contract;
- (d) the interpretation which has already been given to similar clauses by the parties and the practices they have established between themselves;
- (e) the meaning commonly given to terms and expressions in the branch of activity concerned and the interpretation similar clauses may already have received;
- (f) usages; and
- (g) good faith and fair dealing

4—190   Article 5.103—Contra Proferentem Rule

Where there is doubt about the meaning of a contract term not individually negotiated, an interpretation of the term against the party who supplied it is to be preferred.

4—191   Article 5.104—Preference to Negotiated Terms

Terms which have been individually negotiated take preference over those which are not.

4—192   Article 5.105—Reference to Contract as a Whole

Terms are to be interpreted in the light of the whole contract in which they appear.

4—193   Article 5.106—Terms to Be Given Effect

An interpretation which renders the terms of the contract lawful, or effective, is to be preferred to one which would not.

4—194   Article 5.107—Linguistic Discrepancies

Where a contract is drawn up in two or more language versions none of which is stated to be authoritative, there is, in case of discrepancy between the versions, a preference for the interpretation according to the version in which the contract was originally drawn up.

CHAPTER 6: CONTENTS AND EFFECTS

4—195   Article 6.101—Statements giving rise to Contractual Obligations

    (1) A statement made by one party before or when the contract is concluded is to be treated as giving rise to a contractual obligation if that is how the other party reasonably understood it in the circumstances, taking into account:

        (a) the apparent importance of the statement to the other party;
        (b) whether the party was making the statement in the course of business; and
        (c) the relative expertise of the parties.

    (2) If one of the parties is a professional supplier who gives information about the quality or use of services or goods or other property when marketing or advertising them or otherwise before the contract for them is concluded, the statement is to be treated as giving rise to a contractual obligation unless it is shown that the other party knew or could not have been unaware that the statement was incorrect.

    (3) Such information and other undertakings given by a person advertising or marketing services, goods or other property for the professional supplier, or by a person in earlier links of the business chain, are to be treated as giving rise to a contractual obligation on the part of the professional supplier unless it did not know and had no reason to know of the information or undertaking.

4—196   Article 6.102—Implied Terms

In addition to the express terms, a contract may contain implied terms which stem from

    (a) the intention of the parties,
    (b) the nature and purpose of the contract, and
    (c) good faith and fair dealing.

4—197   Article 6.103—Simulation

When the parties have concluded an apparent contract which was not intended to reflect their true agreement, as between the parties the true agreement prevails.

4—198   Article 6.104—Determination of Price

Where the contract does not fix the price or the method of determining it, the parties are to be treated as having agreed on a reasonable price.

4—199   Article 6.105—Unilateral Determination by a Party

Where the price or any other contractual term is to be determined by one party whose determination is grossly unreasonable, then notwithstanding any provision to the contrary, a reasonable price or other term shall be substituted.

4—200   Article 6.106—Determination by a Third Person

(1) Where the price or any other contractual term is to be determined by a third person, and it cannot or will not do so, the parties are presumed to have empowered the court to appoint another person to determine it.

(2) If a price or other term fixed by a third person is grossly unreasonable, a reasonable price or term shall be substituted.

4—201   Article 6.107—Reference to a Non Existent Factor

Where the price or any other contractual term is to be determined by reference to a factor which does not exist or has ceased to exist or to be accessible, the nearest equivalent factor shall be substituted.

4—202   Article 6.108—Quality of Performance

If the contract does not specify the quality, a party must tender performance of at least average quality.

4—203   Article 6.109—Contract for an Indefinite Period

A contract for an indefinite period may be ended by either party by giving notice of reasonable length.

4—204 Article 6.110—Stipulation in Favour of a Third Party

(1) A third party may require performance of a contractual obligation when its right to do so has been expressly agreed upon between the promisor and the promisee, or when such agreement is to be inferred from the purpose of the contract or the circumstances of the case. The third party need not be identified at the time the agreement is concluded.

(2) If the third party renounces the right to performance the right is treated as never having accrued to it.

(3) The promisee may by notice to the promisor deprive the third party of the right to performance unless:

(a) the third party has received notice from the promisee that the right has been made irrevocable, or
(b) the promisor or the promisee has received notice from the third party that the latter accepts the right.

4—205 Article 6.111—Change of Circumstances

(1) A party is bound to fulfil its obligations even if performance has become more onerous, whether because the cost of performance has increased or because the value of the performance it receives has diminished.

(2) If, however, performance of the contract becomes excessively onerous because of a change of circumstances, the parties are bound to enter into negotiations with a view to adapting the contract or terminating it, provided that:

(a) the change of circumstances occurred after the time of conclusion of the contract,
(b) the possibility of a change of circumstances was not one which could reasonably have been taken into account at the time of conclusion of the contract, and
(c) the risk of the change of circumstances is not one which, according to the contract, the party affected should be required to bear.

(3) If the parties fail to reach agreement within a reasonable period, the court may:

(a) end the contract at a date and on terms to be determined by the court ; or
(b) adapt the contract in order to distribute between the parties in a just and equitable manner the losses and gains resulting from the change of circumstances. In either case, the court may award damages for the loss

suffered through a party refusing to negotiate or breaking off negotiations contrary to good faith and fair dealing.

Chapter 7: Performance

4—206   Article 7.101—Place of Performance

(1) If the place of performance of a contractual obligation is not fixed by or determinable from the contract it shall be:
  (a) in the case of an obligation to pay money, the creditor's place of business at the time of the conclusion of the contract;
  (b) in the case of an obligation other than to pay money, the debtor's place of business at the time of conclusion of the contract.

(2) If a party has more than one place of business, the place of business for the purpose of the preceding paragraph is that which has the closest relationship to the contract, having regard to the circumstances known to or contemplated by the parties at the time of conclusion of the contract.

(3) If a party does not have a place of business its habitual residence is to be treated as its place of business.

4—206A   Article 7.102—Time of Performance

A party has to effect its performance:

(1) if a time is fixed by or determinable from the contract, at that time;

(2) if a period of time is fixed by or determinable from the contract, at any time within that period unless the circumstances of the case indicate that the other party is to choose the time;

(3) in any other case, within a reasonable time after the conclusion of the contract.

4—207   Article 7.103—Early Performance

(1) A party may decline a tender of performance made before it is due except where acceptance of the tender would not unreasonably prejudice its interests.

(2) A party's acceptance of early performance does not affect the time fixed for the performance of its own obligation.

4—208 Article 7.104—Order of Performance

To the extent that the performances of the parties can be rendered simultaneously, the parties are bound to render them simultaneously unless the circumstances indicate otherwise.

4—209 Article 7.105—Alternative Performance

(1) Where an obligation may be discharged by one of alternative performances, the choice belongs to the party who is to perform, unless the circumstances indicate otherwise.

(2) If the party who is to make the choice fails to do so by the time required by the contract, then:
(a) if the delay in choosing is fundamental, the right to choose passes to the other party;
(b) if the delay is not fundamental, the other party may give a notice fixing an additional period of reasonable length in which the party to choose must do so. If the latter fails to do so, the right to choose passes to the other party.

4—210 Article 7.106—Performance by a Third Person

(1) Except where the contract requires personal performance the creditor cannot refuse performance by a third person if:
(a) the third person acts with the assent of the debtor; or
(b) the third person has a legitimate interest in performance and the debtor has failed to perform or it is clear that it will not perform at the time performance is due.

(2) Performance by the third person in accordance with paragraph (1) discharges the debtor.

4—211 Article 7.107—Form of Payment

(1) Payment of money due may be made in any form used in the ordinary course of business.

(2) A creditor who, pursuant to the contract or voluntarily, accepts a cheque or other order to pay or a promise to pay is presumed to do so only on condition that it will be honoured. The creditor may not enforce the original obligation to pay unless the order or promise is not honoured.

4—212   **Article 7.108—Currency of Payment**

(1) The parties may agree that payment shall be made only in a specified currency.

(2) In the absence of such agreement, a sum of money expressed in a currency other than that of the place where payment is due may be paid in the currency of that place according to the rate of exchange prevailing there at the time when payment is due.

(3) If, in a case falling within the preceding paragraph, the debtor has not paid at the time when payment is due, the creditor may require payment in the currency of the place where payment is due according to the rate of exchange prevailing there either at the time when payment is due or at the time of actual payment.

4—213   **Article 7.109—Appropriation of Performance**

Where a party has to perform several obligations of the same nature and the performance tendered does not suffice to discharge all of the obligations, then subject to paragraph 4 the party may at the time of its performance declare to which obligation the performance is to be appropriated.

If the performing party does not make such a declaration, the other party may within a reasonable time appropriate the performance to such obligation as it chooses. It shall inform the performing party of the choice. However, any such appropriation to an obligation which:

(a) is not yet due, or

(b) is illegal, or

(c) is disputed,

is invalid.

In the absence of an appropriation by either party, and subject to paragraph 4, the performance is appropriated to that obligation which satisfies one of the following criteria in the sequence indicated:

- the obligation which is due or is the first to fall due;
- the obligation for which the creditor has the least security;
- the obligation which is the most burdensome for the debtor
- the obligation which has arisen first.

If none of the preceding criteria applies, the performance is appropriated proportionately to all obligations.

- In the case of a monetary obligation, a payment by the debtor is to be appropriated, first, to expenses, secondly, to interest, and thirdly, to principal, unless the creditor makes a different appropriation.

4—214   Article 7.110—Property Not Accepted

(1) A party who is left in possession of tangible property other than money because of the other party's failure to accept or retake the property must take reasonable steps to protect and preserve the property.

(2) The party left in possession may discharge its duty to deliver or return:

   (a) by depositing the property on reasonable terms with a third person to be held to the order of the other party, and notifying the other party of this; or
   (b) by selling the property on reasonable terms after notice to the other party, and paying the net proceeds to that party.

(3) Where, however, the property is liable to rapid deterioration or its preservation is unreasonably expensive, the party must take reasonable steps to dispose of it. It may discharge its duty to deliver or return by paying the net proceeds to the other party.

(4) The party left in possession is entitled to be reimbursed or to retain out of the proceeds of sale any expenses reasonably incurred.

4—215   Article 7.111—Money not Accepted

Where a party fails to accept money properly tendered by the other party, that party may after notice to the first party discharge its obligation to pay by depositing the money to the order of the first party in accordance with the law of the place where payment is due.

4—215a   Article 7.112—Costs of Performance

Each party shall bear the costs of performance of its obligations.

Chapter 8: Non-Performance and Remedies in General

4—216 **Article 8.101—Remedies Available**

(1) Whenever a party does not perform an obligation under the contract and the non-performance is not excused under Article 8.108, the aggrieved party may resort to any of the remedies set out in Chapter 9.

(2) Where a party's non-performance is excused under Article 8.108, the aggrieved party may resort to any of the remedies set out in Chapter 9 except claiming performance and damages.

(3) A party may not resort to any of the remedies set out in Chapter 9 to the extent that its own act caused the other party's non-performance.

4—217 **Article 8.102—Cumulation of Remedies**

Remedies which are not incompatible may be cumulated. In particular, a party is not deprived of its right to damages by exercising its right to any other remedy.

4—218 **Article 8.103—Fundamental Non-Performance**

A non-performance of an obligation is fundamental to the contract if:

(a) strict compliance with the obligation is of the essence of the contract; or

(b) the non-performance substantially deprives the aggrieved party of what it was entitled to expect under the contract, unless the other party did not foresee and could not reasonably have foreseen that result; or

(c) the non-performance is intentional and gives the aggrieved party reason to believe that it cannot rely on the other party's future performance.

4—219 **Article 8.104—Cure by Non-Performing Party**

A party whose tender of performance is not accepted by the other party because it does not conform to the contract may make a new and conforming tender where the time for performance has not yet arrived or the delay would not be such as to constitute a fundamental non-performance.

4—220   Article 8.105—Assurance of Performance

(1) A party who reasonably believes that there will be a fundamental non-performance by the other party may demand adequate assurance of due performance and meanwhile may withhold performance of its own obligations so long as such reasonable belief continues.

(2) Where this assurance is not provided within a reasonable time, the party demanding it may terminate the contract if it still reasonably believes that there will be a fundamental non-performance by the other party and gives notice of termination without delay.

4—221   Article 8.106—Notice Fixing Additional Period for Performance

(1) In any case of non-performance the aggrieved party may by notice to the other party allow an additional period of time for performance.

(2) During the additional period the aggrieved party may withhold performance of its own reciprocal obligations and may claim damages, but it may not resort to any other remedy. If it receives notice from the other party that the latter will not perform within that period, or if upon expiry of that period due performance has not been made, the aggrieved party may resort to any of the remedies that may be available under chapter 9.

(3) If in a case of delay in performance which is not fundamental the aggrieved party has given a notice fixing an additional period of time of reasonable length, it may terminate the contract at the end of the period of notice. The aggrieved party may in its notice provide that if the other party does not perform within the period fixed by the notice the contract shall terminate automatically. If the period stated is too short, the aggrieved party may terminate, or, as the case may be, the contract shall terminate automatically, only after a reasonable period from the time of the notice.

4—222   Article 8.107—Performance Entrusted to Another

A party who entrusts performance of the contract to another person remains responsible for performance.

4—223   **Article 8.108—Excuse Due to an Impediment**

(1) A party's non-performance is excused if it proves that it is due to an impediment beyond its control and that it could not reasonably have been expected to take the impediment into account at the time of the conclusion of the contract, or to have avoided or overcome the impediment or its consequences.

(2) Where the impediment is only temporary the excuse provided by this Article has effect for the period during which the impediment exists. However, if the delay amounts to a fundamental non-performance, the creditorr may treat it as such.

(3) The non-performing party must ensure that notice of the impediment and of its effect on its ability to perform is received by the other party within a reasonable time after the non-performing party knew or ought to have known of these circumstances. The other party is entitled to damages for any loss resulting from the non-receipt of such notice.

4—224   **Article 8.109—Clause Excluding or Restricting Remedies**

Remedies for non-performance may be excluded or restricted unless it would be contrary to good faith and fair dealing to invoke the exclusion or restriction.

CHAPTER 9: PARTICULAR REMEDIES FOR NON-PERFORMANCE

Section 1: Right to Performance

4—225   **Article 9.101—Monetary Obligations**

(1) The creditor is entitled to recover money which is due.

(2) Where the creditor has not yet performed its obligation and it is clear that the debtor will be unwilling to receive performance, the creditor may nonetheless proceed with its performance and may recover any sum due under the contract unless:

(a) it could have made a reasonable substitute transaction without significant effort or expense; or
(b) performance would be unreasonable in the circumstances.

4—226　Article 9.102—Non-monetary Obligations

(1) The aggrieved party is entitled to specific performance of an obligation other than one to pay money, including the remedying of a defective performance.

(2) Specific performance cannot, however, be obtained where:
   (a) performance would be unlawful or impossible; or
   (b) performance would cause the debtor unreasonable effort or expense; or
   (c) the performance consists in the provision of services or work of a personal character or depends upon a personal relationship, or
   (d) the aggrieved party may reasonably obtain performance from another source.

(3) The aggrieved party will lose the right to specific performance if it fails to seek it within a reasonable time after it has or ought to have become aware of the non-performance.

4—227　Article 9.103—Damages Not Precluded

The fact that a right to performance is excluded under this Section does not preclude a claim for damages.

Section 2: Withholding Performance

4—228　Article 9.201—Right to Withhold Performance

(1) A party who is to perform simultaneously with or after the other party may withhold performance until the other has tendered performance or has performed. The first party may withhold the whole of its performance or a part of it as may be reasonable in the circumstances.

(2) A party may similarly withhold performance for as long as it is clear that there will be a non-performance by the other party when the other party's performance becomes due.

Section 3: Termination of the Contract

4—229   Article 9.301—Right to Terminate the Contract

(1) A party may terminate the contract if the other party's non-performance is fundamental.

(2) In the case of delay the aggrieved party may also terminate the contract under Article 8.106 (3).

4—230   Article 9.302—Contract to be Performed in Parts

If the contract is to be performed in separate parts and in relation to a part to which a counter-performance can be apportioned, there is a fundamental non-performance, the aggrieved party may exercise its right to terminate under this Section in relation to the part concerned. It may terminate the contract as a whole only if the non-performance is fundamental to the contract as a whole.

4—231   Article 9.303—Notice of Termination

(1) A party's right to terminate the contract is to be exercised by notice to the other party.

(2) The aggrieved party loses its right to terminate the contract unless it gives notice within a reasonable time after it has or ought to have become aware of the non-performance.

(3) (a) When performance has not been tendered by the time it was due, the aggrieved party need not give notice of termination before a tender has been made. If a tender is later made it loses its right to terminate if it does not give such notice within a reasonable time after it has or ought to have become aware of the tender.

(b) If, however, the aggrieved party knows or has reason to know that the other party still intends to tender within a reasonable time, and the aggrieved party unreasonably fails to notify the other party that it will not accept performance, it loses its right to terminate if the other party in fact tenders within a reasonable time.

(4) If a party is excused under Article 8.108 through an impediment which is total and permanent, the contract is terminated automatically and without notice at the time the impediment arises.

4—232   Article 9.304—Anticipatory Non-Performance

Where prior to the time for performance by a party it is clear that there will be a fundamental non-performance by it the other party may terminate the contract.

4—233   Article 9.305—Effects of Termination in General

(1) Termination of the contract releases both parties from their obligation to effect and to receive future performance, but, subject to Articles 9.306 to 9.308, does not affect the rights and liabilities that have accrued up to the time of termination.

(2) Termination does not affect any provision of the contract for the settlement of disputes or any other provision which is to operate even after termination.

4—234   Article 9.306—Property Reduced in Value

A party who terminates the contract may reject property previously received from the other party if its value to the first party has been fundamentally reduced as a result of the other party's non-performance.

4—235   Article 9.307—Recovery of Money Paid

On termination of the contract a party may recover money paid for a performance which it did not receive or which it properly rejected.

4—236   Article 9.308—Recovery of Property

On termination of the contract a party who has supplied property which can be returned and for which it has not received payment or other counter-performance may recover the property.

4—237   Article 9.309—Recovery for Performance that Cannot be Returned

On termination of the contract a party who has rendered a performance which cannot be returned and for which it has not received payment or other counter-performance may recover a reasonable amount for the value of the performance to the other party.

Section 4: Price Reduction

4—238   Article 9.401—Right to Reduce Price

(1) A party who accepts a tender of performance not conforming to the contract may reduce the price. This reduction shall be proportionate to the decrease in the value of the performance at the time this was tendered compared to the value which a conforming tender would have had at that time.

(2) A party who is entitled to reduce the price under the preceding paragraph and who has already paid a sum exceeding the reduced price may recover the excess from the other party.

(3) A party who reduces the price cannot also recover damages for reduction in the value of the performance but remains entitled to damages for any further loss it has suffered so far as these are recoverable under Section 5 of this Chapter.

Section 5: Damages and Interest

4—239   Article 9.501—Right to Damages

(1) The aggrieved party is entitled to damages for loss caused by the other party's non-performance which is not excused under Article 8.108.

(2) The loss for which damages are recoverable includes:

(a) non-pecuniary loss ; and
(b) future loss which is reasonably likely to occur.

4—240   Article 9.502—General Measure of Damages

The general measure of damages is such sum as will put the aggrieved party as nearly as possible into the position in which it would have been if the contract had been duly performed. Such damages cover the loss which the aggrieved party has suffered and the gain of which it has been deprived.

4—241   Article 9.503—Foreseeability

The non-performing party is liable only for loss which it foresaw or could reasonably have foreseen at the time of conclusion of the contract as a likely result of its non-performance, unless the non-performance was intentional or grossly negligent.

4—242   Article 9.504—Loss Attributable to Aggrieved Party

The non-performing party is not liable for loss suffered by the aggrieved party to the extent that the aggrieved party contributed to the non-performance or its effects.

4—243   Article 9.505—Reduction of Loss

> (1) The non-performing party is not liable for loss suffered by the aggrieved party to the extent that the aggrieved party could have reduced the loss by taking reasonable steps.
>
> (2) The aggrieved party is entitled to recover any expenses reasonably incurred in attempting to reduce the loss.

4—244   Article 9.506—Substitute Transaction

Where the aggrieved party has terminated the contract and has made a substitute transaction within a reasonable time and in a reasonable manner, it may recover the difference between the contract price and the price of the substitute transaction as well as damages for any further loss so far as these are recoverable under this Section.

4—245   Article 9.507—Current Price

Where the aggrieved party has terminated the contract and has not made a substitute transaction but there is a current price for the performance contracted for, it may recover the difference between the contract price and the price current at the time the contract is terminated as well as damages for any further loss so far as these are recoverable under this Section.

4—246   Article 9.508—Delay in Payment of Money

> (1) If payment of a sum of money is delayed, the aggrieved party is entitled to interest on that sum from the time when payment is due to the time of payment at the average commercial bank short-term lending rate to prime borrowers prevailing for the contractual currency of payment at the place where payment is due.
>
> (2) The aggrieved party may in addition recover damages for any further loss so far as these are recoverable under this Section.

4—247   Article 9.509—Agreed Payment for Non-performance

> (1) Where the contract provides that a party who fails to perform is to pay a specified sum to the aggrieved party for

such non-performance, the aggrieved party shall be awarded that sum irrespective of its actual loss.

(2) However, despite any agreement to the contrary the specified sum may be reduced to a reasonable amount where it is grossly excessive in relation to the loss resulting from the non-performance and the other circumstances.

4—248   Article 9.510—Currency by which Damages to be Measured

Damages are to be measured by the currency which most appropriately reflects the aggrieved party's loss.

Chapter 10: Plurality of Parties

Section 1: Plurality of debtors

4—249   Article 10.101—Solidary, Separate and Communal Obligations

(1) Obligations are solidary when all the debtors are bound to render one and the same performance and the creditor may require it from any one of them until full performance has been received.

(2) Obligations are separate when each debtor is bound to render only part of the performance and the creditor may require from each debtor only that debtor's part.

(3) An obligation is communal when all the debtors are bound to render the performance together and the creditor may require it only from all of them.

4—250   Article 10.102: When Solidary Obligations Arise

(1) If several debtors are bound to render one and the same performance to a creditor under the same contract, they are solidarily liable, unless the contract or the law provides otherwise.

(2) Solidary obligations also arise where several persons are liable for the same damage.

(3) The fact that the debtors are not liable on the same terms does not prevent their obligations from being solidary.

4—251   Article 10.103—Liability under Separate Obligations

Debtors bound by separate obligations are liable in equal shares unless the contract or the law provides otherwise.

4—252   Article 10.104—Communal Obligations: Special Rule when Money claimed for Non-performance

Notwithstanding Article 10.101(3), when money is claimed for non-performance of a communal obligation, the debtors are solidarily liable for payment to the creditor.

4—253   Article 10.105—Apportionment between Solidary Debtors

(1) As between themselves, solidary debtors are liable in equal shares unless the contract or the law provides otherwise.

(2) If two or more debtors are liable for the same damage under Article 10.102(2), their share of liability as between themselves is determined according to the law governing the event which gave rise to the liability.

4—254   Article 10.106—Recourse between solidary Debtors

(1) A solidary debtor who has performed more than that debtor's share may claim the excess from any of the other debtors to the extent of each debtor's unperformed share, together with a share of any costs reasonably incurred.

(2) A solidary debtor to whom paragraph (1) applies may also, subject to any prior right and interest of the creditor, exercise the rights and actions of the creditor, including accessory securities, to recover the excess from any of the other debtors to the extent of each debtor's unperformed share.

(3) If a solidary debtor who has performed more than that debtor's share is unable, despite all reasonable efforts, to recover contribution from another solidary debtor, the share of the others, including the one who has performed, is increased proportionally.

4—255   Article 10.107—Performance, Set-off and Merger in Solidary Obligations

(1) Performance or set-off by a solidary debtor or set-off by the creditor against one solidary debtor discharges the other debtors in relation to the creditor to the extent of the performance or set-off.

(2) Merger of debts between a solidary debtor and the creditor discharges the other debtors only for the share of the debtor concerned.

4—256 Article 10.108—Release or Settlement in Solidary Obligations

(1) When the creditor releases, or reaches a settlement with, one solidary debtor, the other debtors are discharged of liability for the share of that debtor.

(2) The debtors are totally discharged by the release or settlement if it so provides.

(3) As between solidary debtors, the debtor who is discharged from that debtor's share is discharged only to the extent of the share at the time of the discharge and not from any supplementary share for which that debtor may subsequently become liable under Article 10.106(3).

4—257 Article 10.109—Effect of Judgment in Solidary Obligations

A decision by a court as to the liability to the creditor of one solidary debtor does not affect:

(a) the liability to the creditor of the other solidary debtors; or

(b) the rights of recourse between the solidary debtors under Article 10.106.

4—258 Article 10.110—Prescription in Solidary Obligations

Prescription of the creditor's right to performance ("claim") against one solidary debtor does not affect:

(a) the liability to the creditor of the other solidary debtors; or

(b) the rights of recourse between the solidary debtors under Article 10.106.

4—259 Article 10.111—Opposability of other Defences in Solidary Obligations

(1) A solidary debtor may invoke against the creditor any defence which another solidary debtor can invoke, other than a defence personal to that other debtor. Invoking the defence has no effect with regard to the other solidary debtors.

(2) A debtor from whom contribution is claimed may invoke against the claimant any personal defence that that debtor could have invoked against the creditor.

Section 2: Plurality of creditors

4—260   Article 10.201—Solidary, Separate and Communal Claims

(1) Claims are solidary when any of the creditors may require full performance from the debtor and when the debtor may render performance to any of the creditors.

(2) Claims are separate when the debtor owes each creditor only that creditor's share of the claim and each creditor may require performance only of that creditor's share.

(3) A claim is communal when the debtor must perform to all the creditors and any creditor may require performance only for the benefit of all.

4—261   Article 10.202: Apportionment of Separate Claims

Separate creditors are entitled to equal shares unless the contract or the law provides otherwise.

4—262   Article 10.203—Difficulties of executing a Communal Claim

If one of the creditors in a communal claim refuses, or is unable to receive, the performance, the debtor may discharge the obligation to perform by depositing the property or money with a third party according to Articles 7.110 or 7.111 of the Principles.

4—263   Article 10.204—Apportionment of Solidary Claims

(1) Solidary creditors are entitled to equal shares unless the contract or the law provides otherwise.

(2) A creditor who has received more than that creditor's share must transfer the excess to the other creditors to the extent of their respective shares.

4—264   Article 10.205—Regime of solidary Claims

(1) A release granted to the debtor by one of the solidary creditors has no effect on the other solidary creditors

(2) The rules of Articles 10.107, 10.109, 10.110 and 10.111(1) apply with appropriate adaptations to solidary claims.

Chapter 11: Assignment of Claims

Section 1: General Principles

4—265   Article 11.101—Scope of Chapter

(1) This Chapter applies to the assignment by agreement of a right to performance ("claim") under an existing or future contract.

(2) Except where otherwise stated or the context otherwise requires, this Chapter also applies to the assignment by agreement of other transferable claims.

(3) This Chapter does not apply:
  (a) to the transfer of a financial instrument or investment security where, under the law otherwise applicable, such transfer must be by entry in a register maintained by or for the issuer; or
  (b) to the transfer of a bill of exchange or other negotiable instrument or of a negotiable security or a document of title to goods where, under the law otherwise applicable, such transfer must be by delivery (with any necessary indorsement)

(4) In this Chapter "assignment" includes an assignment by way of security.

(5) This Chapter also applies, with appropriate adaptations, to the granting by agreement of a right in security over a claim otherwise than by assignment.

4—266   **Article 11.102—Contractual Claims Generally Assignable**

(1) Subject to Articles 11.301 and 11.302, a party to a contract may assign a claim under it.

(2) A future claim arising under an existing or future contract may be assigned if at the time when- it comes into existence, or at such other time as the parties agree, it can be identified as the claim to which the assignment relates.

4—267   Article 11.103—Partial Assignment

A claim which is divisible may be assigned in part, but the assignor is liable to the debtor for any increased costs which the debtor thereby incurs.

4—268   Article 11.104—Form of Assignment

An assignment need not be in writing and is not subject to any other requirement as to form. It may be proved by any means, including witnesses.

Section 2: Effects of Assignment As Between Assignor and Assignee

4—269   Article 11.201—Rights Transferred to Assignee

    (1) The assignment of a claim transfers to the assignee:

        (a) all the assignor's rights to performance in respect of the claim assigned; and
        (b) all accessory rights securing such performance.

    (2) Where the assignment of a claim under a contract is associated with the substitution of the assignee as debtor in respect of any obligation owed by the assignor under the same contract, this Article takes effect subject to Article 12.201.

4—270   Article 11.202—When Assignment Takes Effect

    (1) An assignment of an existing claim takes effect at the time of the agreement to assign or such later time as the assignor and assignee agree.

    (2) An assignment of a future claim is dependent upon the assigned claim coming into existence but thereupon takes effect from the time of the agreement to assign or such later time as the assignor and assignee agree.

4—271   Article 11.203—Preservation of Assignee's Rights Against Assignor

An assignment is effective as between the assignor and assignee, and entitles the assignee to whatever the assignor receives from the debtor, even if it is ineffective against the debtor under Article 11.301 or 11.302.

4—272   Article 11.204—Undertakings by Assignor

By assigning or purporting to assign a claim the assignor undertakes to the assignee that:

> (a) at the time when the assignment is to take effect the following conditions will be satisfied except as otherwise disclosed to the assignee:
>
>> (i) the assignor has the right to assign the claim;
>> (ii) the claim exists and the assignee's rights are not affected by any defences or rights (including any right of set-off) which the debtor might have against the assignor; and
>> (iii) the claim is not subject to any prior assignment or right in security in favour of any other party or to any other incumbrance;
>
> (b) the claim and any contract under which it arises will not be modified without the consent of the assignee unless the modification is provided for in the assignment agreement or is one which is made in good faith and is of a nature to which the assignee could not reasonably object; and
>
> (c) the assignor will transfer to the assignee all transferable rights intended to secure performance which are not accessory rights.

Section 3: Effects of Assignment As Between Assignee and Debtor

4—273   Article 11.301—Contractual Prohibition of Assignment

> (1) An assignment which is prohibited by or is otherwise not in conformity with the contract under which the assigned claim arises is not effective against the debtor unless:
>
>> (a) the debtor has consented to it; or
>> (b) the assignee neither knew nor ought to have known of the non-conformity; or
>> (c) the assignment is made under a contract for the assignment of future rights to payment of money.
>
> (2) Nothing in the preceding paragraph affects the assignor's liability for the non-conformity.

4—274 Article 11.302—Other Ineffective Assignments

An assignment to which the debtor has not consented is ineffective against the debtor so far as it relates to a performance which the debtor, by reason of the nature of the performance or the relationship of the debtor and the assignor, could not reasonably be required to render to anyone except the assignor.

4—275 Article 11.303—Effect on Debtor's Obligation

(1) Subject to Articles 11.301, 11.302, 11.307 and 11.308, the debtor is bound to perform in favour of the assignee if and only if the debtor has received a notice in writing from the assignor or the assignee which reasonably identifies the claim which has been assigned and requires the debtor to give performance to the assignee.

(2) However, if such notice is given by the assignee, the debtor may within a reasonable time request the assignee to provide reliable evidence of the assignment, pending which the debtor may withhold performance.

(3) Where the debtor has acquired knowledge of the assignment otherwise than by a notice conforming to paragraph (1), the debtor may either withhold performance from or give performance to the assignee.

(4) Where the debtor gives performance to the assignor, the debtor is discharged if and only if the performance is given without knowledge of the assignment.

4—276 Article 11.304—Protection of Debtor

A debtor who performs in favour of a person identified as assignee in a notice of assignment under Article 11.303 is discharged unless the debtor could not have been unaware that such person was not the person entitled to performance.

4—277 Article 11.305—Competing Demands

A debtor who has received notice of two or more competing demands for performance may discharge liability by conforming to the law of the due place of performance, or, if the performances are due in different places, the law applicable to the claim.

4—278   Article 11.306—Place of Performance

(1) Where the assigned claim relates to an obligation to pay money at a particular place, the assignee may require payment at any place within the same country or, if that country is a Member State of the European Union, at any place within the European Union, but the assignor is liable to the debtor for any increased costs which the debtor incurs by reason of any change in the place of performance.

(2) Where the assigned claim relates to a non-monetary obligation to be performed at a particular place, the assignee may not require performance at any other place.

4—279   Article 11.307—Defences and Rights of Set-Off

(1) The debtor may set up against the assignee all substantive and procedural defences to the assigned claim which the debtor could have used against the assignor.

(2) The debtor may also assert against the assignee all rights of set-off which would have been available against the assignor under Chapter 13 in respect of any claim against the assignor:

   (a) existing at the time when a notice of assignment, whether or not conforming to Article 11.303(1), reaches the debtor; or
   (b) closely connected with the assigned claim.

4—280   Article 11.308—Unauthorised Modification not Binding on Assignee

A modification of the claim made by agreement between the assignor and the debtor, without the consent of the assignee, after a notice of assignment whether or not conforming to Article 11.303(1) reaches the debtor does not affect the rights of the assignee against the debtor unless the modification is provided for in the assignment agreement or is one which is made in good faith and is of a nature to which the assignee could not reasonably object.

A. Transnational Contract Principles

Section 4: Order of Priority between Assignee and Competing Claimants

4—281   Article 11.401—Priorities

(1) Where there are successive assignments of the same claim, the assignee whose assignment is first notified to the debtor has priority over any earlier assignee if at the time of the later assignment the assignee under that assignment neither knew nor ought to have known of the earlier assignment.

(2) Subject to paragraph (1), the priority of successive assignments, whether of existing or future claims, is determined by the order in which they are made.

(3) The assignee's interest in the assigned claim has priority over the interest of a creditor of the assignor who attaches that claim, whether by judicial process or otherwise, after the time the assignment has taken effect under Article 11.202.

(4) In the event of the assignor's bankruptcy, the assignee's interest in the assigned claim has priority over the interest of the assignor's insolvency administrator and creditors, subject to any rules of the law applicable to the bankruptcy relating to:

(a) publicity required as a condition of such priority;
(b) the ranking of claims or
(c) the avoidance or ineffectiveness of transactions in the bankruptcy proceedings.

CHAPTER 12: SUBSTITUTION OF NEW DEBTOR: TRANSFER OF CONTRACT

Section 1: Substitution of New Debtor

4—282   Article 12.101—Substitution: General rules

(1) A third person may undertake with the agreement of the debtor and the creditor to be substituted as debtor, with the effect that the original debtor is discharged.

(2) A creditor may agree in advance to a future substitution. In such a case the substitution takes effect only when the creditor is given notice by the new debtor of the agreement between the new and the original debtor.

4—283   Article 12.102—Effects of Substitution on Defences and Securities

(1) The new debtor cannot invoke against the creditor any rights or defences arising from the relationship between the new debtor and the original debtor.

(2) The discharge of the original debtor also extends to any security of the original debtor given to the creditor for the performance of the obligation, unless the security is over an asset which is transferred to the new debtor as part of a transaction between the original and the new debtor.

(3) Upon discharge of the original debtor, a security granted by any person other than the new debtor for the performance of the obligation is released, unless that other person agrees that it should continue to be available to the creditor.

(4) The new debtor may invoke against the creditor all defences which the original debtor could have invoked against the creditor.

Section 2: Transfer of Contract

4—284   Article 12.201—Transfer of Contract

(1) A party to a contract may agree with a third person that that person is to be substituted as the contracting party. In such a case the substitution takes effect only where, as a result of the other party's assent, the first party is discharged.

(2) To the extent that the substitution of the third person as a contracting party involves a transfer of rights to performance ("claims"), the provisions of Chapter 11 apply; to the extent that obligations are transferred, the provisions of Section 1 of this Chapter apply.

CHAPTER 13: SET-OFF

4—285   Article 13.101—Requirements for Set-Off

If two parties owe each other obligations of the same kind, either party may set off that party's right to performance ("claim") against the other party's claim, if and to the extent that, at the time of set-off, the first party:

(a) is entitled to effect performance; and

(b) may demand the other party's performance.

4—286   Article 13.102—Unascertained Claims

(1) A debtor may not set off a claim which is unascertained as to its existence or value unless the set-off will not prejudice the interests of the other party.

(2) Where the claims of both parties arise from the same legal relationship it is presumed that the other party's interests will not be prejudiced.

4—287   Article 13.103—Foreign Currency Set-Off

Where parties owe each other money in different currencies, each party may set off that party's claim against the other party's claim, unless the parties have agreed that the party declaring set-off is to pay exclusively in a specified currency.

4—288   Article 13.104—Notice of Set-Off

The right of set-off is exercised by notice to the other party.

4—289   Article 13.105—Plurality of Claims and Obligations

(1) Where the party giving notice of set-off has two or more claims against the other party, the notice is effective only if it identifies the claim to which it relates.

(2) Where the party giving notice of set-off has to perform two or more obligations towards the other party, the rules in Article 7.109 apply with appropriate adaptations.

4—290   Article 13.106—Effect of Set-Off

Set-off discharges the obligations, as far as they are coextensive, as from the time of notice.

4—291   Article 13.107—Exclusion of Right of Set-Off

Set-off cannot be effected:

(a) where it is excluded by agreement;

(b) against a claim to the extent that that claim is not capable of attachment; and

(c) against a claim arising from a deliberate wrongful act.

Chapter 14: Prescription

Section 1: General Provision

4—292 Article 14.101—Claims subject to Prescription

A right to performance of an obligation ("claim") is subject to prescription by the expiry of a period of time in accordance with these Principles.

Section 2: Periods of Prescription and their Commencement

4—293 Article 14.201—General Period

The general period of prescription is three years.

2—294 Article 14.202—Period for a Claim Established by Legal Proceedings

   (1) The period of prescription for a claim established by judgment is ten years.

   (2) The same applies to a claim established by an arbitral award or other instrument which is enforceable as if it were a judgment.

4—295 Article 14.203—Commencement

   (1) The general period of prescription begins to run from the time when the debtor has to effect performance or, in the case of a right to damages, from the time of the act which gives rise to the claim.

   (2) Where the debtor is under a continuing obligation to do or refrain from doing something, the general period of prescription begins to run with each breach of the obligation.

   (3) The period of prescription set out in Article 14.202 begins to run from the time when the judgment or arbitral award obtains the effect of res judicata, or the other instrument becomes enforceable, though not before the debtor has to effect performance.

Section 3: Extension of Period

4—296 Article 14.301—Suspension in Case of Ignorance

The running of the period of prescription is suspended as long as the creditor does not know of, and could not reasonably know of:

(a) the identity of the debtor; or

(b) the facts giving rise to the claim including, in the case of a right to damages, the type of damage.

4—297 Article 14.302—Suspension in Case of Judicial and Other Proceedings

(1) The running of the period of prescription is suspended from the time when judicial proceedings on the claim are begun.

(2) Suspension lasts until a decision has been made which has the effect of res judicata, or until the case has been otherwise disposed of.

(3) These provisions apply, with appropriate adaptations, to arbitration proceedings and to all other proceedings initiated with the aim of obtaining an instrument which is enforceable as if it were a judgment.

4—298 Article 14.303—Suspension in Case of Impediment beyond Creditor's Control

(1) The running of the period of prescription is suspended as long as the creditor is prevented from pursuing the claim by an impediment which is beyond the creditor's control and which the creditor could not reasonably have been expected to avoid or overcome.

(2) Paragraph (1) applies only if the impediment arises, or subsists, within the last six months of the prescription period.

4—299 Article 14.304—Postponement of Expiry in case of Negotiations

If the parties negotiate about the claim, or about circumstances from which a claim might arise, the period of prescription does not expire before one year has passed since the last communication made in the negotiations.

4—300   Article 14.305—Postponement of Expiry in case of Incapacity

(1) If a person subject to an incapacity is without a representative, the period of prescription of a claim held by or against that person does not expire before one year has passed after either the incapacity has ended or a representative has been appointed.

(2) The period of prescription of claims between a person subject to an incapacity and that person's representative does not expire before one year has passed after either the incapacity has ended or a new representative has been appointed.

4—301   Article 14.306—Postponement of Expiry: Deceased's Estate

Where the creditor or debtor has died, the period of prescription of a claim held by or against the deceased's estate does not expire before one year has passed after the claim can be enforced by or against an heir, or by or against a representative of the estate.

4—302   Article 14.307—Maximum Length of Period

The period of prescription cannot be extended, by suspension of its running or postponement of its expiry under these Principles, to more than ten years or, in case of claims for personal injuries, to more than thirty years. This does not apply to suspension under Article 14.302.

Section 4: Renewal of Periods

4—303   Article 14.401—Renewal by Acknowledgement

(1) If the debtor acknowledges the claim, vis-à-vis the creditor, by part payment, payment of interest, giving of security, or in any other manner, a new period of prescription begins to run.

(2) The new period is the general period of prescription, regardless of whether the claim was originally subject to the general period of prescription or the ten year period under Article 14.202. In the latter case, however, this Article does not operate so as to shorten the ten year period.

4—304   Article 14.402—Renewal by Attempted Execution

The ten year period of prescription laid down in Article 14.202 begins to run again with each reasonable attempt at execution undertaken by the creditor.

Section 5: Effects of Prescription

4—305   **Article 14.501—General Effect**

(1) After expiry of the period of prescription the debtor is entitled to refuse performance.

(2) Whatever has been performed in order to discharge a claim may not be reclaimed merely because the period of prescription had expired.

4—306   **Article 14.502—Effect on Ancillary Claims**

The period of prescription for a right to payment of interest, and other claims of an ancillary nature, expires not later than the period for the principal claim.

4—307   **Article 14.503—Effect on Set-Off**

A claim in relation to which the period of prescription has expired may nonetheless be set off, unless the debtor has invoked prescription previously or does so within two months of notification of set-off.

Section 6: Modification by Agreement

4—308   **Article 14.601—Agreements Concerning Prescription**

(1) The requirements for prescription may be modified by agreement between the parties, in particular by either shortening or lengthening the periods of prescription.

(2) The period of prescription may not, however, be reduced to less than one year or extended to more than thirty years after the time of commencement set out in Article 14.203.

CHAPTER 15: ILLEGALITY

4—309   **Article 15.101—Contracts Contrary to Fundamental Principles**

A contract is of no effect to the extent that it is contrary to principles recognised as fundamental in the laws of the Member States of the European Union.

4—310   **Article 15.102: Contracts Infringing Mandatory Rules**

(1) Where a contract infringes a mandatory rule of law applicable under Article 1.103 of these Principles, the effects of that infringement upon the contract are the effects, if any, expressly prescribed by that mandatory rule.

(2) Where the mandatory rule does not expressly prescribe the effects of an infringement upon a contract, the contract may be declared to have full effect, to have some effect, to have no effect, or to be subject to modification.

(3) A decision reached under paragraph (2) must be an appropriate and proportional response to the infringement, having regard to all relevant circumstances, including:

   (a) the purpose of the rule which has been infringed;
   (b) the category of persons for whose protection the rule exists;
   (c) any sanction that may be imposed under the rule infringed;
   (d) the seriousness of the infringement;
   (e) whether the infringement was intentional; and
   (f) the closeness of the relationship between the infringement and the contract.

4—311   **Article 15.103—Partial Ineffectiveness**

(1) If only part of a contract is rendered ineffective under Articles 15.101 or 15.102, the remaining part continues in effect unless, giving due consideration to all the circumstances of the case, it is unreasonable to uphold it.

(2) Articles 15.104 and 15.105 apply, with appropriate adaptation, to a case of partial ineffectiveness.

4—312   **Article 15.104—Restitution**

(1) When a contract is rendered ineffective under Articles 15.101 or 15.102, either party may claim restitution of whatever that party has supplied under the contract, provided that, where appropriate, concurrent restitution is made of whatever has been received.

(2) When considering whether to grant restitution under paragraph (1), and what concurrent restitution, if any, would be appropriate, regard must be had to the factors referred to in Article 15.102(3).

(3) An award of restitution may be refused to a party who knew or ought to have known of the reason for the ineffectiveness.

(4) If restitution cannot be made in kind of any reason, a reasonable sum must be paid for what has been received.

4—313   Article 15.105—Damages

(1) A party to a contract which is rendered ineffective under Articles 15.101 or 15.102 may recover from the other party damages putting the first party as nearly as possible into the same position as if the contract had not been concluded, provided that the other party knew or ought to have known of the reason for the ineffectiveness.

(2) When considering whether to award damages under paragraph (1), regard must be had to the factors referred to in Article 15.102(3).

(3) An award of damages may be refused where the first party knew or ought to have known of the reason for the ineffectiveness.

Chapter 16: Conditions

4—314   Article 16.101—Types of Condition

A contractual obligation may be made conditional upon the occurrence of an uncertain future event, so that the obligation takes effect only if the event occurs (suspensive condition) or comes to an end if the event occurs (resolutive condition).

4—315   Article 16.102—Interference with Conditions

(1) If fulfilment of a condition is prevented by a party, contrary to duties of good faith and fair dealing or co-operation, and if fulfilment would have operated to that party's disadvantage, the condition is deemed to be fulfilled.

(2) If fulfilment of a condition is brought about by a party, contrary to duties of good faith and fair dealing or co-operation, and if fulfilment operates to that party's advantage, the condition is deemed not to be fulfilled.

4—316   Article 16.103—Effect of Conditions

(1) Upon fulfilment of a suspensive condition, the relevant obligation takes effect unless the parties otherwise agree.

(2) Upon fulfilment of a resolutive condition, the relevant obligation comes to an end unless the parties otherwise agree.

Chapter 17: Capitalisation of Interest

4—317   Article 17.101—When Interest to be Added to Capital

(1) Interest payable according to Article 9.508(1) is added to the outstanding capital every 12 months.

(2) Paragraph (1) of this Article does not apply if the parties have provided for interest upon delay in payment.

B. Rules of Conflict

Convention on the law applicable to contractual obligations

CONVENTION on the law applicable to contractual obligations (1) opened for signature in Rome on 19 June 1980

4—318   PREAMBLE

THE HIGH CONTRACTING PARTIES to the Treaty establishing the European Economic Community,

ANXIOUS to continue in the field of private international law the work of unification of law which has already been done within the Community, in particular in the field of jurisdiction and enforcement of judgments,

WISHING to establish uniform rules concerning the law applicable to contractual obligations,

HAVE AGREED AS FOLLOWS:

Title I: Scope of the Convention

4—319   Article 1—Scope of the Convention

1. The rules of this Convention shall apply to contractual obligations in any situation involving a choice between the laws of different countries.

2. They shall not apply to:

   (a) questions involving the status or legal capacity of natural persons, without prejudice to Article 11;

   (b) contractual obligations relating to:

   — wills and succession,
   — rights in property arising out of a matrimonial relationship,
   — rights and duties arising out of a family relationship, parentage, marriage or affinity, including maintenance obligations in respect of children who are not legitimate;

   (c) obligations arising under bills of exchange, cheques and promissory notes and other negotiable instruments to the extent that the obligations under such other

negotiable instruments arise out of their negotiable character;

(d) arbitration agreements and agreements on the choice of court;

(e) questions governed by the law of companies and other bodies corporate or unincorporate such as the creation, by registration or otherwise, legal capacity, internal organization or winding up of companies and other bodies corporate or unincorporate and the personal liability of officers and members as such for the obligations of the company or body;

(f) the question whether an agent is able to bind a principal, or an organ to bind a company or body corporate or unincorporate, to a third party;

(g) the constitution of trusts and the relationship between settlors, trustees and beneficiaries;

(h) evidence and procedure, without prejudice to Article 14.

3. The rules of this Convention do not apply to contracts of insurance which cover risks situated in the territories of the Member States of the European Economic Community. In order to determine whether a risk is situated in those territories the court shall apply its internal law.

4. The proceeding paragraph does not apply to contracts of re-insurance.

4—320 Article 2—Application of law of non-contracting States

Any law specified by this Convention shall be applied whether or not it is the law of a Contracting State.

Title II: Uniform Rules

4—321 Article 3—Freedom of choice

1. A contract shall be governed by the law chosen by the parties. The choice must be expressed or demonstrated with reasonable certainty by the terms of the contract or the circumstances of the case. By their choice the parties can select the law applicable to the whole or a part only of the contract.

2. The parties may at any time agree to subject the contract to a law other than that which previously governed it, whether as a result of an earlier choice under this Article or of other

provisions of this Convention. Any variation by the parties of the law to be applied made after the conclusion of the contract shall not prejudice its formal validity under Article 9 or adversely affect the rights of third parties.

3. The fact that the parties have chosen a foreign law, whether or not accompanied by the choice of a foreign tribunal, shall not, where all the other elements relevant to the situation at the time of the choice are connected with one country only, prejudice the application of rules of the law at the country which cannot be derogated from by contract, hereinafter called 'mandatory rules'.

4. The existence and validity of the consent of the parties as to the choice of the applicable law shall be determined in accordance with the provisions of Articles 8, 9 and 11.

4—322   Article 4—Applicable law in the absence of choice

1. To the extent that the law applicable to the contract has not been chosen in accordance with Article 3, the contract shall be governed by the law of the country with which it is most closely connected. Nevertheless, a separable part of the contract which has a closer connection with another country may by way of exception be governed by the law of that other country.

2. Subject to the provisions of paragraph 5 of this Article, it shall be presumed that the contract is most closely connected with the country where the party who is to effect the performance which is characteristic of the contract has, at the time of conclusion of the contract, his habitual residence, or, in the case of a body corporate or unincorporate, its central administration. However, if the contract is entered into in the course of that party's trade or profession, that country shall be the country in which the principal place of business is situated or, where under the terms of the contract the performance is to be effected through a place of business other than the principal place of business, the country in which that other place of business is situated.

3. Notwithstanding the provisions of paragraph 2 of this Article, to the extent that the subject matter of the contract is a right in immovable property or a right to use immovable property it shall be presumed that the contract is most closely connected with the country where the immovable property is situated.

4. A contract for the carriage of goods shall not be subject to the presumption in paragraph 2. In such a contract if the country in which, at the time the contract is concluded, the carrier has his principal place of business is also the country in which the place of loading or the place of discharge or the principal place of business of the consignor is situated, it shall be presumed that the contract is most closely connected with that country. In applying this paragraph single voyage charter-parties and other contracts the main purpose of which is the carriage of goods shall be treated as contracts for the carriage of goods.

5. Paragraph 2 shall not apply if the characteristic performance cannot be determined, and the presumptions in paragraphs 2, 3 and 4 shall be disregarded if it appears from the circumstances as a whole that the contract is more closely connected with another country.

4—323 **Article 5—Certain consumer contracts**

1. This Article applies to a contract the object of which is the supply of goods or services to a person ('the consumer') for a purpose which can be regarded as being outside his trade or profession, or a contract for the provision of credit for that object.

2. Notwithstanding the provisions of Article 3, a choice of law made by the parties shall not have the result of depriving the consumer of the protection afforded to him by the mandatory rules of the law of the country in which he has his habitual residence:

> — if in that country the conclusion of the contract was preceded by a specific invitation addressed to him or by advertising, and he had taken in that country all the steps necessary on his part for the conclusion of the contract, or
> — if the other party or his agent received the consumer's order in that country, or
> — if the contract is for the sale of goods and the consumer travelled from that country to another country and there gave his order, provided that the consumer's journey was arranged by the seller for the purpose of inducing the consumer to buy.

3. Notwithstanding the provisions of Article 4, a contract to which this Article applies shall, in the absence of choice in accordance with Article 3, be governed by the law of the

country in which the consumer has his habitual residence if it is entered into in the circumstances described in paragraph 2 of this Article.

4. This Article shall not apply to:

 (a) a contract of carriage;
 (b) a contract for the supply of services where the services are to be supplied to the consumer exclusively in a country other than that in which he has his habitual residence.

5. Notwithstanding the provisions of paragraph 4, this Article shall apply to a contract which, for an inclusive price, provides for a combination of travel and accommodation.

4—324   Article 6—Individual employment contracts

1. Notwithstanding the provisions of Article 3, in a contract of employment a choice of law made by the parties shall not have the result of depriving the employee of the protection afforded to him by the mandatory rules of the law which would be applicable under paragraph 2 in the absence of choice.

2. Notwithstanding the provisions of Article 4, a contract of employment shall, in the absence of choice in accordance with Article 3, be governed:

 (a) by the law of the country in which the employee habitually carries out his work in performance of the contract, even if he is temporarily employed in another country; or
 (b) if the employee does not habitually carry out his work in any one country, by the law of the country in which the place of business through which he was engaged is situated;

unless it appears from the circumstances as a whole that the contract is more closely connected with another country, in which case the contract shall be governed by the law of that country.

4—325   Article 7—Mandatory rules

1. When applying under this Convention the law of a country, effect may be given to the mandatory rules of the law of another country with which the situation has a close connection, if and in so far as, under the law of the latter country, those rules must be applied whatever the law applicable to

the contract. In considering whether to give effect to these mandatory rules, regard shall be had to their nature and purpose and to the consequences of their application or non-application.

2. Nothing in this Convention shall restrict the application of the rules of the law of the forum in a situation where they are mandatory irrespective of the law otherwise applicable to the contract.

4—326 Article 8—Material validity

1. The existence and validity of a contract, or of any term of a contract, shall be determined by the law which would govern it under this Convention if the contract or term were valid.

2. Nevertheless a party may rely upon the law of the country in which he has his habitual residence to establish that he did not consent if it appears from the circumstances that it would not be reasonable to determine the effect of his conduct in accordance with the law specified in the preceding paragraph.

4—327 Article 9—Formal validity

1. A contract concluded between persons who are in the same country is formally valid if it satisfies the formal requirements of the law which governs it under this Convention or of the law of the country where it is concluded.

2. A contract concluded between persons who are in different countries is formally valid if it satisfies the formal requirements of the law which governs it under this Convention or of the law of one of those countries.

3. Where a contract is concluded by an agent, the country in which the agent acts is the relevant country for the purposes of paragraphs 1 and 2.

4. An act intended to have legal effect relating to an existing or contemplated contract is formally valid if it satisfies the formal requirements of the law which under this Convention governs or would govern the contract or of the law of the country where the act was done.

5. The provisions of the preceding paragraphs shall not apply to a contract to which Article 5 applies, concluded in the circumstances described in paragraph 2 of Article 5. The formal validity of such a contract is governed by the law of

the country in which the consumer has his habitual residence.

6. Notwithstanding paragraphs 1 to 4 of this Article, a contract the subject matter of which is a right in immovable property or a right to use immovable property shall be subject to the mandatory requirements of form of the law of the country where the property is situated if by that law those requirements are imposed irrespective of the country where the contract is concluded and irrespective of the law governing the contract.

4—328   Article 10—Scope of applicable law

1. The law applicable to a contract by virtue of Articles 3 to 6 and 12 of this Convention shall govern in particular:
   (a) interpretation;
   (b) performance;
   (c) within the limits of the powers conferred on the court by its procedural law, the consequences of breach, including the assessment of damages in so far as it is governed by rules of law;
   (d) the various ways of extinguishing obligations, and prescription and limitation of actions;
   (e) the consequences of nullity of the contract.

2. In relation to the manner of performance and the steps to be taken in the event of defective performance regard shall be had to the law of the country in which performance takes place.

4—329   Article 11—Incapacity

In a contract concluded between persons who are in the same country, a natural person who would have capacity under the law of that country may invoke his incapacity resulting from another law only if the other party to the contract was aware of this incapacity at the time of the conclusion of the contract or was not aware thereof as a result of negligence.

4—330   Article 12—Voluntary assignment

1. The mutual obligations of assignor and assignee under a voluntary assignment of a right against another person ('the debtor') shall be governed by the law which under this Convention applies to the contract between the assignor and assignee.

2. The law governing the right to which the assignment relates shall determine its assignability, the relationship between the assignee and the debtor, the conditions under which the assignment can be invoked against the debtor and any question whether the debtor's obligations have been discharged.

4—331   Article 13—Subrogation

1. Where a person ('the creditor') has a contractual claim upon another ('the debtor'), and a third person has a duty to satisfy the creditor, or has in fact satisfied the creditor in discharge of that duty, the law which governs the third person's duty to satisfy the creditor shall determine whether the third person is entitled to exercise against the debtor the rights which the creditor had against the debtor under the law governing their relationship and, if so, whether he may do so in full or only to a limited extent.

2. The same rule applies where several persons are subject to the same contractual claim and one of them has satisfied the creditor.

4—332   Article 14—Burden of proof, etc

1. The law governing the contract under this Convention applies to the extent that it contains, in the law of contract, rules which raise presumptions of law or determine the burden of proof.

2. A contract or an act intended to have legal effect may be proved by any mode of proof recognized by the law of the forum or by any of the laws referred to in Article 9 under which that contract or act is formally valid, provided that such mode of proof can be administered by the forum.

4—333   Article 15—Exclusion of convoi

The application of the law of any country specified by this Convention means the application of the rules of law in force in that country other than its rules of private international law.

4—334   Article 16—'Ordre public'

The application of a rule of the law of any country specified by this Convention may be refused only if such application is manifestly incompatible with the public policy ('ordre public') of the forum.

4—335 Article 17—No retrospective effect

This Convention shall apply in a Contracting State to contracts made after the date on which this Convention has entered into force with respect to that State.

4—336 Article 18—Uniform interpretation

In the interpretation and application of the preceding uniform rules, regard shall be had to their international character and to the desirability of achieving uniformity in their interpretation and application.

4—337 Article 19—States with more than one legal system

1. Where a State comprises several territorial units each of which has its own rules of law in respect of contractual obligations, each territorial unit shall be considered as a country for the purposes of identifying the law applicable under this Convention.

2. A State within which different territorial units have their own rules of law in respect of contractual obligations shall not be bound to apply this Convention to conflicts solely between the laws of such units.

4—338 Article 20—Precedence of Community law

This Convention shall not affect the application of provisions which, in relation to particular matters, lay down choice of law rules relating to contractual obligations and which are or will be contained in acts of the institutions of the European Communities or in national laws harmonized in implementation of such acts.

4—339 Article 21—Relationship with other conventions

This Convention shall not prejudice the application of international conventions to which a Contracting State is, or becomes, a party.

4—340 Article 22—Reservations

1. Any Contracting State may, at the time of signature, ratification, acceptance or approval, reserve the right not to apply:

    (a) the provisions of Article 7 (1);
    (b) the provisions of Article 10 (1) (e).

2. . . . (2)

3. Any Contracting State may at any time withdraw a reservation which it has made; the reservation shall cease to have effect on the first day of the third calendar month after notification of the withdrawal.

Title III: Final Provisions

4—341   Article 23

1. If, after the date on which this Convention has entered into force for a Contracting State, that State wishes to adopt any new choice of law rule in regard to any particular category of contract within the scope of this Convention, it shall communicate its intention to the other signatory States through the Secretary-General of the Council of the European Communities.

2. Any signatory State may, within six months from the date of the communication made to the Secretary-General, request him to arrange consultations between signatory States in order to reach agreement.

3. If no signatory State has requested consultations within this period or if within two years following the communication made to the Secretary-General no agreement is reached in the course of consultations, the Contracting State concerned may amend its law in the manner indicated. The measures taken by that State shall be brought to the knowledge of the other signatory States through the Secretary-General of the Council of the European Communities.

4—342   Article 24

1. If, after the date on which this Convention has entered into force with respect to a Contracting State, that State wishes to become a party to a multilateral convention whose principal aim or one of whose principal aims is to lay down rules of private international law concerning any of the matters governed by this Convention, the procedure set out in Article 23 shall apply. However, the period of two years, referred to in paragraph 3 of that Article, shall be reduced to one year.

2. The procedure referred to in the preceding paragraph need not be followed if a Contracting State or one of the European Communities is already a party to the multilateral convention, or if its object is to revise a convention to which the

State concerned is already a party, or if it is a convention concluded within the framework of the Treaties establishing the European Communities.

4—343   Article 25

If a Contracting State considers that the unification achieved by this Convention is prejudiced by the conclusion of agreements not covered by Article 24 (1), that State may request the Secretary-General of the Council of the European Communities to arrange consultations between the signatory States of this Convention.

4—344   Article 26

Any Contracting State may request the revision of this Convention. In this event a revision conference shall be convened by the President of the Council of the European Communities.

4—345   Article 27 (3)

4—346   Article 28

1. This Convention shall be open from 19 June 1980 for signature by the States party to the Treaty establishing the European Economic Community.

2. This Convention shall be subject to ratification, acceptance or approval by the signatory States. The instruments of ratification, acceptance or approval shall be deposited with the Secretary-General of the Council of the European Communities (4).

4—347   Article 29 (5)

1. This Convention shall enter into force on the first day of the third month following the deposit of the seventh instrument of ratification, acceptance or approval.

2. This Convention shall enter into force for each signatory State ratifying, accepting or approving at a later date on the first day of the third month following the deposit of its instrument of ratification, acceptance or approval.

4—348   Article 30

1. This Convention shall remain in force for 10 years from the date of its entry into force in accordance with Article 29 (1), even for States for which it enters into force at a later date.

2. If there has been no denunciation it shall be renewed tacitly every five years.

3. A Contracting State which wishes to denounce shall, not less than six months before the expiration of the period of 10 or five years, as the case may be, give notice to the Secretary-General of the Council of the European Communities. Denunciation may be limited to any territory to which the Convention has been extended by a declaration under Article 27 (2) (6).

4. The denunciation shall have effect only in relation to the State which has notified it. The Convention will remain in force as between all other Contracting States.

4—349   Article 31 (7)

The Secretary-General of the Council of the European Communities shall notify the States party to the Treaty establishing the European Economic Community of:

(a) the signatures;

(b) deposit of each instrument of ratification, acceptance or approval;

(c) the date of entry into force of this Convention;

(d) communications made in pursuance of Articles 23, 24, 25, 26 and 30 (8);

(e) the reservations and withdrawals of reservations referred to in Article 22.

4—350   Article 32

The Protocol annexed to this Convention shall form an integral part thereof.

4—351   Article 33 (9)

This Convention, drawn up in a single original in the Danish, Dutch, English, French, German, Irish and Italian languages, these texts being equally authentic, shall be deposited in the archives of the Secretariat of the Council of the European Communities. The Secretary-General shall transmit a certified copy thereof to the Government of each signatory State.

In witness whereof the undersigned, being duly authorized thereto, having signed this Convention.

Done at Rome on the nineteenth day of June in the year one thousand nine hundred and eighty.
[*Signatures of the plenipotentiaries*]

4—352 Protocol (10)

The High Contracting Parties have agreed upon the following provision which shall be annexed to the Convention:

'Notwithstanding the provisions of the Convention, Denmark, Sweden and Finland may retain national provisions concerning the law applicable to questions relating to the carriage of goods by sea and may amend such provisions without following the procedure provided for in Article 23 of the Convention of Rome. The national provisions applicable in this respect are the following:

— in Denmark, paragraphs 252 and 321 (3) and (4) of the "Solov" (maritime law),

— in Sweden, Chapter 13, Article 2 (1) and (2), and Chapter 14, Article 1 (3), of "sjölagen" (maritime law),

— in Finland, Chapter 13, Article 2 (1) and (2), and Chapter 14, Article 1 (3), of "merilaki"/"sjölagen" (maritime law).'

In witness whereof the undersigned, being duly authorized thereto, have signed this Protocol.

Done at Rome on the nineteenth day of June in the year one thousand nine hundred and eighty.
[*Signatures of the Plenipotentiaries*]

4—353 Joint declaration

At the time of the signature of the Convention on the law applicable to contractual obligations, the Governments of the Kingdom of Belgium, the Kingdom of Denmark, the Federal Republic of Germany, the French Republic, Ireland, the Italian Republic, the Grand Duchy of Luxembourg, the Kingdom of the Netherlands and the United Kingdom of Great Britain and Northern Ireland,

> I. anxious to avoid, as far as possible, dispersion of choice of law rules among several instruments and differences between these rules, express the wish that the institutions of the European Communities, in the exercise of their powers under the Treaties by which they were established, will, where the need arises, endeavour to adopt choice of law rules which are as far as possible consistent with those of this Convention;
>
> II. declare their intention as from the date of signature of this Convention until becoming bound by Article 24, to consult

with each other if any one of the signatory States wishes to become a party to any convention to which the procedure referred to in Article 24 would apply;

III. having regard to the contribution of the Convention on the law applicable to contractual obligations to the unification of choice of law rules within the European Communities, express the view that any State which becomes a member of the European Communities should accede to this Convention.

In witness whereof the undersigned, being duly authorized thereto, have signed this Joint Declaration.

Done at Rome on the nineteenth day of June in the year one thousand nine hundred and eighty.

[*Signatures of the Plenipotentiaries*]

4—354 Joint declaration

The Governments of the Kingdom of Belgium, the Kingdom of Denmark, the Federal Republic of Germany, the French Republic, Ireland, the Italian Republic, the Grand Duchy of Luxembourg, the Kingdom of the Netherlands and the United Kingdom of Great Britain and Northern Ireland,

On signing the Convention on the law applicable to contractual obligations;

Desiring to ensure that the Convention is applied as effectively as possible;

Anxious to prevent differences of interpretation of the Convention from impairing its unifying effect;

4—355 Declare themselves ready:

1. to examine the possibility of conferring jurisdiction in certain matters on the Court of Justice of the European Communities and, if necessary, to negotiate an agreement to this effect;

2. to arrange meetings at regular intervals between their representatives.

In witness whereof the undersigned, being duly authorized thereto, have signed this Joint Declaration.

Done at Rome on the nineteenth day of June in the year one thousand nine hundred and eighty.

[*Signatures of the Plenipotentiaries*]

4—356 (1) Text as amended by the Convention of 10 April 1984 on the accession of the Hellenic Republic—hereafter referred to as the '1984 Accession Convention' -, by the Convention of 18 May 1992 on the accession of the Kingdom of Spain and the Portuguese Republic—hereafter referred to as the '1992 Accession Convention'—and by the Convention on the accession of the Republic of Austria, the Republic of Finland and the Kingdom of Sweden—hereafter referred to as the '1996 Accession Convention'.

(2) Paragraph deleted by Article 2 (1) of the 1992 Accession Convention.

(3) Article deleted by Article 2 (1) of the 1992 Accession Convention.

(4) Ratification of the Accession Conventions is governed by the following provisions of those conventions:

— as regards the 1984 Accession Convention, by Article 3 of that Convention, which reads as follows:

'Article 3
This Convention shall be ratified by the signatory States. The instruments of ratification shall be deposited with the Secretary-General of the Council of the European Communities.',

— as regards the 1992 Accession Convention, by Article 4 of that Convention, which reads as follows:

'Article 4
This Convention shall be ratified by the signatory States. The instruments of ratification shall be deposited with the Secretary-General of the Council of the European Communities.',

— as regards the 1996 Accession Convention, by Article 5 of that Convention, which reads as follows:

'Article 5
This Convention shall be ratified by the signatory States. The instruments of ratification shall be deposited with the Secretary-General of the Council of the European Union.'.

(5) The entry into force of the Accession Conventions is governed by the following provisions of those Conventions:

— as regards the 1984 Accession Convention, by Article 4 of that Convention, which reads as follows:

'Article 4
This Convention shall enter into force, as between the States which have ratified it, on the first day of

the third month following the deposit of the last instrument of ratification by the Hellenic Republic and seven States which have ratified the Convention on the law applicable to contractual obligations.

This Convention shall enter into force for each Contracting State which subsequently ratifies it on the first day of the third month following the deposit of its instrument of ratification.',

— as regards the 1992 Accession Convention, by Article 5 of that Convention which reads as follows:

'Article 5
This Convention shall enter into force, as between the States which have ratified it, on the first day of the third month following the deposit of the last instrument of ratification by the Kingdom of Spain or the Portuguese Republic and by one State which has ratified the Convention on the law applicable to contractual obligations.

This Convention shall enter into force for each Contracting State which subsequently ratifies it on the first day of the third month following the deposit of its instrument of ratification.',

— as regards the 1996 Accession Convention, by Article 6 of that Convention, which reads as follows:

'Article 6
1. This Convention shall enter into force, as between the States which have ratified it, on the first day of the third month following the deposit of the last instrument of ratification by the Republic of Austria, the Republic of Finland or the Kingdom of Sweden and by one Contracting State which has ratified the Convention on the law applicable to contractual obligations.
2. This Convention shall enter into force for each Contracting State which subsequently ratifies it on the first day of the third month following the deposit of its instrument of ratification.'.

(6) Phrase deleted by the 1992 Accession Convention.

(7) Notification concerning the Accession Convention is governed by the following provisions of those Conventions:

— as regards the 1984 Accession Convention, by Article 5 of that Convention, which reads as follows:

'Article 5
The Secretary-General of the Council of the European Communities shall notify Signatory States of:
(a) the deposit of each instrument of ratification;
(b) the dates of entry into force of this Convention for the Contracting States.',

— as regards the 1992 Accession Convention, by Article 6 of that Convention, which reads as follows:

'Article 6
The Secretary-General of the Council of the European Communities shall notify the signatory States of:
(a) the deposit of each instrument of ratification;
(b) the dates of entry into force of this Convention for the Contracting States.',

— as regards the 1996 Accession Convention, by Article 7 of that Convention, which reads as follows:

'Article 7
The Secretary-General of the Council of the European Union shall notify the signatory States of:
(a) the deposit of each instrument of ratification;
(b) the dates of entry into force of this Convention for the Contracting States.'.

(8) Point (d) as amended by the 1992 Accession Convention.

4—359 (9) An indication of the authentic texts of the Accession Convention is to be found in the following provisions:

— as regards the 1984 Accession Convention, in Articles 2 and 6 of that Convention, which reads as follows:

'Article 2
The Secretary-General of the Council of the European Communities shall transmit a certified copy of the Convention on the law applicable to contractual obligations in the Danish, Dutch, English, French, German, Irish and Italian languages to the Government of the Hellenic Republic.
The text of the Convention on the law applicable to contractual obligations in the Greek language is annexed hereto. The text in the Greek language shall be authentic under the same conditions as the other texts of the Convention on the law applicable to contractual obligations.'

'Article 6
This Convention, drawn up in a single original in the Danish, Dutch, English, French, German, Greek, Irish and Italian languages, all eight texts being equally authentic, shall be deposited in the archives of the General Secretariat of the Council of the European Communities. The Secretary-General shall transmit a certified copy to the Government of each Signatory State.',

— as regards the 1992 Accession Convention, in Articles 3 and 7 of that Convention, which read as follows:

'Article 3
The Secretary-General of the Council of the European Communities shall transmit a certified copy of the Convention on the law applicable to contractual obligations in the Danish, Dutch, English, French, German, Greek, Irish and Italian languages to the Governments of the Kingdom of Spain and the Portuguese Republic.
The text of the Convention on the law applicable to contractual obligations in the Portuguese and Spanish languages is set out in Annexes I and II to this Convention. The texts drawn up in the Portuguese and Spanish languages shall be authentic under the same conditions as the other texts of the Convention on the law applicable to contractual obligations.'

'Article 7
This Convention, drawn up in a single original in the Danish, Dutch, English, French, German, Greek, Irish, Italian, Portuguese and Spanish languages, all texts being equally authentic, shall be deposited in the archives of the General Secretariat of the Council of the European Communities. The Secretary-General shall transmit a certified copy to the Government of each Signatory State.',

— as regards the 1996 Accession Convention, in Articles 4 and 8 of that Convention, which read as follows:

'Article 4
1. The Secretary-General of the Council of the European Union shall transmit a certified copy of the Convention of 1980, the Convention of 1984, the First Protocol of 1988, the Second Protocol of 1988

and the Convention of 1992 in the Danish, Dutch, English, French, German, Greek, Irish, Italian, Spanish and Portuguese languages to the Governments of the Republic of Austria, the Republic of Finland and the Kingdom of Sweden.

2. The text of the Convention of 1980, the Convention of 1984, the First Protocol of 1988, the Second Protocol of 1988 and the Convention of 1992 in the Finnish and Swedish languages shall be authentic under the same conditions as the other texts of the Convention of 1980, the Convention of 1984, the First Protocol of 1988, the Second Protocol of 1988 and the Convention of 1992.'

'Article 8

This Convention, drawn up in a single original in the Danish, Dutch, English, Finnish, French, German, Greek, Irish, Italian, Portuguese, Spanish and Swedish languages, all 12 texts being equally authentic, shall be deposited in the archives of the General Secretariat of the Council of the European Union. The Secretary-General shall transmit a certified copy to the Government of each signatory State.'

(10) Text as amended by the 1996 Accession Convention.

Inter-American Convention On The Law Applicable To International Contracts

4—360   Signed at Mexico, D.F., Mexico, on March 17, 1994, at the Fifth Inter-American Specialized Conference on Private International Law (CIDIP-V)

The States Parties to this Convention,

REAFFIRMING their desire to continue the progressive development and codification of private international law among member States of the Organization of American States;

REASSERTING the advisability of harmonizing solutions to international trade issues;

BEARING in mind that the economic interdependence of States has fostered regional integration and that in order to stimulate the process it is necessary to facilitate international contracts by removing differences in the legal framework for them,

HAVE AGREED to approve the following Convention:

CHAPTER I: SCOPE OF APPLICATION

4—361   Article 1

This Convention shall determine the law applicable to international contracts.

It shall be understood that a contract is international if the parties thereto have their habitual residence or establishments in different States Parties or if the contract has objective ties with more than one State Party.

This Convention shall apply to contracts entered into or contracts to which States or State agencies or entities are party, unless the parties to the contract expressly exclude it. However, any State Party may, at the time it signs, ratifies or accedes to this Convention, declare that the latter shall not apply to all or certain categories of contracts to which the State or State agencies and entities are party.

Any State Party may, at the time it ratifies or accedes to this Convention, declare the categories of contract to which this Convention will not apply.

4—362   Article 2

The law designated by the Convention shall be applied even if said law is that of a State that is not a party.

4—363   Article 3

The provisions of this Convention shall be applied, with necessary and possible adaptations, to the new modalities of contracts used as a consequence of the development of international trade.

4—364   Article 4

For purposes of interpretation and application of this Convention, its international nature and the need to promote uniformity in its application shall be taken into account.

4—365   Article 5

This Convention does not determine the law applicable to:

> a) questions arising from the marital status of natural persons, the capacity of the parties, or the consequences of nullity or invalidity of the contract as a result of the lack of capacity of one of the parties;
>
> b) contractual obligations intended for successional questions, testamentary questions, marital arrangements or those deriving from family relationships;
>
> c) obligations deriving from securities;
>
> d) obligations deriving from securities transactions;
>
> e) the agreements of the parties concerning arbitration or selection of forum;
>
> f) questions of company law, including the existence, capacity, function and dissolution of commercial companies and juridical persons in general.

4—366   Article 6

The provisions of this Convention shall not be applicable to contracts which have autonomous regulations in international conventional law in force among the States Parties to this Convention.

CHAPTER 2: DETERMINATION OF APPLICABLE LAW

4—367   Article 7

The contract shall be governed by the law chosen by the parties. The parties' agreement on this selection must be express or, in the event that there is no express agreement, must be evident from the parties' behavior and from the clauses of the contract, considered as a whole. Said selection may relate to the entire contract or to a part of same.

Selection of a certain forum by the parties does not necessarily entail selection of the applicable law.

4—368   Article 8

The parties may at any time agree that the contract shall, in whole or in part, be subject to a law other than that to which it was previously subject, whether or not that law was chosen by the parties. Nevertheless, that modification shall not affect the formal validity of the original contract nor the rights of third parties.

4—369   Article 9

If the parties have not selected the applicable law, or if their selection proves ineffective, the contract shall be governed by the law of the State with which it has the closest ties.

The Court will take into account all objective and subjective elements of the contract to determine the law of the State with which it has the closest ties. It shall also take into account the general principles of international commercial law recognized by international organizations.

Nevertheless, if a part of the contract were separable from the rest and if it had a closer tie with another State, the law of that State could, exceptionally, apply to that part of the contract.

4—370   Article 10

In addition to the provisions in the foregoing articles, the guidelines, customs, and principles of international commercial law as well as commercial usage and practices generally accepted shall apply in order to discharge the requirements of justice and equity in the particular case.

4—371   Article 11

Notwithstanding the provisions of the preceding articles, the provisions of the law of the forum shall necessarily be applied when they are mandatory requirements.

It shall be up to the forum to decide when it applies the mandatory provisions of the law of another State with which the contract has close ties.

Chapter 3: Existence and Validity of the Contract

4—372   Article 12

The existence and the validity of the contract or of any of its provisions, and the substantive validity of the consent of the parties concerning the selection of the applicable law, shall be governed by the appropriate rules in accordance with Chapter 2 of this Convention.

Nevertheless, to establish that one of the parties has not duly consented, the judge shall determine the applicable law, taking into account the habitual residence or principal place of business.

4—373   Article 13

A contract between parties in the same State shall be valid as to form if it meets the requirements laid down in the law governing said contract pursuant to this Convention or with those of the law of the State in which the contract is valid or with the law of the place where the contract is performed.

If the persons concerned are in different States at the time of its conclusion, the contract shall be valid as to form if it meets the requirements of the law governing it as to substance, or those of the law of one of the States in which it is concluded or with the law of the place where the contract is performed.

Chapter 4: Scope of the Applicable Law

4—374   Article 14

The law applicable to the contract in virtue of Chapter 2 of this Convention shall govern principally:

    a) its interpretation;

    b) the rights and obligations of the parties;

    c) the performance of the obligations established by the contract and the consequences of nonperformance of the contract, including assessment of injury to the extent that this may determine payment of compensation;

    d) the various ways in which the obligations can be performed, and prescription and lapsing of actions;

    e) the consequences of nullity or invalidity of the contract.

4—375   Article 15

The provisions of Article 10 shall be taken into account when deciding whether an agent can obligate its principal or an agency, a company or a juridical person.

4—376   Article 16

The law of the State where international contracts are to be registered or published shall govern all matters concerning publicity in respect of same.

4—377   Article 17

For the purposes of this Convention, "law" shall be understood to mean the law current in a State, excluding rules concerning conflict of laws.

4—378   Article 18

Application of the law designated by this Convention may only be excluded when it is manifestly contrary to the public order of the forum.

Chapter 5: General Provisions

4—379   Article 19

In a State Party, the provisions of this Convention shall apply to contracts concluded subsequent to its entry into force in that State.

4—380   Article 20

This Convention shall not affect the application of other international conventions to which a State Party to this Convention is or becomes a party, insofar as they are pertinent, or those concluded within the context of integration movements.

4—381   Article 21

When signing, ratifying or acceding to this Convention, States may formulate reservations that apply to one or more specific provisions and which are not incompatible with the effect and purpose of this Convention.

A State Party may at any time withdraw a reservation it has formulated. The effect of such reservation shall cease on the first day of the third calendar month following the date of notification of withdrawal.

4—382 Article 22

In the case of a State which has two or more systems of law applicable in different territorial units with respect to matters covered by the Convention: a) any reference to the laws of the State shall be construed as a reference to the laws in the territorial unit in question; b) any reference to habitual residence or place of business in that State shall be construed as a reference to habitual residence or place of business in a territorial unit of that State.

4—383 Article 23

A State within which different territorial units have their own systems of law in regard to matters covered by this Convention shall not be obliged to apply this Convention to conflicts between the legal systems in force in such units.

4—384 Article 24

If a State has two or more territorial units in which different systems of law apply in relation to the matters dealt with in this Convention, it may, at the time of signature, ratification or accession, declare that this Convention shall extend to all its territorial units or to only one or more of them.

Such declaration may be modified by subsequent declarations, which shall expressly indicate the territorial unit or units to which the Convention applies. Such subsequent declarations shall be transmitted to the General Secretariat of the Organization of American States, and shall take effect ninety days after the date of their receipt.

CHAPTER 6: FINAL CLAUSES

4—385 Article 25

This Convention shall be open to signature by the member States of the Organization of American States.

4—386 Article 26

This Convention shall be subject to ratification. The instruments of ratification shall be deposited with the General Secretariat of the Organization of American States.

4—387   Article 27

This Convention shall remain open for accession by any other State after it has entered into force. The instruments of accession shall be deposited with the General Secretariat of the Organization of American States.

4—388   Article 28

This Convention shall enter into force for the ratifying States on the thirtieth day following the date of deposit of the second instrument of ratification.

For each State ratifying or acceding to the Convention after the deposit of the second instrument of ratification, the Convention shall enter into force on the thirtieth day after deposit by such State of its instrument of ratification or accession.

4—389   Article 29

This Convention shall remain in force indefinitely, but any of the States Parties may denounce it. The instrument of denunciation shall be deposited with the General Secretariat of the Organization of American States. After one year from the date of deposit of the instrument of denunciation, the Convention shall no longer be in force for the denouncing State.

4—390   Article 30

The original instrument of this Convention, the English, French, Portuguese and Spanish texts of which are equally authentic, shall be deposited with the General Secretariat of the Organization of American States, which shall forward an authenticated copy of its text to the Secretariat of the United Nations for registration and publication in accordance with Article 102 of its Charter. The General Secretariat of the Organization of American States shall notify the Member States of the Organization and the States that have acceded to the Convention of the signatures, deposits of instruments of ratification, accession and denunciation, as well as of reservations, if any, and of their withdrawal.

IN WITNESS WHEREOF the undersigned Plenipotentiaries, being duly authorized thereto by their respective Governments, do hereby sign the present Convention.

DONE AT MEXICO, D.F., MEXICO, this seventeenth day of March, one thousand nine hundred and ninety-four.

Index

This index covers both volumes. All paragraph numbers prefixed by a number refers to Volume 1: Materials. All paragraph numbers prefixed by 'C' refers to Volume 2: Cases.

Abrogation of jurisdiction
  generally C–045
Ad hoc arbitration
  delay C–055
Admiralty proceedings
  retention of security where stayed 1–012
Agreement to exclude jurisdiction of court 1–088
Ambiguity of awards
  generally C–126
American Arbitration Association's Code of Ethics
  arbitrator in communicating with parties should avoid impropriety or appearance of impropriety 3–006
  arbitrator should be faithful to relationship of trust and confidentiality inherent in office 3–009
  arbitrator should conduct proceedings fairly and diligently 3–007
  arbitrator should disclose any interest or relationship likely to affect impartiality or which might create appearance of partiality or bias 3–004–3–005
    disclosure 3–005
  arbitrator should make decisions in just, independent and deliberate manner 3–008
  arbitrator should uphold integrity and fairness of arbitration process 3–003

American Arbitration Association's Code of Ethics—*cont.*
  ethical considerations relating to arbitrators appointed by one party 3–010–3–016
  generally 3–001–3–016
Anticipatory breach
  arbitration agreements C–127
Anti-suit injunctions
  jurisdiction C–034, C–130
Antitrust law
  application by English courts of C–034
  arbitrability C–009, C–010, C–089, C–109
  security transactions C–113
Appeals against awards
  refusal of permission for C–013, C–104
Appointment of arbitrators
  barristers C–079
  "commercial men" C–101
  generally 1–017
  judges 1–094
  validity C–121
Arab Centre for Commercial Arbitration
  Board of Directors 2–154–2–156
  generally 2–153–2–162
Arab Convention on Commercial Arbitration
  absence of parties 2–177
  application 2–151
  appointment of arbitrator 2–167
  Arab Centre for Commercial Arbitration 2–153–2–162
  arbitral proceedings 2–165–2–179
  arbitral tribunal 2–163, 2–164

Arab Convention on Commercial Arbitration—*cont.*
award 2–180–2–184
Bureau 2–157
challenge to arbitrator 2–168
courts, and 2–176
evidence 2–174
final provisions 2–186–2–191
general provisions 2–150
generally 2–149–2–191
interim measures of protection 2–178
language of proceedings 2–172
place of arbitration 2–171
plea of lack of jurisdiction 2–173
re-opening hearings 2–175
reference to arbitration 2–152
seat 2–161
transitory provisions 2–185

Arbitrability
antitrust law C–009, C–010, C–089, C–109
security transactions C–113, C–128
standard of review C–052
validity of arbitration agreement C–103

Arbitral institutions
immunity 1–075

Arbitral proceedings
arbitrability
standard of review C–052
validity of arbitration agreement C–103
assessors, power to appoint 1–038
concurrent hearings 1–036
consolidation 1–036
delay
ad hoc arbitration C–055
injunctions C–033
want of prosecution, dismissal for C–084
diplomatic immunity C–006
disclosure of documents C–015
evidence
admission, limitations on C–036
failure to submit C–099
generally 1–035
withholding C–031, C–054
experts, power to appoint 1–038
fair hearing, right to C–124
fraud by party C–075
general duty of parties 1–041
general duty of tribunal 1–034
generally 1–034–1–042
injunctions restraining C–033

Arbitral proceedings—*cont.*
legal advisers, power to appoint 1–038
legal representation 1–037
loss of right to object 1–074
multiple parties C–002, C–003, C–076
powers of court in relation to arbitral proceedings 1–043–1–046
see also Court, powers of
procedural matters 1–035
provisional awards 1–040
representation 1–037
rights of person who takes no part in 1–073
State immunity
embassies C–028
nationalisation C–008, C–082
third party debt orders C–006
waiver C–028, C–070, C–081
summary judgment C–063
umpires C–058

Arbitral tribunal
chairman 1–021
competence to rule on own jurisdiction 1–031
decision-making where no chairman or umpire 1–023
determination of preliminary point of jurisdiction 1–033
general powers exercisable by 1–039
generally 1–016–1–033
objection to substantive jurisdiction 1–032
powers in case of party's default 1–042
umpires 1–022, C–058

Arbitration
general principles 1–002
seat
meaning 1–004
signature of award in country other than C–062
small claims in county court 1–093

Arbitration agreements
see also Arbitration pursuant to arbitration agreement
anticipatory breach C–127
choice of law clauses C–122, C–125, C–130
collateral agreements C–098
collective bargaining agreements C–126
death of party, discharge by 1–009

Arbitration agreements—*cont.*
  employment contracts C–027
  frustration C–104
  illegality C–064
  immunity from jurisdiction C–124
  incorporation by reference C–029
  interpretation
    generally C–098, C–104
    multiple meanings, C–119
  meaning 1–007
  pacta sunt servanda C–124
  performance, incapability of
    C–106
  proper law
    charterparties C–042
    choice of law clauses C–125
    insurance contracts C–011
    setting aside of awards C–093
  repudiation C–061, C–127
  separability 1–008, C–105
  standard conditions C–029
  stay of legal proceedings,
    1–010–1–012
    see also Stay of legal
      proceedings
  uncertainty C–119
  validity C–103, C–119, C–130
  writing, in 1–006
Arbitration pursuant to arbitration agreement
  see also Arbitration agreement
  bills of exchange C–095
  binding submission to arbitration
    C–057
  charterparties
    Centrocon arbitration clause
      C–005, C–019, C–099
    comity C–004
    "commercial men", arbitrators to
      be C–101
    consecutive voyages C–005
    costs C–110–C112
    demurrage C–085
    exclusion clauses C–016, C–085
    frustration C–104
    generally 1–002–1–085
    Hague Rules, incorporation of
      C–092
    indemnities C–123
    interpretation C–004, C–059,
      C–099
    jurisdiction C–004, C–020
    paramount clauses C–092
    performance, incapability of
      C–106

Arbitration pursuant to arbitration agreement—*cont.*
  charter parties—*cont.*
    proper law of contract in absence
      of express provision C–042
    salvage expenses C–110–C112
    stay of arbitral proceedings
      C–014
    time limits C–005, C–019, C–092
  collective bargaining agreements
    C–126
  jurisdiction
    abrogation by subsequent
      illegality C–045
    anti-suit injunctions C–034, C–130
    bills of exchange C–095
    choice of law clauses C–094,
      C–130
    collateral agreements C–051
    matters arising under contract
      C–051, C–072
    mistake, rectification on grounds
      of C–020
    proper law differing from seat
      C–091
    public policy C–032
    seat differing from proper law
      C–091
    Sharia law C–094
    unconscionable conduct C–034
  mandatory provisions 1–005
  mistake, rectification on grounds of
    C–020
  non-mandatory provisions 1–005
  partnership agreements C–095
  proper law of contract
    charterparties C–042
    choice of law clauses C–125
    insurance contracts C–011
    setting aside of awards C–093
  rectification
    documents ancillary to main
      contract C–047
    mistake C–020
  security transactions C–096
  scope of application of provisions
    of 1996 Act 1–003
  time limits
    awards, making of C–080
    charterparties C–005, C–019
    generally C–069
Arbitrators
  appointment
    barristers C–079
    "commercial men" C–101

Arbitrators—*cont.*
  appointment—*cont.*
    generally 1–017
    judges 1–094
    validity C–121
  barristers, independence of C–079
  bias C–021, C–041, C–058, C–077
  commitment fees C–077
  court to have regard to agreed qualifications 1–020
  death 1–027
  disagreement between C–058
  evidence, powers to admit C–036
  failure of appointment procedure 1–019
  fees and expenses, joint and several liability of parties for 1–029
  filling of vacancy 1–028
  immunity
    generally 1–030
    negligence C–018
    quasi-arbitrators C–018
  independence C–021, C–041, C–058, C–077
  misconduct
    commitment fees C–077
    special case, failure to state C–097
  power of court to remove 1–025
  resignation 1–026
  removal C–079
  revocation of authority 1–024
  sole, power in case of default to appoint 1–018
  umpires C–058, C–097
Australia
  International Arbitration Act 1974 1–312–3–325/95
    accession to Convention 1–319
    arbitrator, liability of 1–325/15
    definitions 1–315
    delegation by Secretary to the Department of Foreign Affairs and Trade 1–324
    enforcement of foreign arbitral proceedings 1–132
    evidence of awards and arbitration agreements 1–322
    evidence relating to Convention 1–323
    international commercial arbitration 1–325/3–1–325/17
    investment disputes, settlement of 1–325/18–1–325/23, 1–325/75–1–325/96

Arbitrators—*cont.*
  International Arbitration Act 1974—*cont.*
    judiciary act 1–325/1
    Model Law 1–325/4–1–325/9
    Notes to 1–325/97, 1–325/98
    optional provisions 1–325/10–1–325/14
    recognition of foreign awards 1–321
    representation in proceedings 1–325/16
    UN Conference on International Commercial Arbitration Convention on the Recognition and Enforcement of Foreign Arbitral Awards 1–325/24–1–325/39
    UNCITRAL Model Law 1–325/40–1–325/74
Award
  ambiguity C–126
  appeal, refusal of permission for C–013, C–104
  bankruptcy, and C–065–C–067
  clerical errors C–116
  correction 1–058
  court, powers of 1–067–1–072
    appeal, refusal of permission for C–013, C–104
    appeal on point of law 1–070, 1–071
    challenging award 1–068, 1–069, 1–071
    effect of court order 1–072
    enforcement 1–067
    serious irregularity 1–069
  date of 1–055
  different issues, on 1–048
  effect 1–059
  enforcement
    public policy C–115
    State immunity, C–028
    third party debt orders C–046
    trustees in bankruptcy, against C–065–C–067
  evidence, withholding of C–031, C–054
  exclusion clauses C–086
  extension of time for making 1–051
  foreign governments C–072
  form 1–053
  fraud
    evidence, withholding of C–031, C–054

Award—*cont.*
  fraud—*cont.*
    traffic in influence and bribery C–048
  generally 1–047–1–059
  insolvency, and C–065–C–067
  interest
    generally 1–050
    rate C–030, C–038, C–068, C–080
    interim C–086, C–117
  judicial review of C–078, C–104
  jurisdiction
    abrogation by subsequent illegality C–045
    bills of lading C–007
    conduct of parties C–007
    enforcement of awards C–035
    non-parties to arbitration agreements C–017
  notification 1–056
  partial, review of C–031
  place where treated as made
    generally 1–054
    signature in country other than seat C–062
  power to withhold in case of non-payment 1–057
  punitive damages C–075, C–129
  reasoning, insufficient C–056, C–126
  remedies 1–049
  rules applicable to substance of dispute 1–047
  satisfaction, inability of party to make C–065–C–067, C–106
  setting aside
    bias C–021, C–041, C–050
    evidence, refusal to admit C–045
    fraud C–031, C–048, C–054
    misconduct of arbitrator C–012
  settlement 1–052
  special C–097
  time limits C–080, C–120

Bankruptcy
  awards, and C–065–C–067
Barristers, independence of
  appointment of arbitrators C–079
Bias of arbitrators
  generally C–021, C–041, C–058, C–077
Bills of exchange
  arbitration agreements C–095

Binding submission to arbitration
  arbitration agreements C–057
Centrocon arbitration clause
  charterparties, arbitration pursuant to C–005, C–019, C–099
Charterparties, arbitration pursuant to
  Centrocon arbitration clause C–005, C–019, C–099
  comity C–004
  "commercial men", arbitrators to be C–101
  consecutive voyages C–005
  costs C–110–C112
  demurrage C–085
  exclusion clauses C–016, C–085
  frustration C–104
  Hague Rules, incorporation of C–092
  indemnities C–123
  interpretation C–004, C–059, C–099
  jurisdiction C–004, C–020
  paramount clauses C–092
  performance, incapability of C–106
  proper law in absence of express provision C–042
  salvage expenses C–110–C112
  stay of arbitral proceedings C–014
  time limits C–005, C–019, C–092
China
  arbitration agreement 1–341–1–345
  Arbitration Association 1–335–1–340
  Arbitration Commission 1–335–1–340
  Arbitration Law
    general principles 1–326–1–334
    generally 1–326–1–405
  arbitration procedure 1–346–1–382
    acceptance 1–346–1–354
    application 1–346–1–354
    formation of arbitration tribunal 1–355–1–363
    hearing 1–364–1–382
    ruling 1–364–1–382
  execution 1–387–1–389
  generally 1–326–1–405
  recognition and enforcement of foreign awards C–088, C–114
  request to repeal ruling 1–383–1–386
  special provisions for arbitrations involving foreign concerns 1–390–1–398

Choice of law clauses
  arbitration agreements C–122,
    C–125, C–130
  jurisdiction C–094, C–130
Clerical errors
  awards C–116
Collateral agreements
  arbitration agreements C–098
  jurisdiction C–051
Collective bargaining agreements
  arbitration agreements C–126
Comity
  charterparties, arbitration pursuant
    to C–004
**Commencement of arbitral
  proceedings**
  generally 1–013–1–015
  Limitation Acts, application of
    1–014
  power of court to extend time for
    1–013
"Commercial men"
  appointment of arbitrators C–101
**Commitment fees payable to
  arbitrators**
  generally C–077
Common law
  matters governed by 1–082
Consecutive voyages
  charterparties, arbitration pursuant
    to C–005
Consumer arbitration agreements
  application of unfair terms
    regulations 1–090
  consumer legal person, where 1–091
  generally 1–090–1–092
  unfair where modest amount sought
    1–092
**Convention on Law applicable to
  Contractual Obligations**
  applicable law in absence of choice
    4–322
  burden of proof 4–332
  consumer contracts 4–323
  employment contracts 4–324
  final provisions 4–341–4–351
  formal validity 4–327
  freedom of choice 4–321
  generally 4–318–4–359
  incapacity 4–329
  joint declarations 4–353–4–359
  mandatory rules 4–325
  material validity 4–326
  no retrospective effect 4–335
  ordre public 4–334

**Convention on Law applicable to
  Contractual Obligations**—*cont.*
  precedence of Community law
    4–338
  Protocol 4–352
  relationship with other Conventions
    4–339
  reservations 4–340
  scope 4–319, 4–320
  scope of applicable law 4–328
  States with more than one legal
    system 4–337
  subrogation 4–331
  uniform interpretation 4–336
  uniform rules 4–321–4–340
  voluntary assignment 4–330
**Convention on the Settlement of
  Investment Disputes between
  States and Nationals of Other
  States.** *see* **ICSID**
Costs of arbitration 1–060–1–066
  agreement to pay in any event
    1–061
  award of 1–062
  effect of agreement or award about
    1–063
  generally 1–060–1–066
  recoverable
    generally 1–064
    power to limit 1–066
  recoverable fees and expenses of
    arbitrators 1–065
  salvage expenses C–110–C112
  security for
    insolvent parties C–043, C–044
    non-residents C–025, C–043,
      C–044
  settlement offers, rejection of C–049
County court
  jurisdiction 1–106
Court
  agreement to exclude jurisdiction of
    1–088
  meaning 1–106
Court, powers of
  anti-trust law, application by
    English courts of C–034
  award, in relation to. *see* Award
  determination of preliminary point
    of law 1–046
  enforcement of peremptory orders
    of tribunal 1–043
  exercisable in support of arbitral
    proceedings 1–045
  generally 1–043–1–046

Court, powers of—*cont.*
jurisdiction C–122
orders in aid of arbitration
C–122
removal of arbitrators C–077,
C–121
securing attendance of witnesses
1–044
security for costs C–025
service of documents 1–078
want of prosecution, dismissal for
C–084
Crown 1–107
Death
arbitrator 1–027
party 1–009
Definitions
generally 1–083
index 1–084
Delay
ad hoc arbitration C–055
injunctions C–033
want of prosecution, dismissal for
C–084
Demurrage
charterparties, arbitration pursuant
to C–085
Diplomatic immunity
generally C–006
Disclosure of documents
generally C–015
Domestic arbitration agreements
1–086

Egypt
arbitral award 1–449–1–461
arbitral panel 1–425–1–434
arbitration agreement 1–420–1–424
closing of procedures 1–449–1–461
conduct of arbitral proceedings
1–435–1–448
enforcement of arbitral awards
1–465–1–468
generally 1–406–1–468
Law Concerning Arbitration
in Civil and Commercial
Matters
general provisions 1–411–1–419
generally 1–411–1–468
nullity of arbitral award
1–462–1–464
recognition of arbitral awards
1–465–1–468
Embassies
State immunity C–028

Employment contracts
arbitration agreements C–027
Enforcement of awards
public policy C–115
third party debt orders C–046
trustees in bankruptcy, against
C–065–C–067
Enforcement of foreign awards. *see*
**Recognition and enforcement of
foreign awards**
Ethical rules 3–001–3–136
European contract law principles
adaptation of contract 4–173
agents, authority of 4–154–4–168
direct representation
4–156–4–164
general provisions 4–154, 4–155
indirect representation
4–165–4–168
assignment of claims 4–265–4–281
effects as between assignee and
debtor 4–273–4–280
effects as between assignor and
assignee 4–269–4–272
general principles 4–265–4–268
order of priority between assignee
and competing claimants
4–281
avoidance 4–180–4–184
capitalisation of interest 4–317
computation of time 4–132
conditions 4–314–4–316
contents 4–195–4–205
damages 4–185
effects 4–195–4–205
excessive benefit 4–177
exclusion or restriction of remedies
4–186
formation
acceptance 4–141–4–151
general provisions 4–134–4–140
generally 4–134–4–153
negotiations, liability for 4–152,
4–153
offer 4–141–4–151
fraud 4–175
general duties 4–127, 4–128
general provisions 4–120–4–133
generally 4–20–4–317
illegality 4–309–4–313
imputed intention 4–133
imputed knowledge 4–133
inaccuracy in communication 4–172
incorrect information 4–174
initial impossibility 4–170

European contract law
    principles—cont.
  interpretation 4–188–4–194
  mistake 4–171
  non-performance 4–216–4–224
  notice 4–131
  performance 4–206–4–215
  plurality of creditors 4–260–4–264
  plurality of debtors 4–249–4–259
  plurality of parties 4–249–4–264
  prescription
    effects 4–305–4–307
    extension of period 4–296–4–302
    general provision 4–292
    generally 4–292–4–308
    modification by agreement
      4–308
    periods 4–293–4–295
    renewal of periods 4–303, 4–304
  reasonableness 4–130
  remedies 4–216–4–224
  remedies for non-performance
    damages 4–239–4–248
    generally 4–187, 4–225–4–248
    interest 4–239–4–248
    price reduction 4–238
    right to performance
      4–225–4–227
    termination 4–229–4–237
    withholding performance 4–228
  scope 4–120–4–126
  set-off 4–285–4–291
  substitution of new debtor 4–282,
    4–283
  terminology 4–129–4–133
  third persons 4–179
  threats 4–176
  transfer of contract 4–284
  unfair advantage 4–177
  unfair terms not individually
    negotiated 4–178
  validity 4–169–4–187
European Convention on
    International Commercial
    Arbitration
  applicable law 2–130
  final clauses 2–133
  generally 2–123–2–134
  jurisdiction of courts of law 2–129
  organization of arbitration 2–127
  plea as to arbitral jurisdiction
    2–128
  reasons for award 2–131
  right of foreign nationals to be
    designated as arbitrators 2–126

European Convention providing
    Uniform Law on Arbitration—
    cont.
  right of legal persons of public
    law to resort to arbitration
    2–125
  scope 2–124
  setting aside of award 2–132
  Special Committee
    composition 2–134
    procedure 2–134
European Convention providing
    Uniform Law on Arbitration
  appointment of arbitrators
    1–542–1–545
  arbitral tribunal 1–540–1–543,
    1–550–1–553
  arbitration agreement 1–536–1–539
  award 1–554–1–565
  challenge to arbitrator 1–547,
    1–548
  compromise 1–566
  derogation from 1–567
  generally 1–520–1–568
  Uniform Law 1–536
Evidence
  admission, limitations on C–036
  failure to submit C–099
  generally 1–035
  withholding C–031, C–054
Exclusion clauses
  appeals against awards C–086
  charterparties, arbitration pursuant
    to C–016, C–085
Exhaustion of domestic remedies
  North American Free Trade
    Agreement C–083

Fair hearing, right to
  immunity from jurisdiction C–124
Foreign governments
  awards C–072
France
  international arbitration
    1–186–1–201
  enforcement of awards
    1–192–1–201
  meaning 1–186
  public policy C–115
  recognition of awards
    1–192–1–201
  New York Convention
    availability of enforcement
      C–100
    inapplicability C–056

Fraud by party
  evidence, withholding of C–031, C–054
  punitive damages C–075
  traffic in influence and bribery C–048
Frustration
  arbitration agreements C–104

Germany
  arbitration agreement 1–206–1–210
    arbitrability 1–207
    definition 1–206
    form 1–208
    interim measures by court, and 1–210
    substantive claim before court, and 1–209
  award
    additional 1–235
    application for setting aside 1–236
    contents 1–231
    correction 1–235
    decision-making by panel of arbitrators 1–229
    effect 1–232
    enforcement 1–237, 1–238
    form 1–231
    generally 1–228–1–235
    interpretation 1–235
    recognition 1–237, 1–238
    rules applicable to substance of dispute 1–228
  competence of arbitral tribunal to rule on jurisdiction 1–217
  conduct of arbitral proceedings
    commencement 1–221
    court assistance in taking evidence and other judicial acts 1–227
    default of party 1–225
    defence 1–223
    expert appointed by arbitral tribunal 1–226
    general rules of procedure 1–219
    generally 1–219–1–227
    language 1–222
    oral hearings 1–224
    place of arbitration 1–220
    statements of claim 1–223
    written proceedings 1–224
  constitution of arbitral tribunal
    appointment of arbitrators 1–212
    appointment of substitute arbitrator 1–216

Germany—*cont.*
  constitution of arbitral tribunal—*cont.*
    challenge of arbitrator 1–213
    challenge procedure 1–214
    composition 1–211
    failure or impossibility to act 1–215
    generally 1–211–1–216
  costs, decision on 1–234
  court proceedings
    competence 1–239
    legal remedies 1–242
    generally 1–239–1–243
    particularities regarding enforcement of awards 1–241
  extent of court intervention 1–203
  generally 1–202–1–243
  interim measures of protection 1–218
  jurisdiction of arbitral tribunal 1–217, 1–218
  loss of right to object 1–204
  receipt of written communications in case of unknown whereabouts 1–205
  settlement 1–230
  termination of proceedings 1–233
Guidelines on Conflicts of Interest in International Arbitration
  general standards 3–018–3–028
    conflict of interests 3–018
    disclosure by arbitrator 3–019
    explanatory notes, 3–021–3–023
    general principle 3–018
    Green List 3–028
    information known to parties 3–020
    Orange List 3–025, 3–027
    practical application 3–024–3–028
    Red List
      generally 3–021
      non-waivable 3–023
      waivable 3–024
    relationships 3–020
    scope 3–020
    waiver by parties 3–019
  generally 3–017–3–028

Hague Rules, incorporation of
  charterparties, arbitration pursuant to C–092
High Court of England and Wales
  jurisdiction 1–106

IBA Rules on Taking of Evidence in International Commercial Arbitration
admissibility of evidence 3–135
assessment of evidence 3–135
definitions 3–127
documents 3–129
evidentiary hearing 3–134
generally 3–125–3–135
party-appointed experts 3–131
scope of application 3–128
tribunal-appointed experts 3–132, 3–133
witnesses of fact 3–130
ICC Rules
evidence, fraudulent withholding of C–031
exclusion clauses, incorporation of C–016, C–086
independence C–021
interim awards C–086
partial awards, review of C–031
security for costs
  insolvent parties C–043, C–044
  non-residents C–025, C–043, C–044
"step in the proceedings" C–108
ICSID
Administrative Council
  Chairman 2–022
  composition 2–021
  functions 2–023
  generally 2–021–2–025
  meetings 2–024
amendment of Convention 2–082, 2–083
Arbitral Tribunal
  constitution 2–054–2–057
  functions 2–058–2–064
  generally 2–054–2–064
  powers 2–058–2–064
  procedure 2–058–2–064
arbitration
  generally 2–053–2–072
  request for 2–053
award
  annulment 2–067–2–069
  dispatch of copies 2–066
  enforcement 2–070–2–072
  generally 2–065–2–072
  interpretation 2–067–2–069
  recognition 2–070–2–072
  revision 2–067–2–069

ICSID—*cont.*
conciliation
  Conciliation Commission 2–046–2–048
  generally 2–045–2–052
  proceedings 2–049–2–052
  request for 2–045
  settlement 2–051
consent of parties 2–043
cost of proceedings 2–076–2–078
diplomatic protection, and 2–044
disputes between Contracting States 2–081
disqualification of arbitrators 2–073–2–075
disqualification of conciliators 2–073–2–075
establishment 2–018–2–020
final provisions of Convention 2–084–2–090
financing 2–034
generally 2–017–2–091
immunities 2–035–2–041
jurisdiction
  generally 2–042–2–044
  "national of another Contracting State" 2–042
legal personality 2–035
organization 2–018–2–020
Panel of Arbitrators 2–029–2–033
Panel of Conciliators 2–029–2–033
Panels 2–029–2–033
place of proceedings 2–079, 2–080
privileges 2–035–2–041
replacement of arbitrators 2–073–2–075
replacement of conciliators 2–073–2–075
Secretariat 2–026–2–028
Secretary-General 2–027, 2–028
State/sovereign immunity, waiver of C–081
status 2–035–2–041
stay of proceedings C–024
Illegality
arbitration agreements C–064
Immunity
arbitrators
  generally 1–030
  negligence C–018
  quasi-arbitrators C–018
diplomatic C–006
jurisdiction, from C–124

Index

Impartiality of arbitrators
generally C–021, C–041, C–058, C–077
Incorporation by reference
arbitration agreements C–029
Indemnities
charterparties, arbitration pursuant to C–123
Independence of arbitrators
generally C–021, C–041, C–058, C–077
Index of defined expressions 1–084
Injunctions
arbitrators' powers C–118
delay C–033
interim C–117
restraining arbitral proceedings C–033
Insolvency
awards, and C–065–C–067
Inter-American Convention on International Commercial Arbitration
appointment of arbitrators 2–137
award, effect of 2–139
generally 2–235–2–248 1–305–1–311
refusal of recognition and execution of decision 2–140, 2–141
validity of arbitration agreement 2–136
Inter-American Convention on Law applicable to International Contracts
determination of applicable law 4–367–4–371
existence of contract 4–372, 4–373
final clauses 4–385–4–390
general provisions 4–379–4–384
generally 4–360–4–390
scope of applicable law 4–374–4–378
scope of application 4–361–4–366
validity of contract 4–372, 4–373
Interest
generally 1–050
rate C–030, C–038, C–068, C–080
Interim awards
generally C–086, C–117
International Arbitration Conventions 2–001–2–137
International Centre for Settlement of Investment Disputes. *see* ICSID
International Chamber of Commerce Arbitration Rules. *see* ICC Rules

International contractual instruments 4–001–4–390
Interpleader issue
reference to arbitration 1–011
Interpretation of arbitration agreements
charterparties C–004, C–059, C–099
generally C–098, C–104
multiple meanings, C–119
Ireland
adoption of UNCITRAL Model Law on International Commercial Arbitration 1–112–1–166
international commercial arbitration
amendments to Arbitration Acts 1954 and 1980 1–128, 1–129
consolidation of arbitral proceedings and concurrent hearings 1–120
construction of Model Law 1–117
court powers exercisable in support of proceedings 1–118a
effect of award 1–125
generally 1–112–1–166
High Court, functions of 1–118
interest 1–121
powers of arbitral tribunal in relation to examination of witnesses 1–119
recoverable costs of arbitration 1–122
recoverable fees and expenses of arbitral tribunal 1–122
restriction on liability of arbitrators 1–123
time limits for setting aside award 1–124
Islamic (Sharia) law
jurisdiction C–094

Judges
appointment as arbitrators 1–094
Judicial review of awards
generally C–078, C–104
Jurisdiction
abrogation by subsequent illegality C–045
anti-suit injunctions C–034, C–130
bills of exchange C–095

Jurisdiction—*cont.*
  bills of lading C–007
  charterparties, arbitration pursuant to C–004, C–020
  choice of law clauses C–094, C–130
  collateral agreements C–051
  conduct of parties C–007
  courts' powers C–122
  enforcement of awards C–035
  proper law differing from seat C–091
  matters arising under contract C–051, C–072
  mistake, rectification on grounds of C–020
  non-parties to arbitration agreements C–017
  North American Free Trade Agreement C–083
  public policy C–032
  seat differing from proper law C–091
  Sharia law C–094
  unconscionable conduct C–034

Misconduct of arbitrators
  commitment fees C–077
  disclosure, failure to order C–012
  special case, failure to state C–097
Mistake
  arbitration agreements, rectification of C–020
Multiple parties
  generally C–002, C–003, C–076

Negligence of arbitrators
  immunity C–018
New York Convention awards
  agreement or award falling under 1–298
  appointment of arbitrators 1–302
  bankruptcy law, impact on C–053
  compulsion to arbitrate 1–302, C–073
  enforcement
    enforceability C–114
    generally 1–297
    jurisdiction C–037
    jurisdiction, personal C–026
    procedural irregularity C–102
    public policy C–088
  enforcement of agreements to arbitrate 1–302, C–073
  forum non conveniens, C–090

New York Convention awards—*cont.*
  French law, availability of enforcement under C–100
  generally 1–101
  inapplicability under French law C–056
  independence of arbitrators C–050
  interest rates C–080
  jurisdiction
    generally 1–299
    personal C–026, C–037
  local law, propriety under C–040
  new evidence C–050
  non-domestic arbitration C–107
  place of arbitration C–073
  procedural irregularity C–001, C–071, C–102
  procedural law of seat C–068
  public policy C–088, C–102
  removal of cases from State courts 1–301
  res judicata C–040
  State immunity
    generally C–074
    waiver C–070
  stay of arbitral proceedings C–014
  stay of legal proceedings C–074, C–076, C–087, C–107
  third party debt orders C–087
  time limits C–080
  vacation of C–068, C–071
  venue 1–300
  waiver of arbitration C–073
North American Free Trade Agreement
  appointment of arbitrators 2–200
  claim by investor of party on behalf of enterprise 2–194
  claim by investor of party on behalf of itself 2–193
  conditions precedent to submission of claim to arbitration 2–198
  consent to arbitration 2–199
  constitution of tribunal when party fails to appoint arbitrator 2–201
  consolidation 2–202
  definitions 2–215
  documents 2–205
  enforcement of award 2–212
  exclusions 2–214
  exclusions from dispute settlement 2–217
  exhaustion of domestic remedies, C–083

North American Free Trade Agreement—*cont.*
final award 2–211
finality of award 2–212
generally 2–192–2–217
governing law 2–207
interim measures of protection 2–210
interpretation of annexes 2–208
jurisdiction C–083
notice 2–203
notice of intent to submit claim to arbitration 2–196
number of arbitrators 2–200
participation by party 2–204
place of arbitration 2–206
receipts under insurance of guarantee contracts 2–213
report from expert 2–209
settlement of claim through consultation and negotiation 2–195
settlement of disputes 2–192–2–215
submission of claim to arbitration 2–197, 2–216
time when claim submitted to arbitration 2–213
Notices
service of 1–077

OHADA Uniform Act on Arbitration
arbitral award 1–587–1–592
arbitral hearing 1–577–1–586
constitution of arbitral tribunal 1–573–1–576
enforcement of awards 1–598–1–602
final provisions 1–603, 1–604
generally 1–569–1–604
recognition of awards 1–598–1–602
recourse against arbitral award 1–593–1–597
scope of application 1–569–1–572
Orders in aid of arbitration
courts' powers C–122

Pacta sunt servanda
arbitration agreements C–124
Paramount clauses
charterparties, arbitration pursuant to C–092
Partial awards
review of C–031
Partnership agreements
arbitration agreements C–095

Performance of arbitration agreements, incapability of
generally C–106
Place of making of awards
generally 1–054
signature in country other than seat C–062
Procedural rules
generally 3–001–3–136
Proper law of contract
charterparties C–042
choice of law clauses C–125
generally C–011
jurisdiction C–091
seat, differing from C–091
setting aside of awards C–093
Public policy
France C–115
jurisdiction C–032
recognition and enforcement of foreign awards C–088, C–102
Punitive damages
awards C–075, C–129

Quasi-arbitrators
immunity C–018

Reasoning for awards, insufficient
generally C–056, C–126
Recognition and enforcement of foreign awards
evidence to be produced by party seeking 1–103
generally 1–100–1–105
Geneva Convention awards 1–100
New York Convention awards
  bankruptcy law, impact on C–053
  compulsion to arbitrate 1–302, C–073
  enforcement, C–088, C–102, C–114
  forum non conveniens, C–090
  French law, availability of enforcement under C–100
  generally 1–101
  inapplicability under French law C–056
  independence of arbitrators C–050
  interest rates C–080
  jurisdiction, personal C–026, C–037
  local law, propriety under C–040
  new evidence C–050
  non-domestic arbitration C–107

Recognition and enforcement of foreign awards—*cont.*
New York Convention awards—*cont.*
place of arbitration C–073
procedural irregularity C–001, C–071, C–102
procedural law of seat C–068
public policy C–088
res judicata C–040
State immunity C–074
State immunity, waiver of C–070
stay of arbitral proceedings C–014
stay of legal proceedings C–074, C–076, C–087, C–107
third party debt orders C–087
time limits C–080
vacation of C–068, C–071
waiver of arbitration C–073
public policy C–088, C–102
refusal 1–104
Rectification of arbitration agreements
documents ancillary to main contract C–047
mistake C–020
Regional Multilateral Conventions 2–223–2–317
Remedies 1–049
Removal of arbitrators
bias C–079
commitment fees C–077
invalid appointment C–121
Repudiation of arbitration agreements
generally C–061, C–127
Russia
arbitration agreement
definition 1–251
form 1–251
generally 1–251–1–253
interim measures by court, and 1–253
substantive claim before court, and 1–252
competence of arbitral tribunal to rule on jurisdiction 1–260
composition of third party tribunal
appointment of arbitrators 1–255
challenge procedure 1–257
generally 1–254–1–259
grounds for challenge of arbitrator 1–256
number of arbitrators 1–254
substitution of arbitrator 1–259
terminate of authority of arbitrator 1–258

Russia—*cont.*
conduct of arbitral proceedings—*cont.*
conduct of arbitral proceedings
additional award 1–277
commencement of arbitral proceedings 1–265
contents of award 1–275
correction of award 1–277
court assistance in taking evidence 1–271
decision making by panel of arbitrators 1–273
defence 1–267
determination of rules of procedure 1–263
equal treatment of parties 1–262
expert appointed by arbitral tribunal 1–270
failure to appear at hearing 1–269
failure to submit documents 1–269
form of award 1–275
generally 1–262–1–277
hearings 1–268
interpretation of award 1–277
language 1–266
place of arbitration 1–264
rules applicable to substance of dispute 1–272
settlement 1–274
statements of claim 1–267
termination 1–276
written proceedings 1–268
enforcement of awards
generally 1–279
grounds for refusing 1–280
generally 1–244–1–280
international commercial arbitration
authority for functions of assistance and control 1–250
definitions 1–246
extent of court intervention 1–249
generally 1–244–1–280
receipt of written communications 1–247
scope of law 1–245
waiver of right to object 1–248
jurisdiction of arbitral tribunal 1–260, 1–261
power of arbitral tribunal to order interim measures 1–261
recognition of awards 1–279
grounds for refusing 1–280
recourse against award 1–278

Salvage expenses
   charterparties, arbitration pursuant to C–110–C112
Satisfaction of awards
   insolvent parties, by C–065–C–067, C–106
Seat of arbitration
   meaning 1–004
   proper law, differing from C–091
   signature of award in country other than seat C–062
Security for costs
   insolvent parties C–043, C–044
   non-residents C–025, C–043, C–044
Security transactions
   arbitration agreements
      enforceability C–096
      enforcement C–128
Separability of arbitration agreements
   generally 1–008, C–105
Setting aside awards
   bias C–021, C–041, C–050
   evidence, refusal to admit C–045
   fraud C–031, C–048, C–054
   misconduct of arbitrator C–012
Settlement offers
   costs C–049
   generally 1–052
Sharia law
   jurisdiction C–094
Solicitors' costs
   charge to secure 1–076
Sovereign immunity. *see* **State immunity**
Special awards
   generally C–097
Special case, failure to state
   misconduct of arbitrators C–097
Standard conditions
   arbitration agreements C–029
State immunity
   embassies C–028
   nationalisation C–008, C–082
   stay of legal proceedings C–074
   third party debt orders C–006
   waiver C–028, C–070, C–081
Statutory arbitrations
   general adaptation of provisions 1–096
   generally 1–095–1–099
   previous excluded from applying to 1–098
   specific adaptations provisions 1–097

Stay of arbitral proceedings
   enforceability of arbitration agreement C–014
   foreign seat of arbitration C–039
   illegality of arbitration clauses C–060
Stay of legal proceedings
   generally 1–010–1–012, 1–087
   ICSID, under C–024
   interpleader issue, reference to arbitration of 1–011
   repudiation of arbitration agreements C–061
   retention of security in admiralty proceedings 1–012
   State immunity C–074
   "step in the proceedings" C–108
   summary judgment, setting aside of C–063
"Step in the proceedings"
   enforcement of agreements to arbitrate C–073
   ICC Rules C–108
Summary judgment
   generally C–063
Switzerland
   international arbitration
      appointment of arbitrators 1–170
      arbitrability 1–168
      arbitral award 1–180
      arbitral tribunal 1–170
      arbitration agreement 1–169
      certificate of enforceability 1–184
      challenge of arbitrators 1–171
      court of appeal 1–182
      decision on merits 1–178, 1–179
      deposit of copy of award 1–184
      finality 1–181
      foreign arbitral awards 1–185
      further assistance by judge 1–176
      generally 1–167–1–185
      jurisdiction 1–177
      lis pendens 1–172
      procedure 1–173
      protective measures 1–174
      provisional measures 1–174
      seat of arbitral tribunal 1–167
      taking of evidence 1–175
      waiver of appeal 1–183

Third party debt orders
   State immunity C–006
Time limits
   awards, making of C–080, C–120

Time limits—*cont.*
  Centrocon arbitration clause
    appointment of arbitrator out of
      time C–005
    extension, refusal of C–019
    paramount clauses in charter-parties
      C–092
    reference to arbitration C–069
Time periods
  reckoning 1–079
Transnational contract principles
  4–001–4–317

Umpires
  generally 1–022
  impartiality C–058
  special case, statement of C–097
Uncertainty
  arbitration agreements C–119
UNCITRAL Arbitration Rules
  appointment of arbitrators
    3–090–3–092
  arbitral proceedings
    amendments to claim or defence
      3–104
    generally 3–099–3–114
    language 3–101
    place of arbitration 3–100
    pleas as to jurisdiction of arbitral
      tribunal 3–105
    statement of claim 3–102
    statement of defence 3–103
  assistance 3–088
  award
    additional 3–121
    amiable composition 3–117
    applicable law 3–117
    correction 3–120
    costs 3–122–3–124
    deposit of 3–125
    decisions 3–115, 3–116
    effect 3–116
    form 3–116
    generally 3–115–3–125
    grounds for termination 3–118
    interpretation 3–119
    settlement 3–118
  calculation of periods of time 3–086
  challenge of arbitrators
    3–093–3–096
  composition of arbitral tribunal
    3–089–3–098
  further written statements
    closure of hearings 3–113
    default 3–112

UNCITRAL Arbitration Rules—*cont.*
  further written statements—*cont.*
    evidence 3–108, 3–109
    experts 3–111
    generally 3–106
    hearings 3–108, 3–109
    interim measures of protection
      3–110
    periods of time 3–107
    waiver of rules 3–114
  generally 3–084–3–125
  introductory rules 3–085–3–088
  notice 3–086
  notice of arbitration 3–087
  number of arbitrators 3–089
  repetition of hearings in event of
    replacement of arbitrator
    3–098
  replacement of arbitrator 3–097
  representation 3–088
  scope of application 3–085
UNCITRAL Model Law on
    International Commercial
    Arbitration
  additional 1–163, 1–502
  application for setting aside 1–164
  appointment of arbitrators 1–480,
    1–141
  appointment of substitute arbitrator
    1–145, 1–484
  arbitration agreement
    1–137–1–139, 1–476–1–478
  award 1–158–1–163, 1–497–1–505
  challenge procedure 1–143, 1–482
  commencement of proceedings
    1–151, 1–490
  competence of arbitral tribunal to
    rule on own jurisdiction
    1–146
  composition of arbitral tribunal
    1–140–1–145, 1–479–1–484
  conduct of arbitral proceedings
    1–148–1–157, 1–487–1–496
  contents 1–161, 1–500
  correction 1–502
  correction of interpretation 1–163
  court assistance in taking evidence
    1–157, 1–496
  court or other authority for certain
    functions of arbitration
    assistance and supervision
    1–136, 1–475
  decision-making by panel of
    arbitrators 1–498, 1–159
  default of party 1–155, 1–494

UNCITRAL Model Law on International Commercial Arbitration—*cont.*
defence 1–153, 1–492
definitions 1–132, 1–137, 1–471, 1–476
determination of rules of procedure 1–149, 1–488
enforcement 1–165, 1–504
equal treatment of parties 1–148, 1–487
expert appointed by arbitral tribunal 1–156, 1–495
extent of court intervention 1–135, 1–474
failure of administrator to act 1–144
failure to act 1–483
form 1–137, 1–476, 1–161, 1–500
generally 1–131–1–166, 1–469–1–505
grounds for challenge 1–142, 1–481
grounds for refusing 1–166, 1–505
hearings 1–154, 1–493
impossibility of arbitrator to act 1–144, 1–483
interim measures by court, and 1–139, 1–478
interpretation 1–502
jurisdiction of arbitral tribunal 1–146, 1–147, 1–485, 1–486
language 1–152, 1–491
number of arbitrators 1–140, 1–479
place of arbitration 1–150, 1–489
power of arbitral tribunal to order interim measures 1–147
receipt of written communications 1–133, 1–472
recognition 1–165, 1–504
recourse against 1–164, 1–503
rules applicable to substance of dispute 1–497, 1–158
rules of interpretation 1–132, 1–471
scope of application 1–131, 1–470
settlement 1–160, 1–499
statements of claim 1–153, 1–492
substantive claim before court, and 1–138, 1–477
termination of proceedings 1–158–1–163, 1–497–1–505
waiver of right to object 1–134, 1–473
written proceedings 1–154, 1–493

UNCITRAL Model Law on International Commercial Conciliation
admissibility of evidence in other proceedings 1–515
appointment of conciliators 1–510
commencement of conciliation proceedings 1–509
communication between conciliator and parties 1–512
conciliator acting as arbitrator 1–517
conduct of conciliation 1–511
confidentiality 1–514
definitions 1–506
disclosure of information 1–513
enforceability of settlement agreement 1–519
generally 1–506–1–519
interpretation 1–507
number of conciliations 1–510
resort to arbitral or judicial proceedings 1–518
scope of application 1–506
termination of conciliation proceedings 1–516
variation by agreement 1–508

UNCITRAL Notes on Organizing Arbitral Proceedings
administrative services that may be needed for arbitral tribunal to carry out functions 3–043
annotations 3–036–3–083
arrangements for exchange of written submissions 3–051–3–053
confidentiality of information relating to arbitration 3–047
defining points at issue 3–054–3–056
defining relief or remedy sought 3–054–3–056
deposits in respect of costs 3–044–3–046
discretion in conduct of proceedings 3–031
documentary evidence 3–058–3–061
electronic means of sending documents 3–050
experts 3–071–3–073
generally 3–029–3–083
hearings 3–074–3–081
language of proceedings 3–037–3–040

UNCITRAL Notes on Organizing Arbitral Proceedings—*cont.*
  list of matters for possible consideration 3–035
  list of matters for possible consideration in organizing arbitral proceedings 3–034
  multi-party arbitration 3–032, 3–082
  non-binding character 3–030
  order of deciding issues 3–054–3–056
  physical evidence other than documents 3–062–3–064
  place of arbitration 3–041, 3–042
  possibility of meetings outside place of arbitration 3–042
  possible requirements concerning filing or delivering award 3–083
  practical details concerning written submissions and evidence 3–054
  process of making decision on organizing arbitral proceedings 3–033
  purpose 3–029
  routing of written communications among parties and arbitrators 3–048
  set of arbitration rules 3–036
  settlement negotiations, effect on scheduling proceedings 3–057
  Telefax 3–049
  usefulness of timely decisions on organizing proceedings 3–031
  witnesses 3–065–3–070

Unconscionable conduct
  jurisdiction C–034

UNIDROIT Principles for International Commercial Contracts
  content 4–061–4–068
  formation 4–011–4–032
  general provisions 4–002–4–010
  generally 4–001–4–119
  interpretation 4–053–4–060
  non-performance
    damages 4–107–4–119
    generally 4–089–4–119
    right to performance 4–096–4–100
    termination 4–101–4–106
  performance
    application for public permission 4–082

UNIDROIT Principles for International Commercial Contracts—*cont.*
  performance—*cont.*
    at one time 4–070
    costs of 4–079
    currency not expressed 4–078
    currency of payment 4–077
    earlier 4–073
    generally 4–069–4–088
    hardship 4–086–4–088
    imputation of non-monetary obligations 4–081
    imputation of payments 4–080
    instalments 4–070
    order of 4–072
    partial 4–071
    payment by cheque or other instalment 4–075
    payment by funds transfer 4–076
    permission neither granted nor refused 4–084
    permission refused 4–085
    place of 4–074
    procedure in applying for permission 4–083
    time of 4–069
  validity 4–033–4–052

United Nations Convention on the Recognition and Enforcement of Foreign Arbitral Awards
  adjournment of decision 2–006
  "agreement in writing" 2–002
  application 2–001
  "arbitral awards" 2–001
  denunciation 2–013
  federal or non-unitary States 2–011
  generally 2–001–2–016
  multilateral or bilateral agreements, and 2–007
  refusal of recognition and enforcement 2–005
  scope 2–010
  supply of documents 2–004

U.S.A.
  Act of State doctrine, inapplicability of 1–295, C–082
  antitrust law
    arbitrability C–009, C–010, C–089, C–109
    English courts' power to apply C–034
    security transactions C–113
  appeals 1–296

Index

U.S.A.—cont.
  application to court heard as motion 1–286
  appointment of arbitrators or umpire 1–285
  arbitrability
    antitrust law C–009, C–010, C–089, C–109
    security transactions C–113, C–128
    standard of review C–052
    validity of arbitration agreement C–103
  award
    ambiguity C–126
    bankruptcy, and C–065–C–067
    confirmation 1–289
    correction 1–291
    enforcement C–028
    generally 1–289
    grounds 1–290
    insolvency, and C–065–C–067
    interest C–038, C–068
    interim C–117
    judicial review of C–078
    jurisdiction 1–289, C–032
    modification 1–291
    notice of motions to vacate or modify 1–292
    papers filed with order on motions 1–293
    procedure 1–289
    punitive damages C–075, C–129
    rehearing 1–290
    vacation 1–290
    time limits C–120
  collective bargaining agreements C–126
  "commerce", meaning 1–281
  Convention on the Recognition and Enforcement of Foreign Arbitral Awards
    agreement or award falling under 1–298
    appointment of arbitrators 1–302
    bankruptcy law, impact on C–053
    enforcement 1–297, C–026, C–037, C–088, C–102, C–114
    enforcement of agreements to arbitrate 1–302, C–073
    forum non conveniens, C–090
    generally 1–297–1–302, 1–303
    inapplicability under French law C–056

U.S.A.—cont.
  Convention on the Recognition and Enforcement of Foreign Arbitral Awards—cont.
    independence of arbitrators C–050
    interest rates C–080
    jurisdiction 1–299
    jurisdiction, personal C–026, C–037
    local law, propriety under C–040
    new evidence C–050
    non-domestic arbitration C–107
    place of arbitration C–073
    procedural irregularity C–001, C–071, C–102
    procedural law of seat C–068
    public policy C–088, C–102
    removal of cases from State courts 1–301
    res judicata C–040
    State immunity, waiver of C–070
    stay of arbitration C–014
    stay of legal proceedings C–074, C–076, C–087, C–107
    third party debt orders C–087
    time limits C–080
    vacation of C–068, C–071
    venue 1–300
    waiver of arbitration C–073
  employment contracts, incorporation of arbitration provisions into C–027
  enforcement of agreements to arbitrate
    antitrust law C–113
    choice of law clauses C–094
    generally 1–302, 1–282
    international agreements C–109
    security transactions C–128
    "step in the proceedings" C–073
    waiver by conduct C–022, C–023
  failure to arbitrate under agreement 1–284
  fraud by party C–075
  generally 1–281–1–311
  injunctions
    arbitrators' powers C–118
    interim C–117
  Inter-American Convention on International Commercial Arbitration 1–305–1–311

U.S.A.—*cont.*
  irrevocability of agreements to arbitrate 1–282
  "maritime transactions", meaning 1–281
  proceedings begun by libel in admiralty 1–288
  security transactions C–096, C–109, C–113, C–128
  separability of arbitration agreements C–105
  Sharia law C–094
  State immunity
    embassies C–028
    nationalisation, expropriation on C–008, C–082
    waiver C–028
  stay of proceedings
    enforceability of contract C–014
    where issue referable to arbitration 1–283, C–074
  validity of agreements to arbitrate 1–282
  witnesses before arbitrators 1–287

Validity
  appointment of arbitrators C–121
  arbitration agreements C–103, C–119, C–130

Waiver
  State immunity C–028, C–070, C–081

Want of prosecution, dismissal for delay C–084

Withholding evidence
  setting aside of awards C–031, C–054

World-wide Multilateral Conventions 2–001–2–222

WTO Understanding on Rules and Procedures governing Settlement of Disputes
  administration 2–093
  adoption of appellate body reports 2–108
  adoption of panel reports 2–107
  agreements covered by 2–119
  appellate body, communications with 2–109

WTO Understanding on Rules and Procedures governing Settlement of Disputes—*cont.*
  appellate body recommendations 2–110
  appellate review 2–108
  application 2–092
  arbitration 2–116
  compensation 2–113
  complaints 2–117
  conciliation 2–096
  confidentiality 2–105
  consultations 2–095
  coverage 2–092
  expert review groups 2–122
  general provisions 2–094
  generally 2–092–2–222
  good offices 2–096
  interim review stage 2–106
  mediation 2–096
  multiple complainants, procedures for 2–100
  non-violation complaints 2–117
  panel, communications with 2–109
  panel procedures 2–103
  panel recommendations 2–110
  panels
    composition 2–099
    establishment of 2–097
    function 2–102
    terms of reference 2–098
  procedures for appellate review 2–108
  right to seek information 2–104
  Secretariat, responsibilities of 2–118
  special or additional rules and procedures contained in covered agreements 2–120
  special procedures involving least-developed country members 2–115
  standing Appellate Body 2–108
  strengthening of multilateral system 2–114
  surveillance of implementation of recommendations and rulings 2–112
  suspension of concessions 2–113
  third parties 2–101
  time-frame for DSB decisions 2–111
  working procedures 2–121